WEIMAR AND NOW: GERMAN CULTURAL CRITICISM

Edward Dimendberg, Martin Jay, and Anton Kaes, General Editors

THE RED COUNT

The Life and Times of Harry Kessler

Laird McLeod Easton

UNIVERSITY OF CALIFORNIA PRESS

Berkeley / Los Angeles / London

University of California Press
Berkeley and Los Angeles, California

University of California Press, Ltd.
London, England

© 2002 by
The Regents of the University of California

Library of Congress Cataloging-in-Publication Data

Easton, Laird McLeod, 1956–
    The red count : the life and times of Harry Kessler / Laird McLeod
Easton.
        p.   cm.—(Weimar and now ; 30)
    Includes bibliographical references and index.
    ISBN 0-520-23035-3 (alk. paper)
    1. Kessler, Harry, Graf, 1868–1937. 2. Diplomats—Germany—
Biography. 3. Intellectuals—Germany—Biography. 4. Authors,
German—20th century—Biography. 5. Germany—Politics and
government—1918–1933. 6. Germany—Intellectual life—20th century.
I. Title. II. Series.

DD231.K4 E27 2002
943.085′092—dc21   2001007155

Manufactured in the United States of America

10   09   08   07   06   05   04   03   02

10   9   8   7   6   5   4   3   2   1

*To my mother, Annabelle McLeod Easton,
and to the memory of my father, Alexander
Laird Easton (1922–1997)*

Écrire une biographie, c'est définir une force.

Harry Graf Kessler

CONTENTS

ILLUSTRATIONS

ACKNOWLEDGMENTS

Researching and writing this book have taken me more than a decade. Along the way I have accumulated many debts to both individuals and institutions. It affords me great pleasure to be able to repay at least some of these, however inadequately, by thanking those who have helped me.

I wish to begin by thanking Kessler's heirs as well as Dr. Ulrich Ott, Director of the German National Literary Archives in Marbach am Neckar, for the right to cite from the diaries, letters, and other documents in the Kessler Nachlaß. Those who have had the pleasure of working at the Archives know how conducive that magical place, high on a bluff overlooking the Neckar river, is for research, study, and contemplation. I would like to thank all the staff there for making me feel welcome, especially Gerhard Schuster, Margot Pehle, and Hildegard Dieke, as well as the members of the Harry Graf Kessler Projekt, for their expert help and advice. I am also grateful to the administration and staff of the lovely Collegienhaus in Marbach, where I and my family had the good fortune to reside for six weeks in the summer of 1995.

Further afield, I would like to thank the Archives of the Foreign Office in Bonn and the Goethe-Schiller Archive in Weimar for their hospitality and for the right to use documents in their collections. Dr. Peter Grupp in Bonn and Dr. Rosawitha Wollkopf in Weimar, both Kessler scholars, were generous with their time and assistance. For the right to consult and cite from the Henry van de Velde papers, I thank the Bibliothèque Royale, Albert Première, in Brussels. Additional archives that were helpful to me include the Thüringian State Archive, Weimar; the Federal Archive in Koblenz; and the National Archives in Washington,

D.C. For responses to inquiries, I thank librarians at the special collections of the Newberry Library in Chicago, the University of California at Los Angeles, the Harry Ransom Humanities Research Center at the University of Texas at Austin, and the State University of New York at Binghamton. The Houghton Library at Harvard University has generously granted me permission to use the William Rothenstein papers in their collection. Closer to home, I am thankful for the cheerful assistance of the Interlibrary Loan staff at the Merriam Library of California State University, Chico.

Without the generous financial support of the following institutions, I could not have completed this book: the German Academic Exchange Service for the initial yearlong research stipendium that got me started in 1988–89 as well as for a generous Study Research Grant in 1995; the National Endowment for the Humanities for a Travel to Collections Grant in 1992 and a Summer Stipend in 1993; the Office of Sponsored Projects at California State University, Chico, for a CSU Research Award in 1992 and for a full semester's release time in the spring of 1994. To the administration and staff of all these agencies, I am profoundly grateful.

As a professional historian, I owe the most to my mentors Paul Robinson and James Sheehan of Stanford University both for their encouragement and support from the very beginning of this project and for serving as models, in their teaching and in their scholarship, of academic integrity. Vernon Lidtke, Gerald Feldman, Brian Ladd, and Diana Barkan have all commented helpfully at various conferences on earlier versions of this work. Here in Chico, my colleague Larry Bryant has both provided venues for me to present my research on Kessler and prodded me, gently but persistently, into finally finishing. Finally, I should thank the anonymous reader who had the courage to read two monstrously large earlier drafts and helped me whittle them down to a more manageable size.

The following debt can never be repaid. Without the long-suffering patience and the stalwart support of James H. Clark, Director of the University of California Press, I fear it is unlikely that the book would ever have seen the light of day. Many thanks as well to Mari Coates.

Elsa and Jonathan Sands provided much appreciated support at an early stage. Over the last years, I have been grateful for the friendship, support, and intellectual stimulation of Robert and Katherine O'Brien, Ken Rose, and Jeanne Lawrence.

I first conceived of writing a biography of Harry Kessler a number of years ago while sitting in a children's playground in the Richmond district of San Francisco. By my side then and in all the years since has been Maria, whose intelligence, good cheer, encouragement, and love have nourished me throughout the long journey. My daughter Natasha has lived with this project all of her life, enduring its ups and downs, tolerating endless chatter about it, and helping her father remember that one cannot simply write the life of another—one must live one's own life as well. To both of them, I go down on my knees in love and gratitude.

Art and Politics
in Modern Germany

You will write the memoirs of our time. It therefore behooves
you to meet everybody who is important in all walks of life. I
envy our grandchildren who will be able to read this.

Richard Dehmel to Kessler, *Tagebuch,*
September 5, 1901

In the spring 1938 issue of *Maß und Wert,* the émigré journal founded
by Thomas Mann and published in Switzerland, the following obituary
appeared:

Harry Kessler

Sometimes he appeared German, sometimes English, sometimes French,
so European was his character. In truth the arts were his home. For he reacted to everything artistic with a storm like swiftness; even in music, of
which he was an ardent enthusiast, he was always first to make a discovery,
in this so like his friend Hofmannsthal. From this mastery came the glow of
his many-sided being. Through his death a darkness has become palpable,
we have been deprived of a great romance: it is a splendid luminosity for
which we mourn.

Seen purely from a matter of fact viewpoint, he was not, among the intellectuals of his day, isolated: A few kept pace with him. But the sharpness
and delicacy of his artistic sensitivity, like a moat around an old castle,
placed him apart, even within this elite.

Be it that he was writing a travel book, a piece for the stage, a biography,
or his memoirs or whether acting as a Maecenas or simply living as he
wished, it was always art that transpired. Thus he attracted magnetically the

I

best and the brightest, and, wherever he went, they formed his company. Such an intense and seldom interrupted sociability was a danger in itself, one was therefore all the more astonished to recognize in him, the gaze of someone who guarded a certain reserve and inward composure. His path ran evenly, but precisely the harmony between the background and the content of his life had a touch of tragedy due to a deep sensitivity, far less of the nerves than that of a very passionate organism.

He took part fully in the fate of the world, especially in Germany's misfortune at the end of the war. He placed his great speaking talent in the service of reconstruction and in the detoxification of the atmosphere. One could hear Harry Kessler back then in the meeting halls of the small border cities, as, surrounded by great crowds, he explained Germany's situation to the people, who found consolation and hope in his words and could take heart in them.

He was in his seventieth year when he died; those who didn't know that would scarcely have believed it. Sickness often, but never old age, afflicted him. What a lesson such an existence teaches us, and what a worthy exit it was allowed to find! Two hours before his death, delirious and staring into space, he cried out, "What a splendid church! There was never one more beautiful. Lift me up so that I may see it better!" These were his last words. . . .

Now this son of the North rests next to the tomb of Alfred de Musset, in a high spot in Pére Lachaise; his grave borders hard on a tranquil ally planted with trees. They stand now denuded of leaves. In the summer, peopled by birds, they will bloom.[1]

Annette Kolb, the Franco-German novelist and, like Kessler, an intermediary between two inimical worlds, wrote this tribute shortly after Kessler's death on November 30, 1937. For the exiles of Nazi Germany it was late autumn in Europe in more than one sense. In a year's time they would be driven out of one of their German-speaking refuges by Hitler's *Anschluss* of Austria; a few months later the Western powers would sacrifice Czechoslovakia, at first the Sudetenland and then the rest. Less than a year later would come the apocalyptic winter of the world war. The times were not propitious for adequately remembering and honoring such an enigmatic traveler between worlds as Harry Kessler. A few error-filled obituaries appeared in England, France, and America; other news was more pressing, and the editors did not bother to check the facts.

From the land that owed him the most, Germany, came not a word. The kind of cosmopolitanism Kessler embodied was anathema to Hitler's Reich. Two years earlier Joseph Goebbels had banned Kessler's volume of memoirs; its title, *Völker und Vaterländer* (*Peoples and Fatherland*), with its Nietzschean overtones of contempt for philistine chauvinism, did not sit well with those who believed only in *ein Volk*. Out of Berlin, out of Weimar—where twice the Gestapo had ransacked his beloved house—there was nothing but stony silence. In the bleak years that followed a few did find the time to remember him in the midst of their own tribulations. During a despairing moment in his New York exile George Grosz recalled Kessler as perhaps the last great gentleman he had encountered. And during 1944, the darkest year of the war, Max Beckmann read Kessler's memoirs and recalled the man who had brought him his first public recognition thirty-eight years earlier.[2] But mostly Kessler was quickly forgotten, a footnote to an already dim memory.

Kessler had foreseen this fate; he knew that he would not see the end of the Third Reich. Perhaps it is inevitable, even in normal times, that the public memory of someone like Kessler—in the words of Hugo von Hofmannsthal "an artist in living material"—should quickly fade. His influence and activity were, with the exception of the years from 1916 to 1924, largely exercised privately. Still, Kessler's rich sociability, remarked upon by Kolb; his almost limitless connections in the world of European art, theater, literature, and politics during the four decades from 1890 to 1930; his uncanny ability to be present at some of the pivotal events of the first third of the twentieth century—in short, his presence, in the fullest meaning of the word, make the contrast with the ensuing obscurity striking. Kessler, described by W. H. Auden as "probably the most cosmopolitan man who ever lived," was indeed a "Crown witness to his times."[3] The number of individuals mentioned in his diary has been roughly estimated at more than forty thousand. Just the list of those with whom he was more than a passing acquaintance is a who's who of European art, society, and politics: Herbert Asquith, Johannes R. Becher, Pierre Bonnard, Paul Cassirer, Jean Cocteau, Gordon Craig, Lady Cunard, Gabriele D'Annunzio, Maurice Denis, Serge Diaghilev, Isadora Duncan, Albert Einstein, Elisabeth Förster-Nietzsche, André Gide, Eric Gill, George Grosz, Maximilian Harden, Gerhart Hauptmann, Wieland Herzfelde, Rudolf Hilferding, Hugo von Hofmannsthal, Herman Keyserling, Annette Kolb, Richard von Kühlmann, Prince Max Lichnowsky, Max Liebermann, Aristide Maillol, Adolf von Maltzan, Thomas Mann, Edvard Munch, Nicolas Nabokov, Harold Nicolson, Vaslav Nijinsky, Jozef Pilsudski, Walther Rathenau, Rainer Maria Rilke, Max Reinhardt, Auguste Rodin, Ida Rubenstein, René Schickele, Misia Sert, George Bernard Shaw, Hugo Simon, Richard Strauss, Gustav Stresemann, Fritz von Unruh, Henry van de Velde, Eduard Vuillard,

Josef Wirth. In more than fifteen thousand closely written pages covering fifty-seven years, Kessler chronicled his works and days with a truly extraordinary tenacity. Long before Richard Dehmel told him that he would write the memoirs of their time, Kessler had been patiently storing the material for what he instinctively must have known would be the great coda of his life, his autobiography (of which, unfortunately, he would only be able to complete one volume). It is this intersection between the richness of a life and its comprehensive recording, mediated by a keen intelligence, that makes Kessler's diary one of the greatest personal documents of the twentieth century, an invaluable source book not only for scholars of art, literature, and history, but also one that will be read for its own sake, for the vivid depiction of the political and intellectual upheaval of that century as seen by a man uniquely equipped to observe it.[4]

Yet, it is unjust to consider Kessler as simply the "most eminent literary magpie"[5] of his time, a self-effacing Venerable Bede chronicling the deeds and words of others. He was an active and passionate participant in those times as well. Just how active a life is the subject of this book, but the following short summary gives some indication: he was instrumental in the dissemination of modern art in Germany, as a writer, patron, museum director, and, more generally, what the Germans call a "*Kunstpolitiker*" (literally, art politician). He played a pivotal role in bringing French impressionist and postimpressionist painting to Germany. His effort to make Weimar again a center of cultural innovation led to his collaboration with Henry van de Velde, one of the pioneers of modern design and the founder of the school that became the Bauhaus. Kessler's sponsorship of the English theater visionary, Gordon Craig, revolutionized the German stage, helping to make it the most advanced in the world. Similarly, his importation of English book and type designers changed the face of German publishing. His own Cranach Presse would become one of the most famous private presses of the twentieth century. In two notable cases Kessler's friendships led to particularly creative collaborations: with the French sculptor Aristide Maillol and with the Austrian writer Hugo von Hofmannsthal. His interest in modern dance led to his collaboration with Hofmannsthal, Diaghilev, Nijinsky, and Strauss in the ballet, *The Legend of Joseph,* the last great international cultural event before the outbreak of the First World War. Kessler, a close, if not uncritical, friend of Elisabeth Förster-Nietzsche, was also one of the most important figures in the prewar Nietzsche cult.

During the war Kessler was active on the eastern front and in Switzerland and Berlin as a soldier, diplomat, propagandist, and secret agent. At the same time, he kept in touch with the latest developments in modern art. With the collapse of the German empire in 1918, Kessler, after a short stint as ambassador of the new regime in Warsaw, became a noted pacifist and an important supporter of the Weimar Republic. An influential proponent of Germany's entrance in the League of Nations, Kessler lectured widely in Europe and the United States on this issue. He was also a founding member of the German Democratic Party, initially the third largest political party of the Republic and a key member of the Weimar coalition. It was during these years that his enemies on the right branded him "the red count." Eventually his politics compelled his exile when Hitler took over in January 1933.

This list is incomplete. It can scarcely do justice, for example, to his largely private actions in bringing creative artists into fruitful activity with one another. It does suggest, however, the biggest conundrum facing any biographer of Kessler; namely, the metamorphosis of the fin-de-siècle aesthete, whose first published article concerned the decadent poet Henri de Régnier, into the prominent pacifist and democrat of the Weimar period. Although the two stages of Kessler's life appear at first glance to be so distinct as to belong to two different people, there was in fact an inner logic to his evolution: Kessler's overt political engagement after the First World War was an imminent development of his prewar search, under the influence of Nietzsche, for an "aesthetic state." The view that judges politics ultimately by aesthetic standards goes back to Plato's *Republic*. In the modern period, it has played an especially fateful and pervasive role in German political thought.[6] The version that Kessler elaborated in bits and pieces over forty years serves not only to link conceptually the two halves of his life but also to provide a fascinating case study of an approach to politics not untypical of German and European intellectuals during the critical first decades of the twentieth century.

The termini of Kessler's active adult life are approximately 1890 to 1930 or roughly the period that saw the birth and triumph of modern art as well as the rise of mass politics. As it turns out, nowhere were art and politics more fatefully intertwined than in the German-speaking lands of Central Europe. If one considers the entire four decades from 1890 to 1930 and defines art broadly to include such things as industrial design, theatrical staging, and film, as well as the so-called "higher" arts, then a very strong argument could be made for designating Germany and Austria, rather than France and England, as the "crucible of modernity," the arena where the most self-consciously radical as well as the most pervasive and influential modernism took shape.[7] Certainly it was in Germany that the most virulent reaction against aesthetic modernism transpired. Again, it was in the German-speaking lands that the allure of a new kind of politics, one practiced with cultural means to attend aesthetic ends, was greatest. From Winckelmann and Schiller through Wagner and Nietzsche to Lukacs, Adorno, Brecht, and Marcuse, it has been German-speaking artists and thinkers—the few exceptions such as Ruskin and Morris notwithstanding—who have been most preoccupied with the question of art and politics.

Kessler's life offers a rare opportunity to examine the possibilities, limits, vicissitudes, and vagaries of an aesthetic approach to politics. With the recent discovery of the diaries covering the period from 1902 to 1914, it is finally possible to explore in detail both his intellectual evolution and his influence.[8] If these years saw tremendous changes in the practice of politics, the structure of business, and the development of a modern society, nowhere was the transformation greater and more fateful than in the realm of culture. Starting with the discovery of Nietzsche and the rise of naturalism and continuing through to the aggressive explosion of expressionism after 1910, the traditional bearers of culture in Germany, the *Bildungsbürgertum,* or educated middle classes, saw themselves confronted by a series of ever more radical assaults on their basic assumptions about art and culture. These struggles, more intense and ideological in Germany than elsewhere, do not permit an unproblematic application of the traditional antinomies derived from politics; cultural politics made strange bedfellows. That is part of the interest of these years.[9]

Our fascination is also rooted in a kind of nostalgia. For all the ideological tumult and the sense of impending doom that pervades any discussion of art, culture, and politics in Central Europe from 1890 to 1930, one still is tempted to call those four decades "the heroic age of modernism." Now that aesthetic modernism is over, and its failure to change radically the nature of bourgeois life has been sufficiently documented, we turn wistfully back to chronicle the works and days of our modernist forefathers.* There is more than a little irony in this "historicization" of

---

*I refer to the radical political and cultural aspirations of some—not all—avant-garde groups around the turn of the century; nor do I mean to suggest that in other, less political areas, modernism has not had a substantial impact on the way we live. One need only think in this context of how our world is shaped by modern architecture.

the birth pangs of modernism, for, if anything, the modernists were revolting against nineteenth-century historicism. The cry of Stephan Daedalus, "History is a nightmare from which I'm trying to awake," could have been the slogan of Kessler's generation in Germany as well. Yet, now that the often messianic hopes accompanying the birth of aesthetic modernism have been disappointed, it requires a historian to recover and recount the story. The very notion of an avant-garde, determined historically by its opposition to an established and officially sanctioned cultural hierarchy, has lost its meaning for a generation that has never known such an official culture. An effort of historical imagination is necessary to understand those who felt themselves on the brink of a brave new world. Here too Kessler's life, based on the unique resource of his diary, can offer a thread of Ariadne to traverse this labyrinth.[10]

There are some who would assert that Kessler's life is both too fragmented and too opaque to yield any unifying threads. Gerhard Schuster, the editor of his collected writings, has gone so far as to assert that "Harry Kessler's biography lacks guidelines in the same way his diary foregoes all perambulatory justifications. No, to treat him as simply 'a child of his times,' measuring, comparing and ordering is not the way to comprehend such an existence."[11] Again, Annette Kolb had hinted at the dangers facing a biography. The bewildering, almost frenetic intensity of Kessler's social life; his restless, centrifugal energy—so irritating to his more sedate friends—careening from one project to another seems to lack a center of gravity, other than, perhaps, the diary. And yet the diary of this man "of too many properties," at first glance, appears to be a monument of reticence regarding Kessler's private core, the still point around which all else revolved. According to Schuster, Kessler "never reveals his innermost dreams, desires, and fears; one can only guess at the effort of self-censorship. So much of the 'stuff' of life, erected like walls around a center of recognizable loneliness, hints at the dangers of a celibate existence."[12]

Although there is some truth to this assessment, the self-censorship is not watertight. Kessler did not use his diary, in general, for confessional purposes, but there are less guarded passages that reveal the man behind the diary. Certain obsessions, preoccupations, and themes form patterns an attentive reader can hardly miss. From this central, private bundle, more public concerns and themes radiate outward, to some extent linking the apparently discrete and divergent enterprises. As he prepared to write his memoirs, Kessler, aware of the problem of "the overabundance and viscosity of the material," outlined the method he would use to construct it: "To compress the specific atmosphere of an era into a small group of intimately known individuals, and, on this sturdy basis, let the personalities and events of the time emerge. Let nothing simply dangle lifelessly in space, in the hope that the reader may otherwise be interested in some important event or historical personage. Values, values, exactly as in a painting!"[13] There is a dim echo of the young Kessler's reading of Hippolyte Taine here, the idea that from "milieu" arises the character, be it of an artwork, a literature, a nationality, or an individual. To an unusual extent, even for the decisive early years of childhood and adolescence, the material exists for such an approach to Kessler's biography.

The raw material of all lives is chaotic. It is the biographer's responsibility to shape the clutter into an order that is both plausible, in that it takes into account both the limits and possibilities of its sources, and insightful, in that it not only helps explain the subject's life but also, even more importantly, contributes something to what is, after all, the essential adventure of human thought, making sense of ourselves and the world we live in. Despite its superficial fragmentation, Kessler's life demonstrates an unusual coherence. In fact, it is not difficult to discover the story he told himself to make sense of his life, nor is it impossible to judge that story's plausibility. To do so, however, requires two things. One must take his ideas seriously and understand the "vocation" of a man who did not have, in the ordinary meaning of the word, a career. Statesmen, soldiers, writers, entrepreneurs—their biographies, however difficult to write in other ways, have clear institutional frameworks against which to judge the accomplishments of their subjects. Kessler, who was something of a statesman, something of a soldier, something of a writer, and indeed something of an entrepreneur, but who never held for long an official post and whose influence played itself out behind the scenes, cannot be judged by these self-evident standards. In this respect, the biographer of Kessler faces some of the challenges confronting biographers of women. And while it is true that Kessler frequently—but by no means always—failed to achieve his goals, this was often because they were beyond the power of anyone to accomplish— for example, the establishment of a secure democracy in postwar Germany. Many of his projects, doomed to failure in his own lifetime, would come to fruition in later, more propitious times. Besides, his failures were often more interesting than other men's successes.

Alexandre Kojève has written that all important questions lead, sooner or later, to the answer to "Who am I?"[14] Precisely because his life seemed to lack the clear contours given to most of us by our professions, Kessler asked himself that question with more self-consciousness than most. His lifelong obsession with establishing an aesthetic state can be seen as a way of approaching the answer. We who come later, we *Nachgeborene,* may find ourselves in a substantially different world, facing different challenges; nevertheless, to a remarkable extent, Kessler's questions are our questions. They still lead us back to the central question, "Who are we?"

PART ONE

Family and Education

CHAPTER I

Pirates and Philosophers

I am half a Kessler, a metaphysician from the time of the
Reformation, and half an Irishman, with a good sound thirst
for beauty and fistfights . . . a professor of a nebulous kind
of philosophy and a monstrously rich pirate and captain (my
grandfather and the like were truly Vikings).

Kessler, *Briefwechsel*

The assumption that the traits of ancestors somehow play an important
role in shaping one's character was much more widespread in Kessler's
day, with its imperfect knowledge of the genetics of inheritance, than in
our own: Kessler himself liked to imagine he could trace both intellectual and physical characteristics of his friends to their ancestry. In his
own case, however, he probably realized that the importance of his family's history was more fanciful than physiological. Besides offering role
models, his forebears provided him with a convenient way to label and
understand the duality he perceived in his personality, which, following
Thomas Mann, might be labeled the bourgeois and the aesthetic. Family history was important to Kessler.

His father, Adolf Wilhelm Kessler (1838–1895), was the actual
founder of the family fortune. Descended on his mother's side from
an old Hamburg banking family and on his father's from a line of pas-
tors allegedly going back to Luther's friend and ally, Johannes Kessler,
Adolf Kessler appears in his portraits to be a typical representative of
the *Gründerzeit* generation, with muttonchop whiskers and a shrewd,

energetic look. He was passionately fond of hunting, riding, and dancing: "movement in itself gave him joy . . . if there had been autos during his day, he would always have driven at one hundred and twenty kilometers per hour." This restlessness he would bequeath to his son, whose eternal haste was proverbial among his friends and whom the doorman at the Grand Hotel in Paris dubbed "l'homme à vapeur."

Adolf Kessler's vitality was, however, tempered by the strenuous work ethic and prudent judgment native to a member of the Hamburg bourgeoisie. As a German banker in Paris, he was well placed to take advantage of the opportunities offered by the enormous war indemnity Germany imposed on France at the end of the Franco-Prussian war, and he quickly amassed a fortune that stretched across three continents, from Canada to Persia. In Quebec alone he owned three hundred square miles of forest along the St. Maurice River, which he exploited not only for lumber, but also used as a private game reserve in which to hunt bear. Brought in as a young man by a maternal uncle to run the Paris branch of the family bank, he used Paris as his headquarters, although he frequently had to travel to the United States and England to look after business. Only the summer months were spent in Germany, usually at the spas in Ems and in Kissingen.[1]

Kessler's private values and political opinions were firmly rooted in the weltanschauung of a nineteenth-century liberal during the period of liberal ascendancy in Europe. Thirty-two years old at the time of the unification, he retained his identity as a citizen of the Free and Hanseatic city of Hamburg, a city-state that had always enjoyed strong ties with England, and he "often uttered exasperated criticism of the political and social circumstances and prejudices of Prussian Germany." Once, he expressed to his skeptical son the confidence that all nations would evolve peacefully into republics within a century's time. From his son, however, he demanded the strictest obedience and subservience, even in the smallest matters, perhaps in an effort to prevent his wife from spoiling what was long their only child. Affectionate and respectful, the relation between father and son lacked the stormy Strindbergian tension that so often characterized the relations of Kessler's friends with their fathers. Yet it was not without an inherent, although perhaps not explicitly recognized, psychological challenge to the young man.[2] A dynamic, self-confident empire builder, robustly optimistic and yet emblematic of his generation in his restraint, self-discipline, and respectability, Adolf Kessler provided in fact an ambiguous role model for his son, who, in obscure, not entirely conscious ways, sought both to emulate his father's achievements and to liberate himself from the relent-

lessly bourgeois ethos bequeathed to him, an ethos he experienced as
sterile and confining.

. . .

Father and son could agree on one point: the extraordinary presence of
the beautiful and strong-willed Alice Countess Kessler (1844–1919) in
their lives. Kessler describes in his memoirs the fierce pride with which
his father exulted in the loveliness of his wife, the way he "brought her
home like a magical flower, whose aroma, beauty, spirit and taste enchanted him" and how he loved to bring her into society "in order to
experience the triumph of her beauty." The son also echoed this sentiment, "I remember the pleasure I had as a young boy—a pleasure
mixed with childish pride—when the people along the promenade in
Ems would climb onto tables and chairs to watch her drive or stroll
by."[3] Indeed, Alice Kessler's beauty and charm were to bring both father and son more tangible benefits than pride, although the venomous
speculation accompanying these rewards would haunt her son particularly all his life. Perhaps the greatest act of filial devotion he performed
for his mother came at the end of his life as he struggled to evoke,
define, and defend the mother of whom he wrote: "I can say today that
I have never loved another being so utterly, to the point of the extinction of my own self, with passion and all that passion brings in the way
of surprise, jealousy and, from time to time, hate, as I did her. I lay
awake entire nights and hated my mother—and then in tears begged
her forgiveness."[4]

The remarkable and exotic family background of his mother fascinated Kessler. Its spell must have been doubly strong on the young
boy, and it is clear that part of his lifelong obsession with the British
Empire and the British character arose from his strong identification
with this history. Alice Harriet Blosse-Lynch was born in Bombay in
1844. Her father, Henry Finnis Blosse-Lynch (1807–1873), was one of
the energetic and talented young men who helped lay the foundations of the British Empire in the first part of the nineteenth century.
Born into the Anglo-Irish landed gentry—the Blosse-Lynch family seat
was Partrey House in County Mayo near Blarney Castle—the third of
eleven sons, Henry Blosse entered the Indian navy at the age of sixteen
as a midshipman. Employed during survey expeditions in the Persian
Gulf, he "appears to have had a talent for languages, and neither the depressing climate of the gulf nor the miseries of the wretched little sur-
vey-brigs deterred him from a close study of Persian and Arabic."[5] In

the course of an adventurous career—at one point he was shipwrecked in the Red Sea and traversed the Nubian desert alone to the Nile, from there descending to Cairo and thus home—Lynch quickly rose through the ranks to commander and then captain. He founded a navigation company on the Euphrates and Tigris rivers that would later figure in the life of his grandson at the time of the controversy over the construction of the famous Berlin-to-Baghdad railway.

Lynch married the daughter of Colonel Robert Taylor, an almost mythical figure, who, after an adventurous life in the Middle East, became the minister of Great Britain to Baghdad, at the time theoretically a part of the Ottoman Empire, but in reality an independent satrap along the lines of Mehemet Ali's Egypt. Perhaps the most romantic episode in his colorful life, however, was his abduction of and marriage to a twelve-year-old relative of the Shah against the wishes of the Persian royal family, according to family legend. This woman, Kessler's great-grandmother, lived until 1877, long enough to receive a state visit from the Shah during his visit to London in 1873. Kessler remembered sitting on a stool at the feet of his blind great-grandmother while her hands, with henna-dyed nails, caressed his face, proclaiming his features to be those of the long dead Colonel Taylor. Thus did Kessler believe that he had the blood of the Persian royal family in his veins. It may be that this Oriental background in his own family history contributed its part to Kessler's taste for Orientalist settings in literature, music, and dance.

A photograph taken around 1870 shows Alice Kessler to have been a remarkably striking woman, with the softly modeled chin, the fine nose, the dark brown eyes, and the masses of dark blond hair so lovingly described by her son. Her beauty and brash charm appear to have captivated several other men besides her husband and son. The most illustrious was the Prussian king—soon to be the German emperor—Wilhelm I, who simply approached her on the promenade at Ems during the summer of 1870 and declared that he had long wanted to be introduced to her. Although this beginning friendship was interrupted by the famous Ems dispatch that triggered the Franco-Prussian war, it was resumed when the Kesslers returned to Ems in the summer of 1873. The emperor's affection for the vivacious young woman was such that in 1877, on the occasion of the birth of Kessler's only sibling, his sister Wilma, he announced his wish to be the godfather; the baptism in Baden-Baden was a quasi-court event.

Naturally, tongues began to wag at the spectacle of the aged emperor's bestowal of time and affection on the Kessler family. Adding fuel to the insinuations, the emperor ennobled Adolf Kessler, out of "special good wishes." Kessler argued that this was done solely because of his father's services on behalf of Germans living in Paris; nevertheless, it was an unusual step for the emperor—in his long reign, there were hardly thirty such ennoblements. But the imperial grace did not rest there. On May 11, 1881, Prince Heinrich XIV of Reuß of the cadet line, prompted no doubt by the emperor, issued a diploma raising Adolf Wilhelm Kessler and his heirs to the rank of count. This second ennoblement was without precedent in the history of the Second Reich: not only was the intermediary stage of baron skipped, but also the Kesslers became thus the only counts in the tiny Reußian principality. The title was somewhat ambiguous, however. The Prussian *Heroldsamt* did not recognize the title within the kingdom of Prussia; therefore, the Kesslers were counts within the Empire but not in Prussia.[6]

This salient evidence of royal favor could not help but cast a shadow on the family coat of arms, with its motto "Semper adscendens" ("Always ascending"). For the rest of his life, Kessler would be plagued by rumors that he was the illegitimate son of Wilhelm I; rumors that became especially piquant when Kessler achieved notoriety as an implacable opponent of Emperor Wilhelm II's *Kulturpolitik* and again when he embraced the republic after the First World War. In his memoirs, he is at pains to put to rest any doubts not only about his own parentage, but also about that of his sister. Inasmuch as Kessler was born two years before his mother made the acquaintance of the emperor, the cloud surrounding his birth is easily dispersed. About his sister, born at the height of the royal friendship, the truth cannot, of course, be known with certainty, but given that the emperor was eighty years old at the time of Wilma's birth, it is safe to conclude that the rumors concerning her parentage seem equally unfounded. Nevertheless, this last burst of gallantry on the part of the elderly sovereign was enough to provoke the enmity of a certain contingent in the court centered on the Empress Augusta, a development that did not escape the attention of Germany's chancellor and greatest statesman, Otto von Bismarck. Ever watchful for ways to counter the influence of the empress, he surprised the Kesslers in the summer of 1874 by announcing his wish to make the acquaintance of Alice, whose singing, he said, had enchanted him. After the assassination attempt on the chancellor that same summer, the six-year-old Harry was sent to his bedside with a bouquet of flowers.[7]

Yet another future chancellor of Imperial Germany would attempt a rapprochement with Alice Kessler. The first years after the Franco-Prussian war were difficult ones for Germans living in Paris. Mindful of the potential dangers to the Kesslers posed by the *revanchist* spirit prevalent in France, Count Heinrich von Lehndorff wrote to Alice Kessler on behalf of the emperor that a certain Bülow, attached to the German embassy in Paris, had been given special instructions to look out for her and her family. Shortly after his arrival at the embassy in March 1878, Bernhard von Bülow did manage to insinuate himself into the Kessler household—running errands, offering advice, playing the "good uncle" to Harry by taking him to the theater, arriving at the last moment at dinner parties to prevent the guests from numbering thirteen—until he came in and out of the house as if he were a member of the family. He apparently misjudged, however, the extent of the gratitude he had thus earned: fancying himself an irresistible Lothario, he took the opportunity of Adolf Kessler's absence in the United States to try and force himself upon Alice Kessler. Upset by his obtrusiveness, she turned to her only relative in Paris at the time, a devoutly religious great-uncle who once, when she was a little girl, had admonished her to repent for her beauty. Lecturing her again for sinfulness, he proceeded to mail a pile of religious tracts to Bülow, who wrote to Kessler's mother the next day: "Many thanks for the edifying presents. I see that I have erred and you are not like a certain witty woman who chose as her epitaph: 'Here lies a lady who made her paradise on earth, uncertain of the one above.'" This clever way of disentangling himself did not, however, assuage Bülow's thirst to revenge the ridicule he endured. Fifty years later, he took the trouble in his memoirs to portray Kessler's father as a mere bank clerk who traded on his wife's favors in order to attack Kessler for using his—in any case tainted—title while serving under a republican regime, and to accuse Alice Kessler of having been the mistress of General Georges Ernest Boulanger.[8]

It was not the first time someone had imputed improper relations between Boulanger, the most serious political threat to the fledgling Third Republic, and Kessler's mother. In the scurrilous journalistic world of the Third Republic, anyone was grist for the mill of politics. In the spring of 1890, although General Boulanger had already fled France and the high watermark of boulangism had in fact already passed, the upcoming municipal elections in Paris threatened to be a triumph for the exiled general. At the end of April, *Le Parti National* published an unsigned article accusing Boulanger of giving up military secrets to "une dame de Kessler," whose salon he assiduously frequented. Other newspapers of various persuasions picked up the story, *Le Matin, Le Soir, La Patrie, L'Autorité*—eventually reporters from the *New York World* arrived to interview "Madame de Kessler." Kessler happened to be in Paris on vacation from the university at the time and his diary reveals the feverish, desperate life of the Kessler household—like that of a citadel under siege—with lawyers and family friends convening to plot strategy. Letters were sent to the various offending journals asking them to reveal their sources and to print front page retractions upon the threat of legal retribution. *Le Parti Nationale* defiantly dared the Kesslers to sue them; other, more friendly papers printed Alice Kessler's refutation of the accusations that in effect she was an agent of the Germans. With the final discrediting of boulangism in the May elections, the scandal dropped from sight, but not without leaving deep wounds in the Kessler family. Kessler does not directly mention the incident in his memoirs, but he recalls the ugly chauvinism of those years as the first ominous sign of the forces that would doom the cosmopolitan, European world in which his parents moved. At the time, the assault on his mother's honor left him near collapse: "the last fortnight has all but broken me; I often feel as if I could never be happy again; what I have gone through, the agony, the torture I have endured passes description: I have often sat for hours powerless to move, as if every nerve, every muscle had been crushed, without even the force to despair."[9]

Alice Kessler reacted to the increasingly savage public world by withdrawing into a private realm of art, literature, and theater. Her taste, like her temperament, was deeply romantic: at its extreme, it shaded off into a something akin to Baudelaire's pessimism. One of her favorite poets and a personal acquaintance was the late romantic exotic Barbey d'Aurevilly, whose disdain for convention she could safely admire while pitying his abject poverty. Many prominent artists of the day numbered among the guests at her salon: Sarah Bernhardt, Eleonore Duse, Tommaso Salvini, Guy de Maupassant, Henrik Ibsen, the young Auguste Rodin. Some of the actors and actresses among them made guest appearances at the theater she had built in the garden of her Paris house. She was a passionate devotee of amateur theater and a gifted enough actress to enchant the young Maupassant in a private production of his *Musotte*. He sent her a copy of the play with the dedication: "To Madame, the Countess of Kessler in memory of the unforgettable Musotte—such as I dreamed of her, grisette of 18 years. Thus I dreamed of her, such a blooming hawthorn." Her portrayal of Nora in Ibsen's *The Dollhouse* impressed the playwright himself, especially her tempestuous dancing of the tarantella.[10]

What was the source of her dramatic impulse? Kessler asks, "Was there in her an irresistible drive to creativity? Or was it a substitute for experiences that nature promised my mother but which life had denied her? I believe, both . . . mixed with the drive to creativity was something less visible, which sprang out of a deeper, more primitive level of the psyche, a sort of savageness that could not conform to the world such as it is. Quite obscurely and without her ever quite realizing it, something in my mother continually rebelled and, from the depths of her soul, said 'no' to everything that was."[11] This "everything that was" was, in part at least, the patriarchal world of the haute bourgeoisie that raised females to be ornamental, child-women, an attitude almost perfectly expressed in Wilhelm I's comment on Alice Kessler's rooms, "The cage is almost worthy of the bird."[12] There was more than a little of Ibsen's Nora in Kessler's mother, which no doubt accounted for the fury of her tarantella. Unlike Nora, however, she did not leave her husband and family to find herself. Instead, she sublimated this urge for transcendence in her literary interests and acquaintances, in her singing and playacting, even in her gestures and in her vanity. It is not necessary to conclude that she actually ever overstepped the bounds of propriety; some longing in her expressed itself in such a way as to be misunderstood by certain men as perhaps an invitation to dalliance. In lieu of the opportunity to develop an autonomous self of her own, she relied chiefly on her physical beauty to express her individuality, a potentially dangerous and in any case ephemeral substitute.

With approaching age her world started to fall apart. The first major blow was the death of her husband of throat cancer on March 22, 1895. Deprived of her intermediary with the world, her beauty fading, she could only think of the future as a "pathless desert." In 1904 began the long, debilitating illness, quite possibly psychosomatic in origin, that crippled her. She retreated utterly from society, refusing to see old friends except now and then in dimmed light. In the winter, she stayed in her Paris house; summers she spent in a rented, eighteenth-century chateau in Ste. Honorine in the middle of a half-overgrown park by the seashore near Caen in Normandy. There she often sat for hours on the terrace, letting the wind from the sea blow through her hair. Her fragmentary writings are one long, self-pitying lament: "O horrible year, 1904, when a frightful, cunning disease, which crept slowly up, surprised me in the middle of life, and, like a leech sucking the blood from the heart, left a miserable cadaver in place of a beautiful, gay, sensitive woman. . . . Each year a new threat, a new advance of the pitiless disease. . . . And all must be endured silently, buried in an already overburdened heart, in order not to tire those who surround me, whose pity through such a long illness gradually wears thin."[13]

What Kessler calls the "long drawn out final chord (*langgehaltener*

Schlußakkord)" of his mother's life must have been indeed a burden for her children, as she herself foresaw. As her illness progressed, Kessler found himself spending more and more summers at her place in Ste. Honorine. In part, this was of course due to concern for the mother he loved "almost to the extinction of my own self"; in part, it was a useful excuse to flee Berlin, Weimar, Paris, or London when personal or public pressures became too unbearable. Particularly in the last years before the First World War, Normandy, its towns and seacoast, if not exactly Ste. Honorine, became a welcome refuge from the nerve-wracking business of seeing his ballet through production, as well as from the mounting international tensions, which Kessler, as a particularly well-placed and sensitive observer, felt keenly. Nevertheless, some of his letters to his sister suggest that, although often frantic over the state of his mother's health, he was not always eager to endure his mother's increasingly morbid company. He puts off plans to travel to Ste. Honorine or puts strict limitations on his stays there; sometimes he failed to contact his family in person when he came to Paris (and rarely stayed with them in their mansion there). In the end, it was his sister Wilma who, despite her own marriage and young children, spent the most time with their mother in her declining years, tending her as faithfully as she was later to tend her ailing brother.

There are enough hints in Kessler's letters, diaries, and even in the rather hagiographic portrait of his mother in his memoirs to indicate that his relation to her was not without rancor, jealousy, and even hate. This does not dispute his claim that his love for her was the deepest he felt for anyone in his life; rather, these "*Trübungen und Verstimmungen*" (gloomy moments and disagreements) were the shadow side of that love. His later love affairs, however passionate, seem imitative in comparison. Tragically, the First World War was to separate them for the last five and a half years of her life: just on the eve of their long-awaited reunion in Switzerland, on September 19, 1919, she died. Upon hearing the news, he wrote in his diary: "A great, but unhappy woman, gifted with beauty, passion, imagination and wit far above average but lacking worldly wisdom. . . . One of the queenly race of Englishwomen with their mixture of matter of factness, soaring passion and imagination and the irrationality of certain Shakespearian heroines. Her fate was tragic because she could never bring to fruition what was inside her, her personality consumed itself! I lose in her more than a mother: a background for my life that still exerts its power despite all distance."[14] Her death left a void in his emotional life that no one would fill.

CHAPTER 2

From Ascot to Hamburg

Where once a classical education was considered a joyful end in itself, which one pursued with leisure and a cheerful idealism, now the concepts of authority, duty, power, service and career had become all important, and "the categorical imperative of our philosopher Kant" was the banner which Director Wulicke unfurled threateningly in each speech.

Thomas Mann, *Buddenbrooks*

Harry Clément Ulrich Kessler was born in Paris at the corner of the rue de Luxembourg and the rue du Mont Thabor on May 23, 1868. A picture taken in a Parisian studio twelve years later reveals a haughty boy, with his right hand cocked on his hip, staring imperiously at us. This gaze of cool assessment is reflected in the very first pages of his great diary, which he began in 1880. Describing the crowd of holiday-goers in Ems in June, he mocks the colors of the dresses, clearly chosen in order to set "your teeth on edge." The dresses themselves are "most certainly copied from the asseryrian bas reliefs or from the cloaks found with the mummies in the pyramyds [*sic*]." Mannered and precious, the diary at the same time shows the adumbrations of the painterly eye that made Kessler a master depicter of crowd scenes and urban landscapes. There is something of the young Flaubert's diaries in these pages, in the snobbish elitism, the sharp sketching of certain evocative details, and the striking metaphors.[1]

The arrogant and sardonic pose hid the vulnerability of the young boy who grew up a rather lonely child without siblings or friends his own age (his sister was nine years younger). The haughtiness exemplified in the first pages of his diary may have been an exaggerated reaction to the unease the twelve-year-old felt exactly at that moment, for he stood before the first great turning point in his development. In the fall of 1880, he was to enter St. George's School in Ascot, England. What this meant to him emotionally, the first separation from his beloved mother, can be seen in the graphic description of his leave-taking in his memoirs. The two years spent in England at the time of the zenith of the British Empire proved a watershed in the development of his intellectual history, particularly his notions of politics and culture. Even the relatively short duration of his stay has its significance: Kessler was almost an Englishman—had he stayed longer, he may well have become one. This "almost," in its polarity of attraction and repulsion, explains much in Kessler's life.

His parents' decision to send him to school in England may have been due in part to his mother's wish to introduce him more thoroughly to her country and culture; nevertheless, the immediate antecedent was the misery of the French school he attended from 1878 to 1880. In the sheer meanness of the surroundings and the moral and intellectual abasement of teacher and pupil alike, Kessler's Parisian school was the urban counterpart of the preposterously bleak lycée Alain Fournier describes in his novel, *The Wanderer*. Constructed in a former cloister, it was filthy beyond imagination, without any facilities for sport or hygiene. The students wore gray linen smocks that gave them the appearance of "little old men with a touch of girlishness. Despite the gaiety and agility that usually characterizes little French boys, these youths, when they were playing or standing around in the courtyard, had nothing youthful about them; rather they resembled a collection of dwarf-like bureaucrats, especially as many wore medals on their smocks, distributed weekly for industriousness."[2] Each day Kessler had to defend himself, with kicks and bites, against a little "black devil" of a schoolboy; one day he even came home with lice. The daily contrast between the refinement of his family's home and the squalor of his school eventually proved too much for the sensitive boy. On advice from the family doctor, he was removed from school and the decision was made to send him to St. George's.[3]

• • •

Arising from a hill in the midst of a park-like setting, the original red brick Victorian cottages of St. George's, situated in Ascot near Windsor

Castle and Eton, still stand. Allegedly one of the most fashionable and expensive schools in England, St. George's was supposed to be, in the words of a former pupil, "the very last thing in schools. Only ten boys in a class; electric light (then a wonder); a swimming pond; spacious football and cricket grounds; two or three school treats, or 'expeditions' as they were called, every term; the masters all M.A.'s in gowns and mortar-boards; a chapel of its own; no hampers allowed; everything provided by the authorities." For Kessler, coming from the paving stones of his Parisian boarding school, St. George's was a verdant paradise: from the veranda, one could look out over the rolling countryside covered with moors and patches of forest. A part of the original hunting grounds of Windsor served as a refuge for rare flora and rabbits, lizards, and turtles. The boys could grow their own flowers and vegetables in the garden and swim in a pond fed by a waterfall. Sandwiched as it was between the comparatively gray worlds of a Parisian *école* and a Hamburg *gymnasium,* Kessler's experience at Ascot understandably appeared to him as a "happy garden-state." On his English schoolmates, more accustomed to the English countryside, the school, and particularly its headmaster, left a decidedly more ambiguous impression.[4]

Although for years now a girl's school, St. George's was founded in the 1870s by the Reverend H. W. Sneyd-Kynnersley as a preparatory school for Eton. Its function as a training ground for the young elite of Great Britain did not outlast by much his death of heart failure at thirty-eight, but during the relatively brief period of his tenure, a surprising number boys who would obtain prominence as adults passed through its doors. The most famous was Winston Churchill, who spent what were probably the most miserable two years of his young life there.[5] Punishment, whether by flogging with a birch rod or by jolts of electricity (!) or by the removal of privileges, seemed to have played an unusually prominent role in the headmaster's pedagogy, creating, as Maurice Baring put it, "an atmosphere of complete uncertainty. We never knew if some quite harmless action would not be construed into a mortal offence." The future art critic, Roger Fry, who befriended Kessler on his first day, later provided a damning portrait of Sneyd-Kynnersley, depicting the headmaster as a bigoted High Tory churchman with "a pair of floating red Dundreary whiskers which waved on each side of his flaccid cheeks like bat's wings," whose sole intellectual attainment "consisted almost entirely in having as an undergraduate at Cambridge belonged to a Dickens society which cultivated an extreme admiration for the great man." Fry's depiction of the ugly scenes of chastisement in the headmaster's study, which he, as one of the school's top students, was forced to attend, leaves little doubt as to Sneyd-Kynnersley's sadism.[6] In wooing the parents of prospective students, Sneyd-Kynnersley naturally made no mention of this aspect of his instruction, and the boys did not directly mention it in their letters home. Nevertheless, word of this dark side of St. George's eventually got out, and many parents withdrew their children. It may be that such behavior eventually led to the decline of the school and the relatively early death of the headmaster.

Kessler's own recollections of Sneyd-Kynnersley are much more generous. Although he recognizes the severity of the whippings, he asserts that it was not due to any personal sadism but was merely the application of an ancient English formula for turning barbarous young Englishmen into gentlemen. Instead, he chooses to remember how the headmaster took part in all of the games the boys played, how he read aloud to them from Dickens, how they learned Shakespeare by reading and miming the roles. It was at Ascot that Kessler learned how to read both Greek and Latin fluently, a skill upon which he prided himself and that he never lost. As commonly occurred in such an environment, a strong homoerotic bonding developed between the headmaster and his favorite students, who, like Kessler, were invited to afternoon tea at his home. Defending him from accusations of sadism, Kessler argues that Sneyd-Kynnersley was able to seize the imagination of his students, "upon which he played like an artist upon a keyboard. . . . For myself I must admit that, of all my educators, Mr. Kynnersley was the only one whose personality truly influenced me. Despite his methods of punishment, which he had inherited, he was . . . an adventurer in the field of the formation of young modern individuals, guided and driven by empathy for the souls of individual boys, which, in his case, as with many great educators since Plato, may well have been erotic in origin."[7]

The chief aim of the education imparted to the boys at St. George's was not, in Kessler's view, knowledge in itself, but the formation of character, the cultivation of "nobility, poise, and truthfulness," as allegedly embodied in the type of the English gentleman. Rooted in Plutarch's Romans and Castiglione's ideal of the courtier, modified by the English humanists and Puritanism, the gentleman—as an ideal type —had an independent existence, but still required all the cunning and ruthlessness of educators like Kynnersley to mold actual examples out of the raw material of youth. Once formed and turned out by these "factories of character," the gentleman became the most formidable resource of the greatest empire the world had ever known. Kessler never doubted that English gentlemen were trained to serve the class interests of those who ruled the British Empire, the nobility and wealthy bourgeoisie. He recognized that the ideal type was based on a double moral; indeed, hypocrisy, or cant, for Kessler, was almost the quintessential English vice. Nevertheless, Kessler greatly admired the gentlemanly ideal: when the educational system worked, it created splendid human specimens, "the best of the best, like the thoroughbreds raised and trained in English stud farms." Moral fortitude, not material wealth, was the secret of empire, and the real threat to Great Britain came not from the working classes, but from the rise of the lower middle class, philistine shopkeepers without perspective or character.[8]

In Germany (and in the United States), Kessler's manners and appearance struck friends and observers as those of an English gentleman: at Ascot, alas, he was, in the beginning, nothing better than a foreigner. Challenged on this account to a fistfight on his first day, he later became the victim of a band of schoolboys who conspired to persecute him by tripping him during rugby games and the like. Once, when someone he considered his friend joined in the fun, he took a bottle of chloroform from the school pharmacy and swallowed its contents. Recovering from this incident, Kessler eventually became friends with a small clique of talented students, but the experience may have soured him on the prospects of ever becoming a bona fide English gentleman. This clique— which included Roger Fry and Claud Schuster, later permanent secretary to the prime minister—eventually became the center of school life by the clever coup of founding a weekly newspaper, *St. George's Gazette,* for which Kessler, who had previously owned a small hand press in Paris, had sole responsibility for the layout and shared editorial duties. Printed on high quality, wood-free paper, *St. George's Gazette,* with its anomalous motto, "*Mit Gott allein,*" marked the beginning of Kessler's lifelong interest and involvement in fine printing and publishing.

• • •

In July of 1882, the *St. George's Gazette* announced that "Count H. Kessler" would be moving next semester to the *gymnasium* in Baden-Baden in order to prepare for the German diplomatic service. Actually, in accordance with the wishes of his father, who had always intended that his son complete his education in Germany, Kessler arrived in Hamburg in the middle of September to attend the famous Gelehrtenschule des Johanneums. Awakening on the first morning to see from his hotel window the twin lakes of the Alster glistening in the sun, covered with sailboats and steamers and surrounded by colorful gardens and trees, Kessler discovered that Hamburg was in no way the provincial, slightly comic town he had imagined, but a truly cosmopolitan city. Fond of ports in general, he fell in love with Hamburg at first glance: "I have only fallen in love in such a fashion with one other city, Berlin after the war, in its time of deepest need, as I saw it struggle for bread and light. I didn't suspect on this beautiful September morning, that a difficult struggle still lay ahead between this new love and my attachment to England."[9]

This attachment was put to the test almost immediately in the house of Pastor Blümer, where Kessler roomed during his Hamburg years. On his first morning in the Blümer house, Kessler received a lecture on his duties as a student and boarder that made him feel for the first time the generation gap so omnipresent in Imperial Germany. It was in the Blümer household that Kessler first encountered the curious and ultimately pernicious role that Bildung, or education, played in the life of the German middle class. Pastor Blümer accorded the same scorn to those who were *ungebildet* (uneducated) as Mr. Kynnersley felt for those who were not "gentlemen," but there the similarities ended. Unlike the British system of prep and public schools, which educated its students to be self-supporting pillars of the empire and where the welding of "the will to political and commercial power with antique Humanism and the cosmopolitan self assurance of the Renaissance man resulted in an alloy of uncommon strength, tenacity and smoothness," the ultimate aims of German Bildung were more general and fuzzy: "We only knew that the goal of our schooling was to become educated, and therefore our duty was to educate ourselves day and night with never-ceasing studiousness. What the content, not to mention the goal, of this so strenuously acquired Bildung, this veiled idol, was, however, remained unclear."[10]

Accustomed as he was to his grandmother's house in London, full of beautiful old furniture by Sheraton and Adams, covered in light, soft upholstery, Kessler considered the Blümer household a coffee-brown abomination. Besides good taste, other qualities neglected by Bildung included the refinement of the senses through sport (with the exception of gymnastics, considered largely a trivial pastime) and, most importantly, moral character. Kessler's analysis of this last deficiency in his memoirs reflects his mature judgment, but his concern with this aspect of the German national character dates back to his Hamburg years, when in his search for self identity, he continually fell back on comparisons between Germany and England. By contrast with the English "gentleman," where the form, as it were, so perfectly fit the function, "the educated German resembled an object that could serve a thousand different and opposing ends; he lacked the clear and pleasing shape of an object perfectly adapted to its end." The roots of the German educational system lay in the humanitarian idealism of Goethe, Herder, and Humboldt; yet the emerging materialism of the later nineteenth century had not successfully melded with the earlier idealism to create a fruitful synthesis. Rather, it had only undermined the original goals. Without a commonly accepted role model in the manner of the English gentleman, each member of the German educated elite was left to effect his own synthesis of tradition and modernity, idealism and materialism, to create his own personality: "Most failed; they remained with their contradictions a formless mass, over which the few who had succeeded in forging a personality, hovered without any connection." Thus, the outstanding representatives of German intellectual life in the nineteenth century, Schopenhauer and Nietzsche most prominently, felt nothing but contempt for the "formless mass" of the German *Bildungsbürgertum*.[11]

Another aspect of German education that inspired the young man to rebellion was the appalling pedantry, cruelty, and hypocrisy of many of his teachers. He cites two egregious examples: a young martinet, reserve officer, who barked commands at the students as if they were on the parade ground, wore his uniform on every possible occasion, continually exhorted the students to prepare themselves morally for a vaguely militaristic yet undefined form of "service" and yet was discovered by them frequenting a bordello. The second, a sadistic math instructor, hounded a student to suicide with his sarcasm. There was one exception, Julius Bintz, his teacher the last two years and the only educator besides Sneyd-Kynnersley who had any influence on Kessler. Severe, yet just, he called Kessler to order after his first day to warn him to make diligent use of his talent: "We aren't gentlemen here, but Germans, who must work because we are poor. You are socially privileged. Your parents are close to the Emperor. It is therefore all the more incumbent for you to maintain a good spirit. I will be more strict with you than with the others."[12]

Kessler's reaction to the "life-threatening experiment" of the sudden transplantation from St. George's to the Johanneum was to become "a revolting little snob and show-off, vain, pleasure-seeking and smug. I allowed myself to be feted as a Count among the petty-bourgeoisie, dressed fashionably and went to many dances." All together, his fifteenth and sixteenth years he considered as, outwardly, the least interesting of his life; undoubtedly, loneliness and the pangs of adolescence played a role in these years. His voracious reading in his private time provided him with a refuge from outside tensions. The comments on his reading found in his diaries during these years—enthusiastic, critical, comparative—confirm his claim to have read nearly all of the classic English, French, and Greek authors, laying the foundation for the exceptional erudition that so astounded André Gide and others. German literature remained for a while a closed book; Kessler could not remember ever hearing the names of Novalis, Brentano, Hölderlin, Stifter, Hebbel, Büchner, or Keller in the Blümer household. Introduced by a school friend to *Wilhelm Meister,* Kessler eventually discovered Goethe, and through him, the living world of German literature, a revelation that he credits with the ultimate victory of his German blood over his English education. Overwhelmed by Goethe and the German romantic poets, especially Hölderlin and Novalis, Kessler wrote that "every German word, in its beauty and intimacy, its sound and scent, became holy to me." To the influence of German literature was added that of German music. An Easter performance of Bach's *St. Matthew's Passion,* at the time of his greatest identity crisis, moved him to tears and helped convince him that he was, after all, German.[13]

· · ·

What art had begun, love would complete. At Ascot, Kessler had found companionship but no close friends. His German schoolmates, by contrast, seemed much more naive, open, and natural. He became especially good friends with a boy nicknamed Maat, who wanted to become a sea captain and whose dreamy wanderlust appealed greatly to Kessler. In the summer of 1883, they sailed together on Maat's little boat down toward the mouth of the Elbe on the North Sea and made plans, under the night sky still red from the volcanic dust of Krakatoa, to escape to England and ship out as sailors. "Something cosmic was intertwined with our friendship, the stars, the ebb and flood of the tides, the sea— and, like a sharp treble against this music of the spheres, the exultation of our young bodies."[14] It is difficult to assess the exact role that homoeroticism played in these friendships, particularly in Kessler's relation with Maat. The romantic pathos of their conversations, the invocations of eternal friendship and purity, the rituals of swimming naked together and of undertaking expeditions *zu zwein,* are rooted so deeply in the nineteenth-century Romantic tradition that it is hard to distinguish what is merely the conventional idiom of German adolescents and what represents sexual longing. There is no outside evidence, in the form of diary entries or letters, to confirm Kessler's homoerotic attachment to Maat. The nature of his subsequent attachments, however, suggests that, at least as far as Kessler was concerned, there was a strong homosexual component to this friendship, although probably these desires were sublimated and idealized, as the language of his memoirs indicates.

The problematic nature of Kessler's relation to women during his adolescence supports this assertion. In his memoirs, he describes a brief, melodramatic affair during a school vacation with a Parisian *grisette.* Kessler's description of this interlude, the only explicitly sexual experience allusion in his memoirs, reads as if it came straight from the pen of Maupassant, and it is impossible, in the absence of any corroborating evidence, to ascertain its verisimilitude or to what extent a literary imagination colored his recollection. The incident is more an opening chapter in his sentimental education, awakening the social conscience of the young nobleman, than a guide to his future relations with women. As a student at the university in Bonn, he mentions having an "adventure galante" with a woman, but feeling like the innocent Joseph confronted by Potiphar's wife. The same analogy occurs to him while onboard the ship *Normandie* on the first leg of his trip around the world: "Adding a little variety is a comedy in which I play the role of Joseph and an old, retired cocotte the role of Potiphar's wife."[15] The confrontation between Joseph and Potiphar's wife is, of course, the subject of the ballet-pantomime Kessler and Hugo von Hofmannsthal would write for Diaghilev and Nijinsky. As a literary trope, it served the same function for turn-of-the-century literature and art as the stories of Salomé and Judith and Holofernes: in the shape of Potiphar's wife, female sexuality is seen as something menacing and corrupt, threatening to overwhelm male youth, idealism, and chastity. The ease with which this metaphor occurs to Kessler suggests that the same anxiety bothered him.[16]

During a vacation at Norderney in the summer of 1888, a young man Kessler's age, Count Schweinitz, introduced himself and invited Kessler to join a group of his friends vacationing at the beach. Kessler quickly noticed that Schweinitz, blond and slender, seemed to have a special relationship with a handsome elderly man, Count Werthern-Beichlingen, the Prussian ambassador to Munich, "the very image of a Germanic warrior." Kessler was very surprised to discover that they were not, in fact, father and son. "They maintained a certain distance from the others and seemed to share a secret together. The puzzling way they interacted attracted me." Accompanying the pair to the beach to watch the particularly striking sunsets of that season, Kessler would listen as the two, carried away by the spectacle, went into ecstasies of wild nature poetry, "fantasying with each other as if playing two pianos. I was overcome with a desire to hurl myself into nature as into an abyss and lose myself." Despite differences of opinion between the two younger men, "something in our deeper instincts" led to an understanding. Kessler was admonished never to betray the romantic liaison between the two men as long as the old count lived, "for it could only work its mystical effect with the strictest discretion. I thought about Maat and our secret oaths. Romantic Germany! I myself was a member."[17] The liaison between Schweinitz and Werthern bears every mark of a homosexual relation in the manner of the Liebenberg Circle*—the arch-conservative Romanticism, the musical sensibility, the pantheism and mysticism, the language, and the role of secret covenants, all are characteristic. In this light, Kessler's final remark must be read as a coded confession.

Kessler's homosexuality influenced in many ways not only the critique of Wilhelmian culture he later elaborated in his diaries and published writings, but also his own position within that culture. His thoughts on morality and the state, on the culture of ancient Greece, and more generally, on the possibilities of cultural renewal, were all fed, albeit sometimes indirectly, by the spring of a sexuality that he struggled to repress and yet continually strove to justify. Moreover, Kessler's sexual ambivalence, which gave him the sense of being a secret outsider within the gates of Wilhelmian high society, may well have made him more receptive to avant-garde modernity than he otherwise might have been. It certainly echoed the ambivalence of his social position within the Wilhelmian elite: both insider and outsider, his situation was similar to that of many Jews in Imperial Germany—most notably Kessler's good friend, Walther Rathenau—but in Kessler's case, the boundary was much more disguised, fluid, and ambivalent.[18]

At the end of August 1888, Harry passed his *Arbitur* examination, and then, after a brief trip to Paris, Spain, and North Africa, he headed

---

*The Liebenberg Circle refers to a group of conservative aristocrats who sought to influence the young Kaiser Wilhelm II's foreign policy. Two of their principal leaders, Count Philipp zu Eulenberg and Count Kuno von Moltke, were homosexual.

for Bonn to attend the university. It had not been self-evident that he would go on to the university. A university education was not at this time a requirement for a banker's son who wanted to follow in his father's footsteps—a school of commerce or an apprenticeship would also suffice. It appears his parents had wanted him to take over his father's business. Adolf Kessler was having some financial difficulties in the later 1880s and early 1890s and it was felt that the only son should help his father in the crisis. Harry had to make the case for attending the university in a letter to his parents: "It permits me to be useful to Papa and us all in money matters and to earn my own fortune as well; on the other hand it does not preclude me becoming something in Germany later. For it is exceptionally difficult, if not impossible, to enter the Reichstag or play a role in public, without having studied. Certainly there are Reichstag delegates who come from the business world but they have little importance outside of economic questions. In order to achieve something in this direction, it is, as I said, absolutely necessary to have studied." Although they relented, compromising on a program of legal study, Alice Kessler continued to write positively hysterical letters the first year at the university to her son, warning him that "you are *never* going to be a rich man" and chastising him for foolishly abandoning "the brilliant future Papa's son could have had." [19] Upon the restoration of the Kessler finances, these outbursts subsided somewhat, and on November 3, 1888, Harry matriculated at the university.

CHAPTER 3

At the University

The need for art is a sign that men need an ideal but
momentarily find none in the real world.

Kessler, *Tagebuch*

At the time of Kessler's enrollment, Bonn was among the youngest of
the German universities. Founded in 1818, it quickly earned a reputation
as the "Prussian Oxford." [1] Kessler was there to study law in preparation
for the state examinations that were a prerequisite for a career in the foreign service. But, as was the case with many first-year university students
for whom final examinations were still three long years away, he did not
let his studies distract from his real intellectual interests, or from his social life for that matter. Indeed, it was in Bonn that he first was initiated
into the extraordinary social whirlpool—always at its most intense during the winter "season"—that would characterize his life for the next
forty-five years and would become like a narcotic that he both craved
and longed to be free of.

Shortly after his arrival in Bonn, he was invited to become a member
of "Borussia" Corps, or fraternity, perhaps the most aristocratic of the
corps at Bonn; the young emperor had been a member during his student days, as had his father and his son. The mere fact of an invitation
confirmed Kessler's relatively recent status as a count; non-noble members were a very rare exception. With their hurrah-patriotism, their excessive drinking and dueling, and their contempt for outsiders, these
student societies were more like training grounds for conformism than

"factories of character." Some liberal critics even held them responsible for a perceived *Verdummung,* or stultification, of German youth during these years.[2] It was, no doubt, this rather well deserved reputation that caused Kessler's father to forbid his son, as a condition for allowing him to attend university in Bonn, from joining the Borussia Corps. He became instead a "drinking brother," getting violently ill his first night at the pub. Despite the drinking, Kessler found much to admire among individual members. In general, they strove to inculcate a cosmopolitan manner and outlook in their members, many of whom were destined to high office in the army, administration, and foreign service. Among these, several were to play an important part in Kessler's life: Baron Gisbert von Romberg, as ambassador to Switzerland during the First World War, Kessler's immediate superior; Adolf von Maltzan, state secretary of the Foreign Office under Gustav Stresemann and one of the key figures of the Weimar Republic; Count Hans-Albrect Harrach, sculptor and brother-in-law of the future chancellor, Bethmann Hollweg; Karl von Mutzenbecher, later head of the Royal Theater in Wiesbaden; and, most importantly, Eberhard von Bodenhausen, the art critic, patron, and industrialist who was to become Kessler's "brother-in-arms" in the struggle over *Kunstpolitik* in the next three decades.

The way in which Kessler met Bodenhausen sheds some light on the manners and mores of the Borussia Corps. A fellow student, jealous of Kessler's social success, challenged him to a duel (ultimately, the duel was called off when the challenger broke his arm in a riding accident). It was at practice that he met Bodenhausen, there as a referee: "I noticed his cold, but almost ideal beauty. Tall, blond, with a slender, nimble, perfectly proportioned body, with facial features that were sooner English or Greek, than German, he seemed to be a Greek statue, come to life through some inward fire." Kessler noted his calm, grace, and tact, and the respect that the other members of the Borussia paid him. The exact contemporaries had more than the year of their birth in common: both had artistically inclined, English-speaking mothers (Bodenhausen's mother, from an established Philadelphia family, had left her husband and children to become a disciple of the theosophists in Holland), both studied law at Bonn and then Leipzig in preparation for careers in the foreign service, and both were keenly interested in the emerging art and literature of the fin de siècle. Grave, deliberate, and methodical, Bodenhausen possessed a passionate need and capacity for friendship, inwardly self-doubting, outwardly projecting steadfastness and reliability. He was, in the words of his best friend, Hugo von Hofmannsthal, a kind of Calvin returned as Rousseau, a deeply moral pagan. These qualities were in many respects a perfect foil for the mercurial, quick-witted Kessler, and yet the differences in temperament between them, despite many congruences in their intellectual points of view and their political and cultural agendas, ultimately prevented their friendship from reaching the level of intimacy that background, education, and sympathy would seem to have destined. In any case, their real partnership would not begin on the frozen dueling grounds or in the austere classical lecture halls of the university, but rather several years later in the smoky, disreputable tavern on the Neue Wilhelmstraße by the corner of Unter den Linden, dubbed by its habitués "The Black Piglet," the meeting place of the Berlin bohemia.[3]

It was common for German students to attend two or more universities in the course of their studies, and so Kessler, having spent "a happy and lucky year" at Bonn, transferred to the University of Leipzig in the fall of 1889, in order to be able to attend the lectures of the economist Lujo Brentano, the experimental psychologist Wilhelm Wundt, and the art historian Anton Springer. Leipzig was a large industrial city located on a flat, rather featureless plain. Dominated by academics and a prosperous but provincial bourgeoisie, social life here was less aristocratic and carefree than in the Rhineland. At first, Kessler found it difficult to make friends. Eventually, however, he joined another student corps, Canitz-Gesellschaft, an equally aristocratic if somewhat less polished and more hardworking version of the Bonn Borussians. Among the lifelong friendships he formed there were: Gustav (Musch) Richter, the grandson of the composer Giacomo Meyerbeer and the son of the extremely wealthy Cornelia Richter, who kept one of the foremost intellectual salons of Wilhelmian Berlin; Raoul Richter, her other son, who introduced Kessler to Nietzsche's work and became a prominent Nietzsche scholar; Alfred von Nostitz, the future ambassador of Saxony to Vienna and the husband of Kessler's good friend, Helene von Nostitz; and Gerhard von Mutius, a diplomat with philosophical interests. Eberhard von Bodenhausen had also moved to Leipzig to prepare for his state exams. In their company, Kessler would spend two intellectually stimulating years. It was, however, his professors at Leipzig, in general more alert to the modern world than their Bonn counterparts, who provided him with a number of concepts and preoccupations that would last him a lifetime.

In the seminar of Lujo Brentano, the famous *Kathedersozialist*, Kessler was assigned to do research on workers' insurance and factory conditions, an interest first stimulated by reading Macaulay's essays on the ten-hour day and by his private exploration of slums in both London and Hamburg. Brentano was a proponent of using trade unions as a way of ameliorating working conditions, moderating both social and political strife, and thus effecting a reconciliation between workers and the social order. For Brentano the older, nonideological English unions with their faith in arbitration rather than strikes were the perfect models for the fledgling German unions. He taught only briefly, from 1889–1891, at Leipzig, but his period of greatest public influence commenced precisely during Kessler's first semester when, in the spring of 1889, the new emperor took a momentary interest in the social question, intervening on behalf of striking Ruhr miners and drawing up a plan of labor reform to complement the social legislation passed by Bismarck.[4] Despite his interest in these matters, Kessler admitted in his memoirs that he never thought to read Karl Marx or Ferdinand Lassalle because they were considered in his bourgeois circle as beyond the pale. A letter to his sister before the war dismissed socialism as possible but hateful, while claiming anarchism to be a utopia: "Whether it really is a *dangerous* utopia though, except for the individuals it strikes by its bombs, I doubt. I take it, on the contrary, to be a healthy and perhaps necessary foment of our social and sentimental progress. Just as socialism has been and still is."[5]

Art, not politics, however, became Kessler's chief interest. At Leipzig, he attended the lectures of Anton Springer, the first full professor of art history in Germany, whose influence on Kessler's approach to art was deep and abiding.[6] Springer intended to practice art history in the same way that the great nineteenth-century German historians, preeminently Leopold von Ranke, practiced history: as a scientific discipline employing documents that could be subjected to the same rigorous critique of sources and yield the same "objective" results. Springer was also opposed to the increasing isolation of art history from the living arts and crafts of the present, arguing instead for the closest possible cooperation between art historians and art connoisseurs so that they could mutually educate and inform each other. Several of his pupils, notably Alfred Lichtwark in Hamburg and Gustav Pauli in Bremen, went on to become progressive museum directors, sensitive both to the importance of contemporary arts and crafts and to emerging art forms, such as photography.[7]

Kessler's visits with his mother as a young boy to the studios of the artists who frequented their home may have first stimulated his interest in the pictorial arts. Before entering the university, he was an ardent visitor to museums and cathedrals. Indeed, he was well prepared to receive Springer's ideas. Even before attending Springer's lectures, Kessler had demonstrated an aesthetic judgment remarkably free of the shibboleths of nineteenth-century doctrines on the "good and the beautiful," as well as an inclination to ponder the sources of our aesthetic judgments. In the summer of 1889, while admiring some Greek statuettes in the Louvre, he remarks how one has been trained to admire everything Greek and look at it as beautiful and graceful in proportion as it is Greek: "training and persuasion are almost everything in matters of taste and I know of no other way of accounting for the changes of fashion; the beauty of a thing lies much more in our imagination than in the thing itself." At the time, Kessler had just begun to read Immanuel Kant and his influence—so important for the German critical historians of art—is evident here; also the interest in the psychology of art perception. Springer had asserted that one's psychological response to a work of art, from the first perception of the harmonies of line and color to the emotions evoked by this perception, was also an incontestably objective fact, although, of course, variable from individual to individual. Under the influence of Kant and Springer, Kessler increasingly became interested in understanding the way we "read" artworks rather than in elucidating their "meaning."[8]

Kessler had an opportunity to test his ideas and the training he received from Springer during a trip to Italy after his first year at Leipzig. It was not his first visit to Italy, but the two months he spent there in the fall of 1890 were absolutely seminal in the development of his notions of art and history: the themes and metaphors he jotted down in his diaries on this journey reappear continually in the thought of the mature man.

In Florence, while admiring the delicate, dreamy, feminine beauty in the works of Donatello, Kessler first articulated one of the central themes that would preoccupy him for many years, the revolution in human consciousness brought about by St. Francis of Assisi. Like a spring, the Franciscan movement replenished the well of the Western imagination, bringing in its flood two new contributions to art: the ideal of feminine beauty and a fresh enthusiasm for nature. This revival and redirection of human passion was chiefly responsible for the Renaissance, not the rediscovery of Roman sculpture and the importation of Greek literature. For the admiration of strong, graceful bodies in itself would have led only back to the art of the Greek republics, "but the Reformation of the thirteenth century gave the current a new bent; the soul became more important than the body, the expression more important than the form, the face more important than the limbs, and this Reformation made the difference between the art of the fourteenth and fifteenth centuries and the art of ancient Greece."[9] Artistically, the Franciscan revolution represented an advance over antiquity in that God and nature were united by Christian love, an ecstatic and sentimental vision, unknown in earlier medieval art, that overflowed strictly religious boundaries to infiltrate all aspects of life.[10]

By downplaying the role that the imitation of classical models played in the "rebirth" of art during the Renaissance, Kessler saw that a blow had been struck at the very heart of the theory and praxis of art as taught in the art academies of nineteenth-century Europe. Students in the academies were commonly taught that the art of the classical world, particularly of Greece, represented an unsurpassed and unsurpassable cultural achievement, a perfect synthesis of material beauty and moral freedom, which later generations could only aspire to emulate. A very characteristic expression of this theory occurred in the speech of the self-appointed *precepteor Germaniae* in aesthetic matters, Wilhelm II, on the occasion of the dedication of the *Siegesallee,* a series of stiff and clumsy statutes celebrating his ancestors in Berlin's Tiergarten. Looking back on the remnants of Greek art, the emperor, an ardent archaeologist, declared that "here an eternal, ever constant law rules; the law of beauty and harmony, of aesthetics. This law has been expressed by the ancients in such a surprising and overwhelming fashion—in such a perfect form—that we, for all our modern sensibilities and mastery of technique, can be proud if someone should say, of a particularly good achievement, 'That is almost so good as it was done 1900 years ago!'" If, however, the real roots of the Renaissance lay in an upswelling of religious passion provoked by St. Francis that resulted in the evocation of a new kind of beauty, unknown in Greek art, then all of this slavish imitation in the art academies was missing the essential point; namely, that art is a matter of passion as well as of technique. The "naturalness" that Kessler admired in Giotto and others was "something different from our Naturalism or Realism; it did not aspire to depict exact details but rather the impression of an alert, but naive observer: one saw an event, a pose, a face, even the colors and play of the lines as with the eyes of a child for whom the world is still new and full of wonder."[11]

Upon his return from Italy, Kessler was more convinced than ever of the decadence of contemporary painting, especially the German painting of the nineteenth century. After visiting a museum back in Leipzig, he remarked that, "all the modern so-called Realists have managed to do is to make historical-genre pictures . . . out of the grandest, the most important, and the most pathetic events in the history of mankind." In an argument with a friend, who asserted that art should only depict "the beautiful," Kessler pointed out how notions of the beautiful had changed over the years and indeed must change. "Every time must find its own form, for no form is eternally and absolutely valid. Rather every form is only the best, and therefore classic, in so much as it is suitable to express the thoughts that must be expressed." [12]

• • •

Kessler came rather quickly to reject Springer's claim that art history could be a science, but it was decades before he escaped the influence of Wilhelm Wundt's theories on psychology. Photographs of Wundt depict him as a typical nineteenth-century scholar-scientist with a somewhat abstracted expression behind rimless spectacles. A stupendous life of scholarship lay hidden behind this mask.* The institute he founded at Leipzig in 1879 was the first permanent laboratory for experimental psychology in the world; during Wundt's career approximately twenty-four thousand students passed through its halls, many of them Americans destined to found the most influential schools of psychology in the United States. [13]

Wundt's basic premise was the Kantian notion that the only certain reality was experience, an experience filtered by the mind's sensory apparatus. Persuaded that all conscious thought arose ultimately from simple sensations and the feelings that accompanied them, he concluded that they were the irreducible elements, the building blocks of consciousness. Most influential for Kessler's own thinking was Wundt's argument that each sensation was accompanied—but not caused—by

---

* The facts are mind-boggling: from 1853 when he published his first article until a few weeks before his death in 1920, Wundt published close to five hundred books and articles, or nearly sixty thousand pages, on almost every scholarly subject, from neurology and psychology to art, ethnography, linguistics, and philosophy. That amounts to a rate of a word every two minutes, day and night, for sixty-seven years, a feat wonderful to the late twentieth-century reader simply as evidence of faith in the capacity of human reason to explain the world. Not all of his contemporaries felt the same way about this productivity. His fellow psychologist and sometime rival, William James, once remarked that Wundt's daunting oeuvre "could hardly have arisen in a country whose natives could be *bored*."

a specific, irreducible "feeling-tone." These feeling-tones were organized around three polar axes: pleasantness-unpleasantness, arousal-
moderation, and tension-release. Feeling-tones, like the notes of a piano, can be arranged according to different laws to create elementary
feelings, just as notes can be arranged by the principles of harmony and
rhythm to compose melodies. If this process is intensified, then these
feelings will swell, in a mounting crescendo, into emotions strong
enough to compel the human subject to act.

There is something undeniably reductive and implausible about this
reconstruction of the process of volition. Wundt himself was aware of
some of the lacunae in the model. But whatever doubts existed about
its scientific stature, Wundt's explanation offered Kessler a way to the-
orize about the psychological reception of art that avoided, as much as
possible, discussion of the "idea," "content," or "meaning," concentrating instead on the way in which an artwork's sensuous form evokes
an emotional response. Wundt's vocabulary also lent this approach an
aura of scientific authority, thus avoiding, in appearance at least, the obvious danger of falling into an unchecked subjectivism when discussing
art. Kessler's essay "Kunst und Religion" represents his most ambitious
attempt to elaborate an aesthetic based on these principles, yet he applied them to other phenomena as well, such as the origins of national
character. Here too, he thought he discerned an interesting and reveal-
ing connection between form and feeling, which he explores in his
essay on national character as well as in his travel book, *Notizen über
Mexiko*.

In his memoirs, Kessler collated the impact not only of Wundt and
Hippolyte Taine, the French positivist critic, but also of such creative
writers as Dostoevski, Strindberg, Ibsen, and Wilde, and saw the sum as
symptom, and to a lesser extent, cause, of the impending crisis in European culture, the full consequences of which his generation would be
the first to endure. Naturally, the effect is a bit orchestrated by hindsight; nevertheless, there is ample evidence in the young man's diaries
of an acute awareness of crisis, both in a general cultural sense and on
a more personal level. Often the two are conflated, such as when, in attending Sunday services aboard an English ship on the Red Sea on his
way back from India in 1892, Kessler reflected on the growing gap between sentiment and reason: "The great misfortune of our time is that
each of us is forced to sacrifice either his heart or his understanding; to
strangle his feelings, or to send his reason to the Devil. One feels this
when one hears again the old liturgy and the familiar hymns one re-

peated as a child each Sunday. And with what unspeakable bitterness one feels it!"[14] Kessler himself would never be able to fully sacrifice either heart or mind and would instead spend his life searching for some synthesis.

At another level, the crisis manifested itself in the growing sense among Kessler and his contemporaries that their age was an *Übergangszeit,* an age of transition. They knew they stood on the cusp of a new era, the outlines of which they sometimes thought they could dimly perceive. Or was it a hallucination? Again, the psychological effect was a vertiginous sense of exhilaration and doubt. No single question was more central, or vexing, to the intellectuals of Wilhelmian Germany than whether the new age that was clearly emerging would herald renewal or decline. It was easy to reject the morality sanctioned by church and state as outmoded, but what would replace it? How should one behave? Kessler blamed the unnerving effect of this crisis for the personal tragedy of a fellow student and friend who murdered his working-class girlfriend and then tried to commit suicide. At the trial, Kessler actually testified on the deleterious effects of his friend's reading of Dostoyevsky's *Crime and Punishment* on his mental stability. This was but one of a contemporary rash of murder trials where the question of the baleful influence of modern literature and philosophy on the young men, generally students accused of killing their lovers, became an issue. In the wake of these incidents, Kessler and his friends felt compelled to ask themselves whether this kind of literature, this "dangerous knowledge," did not in fact represent the moral danger denounced by conservatives and liberals alike. Caught between the interstices of two eras, they were prey to exaggerated vacillations of chiliastic hope and self-pitying melancholy. It was fertile ground for prophets. "A secret messianism developed in us. The desert which every Messian needs was in our hearts, and suddenly there appeared above it, like a meteor, Nietzsche."[15]

· · ·

If ever there was a person ready to read Nietzsche, it was Kessler in the fall of 1891. His response confirms Gide's remarks that Nietzsche's works fell on well-prepared ground. The parallels between Kessler's and Nietzsche's rejection of the predominant culture of historicism have already been noted. Kessler's interest in the culture and religion of ancient Greece, as well as the importance he increasingly ascribed to art, predisposed him to an understanding of Nietzsche's worldview. The emphasis on psychological insight that Kessler first encountered in Taine and Wundt prepared him well for Nietzsche's relentlessly psychological approach. Finally, something of the pathos of Nietzsche's rhetoric concerning the death of God and the need for a new faith and a new moral code struck a deep chord in Kessler, who had already begun to doubt his ability to conform entirely with the liberal, positivist, bourgeois ethos of his father's generation.

Still, Kessler did not become a Nietzschean overnight. Contrary to the hint dropped in his memoirs that he had read Nietzsche prior to the murder incident, Kessler did not in fact read him until shortly after the trial and before his trip around the world, when Raoul Richter loaned him a copy of *Human, All too Human,* at the end of November 1891. He understood immediately that Nietzsche's chief goal was to teach one to mistrust one's previous judgment, to leave no moral assumption unexamined. Nevertheless, although clearly fascinated by Nietzsche's unfamiliar but exhilarating style, Kessler resisted some of the philosopher's arguments. Nietzsche's polemic against both Christianity and Germany disturbed the admirer of St. Francis and Goethe; he noted quite perspicaciously that there was something nervous in the book, "something unfinished, parvenu-like, almost pigheaded, something as if the feeling did not quite get along with the reason: one could almost think that Nietzsche was struggling with himself." [16] A similar struggle took place in Kessler, and it would take the incubation period of his six-month trip around the world and his year of military service before he emerged the complete Nietzschean.

It is difficult to disentangle from Kessler's life and work a number of ideas directly traceable to Nietzsche and rate them according to a scale of influence, as one might do in the case of Springer, Taine, or Wundt. As with many of his contemporaries, Kessler did not simply acquire a certain quantum of ideas from Nietzsche. Rather, he adopted a whole attitude, a way of first approaching questions, even—oftentimes with unfortunate consequences—a certain rhetorical *furor teutonicus.* Nietzsche's impact on Kessler's generation was much closer to that of a poet like Byron than a philosopher like Kant or Hegel. Indeed, the most important impact Nietzsche had on Kessler was psychological. The sheer independence of Kessler's position—independence from career, family, faith, and even from nation and mother tongue—posed the danger of utter rootlessness, the cynical and demeaning existence of a wealthy, cosmopolitan hedonist. He was acutely aware of this danger:

on one of the anniversaries of his father's death, he noted ruefully his isolation: "My father, the tie that links me backwards with all of past mankind; and I wonder if I won't be the last of this chain, whether something will one day reproduce myself into the future. This old, trivial question becomes tragic when one begins to doubt its confirmation."[17] Nietzsche's argument that a life could be justified by its beauty, not by its usefulness, and his will to confirm the value of life, despite his own isolation, lack of faith, and sickness, served as an important moral reinforcement for Kessler in his own struggle to define a mission that would justify his life.

Aside from this psychological element, two other broad Nietzschean themes pervaded Kessler's thinking. The first was Nietzsche's idea of the superman, especially his investigation of the conditions necessary for the creation of an elite that would justify the misery and squalor of existence. Kessler recognized immediately that in Nietzsche's case, "not his philosophy, not even his poetic force, are the chief things, but rather the human being in his inclinations and disinclinations, in his strivings, and in his dreams, [as] the expression of a new species, the spiritually noble but nervous type in the struggle against the mounting democratization."[18] In Nietzsche's own words, the "coming philosophers" of the future will not offer a new philosophy or a new set of rules, but the chance above all "to *be* something new, to *signify* something new, to *represent* new values!" Kessler had been fascinated with strong characters since his school days at Ascot; for much of the rest of his life, he would be compelled to seek out "great personalities," certain that they held the key to the future, that they were, in fact, the future. In *Beyond Good and Evil,* the book that influenced Kessler the most, Nietzsche describes the supermen as "attempters," playing on the word temptation. Looking back in his memoirs, Kessler recognizes in a number of his future friends these attempters, who, at first isolated, were preparing to become the intellectual adventurers Nietzsche had prophesized: "And because they all were fighting the satiety and smug contentment of this materially and spiritually overweight time and depended mutually on the victory of untimely evaluations, they therefore felt themselves drawn fatefully and secretly together through the bonds of a mysticism of the future, that was still not always clear to themselves; comrades, ready to help each other even before they truly had met." Kessler promises to say a great deal more about these individuals, who "have not only codetermined the direction and content of my own life but exerted more influence on the development of Germany than the intellectual trends officially encouraged from above."[19] He would not, in fact, have the time to write about them, at least not in his memoirs, but it is clear whom he meant: men like Hugo von Hofmannsthal, Henry van de Velde, Walther Rathenau, Richard Dehmel, Gerhart Hauptmann, Aristide Maillol, and Gordon Craig.

Kessler notes the role that art played in the lives of these pathfinders, "not simply music as with the Romantics, but also and perhaps even more pictorial art—and especially the shaping of their daily surroundings, their personal articles, living rooms, and style of life. Perhaps arts and crafts attained among them, and the related circle around William Morris in England, for the first time part of the mystical aura that had always transfigured the *great* arts, architecture, sculpture and painting. While insurmountable obstacles still prevented them for the moment from the transformation of practical life, of the state and science, the accommodation to the new life-feeling ran up against the weakest resistance in art. In it therefore the deep transformation from the old to the new man first manifested itself, which later would shake everything else."[20] This was the second great legacy of Nietzsche: namely, the notion that the purpose of the coming elite would be to creatively shape first their own lives, then their surroundings, and only then the life of the community, the state, and civilization.

· · ·

Kessler claimed that it was Section 256 in *Beyond Good and Evil*—in which Nietzsche excoriates the "morbid estrangement which the lunacy of nationality has produced and continues to produce between the peoples of Europe" and declares that they are unmistakable signs that "Europe wants to become one"—that literally changed him from a boy to a man. The creation of this Europe, one in which each nation would have room to develop to its fullest capacity, but still remain part of a larger whole, gave the young man a philosophic justification to his chosen career as a diplomat. It also offered him a way to transcend the intense personal divided loyalties he felt among the German, English, and French elements of his character and upbringing. If Kessler did not in fact unconsciously backdate the meaning this passage had for him, then he at least chose to emphasize in his memoirs the part of Nietzsche that could justify his career as an internationalist. Other parts of *Beyond Good and Evil* are susceptible to less pacific interpretations, for example, the passage in which Nietzsche prophesizes, "The time for petty politics is past: the very next century will bring with it the struggle for mastery over the whole earth—the *compulsion* to grand politics."[21] "Compulsion to grand politics"—that would be an excellent subtitle for a history of Wilhelmian foreign policy. Kessler himself would not be free from this compulsion. For the young, budding diplomat, the greatest embodiment of the compulsion to grand politics was, of course, Bismarck. As fate would have it, just prior to his discovery of Nietzsche, Kessler would have an opportunity to examine at close hand the Iron Chancellor and determine what vision of the future this "great personality" had to offer the younger generation.

In the summer of 1891, Kessler was invited to give an address as the head of a delegation of students that planned to honor the retired chancellor in Kissingen. Because of his reservations over Bismarck's domestic policies, Kessler refused to serve as head of the delegation but went along anyway, curious to hear the great man's ideas on the future of the Reich he created. Three years had passed since his dismissal by Wilhelm II and already there was a growing feeling that the ship of state needed his firm guidance. The new emperor's increasingly evident instability and poor judgment helped refurbish Bismarck's reputation, which had suffered in his last years in office. Shortly before he traveled to Kissingen, Kessler had heard from a friend that officers in the army spoke about Wilhelm II in the same way that Socialists had three years before: "too much shifting, too much caprice, especially in petty things, too many incautious statements; the high personage himself doesn't seem to know what he wants, rumors concerning psychological disturbances, etc."[22] Kessler dismissed these at the time as the machinations of an aristocratic *fronde,* but these rumors would only increase with the years.

Kessler was clearly fascinated and impressed with Bismarck personally. Page after page of his diary is covered with a detailed protocol of the conversation he had, along with five other students, at an afternoon "coffee" at the Bismarck residence a day after the reception. It provides a very lively portrait of the old man, his squeaky voice—surprising in such a large man—the way tears would emerge from his bulging eyes, and his absolute mastery of language, honed by forty years of parliamentary experience. And yet, "the longer and apparently more freely the Prince spoke, the more a feeling of numb hopelessness grew stronger. . . . His conversation had something ghostlike, as if we had hauled him from the company of his dead contemporaries out of the grave. Up to foreign policy, the outlines of which are valid for centuries, all appeared in a light that was no longer of this world. To us, us youth, he evidently had nothing to say."[23] Bismarck's only political message appeared to be to hold tight, defend what he had achieved, and, above all, do not try to tamper with it.

In his memoirs, Kessler made the legend of Bismarck responsible for the political ineptitude of the bourgeois youth of his generation. Growing up in his shadow, marveling at his tactical skill, overawed by his extraordinary personality, they failed to notice that he was essentially a cynical nihilist, brilliant at exploiting political and diplomatic opportunities but without firm goals, values, or principles, other than a ruthless egotism. As soon as he was gone, no one else proved adroit enough to maintain the same delicate balancing act, largely because the Reich had been deliberately shaped so that only Bismarck could effectively govern it. The most damning legacy of Bismarck was, according to Kessler, that he deliberately rooted out anyone of character in politics who opposed him and thus contributed immeasurably toward creating the nation of obedient lackeys that Heinrich Mann lampooned in his novel, *Der Untertan*. The chancellor's tremendously seductive allure to young Germans was a dangerous trap—in fact, he was the worst possible schoolmaster for a young people without a long and established political tradition as a unified nation. The first sign of this pernicious influence lay in the general lack of character Kessler and his contemporaries believed to notice in their fathers' generation. "Daily reoccurring events showed us that, not only in politics but everywhere men of principle were less common among the generation that grew up under Bismarck than in the older generation that had developed in the 1840s and 1850s before Bismarck." Bismarck did not represent, as the nationalist historians, Heinrich von Treitschke and Heinrich von Sybel, had argued, the culmination and fulfillment of the ideals of the heroic age of German idealism, as exemplified by Schiller, Fichte, Goethe, Scharnhorst, Humboldt, Geneisenau, and Stein, but its betrayal. The fatal flaws in Bismarck's makeup, his inability to tolerate independent thought and behavior and his ferocious hatred for anyone who crossed him, eventually seeped out to poison the entire political structure that bore so thoroughly his imprint. While Kessler's identification of Bismarck as the responsible party for this malaise dates from a later period, ample remarks in his diaries vouch for his discontent with the lack of principle in politics and his ambiguity regarding Bismarck's legacy.[24] The hundreds of little Bismarcks that followed in the original's path—craven men, ruthless toward their subordinates and fawning toward their superiors— would plague Germany's public life, both political and cultural. Kessler himself would be among their victims.

CHAPTER 4

From New York to Potsdam

The degree and kind of a man's sexuality reaches up into the topmost summit of his spirit.

Nietzsche, *Beyond Good and Evil*

In the fall of 1891, Kessler finished his classes and began to prepare for the *Referendar* exam, a state legal examination that one had to pass in order to begin an unpaid apprenticeship in government service. At the same time, he studied for the oral examinations for his doctorate. In November, he passed the *Referendar* with the grade "good," and in December, he learned that his orals had been awarded magna cum laude. Before him loomed the year of military service expected of most university graduates. But before he would enter the barracks at Potsdam, he planned to undertake, in the best tradition of the young English lord, a grand tour around the world. On December 22, after taking his oath as a Prussian official, he departed for Paris to bid adieu to his family and then embarked, four days later, aboard the *Normandie* for New York.

His original plan had been to circumvent the world from East to West, starting in Egypt, then proceeding via India, Indochina, Japan, Australia, New Zealand, and then North America. He changed his plans when, through his father's business connections, he found a place for a few months as an unpaid assistant in a New York law firm. From this vantage point, he hoped to gain insights into the economic and political life of the United States, already the most important industrial power of the world, that would be invaluable for his future diplomatic career.

47

The splendors and sorrows of democracy could be better studied there than in the Old World, where democratic institutions cohabited with aristocratic values and traditions in an uneasy amalgam. The United States posed an interesting challenge to the young aristocrat who had just begun to read Nietzsche.

After nine days at sea, Kessler arrived in New York harbor on the evening of January 4, 1892, and met his father at the dock. Despite his censure of many individual details, Kessler was impressed with the great energy underlying the whole tableau; the sight from the Brooklyn bridge causes him to exclaim over, "the feeling of unlimited wealth, of the daring force of youth, of the grandiose creation of an entire people of millions, and in everything the feeling of the immeasurable life-force that is evident here . . . the sensation of an almost solemn *aesthetic* beauty." [1] In the two months that Kessler spent in New York, he managed to observe at close hand the pinnacle of American society and politics. His entrance into high society during the height of the winter season was, of course, greatly facilitated by his title, looks, and urbane manners. Ward MacAllister, the social kingpin whom Kessler compared to Honore de Balzac's Rastignac, introduced him to the doyenne of American society by whispering, "Mrs. Astor, he is a good dancer and a Count!" This was the Gilded Age, after all, and Kessler witnessed with amusement and some dismay the machinations of the nouveaux riches to attain social status, the conflicts between these parvenus and the established New York knickerbocker society. His natural inclination was to favor the latter in whom he recognized some of the qualities he admired in certain parts of the European aristocracy: reserve, good taste, principles, and character. It was not so much the pretensions of the newly rich, or even their extravagant bad taste, that upset Kessler, but rather how, despite their professed disdain for politics, their vast amounts of money exerted a corrupting influence in politics as well as in society.

He noted that, despite all the evident aping of European taste and customs, the emerging American elite possessed several fundamental characteristics that distinguished it from its Old World counterparts. The first was the position of women. Invited to the greatest event of the season, the New Year's Ball, Kessler remarked that it was not so different from a similar event in Europe, "only that the girls were almost exclusively beautiful, slender apparitions with blond hair, splendid skin, and often dark, glowing eyes. The tone is much freer than in Europe; the girls lead the conversation alternatively instead of, as in Europe, leaving this to their partner, which gives the entire conversation something comradely." In his occasional eugenic musings over the possibilities of improving the physical beauty of a race, Kessler would often mention the example of young American women as worthy of emulation: "One thought, when one saw them ride or dance, of nymphs or Amazons, uncomplicated, but beautiful, healthy to the core, and, in conversation, comfortable, straight, clean, and clever."[2] Later, he would admire the same qualities in the American pioneers of modern dance, Isadora Duncan and, especially, Ruth St. Denis. Second, American men, both young and old, differed from their European peers, suffering considerably in comparison in Kessler's estimation. On the whole, he found them both rawer and more superficial than their European peers. To a surprising extent, they abdicated their power in society to women, interrupting their business affairs only long enough to indulge in more or less crude forms of relaxation.

A third quality distinguishing Americans, even the wealthiest and most aristocratic, from Europeans was their fundamentally democratic sentiments. Kessler in this respect confirmed Alexis de Tocqueville's observation, made sixty years earlier, that the moral and intellectual distance between the poorest frontiersman and the richest tycoon was not nearly so great as that between the European nobility and the peasantry. Even the established families of Philadelphia and Boston for the most part never questioned the belief in democracy. When, in Washington, Kessler mentioned to Vice President Levi P. Morton his concern over the role that money seemed to be playing in undermining the equal rights proclaimed in the Constitution, Morton promised to set him right. The next day he brought Kessler to the White House to observe the common people meeting President Benjamin Harrison. After watching the unprepossessing Harrison come in and shake everyone's hand, Kessler admitted to Morton that the German emperor would not have deigned to perform a similar role, and he noted in his diary, "One feels here, what, in the demagogic sense, it means to be first server of one's people." Such displays did not convince him, however, that the political power of the moneyed classes, as expressed in the powerful lobbies and in the rule of political machines in the great cities, did not present a formidable, potentially fatal, challenge to American democracy. Like another liberal-minded German visitor to America, Max Weber, Kessler judged American politics with two influential examples in mind: one historical, the disintegration through corruption of the Roman Republic, and one contemporary, the relatively efficient and honest German civil administration. Viewed this way, the practice of turn-of-the-century

American politics—if not the theory, which remained seductive—contained much that was deplorable and worrisome.[3] Kessler resembled Weber as well in his almost sociological survey of cities and institutions along the East Coast. Having traveled up and down the eastern seaboard, from Washington to Boston, taking the time to visit steel factories and note the wages and living conditions of the workers, and having journeyed deep into his father's snowbound lands in Quebec, Kessler was ready to undertake the next stage of his voyage. He and his father boarded a train for Florida in March 1892; from there, they would travel to New Orleans and Texas, where his father was to leave him, and then California.

After a fifty-hour trip across the Southwest, he finally arrived in California, and after a short stay in Los Angeles, he left for San Francisco. Apart from its incomparable physical location, San Francisco first appeared to Kessler as a smaller, more provincial New York. But, as his departure for Japan was delayed, he had the opportunity to explore it a little more closely. What struck him most was that here, unlike in New Orleans and San Antonio, two equal cultures, the oriental and occidental, confronted each other. Accompanied by a detective, he toured Chinatown one evening, noting the half-naked prostitutes in the windows of the bordellos in Dupont Street. Again, the matter-of-fact, wholly unromantic approach to sex struck him as proper for an older, not necessarily inferior civilization. The next day, his last in the United States, he went to visit Stanford University in Palo Alto. It had just opened its doors the previous September: "The buildings stand in the middle of a wide park, at the foot of the forested hills that rise soft and dark in the southern sky. The native old-fashioned Spanish mission style has been transformed in the main building. This is the Quadrangle, an enormous, open colonnaded court which surrounds a garden full of palms and aloes; wide projecting red tile roofs rest on low walkways and the golden yellow sandstone of the columns and massive, square tower gates, rise wonderfully soft against the blue sky. It is the most beautiful and original architectural monument I have seen in the United States, with a romantic and archaic shimmer that does not, however, result all too obviously from the intention to be romantic and archaic." He foresaw a great future for American architecture if the architects of the South and Southwest would only stick to their native models. Wandering through the campus, he was impressed by the tanned strong figures of the men playing baseball and tennis, and by their camaraderie with the female students, who had nothing of the bluestocking about them.

The next morning, Kessler's ship steamed through the Golden Gate and passed a lonely lighthouse on the Fallarone Islands around noon; he would not see land again for another eighteen days.

After the long voyage across the Pacific, during which he read Nietzsche's *Thus Spake Zarathustra* and refreshed his knowledge of *The Odyssey,* Kessler arrived in Yokohama on April 13, in time for the cherry blossom festival. What most attracted Kessler's attention in Japan was the role of nature and art in Japanese society. Here, to a much greater degree even than in Italy, he thought he discerned the realization of an aesthetic state, one in which a uniquely suggestive art pervaded all spheres of life, or at least all that had not already become corrupted by European influence. Upon visiting a temple, he remarked upon the very careful integration of the landscape into Japanese architecture; whereas in the West, a beautiful setting for a church was mostly a matter of coincidence: "In this connection between art and landscape lies perhaps a fruitful thought for our stagnate European architecture; enough themes and inspirations may be found in the villas and designs for villas of the Cinquecento, but the important thing would be to learn to consider landscape and architecture together as one whole; in this the Japanese surpass us immeasurably."[4] Later, in planning the Nietzsche monument, Kessler would draw upon this insight to argue for the closest integration of landscape and monument.

Departing Japan on May 9, Kessler briefly visited Shanghai, where he sampled opium, Hong Kong, Saigon, and Singapore before embarking on a miserable voyage through the Malaysian straits and then up to India. Aboard ship he read Mark Twain's *Innocents Abroad* and Schopenhauer's *The World as Will and Idea.* Arriving in Calcutta on June 12, he depicted India as a vast, incomprehensible, and colorful tableau, the secrets of which defy European reason. He was amazed at the multitude of human types in India, where no two are alike, and contrasted this with the West and its ever greater trend toward uniformity, as if humans could be cultivated like fruit trees. Still, he found the sculpture grotesque, the music uncomfortably strange, the temples—with the notable exception of the Taj Mahal—soulless, and the dancing of the girls utterly without fantasy. In the end, the lesson India seemed to offer Kessler concerned the moral roots of empire: how, through the superior will, unity, and morale of its people, a small island nation like Britain could dominate an entire, teeming subcontinent. Intellectual without moral dominance is like a Christmas tree with beautiful bulbs but no roots or sap.

Kessler then traveled to Egypt, before returning eventually to Italy and then continuing on to Plombières to meet his family at the end of July. By August 1892, he was back in Leipzig and then, at the end of September, he reported to his regiment to serve his year of military service.

• • •

"Every social class today, every household, has a certain idol. In general, however, one can say that in Prussia there are only 6 idols, and the chief idol, the great god of the Prussian cult, is the lieutenant, the reserve officer." So wrote the novelist Theodor Fontane to a friend in 1893, confirming an increasingly evident aspect of Wilhelmian Germany: namely, that there was no more coveted position for an educated member of the bourgeoisie than that of reserve officer in the Prussian army. Not the doctorate, not even the title of privy councilor, could compete in prestige and in social leverage with that of Prussian lieutenant. By the end of the nineteenth century the reserve officer had become one of the principal tools of socialization in the army's struggle to preserve its privileges as a "state within the state" in Germany and to stem the tide of democratization. Indeed, increasingly in the course of Wilhelmian Germany, any sign of deviation from strict, conservative orthodoxy—writing for a liberal newspaper, say, or even eating outside of the officer's club—was frowned upon and resulted in either one's dismissal or the frustration of one's advancement. Kessler, as a count, even if coming from a recently ennobled family, was able to join one of the most prestigious regiments in the Prussian army, the Third Guard-Lancers. As a cavalry regiment based in Potsdam, the Third-Guard Lancers had enough social cachet to insist that all of its officers come from the nobility. Kessler, in fact, was the only one-year volunteer in his class and thus came into close contact from the very beginning with the regular officer corps.[5]

In looking back at this year, Kessler considered that he had been fortunate to learn about military life from the most favorable side. The notorious Prussian *Kommissgeist* then prevalent in much of the army, where the officers attempted to break the spirit of their men through rigid discipline and much shouting, was frowned upon in his regiment; rather, the officers strove to maintain the best possible relations with their men. In this respect, as well as in the lively interest in intellectual life, as manifested by various reading groups, Kessler thought to discern the virtues of the old Prussian army of the Napoleonic period. What he could not mention about this year, however, was how his recollections were indelibly stamped by the memory of his first great love affair.

In 1892, Otto von Dungern was a nineteen-year-old cadet officer from a noble Bavarian family. Slender, blond, handsome, and *bête comme un héros de Corneille*, Dungern was also a first-rate horseman, who won many races for the regiment. Entering the army about six months after Kessler, he became Kessler's roommate and during the fall 1893 maneuvers, they took morning horseback rides together, swam in streams and lakes, and bivouacked or boarded across the sandy plains and pine forests of Brandenburg. Besides admiring the young man's looks and his horsemanship, Kessler approved of his idealism or, as Kessler would put it later, the way his will exceeded his strength. The older, university-educated Kessler, filled with the ideas and experiences gleaned from his reading and his travel, no doubt saw the blissfully ignorant but idealistic Dungern as a young Alcibiades waiting to be educated.

It was, however, a relation that depended very much on its background, the initiation into military life, for its homoerotic overtones; outside of that background it could not survive. Years later, in 1907 when the Moltke-Eulenberg scandal had focused public attention on the issue of homosexuality, Kessler would argue that behavior that seemed overtly homosexual to the outsider may well only be the innocent conventions of an insider group. As an example, he recalled the way officers and young cadets danced together or tossed flowers to each other, or how handsome cadets were made drunk and then ordered to strip. All of this was merely "empty phrases" Kessler asserts, but to a generation more open to the discussion of homosexuality, it would appear evident that this kind of behavior is at least homoerotic in form even if, as with other forms of male bonding such as English public schools, it only represents a passing phase for many men, who later go on to marry and lead heterosexual lives.[6]

Such was indeed Dungern's case. Shortly after Kessler completed his year of service, Dungern wrote to him of his flirtations with women, letters that must have been galling for Kessler to read at the time. In October 1896, Dungern married, and if his extramarital activity would in fact compel him to interrupt a promising career as an aide to the crown prince, there is nothing to indicate that, after his military service, he was anything but heterosexual. Kessler remained friends with him for several decades: it was Dungern to whom Kessler turned when he needed someone presentable as a second to challenge his archenemy at Weimar to a duel. Kessler used his connections to secure unlikely venues for

Dungern's articles on hunting, one of his passions. At the time of the mobilization in 1914, the two exchanged enthusiastic telegrams and they even met during the war in Berlin, but by then their paths had begun to diverge too sharply to permit their—in any case—formal friendship to survive. Dungern's idealism was, unfortunately, of the narrow-minded kind that led him straight to the ultra-right chauvinism of the Weimar period; eventually he became a low-level functionary of the Nazis in the Berlin area. By that time, he had every reason to forget his youthful friendship with the exiled "red count."[7]

Kessler would suffer greatly in the three years between his taking leave of the army and Dungern's marriage. As always, when he recorded his feelings in his diary, he moved quickly from the personal mood to the general insight. For example, having compared his love for Dungern to his love for his mother, he notes bitterly how little he does consciously day by day for either and reflects that "it is the difference between the content of conscious thought, the hasty, loud, crashing of the waves of the surface that force themselves upon the perception, and the still, dark abysses which, threaded by powerful, never-changing currents, elude consciousness; it is this contradiction which brings the disharmony, the feeling of discontent, the *Weltschmerz* in our souls." The next day, Kessler notes how carefully the loved one must move in order not to destroy the image that one has of him. There was little Kessler could do about his feelings for Dungern in any event, and when the latter announced his engagement, Kessler decided to put the best face on it: "the way in which he conceived marriage has brought him *even* closer to me, if that was even possible. He is truly the most unaffectedly and unconsciously noblest and purest nature that I know." The following day, he mused further, "In this new intimacy, created by his sharing the secret of his love, he grows ever deeper in my heart; it is as if a second, new feeling for him overcomes me. Nothing of the raging, burning jealousy which overcame me before when he was friendlier to other acquaintances than to me, but a deep, holy happiness in his happiness." Nevertheless, as the marriage loomed closer, Kessler notices "a certain *serrement de coeur*. In the end marriage does effect a deep breach in friendship and it is painful to give up habits of the mind and heart that for almost four years have been the one constant factor in all matters of the soul. . . . There ensues for friendship a kind of death, from which it is doubtful whether a resurrection will follow."[8] The day after attending his friend's wedding ceremony, Kessler departed hastily on a long trip to the United States and Mexico.

Kessler overcame gradually his passion for Dungern. In later years, he would note how the man he had known was so swallowed up by wife and children as to be practically unrecognizable. The episode nevertheless marked him deeply. Fully aware now of the emotional and sexual frustrations that he would face, Kessler began to foresee that he would lead, at its deepest core, an isolated and lonely existence, a realization that expressed itself in his fancy of writing a play called *Der Einsame,* or *The Loner.* From this point probably dates that ultimate reserve that even a close friend like Henry van de Velde felt he could not breach after forty years of friendship. There would be other, more satisfying liaisons, but nothing that could permanently assuage his solitude. It was with the experience and knowledge of this that Kessler always looked back upon his year of military service. Upon revisiting St. George's in 1902, he noted, "Ascot, and Potsdam in the summers of 1893 and 1894 are the two most happy remembrances of my life. Everything else, even Bonn and Leipzig, by contrast, mean nothing to me. And nevertheless it was precisely in Ascot and Potsdam that I experienced my stormiest and most intimate sorrows. But I would give up all the undisturbed and even holy moments of my life, to grope through, just once more, these sorrows and joys. And I hope that it is these images that appear before me in my last hour."[9]

In the fall of 1893, Kessler's year of military service was over. Of average height, he was slender and well proportioned. Van de Velde noticed Kessler's sharp, bright, yet not hard, eyes and the way sometimes an authoritarian streak would come over the handsome face. Clean shaven in later years, he sported in his youth an elegant moustache, as may be seen in Edvard Munch's famous portrait of Kessler as a dandy, complete with canary yellow, broad-brimmed hat and cane. He attached great importance to dressing well, considering his friend Richard Dehmel's predilection for gaudy ties to be something of a moral failing. He was famous for his impeccable manners and for his elegant bearing, "half diplomat, half Prussian officer" in the words of Nicholas Nabokov. John Rothenstein recalled that Kessler's "correctness of deportment—more correct and less relaxed than that of an Englishman of similar origins (he was apt to raise his head in an abrupt gesture of disapproval at the slightest breach of taste)—masked a passionate nature and deep convictions."[10] The surviving photographs show him as a somewhat reserved figure; there always appears to be some distance between him and others even when he is bending toward someone solicitously as if to respond to a query. His was not, however, a completely phlegmatic temperament: when excited, whether by a work of art or by a conversation, he could become animated in a way that others found either exciting or, in some cases, profoundly irritating. Van de Velde, searching for literary comparisons, came up with Des Esseintes in Joris-Karl Huysman's *Against the Grain* or Oscar Wilde's Dorian Gray.

His formal education over, Kessler prepared to move to Berlin and start his unpaid apprenticeship as a legal assistant in the court at Spandau. From there, he expected in a few years to be admitted to the diplomatic corps, a career for which he felt suited in every way. As it turned out, the few years would stretch into nearly a decade, during which his official career would be in limbo. Yet during these years of waiting, he was hardly idle. It was a time of great ferment, especially in the arts, and Kessler would plunge directly into the thick of the action, not just in Berlin but in Paris and London as well.

PART TWO

Apprenticeship

CHAPTER 5

Berlin in the 1890s

In the end what came out of it? What did *Pan* achieve? It revived the craft of bookmaking, of decoration, etc. Oh, if one of us had said back then that we would revive the craft of bookmaking—Dehmel would have hit him with a bottle of Burgundy.

Julius Meier-Graefe, "Der Pan"

By 1893, Berlin was already, by nearly every standard, the predominant city in the Reich. Its population more than quadrupled in the second half of the nineteenth century; by 1900, it had considerably more than twice the number of inhabitants as Hamburg, the next largest city.[1] Yet, despite its overwhelming political, economic, and intellectual presence, it still had not achieved the same cultural position in Germany that Paris and London had enjoyed for centuries in France and England, as a school for politics and manners and as a magnet for young, ambitious talent. The legacy of Germany's centuries of political fragmentation weighed heavily even after the founding of the Reich: cities with proud pasts as independent city-states or commercial centers such as Hamburg, Frankfurt am Main, and Cologne could not be relegated so easily to the status of provincial centers of mere regional importance. Indeed, much smaller towns had shaped German culture to a degree unimaginable in France, England, Spain, or Russia. Just as the capital had finally achieved something like a style of its own in the first decades of the nineteenth century—embodied by the elegant, austere, albeit cold, neoclassicism of the architect Karl Friedrich Schinkel and the sculptor

Johann Gottfried Schadow—its contours were overwhelmed by the rapid, virtually uncontrolled growth stimulated by industrialization and urbanization. In 1901, the journalist Maximilian Harden, commenting on Madame de Stael's disparaging description, a hundred years previously, of Berlin as a city without a deeply impressed character, argued that such a judgment still applied in his day: "Berlin in 1901 still has no physiognomy. Nowhere the impression of quiet organic growth, hardly a corner in which the history of the city is evident." In Walther Rathenau's famous jibe, "Athens on the Spree" had become "Chicago on the Spree."[2]

Into this booming, nervous, boastful, insecure *Parvenupolis* the young Kessler moved in the fall of 1893. As early as his military service, he had found the time to travel from Potsdam and take part in Berlin's social and cultural life, attending performances of August Strindberg's *The Creditors* and Gerhart Hauptmann's *The Weavers,* visiting exhibitions of the paintings of Arnold Böcklin and Max Klinger, and frequenting the salon of Cornelia Richter. His duties as a law clerk in the court at Spandau did not prevent him from immediately entering the maelstrom of social life. The very scarce comments on his work in the diary indicate that, like many young *Referendars* and *Assessors* hoping to start careers in the civil or foreign service, he found his legal apprenticeship dull and sought to escape as much as possible its tedium. On the occasion of his first legal session, for example, Kessler noted in his diary, "A mistaken vocation. . . . The moment when striving stops, when one is (surrounded) by fluttering prospects of the future repugnant to his being, one is lost to the devil."[3]

One refuge was the salons of Berlin society. As much as the official rhythms of high society were determined by a formal calendar—the dates of the subscription balls and the arrival and departure of the kaiser, for example—the real social life of the capital took place in the salons, where young and old, men and women, bourgeois and aristocrat, artists and statesmen could meet and speak freely with each other, constrained only by respect for the hostess and by an etiquette of mutual tolerance. Although originally inspired by the great French models of the eighteenth century, the Berlin salons had, by the end of the nineteenth century, established their own more intimate brand of sociability. Wilhelmian Germany witnessed the last flourishing of the salon: in its classic form, it did not survive the social upheaval following the war and the competition with new forms and places of entertainment, the cinema, nightclub, and café. But in their heyday, the salons offered the quickest and surest route for a young, ambitious man, whether a budding artist or diplomat, to become known, to make connections, and to polish his manners. The best of them served as a kind of clearinghouse for new intellectual trends, diplomatic and political information, and artistic developments.[4]

The most important literary and artistic salon in Berlin around the turn of the century was that of Cornelia Richter, the very wealthy youngest daughter of the composer Giacomo Meyerbeer. As a young girl, she had experienced the late-Romantic salon of her grandmother, Amalie Beer. After withdrawing from society for a few years following the early death of her husband, Richter began holding a salon again in her home in the Bellevuestraße starting around 1890. Two different generations gave her salon its distinct tone. The older generation cultivated a rather pallid, self-consciously aristocratic, late-Romantic aesthetic sensibility.[5] Cornelia Richter's four sons, especially Raoul and Gustav, were responsible for bringing Kessler and other members of the younger generation into her salon. They shared an elitist aestheticism with the older generation as well as a love for music, especially Richard Wagner, whose widow often visited the salon when in Berlin. They too admired Goethe but were also enthusiasts of Nietzsche, whose sister Elisabeth Förster-Nietzsche, as a friend of Raoul's, was often a guest. Hugo von Hofmannsthal admired the Richter salon and wrote a remembrance of Raoul on the occasion of his early death. Other guests included the eccentric Baltic philosopher and aristocrat Count Hermann Keyserling, whose path would intersect with Kessler's from time to time over the next forty-five years, and Walther Rathenau. Kessler brought the salon a measure of public notice when he arranged in February 1900 for three lectures by Henry van de Velde, in front of a bemused and rather skeptical audience, on the rebirth of arts and crafts.[6]

With his good looks and his cosmopolitan air, Kessler quickly became *salonsfähig* everywhere in Berlin, including the court events that he describes in detail in his diaries. The spectacle of society fascinated Kessler in much the same way it did Marcel Proust. Like Proust, Kessler had the ability to view social events as a detached observer whose sensitive eye could make fine distinctions in gestures and costumes and whose imagination could provide the smallest nuance with an abstract meaning: "A handshake can decide the fate of thousands. All these people are simply symbols, algebraic signs for forces, the application of which, in one sense or the other, the tone of an expression can determine. This symbolism of every individual for a world of connections and powers determined by fate distinguishes the crowd in a ballroom from a mob of people much more than do the white necks of the women or the fine hands and shining frontshirts of the men."[7]

Nevertheless, Kessler admitted to often being bored with society. Fortunately, Berlin in these years offered more exciting spectacles than royal receptions in the White Room of the imperial palace. Everywhere there were signs that a new art and literature—more youthful, more contemporary, in short, more modern—was breaking through the crust of the tired conventions and genteel historicism that had dominated the *Gründerjahre*. The signs of this ferment were particularly strong in the theater. Organized in 1889 to perform for a subscription audience, the *Freie Bühne Verein* produced plays that could not be performed in the official or commercial theaters of Berlin. Its premieres of Ibsen's *Ghosts* and Gerhart Hauptmann's *Before Daybreak* in the same year provoked much controversy and were seminal events both in the history of German theater and in the rise and brief triumph of German naturalism. In a deliberate attempt to shock their audiences into a confrontation with the contemporary world, the naturalists introduced into their own literary works previously taboo subjects, such as sex, alcoholism, unemployment, hunger, the misery of the working class, and the hypocrisy of the bourgeoisie. The mere depiction of such ugly facts of life in modern life was enough to brand the naturalists as revolutionaries: their open debt to foreign influences, such as Emil Zola and Ibsen, and their sympathy with the working class compounded their sins in the eyes of those in the educated middle classes who felt such inclinations were "un-German." The fierce resistance to naturalism foreshadowed the virulent opposition to aesthetic modernism that would later develop in Wilhelmian Germany.[8]

Naturalism, although it celebrated its greatest "succès de scandale" in 1893 with the public performance of Hauptmann's *The Weavers* at Deutsches Theater, Berlin's most prominent theater, an event Kessler attended, nevertheless stood before a steep and precipitous decline. It was replaced by a variety of aesthetic modernisms, the most important of which was Jugendstil, the German variant of the international movement in arts and crafts most commonly referred to as art nouveau. However the movement is labeled, its example and doctrines were of immense importance for Kessler's ideas on art and culture. Even when they claimed to have transcended it, the members of Kessler's generation—including his closest friends and associates such as Maillol, Craig, and van de Velde—all were stamped by art nouveau.[9]

Three basic qualities characterize most of art nouveau. First, it abandons the illusion of depth created by three-dimensional perspective and so fondly cherished by academic artists as the acme of Western art. Even in artists who retain some degree of three-dimensionality, the difference between the foreground and the background is reduced to a minimum. Second, art nouveau artists increasingly favored the expressly ornamental instead of the realistic representation of figures. In art nouveau, as space is squeezed into two dimensions, the artist creates chains or friezes of ornamental figures with certain, often very complex, repetitions comparable to the sequential rhythms of music. Third, art nouveau is characterized by a preference either for linear expression—for flowing lines that curl back upon themselves only to spring forward once again, carrying the observer's eye with them—or for blocks of startling asymmetrical shapes such as are found in the posters of Henri de Toulouse-Lautrec or Jules Chéret. At one extreme then art nouveau tended toward a wild profusion of organic shapes best represented perhaps by the extraordinary zoomorphic forms of the Catalonian architect Antoni Gaudí. This playful style lent itself to parody, and within a few years of its heyday, what one might call "organic" art nouveau was dead, killed by caricature and ridicule. At the other extreme, however, art nouveau merged into a rigorously streamlined and geometric style most prominent in the work of Kessler's friend Henry van de Velde, the Scottish architect Charles Rennie Mackintosh, and his Viennese colleague Josef Hoffmann. This school was tremendously influential in the development of modern architecture and design.[10]

Perhaps the longest lasting achievement of the art nouveau and Jugendstil artists and designers was to resurrect the crafts traditions by erasing the firm distinctions between the arts and crafts that had developed since the Renaissance and were so firmly lodged in the curricula of the nineteenth-century art academies. The integration of arts and crafts found in art nouveau owes something to the spirit of fin de siècle "life-philosophy," a phenomenon that transcended Germany. Preferring the dynamic to the static, the ornamental to the figurative, the rhythmic to the harmonic, young artists no longer felt bound by the compartmentalization of art into the fine arts—embracing painting, sculpture, and architecture—and the applied arts—encompassing crafts such as weaving, glass and iron work, printing, papermaking, ceramics, and jewelry. Just as life itself was too vital to yield to the categories of nineteenth-century positivism, so too would genuine art, by virtue of its own innate dynamism, break down the divisions taught in the academies.

The original, and most explicit theoretical expression of this idea, as well as its first practical application, came, of course, from William Morris and the English arts and crafts movement. Morris, following in John Ruskin's footsteps, argued for the reintegration of art into life, a unity he assumed existed in the Middle Ages. Behind this ideal lies the assumption that an integrated art could shape our environment so thoroughly as to effect a moral—and eventually a social and political—revolution. The influence of Morris's example and writings on the Continental exponents of art nouveau is well known. Henry van de Velde credited him with the decision to abandon painting in favor of a career as a omnivorous designer.[11] There is an obvious affinity between the ideals pursued by Morris and the Wagnerian notion of a total art-work or Gesamtkunstwerk. One example of the pursuit of a Gesamtkunstwerk was the revival of interest in fine printing, combining the crafts of papermaking, type design and setting, illustration, binding, and literature. The famous books of Morris's Kelmscott Press are examples of the ideal of the Gesamtkunstwerk writ small. It was an aspect that appealed especially to the young Kessler, who visited Morris twice and thus made the first contacts with English book designers that he would cultivate all his life. It was also the governing principle behind the literary/artistic endeavor that absorbed Kessler's attentions for five years, from 1895 to 1900, the seminal German arts and letters journal, *Pan*.

• • •

Pan was a product of the Berlin bohemia: this much, at least, it owed to the naturalists despite the avowedly anti-naturalist intentions of its founders. A major legacy of the naturalist movement was the creation of a vigorous bohemian culture in Berlin, a city that, in comparison to Paris and Munich, never enjoyed much of a bohemian life throughout most of the nineteenth century. Now in the bars, coffeehouses, and suburban communes of Berlin, young men and women met to plan new journals, theaters, and galleries. Among the most interesting of these new groupings was the odd and picturesque circle of individuals whose meeting place was located in a crowded two-room wine tavern on the corner of Unter den Linden and the Wilhelmstraße, dubbed "Zum Schwarzen Ferkel" (At The Black Piglet). It had been discovered in the winter of 1892–93 by August Strindberg, then in exile from his native Sweden. Around Strindberg gathered a number of aspiring artists and writers, many, like him, exiles from Scandinavia. Among their number was a young Norwegian painter who was unwittingly to play a major role in the assault on academic art in Germany, Edvard Munch. Another habitué of Strindberg's circle was a young Polish mystic, Stanislaw Przybyszewski, whose febrile novels, heavily influenced by Nietzsche and occultism, enjoyed a wildly inflated reputation among German intellectuals around the turn of the century. With the departure of Strindberg for Paris, Przybyszewski took over as the presiding luminary, and the dyspeptic influence of the Swede gave way to an equally alcoholic but rather more ecstatic and mystical camaraderie induced by the Pole. The gatherings became less heavily composed of Scandinavians with the arrival of many German writers and artists, the most important of whom were Richard Dehmel, Otto Julius Bierbaum, and Julius Meier-Graefe. It was within this circle that the idea for a new and exciting journal, unlike anything Germany had known previously, was first bruited about.[12]

A compromise at the very beginning of *Pan* preordained its destiny. Eberhard von Bodenhausen, Kessler's fellow student and fraternity brother from Bonn and Leipzig, had been part of the *Pan* enterprise from the start. To his skeptical father, he explained that the initiative for the founding of a journal was due largely to his wish to help alleviate "the cruel poverty prevalent among the young—and in part—wonderfully gifted artists." He suggested to the interested members of the Schwarze Ferkel circle that they should form a limited corporation in order to raise the 100,000 marks they felt was the minimum amount necessary to launch the journal and other projects. The price of a share in the enterprise ranged from a minimum of 100 marks to a maximum of 10,000 marks, in return for which the stockholder received a proportionate reduction in the list price of each edition. Compared to a typical subscription rate of 12 to 20 marks for journals of arts and letters, *Pan's* yearly subscription rate ranged from 75 marks to as much as 160 marks for the luxury edition printed on handmade paper and containing inserted original prints. Clearly, as a review of the new journal put it, *Pan* "has not been intended to influence the working classes."[13]

The founders had a number of reasons for this elitist conception of their journal. Certainly, a reaction against the more popular and political strand of naturalism played a part, as did the general revulsion toward the aesthetic and literary level cultivated by such mass publications as the notorious *Gärtenlaube* or *Die fliegende Blätter*. A further consideration was the desire to insulate the journal as much as possible from the pressures of the marketplace—pressures that, it was felt, inevitably led to the decline of artistic standards. In short, the founders doubted that a large enough audience existed for their publication to rely exclusively on subscriptions and bookstore sales; hence the cultural philanthropy implicit in the corporative model. Dehmel justified the high costs in a letter to a friend, arguing that the desire to create something for posterity demanded the very best; "Or does one think that Dürer's woodcuts were cheaper in his day?"[14]

Nevertheless, Dehmel believed that, just as occurred in antiquity and in the Renaissance, the genuine art cultivated by the *Pan* circle would eventually find its way into society as a whole: "It is precisely the thought behind the corporative nature of our enterprise to turn to the unpropertied masses—as soon as the support of the wealthy allows us—in that we hope, from our profits and the collection of art we gather, to reach a wider audience." The idea that avant-garde art and culture would "trickle down," as it were, from a small coalition of artists, writers, critics, and wealthy patrons, into the masses at large— to the extent that they were in any way capable of appreciating art—was a very characteristic assumption in Wilhelmian Germany. Again and again Kessler's life and activity would be marked by this effort to create a "web" of circles from which the creative and rejuvenating impulse would infiltrate the society as a whole, as if by a process of osmosis.[15] At any rate, Meier-Graefe enthusiastically pursued wealthy patrons, members of the nobility, and established artists to lend their money and their name to the enterprise. One method of enticement was to make them members of the board of control of the corporation, an organization conceived by Meier-Graefe and Bierbaum as a mere fig leaf, useful for attracting other moneyed members of the elite, but without any authority over their editorial activities.

This was their mistake, as they quickly discovered. Among the men who joined the board of control were several of the most famous and prestigious of Germany's museum directors, including Alfred Lichtwark, the ambitious director of the Hamburg *Kunsthalle;* Woldemar von Seidlitz, director of the Saxon Art Collections in Dresden; and the formidable Wilhelm von Bode, the "Bismarck of the Museums," soon to be the general director of Berlin's famous Museum Island. These gentlemen, mostly of a generation older than the Schwarze Ferkel crowd, had substantially different ideas about the role of *Pan* and would not hesitate to use their predominant position in the governing board and editorial committee to push the enterprise in the direction they preferred.

The latent conflict between the editors and the board of control was not long manifesting itself. The libertine element in much of the poetry and the—in their minds—excessive worship of French art and literature annoyed the so-called "museum bosses" who wanted to make *Pan* into a publication dedicated to the fine and applied arts in Germany. Lichtwark especially harbored pedagogical ambitions, hoping that a publication devoted to the renaissance in native German arts and crafts would both free Germany from the dominance of the English in this area and provide the moneyed public with an aesthetic education worthy of a great power. Matters came to a head over a controversy regarding the unauthorized acquisition and publication of a lithograph by Toulouse-Lautrec. Considering the picture not just technically startling with its bold colors and flat surfaces, but immoral as well, the board of control, supported by Bodenhausen in this case, both rejected the lithograph and used the incident as a pretext to reverse what they increasingly felt was a pernicious and dangerous editorial direction. On September 17, 1895, the board of control voted to dismiss Meier-Graefe and Bierbaum as editors. The "museum bosses" had won; the new editor, a Swabian writer named Cäser Flaischlen, not only shared in general the views of the board of control, but also was reduced effectively to its instrument. Among the newcomers elected to the board of control in the aftermath of this "palace coup" was Kessler.

. . .

Kessler, although never a regular at the Schwarze Ferkel, met the key members early in 1894 as they were planning their journal. On the first of December in that year, he attended a fundraising supper for *Pan;* afterward, he went to the famous café Josty's with Bierbaum, Bodenhausen, Meier-Graefe, Dehmel, and Przybyszewski. The Polish poet impressed Kessler as a genuine mystic, and a few days later he visited him in his furnished rooms. The contrast between the conventional furnishings provided by the landlady and Przybyszewski's own collection of art—a landscape by Munch and etchings by Félicien Rops—struck Kessler as somewhat uncanny evidence for the close and contemporaneous existence of two completely different worldviews. The Pole, noted for his frenzied piano playing, played a Chopin mazurka while his lovely, blond, aristocratic wife danced;* the performance very much moved Kessler who, moving always from the specific to the general, commented that it was the "secret of love that man and woman could

---

* This was the lovely Dagny Przybyszewska, the Norwegian-born femme fatale of the Schwarze Ferkel crowd, whose murder a few years later would lead to her husband's arrest and subsequent acquittal when it was proven that the real murderer was a Polish student.

never quite understand each other and therefore desire always remained."[16] No doubt the wealthy young count left some money for the impoverished, if soulful, bohemians, although he was too discreet to mention it in his diary.

Besides Przybyszewski, Kessler—enlisted by the comparatively poorer Bodenhausen—was providing financial support for Edvard Munch. Munch had been at the center of a scandal nearly three years earlier when he had been invited by some independently minded artists in Germany to show his work in Berlin. The ensuing controversy was responsible for the creation of the Berlin Secession, an umbrella organization for artists dissenting from the official culture endorsed by the emperor.[17] Only a few years later, a similar controversy would ensure a young artist at least some financial support from art dealers interested in the avant-garde; Munch, however, was still on the brink of starvation. In April 1895, as Kessler sat for the first of the series of portraits Munch would do for him, culminating nine years later in the great full-length painting in the National Gallery, an energetic shop girl and a burly assistant hauled away Munch's easel because of an unpaid debt of twenty-five marks.[18]

Kessler's impressions of the artists he met during his first foray into patronage during the fall of 1894 and the spring of 1895 belie any notion that he belonged to any so-called "bohème dorée," that is, wealthy bourgeoisie and aristocrats who sought diversion by slumming amongst the impoverished bohemians.[19] At a dinner for *Pan,* for instance, where he met the old naturalist Heinrich Hart, Kessler noted, rather uncharitably, the desperate way in which Hart glanced at Meier-Graefe, hoping that he would accept a contribution. The misery of bohemia did not appeal to Kessler. Unlike his friend Alfred Walter Heymel, the wealthy adopted son of a Bremen merchant who became a fixture in the Schwabing district in Munich, Kessler did not immerse himself in bohemian life. Nevertheless, he visited the ateliers of many young artists and either bought finished works or commissioned new ones: among those he helped in this way, besides Munch, were Josef Sattler, a typical Jugendstil artist who designed Kessler's ex libris, and Fidus, the professional name of Hugo Höppner, whose excruciatingly kitschy drawings of nude young sun-worshipers enjoyed a vogue before the First World War, even among those who ought to have known better.

Kessler had been active for *Pan* even before he officially joined, attending their banquets and undertaking errands. He was commissioned to recruit friends of his from the Richter salon, including Count Kuno

Moltke of the Liebenberg circle, to join the board of control; there was even talk of the kaiser himself joining. Kessler also visited artists and writers to ask for contributions. These duties accelerated and added to them was the task of keeping the ambitious journal financially afloat. Kessler's energy and enthusiasm soon became indispensable to the enterprise. Bodenhausen relied on him increasingly, especially inasmuch as the new editor Flaischlen, a good-natured writer, seemed to Bodenhausen to lack sufficient drive. During his frequent trips in these years, Bodenhausen let people know that they should approach Kessler regarding *Pan* business. By the end of October, Bodenhausen wrote Lichtwark to ask: "Don't we want to make Kessler vice-chairman? We need someone and he is so engaged body and soul." A few months earlier, Bodenhausen had even asked Kessler if he would like to take over "the direction of *Pan*" (it is not clear exactly what he meant by that); Kessler, perhaps because he expected to join the diplomatic corps imminently, declined. Nevertheless, for the next five years, until the final liquidation of *Pan,* Kessler remained one of the principal forces behind the journal.[20]

Although he only officially became a member of the board of control after the departure of Bierbaum and Meier-Graefe, Kessler did not subscribe completely to the program of Lichtwark and Bode, any more than did Bodenhausen. His reservations concerning the two previous editors did not preclude maintaining their friendship, especially with Meier-Graefe. He admired Lichtwark as a rare example of a scholar who had not lost his living connection with art. He also agreed with much in Lichtwark's programmatic statement in the third issue concerning the new direction the journal would follow, especially with the thought that "all culture begins as aristocratic, and one doesn't raise its level like that of a pond in that one lets more water in. The essence of education is quality, not mass."[21] Neither would he have disagreed with Lichtwark's emphasis on the need to make up the aesthetic gap between Germany and England. Where Kessler diverged from Lichtwark was in the need for the journal to introduce the German audience to the latest developments in Western Europe: in this matter, Kessler was closer to the viewpoint of Meier-Graefe.

Kessler also assumed the role of the departed editors when it came to the literature section. Here he often found himself in conflict not only with Bode, Lichtwark, and Seidlitz, but with Flaischlen as well. One such controversy took place when Kessler accepted for publication the poems of Ludwig Derleth without consulting the editorial committee. Derleth, whom Kessler first met in Munich and whom he visited frequently there and later in Paris, is one of those forgotten writers who sometimes define their age far better than their more famous contemporaries. Thin, gaunt, and pale, Derleth cultivated a completely unworldly, ascetic, asexual, and prophetic appearance. Guarded, fed, and clothed by a sister convinced to the point of mania of his genius, he gave elaborately rehearsed readings of his incantatory poetry to select audiences. It is not his verse, however, that has immortalized Derleth, but rather the ironic portrait Thomas Mann provided in his very amusing story, "At the Prophet's."

Kessler fell for a while under his spell, almost in spite of himself. He records the conversation of the mystic poet for pages. At one point, Derleth confesses that it was a mistake to go to Paris: "Now I will go to the sea in order to wash myself clean; and then into the solitude for many years. I wish to take the sea with me into my solitude the way one puts on white robes. I shall go to the Belgian coast; there all will be fog and sunsets and the tremendous melancholy of the sea." And when Kessler asks him what will happen when he returns: "Then I will be a different person from today: I imagine it as if on a warm night I enter through the Victory Gate in Munich drawn in a wagon pulled by white horses, in a night where all the people were on the streets and they came with torches in their hands, and I would ride through them on a wagon drawn by white steeds, *without seeing them*." Kessler was fascinated by the hypnotic quality of Derleth's conversation. "What is attractive about Derleth is *his way of being*. He is not a writer, not a scholar, not a philosopher, not even an artist, but rather here is once again an *individual* of the greatest possible style; his own appearance is actually his art, his gestures and his spoken word." Kessler's attitude is perhaps an example of his susceptibility to the prophetic gesture, to an art that was both intensely personal and religious in overtone. His interest in Derleth would fade, but something akin to it would reawaken years later when he met Johannes Becher during the First World War. At any rate, the editorial committee gave an indication of Kessler's power when it backed down after he threatened to resign if they did not publish Derleth's poetry.[22]

One of the benefits Kessler drew from his experience with *Pan* was a growing acquaintance with modern French art and literature. Given his family connections and his interests, he of course would have encountered French modernism anyway, but the missions he undertook on behalf of *Pan* accelerated the process. Concerning modern painting, he had quite early expressed his disdain for the naturalist school in

German painting. The precise copying of nature cannot disguise the lack of fantasy even in such exceptional works as the portraits of Max Liebermann.[23]

It would take repeated visits to the Durand-Ruel gallery, chief venue of the impressionists, for Kessler to undergo the same aesthetic education. While he was, from a very early age, disgusted with the historical school of painting best represented by Anton von Werner, it took longer to wean him from painters such as Anselm Feuerbach and Arnold Böcklin, and of course also from the German symbolists such as Max Klinger. At first, he found it hard to believe that Manet had initiated a revolution in the use of color because he found that artist's colors to be harsh and unpleasant. Soon, however, he was beginning to build the foundations of his private collection of impressionist masterpieces. At the end of May 1896, he bought Renoir's *Marchandeuse des pommes* for 3,000 francs. Paintings by Cézanne, Van Gogh, Signac, and Seurat soon followed. Kessler began to muse about tracing the history of the extraordinary evidence of the impressionist revolution spread out in the Durand-Ruel gallery: "One must sometime describe the capture of color, shimmering and changing in the light, for art."[24] By the end of the decade, Kessler was visiting the studios of Paul Signac, Maximilien Luce, Henri-Edmond Cross, and others, taking notes on their palettes with the thought of writing a history of modern art.

About the same time, Kessler discovered the great English artists of the first half of the century: William Blake, John Constable, and J. M. W. Turner. During a trip to the National Gallery in London, he noted that, "Turner in his last pictures, and especially in his watercolors, stands at the point where the impressionists, and above all, Monet, are striving for. . . . I hardly know another picture that I would like to compare with *Téméraire* in its magnificent color." Compared to Turner, the paintings by Dante Gabriel Rossetti that he viewed then for the first time pale in significance. The next day, without expecting much, he viewed Blake's drawings at the South Kensington museum; it was an overwhelming experience: "Already here is the original genius from which the entire modern English decorative art—the only modern decorative art which even exists in Europe—descended. . . . Blake even anticipated Beardsley's powerful contrasts in light and dark." That same trip Kessler traveled to Kelmscott House to meet William Morris, who struck him more as a country gentleman than an artist. Morris laid out his collection of prints for his young German visitor, providing a short history of fine printing. Kessler was impressed with the Englishman's practical and sensible appearance, free from any Pinafore-esque mannerisms.[25]

All the while Kessler was embarked on this apprenticeship in modern art, he was at the same time fulfilling duties for *Pan*, without receiving a salary. It was a doomed enterprise. Without ever being able to transform the journal into one devoted strictly to German art and to art history, Lichtwark, Bode, and Seidlitz did manage to dampen its connection to modern literature. The extraordinarily high standards *Pan* set regarding the quality of its paper and its typesetting, while pathbreaking for German printing and publishing, proved enormously expensive, especially for a journal with a very limited subscription.[26] Even Kessler, a perennial optimist when it came to these matters, was forced to see that the journal would not survive its fifth year. When plans for a fusion between *Pan* and a new journal, *Insel*, founded by Heymel and Rudolph Alexander Schröder, fell apart, the last glimmer of hope was gone.

"What in the end did *Pan* achieve?" asked Meier-Graefe in 1910 in the preface to a new journal by the same name published by Paul Cassirer. His answer, tinged by his own bitter experience, was on the whole negative. "We carried too much art in our—in themselves— praiseworthy thoughts. Art should be connected with life. We thought of all possible connections, but they were all too artistic, not to say, artificial. And the more we invented them, the more our beautiful project diverged from life. I almost want to end this sermon with the warning—beware of art!"[27]

Looking back from a greater distance than Meier-Graefe, we can recognize perhaps the achievement of *Pan* more objectively than he could. The founding of the journal has been called one of the four seminal events—along with the creation of the *Freie Bühne Verein,* the start of the Berlin Secession, and the foundation of the Fischer Verlag—that turned Berlin, twenty years after the creation of the Second Reich, into a cultural *Weltstadt*.[28] Its bibliophilic aspirations were a direct inspiration to the journal *Insel,* out of which the Insel Verlag, one of the innovators in the field of German publishing, would emerge. Finally, many of the leading writers and artists of the period between 1890 and 1910 found a much-needed outlet in the journal's pages. Among these was Kessler himself, whose first reflections on art and culture were published there.

CHAPTER 6

Decadence and Renewal

Apart from the fact that I am a decadent, I am also the opposite.

Nietzsche, *Ecce Homo*

The shortest path to one's self lies around the world.
Herman Graf Keyserling, *Reisetagebuch eines Philosophen*

Kessler's first published writings all deal, in one way or another, with the theme of decadence: its definition, its causes, its consequences, its pitfalls and its pleasures, and the possibilities of escaping it and finding renewal. Decadence was very much in the air in the 1890s. So it comes as no surprise to find the subject pervading his thinking, but there were profound personal as well as generational roots for his reflections.[1] His first decade in Berlin, from the time of his arrival in 1893 until his nomination to be director of the Grand Ducal Museum of Arts and Crafts in Weimar in 1903, was a time of uncertainty, of self-doubt, of confusion over identity and purpose, of searching, of crisis. His career plans remained in limbo: while he had definitely abandoned any thoughts of following in his father's footsteps by the time he graduated from college, neither did he seem to have pursued the alternative of a career in the foreign service with single-minded enthusiasm. On his father's last visit to Berlin in the fall of 1894, they approached the new chancellor, the aged Prince Hohenlohe, who, as German ambassador to France, had known the Kesslers well in Paris. The prince, after making inquiries regarding Kessler's family and education, promised to bring the matter to the attention of State Secretary Marschall. A few days later, the state secretary himself promised Kessler an appointment in a few months. No such call came forth, however, and it was not until the summer of 1897, as the fall of Marschall appeared imminent, that he approached Hohenlohe again about the matter. The prince was very friendly and promised to bring the matter up again in writing. Still, the appointment remained stalled—whether because of opposition within the Foreign Office or because Kessler did not pursue it actively enough is not clear. In any case, the years of drifting were made more supportable by the fortune he inherited upon his father's death in May 1995.[2]

Not only his professional life but also his personal life was left in limbo. He never considered marriage a serious option, although of course many homosexuals did start families. In the winter of 1894–95, as his relation with Dungern was unraveling, he filled his diary with bitter, searching remarks on love.

In this mood, he wrote his article on the most popular of the French symbolist poets, Henri de Régnier (1864–1936), for *Pan* in December 1895. His first encounter with symbolism came two years earlier and he was deeply impressed: "Works of an old and rich speech and culture: they play with associations, with reawakened sensations and moods from other poems that cling like perfume to the words; the whim of a jaded Sultan who contents himself by letting the same rubies and pearls slide through his fingers over and over again, rather than collecting new ones."[3] In the summer of 1895, he visited Paul Verlaine three times in Paris, obtaining autographed copies of his poems. Although he admired Verlaine more as a poet, he chose to write about Régnier precisely because he was a less original and therefore more representative example of fin de siècle decadence than either Verlaine or Stéphane Mallarmé. His review of the Frenchman's collected poems is in many ways an affirmation of his own attraction to decadence. Its descriptive part offers a remarkably concise and pithy diagnosis of the state of the late nineteenth-century psyche in which Kessler's own experiences and situation are mirrored. At the same time, however, Kessler is aware of the limitations of this melancholy affectation, and his remarks contain an immanent critique of aestheticism and especially of the doctrine of "art for art's sake." The tension between Kessler's attraction to and his rejection of the languid decadence represented by Régnier not only marks this review, but is a recurrent cleavage throughout his early writings on art and culture.

In addressing the way in which the more or less constant persona of Régnier's poetry suffers, Kessler mentions that all of us suffer and have always suffered from a dangerous excess of fantasy. Precisely those with the greatest imagination, the great artists and religious figures, have suffered the most. Yet, although the disproportion between our fantasy and the world we must live in is a constant of the human condition, our response to the dichotomy varies throughout history. For the modern generation, for those "who have already tasted the future, life is a drama already seen once and played by better actors; it is not worth watching again."[4] As with all of his published writing, this metaphor has its roots in one of Kessler's journal entries. It is the preemptive enjoyment (*Vorwegsgeniessen*) of the imagination that sours the actual enjoyment of life for the person endowed with too much fantasy. The peculiar melancholy of the fin de siècle stems from the conflict between the ideal and reality, between dream and act, between text and life, between fantasy and sensuality that a hypertrophic intellectual culture has nourished. Kessler goes on to exclaim, "for the man with too much fantasy life is a novel whose last chapter he already knows; it doesn't pay to read the rest."[5] Kessler wrote this at the time he was struggling with his own feelings for Dungern, and his personal frustration undoubtedly lay behind his assertion that we suffer "because the satisfaction of our desire is impossible or rendered worthless through its transitory nature."[6]

Yet, there were also objective causes, Kessler argued, for the state of the soul that he discerned both in Régnier and himself, reasons inherent in their particular time and place. The laming of desire so apparent in fin de siècle literature is rooted in the attrition of the personality, a dissolution occasioned by the decline of faith and accelerated greatly by the steady assault of science during the nineteenth century upon the anthropomorphic presumptions of the human ego. Here, Kessler drew upon the vertigo he experienced in Wundt's lectures. "Everything that man learns today about himself or the world, all that he does to increase this knowledge, everything that is preached to him as his duty, has the effect of weakening his personality."[7] Charles Darwin had already dealt a blow to Western anthropomorphism: now, if the theories of experimental psychologists like Wundt were true, even human consciousness was mere shorthand for a momentary confluence of forces. If the dissolution of the boundaries between the ego and the world facilitated the spread of pantheistic ideas, it also paralyzed the will. Uncertain if he is even the instigator of his actions, modern man is left wondering: what is worth striving for?

There are several possible ways to react to this dilemma. Like Nietzsche, one can hope to create one's own ideals in which to believe. Or, one can seek to end one's suffering by returning to the old ideals as

Kessler—following Nietzsche's critique—claims Wagner did. One can simply and stubbornly persist in the struggle as does Verlaine, "whose whole poetic work is a confession of a shipwrecked soul tossed between skepticism and the longing for peace, between sensuality and the need for faith." Or, one can simply give up, as does Régnier, the poet of resignation, of twilight, of dreaming, and of autumn. Modern pessimism of this last variety comes very close, Kessler asserts, to Buddhism. What prevents it from sliding ultimately into nihilism is the striving to "dream the dream that must be dreamt as harmoniously and completely as possible."[8] This urge is what explains the extraordinary thirst for art that had emerged in the last twenty years, not just in music and literature, but in the pictorial arts as well.

As indulgent and remote from the life of the world as this aesthetic may appear, it is not, Kessler maintained, in the end completely divorced from ethics, religion, or philosophy. Even the most resolutely sensual and amoral art employs symbols that must—in order to be effective—evoke some kind of ethical or philosophical response: a completely closed and hermetic art cannot exist. Because art, unlike science, restores, however momentarily, the personality to the center of the psychic stage, it has inherited the mantle that religion once carried. The true task of poets such as Régnier, whether they acknowledged it or not, was to awaken the symbolic art that had slumbered since the decline of religion, only this time without the aid of religious dogma. Thus, Kessler endeavored to prove that the tired pessimism of symbolism really represented but a stage in the search for new ideals to live by, "a vision of a deeper, more passionate, and more painful world view." This evolutionary view of decadence owed much to Nietzsche, who also spoke of "ennoblement through decadence" and who called himself both a decadent and its opposite.[9]

When commenting on Régnier's fondness for musically evocative word games, Kessler remarked that in this, as in much else, he resembled the young Austrian poet Loris. Loris was, of course, the pseudonym of Hugo von Hofmannsthal, with whom Kessler was destined to enjoy a particularly creative and, at the same time, difficult relationship. The allusion in Kessler's review is his first mention of Hofmannsthal, whose poetry he had encountered in his work for *Pan*. The two men met for the first time on May 11, 1898, when Hofmannsthal traveled to Berlin for the premiere of his verse play, *The Woman at the Window*. Kessler's opinion of his new acquaintance oscillated wildly during this first visit. At first, he described Hofmannsthal as a "short, jolly Viennese with a high-pitched voice but thoroughly agreeable and natural . . . in his style and manner." After showing him Berlin in the afternoon, however, Kessler noted that, "while he had a sharp eye for the surface of life and expressed his discoveries in a pointed and picturesque manner, his philosophical talent seems more elegant than is desirable in the long run." A few days later, after inviting him to breakfast following the premiere, Kessler revised his opinion yet again, beginning the long chain of revisions of his relation to Hofmannsthal that accompanied their friendship as a running commentary: "Above all he is vain and *socially* ambitious; he is in danger of becoming like Heyse or Bourget, a tea circle poet and philosopher of the boudoir: his temperament is completely unrevolutionary. . . . Moreover a writer is apparently quite an exceptional being for him, separated from all others by great chasms." [10]

The Austrian for his part wrote to Bodenhausen about Kessler, "I found him very pleasant, different from the young society people among us. . . . I would almost say more West European." He stayed with Kessler upon his return visit to Berlin the next year. It was during this visit that he complained to Kessler of never finding subjects for plays and asked Kessler to send him any suitable material he might find in memoirs and the like. He wanted to make money, lots of money, in the theater, Kessler remarked rather uncharitably. Nevertheless, he would take up Hofmannsthal's suggestion and from the summer of 1898 begins the long correspondence in which Kessler sends books, offers reading lists, suggests topics, criticizes drafts, makes introductions, and sends addresses. The final fruits of this collaboration would be *The Rosenkavalier* and *The Legend of Joseph.*[11]

Given the importance of each in the other's life, it is interesting to see how both Kessler and Hofmannsthal arrived, approximately around the same time, at a similar diagnosis of decadence. One of Kessler's favorite works by Hofmannsthal, *The Fool and Death,* offers a strong, if plaintive, critique both of the author's own aestheticism and of the dangers of an overly intellectual culture. Claudio, the wealthy aesthete protagonist, finds that not only has a relentlessly rationalizing intellect stepped between him and the direct experience of life, as it were, but also that the entire cultural accumulation of centuries intervenes as well, serving as an unwanted filter, a screen between his consciousness and his experience. His life, he feels, is like "a book, some twice-told tale partly not yet intelligible, partly no longer so."

Both the anxiety that they might never escape the black-and-white world of the text and savor some more sensuous, colorful, and immediate experience of life, and the sense of inheriting from their fathers a world already made, already known, gave not only the early work of Hofmannsthal and Kessler, but also the entire fin de siècle its peculiar underlying strain of despair. It was the kind of crisis that defines a generation: both men would spend much of the rest of their lives in the attempt to transcend it; by defining for themselves a mission worthy of their efforts and by seeking, by however a circuitous route, a connection to life, a detour around pure intellect. Part of this path they traveled together. When they began to diverge, their friendship, for which they had both harbored many illusions, would not withstand the strain.

• • •

One of the first volumes Kessler sent Hofmannsthal was a copy of his first book, *Notizen über Mexiko,* published in May 1898. Essentially a rewritten version of the impressions he recorded in his journal during his trip to North America and Mexico in the late fall and winter of 1896, *Notizen über Mexiko* is a minor classic of fin de siècle travel literature. A compendium of many of Kessler's abiding obsessions—the relation between art and religion and the influence of climate and culture on national character—it is a fine example of Kessler's painterly eye, the way he could seize the significant feature in a new landscape, evoke its singularity, and use it as a bridge to interesting speculation. But above all it offers an anthropology of decadence.[12]

In a foreword that he had printed separately, Kessler mused over the special role of travel literature in the age of imperialism: "Ours is perhaps the last age in which one can still travel. Already we can barely escape our civilization. The picture remains astonishingly the same from one part of the world to the next." After the explorers and the artists, the geographers, economists, and journalists have made the strange familiar. The exotic, when pictured daily in the magazines and newspapers, becomes routinized. Only the traveler who can tear himself away from the numbing web of familiar associations will know how to refresh his "tired spirit, made superficial by disappointments."[13] The reader of travel literature can also transform his apprehension of the world, but only if he accepts the inherent incompleteness of the genre: anything too finished destroys the momentary impression that is at the core of this kind of writing.

Kessler's thoughts echoed those of many of his contemporaries, who finding, in the words of Hermann Graf Keyserling, "Europe doesn't challenge me anymore," fled to the four corners of the world and sent back their impressions of China, Japan, Russia, South and North America, and Africa. Eager to discover for themselves those realms still relatively untouched by the high tide of European imperialism, these travelers yearned for an encounter with the non-European Other before the future foreclosed the possibility. The impulse was another expression of *die Flucht aus der Bürgerlichkeit,* the flight from bourgeois respectability. Even the relatively sedentary Hofmannsthal, who never left Europe, enjoyed tremendously the books describing Japan by the American expatriate, Lafcadio Hearn. The motivation for much turn-of-the-century travel literature was not so much scholarly or even escapist, at least in the narrow sense of the word; rather, travel served as a means of self-discovery. This explains the fragmentary, deeply subjective, and impressionistic character that Kessler insisted was an integral part of the genre.[14]

The first pages recounting the results of Kessler's random wanderings around Mexico City read as if he had spent the time dazed by the subtropical sun and numbed by the heat. Following Wundt he speculated on the effect of this climate upon the nervous system of those who must endure it. The answer, Kessler asserted, can be found in the art and architecture, both religious and popular. The constant, intrusive vivacity and intensity of light and heat compel a corresponding torpor of the nerves, which must protect themselves from overstimulation. This torpor has the paradoxical effect of making the nerves susceptible only to either the loudest and strongest stimuli or the subtlest; the middle range, common to more temperate climates, is entirely missing; thus, the profuse baroque ornamentation found inside the churches, as well as the garish, larger-than-life advertisements for taverns. These abnormally strong stimuli were accompanied by sensitivity to the finest shades of light and color usually found only in the most cultivated European aesthete. Indeed, in Mexico the sun and the climate by themselves had produced what it took Europe centuries to achieve—and then only in a few individuals; namely, the twin characteristics of decadence: a predilection for the grotesque and savage and the most nuanced appreciation of aesthetic tones.[15]

Having introduced the notion of decadence, Kessler proceeded to use it to characterize both Mexican civilization and the Mexicans themselves. His use of decadence in this context became, in the course of his trip, less and less pejorative until it echoed his application of the term to describe the poetry of the symbolists. He ascribed a pair of seemingly contradictory traits associated often with decadence, indifference and sudden caprice, to Mexican society. Against a background of general indifference, the relatively few desires that manage to seep into the consciousness take on a correspondingly greater importance: they become obsessions. These sudden, violent, and seemingly irresistible seizures of desire subside quickly, however, as their immediate stimulus passes. The tropical mind, Kessler asserted, was incapable of the tenacity of will found in more northern climates.[16]

Kessler was perfectly clear about the difficulties of this kind of speculation. Nor was he unaware of the possibility that the lethargy he notes may be a product of a social system and not simply of the climate. Speculating about the stoic indifference of the Mayan peasant, he admitted that "in how far the natural indifference has been reinforced by the old experience that the Spanish landlord takes every service, every surplus, by whatever means, either as theft or as interest, for himself; to what extent the hacienda system is guilty of the sluggishness which they claim to suffer, cannot be measured exactly: certainly this too had its historical cause and to be sure in the same way that the older, the climatic, influenced the development of the Mayans."[17] At any rate, it is certainly not from the economic life, which, precisely because of this indolence, is mostly in the hands of the Yankees, that one may draw conclusions about Mexican culture, but from the role of the church, of nationalism, and of political authority.

The second part of the book discusses Kessler's excursions to the various ruins of pre-Columbian civilizations. Having first taken the time to ascend Popocatepetl, the ancient volcano that towers over Mexico City, he then traveled by boat to Yucatán to see the Mayan ruins.

In a short, brilliantly suggestive essay first published in 1911, Georg Simmel, the famous sociologist, meditated on the attraction of ruins for the modern spirit. A ruined structure no longer fulfills the original purpose spirit imposed upon it, but nevertheless acquires a new unity, impossible for other damaged art forms, a configuration that, by pitting the decay of human endeavor against the ever present entropy of nature, points to the common ground of both, the life-force. In a ruin, nature, once subordinate to art, now achieves dominance and yet works upon the ruin almost as if it were the artist, molding the color and shape of the stones to meld harmoniously with the surroundings. The profound peace surrounding ancient ruins induces in us a nostalgic sense of return to what Goethe called "the good mother," the life-stream from which both art and nature emerge. It also reflects the same incessant struggle that transpires within our soul. According to Simmel, this struggle can never reach equipoise within us; it constantly threatens to break out of any frame, to upset any balance. Simmel concludes: "Perhaps this is the reason for our general fascination with decay and decadence, a fascination which goes beyond what is merely negative and degrading. The rich and many-sided culture, the unlimited *impressionability,* and the understanding open to everything, which are characteristic of decadent epochs, do signify this coming together of contradictory strivings."[18]

Nothing could better describe the elective affinity Kessler felt for the ruins of pre-Columbian civilization, or the logic behind his description of them. In this respect at least like his emperor, Kessler was fascinated by the archaeological discoveries of the end of the nineteenth century. In Mexico, he visited practically every site of pre-Columbian ruins then known. Their ornamentation, the cascades of demons and snakes— some with bits of their once striking pigmentation still clinging to them—surrounding their temples, speaks a strange language with un- fathomable associations for Europeans. In *Notizen über Mexiko,* Kessler first addressed an aesthetic problem that engaged his attention over the next decade: how what we call realism in art arose, not from the correct depiction of form and color, but from the increasingly sensitive repro- duction of rhythmical movement found in ornamental art. In certain parts of pre-Columbian ornament he claimed to notice the gradual evo- lution of an independent artistic vision out of the strictly regimented ornamentation, a subtle increase in the attention to movement.[19]

As his senses became acclimated to the Mexican climate and land- scape, Kessler fell, at least partly, under the charm of its art and archi- tecture. The disdain resurfaced briefly at the end when he visited the execution site and tomb of Maxmilian, the Habsburg Napoleon III hoped to establish as emperor of Mexico. Maxmilian failed, Kessler notes, because he tried to rule a non-European country with European methods. Precisely the success of Porfirio Diaz's brutal regime illustrates the depravity of Mexican political life. Yet, even this judgment was mixed with admiration for the expressive and colorful street life. Read- ing his loving descriptions of this, one senses how much Kessler had been seduced by Mexico, despite his contempt for its politics.

He arrived back to Europe via New York at the beginning of 1897. The book was published in Berlin in May 1898 after the foreword had appeared separately a month before in the journal *Die Zukunft.* It was the impressionism of the book that struck its readers. One review be- gan, "This is a modern man with the finest feeling for style and a painter with an innate talent for the impressionistic art of description. The sci- entific ethnologist will admittedly find little in his work. But he who knows that travel writing, seen purely formally, must have a relation to the poetic style of its epoch, will recognize that such a work could be written only by a completely modern man."[20] And Bodenhausen, in a letter to his father, mentioned how he and Lichtwark had agreed that Kessler's book was one of the most important and original they had read. "From now on travel descriptions will have to be written like this or they will cease to be of interest. It is not the spectacle in itself that interests him, but the (psychological) process that the spectacle evokes. But one must be an acute psychologist to attempt such an ethnography. . . . The thoughts are fully new and they demonstrate above all the capability, which one normally associates with genius, to disassociate everything that is a mere ratiocination (*Gehirnformel*), to turn off learning and speech, the heavy shackles and formulas of learning, in order to see and to think with one's own eyes, the eyes of a child."[21] Bodenhausen's encomium suggests one way out of the impasse of decadence; namely, to learn to see again with "the eyes of a child." In his next project, Kessler would employ "the heavy shackles and formulas of learning" that Bodenhausen praised him for rejecting to forge another way out of the same impasse.

• • •

The trip to Mexico did not exhaust Kessler's wanderlust. A restlessness—compounded of boredom with his life as a legal intern, anxiety over his career plans, and sexual tension—drove him beyond his usual triangular itinerary of Berlin, Paris, and London during the next few years. His favorite destination was the Mediterranean, especially Italy and Greece. In the summer of 1898, after he had finished correcting the proofs for his Mexico book, he spent two months in Italy. He returned in May 1899 and then in September of the same year left for his first trip to Greece, where he fell immediately in love with the play of light and shadows in the Attic landscape. In 1900, he visited Greece again and went on to Turkey in time to witness the beginning of the new century in Constantinople. Kessler's travels to Greece especially resemble pilgrimages, and he was responsible for encouraging a number of his friends, Richard Dehmel and Gerhart Hauptmann among them, to undertake their own pilgrimages there: finally, in 1908, after a long absence, he took both Hofmannsthal and Maillol with him to drink at the well of the Delphic oracle, a trip with consequences we will examine later.

The trips to Italy and Greece in 1898–99 were also, in many respects, working trips. After returning from Mexico in the winter of 1897, he found himself once again drawn into the whirlwind of the social season, unable to write anything. In addition to his book on Mexico, he was mulling over another project on a subject that had long been on his mind, the relation between art and religion. His concern with this issue grew out of a concatenation of influences: his interest in the Italy of St. Francis and Giotto, the Nietzschean search for a new ideal to replace Christianity, the pantheism he discerned in modern art, his hopes of escaping the cul-de-sac of decadence, and finally, his recent impressions of Mexico. Unable to work seriously in Berlin, or Paris, or London, he went to Italy, in part to find the repose and solitude he needed, in part to find confirmation, in situ, of intuitions he had been brooding over for a number of years. The results of this labor were published in *Pan* in April 1899: Kessler's article "Art and Religion: Art and the Religious Multitude" (*Kunst und Religion: Die Kunst and die religiöse Menge*), besides being his last contribution to the journal, is his most ambitious theoretical discussion of aesthetics.

In response to a letter from Bodenhausen that asserted that all aesthetics are subjective, Kessler outlined the intentions behind his essay. Bodenhausen, Kessler argues, has mistaken the subject of aesthetics for the science itself. Undeniably, our responses to works of art are subjective but if aesthetics is not to lapse into mere personal effusion, it must concern itself with what is common to all or most of our individual responses: "I have just attempted in my essay on art and religion to link aesthetics in a new way to science, and specifically to psychology. I consider this important because, according to my view, only an aesthetic that rests on sound foundations and not in the clouds can save us from the degeneration of aesthetic sensibility caused by the unrestrained reign of art *history*. Art history absolutely needs an independent aesthetics to prevent it from pulling the aesthetic sensibility to pieces." But aesthetics of this kind, based on the principles of psychology, can never be subjectively true for the individual; it—like any scientific theory—can only be objectively true or false. The kind of aesthetics Bodenhausen had in mind is, at best, "an attractive and useful half-art which consists in making the psyche receptive for an artwork, that seeks to enhance its effect so to speak." A more ambitious aesthetics must present its ideas in a manner accessible to human thought, and submit them to the winnowing of reason.[22]

The influence of the positivism he imbibed at the feet of Wundt and

Springer is evident here, as well as the Nietzschean disdain for history. Yet, at the same time that he wants to construct a theory of aesthetics with scientific pretensions, he also hopes to restore the degenerate aesthetic sensibility of the nineteenth century by emphasizing the role of feeling, and particularly of religious emotion, in our appreciation of art. Kessler tries to resolve the apparent contradiction by anchoring his discussion in the psychology of art perception. Already in his essay on Henri de Régnier he had argued that the essence of art resides in its effect on the observer/listener; a work of art without a recipient is meaningless. Because he believed that science had advanced far enough to give him at least the basic tools to discuss the psychology of art perception, he thought it might be possible to propose the outline of a scientific aesthetics.

Kessler begins the essay by asserting what he has yet to prove: that religion has always been the most inexhaustible source of art. The whole argument depends on the parallel between the relation between the priest and the religious community and the artist and his audience. Both the priest and the artist seek to evoke in their respective audiences emotions that will fuse with the idea they are trying to communicate. The priest seeks to play upon the religious emotion present in the community of believers by using the sensuous means of ritual and liturgy to reinforce the bond between this emotion and the idea of God. The community serves as a kind of resonating chamber for the priest. The artist too, Kessler asserts, seeks to evoke emotions in his audience and link them to ideas through the means of sensuality and fantasy. There are three major ways for an artist to bind an idea to a feeling in a community: rhythm, harmony, and what Kessler somewhat unhappily calls poetry.

Rhythm is the most primitive method of exciting feelings through sensation. From his reading of Wundt, Kessler notes that certain repeated patterns of sensations—spatial as well as temporal—have the power of releasing emotions, behaving like waves, sometimes canceling, sometimes reinforcing each other. Harmony, to use Kessler's vocabulary, is the "color" of the feeling. Rhythm and harmony are methods of organizing raw sensation so as to unleash specific emotions. Besides pure sensation, however, the psyche reacts to fantasy in art as well. Fantasy also releases emotions or feelings. What Kessler calls "poetry" then is the principle that organizes not only fantasy and its accompanying chain of feelings, but also the sequence of feelings released by the senses as well. It bridges the gap between idea and feeling by weaving a web of sensation and feeling that results in a clear feeling and a clear idea, side by side as it were. This "play of feelings" is unique to every poetic conception; it is the heart of every revelation. We may correctly call it the "meaning" of an artwork, or of a religious epiphany.

Idea and feeling must be united during this mystical moment, separate but equal, or, as Kessler puts it, "next to each other" not "one after the other." He insists on this equal partnership because he hopes to distinguish with its help art from other kinds of communication and from propaganda. If the idea prevails in a work that aspires to be art, then it threatens to become merely allegorical, or a hieroglyph, which Kessler defines as the linkage of sensation to an idea without the mediation of feeling. It can communicate ideas but loses the power of evoking feelings. On the other hand, a work that neglects too emphatically the idea in order to evoke an emotion degenerates into propaganda, whether political, moral, or commercial. Or, as Schopenhauer put it, "Art stops where the motive begins."[23]

With this theory in hand, Kessler proceeds to attack both extremes of contemporary aesthetic theory: German academic idealism and the French notion of art for art's sake. German idealism neglected almost completely the component of feeling by defining art as a Platonic search for ideal forms in an ugly world. At its core was the mimetic goal, first formulated by Benvenuto Cellini, of reproducing the perfect human body. Kessler points out that, in practice, this leads to either exaggeration or caricature, or to the mere average, an anatomic schema. As he wrote in his diary, "No one would call the correct anatomical drawing of a human body free of any contingencies in itself an artwork, and no one would place an academic nude higher than even an anatomically incorrect sketch of a naked body by Leonardo." Authentic art was subversive of this stiff idealism. It induced the subjective feelings of the observer and brought him into the picture; not only his thoughts, but also his emotions, were inextricably mixed with the content.

Kessler was also eager to defend art from the definition that Baudelaire proffered: that the only purpose of art is to evoke a feeling of beauty. The famous phrase, "Art for art's sake" was inadequate for three reasons. First, because, followed strictly, it neglected whole genres of art, such as drama, and led such an otherwise astute critic as Baudelaire to consider the sonnets of Théophile Gautier a higher achievement than Shakespeare's tragedies. Second, it was a tautology. To define art as that which evokes a feeling of beauty presupposed a definition of beauty. But different epochs and cultures have obviously experienced radically different sensations and objects as beautiful. Third, it leads to at most a precious and desiccated refinement of taste among a few individuals. This cannot substitute for the waves of feeling that religion can generate for art.[24] Once again, Kessler comes to the conclusion that pure aestheticism represents a dead end: there must be a way to connect with modern life if art is to be reborn.

After illustrating the evolution of the relation between art and religion, using the Greek temple and the Gothic cathedral as examples, Kessler concludes the essay with a dispiriting admonition that aesthetic education alone can only strengthen the perception of one half of the duality underlying the enjoyment of art; namely, the idea. It cannot provide the feeling. "Pale aesthetes" are not really capable of enjoying, let alone creating, art. Rather, an authentic art requires equal portions of sensuality and fantasy, such as were found among the artists of the Renaissance. "While non-religious art finds it difficult to discover and excite feelings that are sufficiently deep and attractive, religious sentiment creates and employs feeling-tones which are aroused powerfully by the slightest sensation and illuminate the innermost part of the ego."[25] The reader is left with the implicit question, if modern art is not to be at the mercy of academicians or aesthetes, then what will provide the indispensable religious groundswell? To what community of believers can the modern artist, in his capacity as priest, preach?

How does "Art and Religion" measure up against the intentions Kessler outlined to Bodenhausen? Kessler himself remarked that he felt like a mole emerging from the dark after completing it and worried that it was "frightfully gray."[26] Bodenhausen thought it was "wonderfully constructed and, so far as I can judge such abstract matters, deeply thought out," but confessed that, in fact, he found the argument hard to follow. Hofmannsthal read it "with increasing pleasure in parts three or four times" and found the rich background of the essay particularly gratifying.[27] It does not seem to have found much of an echo beyond his immediate friends, however. Kessler's own awareness of the essay's faults probably caused him to abandon the announced continuation, although the ensuing demise of *Pan* may also have deprived him of a venue. The weaknesses are obvious. Although wishing to make a scientific contribution to aesthetics, Kessler quickly fell back on metaphysical assertions quite beyond the possibility of verification or falsification. In important passages an exalted and lofty prose seems to cloak imprecise definitions and thinking. The reliance on concepts drawn from Wundt's psychology strikes the present-day reader as outdated, and even in Kessler's time, it was probably a clumsy and inadequate attempt to address the issues he adumbrates. The examples Kessler adduces to support his argument often remain impressionistic hints: the reader needs to summon up much good will and imagination to find them convincing.

For all this, Kessler's essay was a serious effort to grapple with a core aesthetic problem, namely, how to define and discuss form and content in a work of art. His emphasis on the psychology of the observer anticipates, in an interesting way, the work of Ernst Gombrich, Rudolf Arnheim, and others, who, armed with a more sophisticated psychological arsenal, would later develop the psychology of art perception into the most intellectually compelling subdivision of aesthetics. Kessler does not really succeed in convincing one that art and religion are quite the same phenomenon, perhaps in part because he was planning to address that question more completely in his proposed sequel. Nevertheless, the parallels he points out are suggestive. At the very least, they hint at the conditions Kessler felt were necessary for the revival of the arts for which he, and the circle of friends and apostles gathered around him, so ardently prayed: namely, the emergence of a groundswell of religious feeling, but one forward-looking, fructifying, and new.

CHAPTER 7

A Change of Plans

I spoke of my plans during a walk with Camille Lemonnier, whom all progressive Belgian artists regarded as the leader of the rebellion against official art. Lemonnier, the "Marshall of Literature," as the Belgian writers called him, stopped by the great circle of the Avenue Louise, where today one finds his monument, took me under the arm energetically and cried out: "One must convert them!" "Who?" "The young people!"

Henry van de Velde, *Geschicte meines Lebens*

That Kessler was susceptible to "the prophetic strain" has already been seen in his reception of Nietzsche and his fascination with Derleth. It was a susceptibility shared with many in his generation, but in Kessler's case, it was augmented by his need to find a way into the twentieth century, as it were, to confront and overcome the fin de siècle malaise engendered by the long, melancholy withdrawal of Christianity. This need was further compounded by his anxiousness to find a personal role in the impending transformation, signs of which he saw in the art and literature of his day. Of course, Kessler did not imagine himself in the role of the unquestioning disciple whom Derleth, for example, seemed to require. Rather, he wished to serve as an equal partner, using his wealth, his connections, and his pen. Increasingly, the idea that he could aid this transformation as a public servant of the German government, even in the comparatively freer and more cosmopolitan realm of the diplomatic service, seemed implausible. Although he did not know it at the time, both his desire to find a partnership with a worthy "prophet" of transformation and his hopes of discovering a career in the service of the ideals he was outlining in his diaries came to a decisive turning point when he met the Belgian artist, architect, and designer Henry van de Velde (1863–1959).

Van de Velde's passionate temperament coupled, to use the vocabulary of Kessler's essay on art and religion, idea and feeling in a remarkable synthesis. The idea—or better, the vision—was of a revolution that would harness the socialist idealism of William Morris and the aesthetic of the arts and crafts movement to the machine age. The ideals of beauty would neither retreat to an ivory tower, as in fin de siècle aestheticism, nor be employed to compel a return to an idealized middle ages as Ruskin and, to some extent, Morris desired. Rather, these ideals would intermingle with and fructify the technological civilization of the emerging century. Ultimately, for van de Velde, reason and feeling were not incompatible. In his own work and especially in his numerous articles, lectures, and books, written in the vatic, evangelical style characteristic of turn-of-the-century reform movements, he preached on behalf of the "Cleansing of Art" and "The New Style." Because he sought to embrace the modern world, indeed to compel it to conform to his vision, van de Velde was for Kessler a more promising "priest" of the new religion of art, beating on the drums to summon up a corresponding feeling in his audience, than someone like Stefan George, whose proselytizing urged withdrawal from the world.[1]

The second youngest of eight children of a prosperous pharmacist, van de Velde grew up in Antwerp. Wanting to become a painter, he went to Paris where he discovered Manet and the impressionists. Eventually, he came into contact with a group of Belgian avant-garde artists known as "Les Vingt" and began painting pointillist canvases. An exhibition of the products of the English arts and crafts movement changed his life. Realizing that here was a path where he could combine art with a social consciousness, he threw himself into the study of crafts and design and began lecturing on the redemptive world of the arts and crafts movement at the newly organized "Université Libre" in Brussels.[2] His first project was to build his own house on an open plan, bold for the time. The compartments of bourgeois life were to be overcome by an essential living unity, uniting working, eating, playing, and all the functions of family life. After the house was completed, van de Velde relates in his autobiography that funeral processions on the way to the nearby cemetery would often break down in laughter as they passed by, so struck were they by its unusual appearance. Others were equally taken aback, but in a more receptive manner. Among the visitors were the famous Parisian art dealer Samuel Bing, the art critic Julius Meier-Graefe, and Kessler's friend Eberhard von Bodenhausen, who immediately engaged van de Velde to design the advertising for the company he had founded. When Bodenhausen discovered the difficulty van de Velde had finding enough workers to complete the contracts that were beginning to come in from Germany, the genial baron quickly amassed enough capital for van de Velde to form his own company. He also hired van de Velde to design the furniture for the apartment in Berlin he had bought for his new wife and himself. As his reputation grew in Germany, van de Velde began to contemplate moving there simply to save shipping costs.

Kessler first arrived at van de Velde's house in October 1897. He had seen van de Velde's work at Bing's gallery in December 1895; he had also read the two essays that van de Velde had published in *Pan,* the last of which, "A Chapter on the Design and Construction of Modern Furniture," explained the principles behind his furniture design. Kessler was interested in hiring him to furnish his new Berlin apartment, 28 Köthnerstraße next to the Potsdam train station, as well as in the possibility of van de Velde designing a deluxe edition of Nietzsche's *Thus Spake Zarathustra.* The next month van de Velde and Belgian sculptor Constantin Meusnier arrived in Berlin where Kessler acted as their cicerone and introduced them to high society. In his diary, Kessler noted that when van de Velde spoke about his own work and theories, he was always fresh and interesting, but that as soon as he ventured out of his field he became "capricious and narrow." Despite this reserved judgment, Kessler, after visiting van de Velde and seeing his home, immediately recognized that here was an artist with the energy, will, and talent to confront the future. Within days of van de Velde's arrival in Berlin, Kessler was estimating the funds that would be needed to establish him there. Van de Velde himself credited Kessler with finally persuading him to leave his beloved house and move his family and his work to the capital of the country that seemed most receptive to his ideas.[3]

Before his move to Berlin, van de Velde completed his work on Kessler's apartment. Kessler had asked that his furniture be more elegant than that which van de Velde had designed for Bodenhausen, a request that at first took van de Velde aback but that in the end he fulfilled. The unified, uncluttered style of the furnishings bespoke a dignified elegance, all the more appealing because of its restraint. Van de Velde took special pains to highlight Kessler's rapidly growing collection of impressionist and postimpressionist art. In one instance, he was compelled to an act of ingenuity that would make a curator today blanch. At the end of 1897, Kessler had purchased from Ambroise Vollard the famous painting by Georges Seurat, *Les Poseuses,* one of his four masterpieces, for a mere 1,200 francs.* Excited by his coup, Kessler neglected to consider where in his relatively small apartment he could hang a painting two meters tall and three meters wide. Van de Velde solved the problem by rolling each end around a large pin and displaying only the middle figure in the frame. He assured the nervous Kessler that, because of the pointillist technique, this would not damage the painting. At any rate, Kessler's apartment soon attracted curious visitors, many of them unknown to the owner, drawn in part by the Cézannes, Renoirs, van Goghs, and Seurat's great painting and in part by their carefully designed setting. In this regard, 28 Köthnerstraße was a dress rehearsal for Kessler's later abode, 15 Cranachstraße in Weimar.

It was through Kessler that van de Velde met Elisabeth Förster-Nietzsche. Commonly considered today as the profoundly banal, but nevertheless baleful culprit whose incompetent, capricious, and deceitful handling of her brother's manuscripts, letters, and papers resulted in a completely distorted reception of his philosophy, Elisabeth Förster-Nietzsche nevertheless exerted a personal charm on her contemporaries that is all the more remarkable considering how evident her faults were. Part of the pious respect Wilhelmian intellectuals paid to the "martyred" genius rubbed off apparently on the sister, who so jealously and with such great devotion tended him during the pathetic last twelve years of his life and then fanned the flame of his memory after his death. She exploited these refracted sentiments cunningly and used every bit of the emotional capital it earned her to build up her position as guardian of her brother's legacy and to ward off any potential rivals. Looking back in his memoirs, van de Velde, summons up a devout and respectful image of her, even with the evidence of the disgraceful reception she gave to Hitler at the Nietzsche archives during the last years of her life. In truth, van de Velde had reason to be grateful to her, as will be seen.[4]

Kessler first made the acquaintance of Förster-Nietzsche when he visited her newly established Nietzsche Archive in Naumburg in October 1895 in order to gain permission to print Nietzsche's hymns to

---

* Kessler was forced to sell it for financial reasons in 1926 for 100,000 marks. It is now at the Barnes Foundation in Merion, Pennsylvania.

friendship in *Pan*. There he also met the man she had chosen to oversee the editing of her brother's remaining manuscripts, Fritz Kögel, a
rather vain musician who later that evening sang some of Nietzsche's
compositions. In May 1896, Kessler returned again with his friend Raoul
Richter to discuss the publication of *Ecce Homo*. Kessler and a young assistant at the archive, Rudolph Steiner, later to become known as the
founder of anthroposophy, advised against publication due to what they
considered clear signs of madness in the manuscript. When Förster-
Nietzsche decided to move the archive to the Villa Silberblick in
Weimar, Kessler helped with a generous financial donation. Earlier, he
had put up one-fifth of a loan in the amount of 30,000 marks so that
she could secure the copyrights to her brother's writings, an essential
first step in the creation of the influential Nietzsche Archive.[5]

In August 1897, he arrived in Weimar for a short visit to discuss a
deluxe edition of *Also Sprach Zarathustra*. The decoration of the villa
reminded Kessler of that of a well-to-due university professor or civil
servant, an impression that Förster-Nietzsche's appearance seconded:
"When she becomes excited she begins to speak with a Saxon accent
and often becomes mawkishly sentimental; *how* she says things often
sounds inane but *what* she says is mostly good."[6] For her part, Förster-
Nietzsche was impressed enough with her wealthy young patron to offer Kessler the editorship of the Nietzsche papers replacing Kögel, from
whom she was now estranged. Aware perhaps of the difficulty of working with her and not wanting to become entangled in such a scholarly
enterprise, Kessler refused as he had when offered the directorship of
Pan. The next day she led him to see Nietzsche himself, asleep on a sofa:
"the powerful head rested sunken on his breast, as if it were too heavy
for his neck. The forehead is quite colossal; his hair, like a mane, still
dark brown and likewise his thick, shaggy mustache; under the eyes are
wide, black-brown rings sunk deep in the cheeks; one sees still in the
tired, loose face some deep lines, engraved by thought and will but soft-
ened and gradually flattening out. His expression is of an endless fatigue. He was exhausted by the sultry thunderstorm atmosphere, and
although his sister caressed him several times, fondly whispering "Darling, darling," he did not awaken. Thus he did not resemble an invalid
or a lunatic, but rather a dead man." On subsequent visits, Kessler
would look in on Nietzsche and hold his hand while the sick man would
look up at him, "earnest and peaceful like a beautiful, loyal animal."
Once, when he stayed overnight, he was awakened suddenly by loud
groans: "I stood half up and heard two or three times the long, raw,

moaning sounds which he screamed into the night with all his might; then all was still again."⁷

Nietzsche's long martyrdom was ended a few years later. On August 25, 1900, Kessler received word that Nietzsche had died that afternoon and he rushed to Weimar. Because Max Klinger could not make it to the funeral, Kessler helped prepare the death mask. Later, upon Förster-Nietzsche's request, he opened the coffin one last time and, finding Nietzsche's eyes opened, closed them again. The ceremony commenced on the wrong note due to the long and boring speech of a professor from Berlin, but it closed with Giovanni Pierluigi da Palestrina's magnificent "Quare fremuerunt gentes," sung by an a capella women's choir. At the end of the day, Kessler noted not only the lack of famous, recognized people at the funeral, but also the mediocrity of those present: "No one who stands out in either spirit or character, and nothing of the powerful unity of a coming generation."⁸

Kessler's devotion to the work and memory of Nietzsche proved stronger than either his disdain for the Nietzsche acolytes or whatever misgivings he may have had concerning the philosopher's sister. She soon began calling him her "bibliographic advisor," and Kessler threw himself into work on a luxury edition of *Zarathustra*. He originally intended to have Charles Ricketts design the book using one of the typefaces cut by William Morris. However, after he became familiar with the work of van de Velde, Kessler convinced Förster-Nietzsche that the Belgian would help make *Zarathustra* into the most beautiful book in the world, leaving the books of Morris and Ricketts behind. Van de Velde was hired to design the cover and a hundred woodcuts to serve as text decorations; another Belgian artist, Georges Lemmen, who had done the decorations for *Notizen über Mexiko,* was to design a completely new typeface. From December 1898 until the end of January 1900, Kessler cajoled and encouraged Lemmen, sending him samples of typefaces he admired, urging that he combine great stability with absolute clarity in his design, and explaining his ideas about encouraging a revolution in German printing typography, based in part on the abandonment of the Gothic "Fraktur" script. By the spring of 1901, the new and quite beautiful typeface had been cast. But the immensely complicated copyright problem and the difficult temperament of Elisabeth Förster-Nietzsche caused the project to go through four different publishers before *Also Sprach Zarathustra* was finally published by Insel Verlag in 1908.⁹

Despite the whirlwind of his activity and his travels during the succeeding years, Kessler still frequently felt depressed and bored. Unable either to make headway in his original career choice or to find an attractive alternative, he increasingly felt beneath all his restless activity a strange listlessness. In September 1900, he confided, "I have times in which nothing in my entire life, future and past, interests me, *while the momentary interests attract me as much as ever.* . . . Fragmentary flashes of joy in life against a monotone gray background." A day after this entry, Kessler volunteered for service in the German contingent of the international force that was sailing to China to put down the Boxer rebellion. As it turned out, the experience of war would still elude him for fourteen years; the expedition had already been filled, and Kessler had to content himself with a trip to Greece and Turkey.

Just as he had reached this impasse, however, two possibilities loomed over the horizon: the first was a renewed interest on the part of the Foreign Office in his candidacy and the second was the possibility of becoming director of the art museum in Weimar. The latter alternative had first come up in the aftermath of the death of the grand duke of Saxony-Weimar, Karl Alexander, and the ascension of his twenty-five-year-old grandchild, Wilhelm Ernst. Among those who saw in this event the possibility of a "third golden age" of cultural innovation in Weimar was Elisabeth Förster-Nietzsche, who first suggested that van de Velde be hired as head of a "Kunstgewerblichen Seminar" in order to improve the design and quality of the local arts and crafts industry.

Van de Velde and Kessler had just returned from a visit to an exhibition of Jugendstil art in Darmstadt, sponsored by the grand duke of Hesse. Both men were very disappointed by the work of Peter Behrens, Hermann Obrist, and others, finding in them a romantic rejection of modern life. "Architecture for a bordello, and what's more, a bad bordello" was van de Velde's reaction; Kessler's own response was equally scornful. Against this background, the prospect of van de Velde's official appointment to the post at Weimar seemed like a godsend. Kessler, in a letter to Bodenhausen urging him to use his connections to the Weimar court to help, laid out the advantages: "What van de Velde could accomplish there is beyond imagination if he brings the entire industry of the little state (ceramics, toys, cabinetry, etc.) under his influence. The whole thing would be a wonderful piece of luck for Germany. And how nice that once again Weimar would march at the front. Precisely the risible Darmstadt fiasco has proven that it takes time and patience in order to create something worthwhile, the gradual development of an entire industrial complex; that a sudden caprice cannot create something from nothing; and that success can only lie in the acceptance of modern life with its technology etc., and not in escapism and rubbishy nonsense with so-called beauty."[10]

With this prospect before them, both Bodenhausen and Kessler went to work. The principle resistance they had to overcome was from the *Oberhofmarschall* of the court, General-Lieutenant Aimé von Palézieux, who had been in charge of the art museum of the duchy, a strictly provincial collection. Bodenhausen worked on him through his wife, who was the sister of one of Bodenhausen's friends. Kessler went to Weimar several times to assure him of van de Velde's talent and intentions. One of the first questions Palézieux asked him was whether van de Velde despised all the old styles. He was also concerned about whether van de Velde's wife would be presentable at the court. After two days with this man, Kessler noted in his diary: "An unstoppable self-satisfied pedantry: Polonius." A few months later, he commented on the endless, petty feuds of the *Oberhofmarschall* and noted how typical such intrigues were of the small town where so many idle people have nothing else to do. Nevertheless, he persisted. In a letter to Förster-Nietzsche, he addressed the main concern of the court circle: "The greatest difficulty which must be overcome is that everyone seems firmly to believe that Van de Velde wants to break with all traditions and *import* a completely new style, whereas, just the opposite, he would give the Thüringian crafts the knowledge to *continue* their *own* traditions in an artistic manner; would do this in that he would teach them what *rhythm* is; for this lies at the heart of *every* art practice and it is precisely the essence of this that Van de Velde understands intuitively as well as with his reason as only a few have in the history of art." The influence of Kessler, Bodenhausen, and Förster-Nietzsche proved successful: van de Velde was appointed as head of the arts and crafts school in Weimar on December 21, 1901.[11]

In the course of the negotiations over this appointment, it was suggested that Kessler too should accept a position at the court, as director of the Grand-Ducal Museum for Arts and Crafts. In December 1901, Förster-Nietzsche informed him that "the court circle is still more interested in you than van de Velde and I am truly curious what this circle will put together to attract you here." A month later, however, she sent him a strangely ambivalent letter, informing him that an official decision had not yet been made, but that she was nervous about the thought of him accepting a position: "My impression is now the disturbing feeling that one wishes to lock a young eagle in a cage; in general eagles prefer to fly free. What is fortunate about this situation, however, is that the eagle can open his cage at any time he wants."[12] This may have been a sly way of acknowledging and overcoming Kessler's own fears of entanglement in small town affairs. Ironically, it was Palézieux who informed Kessler, in April 1902, of the plan to open up an entire new building for the permanent collection and asked him whether he cared to join the curatorship. Kessler responded positively but said he was still negotiating with the Foreign Office.

In February 1902, Kessler had tried to learn who was thwarting his appointment to the diplomatic core. Kessler suspected it was Bernhard von Bülow, the jilted suitor of his mother, whom the kaiser had appointed the fourth chancellor of the Reich in October 1900. An informant told him that Bülow never bothered with personnel questions and presumed it was the "eminence grise" of Wilhelmstraße, Friedrich von Holstein, whom everyone feared. Then in March, Kessler was informed through the Richters that Prince Max Lichnowsky, the former ambassador to Washington, wanted to discuss his career with him, evidently in response to Kessler's entreaties. The meeting took place on April 15, 1902. Lichnowsky told Kessler that, although he recognized fully his qualifications for the diplomatic service, the Foreign Office was overfilled and he could not guarantee a position would be free. Because the prince seemed to be full of good will personally, Kessler was emboldened to suggest that he could be useful at the London embassy due to the sickness of the Second Secretary, the upcoming coronation of Edward VII, and his personal connections in England. Lichnowsky seemed intrigued by this suggestion and implied that, if all went well, Kessler might become attached as Secretary to the embassy in little more than a year. He promised to give a definitive answer in eight to ten days.

In the event the answer came sooner, Lichnowsky wrote to Cornelia Richter: "At the moment too many people are against it."[13] Kessler was left to speculate on who was behind the decision. Two days later, on April 22, 1902, he met with Alfred Lichtwark to discuss his plans for the museum in Weimar. In October 1902, Kessler was appointed honorary director of the curatorship; the following March, he officially took over the Grand-Ducal Museum for Arts and Crafts. His long apprenticeship and his years of waiting were over. Now it was time to build "the new Weimar."

PART THREE

The Third Weimar

CHAPTER 8

The New Weimar

Only please do not imagine Weimar and the court as a
museum full of intrusive, dead memories. Quite the contrary.
It is so lively, so animated and *rerum novarum cupidus* as
no other place now in Germany. I hope that we will, here at
the court, gradually build up a real *Public,* what Germany
otherwise lacks.

Kessler to Hofmannsthal, Briefwechsel

What kind of trouble is Kessler making in Weimar? Well, you
can be sure I won't forget what he has done. He will have
cause to remember me in his lifetime.

Wilhelm II

Weimar in 1902 was a somnolent, small city of about 30,000 inhabitants located on the Ilm River, the capital of the duchy Saxony-Weimar-
Eisenach, one of the smaller states that made up the German Empire.
Despite its size, Weimar is unique as a cultural phenomenon: no other
European or American small city has played an equivalent role in the
history and development of its nation's culture. During its "golden
age," from the accession of Karl August and the arrival of Goethe in 1775
to the death of Schiller in 1805, most of the greatest men in German
letters resided there, taught at the nearby Jena University, or visited
frequently—most prominently, Christoph Martin Wieland, Johann
Wolfgang von Goethe, Friedrich Schiller, Johann Gottfried von Herder,
Wilhelm von Humboldt, Johann Gottlieb Fichte, and Friedrich Wilhelm
Joseph von Schelling. The use of German as a literary and philosophical

language was, at the time, hardly two generations old; it is only a slight exaggeration to claim that the German language, as Kessler and his contemporaries knew it, and the specialized vocabulary that distinguished it from its neighbors was forged largely at Weimar. Certainly, this is true for the German ideas of culture and of Bildung. Although the aesthetic ideal that became known as Weimar classicism would soon give way before the Romantics, much of the philosophy of culture developed at Weimar influenced German arts and letters, for better or worse, until at least the end of the Second World War.[1]

Long before Goethe's death in 1832, the name of Weimar had begun to acquire that numinous aura that made it a metonym for all German culture. Its peaceful parks, laid out in the English fashion along the banks of the Ilm, the Belvedere palace, the ducal library, and the court theater, the homes and studies of Schiller and Goethe, above all the simple garden house where Goethe worked—all were encased, as it were, in amber so they could become the site of inspiration for succeeding pilgrims.[2] Weimar became a favorite residence for retired couples of the educated middle classes or for well-to-do families with children to educate.[3] At the same time, however, as the picture of these great men living and working together in harmony became more and more idealized, the legacy of Weimar became an irresistible magnet for those who dreamed of creating a "second" Weimar to build upon the achievements of the first.

What is sometimes called "the silver age" of Weimar began with the arrival of Franz Liszt in 1848 to direct the court theater. Liszt proceeded to stage the first productions of his friend Richard Wagner's operas, as well as to compose many of his most important works. Liszt and his friends and students formed an association, the *Neu-Weimar-Verein,* to attract other artists to Weimar and promote culture there, but eventually these initiatives ran into two problems: the lack of public monies from the financially strapped duchy and the vehement opposition of those who feared that Weimar's legacy would be soiled by upstarts.[4] Eventually, the opposition of offended burghers and self-appointed guardians of "the Weimar spirit" had their way. The last decades of Karl Alexander's forty-eight-year reign were a long, undistinguished twilight. Weimar became truly a provincial *Museumstadt,* vegetating peacefully with its memories, undisturbed by any contact with living culture.[5]

Perhaps if Kessler had considered the example of Liszt's efforts more carefully, he may have entertained less ambitious plans for a "third Weimar." As early as 1891, he had visited the city and was surprised by the unexpected poverty of the houses and furnishings of Schiller and Goethe. It pained him to see the tombs of Germany's two greatest writers next to the remains of all the princely "nullities" of Weimar: "it reminds one a little too strongly of the Privy Councilor" (the official title bequeathed to both Schiller and Goethe).⁶ Now, eleven years later, he was about to follow in their footsteps.

He did not entertain many illusions about the Weimar court. In November 1901, as he was assessing van de Velde's chances of being called to Weimar, he catalogued their motivations: "Palézieux seems to want strongly that his life's work [the so-called "Permanent Exhibition"] will be revived and receive recognition through van de Velde's activity. This is what motivates him. With Rothe [Karl Rothe, state minister] [it is] more the common weal of the state and the influence of his wife. . . . With the grand duke it is the wish to do something to inaugurate his reign in a grand way. Among the court society it is boredom and the search for a toy that can amuse them." About the best thing he could say about the grand duke's character was that he was refreshingly open about his lack of education. Yet, with the hopeful optimism that was an inextinguishable part of his character, Kessler, mindful of his family slogan *Und doch,* ("And nevertheless") approached the task before him in a combative and challenging spirit. In October 1902, he wrote to van de Velde: "I will come to Weimar and will come especially eagerly if there are fights, and intrigues and dangers which are aimed against the tasks that you must accomplish. But I am less pessimistic than you. What do we actually want to do? To create—how can intrigues hinder us in this? You are master in your studio, I in my museum. We will build what we have in mind: a clear, clean, healthy, invigorating and productive apprenticeship. Let the others follow with sour expressions. It won't change anything."⁷ The chief thing, he argues, is that both van de Velde and he be productive.

How did Kessler conceive of his mission in Weimar? For years he had been jotting down thoughts about the task of culture, thoughts provoked by his painful sense of the inferiority of the culture of Imperial Germany compared to that of its western neighbors and political rivals, France and England. Most of these remarks are in the spirit of Nietzsche's aphorism that "a people is a detour of nature to get to six or seven great men."⁸ For example, Kessler posited as a goal the creation of personalities that would combine, effortlessly and naturally, the philosophical culture of Goethe's time with the political culture of Bismarck's day, and the aesthetic culture of the fin de siècle. It is this natural, manifold culture that one admired so much in English statesmen and thinkers, but there, Kessler noted, it was the product of a three-hundred-year development.[9] Kessler's conception of culture remained, however, elitist. He still subscribed to the "trickle down" theory of cultural dissemination that inspired *Pan*. The growing enthusiasm for *Heimatkunst* (roughly, "art of the homeland") in Germany and the interest in the *völkish* arts and crafts of the peasants and small towns left him cold. Industrialization had obliterated the culture of the peasants and of the Mittelstand: what remnants there were would soon be swept away. The lower classes could never achieve anything positive culturally by themselves; they needed an aesthetic elite to serve as an example: "Everything else, the sentimental enthusiasm for folk culture, folk art, folk literature, is pure fantasy . . . . The exact opposite of England and America, where the culture of the upper estates are truly suitable for the rest of society." [10]

The hope that Weimar could become the seedbed of a new culture, suitable for the modern age and for a great nation, originating, to be sure, in an aristocracy of artists and patrons, but whose influence would radiate into all levels of society, began to take hold in Kessler's mind. He nourished it with his customary energy. Soon his plans encompassed not simply van de Velde's activities, or his own as head of the Permanent Exhibition, but also proposals for the revival of the theater at Weimar, long since moribund; for attracting—on a more or less permanent basis—artists, poets, and playwrights to Weimar; for expanding the influence of the Nietzsche Archive; and even for creating an elite school on the model of Eton. For himself, Kessler hoped for the creation of a position from which to overlook, coordinate, and direct this array of enterprises, a podium from which to direct the symphony.[11]

In the meanwhile, Kessler had to content himself with the direction of only one of the two museums of Weimar, the so-called "Permanent Exhibition," a collection of miscellany begun by Palézieux in 1880 and stored in a museum with a hall in which, from time to time, local artists and members of the art school displayed their work. The other museum, the art museum, featured the work of local artists as well, especially the historical pictures of Friedrich Preller. Kessler hoped to induce the grand duke to invite Bodenhausen, after the latter had completed his doctorate in art history, to take over the art museum when its current director retired. Meanwhile, he launched into plans for the reorganization of the Permanent Exhibition into the Grand Ducal Museum for Arts and Crafts. Other than turning the private collection, originally funded by a lottery, into a state enterprise, Karl Rothe, the state minister, could do nothing financially for the new museum. Kessler intended to raise money in part by selling off part of the collection to pay for new acquisitions. He planned to organize what was left into six groups, according to style and geographic origin: Gothic, Louis XV, Sheraton and the period from 1800–1840, oriental carpets and pottery, Japan, and the moderns. The moderns section was to be subdivided into impressionist painting, modern pottery and glass, and furniture (mostly by van de Velde). The arrangement was meant, of course, to be pedagogical, but for the aesthetic sensibility, not for the art historian. "We do not want to create historians," Kessler warned.[12]

The real centerpiece of Kessler's program was the exhibition room. Here he intended to introduce the Weimar public to the world of contemporary French and English art that was otherwise so difficult to find in Germany, outside of a few large cities. The focus was on French impressionist and post-impressionists, but Kessler also wanted to provide a venue for the work of German modernists. To accomplish both of these aims, he diplomatically included exhibitions of the works of older, established German artists such as Adolf Menzel, the local Weimar artist Theodor Hagen, and Wilhelm Leibl. Kessler had another reason for including older works alongside the contemporary: he hoped to show the German public that modern art did not spring like Minerva from the head of a French boulevard journalist, but had a prehistory. Such an evolutionary view could serve to legitimize modern art by placing it squarely within a recognized tradition.

With these principles in mind, Kessler began his exhibition campaign. His first show featured the paintings, graphics, and sculpture of Max Klinger. Immediately following came an exhibition of mostly French impressionist and neoimpressionist painting, most prominently featuring Pierre Bonnard, Maurice Denis, Maximilien Luce, Odilon Redon, K. X. Roussel, Theo van Rysselberghe, Paul Signac, and Eduard Vuillard. Kessler wrote a brief introduction to the catalogue accompanying the show to help explain the intentions of the neoimpressionists. It was only through his good contacts with such art galleries and dealers as Durand-Ruel and Ambroise Vollard that Kessler was able to mount these shows, since there was little hope of selling much of the work and the risks of transportation were great.[13] There followed the same year an exhibition of paintings by Hans Olde, a more conservative painter who had been called to Weimar to lead the Art School, Max Liebermann, Theodor Hagen, Wilhelm Trübner, and Wilhelm Leibl.

Of these, only Liebermann and Trübner were in any way still controversial. Finally, at the end of the year, Kessler exhibited the arts and
crafts that van de Velde had produced over the past year and a display of
photographs of his interior designs. By this time, the latter included van
de Velde's designs for Kessler's new home in Weimar (he kept his Berlin
apartment as well), 15 Cranachstraße.

Van de Velde, for his part, was deeply engaged in his effort to invigo-
rate the slumbering arts and crafts of Weimar and the surrounding
countryside of Thuringia. Unlike earlier reformers who had founded
their own businesses and attempted to compete in the marketplace, van
de Velde, as a state official, could develop his designs, with the students
in his arts and crafts seminar, free from commercial concerns. He then
would offer both the designs and instructions on how to execute them
to interested local firms, free of charge. He conceived of his seminar as
a laboratory, devoted to the pure theory of design, but with spin-offs for
industry. As Kessler reported enthusiastically to Bodenhausen: "Here
for the first time a truly practical, modern form of the position of the
artist to industry has been discovered; a derivation, it is true, of the
wonderfully successful arrangement, invented in Germany, of scientists,
chemists and physicists etc., with industry. A kind of art laboratory in
the service of industry will be established, that will work on the artistic
problems facing industry and offer solutions for exploitation; exactly as
the chemical laboratories [did] with their artificial indigo or Bremer
burners. If the experiment in Weimar succeeds, I am convinced that it
will be path breaking in Germany." The experiment began with a grand
tour through the duchy in the company of the grand duke's mother
Pauline, who had taken an interest in van de Velde's efforts. In two
coaches, drawn by servants in livery, they visited ceramic and porcelain
factories, leather and woodworking shops, weavers, carpet and toy man-
ufacturers, and at each stop van de Velde would descend and preach the
gospel of functional design. It was a strange procession: half a throw-
back to the seventeenth-century mercantilism of Louis XIV's minister,
Jean-Baptiste Colbert, and half an anticipation of the activity of the
Werkbund and the Bauhaus.[14]

Van de Velde, in his first report to the grand duke, avowed that he
conceived his mission as being no less than "to shape the style of the
twenty-first century."[15] The promising results of his grand tour may
have encouraged this ambition. In the shops of Weimar soon were seen
some vases and a small tea service from the revitalized firm of Bürgeler,
furniture by the cabinetmaker Scheidemantel, jewelry by the goldsmith
Müller, and leather bindings, all of them based on designs by van de

Velde. One of his greatest early successes was convincing the cooperative basket-making firm, Tannrodas, to expand into making cane and rattan furniture according to his designs. Their elegant products were soon found in all the major cities of Germany and made their way as well into Kessler's sitting room.

Sometimes van de Velde overreached himself, unintentionally treading on taboo sensibilities of Germans uncertain of the reason for this Belgian's presence in the city of Goethe and Schiller. A remark of his made at a dinner party was distorted through malicious gossip into the phrase, "Piety? I have no piety!" and then brought into play when he proposed replacing the extremely high wall that surrounded Goethe's garden house with an iron fence. Although his intention was simply to let pedestrians see the house and its grounds, the outcry reached the national press. One satirical journal printed a cartoon showing van de Velde, looking like a frivolous French elf, working on a wrought iron fence encompassing vaguely poodle-like shapes, when he is interrupted by a statue of a glowering Goethe. His reputed remark on piety is contrasted with Napoleon's respectful, "*Qu'en dit Monsieur Goethe?*" ("What does Monsieur Goethe think about it?") Van de Velde was forced to deny publicly ever saying that he had no piety, and his plans were quietly abandoned. It was a foretaste of things to come.

Nevertheless, despite this one reversal, "the new Weimar" seemed to have begun propitiously. Van de Velde's previous reputation in Germany, coupled with Kessler's connections to the progressive art establishment and to the press, ensured that their efforts were noticed. One glowing report, by Hans Rosenhagen, a prominent art critic and, at the time, a warm supporter of modern art, was published in the conservative *Der Tag*, one of the most widely read newspapers of Berlin. Responding directly to the brouhaha over van de Velde's "lack" of piety, Rosenhagen praised the young grand duke effusively for recognizing that time cannot stand still, even in Weimar, and for having the courage to appoint a foreigner to revive the art and industry of his state. After explaining van de Velde's mission, he expressed the greatest hopes for its success, particularly noting how van de Velde's style had evolved, shedding its *Jugendstil* excesses in favor of a restrained functionality. Although stressing the contribution of van de Velde, Rosenhagen also praised the grand duke for calling Hans Olde to the Art School and for assigning Kessler, "known through his sensitive articles on aesthetics and for role in the leadership of *Pan*," to the task of reorganizing the art collection: "Count Kessler intends to present in these exhibitions only selected and original works of contemporary art, so that one can soon learn as much about modern artists and their achievements in Weimar as in Berlin. Nothing will be left to chance. Following the Klinger exhibition will be presentations of the works of Leibl, Liebermann, Menzel, and Trübner. The paintings of the French impressionists and neo-impressionists, the best of the Belgians, the finest English artists will appear in Weimar, so that both the residents and especially the young art students of this museum will be able to profit from the many-sided stimulation." [16]

Rosenhagen's article was typical of the response of those interested in the advancement of modern art. Those opposed to this development expressed sharply contradictory opinions of the effort to build a new Weimar. In Weimar itself, the opposition did not take long to emerge. The day of the opening of the van de Velde exhibition, November 8, 1903 — a mere eight months after his official appointment — Kessler's Polonius, General-Lieutenant Palézieux, complained that Kessler was ruining his life's work. A few days later, the state minister Rothe took Kessler aside and warned him of Palézieux's grievances. Although Kessler dismissed this news with the contempt he felt it deserved, he had more powerful enemies than the chamberlain Palézieux. The most highly placed of these opponents kept a close eye upon the events transpiring in the duchy of Sachsen-Weimar-Eisenach. The kaiser perused the reports of his ambassador at the court in Weimar with outraged interest, making marginal comments, as was his custom. Already he had insulted van de Velde by refusing, at an industrial fair, to enter a room decorated by the Belgian for fear, as he put it, of "becoming seasick." When he learned of how Kessler's opponents accused him of using all his means to favor van de Velde and modern art, going so far as selling the paintings of Franz von Lenbach to create room and raise money for the "hypermoderns," the kaiser jotted down an explosive, "Jackass!!!" in the margins. The enemies of "the new Weimar" had a powerful ally. [17]

· · ·

Kessler would learn of the Kaiser's personal animosity toward his activity a few months after the Weimar experiment was over. Of the Kaiser's disdain for modern art and his willingness to intervene where possible to support his views, Kessler had long been aware. It was during the campaign to have van de Velde appointed to the position in Weimar that the *Siegesallee* was dedicated, an occasion that the kaiser used to try to impose his definition of art on the entire German public. Reading of his speech in the newspapers the next day, Kessler remarked on how the kaiser's thoughts were naive, poorly informed, and full of illusions. He went on to comment, "The basic character of his being comes through clearly; temperamental ignorance, crowned dilettantism, Friedrich Wilhelm IV [referring to Wilhelm's hopelessly inept great uncle], only more of a windbag." On both sides of the debate over modern art in Germany, a rancorous vocabulary threatened always to conflate a matter of taste into an affair of state. This might appear strange to a reader today, but the investment of aesthetic questions with a charged political content was one of the characteristic marks of Wilhelmian culture.[18] In a way that—with the exception of the occasional scandal over funding choices of the National Endowment for the Arts—we have difficulty recalling, art mattered.

The man who served as a lightning rod for the attacks of those, like Kessler, who were interested in modern art was Anton von Werner. As the director of the Institute of Fine Arts, the premier art school in the Reich, and chairman of both the *Verein Berliner Künstler* and the *Allgemeine Deutsche Kunstgenossenschaft,* an umbrella organization of Austrian and German artists, Werner dominated the official art world of Wilhelmian Germany. Bismarck once remarked that if he had not become an artist, Werner would have made an excellent diplomat. His own paintings were competent but lifeless showcase examples of historical genre painting in the glossy, academic mode. His most famous work, *The Proclamation of the German Empire,* depicted the coronation of Wilhelm I as emperor of the new German Empire in the Hall of Mirrors at Versailles. In a savage polemical piece, written at the height of controversy over official sponsorship of art, Kessler dismissed his opponent's art:

One knows the pictures of Herr von Werner. Their subjects have insured them a wide distribution, that corresponds somewhat to that of the state handbook on the Prussian monarchy. They provide ministries and the homes of lesser civil servants with atmosphere. They are considered there history pictures. Usually twelve to sixty uniformed, expressionless gentlemen stand around utterly dry and stiff. One thinks, a fashion illustration for military tailors, but the signature reads: a historical picture, a great moment from a great time; King William's war council, the capitulation of Sedan, the imperial proclamation at Versailles. Before one wanted to laugh; now one would rather cry, if boredom did not foreclose any expression of emotion.[19]

Kessler went on to remark how Werner failed to answer his own rhetorical question, posed in one of his speeches; namely, what would happen to artists once photography succeeds in developing color pictures? Werner's silence, Kessler asserted, proved the utter poverty of an art theory that aims simply to reproduce, as accurately as possible, a scene from life. The stale quality of the paintings that result from the rigorous application of this theory offered sufficient evidence to contradict it.*

The first major challenge to the official, academic conception and practice of art favored by Werner was the formation of the Berlin Secession. Among the major secessions that marked the beginning of modern art, Berlin's was the last. Ironically, although the Berlin Secession, compared to its rival in Vienna, was more eclectic aesthetically, less self-consciously modern, and less concerned with the aesthetic improvement of everyday life, its struggle for existence was more bitter, and ultimately, ideological. Because it occurred in the capital of the German Empire, right under the nose of a fundamentally hostile—with a few exceptions—official art establishment, whose opposition was reinforced by a monarch able and willing to intervene in these matters, the birth, struggle for recognition, moment of triumph, and final decline of the Berlin Secession was accompanied by political reverberations of a vehemence unknown in Vienna or Munich.[20]

Von Werner and his allies provoked the creation of the secession by their successful effort to close an exhibition by Edvard Munch in 1892 before it had opened; ironically, it was *Verein Berliner Künstler* itself— acting on the basis of recommendations and without having seen his work—that had invited Munch to display his paintings. When some seventy members protested, Werner reacted strongly against the insubordination by forcing the resignation of a number of the ringleaders from their positions as teachers at the Institute for the Fine Arts. The hostility against Werner on the part of an influential minority was so great now that it was only a matter of time before a new secession resurfaced—this time with effective leadership and a financial basis—in May 1898 with the foundation of the Berlin Secession.[21]

The principal personality in the leadership of the Berlin Secession was Max Liebermann. Famous for his wit, delivered in the inimitable

---

*From Werner's point of view, of course, art self-evidently was mimesis, and it was precisely the fault of modern art, beginning with impressionism, to neglect the accurate depiction of nature that damned it in his eyes. One of his proudest achievements was the supervision of the creation of a vast panoramic depiction of the battle of Sedan, a laborious piece of work, employing many painters working according to the most detailed and painstaking instructions. Its purpose was to give the viewer, perched on a platform in the center of the circular building, the complete illusion of being in the midst of the battle. The immense popularity of the Sedan panorama, in an age before cinema, was a source of satisfaction for Werner and confirmation of the value of his art; see Dolf Sternberger, *Panorama of the Nineteenth Century* (New York: Urizen Books, 1977), 7–16.

Berlin dialect, Liebermann was, according to temperament and background, a member of the liberal, Jewish, upper middle class. He was far from a bohemian—even the transformative goals of the *Jugendstil* remained alien to him. Of van de Velde's interior design, he is alleged to have remarked, "From my furnishings I want my own amusement, not van de Velde his." A man sure of his talent, ambitious, and utterly devoted to painting, Liebermann resented his exclusion from the Academy and its domination by a mediocrity like Werner. His energy, presence, and prestige made him a formidable leader of the secession.[22]

The secession was able to survive without state support due largely to a pair of cousins from a well-to-do Jewish family. Bruno and Paul Cassirer had already opened a gallery of their own, designed by van de Velde as one of his first Berlin commissions, where they presented carefully planned exhibitions of modern French and German art. What distinguished the Cassirer gallery from the other Berlin galleries that from time to time displayed modern art was the programmatic intent of the former. The Cassirers did not simply scatter a few modernist pieces among a plethora of more saleable traditional works; rather, like Kessler in this respect, they planned their exhibitions around thematic principles. Seen against the background of the marketing of art, the Cassirer gallery represented the increasingly successful challenge of exclusive private art dealers over the older, state-supported and -sanctioned system of annual public salons. In return for a number of privileges, including a say in the selection of art, the Cassirers agreed to organize, administer, and help finance the secession. With their energetic assistance, the secession was able to build its own gallery and offices and open its first show a mere year after the foundation of the secession.[23] From the beginning the exhibitions of the Berlin Secession in the Kantstraße were a social, cultural, and financial success, helped by the participation of a number of Germany's most prominent modern artists, most notably Max Slevogt and Lovis Corinth, both of whom were elected to the executive committee of the secession. The art of the Berlin Secession was sufficiently challenging to meet the demands of this new audience, yet conventional enough not to alienate it.[24]

The struggle between the secession and Anton von Werner reached its climax in the controversy over Germany's plans for the 1904 World's Fair in St. Louis. Irritated by an initial decision by the nominating committee to grant more exhibition space to members of the secession than he deemed proper, Werner complained to the kaiser, who needed no further provocation. He quickly cashiered one of the officials responsible for the new committee and ordered that control over the exhibition be returned to von Werner. The kaiser's heavy-handed intervention in the controversy—the way he presumed to speak for all of Germany in aesthetic matters as in other affairs—created a backlash that he probably did not foresee. One consequence was the final alienation of the secession whose members realized that the state, in the final analysis, would always be hostile to them. The solidarity induced by this hostility enabled them to organize to defend their interests. Having rejected the feeble efforts made by the *Kunstgenossenschaft,* after July, to appease them, secession members finally met in Weimar in December 1903, under the protection of the grand duke, to form the *Deutsche Künstlerbund,* an alliance of secessions meant to act as a countervailing force to the *Kunstgenossenschaft.*

Kessler was instrumental in the founding of the *Deutsche Künstlerbund.* At the beginning of 1903, before the controversy over St. Louis, he had been meeting regularly with Liebermann and with Georg Simmel to discuss plans for the secession. They informed him that the aim of the secession should be to organize "the pair of *Kulturmenschen*" living amidst the barbarians. Above all, it should combat all official art as represented by the *Siegesallee.* Then in October, after the St. Louis incident, Kessler discussed the plans for the *Künstlerbund* with Liebermann and others. The goal, they agreed, should be freedom from moral constraint in art; the method would be the boycott of official salons, the creation of their own exhibitions, and eventually, a museum and studios of their own as well.[25] It was meant to be smaller than the secession and not represent any particular party, simply the strongest talent active in Germany. Membership was to be chosen on an individual basis.

Throughout November, Kessler canvassed the leading German artists for their help. He traveled to Munich, Stuttgart, Düsseldorf, Karlsruhe, and Leipzig to drum up support; among the artists he consulted were Fritz von Uhde, Franz von Stuck, Adolf von Hildebrand, Max Slevogt, Lovis Corinth, Max Klinger, and Leopold Graf Kalckreuth. When the founding session of the *Künstlerbund* was opened on the 15 of December 1903, nearly every important artist and museum director in any way connected with modern art was present. Kalckreuth, a rather conservative but independent-minded artist, was elected president and Kessler first vice-president. The daily business of the organization was in Kessler's hands.

After meeting all the first day and then attending a banquet, the dignitaries were accompanied by students of the nearby university of Jena, marching with flags and torches, on their way to meet the grand duke in the palace courtyard. The overwhelming favorite of the crowd was Max Klinger, whose brief, stuttering address to the grand duke was received with great enthusiasm. Later, according to van de Velde, the students accompanied the leaders of the *Künstlerbund* to the restaurant Kunstverein, the meeting place of those who disapproved of "the new Weimar." In the smoky den, the classic example of Auerbach's cellar in *Faust,* the students drove the regulars out, drank toasts to the artists gathered in Weimar, and made the rafters sing when they shouted out the names of Kessler and van de Velde. It was a heady way to celebrate the foundation of the *Künstlerbund* to carry the fight to the enemy, but it cannot have won Kessler or van de Velde any friends among the regulars at the Kunstverein.[26]

Even before the *Künstlerbund* was officially founded, Kessler had been planning for a public debate on the St. Louis exhibition debacle. In October, he met with Hugo von Tschudi, the director of the National Gallery, to outline possible strategies. To their indictment of the government for favoring one kind of art over another, they anticipated the response that the government was only legitimately interested in art that furthered the interests of the state; all other art was free to find private patrons if it could. Kessler advised, as a counterthrust, to raise the ire of the educated philistines by arguing four points: first, the state did spend money on art that did not glorify it; namely, old art, Italian masters, and so forth. Two, the state could not patronize one kind of art exclusively without driving all other kinds to the wall. Three, by forcing art to be "patriotic," the state would end up killing genuine art and thus undermine its purpose. Four, such a step would also harm Germany materially by completely destroying her—in any case diminishing—market abroad, especially in the United States.[27]

The evident tenuousness of these responses to the question of why the state should support modern art points to the difficulty, replete with irony, of the *Künstlerbund*'s position in any public debate. The very act of bringing the issue to the Reichstag implied the right of the majority, as expressed by the representatives of the people, to discuss and decide the question. But the content of the *Künstlerbund*'s complaint and the principle of its organization were thoroughly elitist. To mount an effective political attack in the Reichstag, the *Künstlerbund* absolutely needed the support of the democratic opposition, principally the Socialist, Catholic Center, and Progressive Parties. At the same time, however, to avoid being branded as part of the political fringe, it needed at least the partial support of the government coalition, the National Liberals and the Conservatives, to whom the elitist philosophy of the new organization was inoffensive but who distrusted modern art as an ideologically suspect, foreign import. As the chief strategist of the *Künstlerbund* in the forthcoming debate, Kessler was confronted with bridging this apparently insuperable gulf.

His most successful political move was the pamphlet he wrote, "Der Deutsche Künstlerbund," which was distributed to the Reichstag before the debate on February 16 and 17, 1904 (and later published as an article with revisions in response to the debate). With it, Kessler defined the terms of the debate in a way that avoided discussion of the most vulnerable points of the *Künstlerbund*'s position. The first part seizes the high ground by declaring the enthusiastic support of the press for the new organization, which promises, above all else, "to guarantee the artist his freedom." Then he brands the opponents of this worthy and unobjectionable goal as a Berlin clique, composed of mediocrities who wish to crush individual talent through the rule of the majority. If this clique is a party representing special interests that have somehow acquired an unfair influence on the state bureaucracy, then the *Künstlerbund*, by contrast, is *parteilos,* belonging to no special school but open to all with talent. Kessler makes great use of the presence of a number of famous, conventional artists in the new organization, particularly Arthur Kampf, a highly successful portrait painter, to prove the openness of the *Künstlerbund* to any artist regardless of his style, the only criterion being his talent. It is not the *Künstlerbund*, Kessler argues, but the unnamed Werner and the *Kunstgenossenschaft* that represent a single style and persecute relentlessly anyone who deviates from it, going so far as to reject paintings for an exhibition in Chicago that were recommended by Professor Kampf, a respected member of the Royal Prussian Academy, simply because the artists belonged to secessions. This kind of high-handed, narrow-mindedness has actually harmed the state by destroying the reputation of German art abroad. In the United States especially, the import of French modern art, from Millet to Cézanne, has reached the annual figure of 4 million marks, nearly ten times that of Germany.[28]

Expressing the conflict in this way helped make the *Künstlerbund* more appealing to educated Germans, who, even if they were politicians, believed that the state should be above politics, a neutral arbiter, a promoter of all that was best in German culture, and a protector of the free personality. Kessler emphasized that his opponents practiced a politics based purely on numbers without regard to quality, a practice that many educated Germans felt was inappropriate even in public life, let alone in aesthetic matters. Kessler played upon this sentiment masterfully. Anton von Werner and his allies had only one eternal goal, "to eradicate personalities in art in order to make room for others and for the masses." In art, only the exceptional was important. No amount of industry, good intentions, or schooling could make up for the individual talent. And only the *Künstlerbund* was capable of giving the individual artist his freedom to develop himself and contribute to German culture; the *Kunstgenossenschaft* represented a spirit that was, in its essence, antithetical to individuality.

The second part of the pamphlet called for the establishment of a new museum of modern art that would be organized along the principles of all successful museums, that is, under the firm leadership of a museum director who would build the collection according to aesthetic principles and aesthetic principles only: no inartistic criteria such as subject matter, or the artist's good intentions, or official position should apply. And the aesthetic form, clearly, must be both artistically exceptional and personal; nothing merely average and nothing impersonal, in a style simply copied from someone else. Such a museum would have an inestimable value for contemporary German art. For modern art, despite the sneering accusations by Werner and others, is firmly rooted in the past: Degas was deeply indebted to his studies of Nicolas Poussin, and Cézanne, the most radical French artist of his day, spent hours in the Louvre copying the works of Luca Signorelli and Eugene Delacroix.[29] Kessler closes the pamphlet with the admonition, mentioned in an earlier chapter, that the state is necessarily concerned with art. The whole mighty apparatus of the state is only there to permit the flowering of a nation's culture. Despite the chicanery of certain officials, Kessler prophesizes the emergence of a new generation of *Kulturpolitiker* devoted to this higher end.[30]

The Reichstag debate on the St. Louis exhibition controversy took place on February 15 and 16, 1904. The result was a triumph for the artists represented by the *Künstlerbund* and a political embarrassment for the Bülow administration. The fact that at least one member of each political party of any importance in the Reichstag spoke against the government, thus undermining the minister of the interior Count Arthur Posadowsky's defense, was due in large part to Kessler's connections and political savvy. Most speakers addressed themselves to the main issue as defined by Kessler, the self-serving and unfair intervention by a clique, abetted by an irresponsible head of state, in the composition of

the German art exhibition at St. Louis. Against the assault from all sides
on this matter, the government could only weakly defend itself, in the
end promising vaguely never to mount a similar exhibition without
consulting the other states of the Empire. The same debate in the Prussian legislature, the Landstag, although less sharply cast than in the
Reichstag due to the more conservative composition of the members,
reached roughly the same conclusions. The echoes from the debate
reached beyond Germany: both the *London Times* and the *New York
Times* reported the incident as a setback to the kaiser.

While apparently chastened by the criticism he received in the debate, Wilhelm II by no means refrained thereafter from interfering in
cultural politics. In 1908, he would create another scandal by his forced
dismissal of Hugo von Tschudi from the directorship of the National
Gallery. Still, the personal attack on Anton von Werner did represent a
blow from which the Director of the Institute of Fine Arts never recovered. The narrow brand of idealistic, heroizing, academic art he represented fell increasingly into ridicule and discredit, even among more
conservative circles. In Berlin at least, and in the other major art me-
tropolises, the secessions and their umbrella organization, the *Deutsche
Künstlerbund,* achieved a position of hegemony that ended only
with the emergence of expressionism and the outbreak of the First
World War.[31]

Kessler remained a leading force behind the scenes for the duration
of the *Künstlerbund* until its disbandment in 1914. Just as it owed its
birth largely to his constant diplomacy, so it surmounted several other
crises due to his personal mediation. When Fritz von Uhde, upset by an
article in *Kunst und Künstler* that only mentioned Max Liebermann's
name in connection with the *Künstlerbund,* threatened to bolt the organization because it was becoming, in his opinion, an association of
Jews on behalf of Jews, Kessler smoothed his ruffled feathers by praising
his paintings. Later, he helped sort out differences between the artists
Franz von Stuck and Leopold Graf Kalckreuth. He was also instrumental in the leasing of the Villa Romana outside of Florence on behalf of
the *Künstlerbund,* where promising young German artists could live for
a year on a stipend. In June 1906, he helped organize the third annual
exhibition of the Künstlerbund in Weimar, the last exhibition he gave
there. Among the most interesting artists invited was Max Beckmann,
a young man working in a style quite different from the "north-
German" impressionism of Liebermann, Slevogt, and Corinth. After
visiting his studio where he saw Beckmann's large work-in-progress de-

picting the crucifixion, Kessler commented, "He is through and through a *painter,* something rare for a German." Kessler managed to secure a year-and-a-half stipend for Beckmann at the Villa Romana, and he purchased the artist's picture, *Young Men at the Sea,* for the museum in Weimar. His sympathetic interest in the emerging expressionist art distinguished Kessler from many of his friends—Bodenhausen, Liebermann, and Meier-Graefe, among them—in the *Künstlerbund* who soon would find themselves in the uncomfortable position of resisting the next wave of modernism. In 1910, when the Berlin Secession rejected the work of young expressionist painters, who reacted by forming a new group, the New Secession, Kessler was already a so-called passive member of *Die Brücke,* the seminal expressionist organization featuring the artists Erich Heckel, Ernst Ludwig Kirchner, Max Pechstein, and Karl Schmidt-Rottluff.[32]

CHAPTER 9

The Culture of the Eye

Personalities whom I don't even know, Druet, Denis-Cochin,
Octave Mirabeau, have let me know that they wish to get
in touch with us. I see that today we already have the same
strong backing in England and France that we possess in
Germany. We hold the world of art in our hands. Above all
we must not lose the wonderful pivotal point that is Weimar.
In this respect, Bonnard will come to Weimar. . . .

Kessler to van de Velde, van de Velde Archives

For all of his ambitions and dreams of turning Weimar into the pivotal
point of modernist culture in Germany, Kessler could not abide the
small town atmosphere on the banks of the Ilm for any extended length
of time. The mounting signs of a backlash against his efforts, expressed
at the time mostly in the ill-concealed resentment of certain individuals
at the court, also discouraged him. In April 1904, a little more than a
year after taking office, he recorded this resolution: "How one, as a
practical matter, can best proceed: *stubbornly* and *without bitterness*. So
I in Weimar, if it were only possible." [1] Paris, London, and Berlin always
loomed as refuges of cosmopolitanism, and Kessler shuttled regularly
among the Grand Hotel in Paris, the Cecil in London, and his Berlin
apartment. His activity as director of a museum devoted to modern art
required, of course, that he visit Paris and London frequently. By building upon the connections he had made during his *Pan* years, he soon
established himself not simply as a patron but also as a personal friend
of the leading French and English artists.

Although his closest acquaintances, outside of his family, in both England and France were initially creative artists, London and Paris appealed to different parts of Kessler's personality and interests. Because of the growing political rivalry between England and Germany, political and diplomatic questions often preoccupied Kessler while in London. In France, by contrast, he mentions politics infrequently in his diary, concentrating instead on observations about the theater, literature, and above all, art. It was the art world that drew Kessler to Paris repeatedly. Eventually he met, through the art dealers Durand-Ruel and Ambroise Vollard, most of the great French modernist painters then living, including Monet, Renoir, and Degas, all of them famous by the time he met them. In November 1903, he traveled with the Belgian painter Theo van Rysselberghe to Giverny to visit Monet, whom Kessler had met earlier at Durand-Ruel's gallery. One of the remarkable qualities of Kessler as a diarist was his ability to record, sentence by sentence, the conversation and monologues of someone like Monet, filling page after page with an evocative *procès-verbal* of his visit. A few years later, the art dealer Ambroise Vollard arranged a dinner especially so that Kessler could meet Degas. Among the guests were the painters Jean-Louis Forain, Pierre Bonnard, and the decorator José Maria Sert. Kessler's detailed account of the witty but malicious conversation that ensued, capturing every sally and every nuance, offers a wonderful and rare record of the style of conversation of an epoch. He was rather shocked by Degas's vicious anti-Semitism and misogyny, calling the artist "a frenzied and maniacal innocent." Another dinner at Vollard's a few days later brought him together with Renoir, who made a much more agreeable impression, especially when the old man began to speak "with the spirit, tempo, and voice of a twenty-year old."[2]

If Monet, Degas, and Renoir were already legendary figures, the succeeding generation of French artists, many his contemporaries, offered Kessler the opportunity to form personal friendships, some of which lasted decades. Kessler was first introduced to the pointillists at the gallery of Durand-Ruel. Soon he was visiting Paul Signac, Henri-Edmond Cross, and Maximilien Luce in their studios to discuss their theories and purchase their paintings: his growing collection of post-impressionist masterpieces now included, besides Seurat's *Poseuses,* Luce's shimmering Parisian landscape, *Le Quai Saint-Michel,* which Kessler later donated to Munich's Neue Pinokothek, and Signac's harbor scene, *Brume du Matin,* which he bought in May 1902 for 1,000 francs.

Kessler's familiarity with the goals and theories of the pointillists served him well during the polemics over this new direction in modern art that were unleashed in Germany. In February 1903, shortly before Kessler's exhibition of postimpressionist art in Weimar, he responded publicly to a clever but on the whole moderate attack on pointillism by Wolfgang von Oettingen, the standing secretary of the Academy of Art, who had objected to the presentation of what he considered "studio exercises" before an untutored public in museums and galleries.[3] Kessler argued that Oettingen had conceded more than he intended when he allowed that the pointillist method had antecedents. Not only Jean-Baptiste-Siméon Chardin practiced a form of optical color analysis, Kessler pointed out, but also Jacopo Robusti Tintoretto, El Greco, Peter Paul Rubens, Jean-Antoine Watteau, Jean-Honoré Fragonard, Francisco de Goya, Joseph Turner, John Constable, and Eugene Delacroix, to name only a few. Furthermore, Oettingen's complaint that the "radical" pointillists used tiny squares of color was patently absurd when one considered that for centuries artists had used various brush strokes that—in themselves—bore no more "natural" relationship to reality than the pointillist squares. The main thrust of Kessler's polemic was to argue that the various styles of art represented different systems of signs, each with the power to evoke a reality for those prepared to learn their conventions, and none of them being somehow more "natural" than the others. Our preference for one system or the other should not depend on a thoroughly spurious assumption of what is more natural, but on the aesthetic advantages of each system—to put it succinctly, on what new beauty a new style of art can offer. As far as the "charm of detail" that Oettingen complained was missing in modern pointillism, Kessler retorted that in all honest painting, this should consist "not in the correctness of the copied, anecdotal details of the model or the landscape, but rather in the harmony and the rhythmically effective arrangement of dabs of color."[4]

Kessler's insistence that the essence of art was found not in the interpretation of the artist, but in his means of expression, was rooted in his conviction that art history was best conceived as the history of the response of individual artists to certain aesthetic problems. A truly interesting art history would discuss how these problems, such as the possibility of expressing light through contrasting values, were raised, addressed, and developed by artists working within a specific tradition. Everything else—biography, history, and philosophical aesthetics—should be secondary.[5]

Curiously, although Kessler employed this principle to defend the practice of pointillism, it was Pierre Bonnard, Maurice Denis, and Edouard Vuillard—painters for whom Oettingen expressed admiration—who represented for Kessler the epitome of a true artistic culture. He had developed especially close ties with this circle of artists, known as the Nabis after the Hebrew word for prophet, just before becoming director of the museum in Weimar. The decisive influence on this group of unusually close-knit friends was the art and teaching of Paul Gauguin. Seeking to define where his art differed from the impressionists, Gauguin wrote to a friend, "Art is an abstraction. Take inspiration from nature, let it play on your imagination, but think more of the original work you can create from it; the only way to move closer to God is by doing as our Lord did: by creating." In their early years, all the Nabis followed Gauguin's example of using bold swatches of complementary pure colors—similar to those used in posters (indeed Toulouse-Lautrec was a friend)—compressing the foreground and background, creating odd, tilted or angular perspectives found in Japanese prints, and emphasizing a simplified and rhythmic use of line. As Kessler argued in the catalogue accompanying an exhibition featuring the artist that he mounted in Weimar, Gauguin achieved his powerfully mysterious and symbolic effects not by his choice of subject matter, but by the novelty and strangeness of his color harmonies. Although he did not mention it, Kessler may have had in mind an implicit contrast with other symbolist painters, such as Klinger, whose art depended almost entirely upon its subject matter for its symbolic effect. At any rate, this concentration on the formal aspects of art pervaded all of Gauguin's followers; so much so that Maurice Denis, the most theoretical of the Nabis and for a time their unofficial spokesman, formulated this famous doctrine: "Remember that a picture, before being a war horse, a nude woman or some anecdote, is essentially a flat surface covered with colors and assembled in a certain order."[6]

The art of the Nabis, at least in their early period, has much in common with Art Nouveau, notably the rejection of the distinction between fine and applied art, the interest in reviving ornamental art, and, in general, the desire to make art once again a part of everyday life. A decorative panel by Denis, *The Ladder in the Foliage,* depicting four female figures draped in gowns, with long flowing hair, ascending, as in a dream, a precariously perched ladder against a tangled background of serpentine branches and foliage, is easily classifiable as Art Nouveau. The same can be said for his panel that graced Kessler's living room, *The Hyacinth Forest,* wherein satyrs chase laughing maidens in various states of undress through unreal, moonlit woods. Nevertheless, these compositions by Denis lack completely the ominous or grotesque effects or the tormented sexual anxiety found in much Art Nouveau and symbolist art. All the Nabis shared the same extremely serious—almost religious—devotion to art that characterized most Jugendstil artists, but somehow their art was, generally, more serene and sunnier.

The peculiar serenity and calm of the Nabis reached a culmination in the work of Bonnard and Vuillard, especially in the large decorative panels they painted for their patrons. Simply the names of Vuillard's Desmarais Panels—*Nannies and Children in the Park, Stroking the Dog, Gardening, The Game of Battledore and Shuttlecock, The Dressmaker's Shop*—evoke the confident and nonchalant pleasures of the upper middle classes *en famille.* The use of patterns of prints in the last composition, resembling the swatches of material used by a seamstress such as Vuillard's mother, served the artist as a way to explore textures in painting: their collage-like quality seems to hint at the work of Braques and Picasso. When seen against the background of their contemporaries—not simply Jugendstil artists like Klinger, Gustav Klimt, and Munch, but even their more mystically and religiously inclined Nabis colleagues such as Denis, Paul Ranson, and Paul Sérusier—Bonnard and Vuillard are remarkably free from any straining after profundity or depth, from any hint of *Ideengeschichte* (intellectual exposition). Although capable of speaking at length about their art, they were far more interested in questions of form rather than content. With its intense concentration on texture, composition, and color, the art of Bonnard and Vuillard was the product of an aesthetic culture peculiar to France. It was this aspect that attracted and fascinated Kessler.[7]

He had first encountered the Nabis when he attended the same Bing exhibition of Art Nouveau in 1895 that featured van de Velde's interior designs, and then again some years later at the Exhibition of Independent Artists in 1902. In the fall of 1902, accompanied by Hugo von Tschudi, he visited Denis in St. Germain and Vuillard in his home in Paris, where he immediately bought two sketches. He returned again in December of that year to invite Denis, Vuillard, and Odilon Redon to visit Weimar. Denis eventually came twice to Weimar, where he admired the way in which van de Velde had incorporated his panels (two others besides *The Hyacinth Forest*) in Kessler's home, if he found little else there to his liking. Kessler, for his part, began to frequent studios, especially those of Vuillard and Bonnard, during his trips to Paris. It was through these artists that he was introduced to the salon of the

Natanson brothers, the wealthy Jewish patrons of the Nabis. Thadée Natanson had founded *La Revue Blanche* (1891–1903), a journal that published the early work of Marcel Proust and André Gide, among others, as well as offering its subscribers original prints mostly by Nabis artists. Kessler became not only friendly with him, but with his striking wife, Misia, who was well on her way to becoming one of the fixtures of the European social and artistic scene before the war. Another frequent guest of the Natansons was Felix Féneon, the anarchist art critic, editor of *La Revue Blanche,* and champion of the neoimpressionists. Féneon advised Kessler on the purchase of a number of paintings.

Stimulated by this environment, Kessler began to fill his journals with notes and outlines for a book on the emergence of modern art in France. As he became more intimate with the Nabis, especially Bonnard and Vuillard, he felt compelled to revise his opinions about the Jugendstil artists he had once admired. In Dresden, after seeing an exhibition of paintings by Gustav Klimt, for whom he had in truth never really cared, he let out a melancholy sigh: "Everywhere one looks, the German art of the nineteenth century hardly got beyond the beginnings. Just compare Overbeck with Ingres, Feuerbach with Puvis de Chavannes, Böcklin with Delacroix, Leibl with Manet, all second best (*lauter zweiter Garnitur*). The question is whether it is any different today with Liebermann, Slevogt, Klinger, Ludwig von Hofmann? What is the originality of *their* means of expression?" Shortly after returning from a visit to Paris, Kessler visited his friend and ally in Weimar, Ludwig von Hofmann, a more typical than outstanding artist of the Jugendstil. Appalled privately by Hofmann's new canvases, Kessler advised him to go to Paris to study the painting of the masters. Hofmann was simply another example, in Kessler's view, of the tragic lack of a true aesthetic tradition in the pictorial arts in Germany.[8]

· · ·

The artist with whom Kessler would have his most productive relation as a patron came from a region rich in the tradition Germany lacked, the Mediterranean littoral. One day, while Kessler visited Rodin in his studio in Meudon, the great sculptor, a friend of Kessler's family for years, reached into one of the large drawers in which he kept his sketches and withdrew a small clay figure: "'Do you know who made this? He is our strongest sculptor.' Thus I was introduced to Maillol." This may have been the same clay model that Kessler noted, on New

Year's Day 1903, he had been carrying around with him for more than a week: "A curious, growing magic from its simple forms, which everywhere offer pure, soft profiles. It captivates me more and more." Nevertheless, it was not until a year and a half later, in August 1904, that he actually met the sculptor, traveling to his studio in Marly outside of Paris: "He lives in quite a small and very primitive and rural house in the midst of large open orchards. When we knocked on the door (there was no bell), a woman appeared on the small balcony and cried towards the garden: Aristide! Aristide! Whereupon a farmer in a blue blouse, the wide-brimmed worker's straw hat on his head, came and greeted us in a very broad and rustic patois. He didn't introduce himself, and didn't bother much about our names either; he was simply Maillol: appearing to be about forty years old with a long, uncut, and full black beard, very expressive and sparkling blue eyes, lean and with a pronounced Spanish nose." Kessler quickly made up for lost time by buying a model of a crouching woman for 800 francs and then commissioned, from a sketch the artist had shown him, yet another sculpture of a squatting woman, this time in stone. This last project, known to Maillol and Kessler as "Statue pour un parc tranquille" ("statue for a tranquil park"), was eventually displayed publicly in 1905 under the title *Mediteranné,* an exhibition that earned Maillol his first widespread public and critical acclaim. For years, this sculpture served as the centerpiece of Kessler's Berlin residence.[9]

Kessler was overcome with enthusiasm for his discovery. Here was an artist whose work was utterly free from any hint of artifice; the most classically perfect forms seemed to flow from him as from a spring in his native Banyuls, a fishing village on the Mediterranean quite close to the Spanish border. A few days after his first visit, Kessler invited Maillol to breakfast in Paris and watched in wonderment as he sketched his likeness on the tablecloth with his fingernail, and did it so well that he asked for paper and a pen to finish it. Two days later, Kessler again traveled to Marly where Maillol showed him his sketches for illustrations of Virgil, Pierre Louys, and others. Kessler, who had been tinkering with the idea of establishing his own private press, realized instantly that here was a born illustrator. At the beginning of September, only eleven days after first meeting him, he invited Maillol to accompany him to London for a week. There, perhaps in response to Maillol's earlier remark that he never sculpted male nudes because he could never find models, Kessler took him to the ring in the East End so he could sketch the boxers: "He sketched with unbelievable swiftness the fighters, sketches which are comparable to the most beautiful of Delacroix." Maillol, partly out of enthusiasm, and partly, it would seem, from an incipient sense of what would please his new patron, compared the boxers to a "young race who fight to exercise like the heroes of Homer." Kessler then took Maillol to meet the preeminent British book designer, Emery Walker, and together with the German printer Carl Ernst Poeschel, they visited the British Museum to examine various typefaces. The immediate goal was to go over the designs for the new edition of the German classics, to be published by Insel Press, that Kessler was supervising. But in the back of his mind, Kessler was no doubt beginning to spin out the idea of commissioning Maillol to illustrate a work of Virgil's, an idea that finally came to fruition after many years of labor by Maillol, himself, and others. Just before his departure for Paris, Maillol declared that the trip to London had been "an illumination for me. I better understand sculpture and art in general." [10]

It was a strange attraction of opposites that drew the nervous, refined, Anglo-German cosmopolitan to the Franco-Spanish sculptor whose somewhat misleading rusticity went hand in hand with a supreme artistic self-assurance. Maillol (1861–1944) had studied at the École des Arts Décoratifs in Paris, where he encountered the work of Gauguin in 1884. His surviving paintings from this period show the influence both of the Nabis and of the pointillists, but he soon turned to the design of tapestries in keeping with the current trend toward decorative art. His efforts were rewarded by the attention and praise of Gauguin himself when his tapestries were displayed at the exhibition of Les XX in Brussels. But for Maillol, who had married one of the seamstresses who worked on his tapestries, the 1890s was a period of dire poverty. Temporary blindness prevented him from continuing with his tapestry work and, in his forties, he made the final transition to sculpture. In 1900, Vuillard brought the art dealer Ambroise Vollard around to see Maillol's collection of terra cotta sculptures. From then on, his work began to gain admirers beyond his immediate circle, but it was Kessler's patronage that, once and for all, rescued him from poverty and obscurity. [11]

In an essay published years later, Kessler made much of the fact that it was Maillol's great antipode in sculpture, Rodin, who had first mentioned him: "Rodin, the continuation of the French late Gothic, of the 'Dix-huitième,' the master of details, of realistic observation, of the soft or stormy fluctuating surfaces, the dramatic silhouette; Maillol, the Greek, the master of masses, of the round fullness of physical health, which strives for the light, and for whom detail has only as much worth as has the white veil of blossoms for the fruit tree, serving to momentarily illuminate its structure and the powerful thrust of its sap." This way of conceptualizing the differences between the two sculptors was encouraged by Rodin and Maillol themselves, who continually reflected on what differentiated their work. In part, this served to diffuse and manage the rivalry that underlay their real admiration for each other (although Maillol was not above a certain subtle, but persistent, criticism of Rodin, born perhaps from envy of his more famous colleague). Nevertheless, the antithetical relation of Rodin and Maillol is immediately evident if one visualizes their work or if one is so lucky, as Kessler was, to have sculptures of both in one's study. There is no getting around the famous distinction between romantic and classical art in this case. Rodin's typical gesture is theatrical: attention is directed toward the tension in the clenched hand or the distorted face; the literary analogues, as Kessler noted, are Dante and Baudelaire; and his sculptures are instantly identifiable. With Maillol, the face and hands—even the head—scarcely matter, it is the form of the torso, the relation between the masses of the neck, shoulders, back, belly, thighs, and buttocks that is important. Maillol strove to find the center of gravity for these masses, to bring them into harmony. The thought of sculpting someone famous, either dead or living, would not have occurred to Maillol, who worked constantly to simplify his forms to their most irreducible type. Once while standing before an antique Venus in the Louvre, whose forms had been gradually smoothed and simplified by the erosion of centuries, Maillol remarked to Kessler: "You see, this figure has been my teacher. If a Rodin had made this, nothing would be left. This statue has taught me what sculpture is. A statue must be beautiful even when its surface is destroyed and polished as flat as a pebble." [12] Even in his own day, Maillol was often attacked for always choosing heavyset women as his models.* The criticism misunderstands, according to Kessler, Maillol's intentions: the model is a matter of indifference as long as it supplies a sculptural motif. This concern with the abstract qualities of

---

* Once Maillol complained that Misia Sert had told him that, while she admired his sculpture, she did not like his women, his *"grosses femmes."* She does not understand that I am sculpting surfaces, he told Kessler, whereupon Kessler responded that nevertheless, when one looks at a statue of a woman, one thinks of the woman. "Maillol laughed. 'Obviously one thinks of the woman! If I didn't have anything between my legs, I would not perhaps sculpt women.'"

form, volume, mass, and harmony makes Maillol's statues an important transitional stage on the path to modern abstract sculpture. Never ceasing to be realistic, they nevertheless point to the abstract shapes of Hans Arp or Henry Moore.

For Kessler, Maillol represented almost an atavism, an unselfconsciously archaic modern, a Homeric figure in the age of the locomotive and the telephone. All the tensions that Kessler felt so keenly within himself, "the oppositions that divide the modern artist and make him a problematic figure, between man and nature, between morality and sensuality, are not present to Maillol." It was only after he had traveled to Banyuls to see Maillol in his milieu that Kessler felt he could understand this paradox. Only against the background of this border region, Catalonian more than French, but really older than that, the relation between man and nature, the social intercourse of its inhabitants, its forms of life, all dating back to antiquity, could an apparition like Maillol make sense: "The men fish or alternatively in spring and fall tend their vineyards. The women wash their clothes like Nausica in the mountain brook just before it flows into the surf. The older matrons, austere, dark women, wander in black robes and black veils like priestesses. At the well in the evening stand the girls with jars on their broad shoulders. . . . If Odysseus landed here, he would have recognized a home like his own: and this home is Maillol's." [13]

In a way Maillol posed a challenge to Kessler's ideas about aesthetic education, the value of a genuine artistic tradition, and the possibilities of cultivating artists through museums and schools. In a letter to Hofmannsthal on the occasion of his first visit to Banyuls, he noted the surprising social position of Maillol, who, it turned out, was more of a sturdy yeoman, possessing rather large vineyards, than he had imagined. The society there was completely undifferentiated, all the families were alike, the conditions pre-Homeric: "That from this a fine strong art, indeed an entire artist family (for he has painters and poets as nephews) could suddenly spring forth, is a very curious phenomenon. To be able to witness so concretely the sudden refinement (mutation) of an entire family from simple peasant and sailor to an artistic refinement that borders on over cultivation, has interested me enormously. . . . One becomes quite skeptical about any kind of aesthetic education." [14] In the end, Kessler dealt with the challenge by turning Maillol into the exception that proved the rule.

The relation between two such different men was bound to encounter tensions, especially when they were tempted to see too much of each other.[15] This became evident at the end of their trip to Greece in the spring of 1908. Still, precisely the enormous differences in nationality, social origin, education, and vocation prevented the kind of misunderstandings that vexed Kessler's relationship with Hofmannsthal. With Maillol, Kessler was always first a patron and only then a friend. Nevertheless, Kessler's relation to the sculptor was among the most enduring and affectionate he enjoyed with anyone. This is in part due to an endearing comic undertone that announces itself almost from the first, when, shortly after they met, Kessler, the cosmopolitan "nighthawk" who rarely turned in before midnight, especially in Paris, awoke at the uncomfortable hour of eight o'clock to the sound of heavy knocking and shouting: "*C'est moi, Maillol, ouvrez, c'est moi, Maillol!*" Outside the door of his room at the Grande Hotel was the sculptor, wife and child in tow, waiting impatiently for his breakfast.[16]

. . .

Long before Maillol was to visit Weimar, an entirely different sort of Frenchman was invited by Kessler to give a talk before the court. Kessler had probably heard of André Gide first through his connections with *La Revue Blanche*. Later, he read and admired Gide's novel, *Les Nouritures Terrestes*. They had a friend in common, the Belgian post-impressionist Theo van Rysselberghe, who had known van de Velde for many years and whose wife, Marie, was one of Gide's closest friends. Gide was a great admirer of Goethe, so when Kessler invited him to visit Weimar for the opening of the post-impressionist exhibition, he accepted with enthusiasm. As the date approached, he began to have second thoughts, especially about giving his talk in French before a select audience composed of high Weimar society. After arriving in Weimar and visiting the sites connected with Goethe, as well as the Nietzsche archive, Gide gave his lecture, entitled "The Importance of the Public," on the evening of August 5, 1903.[17]

It was a fascinating and provocative speech, at places quite awkward for some members of the audience. Gide's topic was the duties of the public toward the artist, not just any public but those *honnêtes gens,* who—situated between the vulgarity of the mob and the rigid formalism of court society—have always been, according to him, the guardians of good taste. This public, however, which Gide explicitly identifies with the Weimar of Goethe's day, no longer existed, replaced, it appeared, by a vulgar and heterogeneous mob, against whose tastes the "art for art's sake" school reacted. In a plea for a Nietzschean inspired paganism, Gide argued that the gods must return to earth for art to revive. No art has ever sprung from an abstract monotheism that drew too great a distinction between heaven and earth. Technically speaking, there is no such thing as Christian art (here he must have heard the uncomfortable coughing and scraping of feet among the twenty members of his audience). Rubbing salt in the wound, he rejected the current vogue for sincerity in art, arguing instead that hypocrisy was the necessary precondition for any genuine art.[18]

Few in his audience could have appreciated Gide's playfully paradoxical defense of classicism with its oblique attacks on naturalism in the theater and its rather ironic gestures of respect toward Weimar, past and present. The grand duchess protested the passage about the cloak of Catholic hypocrisy thrown over the art of the Renaissance, and the wife of the kaiser's favorite playwright, Ernst von Wildenbruch, found the whole thing "incongruous." In Kessler, however, the Frenchman found an interested listener, even if the personal impression he left with his host was rather sinister.* The aesthetic theory Kessler had worked out emphasized the role of the public, and increasingly he was becoming aware of the need to cultivate a public for modern art in Germany. With the growing fragmentation of the audience for art, those museum directors interested in supporting modern art were naturally concerned with identifying its potential public. As early as 1893, Tschudi had addressed the problem and conceded that the public for modern art would always be an elite, those who were able to appreciate that art is not reducible to its content. Kessler, at least publicly, was not quite so pessimistic.[19] In his own lecture on "Art and the Public," which he first delivered in Jena in 1904 and then, in various forms, in other German, Belgian, and Austrian cities over the next few years, he returned to the question he had left pending at the end of this essay on art and religion; namely, to what community of believers could the modern artist find a relation?

Certainly the false traditions of the art academies or of the "aesthetic

---

* Kessler, perhaps alerted by Gide's hint at his contempt for sincerity or perhaps sensing the unspoken homosexuality shared by both men, wrote the following: "A kind of not quite normal sensuality, which he does not have the courage to acknowledge, appears in the background of his entire being. It gives him a somewhat weak, almost fearful appearance that is paired with an oddly lively curiosity as soon as abnormal cases of murder are mentioned." *TB,* July 31, 1903.

tea circles," which the English, under the influence of Ruskin, fabricated were not adequate substitutes for a cohesive community with uniform standards. As an example of the latter, Kessler pointed to the European court societies from the Renaissance to the eighteenth century, that, whatever their limitations, served both to appreciate pure art and to train connoisseurs who could make "the short life of genius fruitful." Rather, a circle of connoisseurs must be created whose "eyes" are trained like a music lover's "ears." Alfred Lichtwark's promotion of dilettantism is a step in the right direction, according to Kessler, but dilettantism is not actually necessary; all that is necessary is to train and use one's senses. Taste must be the substitute of tradition, a taste we can no longer inherit from a living tradition, but must acquire through training. If the modern public applies itself to acquiring this taste, then it can fulfill the function of the old court societies by supporting deserving artists. Kessler finishes with a lament over how small the public for contemporary art is: "Living taste always feels drawn to the art of its own time and fulfills instinctively its duty."

After Gide left, Hofmannsthal arrived for a week. Kessler took the opportunity of asking him whether he wished to come to Weimar as Intendant of the theater, the same position Goethe held. Hofmannsthal did not respond positively but did not reject the notion entirely. At the residence of the grand duchess, the famous Belvedere palace, he read some of his poetry as well as part of his verse play, *Das kleine Welttheater*. In a letter to his sister, Kessler praised Hofmannsthal as one of the finest readers he knew and mentioned his hopes of having him come permanently to Weimar: "He has most interesting ideas about the staging, the mise en scène, of pieces and great talent en détail also, I think, by the way he talks. But there is an old man we shall have to poison before this can be realized." Kessler, too, had some exciting new ideas about the theater, based on the revolutionary performances of *Much Ado about Nothing* and Ibsen's *The Vikings* that he had witnessed earlier that year in London. And, once his troublesome guest, whose poetry he admired but whose personality irked him, had finally left, Kessler dashed off for London.[20]

CHAPTER 10

A Theater of Dreams

The "crazy Englishman" is only an exaggeration. The English spirit does indeed have a touch of madness. That and physical beauty are the charm of the English.

Kessler, *Tagebuch*

London offered Kessler, if anything, even more of a refuge than Paris, at least during the first years of the century. Edwardian England intrigued Kessler as the supreme example of an empire and a culture at its peak that, at the same time, displayed unmistakable signs of decadence. Whereas Kessler saw very little to admire or emulate in French—or, for that matter, American—politics, the British parliamentary system, with its web of compromises between authority and freedom, aristocracy and democracy, tradition and innovation, seemed to him to be the very model of a successful political tradition, an example from which Germany could profit. So too he admired the apparent aplomb with which the island nation ruled its vast empire, for it seemed to prove to the anxious aristocrat that numbers did not account for everything in the modern world, that a superior moral will would, in the end, carry the day.

Still, there were cracks in the edifice: the Boer War presented the sordid spectacle of a middle class aping the mores of an earlier, warrior class. To Kessler, this jingoism represented an analogous phenomenon to the Dreyfus affair in France; both were signs of decadence. Then, too, Kessler began to be alarmed at the degree of anti-German hostility evident in the British press, which he assumed was controlled by the financial interests of the City. He attributed the campaign waged against Germany in the press to the city's fear of the rising economic clout of Germany, a supposition, that, although widely held by Germans, was nonetheless quite incorrect: in fact, the British financial interests stood the most to lose from a war and were therefore eager to avoid a conflict with Germany. Ultimately, Kessler predicted as early as 1902, the trade rivalry between England and Germany would become as intractable an issue as the struggle over Alsace-Lorraine between France and Germany. Kessler did not blame Germany for inspiring fear in the British; he took the emerging predominance of the German economy in Europe for almost a natural force, to which the British should learn to accommodate themselves. Such an accommodation might be conceivable if the City did not prevent it by fueling the British fear of Germany. For Kessler, the power of the press was a sign of the penetration of money interests into politics, an example of political degeneration. He seemed to assume that Germany was relatively safe from a similar phenomenon due to the supposedly neutral German civil service and its devotion to the state, an assumption that ignored the pervasive impact of organized interest groups in Germany.

If British industry and commerce were clearly slipping, British culture, in Kessler's opinion, remained in many respects exemplary. As important as the French contribution to modern art was, Kessler considered that, taken as a whole, modern culture owed more to England than to any other country. "The English between 1750 and 1850 created the modern house, modern clothing (Beau Brummel), modern painting, and moreover the modern constitution and the (entire?) white world. The influence of this English century, if one adds that of literature, industry, science, and philosophy (Locke, Berkeley, Hume), has in the whole of history only two or three equivalents: Greece, Rome, France in the thirteenth century." In comparison with the golden age of Great Britain, the century from 1750 to 1850, the subsequent fifty years represented, in Kessler's view, at best a silver age. While acknowledging the pedagogical importance of the Pre-Raphaelites, he considered their artistic worth to be negligible. In addition, he had qualms about the latest direction taken by the English arts and crafts movement. Finally, with a few exceptions, he found modern English painting and sculpture to be weak; like German art, it suffered tremendously in comparison with its French counterpart. Considering culture in a broader sense, however, including manners, conversational style, grace, poise, and comfort, Kessler found the upper-class British way of life an admirable achievement. He even contemplated at one point writing a book on English artists and writers; the theme would be "the possibilities of culture under modern living conditions."[1] Although some aspects of English culture were undeniably the inimitable result of hundreds of years of evolution, nevertheless, he felt that there was much Germany could learn from England's example. In two areas close to his heart, Kessler did prove to be an important agent in Germany's successful attempt to overtake the English: the craft of fine printing and the theater.

Kessler's efforts to publish a deluxe edition of Nietzsche's *Zarathustra* first brought him into contact with the English book designers around William Morris and his Kelmscott Press who had revived the art of fine printing. As museum director in Weimar, Kessler took unusual pains to publish his exhibition catalogues in a typographically distinguished way. At the same time, he gained an important foothold in the German publishing world when his friends Alfred Walter Heymel and Rudolph Alexander Schröder founded the Insel Verlag in 1901. The first director of the Verlag, Rudolf von Poellnitz, began publishing books with features that had long been commonplace in England: thin but strong, wood-free India paper, legible typefaces, a thoughtful compositional design, and flexible, sturdy bindings. In the beginning of May 1904, Kessler, with the financial backing of Heymel, who was heir to a large fortune, won the approval of the grand duke to serve as the patron of an ambitious collection of classics to be published by Insel. The plan called for publishing Goethe and Schiller, Schopenhauer, Lessing, Herder, Hölderlin, Novalis, Kleist, Hebbel, and Wieland. Kessler traveled to England to hire the best English experts to create a format that would distinguish Insel's editions from the others that flooded the market. His contact there was Emery Walker, "perhaps the greatest printer since the Renaissance," who had directed Morris's Kelmscott Press and helped found, along with Thomas J. Cobden-Sanderson, the Doves Press. Walker agreed to serve as the overseer for the Grand Duke Wilhelm-Ernst Edition and directed Kessler to the calligrapher Edward Johnston and his pupil Eric Gill, who agreed to design the titles for the edition. Douglas Cockerell, a student of Cobden-Sanderson, designed the cord-free, flexible bindings with tomato-red leather covers. These were produced in Britain, as was an unusually light brand of Oxford India paper. Further distinguishing this edition from earlier ones was the easily readable Antiqua type, a bold move considering the common assumption that the German classics should be published in a *Fraktur* rather than a Latin script. The design was fully free of any ornament, and the texts, although carefully edited, were presented without commentary and scholarly apparatus in order to facilitate reading.[2]

The first volumes, *Goethe's Romanen und Novellen* and *Schillers dramatische Dichtungen,* appeared in time for Christmas 1904. The praise was not unanimous. Some of the criticism was legitimate; the margins were too narrow and the paper was too transparent. These errors were soon corrected just as the leather covers gave way to linen in order to increase the affordability. Other criticism was of a kind that Kessler was coming to expect: in February 1905, Heymel wrote to him about the reception of the initial volumes: "As I hear, in Berlin, especially in the arts and crafts museum and among the directors, the naming of so many Englishmen has caused bad feelings, something I consider laughable and in poor taste, yet not completely without weight since these professors are making a fuss and can hurt us with their judgments."[3] Despite these cavils, the Grand Duke Wilhelm-Ernst Edition represented a landmark in publishing history, and not just in Germany. Other German publishers began using similar formats, and in France the famous Bibliothèque de la Pléiade imitated Insel's format, typography, and paper. Only in Britain, oddly enough, was the example not followed.

Kessler's relation with Insel continued after Poellnitz's death in 1905. He became a close friend of and unofficial artistic advisor to the succeeding director, the energetic Anton Kippenberg.[4] In the spring of 1905, Kessler devoted an entire exhibition to the art of modern printing. It was a comprehensive introduction to both the history and the present state of fine printing. Besides books from the Kelmscott and Doves Presses, the exhibition included illustrated books of Beardsley and Laurence Houseman; first editions of Klopstock, Wieland, and Schiller; and copies of *Pan, Insel,* and *Blättern für die Kunst*—examples of the latest Belgian, Scandinavian, American, and French publications, as well as Italian and German incunabula. As his experience, knowledge, and contacts in this field grew, Kessler began to plan seriously the establishment of a private press that would continue and advance the work commenced by the great private English presses.

· · ·

In London as in Paris, Kessler's introduction to society was through artists. He had influential family connections, among them his cousin

Henry Finnis Blosse-Lynch who became a member of Parliament in 1906, but he did not seem to have used them much. His friendship with the well-connected painter William Rothenstein provided him with his real entrée into the world of English arts and letters. Described once as a "superbly intelligent bee" who "always knew where to find the finest nectar," Rothenstein knew most of the leading artists and writers in late-Victorian and Edwardian England; in this regard, he played a somewhat similar role to Kessler's in Wilhelmian Germany. Rothenstein had already heard of Kessler from Rodin and others by the time of their first meeting in 1902, at a dinner party in Berlin given by Max Liebermann. Their friendship lasted a lifetime, and later, in the 1920s, Rothenstein's son, John, also became friends with Kessler.[5] One of the young artists to whom Rothenstein introduced Kessler was the painter Augustus John. Together, they visited the boxing matches in Whitechapel. The next summer Kessler displayed some of John's sketches at Weimar and wrote a short piece for *Kunst und Künstler* praising the young artist as the best hope of refuting the prevalent assumption that English painting was dead.[6] John, for his part, introduced Kessler to the work of William Hogarth, a revelation that bore fruit a few years later in Kessler's collaboration with Hofmannsthal.

Yet it was another young Englishman, very much in the same mold as John, with whom Kessler was to establish a lasting relationship as a patron, the English counterpart in some ways of his association with Maillol. In April 1903, Kessler visited an exhibition of *ex libris* in London. He found the most striking—powerful and simple designs, very suited for an *ex libris*—to be those by Gordon Craig. The next day, Kessler attended a performance of Ibsen's *The Vikings,* a rarely performed early play. In the lead role was Ellen Terry, the most famous English actress of her day. Responsible for the direction was her son Gordon Craig. What Kessler saw that evening remained fresh in his memory all his life; decades later, he could still describe it in detail to Craig's son.[7]

Craig had broken entirely with the conventions of nineteenth-century theatrical realism by creating a *mise en scène* that relied on suggestion, rather than on historical depiction, and on the atmosphere created by abstract elements of light, shadow, movement, and masses, rather than on the painstaking, almost archaeological, accumulation of stage props and decoration that had been common to European theater for a quarter century. In so doing, he had not hesitated to ignore, when necessary, the detailed stage directions of Ibsen himself. In the second act, for instance, instead of constructing, according to the playwright's instructions, a banqueting hall—complete with tables, benches, fireplace, doors, and seats of honor, exactly as it might have looked in ninth-century Norway—Craig hung, from an invisible height, a semicircle of backcloths, parted in the middle to reveal an imposing doorway. On a mound in the middle of the stage, which was tilted slightly to bring the actors closer to the audience, stood a circular table with the two seats of honor in the center foreground. Suspended above was an immense wrought iron circle bearing lights. The impressive monumentality of the scene owed something, it is true, to the Bayreuth productions of Wagner, especially those for *Parsifal*, but Craig's stage was much more simplified, concentrated, and free of the clutter found in Bayreuth. It has been persuasively argued that Craig's production of *The Vikings* anticipated by fifty years the productions of the so-called "New Bayreuth," staged by Wagner's grandson Wieland Wagner.[8]

It is possible that Kessler may have seen Craig's earlier amateur productions of Henry Purcell's masques that had caused William Butler Yeats to exclaim, in a letter to the *Saturday Review,* "they gave me more perfect pleasure than I have met with in any theatre this ten years."[9] Now, however, the full novelty and magic of Craig's efforts struck Kessler, despite some misgivings about the production itself, as "a very original attempt at the reform of the stage. . . . The fundamental ideas seem to me very important and the impression is in any case much stronger than with the usual paper-mâché decorations; because the fantasy has a much freer reign and the attention is concentrated." In effect, Craig had proven that the same principles that apply to music, painting, sculpture, architecture, and design, belong on the stage as well: rhythm, light, and color.[10]

Craig's family and education were deeply rooted in acting and the theater. He was born out of wedlock in 1872 to Ellen Terry, just then at the beginning of her career, and Edward William Godwin, a pioneering architect and close friend of the Pre-Raphaelites. From an early age, he had begun a promising career as an actor, aided by Ellen Terry's lover and his adoptive father, the great Shakespearean actor Henry Irving. Craig, however, quickly grew bored with acting, and in 1897, in a move that reminds one of the young Hofmannsthal's decision to stop writing poetry, Craig quit the stage, never to play a role again.[11]

During his last years as an actor, he had begun to learn how to draw and make etchings. Craig learned how to concentrate on the most powerful and characteristic elements of a design, ignoring all else. Especially important in wood engraving were the striking effects of chiaroscuro;

Craig's etchings almost always show his attempts to capture the drama of light.[12] As he became more proficient, Craig began to design and sell *ex libris*, as well as to sketch out his favorite scenes from Shakespeare, again always aiming for the greatest simplicity and the greatest emotive force. Slowly his imagination began to conjure up another kind of theater, quite different from Irving's Lyceum, and he began to look for ways to turn his private imagery into reality. The first opportunity came with the amateur productions of Purcell that he and his composer friend, Martin Shaw, staged. He reveled in the freedom and complete control he enjoyed as director of these productions and, conversely, found it dispiriting to watch his ideas compromised or diluted in the next professional productions he directed, *The Vikings* and *Much Ado About Nothing*. Firmly convinced of his redemptive vision of the theater, Craig found it exceedingly difficult to compromise. This quality, coupled with a complete disdain for any commercial considerations, made him a very difficult man to work with and, like a visionary architect's blueprints, most of Craig's creations never were produced for one reason or the other.

When Kessler finally met him at the Café Royal at the end of April 1903, Craig was an extraordinarily handsome thirty-one-year-old man with a thick mane of hair and a boyish charm, neither of which left him his whole long life. He was fond of large, broad-brimmed hats, cloaks, and canes, and this theatricality was complemented by an innate naiveté and a selfless love for the theater. His combination of charm and good looks was irresistible to many women. When Kessler met Craig, he had already fathered six children by three different women and was just about to embark on his famed love affair with Isadora Duncan.* At

---

* An amusing incident Kessler recorded in his diary just before the war must have been repeated often in Craig's life. Craig, Kessler, and the unspeakable Aleceister Crowley, self-proclaimed black magician, were at a dancing hall in Montmartre when Crowley, whom Kessler describes as a "fat, disgustingly dressed bohemian, an Englishman without collars," suggested an orgy with some new, intoxicating drinks. Craig and Kessler managed to shake him off and around 2:30 A.M. found themselves in a nightclub called "Maniko." A young girl in the company of sailors rushed up to Craig and exclaimed: "Monsieur resembles Alfred de Musset. Of course I didn't know Alfred de Musset, I am not old enough, but I have seen him on prints, he was a great poet." The sailors apologized for her behavior but the girl kept insisting that Craig must be a great painter or poet. "I wish to kiss the hands of Monsieur." Craig, who in fact had very ugly hands, "like those of a psychopath" according to Kessler, tried to hide them under the table but the girl kissed them anyway. Later, Craig tried to find her address; he would have liked to go home with her. See the *TB*, February 1, 1912.

the time, he was professionally at a loss, realizing that the only work he could find in the English theater would involve compromising his beliefs to a degree he found repugnant. Therefore, when Kessler told him of the reception he would receive in Germany and of "the new Weimar," Craig was intrigued although he had reservations, writing to Rothenstein, "I can do nothing talking to Dukes and Grand Duchesses & Poets with a court actress or two thrown in—I have had so much experience of these *discussions* about a production. If only he or the duke would make me a definite offer I would then make a definite answer."[13]

Kessler was working on it. The theater has always held a special place in German cultural life; the great *Bildungsroman* by Goethe, *Wilhelm Meisters Wanderjahre,* concerns a theater company that wanders around Germany, and Goethe himself directed the theater established at Weimar. Schiller believed that the theater could provide a divided Germany with a national experience. One can therefore imagine Kessler's excitement when he began to toy with the notion of finagling Hofmannsthal an appointment as *Intendant* and bringing Craig to Weimar to introduce his revolutionary theater design. His enthusiasm must have been redoubled when, in his conversations with Hofmannsthal in August 1903, he learned that the Austrian had been thinking about the theater in much the same way as Craig. It seems that Kessler's description of Craig's productions influenced Hofmannsthal's essay, "The Theater as Dream Image," published in October, for it calls for a theater that in every way reminds one of Craig's vision: "Who constructs the image of the theater, must know . . . that there is nothing in the world fixed and motionless, nothing without a relation, nothing that lives for itself alone. His dreams must have taught him that, and he must see the world thus; the power of dreaming must be strong in him and he must be a poet among poets. His eye must be creative like the eye of a dreamer who sees nothing without meaning. To create an image, in which not an inch is without importance, that is all."[14] A better description of Craig's intentions could scarcely be found.

Hofmannsthal, among other projects, was working on a free translation of Thomas Otway's seventeenth-century play, *Venice Preserved*. It was an important period in his development. Having ceased to write lyrical poetry, he was trying to master the art of writing full-length dramas. The reworking of Otway's play, for which he traveled especially to Venice, would prove to be his breakthrough on the stage, he hoped. Otto Brahm, the old warhorse of German naturalism and then head of the Lessing Theater, had been pressing him to complete the play. Originally, Hofmannsthal had considered Mariano Fortuny as stage designer, a natural choice as the Spanish painter lived in Venice. But Kessler convinced him to insist upon Craig instead.[15]

Craig first came to Weimar the following spring in May 1904. There he could see nine of his drawings and woodcuts on display in an exhibition entitled "New English Art." Kessler introduced him to van de Velde with whom he exchanged ideas about the design of theaters. Kessler also arranged to have him interviewed by the editor of *Kunst und Künstler,* which dedicated an extensive piece, including many illustrations, to Craig in its November 1904 issue. This was to be the first of many visits over the years to Weimar, which later Craig would recall as, "always so full of happiness—light free spirit days." That July he traveled to Berlin for preliminary discussions with Otto Brahm. The dynamism of Berlin and the apparent German respect for its artists appealed to Craig who began to think that here was a country receptive to his ideas.[16]

Craig's plans, however, were running into resistance from Brahm. For one thing, the great proponent of naturalism proved utterly incapable of understanding Craig's intentions. He complained, for example, that in a scene that called for a door, there was no door to be seen. When Craig pointed out that there was a way out and a way in, Brahm replied, "Yes, but I see no door handle or lock. You cannot have a door without a handle." Craig finally convinced him by reassuring him he had found this same scene in an old Italian manuscript.[17] For his part, Craig seems to have been a bit dilatory with his instructions, due in part to his fervent imagination, which, unencumbered by mundane concerns of money and schedule, was busy inventing new machinery up until the very last minute. Finally Brahm, who had been interested in staging a Hofmannsthal play in the first place because of his growing anxiety over the emergence of a young rival in the Berlin theater world, Max Reinhardt, began to feel threatened by Craig's demands for complete control over the stage production. The rift grew too large to bridge and Brahm terminated Craig's contract shortly before the premiere of the play in January 1905. Mutual recriminations followed and Craig sent an open letter to the *Berliner Tageblatte,* explaining his point of view. Hofmannsthal, outraged over Craig's lack of tact, declared himself absolutely finished with the Englishman, seized by an antipathy "as mysterious and irresistible as love." It was left to Kessler to plead with Hofmannsthal not to give up on the designer so soon and to try and find a more suitable project for the gifted, but stubborn Craig. As it turned out, Brahm probably should have paid more attention to Craig; *Das gerettete Venedig* was a failure, the only silver lining being the critical applause for the two scenes based on Craig's drawings.[18]

A whole book, it has been noted, could be written about the unrealized plans and projects of Craig. In fact, a memorable production of Ibsen's *Rosmerholm,* performed in Florence in 1906, and his famous 1912 Moscow *Hamlet,* produced with Konstantin Stanislavsky, were the last two plays that Craig would have a direct hand in designing. Nevertheless, his influence was growing, in large part due to Kessler's relentless patronage and personal politics. If Brahm proved incapable of appreciating his art, Max Reinhardt, who had just taken over the Deutsches Theater and was on the verge of his extraordinary career as an impresario, was very eager to meet Craig. In 1905, again with Kessler acting as the ever-patient, ever-hopeful mediator, Reinhardt and Craig discussed working together on *Tempest, King Lear,* and Shaw's *Caesar and Cleopatra.* Despite Reinhardt's good will, these discussions faltered because of Craig's insistence upon "absolute unity and control." Reinhardt's gentle reminder that Craig's German was not up to the task of directing Shakespeare at the Deutsches Theater met deaf ears. Reinhardt, however, had a good opportunity to absorb the ideas of Craig, and many of his productions—particularly his famous *König Ödipus* (again, an adaptation by Hofmannsthal) and *Sumurûn,* a pantomime incorporating dance and music—reveal Craig's influence. Craig at first resented what he considered Reinhardt's unacknowledged use of his ideas, a feeling reinforced when he came upon two of Reinhardt's assistants sent by the director to "drink in" Craig's sketches, displayed at a gallery in Berlin. This did not prevent him, however, from producing designs in 1908 for Reinhardt's production of *King Lear,* a collaboration that again collapsed on Craig's refusal to make compromises.[19]

His first and most influential book, *The Art of the Theatre,* first published in a German translation in 1905, also spread Craig's ideas and influence. Kessler's introduction to the catalogue accompanying Craig's show in Berlin was used as a preface. In this succinct précis of Craig's ideas, it is interesting to note Kessler's comparison of Craig's art with dance and pantomime: "The dream, the possibilities of an art of fantasy on the stage have been made clear to us by the dances of Loîe Fuller— not to speak of the sudden . . . appearance, out of an alien world, of the Japanese (dancer) Sada Yacco."[20] For Kessler, who with van de Velde had marveled over the dances of Sada Yacco, Craig's interest in a theater of movement, pantomime, and dance helped prepare him for the reception of modern dance, first in the form of the American dancer and choreographer Ruth St. Denis and then for Diaghilev's Ballets Russes.

Kessler remained loyal to his difficult friend, even after Craig left Germany and moved to Florence. There he opened a school for the theater and began publishing *The Mask,* a journal on the theatrical arts that Craig—using nearly seventy pseudonyms to make it appear as if he had many supporters—published almost single-handedly from 1908 to 1929. When he visited Craig in 1911 in London, Kessler was particularly interested in the striking black cut-out figures the designer had made to explain to the Russian actors his ideas for the Moscow *Hamlet*. After showing him proofs of the edition of Virgil that Maillol was illustrating for his newly founded Cranach Presse,* Kessler suggested that Craig might illustrate Shakespeare's *Antony and Cleopatra* or Milton's *Comus* or *Faust*. Whereupon Craig replied that they might as well do *Hamlet*. The very same day Kessler commissioned a new italic print for the project from Emery Walker and, a few months later, when Craig had returned from Moscow, agreed to pay him two hundred pounds immediately and forty pounds for the next ten months to complete the illustrations.[21] Thus was born the famous Cranach Presse edition of *Hamlet,* a project that took seventeen years to complete.

• • •

As if mediating between such sensitive temperaments as those of Craig and Hofmannsthal were not enough, Kessler also took upon his plate an interesting project of international reconciliation. Toward the end of 1905, he enlisted William Rothenstein in a plan to help counter the mounting distrust and hostility between England and Germany that was evident in the popular press of both countries. Leading English and German intellectuals and artists would agree to support, with their signatures, an exchange of open letters, each group expressing their admiration for the other's culture and disavowing any hostile feelings. The gesture was similar to those undertaken by American and Russian intel-

---

* Kessler introduced Craig to Maillol in April 1912. Somehow it is not surprising to learn that they were enchanted with each other. Craig showed Maillol his woodcuts for *Hamlet* and discussed (with Kessler translating no doubt) his ideas for a marionette theater with larger-than-life marionettes. After his departure, Maillol said of his English counterpart, "He's a great artist. He calculates everything; nothing is left to chance." *TB,* April 13, 1912.

lectuals during the last decades of the cold war. It would have been difficult to find two men more suited to the task than Rothenstein and Kessler. Besides the inherent interest in the story, especially the details of how the letters were modified and who refused to sign, the incident sheds a light upon the ambiguous motivations of Kessler and his approach to international politics.

The immediate diplomatic background for the effort was the first Moroccan crisis of 1905–1906. Provoked by the German Foreign Office in an effort to break Germany's growing diplomatic isolation, the crisis had the opposite effect. The perception of German aggression strengthened the Triple Entente of England, France, and Russia, and thereby heightened German fears of isolation, ultimately resulting in a resigned and fatalistic belief among German elites in both the inevitability and desirability of a war to break the chain of enemies. Against this background, the efforts of some intellectuals and artists to foster Anglo-German understanding appears quixotic, a feeble attempt to forestall the inevitable. The mere need for a demonstration of Anglo-German amity indicated the presence of a deep hostility. At the time, things were not yet set in stone, of course, but, as the negotiations over the drafting of the letters proved, attitudes, even among the educated elite, were hardening.[22]

During the fall of 1905, Kessler was busy enlisting support. One sentence in the draft of the proposed German communication read, "We deeply regret the form in which certain papers in Germany, as in other countries of the Continent and America, gave vent to their feelings during the late war in South Africa." Both Richard Dehmel and the playwright Hermann Sudermann raised objections, although they eventually signed. Kessler also asked Gerhart Hauptmann, with whom he had become quite friendly, who requested and was rewarded with the striking out of the "deeply" in front of "regret." Kessler had more problems with Richard Strauss. Although the composer eventually signed, Kessler was exasperated with Strauss's fear of "giving something away, or appearing subservient, etc. Everywhere this same feeling, to which the German middle class owes its bad manners, its readiness to take offence, its sensitivity, the tails at noon, etc. They do not notice that exactly *that* is subservient, a remnant of the old slave chains that they dragged along the Rhine."[23] Meanwhile, Hofmannsthal was having less success convincing his old admirer, the poet Stefan George to sign. Before he reconsidered and decided a lofty silence was the best response to Hofmannsthal's letter, George drafted a written response. "War," he wrote, "is only in the end the consequence of a long, senseless, and relentless economic growth on both sides, the attempt to patch things up on the part of a few men would seem to me ineffectual. Furthermore: who knows if a true friend of the Germans should not wish them a mighty defeat (*See Schlappe*, meaning, literally, "a setback at sea," referring to the naval arms race) so that they would regain their folkish modesty and be capable once again of spiritual values." After Kessler encountered George at a concert and heard the same thoughts uttered in person, he noted, "He speaks so forcefully and monumentally and with such a Dantesque thrust of the head that one almost doesn't notice the nonsense; almost."[24]

On the other side of the channel, Rothenstein was also encountering resistance and responded by diluting the strength of the letter. G. W. Porthero, the editor of the *Quarterly Review*, who had attended the university at Bonn, refused even to sign the final, anaesthetized version on the grounds that the time was inopportune. Neither would Bernard Shaw sign the letter; a decade later, when the war broke out, he claimed to have drafted the letter himself, deliberately including a phrase he thought would force each potential signer to reveal his real colors: "That sentence was to the effect that far from regarding the growth of the German fleet with suspicion and jealousy, we saw in it only an additional bulwark of our common civilization." When nearly everyone balked at endorsing such a statement, Shaw, quite typically, concluded, "our Imperialists were waiting for The Day as much as the Prussian Junkers." At the time, however, Shaw replied to Rothenstein merely that "I will not be a party to a display of silly vanity by which the three tailors of Architectooley Street will come forward to assure the public that all's well with Europe because they appreciate Strauss & Helmholtz, etc. etc." Kessler expressed the concern to Rothenstein in several letters that both the quantity and the quality of the English signatures should not fall too conspicuously below the level of those of the Germans, which he described as "exceptionally brilliant . . . . I do not believe that ever before in Germany so many names of the very first rank have been seen together under any paper or proclamation."[25]

At any event, the letters did appear together in the *Times* and several German newspapers on January 12, 1906. The German letter, drafted by Kessler, urged the English, particularly the press, to stop misconstruing every act of the German government as anti-English. It went on to assure the English that: "None of us, though living in widely distant parts of Germany and moving in different spheres of German society and party life, has ever heard an attack on England seriously discussed or approved of by any man or section of the German public worth noticing; nor have we met anybody in Germany who credited the Government with intentions or plans for a war on England. The naval policy of the Government, whether approved of or resisted, is everywhere in Germany understood and manifestly seen to be directed solely to providing what the Government consider [sic] adequate protection for the growing mass of German shipping, and certainly not at entering wantonly on any contest at sea." It was signed by forty luminaries, who included— besides the names already mentioned—Wilhelm Bode, Lujo Brentano, Ernst Haeckel, Adolf Harnack, Max Klinger, Karl Lamprecht, Max Liebermann, Elizabeth Förster-Nietzsche, Werner Sombart, Siegfried Wagner, and Wilhelm Wundt. The English counterpart responded by professing, "between England and Germany, there is no frontier to be defended," and expressing English indebtedness to German literature, music, and science. Signing on the British side were Walter Crane, R. B. Cunninghame Graham, Edward Elgar, Thomas Hardy, Lord Kelvin, Gilbert Murray, Charles Ricketts, C. H. Shannon, Emery Walker, Alfred Russel Wallace, and Philip Webb, among others. There were also articles about the letter published in the *Standard, Morning Post,* and *Pall Mall.* Three days later, Bernhard von Bülow sent a telegram expressing his approval of the joint letters, a move that probably reinforced British suspicion of German motives, because Bülow was, quite rightly, suspected of being anything but a friend of England.[26]

A few days later, the international women's organization, the Lyceum Club, whose founder Constance Smedley had become good friends with Kessler, honored him with a banquet, where it was agreed that an exhibition of German art should be mounted at the London Lyceum the following May. Smedley describes Kessler in her memoirs as the perfect diplomat and internationalist, whose help in setting up the exhibition was invaluable: "He was never annoyed, never pessimistic, never unduly enthusiastic: he preserved the most helpful poise between all the conflicting schools of thought and yet there was always something strong, sincere and dependable in his decisions and opinions. He was an ideal Ambassador of Art." The exhibit, designed by van de Velde and held at the Princes' Gallery in London, was opened on May 23, Kessler's birthday. Among the guests at the opening banquet held at the Savoy Hotel were Philip Snowden, a leading Labour politician but also Alice Keppel, the mistress of Edward VII, Lord Haldane, George Bernard Shaw, and Kessler himself. According to embassy reports back to Berlin, however, the prevalence of modern art turned off the English audience, an opinion that caused the kaiser to jot in the margins "The Englishman has too fine and good a taste to bother himself about such horrors."[27]

An ambassador of art Kessler certainly was, but was he, at this time, an ambassador of peace? Both Smedley and Rothenstein would have been shocked had they overheard a conversation Kessler had with Arthur von Gwinner, the powerful head of the Deutsche Bank, Germany's largest, a day after George refused to sign the letter. It was Bodenhausen who brought Kessler together with Gwinner, the first of the many introductions to Germany's power elite that he provided his friend.[28] The Deutsche Bank was the chief German partner involved in the financing and construction of the famous Berlin-Baghdad railroad. Gwinner was the director of the organization founded in 1903 to complete its construction and one of the principal German figures in the exceedingly complex negotiations concerning the railroad. Kessler was brought in because his cousin was Henry Finnis Blosse-Lynch, head of Lynch Brothers, the steamship company that since 1861 had enjoyed a monopoly on the Tigris and Euphrates rivers. One of the steamers, in fact, was named after Kessler's maternal grandfather. Naturally, the firm opposed any railway in German control ending either in Baghdad or further on in Basra. Kessler's mission appears to have been a purely private one, to sound out his cousin about the possibilities of striking a deal.[29] He met Lynch in London in August 1905 and heard from his cousin the warning that it would mean war if Germany went ahead with the construction of the railway without English capital. Instead, Lynch proposed a de facto division of the interests in the Ottoman Empire, Asia Minor for the Germans and Mesopotamia for the English.[30]

A month later, Kessler met with Gwinner for the first time to discuss the possibilities of reaching an arrangement with England. To Kessler's suggestion of forming a committee of businessmen and "grands seigneurs" to promote Anglo-German unity, Gwinner demurred, saying that Bülow was against too great a rapprochement. Kessler's idea of a joint letter, on the other hand, seemed to him just right. Kessler, at one point in the conversation, expressed the opinion that "our relation to England can only in the long run be improved by exerting pressure against her; this involves in the first instance the enlargement of our fleet, in the second the achievement of a flanking position against India. Until then we must prevent war through palliative measures such as the letters; afterwards it will self evidently not come to that (meaning the

British, aware of their vulnerability, would reach an arrangement with Germany)." [31]

The idea of achieving an understanding with England through threatening her was a widely spread illusion in Wilhelmian Germany. It formed the rationale for the disastrous naval race initiated by Admiral Tirpitz, the single most important factor leading to Britain's entry into the war against Germany. A few years later, the new chancellor, Theobold von Bethmann-Hollweg, was to repeat the same argument privately to Kessler. Nor is it surprising that Kessler, who was about to deliver a lecture in Berlin on "Art and Patriotism" in which he essentially dismissed the possibility, so dear to German chauvinists, of a *Heimatkunst,* should, when it came to international relations, use the rhetoric of Wilhelmian *Weltpolitik*. An admiration for English manners or French art did not by any means preclude the support of an aggressive German foreign policy, any more than having studied at German universities prevented a diplomat like Sir Eyre Crowe from being deeply suspicious of the kaiser and of Bülow. The ghosts of Goethe and Shakespeare could not conclude peace. [32]

Nevertheless, Kessler's remarks do cast his motives in the whole affair of the letters in a unfavorable light. The most charitable interpretation would be that he sincerely believed he was serving the cause of peace by giving the German fleet a breathing space to expand until it reached a size that precluded an English attack upon it. Is that what he really meant, however, when he wrote to van de Velde about the proposed exhibition of German artists in London, "I am happy to be able to serve the two tasks which mean the most to me, art and peace," a phrase reminiscent of the kaiser's assertion that "the German Fleet is built against nobody at all. It is solely built for Germany's needs in relation with that country's rapidly growing trade." He was not believed and for good reason: only months before he had approved the measures to ensure that the fleet reached the magical number of sixty capital ships by 1918, which Tirpitz assured him, would force the British into submission. [33]

CHAPTER II

The Rodin Scandal

Now, honorable Count, which of us has killed Palézieux?
Maximilian Harden to Kessler, *Tagebuch*

In the middle of his multitudinous projects, Kessler paused for a moment in mid-November 1905 to take stock of his position: "Consider what means of influence I have in Germany: the German *Künstlerbund*, my position in Weimar, including the prestige despite the grand duke's stupidity, the connection with Reinhardt's stage, my intimate relations with the Nietzsche Archive, with Hofmannsthal, with van de Velde, Ansorge, Gerhard Hauptmann, moreover with the two most influential journals, *Die Zukunft* and *Die Neue Rundschau,* and—on the other side—with Berlin society, the Harrachs, Richters, Sascha Schlippenbach, the Regiment and finally my personal standing. The balance sheet is rather surprising and certainly unique. No one else in Germany has such a strong position, reaching out to so many sides. To use this in the service of a renewal of German culture: mirage or possibility? Certainly one with such means could be a *princeps juventutis.* Is it worth the trouble?"[1]

It was a remarkable assessment considering that only five days before he had endured a very unpleasant dinner at the ducal palace: "The grand duke as usual sullen and awkward. To me he said, as a special favor, that neo-impressionism was dead and he hoped that the *Künstlerbund* would also soon disappear. I took it as a joke and laughed which completely bewildered him, he blushed, stuttered, and then left." The growing evidence of the grand duke's boorish hostility no doubt lay at the root of Kessler's stocktaking. When Hofmannsthal arrived at the end of November, Kessler warned him of Wilhelm-Ernst's miserable character and mentioned the possibility that he might have to break off relations with the court. In that event, he asked Hofmannsthal for his support in making Weimar the cultural center of Germany, regardless of the support of the court.[2] The only real support for the forces of the "Third Weimar" within the court was the young Grand Duchess Caroline. When she died suddenly of pneumonia in January 1905, Kessler's whole enterprise rested solely on the grand duke. It would soon be clear what a slender reed that was. Although Kessler had few illusions about his patron, he nevertheless underestimated both the enmity his *Kulturpolitik* had aroused in court circles and the influence these critics had on the grand duke.

Almost from the very beginning, a covert war had raged between the forces of the "old" and "new" Weimar. At the very start of Kessler's tenure, he ran afoul of Karl Ruhland, art historian, president of the Goethe Society, and director of the art museum (as opposed to the arts and crafts museum led by Kessler). When asked by Kessler in November 1905 if his museum would have a few rooms available for the *Künstlerbund* exhibition the following spring, Ruhland lost his temper: "He fell into a wild rage, waved his arms and banged on the table, screamed at me, what did I think, that he would leave his museum to someone who had shown 'Gauguin, such *rubbish*, to a respectable German city,' and an organization like the *Künstlerbund* after its disgusting exhibition in Berlin." Kessler concluded: "So it is a matter of life and death between us. One of us must bite the dust in this tragi-comic *Froschenmäusekrieg*."[3]

Ruhland was typical of those established Weimar officials who feared that Kessler's activities, especially his prominent role in the *Künstlerbund*, were threatening their own positions and incurring the wrath of Wilhelm II. Subsequently, this nagging anxiety ended up affecting the nerves of nearly all of "official" Weimar, especially as the date of the third *Künstlerbund* exhibition in Weimar, grew near.[4] In 1905, more than a year before its scheduled opening, Kessler had an unusual interview with the normally calm Karl Rothe, the state secretary and the principal political figure in Weimar. Sobbing and waving his arms, he told Kessler that he did not plan to be the scapegoat if the exhibition led to trouble. Then he suggested that van de Velde try and design the new rooms for the exhibition so that for once the grand duke would enjoy them. His cravenness disgusted Kessler: "These little Philistines here begin to take themselves seriously since one has sent them so many famous people." But it was an unmistakable sign of the limits of the court's independence from Berlin, and of the fear that the protection Weimar offered modern art was paid for with the displeasure of Wilhelm II. That the kaiser was well informed about Kessler and van de Velde's activities can be seen from the lengthy reports back to Berlin by the Prussian ambassador in Weimar, which emphasized the fear that Kessler and his allies could capture the weak grand duke for their cause. "The danger seems to me no small one, that with the known aversion of His Majesty the Emperor and King against the 'modern,' the intriguers will attempt to play the grand duke against our All Gracious Majesty in favor of their party interests. I trust that the sharp attention of Our Royal Highness will not tolerate this either and that an artistic opposition can, at times, easily lead to a political [one] . . . ."[5] The kaiser read the reports on Kessler's activities carefully, and there can be no doubt that the same source served as a conduit for the expression of Berlin's displeasure.

Oddly enough, the man whose resistance to Kessler would be most fateful, both for the Third Weimar and for himself, was the very man who had offered Kessler his position in the first place, Aimé von Palézieux. One can only surmise that it was pressure either from the grand duke himself or from other members of the court that compelled Palézieux to help negotiate, first van de Velde's appointment, and then that of Kessler. Be that as it may, as early as November 1903, as he was making plans for the foundation of the *Künstlerbund,* Kessler was accused by Palézieux of destroying his life's work and had learned from other sources of the chamberlain's virulent campaign of slander and innuendo. Aside from his disapproval of modernism, the chamberlain appears to have been motivated by an obsessive fear that Kessler would come between him and the grand duke. To van de Velde he once said, "You, my dear Professor, are to be envied. You are the only one at the court that need not fear being dismissed. I, on the other hand, must ask myself, each morning, whether I am still court chamberlain." Despite the virulent pettiness and paranoia characteristic of a small court in Germany, observers must have found it difficult to understand the chamberlain's extreme touchiness on the subject of Kessler. It was left to Kessler to discover a possible reason for it in the question of financial irregularities associated with the administration of the lottery. Finally, adding a strange, almost fratricidal air to their conflict, were the rumors, allegedly well known to both of them, that they both were the illegitimate children of Kaiser Wilhelm I.[6]

The friends of Kessler and the Third Weimar were well aware of these intrigues and worried about Kessler's long absences from the court. Often they were in the dark about his whereabouts, and letters addressed to his various addresses in London, Paris, and Berlin were all too frequently returned with an *addresse inconnue* stamped on the envelope. Van de Velde once admonished his friend to lead a life "less ambulatory, more withdrawn, more healthy!" The following January he again wrote to the absent Kessler, this time about the scandal caused by some nudes in the exhibition of the German impressionist painter Lovis Corinth. Van de Velde, who did not really care for Corinth, had to defend the painter by arguing that if the newspapers in Berlin learned that the most cultivated circles in Weimar were discussing the morality of a painting of nudes, "that would make people talk." Again, he complained of Kessler's absence, urging him to return and undertake a series of lectures to educate the good citizens of Weimar.[7]

The peripatetic cosmopolitan, however, was not about to settle down permanently by the banks of the Ilm and parry the moves of Palézieux. For years he had rejected this kind of entanglement, declining the directorship of *Pan* as well as the offer of a professorship at the university of Jena in favor of his freedom to travel. He preferred to serve without remuneration than to be bound to a bureaucratic position. He recognized in himself a disturbing restlessness but attributed it to the many sides of his personality. An entry in his diary a few years later offers some clues to the rootlessness that sometimes perplexed his friends: "In the afternoon I traveled to Germany where I have not been for nine months. I appreciate more each year the isolation of living abroad. Nevertheless I cannot decide to give up Berlin and Weimar. They are for me the background of my life, a sort of mythical background, something like 'heaven' for Christians; yet I am not eager to arrive there too soon either. But if this peaceful house full of books and pictures were not behind it, the view of my life would be different for me, more scattered, more impulsive, more uncertain, whereas this background provides me at least with the illusion of unity."[8] Kessler therefore left himself open to the intrigues of his enemies. An exhibition of Rodin's watercolors in January 1906, at a time when the grand duke was away on a visit to India and Kessler was in London, offered Palézieux the chance he needed.

It was not the first time that Rodin's work had been shown in Weimar. In the summer of 1904, Kessler had exhibited sixteen statues, thirty-three "movement and silhouette studies," and fifty photographs of Rodin's work. Kessler, in a foreword to the catalogue that was filled with the language of "life philosophy," stressed the artist's attempt to capture movement in his studies. Rodin's sculpture, he asserted, was a celebration of chiaroscuro. And this search for light and shadow was nothing less than a search for life itself. "He found in light, in the gentle fleetingness of light, the most perfect means of expression for the transitoriness of life, for the eternal becoming of things, and above all for the blossoming and fading of the human body and flesh." Kessler warned his public not to expect "here the anatomically correct form, which is the A-B-C of art and which he naturally has mastered." Rather, Rodin's work went beyond such rudiments to establish "how and through what the manifestations of life differ from those of the body in rest and the lifeless academic form."[9]

The second exhibition featured Rodin's drawings and watercolors. The artist, a personal friend of Kessler's, had just been granted an honorary doctorate by the University of Jena and in gratitude had donated these sketches to serve as the core of a collection of drawings and statues to be on permanent display in a special room at Kessler's museum. Mistakenly believing that the grand duke was behind the recent honor, Rodin dedicated the sketches to Wilhelm Ernst and thanked him in his official response to the university.[10] However, for a certain segment of the Weimar audience, both the decision of the university to honor Rodin and Kessler's explanation of the philosophical underpinnings of his art were irrelevant. Expecting to see chaste, academic nudes, the viewers were instead confronted by Rodin's very free sketches of nude and partly clad women, some depicting pudenda. For the provincial Weimar audience of this time, such an exhibition was nothing better than pornography. This time, the angry defenders of public morality let their discontent be known. One local painter, Hermann Behmer— whose son Marcus ironically would many years later provide Kessler with erotic illustrations for an edition of Petronius's *Satyricon*—thundered in the local newspaper:

It is to be deeply regretted from time to time we encounter in the new museum on the Karlsplatz exhibitions of paintings and drawings that deeply offend our feelings. It displays a lack of morality on the part of the artist and a laxity of understanding on the part of the exhibition committee, that such exhibitions are offered to art lovers in Weimar and many in all circles are greatly upset. What is displayed is so revolting that we must warn our wives and daughters not to visit the museum. That at this very time a series of sketches by the French sculptor Rodin have for weeks been exhibited with the dedication of the artist to His Royal Highness, our Grand Duke, is such a scandal for us that we must raise our voices in protest. It is an impudence of the foreigner to offer such things to our high lord, and irresponsible of the committee to display these disgusting drawings and tolerate such an exhibition.[11]

Against such outbursts of provincial prudery, supporters of Rodin and of the museum rushed to defend the exhibition. Some newspapers pointed out that it was the philosophical faculty of the University of Jena that had given Rodin an honorary doctorate and queried whether the opinion of Behmer et al. was to be preferred over that of such a distinguished body. The controversy spread to the national press; the journal *Jugend* published a savage caricature of Behmer as an enraged Philistine hurling a chamber pot at the exhibition. Ferdinand Avenarius, the editor of *Kunstwart,* typically tried to strike a middle ground in the controversy. While claiming himself to be a defender of artistic freedom and an admirer of Rodin, he accused the direction of the museum of a lack of pedagogical sensitivity; they should have known better than to show to the public what only a true expert on sculpture, and particularly on Rodin, could appreciate. His language, however, belied his lukewarm profession of open-mindedness: he described the sketches as "naked female models of blowzy whore types in repulsively common positions apparently incompetently smeared on the paper."[12]

Kessler had not regarded the opening of the small exhibition of fourteen watercolors as significant enough to interrupt his current business, which was to organize the German art show in London.[13] Friends sent press clippings to him, but he apparently thought the controversy would blow over. At the end of January 1906, he briefly passed through Weimar, then went to Paris, and finally back to Berlin to attend the premiere of Hofmannsthal's *Oedipus.* He gave a lecture on the design of books in Dresden and only returned to Weimar with Hofmannsthal in the middle of the following month. Not until February 20 did he make note of the "Behmer affair" in his journal.

That evening he had dinner at the home of the Prussian ambassador to Weimar, von Below. After commenting on the ambassador's nice wife and daughters, he remarked that "society as well as the public is against Behmer." Had he known what his host would write about the affair to his superiors two days later, he might have been less sanguine. In a long report, upon which the kaiser made annotations, von Below took pains to heap scorn and contempt upon Kessler and depicted the opposition against him as a vigilante band of outraged citizenry justifiably seeking to lynch the man who brought this scandal to the home of Goethe and Schiller. The crowning insult, the report went on, was one of the sketches that "depicted an unclothed female figure, distinguished neither by beauty or youth, which was painted from behind and presented to the viewer in a position that can be interpreted in no other way than that she wished to relieve herself. The Gaul apparently values this piece of hackwork most highly, for he has considered it appropriate to dedicate the same, with an ornate inscription: 'Dédiée à Son Altesse Royale, to the *Landesherren* now abroad in India.'" The ambassador then went on to relate how Kessler, "just returned from one of his many tours abroad, is supposed to have sworn by all the gods that the so despised sketches must have been switched in some inexplicable way, for the ones that he, Kessler, had been shown by Rodin, were different and better. He also had not seen among those shown to him the one with the dedication that is considered offensive." The report concluded that Kessler, after stormy debate, had agreed to hide the dedication in the passepartout of the frame, but that his opponents were determined to force the man who had "protected the new direction in art in general and van de Velde in particular in an inappropriate manner" from office, or at the very least compel him to exhibit traditional as well modern art.[14]

Kessler, in fact, was eventually forced to remove the offending sketch. Nevertheless, he felt that the tide was turning against Palézieux and his allies. Having formed an association with the heroic title "League for the Protection of the Absent Grand duke," they had overplayed their hand through an additional intrigue. On March 2, 1906, Palézieux demanded to see the letter Kessler had received from the cabinet secretary of the grand duke, acknowledging and thanking Rodin in the grand duke's name for his gift. When asked by Palézieux, the cabinet secretary— a man named Hermann Freiherr von Egloffstein, the very model of a craven small court courtier—had denied ever writing it.[15] Now the pressure was on Kessler to produce the evidence. For five anxious days he searched. Fifty years later van de Velde wrote, "I still feel our anxiety for we knew the disorder of his correspondence, his notes, and manuscripts; had often enough seen the masses of paper piled high on his desk." At last, however, he found the letter thanking Rodin on behalf of the grand duke. "I won't produce it yet," Kessler noted grimly, "to give the people time to commit further stupidities." To Hofmannsthal, he wrote with glee of his anticipated coup: "For the last eight days I am like Eleonore, I smile and smile again; the comic effect when the letter appears, will be grandiose." Two days after Kessler had recovered the letter, Egloffstein, clearly a member of the court cabal and thinking apparently that Kessler had lost the document, denied officially and in writing ever having written it.[16]

Kessler thought he had his enemies where he wanted them. After carefully going over the correct etiquette with friends in the regiment in which he served as a reserve officer, he sent one of them to see Egloff-stein and Palézieux, to demand an explanation for their behavior and, if necessary, to challenge them to a duel. Although Egloffstein agreed immediately to sign the letter of public apology that Kessler had dictated, Palézieux, made of sterner stuff, would only give an oral retraction. Disappointed, Kessler discovered the next day that the army's code of honor made it impossible to compel a Prussian general to give a written retraction. This time Kessler had gone too far, for the wily Palézieux did not hesitate to inform State Secretary Karl Rothe of Kessler's challenge. The whole affair rested on the ambiguous attitude toward dueling in Wilhelmian Germany. Although officially illegal in civil society, an exception could be made for affairs of honor between officers. In the army, a refusal to defend one's honor could lead to discharge from the service.[17] Civil society, however, frowned on officials challenging each other to duels. Kessler's challenge to Palézieux was intended as a private affair between two officers of the army; once word of it came to Rothe, he had no choice but to inform the grand duke upon the latter's return from India. At the end of May, Kessler was officially informed of the grand duke's displeasure with having officials of his court challenged to duels.[18]

Kessler, fresh from a triumphal appearance at the opening of the German art exhibition in London, returned to Weimar at the beginning of June to open the *Künstlerbund* exhibition. Rothe tried to prevent him from speaking as planned at the opening, but Kessler refused to be budged, noting that he, besides being president of the exhibition committee, had put up the 25,000 marks to guarantee the exhibition. Members of the court clique tried to offer a compromise if Kessler would only return the written retraction of Egloffstein. Kessler declined unless he were approached directly by the grand duke and asked to remain in his post. Instead, he was snubbed in a particularly rude manner by the grand duke at the opening of the exhibition. Van de Velde describes the scene in his memoirs: "The dignitaries, the high officialdom, and some artists stood in a reception line. The grand duke walked down the row, shaking each one's hand, and exchanging a few words with each. He came to Kessler, stopped without offering his hand, pulled his face into an expression of open contempt, and continued silently on."[19]

It was the last straw for Kessler. He submitted his resignation and on July 13, 1906, it was accepted. Just two days before, Edvard Munch had completed the famous full-length portrait of Kessler now in the National Gallery in Berlin, perhaps the greatest picture of a connoisseur ever painted. An elegant dandy who dispassionately assesses his viewers as if they were works of art themselves, which may or may not meet his standard, Kessler recorded his relief in his diary: "I have only one feeling: the happiness after a dangerous adventure to feel *free* again."[20]

The tale has an epilogue. Palézieux, confident of his victory, secured the dissolution of the curatorship of which Kessler had been president and retrieved full control of the museum. He then announced the eviction of the *Künstlerbund* from its offices in the museum. Van de Velde, at Kessler's urging, did not resign, but his position was evidently more vulnerable than ever before. The chamberlain, however, had not counted on Kessler's connections with the press. At the news of his departure, even the local newspaper had called the episode a loss to Weimar's cultural life. Then in November, a commentary in *Kunst und Künstler* reported the incident in detail, laying bare the role of Palézieux in the intrigues that had led to Kessler's resignation. Finally, in the beginning of December, Kessler had a long interview with Maximilian Harden, the editor of *Die Zukunft*. The outcome was a series of articles attacking Palézieux publicly as an "Intriguant" and placing particular emphasis on the thousands of marks missing from the museum's coffers when Kessler had taken over its direction. Immediately after leaving Harden, Kessler used his contacts to mobilize the newspaper *Kreuzzeitung,* mouthpiece of the conservatives, to put further pressure on his enemy, "so that it is not simply the liberal, disreputable papers that let loose." Pursuing this plan a few days later, he received a card of introduction from a Conservative Reichstag deputy to the editor-in-chief of the *Kreuzzeitung*. The same day he spoke to Konrad von Kardoff who agreed to speak to his father, Wilhelm von Kardoff, the head of the Conservative Party, about the matter.[21]

The circle was closing around Palézieux. Harden's articles had thrown him on the defensive by raising the question of missing museum funds, an insinuation made more damaging by earlier rumors. In a letter from London imploring van de Velde to circulate the *Zukunft* articles, Kessler outlined his strategy for destroying his enemy. He intended to continue the attacks while at the same time letting court circles in Berlin and the guard officer corps in the capital know that Palézieux was not responding in the honorable manner demanded of a Prussian officer, that is, by accepting Kessler's challenge to a duel. At some point, if he continued to allow Kessler and his allies to vilify him, Palézieux would be compelled to go before a military court of honor in Berlin to explain his conduct. Kessler took pains to assure van de Velde that the entire campaign was intended to remove a deadly enemy of the Third Weimar, but the vindictive energy with which he pursued his prey indicates a barely acknowledged bitterness stemming from his forced resignation.[22]

Alarmed at the tepidness of Palézieux's defense, the Prussian ambassador reported of the general dissatisfaction with the chamberlain's behavior as well as of the reluctance of either the Weimar government or the grand duke to defend him. Meanwhile, Kessler responded with yet another volley on January 26, 1907. When he received a letter from one of Palézieux's allies asking Kessler to retract publicly his accusation about the chamberlain's "misuse of a letter," referring to Palézieux's denunciation of Kessler's challenge, Kessler responded that he was surprised at the silence regarding his other accusation, the matter of the missing funds. He wrote this final letter in a "curious, wonderful *Nebelstimmung* on the Tower Bridge. . . . So I have Palézieux at last where I have tried for a year to get him: before the court of honor."[23]

In the end, Palézieux found a way out. On February 10, a few days after the receipt of his letter, Kessler heard that the chamberlain had died the evening before, apparently of a sudden pneumonia. The kaiser sent a telegram of condolence to the grand duke. Later, Kessler learned of rumors that Palézieux had poisoned himself; his screams and groans that evening were supposed to have been heard throughout the neighborhood. Kessler wrote to Hofmannsthal: "The darkness that shrouds this death will never lift. The man has eluded me, that is what remains, an emptiness and a kind of disbelief in the reality of his disappearance, . . . I would rather have dueled, which would have been cleaner than this *Schauerdrama*. Now an odor remains, an atmosphere that will only slowly dissipate. . . . What is ugly about life is that it so often only provides uneasy half-solutions, that are so seldom pure and tragic ones; in the end one has only raised more dust where one wished to sweep with an iron broom."[24]

Kessler's experiment of building a Third Weimar effectively came to an end with the Rodin scandal. Despite his avowal—in letters to Bodenhausen, Hofmannsthal, and others—to continue to strengthen privately the cultural circle started in Weimar, this goal quickly receded. Without the public position as head of the Grand Ducal Museum for

Arts and Crafts, Kessler's ability to serve as a leader—and sometimes lightning rod—of modernism diminished.[25] Besides, there was no longer any real reason to make Weimar rather than Berlin the focus of these efforts. With the *Künstlerbund* banished from Weimar, only the Nietzsche Archive and van de Velde's school were left as institutional foundations for modernism. As for van de Velde, Kessler could no longer help defend or promote him in Weimar, although he continued to try and obtain commissions for him elsewhere. Only the ambitious plans for a monument to Nietzsche and the founding of his private press, the Cranach Presse, required Kessler's presence in Weimar in the last years before the war. The former project would ultimately run up against the same problem Kessler's plans for the Third Weimar encountered, the fickleness of a patron; the latter project would be interrupted by the war.[26]

What in the end did the Rodin scandal and the sad denouement of Kessler's Weimar indicate about cultural politics in Wilhelmian Germany? The first thing that strikes one is how charged aesthetic issues *could* be; how quickly in those days, such issues became not simply questions of morality, but also of patriotism. In 1906, Rodin was, after all, an established artist and well respected in most of the Western world. That fourteen of his drawings could ignite such a brushfire in Germany proves how thin the line between culture and politics was. Of course, the Rodin scandal was only the last battle in the war that Kessler and van de Velde had ignited when they came to Weimar. With a patron who was genuinely interested in modern art, such as the grand duke of Hesse, they might have fared better.[27] But the numerous instances on the part of state officials of cringing before the dreaded displeasure of the kaiser corroborates what is known of the Byzantine character of Wilhelmian officialdom. The anxiety of the state secretary of Weimar about the consequences of staging a Rodin exhibition in what was, after all, a nominally independent state in cultural matters speaks volumes about the politicization of aesthetic issues in imperial Germany.[28] The danger may have been more imagined than real but the effect was still often chilling, sometimes in ways that remained hidden.

The balance of the "Third Weimar" was not entirely negative. For nearly three and a half years, Kessler and van de Velde made Weimar into a cultural center as a venue for modern art second only to the much larger cities of Germany. Van de Velde's school would eventually become the Bauhaus; van de Velde himself would appoint his successor, Walther Gropius. The *Künstlerbund* thrived for a few years longer and provided an invaluable function as an umbrella organization for modern artists. But ultimately the choice of Weimar as a *point d'appui* for modernism was a mistake. There it was too easy for the enemies of modernism to wrap themselves in the mantle of the past. Weimar provided a far more congenial platform for the proponents of an anti-modernist *Heimatkunst,* men like the *völkische* novelist Friedrich Lienhard, the critic Adolf Bartels, and the architect Paul Schultze-Naumburg.[29] The spirit that triumphed over Kessler in 1906 would compel van de Velde's eventual resignation during the war. It would attack Gropius relentlessly, eventually compelling the Bauhaus to move to Dessau.[30] In the end, nothing of Kessler's dreams of a cosmopolitan, internationalist Third Weimar would remain except a grotesque parody of Nietzscheanism in the Weimar of the Third Reich. The final desecration would come with the "cleansing" of the "degenerate" artists in the Weimar museums and with Weimar hosting the "Degenerate Art" exhibition in 1939.

PART FOUR

The Fever Curve

CHAPTER 12

Greek Idylls

We hardly know what kind of a spring we are experiencing—
everywhere things are stirring!

Eberhard von Bodenhausen, *Aus dem alten Europa*

Free from "the Serbian conditions" at the Weimar court in the middle
of July 1906, Kessler felt he needed to use the energy liberated to
redefine his life. In a series of long, affectionate letters written to Hofmannsthal, he outlined his plans. The first was to continue to cultivate
his much-cherished cultural circle in Weimar. "At the center stands for
me," he wrote in a postscript, "for the future that, twice or three times
a year in Weimar a few important artists, writers, etc. can *meet and mutually stimulate each other* in our houses in the Weimar atmosphere. . . .
It seems to me that this is one of the most important preconditions for
a balanced culture in Germany, and that Weimar is the only place where
it is possible." In a similar vein, he wrote to Nietzsche's sister that he
was looking forward to the development "of our circle in Weimar in the
next years with unclouded joy now that every concern about the philistines in the court has disappeared." "But that," he wrote in another letter to Hofmannsthal, "cannot be my only goal in life, at least as far as I
am concerned. I would like also, if only in my own modest way, to produce something myself. I have neglected this far too much and would
like to catch up now. For me personally, at least for the next few years,
this direct production must be the chief aim of my life. I need for my psychic health a work under my feet." [1] Kessler had two personal projects in
mind, a book on modern art and one on the issue of national character.

As early as 1903, Kessler had had discussions with the Munich publisher Bruckmann on a book to be entitled *Die Meisterwerke* (of modern painting). It was settled that the publisher would pay Kessler 2,000 marks for traveling expenses. Unfortunately, his friend and erstwhile colleague Julius Meier-Graefe seized the field first with his two-volume *Entwicklungsgeschichte der modernen Kunst* (*The History of the Development of Modern Art*), one of the first important works on modern art. Kessler noted, not without jealousy: "Purely playing with atmosphere (*Stimmungsmacherei*); very good but nevertheless playing with atmosphere. For the German seriousness stops where art begins, for the German artist, for the German critic, and for the German art historian. That is why he believes it necessary to add something extra in order to remove any doubts about his earnestness, a little philosophy, or something tendentious, or worst of all, when nothing else occurs to him, a little poetry or folklore."[2]

The appearance of Meier-Graefe's book compelled Kessler to take a different tack in his approach. Speaking of modern French painting, he wrote, "I can only think of it in the context of modern French culture. I hope to write something fundamental but not boring. A certain way of handling this subject has been exhausted by Meier-Graefe and Muther,[3] another not yet attempted, I mean the approach from a viewpoint within French culture. This field belongs to me, because already as a child I was familiar with France, and, on the other hand, I *think, judge* overwhelmingly in a German way!" In November 1906, he reached an agreement with Bruckmann to deliver a manuscript in about three years. For what was originally entitled *History of European Color since Giotto,* that was anything but a generous amount of time. To write such a book required, he told Hofmannsthal, that he visit nearly all the museums and monuments of Europe: three months in Italy, one in Spain, one in Holland and Belgium, two to three in England, and five or six in Paris.[4]

Alas, Kessler suffered from an inability to define his subject. His diaries from these years are stuffed with false starts, brilliant aperçus on dozens of issues: the baroque, sentimentality, the ideal of the human body, sexuality, the "Nordic fantasy," the role of the line, chiaroscuro, color in European painting. His definition of the "modern" kept expanding, beyond Courbet and Delacroix, beyond Rousseau and Voltaire, beyond Velasquez and Rubens, past the Renaissance, St. Francis, the Greeks. He created vast flow charts of influences, of aesthetic traditions but did not stick with any one schema; rather, he constantly reshuffled them. The beginning stumped him. Immensely complicated, unanswerable questions—How is drawing related to chiaroscuro? When did painting separate from architecture? How does Giotto fit in?—piled up before him like the papers van de Velde described on his desk. From a book about color the theme became "the possibility of an art in relation to the bourgeois. Only two directions of art can help here, German music and French painting of the nineteenth century. . . . The problem in my book is, in essence, that of Ruskin, Morris, Nietzsche, only in an experimental, rather than utopian or philosophical light. Namely: to what extent is art possible in our time, and in a broader sense culture? . . . The failure of the academic, romantic, idealistic, patriotic-*heimatlichen,* is also instructive and should be included. *Why* have these directions remained sterile?" [5]

It was too much. As he confessed to his sister, after outlining a typically optimistic writing schedule, "I *have* the ideas, but my ideas are like badly trained horses. They always carry me to unexpected things and places before I can get them into shape; and then there is my article all dead and far away in the distance behind me somewhere." What he needed was a good editor. What he got instead was Hofmannsthal's critique of his writing. Literary products like those of Kessler, in between literature and a lecture, must have the force of a deed, the Austrian told him. Kessler's style, he argued, was not popular enough; he presumed too much on the part of his audience. He should also be cautious with metaphors and images in such difficult-to-understand things.[6] All of this, while true enough, served only to undermine Kessler's confidence further. Yet another obstacle to Kessler's concentration was the social life that seemed to suck him up wherever he went. When he wrote to Hofmannsthal in 1906 of spending the next years "in reserve," he realized he would have to force himself to do so, "since my natural temperament is quite different. But only when I have again worked through something serious, will I let the reins go (and enter the public arena). That I will take part *too little* in public affairs, is at any rate not a danger; much more so the contrary."[7] Partly because of his temperament and partly because his desire to be of assistance to his friends came into conflict with his writing, this plan of living and working in semi-seclusion remained, for the most part, a mirage.

In the end, something rather modest emerged from the mountain of expectations and note-taking. What Bruckmann ended up publishing in 1909 was *Impressionisten: Die Begründer der modernen Malerei in ihren Hauptwerken* (*The Impressionists: The Founders of Modern Painting as Seen in Their Chief Works*), a collection of sixty reproductions of European paintings, ranging from Turner, Constable, and Ingres to van Gogh,

Signac, Cross, and Denis, a catalogue raisonné, and Kessler's short in-troduction. Employing a vaguely Hegelian scheme, whereby each suc-ceeding school seeks to complete the unfinished work of the earlier, he attempted to show how the impressionist art arose as a merger of the two prevalent schools of painting in the nineteenth century, romanti-cism and realism. The essay clearly suffers from the flaws that marred his essay on art and religion. His ambition compelled him again to spill over the boundaries of his proper subject by dragging in literature and mu-sic in a confusing and unconvincing way. It is the fault of a brilliant con-versationalist who, when writing for an unseen audience, does not quite know how to address it.[8]

Kessler's second writing project, on the causes of national character, is a more interesting work, although it too remained only a fragment of what he had originally planned. In April 1906, a few months after the Anglo-German letters campaign, Harden's *Die Zukunft* published Kessler's essay, "Nationalität." An attempt to address the fascinating, if perhaps intractable, question of national character through a psycho-logical approach, Kessler was pleased enough with it to reprint it in 1919, albeit with a few short, but significant cuts for political reasons. He began with the problem of defining national differences. To say with Fichte, "German is such and such," was to fall prey to a vacuous intel-lectual patriotism. Ideas have no boundaries. If nationality were a ques-tion of intellectual content as expressed in history books or historical pictures, then "how difficult it was for the Greeks to be Greek!" But even more serious explanations of national character lacked credibility upon close examination. Kessler had long recognized that the race the-ory, as propounded by Julius Langbehn's *Rembrandt als Erzieher* or Houston Stewart Chamberlain's *Grundlagen des XIX Jahrhunderts,* was unproven and improbable. The idea of a nation composed of pure Ger-mans was a phantom, given the mixture of races within Germany's bor-ders. Nor was the argument that a shared community of material inter-ests defined a nation any more plausible, at least in the age of capitalism when banks, cartels, and labor organizations often had material inter-ests that transcended national boundaries. Finally, the notion that lan-guage defined a nation fell apart when one considered, for example, the growing differences between an Australian and an Englishman, or a French Canadian and a Frenchman.[9]

One could dismiss the idea of a national character, Kessler asserted, as so much verbiage were it not for the kinship that an Australian, for example, suddenly felt with his fellow countrymen upon visiting En-gland. This feeling of kinship, although arrived at negatively as it were, was nonetheless real and could not be dismissed. Such sentiments had deeper, more subtle, and hidden roots than those of friendship or love; they came closest to the feelings between siblings. Following Wundt's theories, Kessler asserted that it was not the quality or strength of the individual impressions that created a national character, but the way these impressions were processed and the way the mind related them that defined individuals as belonging to one group or another.[10] Among the factors that determined how different nations processed impressions were climate, sexual inheritance (although Kessler was quick to point out that races were constantly changing), the heroes they chose to emulate, and the vocations they practiced. Interestingly, this approach led him to stress the importance of the regional identities that had survived every attempt to stamp them out. Just like one could be a "good" German and still speak *Plattdeutsch,* so one could be a "good" European without thereby ceasing to be a "good" German, or Spaniard, or Frenchman.

This vision of Europe formed the basis of Kessler's later activity as a pacifist and an internationalist, even if he struck from the 1919 reprint of the essay the last three lines, which asserted that a sergeant was more valuable than a whole bench of university professors for understanding the Prussian character because "he at least takes hold there where nationality is really rooted, in the gears of the personality."[11] Kessler never believed that the regional and national differences would disappear, nor did he want them to. The contradiction between this humane vision and the chauvinism expressed in some of his private conversations before the war, although real, was ultimately a more or less technical matter rather than a deep-seated incompatibility. The experience of war taught Kessler that there were limits beyond which being a "good" German meant being a bad European.

As far as the first goal that Kessler mentioned to his friends, Helene von Nostitz—the only woman, Kessler once confessed, he ever dreamed of marrying—provided a full description of "the Weimar atmosphere" as it could be found in 15 Cranachstraße in the years between 1908 and 1910. Her depiction of Kessler's rooms, of the "temple of art" he created and the spirit that reigned within it, evokes a cultural style that was doomed to disappear within the next decade.

The fire burned in the hearth and threw its light upon the festive rider of the Parthenon frieze. Light yellow books stood in white bookcases. In the glass vitrines, however, the lovely, small figures of women by Maillol stared in the mirror which reflected their pure, restrained forms. Over a matted violet divan the nymphs of Maurice Denis ran through a fantastic forest. Before the window stood an ancient bronze Chinese vessel, a gift from the artists of three nations to the head of the house, Harry Kessler. I remember still the evening when Gerhart Hauptmann sat before it and read one of his dramas while Rilke listened with us, attentive and silent. But the door to the study is open, this long, reflective room, where, over rows of costly books, glowed pictures of the French impressionists like colorful flowers. On the desk again a statue of a woman by Maillol rose like a tree and caught the sunlight, which kissed her wistful and yet austere movement. Under the pictures a few of Rodin's bronze sketches stood on wide bookshelves. In the corner a terracotta bust of the painter Terrus by Maillol.

. . . The urge to understand and to unite everywhere that which is essential, created around Harry Kessler this atmosphere full of energy and movement, in which heat and coolness, distance and intimacy, purity and multi-colored splendor, renunciation and envelopment, and everything contradictory, was contained. We enter again a moment in the Cranachstraße, where in the morning sun the young boy of Maillol stands full of anticipation and dreams of the future, while a cool serenity pervades the rooms.[12]

Van de Velde, whose interior design helped created this atmosphere, "which had nothing of *Gemütlichkeit* in the narrow German sense, but rather embodied the spirit of restlessness, of multiplicity, of universality that belongs to Germany's other and larger soul," also recalled the conscious *mise en scène* of meals at Kessler's home: "Harry prepared each lunch, each tea with great deliberation and sensitivity. Like a clever and experienced director he let the gatherings run according to a well-planned program whereby none of the participants realized that he was also an actor. All took place in a ceremony in which a false word, a false gesture would have ruined the atmosphere like an insult whose perpetrator subjects himself to the disdain of all. For the spirit of aesthetic perfection pervaded Kessler's house like the morning freshness of a dew covered meadow or the salt breath of the sea."[13]

One person's "cool cheerfulness" or "salt breath of the sea," however, was another's "cold and inhuman paganism." The same Maurice Denis, whom Nostitz praised as a "well-to-do French bourgeois, not without the sentimental element which other nations find so irritating in Germans," found the spirit of Goethe and Nietzsche that prevailed in Weimar unhealthy and alarming.

The state of soul of this small world is very far from mine. Paganism, curiosity for sickly art, prideful classicism, no submission to the laws of the West: cosmopolitanism, boredom, immorality, the need for new sensations. Nietzsche is the man for this milieu. And how I understand that this madman, occasionally lucid, would have made fun of the hellenism of the bourgeoisie of Leipsick [*sic*]! What effort they make to be true Hellenes! from the cult of Maillol to the dances of the little naked girls of Isadora Duncan and the contortions of Ruth Saint Denis. . . . Despite the charm and distinction of spirit of Kessler, I could not live in this society so far from the idea of Germany I had from the *Lieder*, the ballads, of Schumann and even Wagner. How they have smothered the old German sensibility, the *Stimmung*, and the legendary familial virtues of the Germans![14]

If Denis had gone to Weimar in search of a romantic, *Biedermeier* mood, he was bound to be disappointed. It is not surprising that his mystic, reactionary Catholicism recoiled from Kessler's Weimar: he must have instinctively intuited that the Hellenism he mocked was incompatible with the doctrines of any church. Nevertheless, both Denis's criticism and the almost sacerdotal description of Nostitz have common roots. One of these was the unity of art and life aimed at in van de Velde's interiors. Karl Scheffler, the editor of *Kunst und Künstler*, noted the peculiar strain of living in such rooms: "For the mood in van de Velde's rooms is heavy, even a bit sombre and nowhere ingenuous. While the total atmosphere compels a spiritual attitude, an earnest diligence, it oppresses one a little; while it arouses pathos, it precludes much naturalness. For all the sensuous richness it has something monastic; for all its refinement, something ascetic; for all its cultivation, something primitive; and for all its aristocratic, haute bourgeois fastidiousness it does not lack in Puritanism. To live in such rooms requires especially educated and even especially clothed people. . . ." In all of this exclusiveness reigned a tyrannical restraint that most people could not tolerate. Indeed, there was something parvenu in itself, Scheffler argued, in this dictatorial opposition to the parvenu; "nevertheless something also of a cultural ambition among the best today that borders on reverence."[15]

Scheffler was writing of the house van de Velde designed for Karl Ernst Osthaus, a different man entirely from Kessler. Kessler himself noted the "melancholy *fin de race*, tubercular" atmosphere of Osthaus's home in Hagen when he visited. From the pictures at least, 15 Cranachstraße seems in contrast much lighter and cheerier. Still, what unites the accounts of Nostitz, van de Velde, Denis, and Scheffler is a clear intentionality that imbued Kessler's surroundings. The strains of Beethoven, as played by the virtuoso Conrad Ansorge, echoing through the light rooms filled with art and books, the thick reed matting covering the floor and muting the sound of boots and shoes, the fireplace with the Parthenon frieze upon which Hofmannsthal or Rilke or Dehmel would lean while reading his poetry—all of these were parts of a program, a mosaic composed of many elements. Heymel had once written to Kessler expressing the hope that the two of them should contribute to German culture "if only through the example of our way of life." [16] Kessler was not likely to have been enamored of the comparison between his way of life and that of the unstable Heymel, but he also cherished the idea of *Lebensführung* as a moral and aesthetic example. The concept should not be dismissed as pure snobbery—although it was definitely elitist—for it was a concept shared by many in the modernist movement in Germany and elsewhere. In Germany, in particular, a certain understanding of ancient Greece informed this attitude. The evocation of Greece, especially the culture of Periclean Greece, as a model for the future had an added personal attraction for Kessler: it provided a way for him to think of his sexuality as, at the least, not a hindrance, and at the best, a positive contribution to the creation of a modern way of life.

• • •

Immediately after the acceptance of his resignation in July 1906, Kessler went on August maneuvers in the company of Otto von Dungern. In a riding accident, he broke his knee, which laid him up in Berlin for the rest of the autumn, thus postponing his hopes of getting away to the shore for three weeks and recuperating from the stress of his "unclean" separation from the court in Weimar. The sudden flare-up of his struggle with Palézieux in the winter again played havoc with his nerves. After the depressing denouement of that affair in February, he occupied himself with *Künstlerbund* business; prepared a lecture on "New Tendencies in Art, Paul Gauguin and his Circle," which he delivered in Vienna on March 19, 1907; and negotiated with Miss Patrick Campbell, Shaw's friend, about an English translation of *Elektra*. At the end of May, Kessler visited Maillol, who showed him a series of twelve sketches for reliefs. One in particular struck Kessler's fancy, a man and a woman embracing. He immediately commissioned it for 4,000 francs. Toward the end of June, Kessler returned to Maillol's study to see the progress. At the same time, he sent a young bicyclist and jockey, Gaston Colin, to the artist to serve as a model both for the relief and for a separate statue. "Since Maillol only pays five francs," noted Kessler, "and finds it difficult to find a decent model for that price, I am giving the boy the rest." [17]

For the next two months, Kessler whiled away his time watching Maillol work on his two projects, chatting with him and occasionally photographing his progress. Now and then, work would be interrupted to allow Maillol to rip open the door of his studio and reveal his jealous wife eavesdropping while he worked with the female model. To avoid such distractions, it was agreed that Kessler would travel with the model to Maillol's studio. The conversations between patron and artist sometimes approached intellectual vaudeville. Once, after Kessler explained the goal of the new philosophy, to unify and place on a firm foundation all of knowledge, Maillol responded that it seemed rather complicated to him; "It seems to me that a good philosophy, a simple man like me should be able to understand it. A good philosophy should provide serenity." Complicated thoughts and investigations, Kessler replied, cannot be avoided any more than complicated procedures can be avoided in art. Ah, countered Maillol, but then the conclusions should be simple, as in sculpture. Turning toward the relief, he continued: "Nature is so beautiful. The buttocks are as round as apples and the apples as round as buttocks. There is nothing more beautiful than the buttocks of a woman or of a young man." When not discussing such lofty matters with Maillol, Kessler toured the area of Normandy near his mother's chateau and visited the Channel Islands, finally finding the rest and solitude he needed. "This combination of genius and naked beauty," he told Hofmannsthal later, "became through the contrast with the preceding Palézieux catastrophe a deeply intoxicating idyll." [18]

Maillol's model, Gaston Colin, is not specifically mentioned, outside of references to the work in the studio, in Kessler's diaries. It was during this period, however, that the boy's relationship with Kessler began. It was inevitably an asymmetrical relation, at least in terms of social class, wealth, and education.* In a letter to his sister Wilma, Kessler inquired about the bicycle given to her son by Colin: "He was the boy who stood for the statue and I have helped him on a little in different ways. He is a very nice, clever young fellow who is building an aeroplane on his own. . . . He is quite well off and something of a Casanova, some of his love affairs have been comical and sensational . . . ." Later he is at pains to reassure her of Colin's character and social position: "Young Colin . . . is *absolutely devoted to me.* You can trust Jacques (Kessler's nephew) to him as you would to me. He is a splendid young fellow, ex-

---

*One day Colin, perhaps to stimulate Kessler's jealousy, remarked to him: "You know Michelangelo? Well, when you were gone he asked me to pose for him."

"No kidding! But he's been dead for three hundred years."

"It's true, I made a mistake, it was the other one you speak about all the time with Maillol, what's his name now? Phi . . . Phi . . ."

"Phidias, perhaps?"

"Yes, that's it, it was Phidias; he asked me." *TB,* December 24, 1907.

tremely courageous, adroit in all sports and *manly*. He has risen by his
own means (although he comes from a good middle class family) and
has married his sister to a doctor." Still later, he suggests that she and
her husband take him to the theater as he "dresses very decently and is
presentable." [19]

The adventuresome Colin, bicyclist, jockey, and later a member of
France's first military air division, became Kessler's chauffeur as well,
racing together through the Norman countryside at up to sixty miles
per hour and leaving the occasional dead chicken or goat along the
way. They traveled together to England, so that Colin could race at New
Market, and later to Denmark, but they met most often in Paris and
Normandy. Kessler's letters were destroyed in later years by Colin's wife,
but Kessler kept the correspondence sent to him. The letters and post-
cards, the bulk of them dating from 1908 and 1909, testify to the passionate but unequal nature between the forty-year-old German aristocrat and the seventeen-year-old French boy. From the various stages of
the Tour de France and other cycling events, for which Kessler provided
the funding, Gaston writes of the various accidents that befell him or his
bicycle, expresses his gratitude to his patron, but also says how much he
misses his lover and how he longs to see him again. From Marseilles, he
writes in November 1908 that Kessler should send news "because I too
I am enormously bored without you . . . . I can no longer live without
you. Think of the good times spent together: Naples, Rome and especially along the coast of the Channel, our billiard games, our little disputes. *Enfin* I long to see you. Tell me what you are doing tomorrow
evening. All the time I think of you. I only live for you." Not above the
occasional desire to inspire jealousy—"I hope that you have entertained
yourself well with Maillol. I for my part have amused myself nicely with
the little English girl"—he nevertheless dutifully arranges assignations,
near Caen at a haystack, in a Paris apartment. Once Colin went so far as
to make an orthographical joke, adding an "e" to the end of "ami" in
"vôtre eternal ami" to suggest he was Kessler's girlfriend. In his most
intimate letter, written evidently after a number of quarrels, he expati-
ates on the nature of their relationship: "You believe that I have only
friendship for you as for a father. For myself I consider the little troubles
I've had will no longer be the case because I love you with all my heart,
believe me. Send me your photo that you have promised also. If one day
I am happy it will be thanks to you. I hope that you understand me because it is not me who speaks to you but my heart." [20]

Although the high point of their affair was 1908–1909, their relationship lasted until the war forced them into opposing armies. Kessler

sent him (and his wife, for his relation with Kessler did not prevent him from marrying) money during the war and constantly inquired through his sister after his welfare. "I should be very cut up if anything happened to him. And if he should be in want of money . . . I should be very glad if you could let him have some at my expense." They saw each other infrequently in the postwar years, Kessler still sending Colin money from time to time. In 1928, Colin sent a note commemorating the twentieth anniversary of their affair: "I am greatly troubled and regard the new year with sadness. When I think that it was twenty years ago this pains me greatly and I recall especially many days of happiness." [21]

Too discreet to record in his diary any intimate details of his relation with Colin, Kessler nevertheless mused, in a very impersonal and theoretical way, over the role of sexuality, and particularly of homosexuality, in modern culture. These passages revolve generally around a debate on the rationale for social constraints on what is sexually permissible, a debate that almost always takes place with the example of ancient Greece in the background. The greatest lesson of Greek antiquity for Kessler was that there was no hateful sensuality, that sensuality lay at the heart of a genuine culture. "A beautiful body of a boy and the great love that Plato provided the world as its axis, are both cause and effect. . . . Sensuality is the axis and the pole of all else; perhaps even its *raison d' être*, thus its importance. Thus too the absurdity of the attempt to wish to proscribe precisely for sexual sensuality a law, a generally valid truth." Such a revival of an uninhibited sensuality would require, however, that society shrug off its "hypertrophy of shame," the result, Kessler argued, of the modern woman, of syphilis, and of the church. Without their pernicious influence, no sexual act would cause, or be considered to cause, "psychological" damage: even prostitution would be a work like any other. "We should lead our lives," he concluded, "between the boundaries of what each of us privately considers immoral and what science has as exactly and as narrowly as possible defined as unsocial. In that case, of course, sexuality as well as many other things will have quite a different appearance." [22]

The promised land of sexual liberation, however, still lay a few years ahead as was made vivid to Kessler at the end of 1907, the time of the Kuno von Moltke–Philip von Eulenburg scandal and the libel trial of Maximilian Harden, who had accused the two men of being homosexuals. (Harden's real target was not homosexuality but rather what he considered the unhealthy influence the two aristocrats had exercised on German foreign policy.) Upon hearing of Harden's acquittal, which effectively destroyed the reputations of Eulenburg and Moltke, Kessler, who was politically close to Harden and personally close to Eulenburg and Moltke through the Richter salon, had mixed feelings. On the one hand, he felt that, with the affair's conclusion, "a sea of dirt and contempt has crashed over what, during the ten most happy years of my life, was my society: Potsdam and the Richter salon. . . . One will never be able to wear the uniform with the same feelings." Kessler found Harden's use of a public prejudice, which he himself did not share, not only to destroy an opponent politically, but also to ruin him personally, objectionable.[23] Nevertheless, he did not want to condemn Harden completely. When, in December 1907, the journal *Morgen* asked a series of leading intellectuals—including the Mann brothers, Hofmannsthal, Frank Wedekind, Strindberg, Liebermann, Bierbaum, Georg Brandes, and Dehmel—what they thought of Harden, Kessler's response was a very careful endorsement of the man, not his tactics. For the rest of the year, Kessler tiptoed back and forth between the two antagonists, visiting both Harden, to talk of politics,* and the Richter salon, whose regulars compared the affair to a Socrates trial in reverse, this time the younger generation trying the older.

The Moltke-Eulenburg scandal brought home to Kessler the vulnerability of homosexuals in high office. Still, all in all, he thought the immense publicity concerning a once taboo subject would, after the "indignation" had dissipated, be of benefit. In ten to twenty years, he predicted, there would be "a kind of sexual revolution, through which Germany, in the clear light of day very quickly would overcome the headstart in these things which France and England had taken. Around 1920 we—which is *not* the case today—will hold the record in pederasty, like Sparta in Greece."[24] Considering the Berlin of the 1920s, the Berlin of Christopher Isherwood and W. H. Auden, that was not a bad prediction.

• • •

If *Griechentum* still had to wait as much as twenty years to come to Germany, then the least Kessler could do was to go to Greece. He had not been there since his trip at the turn of the century. For quite some time,

---

*When Kessler mentioned his sympathy for Moltke as a personal friend, Harden replied that the trial had been Moltke's fault and said, "It's a real pity that you and I should have to undo two such wonderful guys like Palézieux and Phili Eulenburg." *TB,* November 8, 1907.

he had been discussing the possibility of traveling there together with Maillol and Hofmannsthal. In April 1908, after long correspondence, the three set out.

What, one wonders today, could have been going through Kessler's mind when he dreamed up the notion of forging this unlikely troika? Did he imagine that the earthy sculptor and the high-strung poet would, joined by their cicerone, drink deeply together from the well of European civilization? Kessler was of the firm conviction that any serious artist, or writer for that matter, could only benefit from contact with Aristide Maillol, as close to a living ancient Greek as existed.* After some delays and mishaps, the Austrian met up with Kessler and Maillol in Athens at the beginning of May.

The sirocco wind, the sultry air, and the blinding sun discomfited Hofmannsthal on his journey. Upon his arrival, he said that if Goethe had landed on Greek soil he probably would have kissed the ground, and he wondered why Kessler and Maillol did not feel the same way. "*Mais mon cher,*" replied Kessler, "I always feel a little like that." When Maillol chimed in with the same sentiments, there ensued a conversation over the nature of *Griechentum,* something in which Hofmannsthal professed to have lost faith. For Maillol, it was simply the place in the

---

*A few years later Kessler would again attempt to bring an artist into Maillol's fructifying presence; this time, Eric Gill, the third of the English originals Kessler cultivated, besides John and Craig. Full of the conviction that Gill, who had been designing title pages for Kessler and was now beginning to sculpt, would profit immeasurably from an apprenticeship under Maillol, Kessler convinced him to leave England and work as the Frenchman's assistant. Kessler signed a three-year lease on a house in Marly for Gill and his family, brought him over to the Grande Hotel in Paris, and then together they went to visit Maillol. Gill could not speak French, or Maillol English, so Kessler had to do all the translating. Believing that all was to everyone's satisfaction, Kessler sent Gill back to his luxurious suite in the Grande Hotel (where the reception desk could not quite believe that someone dressed like Gill could belong). Gill, however, was wondering what he had got himself into. As much as he admired Maillol, he was appalled at the thought of three years in the French suburbs. He decided to take the night train back to England immediately; "if I delayed to see Kessler I should be trapped; for I couldn't stand up against his overmastering confidence in his own schemes, or, for that matter, against my sense of his extraordinary kindness and generosity." Only when he reached the safe haven of England's green hills did he write Kessler a letter explaining his behavior. "I must say Kessler was angelic about it and so was Maillol. And in neither case did I suffer any loss of friendship. And I had the satisfaction of hearing that the grand gentry of the Grand Hotel got a proper dressing down for their snobbish stupidity, though I can't really blame them; for, according to their lights, I must have appeared an extremely ill-dressed and unworthy denizen of such a high-class establishment." See Gill, *Autobiography* (London: J. Cape, 1945), 178–82; for another description of the incident, including a copy of the letter Gill sent Kessler, see Rothenstein, *Summer's Lease,* 195–200.

world where all the art that he admired was created; for Kessler, it was the worldview, so much more embracing and universal in spirit than Christianity. Hofmannsthal claimed that he had once had a firm vision of what Greece was, but at the age of sixteen or seventeen he had read too much contradictory philology and his image had become blurred. Looking back now on his *Elektra,* his *Oedipus,* he realized that he had "orientalised" too much the picture of Greece. They talked deep into the night. "Towards the end Maillol was completely silent, as is his cautious, peasant-like habit when a stranger says something which he disapproves of."[25]

Everyone's mood plummeted the evening of the next day. On the way to an Athens theater to see *Oedipus at Kolonos* the cab, which had been racing along, struck a child. After he carried him to his home and left their address, Kessler and his friends wandered "aimlessly through the streets for a while, Maillol very calm and detached, Hofmannsthal nervous and disturbed. Finally we entered the theater, but without being able to follow the presentation, and left at the first pause." The next day Kessler went to inquire after the child and learned that he had suffered a skull fracture and was not expected to live. The news further distressed Hofmannsthal, who repeated to Kessler continually that only a father could understand what this meant, what a world in itself a small child is, and so forth.[26] The child eventually recovered—Kessler visited him again alone the next morning—but Hofmannsthal could not get over the incident. Hofmannsthal told Kessler that he had to leave, that, in fact, he never wished to leave any place as much as Greece right then. When Kessler responded that it was too bad Hofmannsthal had compelled Maillol, who had been sick, to come, Hofmannsthal said that he did not feel guilty about that since they obviously were enjoying themselves so much. It was agreed that after a trip to Delphi Hofmannsthal would leave from Piraeus by steamer.

The next day Hofmannsthal wrote to his wife, "The air and light are like a paradise here, Harry naturally charming, the gathering *à la trois* not exactly ideal however. Had a beautiful swim with Harry today in the glowing sea." During this swim, he returned to his theme; namely, that it was the language that he missed so much, that only a poet could understand what language meant, how it was his skin—and now here he found himself murmuring French instead of German. Finally he asked Kessler if it was possible to leave Maillol behind for a few days in order to ride together through the landscape; then, perhaps, he would recover his bearings. Kessler, whose patience was understandably wearing thin after five days of this, suggested that a ride through the Greek country-side with someone who was not sure if he liked Greece did not especially appeal to him. Perhaps if Hofmannsthal came around to another point of view in Delphi, such a trip would be possible. They parted that afternoon, and after dinner, Hofmannsthal told Kessler that he had spent a wonderful day at the Acropolis museum. "He appeared quite cheerful again."[27]

They traveled by boat the next day to Itea and from there, by land to Delphi. There transpired what Kessler called "the most unpleasant incident that has ever occurred between us." Hofmannsthal quite casually told Kessler that he had searched through Kessler's suitcase, looking for a book to read, and finding a wrapped package, had opened it and discovered two brochures, both of them worthless. "As he spoke, it was as if someone was slapping me, for allowing into my presence someone who was so far from a gentleman. I told him: 'I am astonished,' and returned to Maillol who was ahead." At dinner, Hofmannsthal excused himself and went straight to his room. When Kessler went upstairs and knocked on his door, Hofmannsthal opened it in his nightshirt; he was crying and completely agitated. Kessler tried to put the matter aside. Hofmannsthal thanked him and made excuses, finally asking "'whether it was truly so bad to look into the suitcase of a traveling companion?'" As Kessler said that he did not want to discuss the incident, but simply to tell him that he had forgotten it, Hofmannsthal threw his arms around Kessler in gratitude and blamed his whole behavior during the trip on fate. "Since I did not wish to prolong this painful and grotesque scene," wrote Kessler, "I gave him my hand and left. Somewhere there is a difference between us in the matter of tact, perhaps a racial difference."[28]

From this absolute nadir, the trip could only get better. Two days later Hofmannsthal and Kessler left Maillol in Delphi for an overnight trip to the monastery of St. Luke. There the solemnity, the scent of thyme and camellias, the singing, and the night fires of the shepherds spread out in the valley below acted as a much needed soothing balm on the raw feelings of the preceding week. They left very early the following morning on the seven-hour trip to the nearest train that could bring them back to Athens. The heat was nearly unbearable. On the way, wrote Kessler, "We spoke of traveling, of wandering, of the weariness of wandering." Hofmannsthal, in his fictionalized description of the journey entitled "The Wanderer," written and published years later, recalls their talk as "one of the strangest and most beautiful conversations that I can remember. There were two of us, and while talking it seemed as if each were following only his own memories, many of which we shared." Both men were struck by the appearance of a barefoot, hatless wanderer, who turned out to be a young man from Bavaria, obviously hungry, exhausted, and feverish. In the end, they gave him a mule, money, food, and a guide. Both travelers noted that the appearance of the wanderer incarnate coincided with the moment when they had been speaking of Rimbaud and wandering. Hofmannsthal said at the time that saving his life served in some way as payment for the child (who he presumed had died).[29]

In Athens, as he prepared to leave, Hofmannsthal assured Kessler of what the trip, his first visit outside of his culture, had meant to him. In a letter to his father, he wrote, "I only hope that you don't believe that my Greek trip was a disappointment or something the like. On the contrary, they were the most remarkably compressed and varied impressions and experiences, which one can imagine; for the first time in my life I had the feeling to truly travel, to truly be in a strange land. I had quite falsely expected a kind of Italy, and found the Orient." Kessler, as might be expected, had a different impression. "Hofmannsthal in Greece was a failure," he wrote to his sister, "*il ne se retrouvait pas*. He was almost always out of sorts, or out of temper, or out of feeling with the surroundings. . . . He said he could not stand the barrenness of the country; woods, and rivers and green fields were his lifeblood etc. . . . I was glad when I had got him into his train for Patras. Maillol has been just the contrary, like a fish in water."

Indeed, Maillol, who had believed to recognize his home town Banyuls as soon as he got off the boat, wandered enchanted through the countryside. Once, carried away with admiration, he clambered up to embrace one of the female statues of the Erechtheion, only to be ordered down by a guard. He filled a large school notebook with sketches, and, between each leaf, he pressed a flower from the places they visited. For Maillol, it was an epic trip, a confirmation of the path he had chosen in sculpture.[30] They decided to stay an extra week in Athens so that he could sculpt one of the local boys; Maillol constructed the base, armature, and whatever else he needed from scraps.

Then they embarked at the beginning of June. In Naples, the two companions separated, Maillol sailing for Marseilles and Kessler staying in Italy. Exhausted and about to become deathly ill, Kessler by this time was glad to see Maillol go as well. Over the long run, he had found the artist's company tiresome: "*Conversation* with him is impossible. He speaks his opinion and finds all that deviates from it *bête*. His opinion is often on the mark and mostly amusing and picturesque; but the impossibility to add anything other than a flat, 'Yes,' is, over the long term, unbearably fatiguing." Kessler attributed Maillol's inability to tolerate contradiction to his insecurity about his education. He then listed Maillol's other faults, the way he ate with his fingers, spitting fish bones on the carpet, the way he walked slowly and cautiously, and the way he looked at the sky to check the time. Kessler especially disliked Maillol's miserliness. "But in the end," wrote Kessler, "one feels very sharply that he belongs to another social class, whose conventions of social intercourse are so different, that it requires a constant effort, in order not to feel hurt by them. It is a *mésalliance* that the intellect alone cannot elide over in daily contact." [31] Exhausted by several weeks in the intimate company of two men, who, however artistically gifted, were "very far from gentlemen," Kessler succumbed to gout and articular rheumatism in Rome.

CHAPTER 13

Hofmannsthal and
Der Rosenkavalier

What sort of nervous, touchy creatures we are anyway.
Kessler to Hofmannsthal, *Briefwechsel*

"Dear Graf Kessler, We wish to record our recognition of your generous services in the cause of what seems to you noble and sincere art
of every kind, and we beg your acceptance of a small token of our
appreciation of your energy, sympathy and unfailing courage." So read
the message, written by Eric Gill, that accompanied the gift of an ancient Chinese bronze bowl to Kessler on December 20, 1908. It was the
gift of artists and writers of three nations.* "My joy was great," noted
Kessler, "but would have been greater had the address been written
in German." What he did not know was that Hofmannsthal had in
fact drafted an address in German, which was not used because Gerhart
Hauptmann found it too devout and sentimental and refused to sign it.
As might be expected, Hofmannsthal's draft was more personal, more
philosophic, more vague in an intriguing way than Gill's rather per-
functory note. Hofmannsthal places Kessler's "unforgettably substantial and loyal support" for the artists of three countries in the context
of a world marked largely by indifference to art: "In a world where the

*On behalf of Germany: Ansorge, Dehmel, Hauptmann, Hofmann, Hofmannsthal,
Klinger, Liebermann, Trübner, Tuaillon, van de Velde; for England: Conder, Gill, John-
ston, Ricketts, Rothenstein, Shannon, Shaw, Steer, Walker; for France: Bonnard, Cross,
Denis, Gide, Maillol, Redon, Rodin, Rysselberghe, Signac, and Vuillard.

masses confront us apathetically, and the aesthete leaves us cold, what greets us in you is not 'the educated,' but rather the *living*. Your being, all temperament and fantasy, answered each cry of our art and there where a world had remained deaf to us, another world appeared from out of a single person to echo back to us." According to Hofmannsthal, it is not merely as an echo, however, that Kessler relates to art: he too is, in a way demonstrated by his Weimar experience, a martyr to art: "You are as lonely as we, and in that you seem to seek us out, you simply follow the course of your fate. But you have always drawn the consequences, and to you, for whom art and religious emotion are one and the same, the experience of art had to become the dramatically intense content of your life (*tragisch gespannten Inhalt*). The abuse, the resistance of the world became in your fate visible to us in a moving way, and we will never be able to express it other than through a symbol, how much we feel connected to you."[1]

Kessler, one assumes, would have appreciated Hofmannsthal's subtle characterization of his relation to art and to the artists he admired. Had he not written to Hofmannsthal that "you are for me . . . something that justifies to me my life. You, van de Velde are for me *the* content of my life, in somewhat the same way your works are for you, that which offers me the possibility in life to participate in creation." There was, Kessler asserted, after all, a difference in the degree of their mutual interdependence: in what concerned their cooperation, "so it is clear as day that I must always be *the one* who helps you as far as it is in my power; you are only permitted from time to time to turn your energies towards my goals." For a planned essay on his friend "with the ten thousand connections," Hofmannsthal jotted in his notebook: "Why is Kessler not an artist? He would not be a great one and this way he is something more: he is an artist in living material: provides souls with an outlook, leads appearances to each other. . . . Expect from Kessler: a path to enjoying strange and new characters."[2] The asymmetry of such a relationship, perfectly tolerable when differences in language, in background, and, especially, in the field of creative ambition, were great enough to preclude ambiguity—as was the case with Maillol, van de Velde, and Craig—proved much more volatile with Hofmannsthal.

Ever since Hofmannsthal had asked him to provide ideas and materials for dramas, Kessler had dutifully sent off a stream of books and suggestions from London, Paris, Berlin, and Weimar. After receiving one such gift, which inspired him to begin a comedy, Hofmannsthal concluded generously, "I would never have thought that one could owe a person so much and so many things, as I do you and not experience it, as one reviews it in the mind's eye, as oppressive, but rather inspiring."[3] While that project remained unfinished, Hofmannsthal was already at work on a version of what later would become *Christinas Heimreise,* for which Kessler was providing him with material on early sea captains and explorers, as well as dramatic and textual criticism. The two looked forward to their meeting in Weimar in February 1909, a few months after the presentation of the Chinese bowl to Kessler, to discuss the play in person. They did, in fact, during this stay, revise substantially *Christinas Heimreise,* but of far more importance to both men, and to the history of both literature and music, they also plotted out together, in three days of excited conversation, the scenario of what would become *Der Rosenkavalier.*

Kessler had returned from Paris—where Felix Féneon had introduced him to Henri Matisse—to Dresden at the end of January to attend the premiere of Hofmannsthal's *Elektra* in the company of the author and the composer. Then at the beginning of February, Hofmannsthal arrived in Weimar to stay for a week. On the second day, Kessler informed his guest of a new Parisian opera *bouffe,* a light comedy based on the eighteenth-century erotic novel *Les Aventures du Chevalier de Faublas.* Hofmannsthal was enchanted and said that was exactly the material he wanted in order to create a light-hearted opera with Strauss that would bring in lots of money and thus free him from financial worries.[4] The other main source for the plot and scenes of *Der Rosenkavalier* was Molière's three-act play, *Monsieur de Pourceaugnac,* with music by Jean-Baptiste Lully. The inspiration for the famous levée scene in the first act with the hairdresser, the Italian tenor, various lackeys, and the blackamoor came from the fourth plate in Hogarth's engraving *Marriage à la Mode,* as found in a German copy with witty commentary by Georg Christoph Lichtenberg.

Hofmannsthal and Kessler began weaving these elements together, occasionally leaving Kessler's house to ride in a carriage through the snow-covered Belvedere Park. Even when writing down their discussions the same evening they occurred, Kessler found it difficult to remember who had invented what: "Hofmannsthal's contribution and my own merge so thoroughly that it is impossible to separate the parts. One gives an idea, a direction, the other criticizes, then in the to and fro something quite different emerges; often neither he nor I can say ten minutes later who had actually invented the scene." In a letter to his sister, Kessler repeated this point and added that "in three days we thus managed to set down the scenario *dans ses plus petits détails jusqu'aux jeux de scène,* so that only the words are still missing." Hofmannsthal seemed to agree. "Strauss is completely charmed by the scenario that I finished in Weimar with Kessler (to the smallest detail). He hopes to be finished with this three-act opera of the lightest sort in 1½ years." To Kessler, he said that making a scenario with another gave him the same security as if the scenario had come from a foreign play.[5] Two years later, in an angry letter to Bodenhausen, Kessler even claimed that Hofmannsthal had said to him in his study that "in view of my contribution on *Der Rosenkavalier,* my name should actually be listed too as author of the play." But Hofmannsthal, Kessler went on, feared that an unknown name would perhaps disturb the public, even Strauss himself, and he and Strauss depended so much on the success that he would be thankful if Kessler would forego the privilege this time.[6]

In any case, both men knew that the scenario they had invented would work, and they were not surprised at Strauss's immediate acceptance. The experiment of working together had gone so well that they proceeded to do the same for *Christinas Heimreise.* Hofmannsthal left for Rodaun, his home outside of Vienna, to work on both pieces, while Kessler left for the south of France to visit Maillol in Banyuls before traveling to Paris to witness the debut of Diaghilev's Ballets Russes. In Paris, he waited impatiently for news of Hofmannsthal's progress in writing out the opera.

Paul Robinson has called *Der Rosenkavalier* an opera "of romantic sacrifice," referring to the decision of the central figure, the aging but still beautiful Marschallin, to relinquish the boyish lover Octavian to her younger rival. "The intellectual and emotional center" of the opera, he quite rightly asserts, is the final scene of the first act in which the Marschallin, alone, contemplates the passing of time, and realizes that, sooner or later, Octavian's love for her too will pass. The modernity of *Der Rosenkavalier,* Robinson goes on, lies in its purely subjective and psychological concentration on time and aging; society, politics, the community—important themes in the great nineteenth-century operas—are reduced here to mere background. Most of the characters are caricatures of social types for whom the audience feels no special sympathy. "The Marschallin, Octavian, and, in her less sophisticated way, Sophie are the only genuine characters in the opera, since they care about nothing except what is in their hearts."[7]

How did what was quite clearly intended as a light opera based on Molière's "objective" comedies come to have at its heart an intensely lyrical and subjective moment? The answer lies perhaps in a remark Hofmannsthal made when he first arrived in Weimar: "What I want is something quite special; namely, as the warp and the woof of a fabric are intertwined, so to weave the well-made French scenario with something that lies in me, call it temperament or ideal, or what you will." The work of the early Hofmannsthal, the poet of "Life, Dream and Death" and the author of *The Fool and Death*, is obsessed with death and the passage of time. Later, as is well known, he felt the need to overcome the aestheticism of his youth. As late as 1907, he had complained to Kessler of his labeling as an aesthete; "precisely I who not only do not close myself off from the world, but rather have a *need* for an activity that transcends the purely artistic."[8] The turn to the theater was motivated by the need to transcend the purely subjective, the purely lyrical. Nonetheless, the transformation was not complete. Through the woof of the *braves Scenarium*—burlesque, ribald, a little *libre*—developed in February, Hofmannsthal threaded the warp of subjective lyricism as he wrote the first draft that spring.

When at last the long-awaited draft arrived on May 17, 1909, Kessler had a chance to discover the changes in emotional accent the scenario had undergone. On the whole, he found it quite wonderful, and laughed aloud often. He did have major reservations about Ochs, a character he found to be far too reflective and philosophical. Kessler's real affection, it seems, was with Octavian; here, he was concerned that this character not become too passive, too effeminate, which would lessen the charm of seeing him dressing and behaving as a chambermaid. Hofmannsthal responded to Kessler's criticism of Ochs by adopting many of his suggestions and making the character more Rabelaisian and less reflective. Nevertheless, he wrote, "My Lerchenau, whom I see, hear, and smell very clearly, is not a dumb yokel, *pur et simple*—in no way a Philistine, but rather a *Kerl*, a rustic, petty noble Don Juan, with a little bit of Falstaff, or, if then a Philistine, in any case a heightened Philistine, a demi-god Philistine and *not a pig*. Otherwise he would be (to me at least) intolerable as a main character." About the Marschallin he noted that "it is she and Ochs, as antipodes, who are the main characters, Octavian and Sophie, the love-pair, *de second plan*. . . . The love-pair as the center, as in Wagner, does not appeal to me; as we worked out the scenario that was not yet so clear to us."[9] In his response, Kessler approved of the new tone, while at the same time praising the ballet- or dance-like qualities of the first two acts. If, however, he acknowledged and approved the change in tone, Kessler did not seem to fully recognize how much the emphasis had changed between the February scenario and the final libretto. This misunderstanding lay at the root of the controversy over the dedication of the opera that began in the summer of 1910.[10]

Before Hofmannsthal's letter of July 5 sparked the disagreement, bad feelings had been accumulating. When Kessler had enthusiastically proposed himself and Thadée Natanson as the translators of *Der Rosenkavalier* into French, Hofmannsthal had written a rather abrupt reply, mentioning that he had ceded the right to choose a translator in the contract and that Kessler underestimated the difficulty of the task. Kessler's criticism of the last act of *Christinas Heimreise,* thoroughly justified by the play's poor reception in its Berlin premiere, appears to have irritated Hofmannsthal as well. Most important, the argument over Craig's staging of *Oedipus* in Munich had stretched the nerves of both men. So when Hofmannsthal wrote to ask Kessler whether he preferred as a dedication, his initials followed by *dem verborgenen Helfer* (the hidden helper), or simply his name, the pot boiled over.

He had thought, Kessler responded, that his name would simply be left out, as they had agreed; if, however, it was to be mentioned then he objected to the word "helper." "Helping" is what he had done with *Christina* or what he and Hofmannsthal had done for Rudolf Alexander Schröder's Homer: "With the *Rosenkavalier,* however, the conception itself and the working out of the pantomine-parts, the fundamentals, that is, the *substance* of the work came in part from me, as the other part came from you. If you afterwards erected upon this foundation a light and charmingly poetic structure so I am nevertheless not reduced to 'Helper' anymore than you are after Strauss has decorated your poetry with music. We are all three in the completely normal and usual sense *co-authors* (*Mitarbeiter*) and as such, and only as such, can I allow myself to be mentioned."[11] It is not necessary to trace the entire *pas de deux* of wounded feelings and expressions of strained politeness that followed this letter. The depth of emotion, however, is surprising. Hofmannsthal, whose handwriting on occasion betrays great agitation, went so far at one point to write bitterly that he had come to the decisive knowledge, "that between us, that is from you to me, a friendship can never have existed, but rather something else: human good will and respect for my artistic talent, both feelings, in accordance with your lively and generous nature, in such a strong measure that you perhaps could consider it friendship."[12]

Kessler tried to put the matter behind him, now that he had expressed feelings that had been building up through the summer. "I cannot," he wrote, "offer you a declaration of love naturally, either by letter or in person: emotional conversations between men are extremely repugnant to me. But truly, if you mean that I could dedicate myself to someone (I did not think of as a friend), no matter how much I respected him as an artist, as I have for the last ten years for you in all matters, then you must in fact very much overestimate me as a friend of art and humanity." Finally, in the letter that seemed to settle the matter, he appealed to their good sense: "Really, my friend, there is so little warmth in the world, one has so few people with whom one experiences unforced sympathy, and still more seldom does such an elective affinity permit a truly human relationship to grow. We have known each other now over half a lifespan, we know approximately what to expect from each other, what we can give to each other. Should we risk all of this because in an emotional moment, in a moment where we both had been made sensitive and touchy through other things perhaps, we unintentionally hurt each other?"[13]

The final wording of the dedication read: "I dedicate this comedy to Count Harry Kessler, whose cooperation it owes so much." Kessler actually missed the first act of the premiere of *Der Rosenkavalier* in Dresden on January 26, 1911, but was treated as a guest of honor at the reception. About the opera, he wrote to his sister that it was one of the most beautiful and exquisite operas existing, that the Marschallin was the great role, and that "the whole opera is *steeped* in an atmosphere of love and silvery light and wit and brightness, such as no composer, except Mozart, has ever achieved." About the dedication, he said, "It is unmistakably cold, but I prefer that to his first wording which simply took the whole book away from me (*sous prétexte* of being cordial). However, we are quite friendly again and he did what he could in Dresden to give me the *"place d'honneur"* everywhere, I must say."[14]

As much as both men would have perhaps liked to believe otherwise, the *Streit* between them had not been laid to rest, either in their own hearts or in the world at large. Rumors about the controversy continued to be bandied about, so much so that Moritz Heimann had to reassure the publisher Samuel Fischer about the book: "I don't believe that *a single* line that went under Hofmannsthal's name is by Kessler; ideas, thoughts, inventions to be sure which Hofmannsthal used (and justifiably, despite everything!) unscrupulously, as he has always taken from every page that he reads, from every mouth that he hears."[15] Finally in June, the two men decided only a personal meeting could stifle the animosity before it overwhelmed what only a year before had seemed like a very promising productive collaboration.

As Kessler reported it, the talk "took a calm and in part joking course." Kessler quite perceptively argued "that a doubtless sympathy which exists between us, which is even stronger than our will, comes always into conflict with some sort of unalterable and forever colliding qualities of our personalities." He could not identify the part of him that offended Hofmannsthal, but for his part, it was the gap he perceived between Hofmannsthal's warm words and his personal indifference. For example, although he had urged Kessler very strongly to write, he had then foregone each time a thoroughgoing criticism of his work. He then ticked off the incidents with Craig, with the Greek trip, and with *Der Rosenkavalier* and *Christinas Heimreise*.[16] Hofmannsthal's turn came next. He could not formulate what it was about Kessler's behavior that disturbed him, he said, but could only give examples. It was the way Kessler suddenly became enthusiastic about someone and then just as suddenly dropped him; it had something "jumpy, exaggerated, absurd in the movement, as if a perfectly normal man started eating matches." Furthermore, Hofmannsthal felt that their forms of fantasy were different, his being more complex, more two-sided, less enthusiastic. In response, Kessler admitted that he was perhaps too sudden and too forceful in his likes and dislikes; there was not much he could do about it, he felt, except try to moderate the expression and bear the effect of his emotional swings in mind.[17]

The real source of the antagonism between the two men, however, lay deeper than that. Hofmannsthal—perhaps due to the *egoisme sacré* of the artist, perhaps because of some other personal defect—was never able to understand that his friend was not in fact content with the selfless task of patronage, of cultural mediation, with being "an artist in living material." Kessler was clear that he was not a sculptor like Maillol, or an engraver and stage designer like Craig, or an architect like van de Velde; he was even clear that he was not a lyric poet like Hofmannsthal, but he did feel that there was more in him than an occasional essayist. For years, as he mentioned, the thinly cloaked dismissive attitude he discerned beneath Hofmannsthal's polite recognition of his writing had irked him, especially inasmuch as a constant theme of Hofmannsthal in person was the exalted and very special nature of the writer, a claim, that however he mocked it, at some level Kessler believed. Finally, the collaboration on *Der Rosenkavalier* and on *Christinas Heimreise* had presented him with the possibility of exercising the one creative gift he felt he had, his dramatic imagination. In a letter to Bodenhausen, explaining his role in the creation of the *Der Rosenkavalier,* he responded to the question why he did not simply write plays and ballets himself: "Hofmannsthal lacks as a dramatic writer *precisely that* which I possess, and *the contrary.* Hofmannsthal had absolutely no constructive talent, he has even only a very limited talent for the further development and dramatically effective ordering of a material already present; that is why he has, with the exception of purely lyrical dramas, relied on already available scenarios. If an effective scenario is available, however, that he can make it alive lyrically in a wonderful way, breathing life into the figures and situations through poetry. I lack *this* gift; I *cannot* bring the figures to speak, so that the speech sounds like *their* voice (the great gift of the lyricist), but I can, and to be sure in a much more certain and clearer way than Hofmannsthal, *invent* and *order* a dramatic plot." [18]

When Hofmannsthal's dedication arrived, Kessler realized the limits to this dream of collaboration. *The Legend of Joseph* is proof that he did not abandon it completely. But the more the prospect of Hofmannsthal as a collaborator faded, the more the many aspects of the Austrian's personal character he had always, from the first time they had met, found objectionable began to grate. This process was accelerated as the magic of the young poet diminished with age, with personal acquaintance, and with Hofmannsthal's move into the theater. As he began to watch with interest the signs of a new art and literature emerging in Germany after 1910, Kessler began to realize how fragile Hofmannsthal's attempt to connect with the modern world was. Hofmannsthal himself dimly perceived this and resented Kessler's interest in expressionist art and literature. The three days together in February 1909 represented then a summit and a turning point. [19]

CHAPTER 14

A Monument for Nietzsche

> The *architect* represents neither a Dionysian nor an Apollonian condition: here it is the mighty act of will, the will which moves mountains, the intoxication of the strong will, which demands artistic expression. The most powerful men have always inspired the architects; the architect has always been influenced by power. Pride, victory over weight and gravity, the will to power, seek to render themselves visible in a building; architecture is a kind of rhetoric of power, now persuasive, even cajoling in form, now bluntly imperious. The highest feeling of power and security finds expression in that which possesses *grand style*.
>
> Nietzsche, *Twilight of the Idols*

A few days after the premiere of *Der Rosenkavalier*, Kessler became involved in another project, shifting his attention back to the first of the four chief benefactors of his patronage, Henry van de Velde. In the beginning of February 1911, he traveled to Weimar to discuss the plan of building a monument to Nietzsche. Van de Velde outlined the two possibilities: a simple renovation of the Nietzsche Archives and the construction of a reception hall or the construction of an entirely new memorial. He favored the first; there was never any question which alternative appealed to Kessler. What is surprising is how he managed to overcome the opposition of Elisabeth Förster-Nietzsche, who had originally favored the first modest proposal, chiefly on financial grounds.[1]

Few, however, could resist the force of Kessler's conviction and the imagery of his imagination, and this project especially inspired in him a

crusading zeal. In a crescendo of enthusiasm, he wrote two separate letters to Nietzsche's sister in response to her invitation to join the memorial committee. The first letter, written on February 1, 1911, suggested
broadening the committee to include Englishmen (George Bernard
Shaw, George Moore, William Butler Yeats, Gilbert Murray, William
Rothenstein, Walter Raleigh, Granville Barker, and Eric Gill) and
Frenchmen (Auguste Rodin, Aristide Maillol, Maurice Denis, Anatole
France, Henri Bergson, Charles Maurras, Maurice Barrès). Kessler then
went on to propose that, in lieu of a portait of Nietzsche, a statue be
erected of a naked male youth as the "Overman" to be sculpted, naturally, by Maillol, with perhaps Klinger employed in providing a relief for
the interior of the temple, the latter to be designed by van de Velde.
Thinking on his feet as he wrote, Kessler went on to promise 5,000
marks of his own money as part of the 50,000 marks in guaranteed
funds that he estimated was necessary to launch the project in a style
adequate to the memory of the great philosopher. In the second letter,
written the same day, he elaborated his idea, arguing that in order to
avoid wounding the sensibilities of either Maillol or Klinger—in truth,
he was only concerned about finding some role for the latter, who was,
in his view, much the inferior sculptor—the task should be divided.
Maillol's statue of a naked youth outside the temple would represent the
Apollinian principle; only an artist with deep roots in classical antiquity
could provide the clear outlines required to incorporate this principle.
Inside the temple would be the bas-reliefs, illustrating inscriptions from
Nietzsche's texts and representing the formless, murky, musical Dionysian principle, a fitting task for a German sculptor. "And Van de Velde,"
he continued, "as a Belgian, romano-German" would unite both in his
architecture. Kessler brushed aside both Förster-Nietzsche's fears that
Klinger could be upset by the prominent role assigned to Maillol and
her concerns about how the money was to be raised, confident in his
ability to persuade her in person if not through correspondence.[2] At this
stage, the proposal called for a temple in Nietzsche's honor: inside
would be bas-reliefs by Klinger illustrating the Dionysian principle, in
between would be tablets carved by Gill. Out in front would stand a
monumental statue of a young man representing the Apollinian principle; Maillol, of course, would provide it, based on his designs for the
Blanqui Memorial. The land in front of the temple would be turned
into a park. He explained to Förster-Nietzsche, "I am assuming that we
don't want to erect in honor of your brother, who loved life so much,
a dead memorial but rather a living one. A simple bust, even a simple

temple like that of Abbé in Jena, is, however, something dead, which only through the quality of its execution but not in its essence, differs from the thousands of superfluous Goethe, Bismarck, Emperor and other monuments." [3]

This proposal was adopted and an informal committee was formed. Money would be raised by subscriptions in the amount of 8,000 marks each, by concerts and lectures throughout Europe—Reinhardt in Berlin, Strauss and d'Annunzio in Paris, Mahler in Vienna—and finally by the sale of facsimile editions of Nietzsche's texts. On March 12, 1911, the official committee was named: Kessler as president; the director of the Insel Verlag, Kippenberg; Privy Councillor Kohler; the mayor of Weimar, Richard Öhler; Walther Rathenau; Professor Raoul Richter; and *Generalkonsul* Paul Schwabach. Missing notably from the committee was Nietzsche's sister, perhaps because she had preferred the choice of the German sculptor Georg Kolbe (who would later carve Kessler's bust) to Maillol or perhaps because Kessler feared granting her too great an influence. The committee also offered the honorary presidency to Bernhard von Bülow, the former chancellor, as of 1909 unemployed. It was agreed that the honorary membership should eventually number 300, including most of the prominent names in European culture. [4] Kessler began work immediately. When van de Velde replied that the proposed site was not large enough for the plan, Kessler agreed enthusiastically and proposed placing the monument at the top of a large hill with a view.

Ambitious as it was, such a scheme was within the realm of the possible. And then hubris tipped the scale. In a sketch, Kessler added a new element, a stadium. Breaking the news to Nietzsche's sister—"Again, I beg you, don't be frightened!"—he made his case: "Your brother was the first . . . to teach joy in one's body, on physical strength and beauty; the first who brought physical culture, force, and grace back into relation with the spirit and the highest things. This relation I would like to see realized in this monument." [5] Two days later, Kessler informed Hofmannsthal of the plan. First, he reported his success in winning Prince Lichnowsky over to his idea; the way is open to high society, he wrote. Then he described in detail the way he pictured the project:

First of all: we wish to unite art and nature (vegetation, vista) as the Greeks and the Japanese have done in their *Heroa*. We wish therefore to create on the slope of the hill, which offers an overview of Weimar, a kind of woods through which a *Feststraße*, a solemn allee leads to a sort of temple. Before this temple, on a terrace, from which one can look over Weimar and its valley, Maillol is supposed to incorporate the Apollinian principle in the form of a greater-than-life size figure of a young man.

In the interior we imagine the temple thus: right and left upon the walls three stone steps, upon which cushions can be laid for festivals, performances, etc. (as back then in Athens). During such occasions chairs can be placed in the middle space. At the front end a kind of low "stage," like those upon which the altar stands in churches, and upon that a large Nietzsche *Herme.* Over the steps the side walls will be divided into three sections by pilasters, in the middle of each section a large relief of Klinger, and right and left of each relief, great tablets with inscriptions (Nietzsche citations). All in all, six reliefs (three on each wall) and twelve tablets. Lighting through a large window over the entrance gate and through low side windows above the reliefs (no skylight). I imagine room for 200 to 250 people and that there memorial celebrations for Nietzsche, but otherwise *as little spoken (lectures) as possible* will take place; rather from time to time music, quartets, song and above all dance (Ruth St. Denis and the like). Since the reliefs in the interior should also incorporate the Dionysian in Nietzsche's world view, so music and living dance belong there. The Apollinian, as I already said, will be expressed *outside:* at first in Maillol's figure; but then also in *living form.* And this is what will give the entire project its most original and innovative character. . . .

Behind the temple I picture a *stadium,* in which annual foot races, gymnastics, contests of all kinds—in short the beauty and strength of the body which Nietzsche as the first modern philosopher, has brought into contact with the highest, most spiritual things—can be presented. As it was fitting that one built hospitals next to Christian churches, so it is fitting that a place dedicated to youth and force arise next to a memorial for Nietzsche. He has spiritualized this part of life again, just as Christ did for suffering.[6]

The stadium, Kessler went on to add, also offers financial advantages, which is why financiers like Rathenau and Julius Stern approved of it. The hundreds of thousands of members of gymnastic clubs and other amateur sports organizations could then be enlisted in the project. That the site would be one of the most majestic and beautiful realized since antiquity would also help gain the stadium project support. The cost he estimated at between 800,000 and one million marks. Stern and Rathenau thought raising the money would not be a problem, he reported; what was needed was to bring everyone possibly interested in the project together. To that end, he requested that Hofmannsthal send him a list of people who might want to support its realization.

The idea of building a stadium was in the air in 1911, of course: the modern Olympic games, which had begun in Athens in 1896 and then degenerated into a sideshow at the World's Fairs of Paris and St. Louis, were about to gain a new lease on life at the 1912 games in Stockholm, generally conceded as the first modern Olympics. For this event, Swedish architect Torbern Grut was building a large outdoor stadium, acclaimed as the best example of a modern stadium. Kessler sent a positive review of the plans for this stadium to van de Velde. The revival of the Olympic games, it has been pointed out, did not serve just the purpose of glorifying the modern world's quest for speed, strength, agility, and records; they also represented a return to the past, to Olympia, the city of athletics, art, and prayer. A greater theater for the revival of Kessler's *Griechentum* could not be envisioned. Here the youth of Germany would relearn the physical grace and rhythm that a hundred years of Bildung had drummed out of them. A swimming pool was added to the plans, to be discreetly screened so as to dispense with "hateful bathing suits." Kessler even mused about the possibility of adding an institute for "genetic beautification of the race," if there was enough money.[7] Presumably here too freer and more universal sexual mores would reign.

More generally, Kessler's letter offers a remarkable *summarium* of his cultural preoccupations. His plans were steeped in the notion of a Gesamtkunstwerk, the lingering ideal of the Jugendstil. Practically all of Kessler's favorite artists were to be enlisted: Maillol for the great statue (with Nijinsky as his model), Klinger for the reliefs, Gill for the tablets, van de Velde to build the temple and the stadium, Ruth St. Denis to dance, Craig, surely, to arrange the magnificent processions, Reinhardt to produce Hofmannsthal's *Oedipus*—who knows, perhaps Colin would take part in the games. Undoubtedly, given time, Kessler would have found a task for Pierre Bonnard and Edouard Vuillard as well. All of these elements were to be so arranged that the two hundred or so *élus* (the spectacle of games and sports in the stadium would be religious instruction enough for the masses, it can be assumed) would enter up the long, ascending avenues, through the sacred woods, up the steps under the shadow of the Apollinian principle, and through the gates of the temple, and, resting on cushions, enter a seamless web of music, dance, and art, of *Einfühlung*—and with as little talking as possible.

It was an intoxicating vision, so much so that when the sister of the great philosopher-prophet wrote an excited letter, opposing the idea of a stadium, Kessler exploded in impatience: "She is fundamentally a little Philistine pastor's daughter, who to be sure swears upon her brother's words, but is incensed and upset as soon as one converts them into deeds. She justifies much of what her brother said about women; she was, after all, the only woman that he knew well." With that off his chest, he hurried out to Weimar to persuade her to change her mind. It turned out that she had feared that van de Velde and Kessler were plotting something behind her back; faced with Kessler's torrent of eloquence, she backed down and appeared very agreeable. Having had experience with a fickle patron already, Kessler should have been more wary, but instead he lunged ahead with his plans. Julius Stern and Paul Schwabach, two Jewish financiers—a fact that did not go unnoticed by right-wing critics of the plan—offered 30,000 marks each for the purchase of the land. Meanwhile, the honorary committee had been expanding rapidly: eventually André Gide, Anatole France, Edvard Munch, Gabriele d'Annunzio, Hofmannsthal, Gustav Mahler, Richard Strauss, and Gilbert Murray, among others, would join.[8]

Kessler had also convinced Diaghilev and Nijinsky to let Maillol do some preliminary sketches that August. After he and Diaghilev returned to Maillol's studio, they found the sculptor showing the dancer his sketches: Maillol's comment was that Nijinsky did not need to pose, he was simply like a god.[9] But the most important artist at this stage was van de Velde. Having explained what was desired and settled on the site and the dimensions, Kessler awaited van de Velde's design.

· · ·

In his lecture "Science as a Vocation," Max Weber wrote that modern life is characterized by the "disenchantment of the world," the process of intellectualization and bureaucratization that had ineluctably eliminated the place of magic, charismatic religion, and religious awe. Our highest values have retreated in the face of this onslaught to the private sphere. "It is not accidental," he continued, "that our greatest art is intimate and not monumental, nor is it accidental that today only within the smallest and intimate circles, in personal human situations, in *pianissimo,* that something is pulsating that corresponds to the prophetic *pneuma,* which in former times, swept through the great communities like a firebrand, welding them together. If we attempt to force and to 'invent' a monumental style in art, such miserable monstrosities are produced as the many monuments of the last twenty years."[10] The Nietzsche memorial was, in many ways, a transcription of the private spirit that pulsated within Kessler's circle to a monumental, public sphere. Van de Velde's difficult task was to see that what resulted was not one more monstrosity.

An inclination toward monumental projects developed in van de Velde as he felt he had come to master the intimate; it was an essential component of his tremendous pedagogical and prophetic drive. He had just finished his first project in this vein, the memorial in Jena for Ernst Abbes, the physicist, industrialist, and philanthropist. The Nietzsche project, however, seemed to stump him at first. A few years before, he too had visited Greece, and perhaps the manifest elements of *Griechentum,* as outlined by Kessler, constricted his imagination. In any case, he delivered a conservative drawing not far removed in spirit from the neo-classicism of Leo von Klenze and Friedrich Gilly. In response to Kessler's criticism that the sanctuary was not situated high enough to take advantage of the view and that no colonnade connected the temple to the stadium, van de Velde went back to work. His second design showed more independence from Greek models, replacing the flat pediment with an arched front supported by long thin columns against which the statue gained more relief. Nevertheless, it resembled a little too strongly a train station and the proportions of the *Feststraße* were too short. Kessler pressed van de Velde to prepare new plans by early November. The architect worried that the stadium project was too enormous, asking Kessler if he knew of modern games that would fit into the dimensions of a Greek stadium (33 × 50 meters).[11]

The unsinkable Elisabeth Förster-Nietzsche chose precisely this point to intervene again. Almost immediately after the initial proposal of a stadium, she had expressed her opposition, complaining that rumors about a Nietzsche stadium were circulating and that she had been visited by a "Berlin Jew" who wanted to stage a number of spectacles at the proposed venue; "he was even so educated as to propose that the Greek dances be accompanied by genuine old Greek music." Perhaps her otherwise opportunistic anti-Semitism was provoked by the prominent role played by Jews in the financing of the project. In any case, she must decline to associate her brother's memory with such a louche business. Responding with a flurry of letters—three in one day!—Kessler protested that she must have misunderstood his intentions, that the stadium would only be used once or twice a year and only in the most solemn and fitting manner and that, in all events, would it not be more serene to have a temple, stadium, and park that belonged to the Archives than to have a modest little temple surrounded by middle-class villas? With these and other arguments, he managed to quiet her fears.[12]

It proved only a respite. The number of foreigners working on the project had raised the hackles of some local patriots, who found a clever way to attack it. They discovered a letter from Nietzsche wherein he exclaimed that "the aping of *Griechentum* by this rich, leisurely mob from all of Europe is revolting to me. The people do not suspect, from what depths of religious and political ideas the Greek festivals originated. I flee before this hollow noise of sensation hungry actors and spectators into the solitude and quiet." His sister then begged that Kessler desist from his plans at least for ten years, by when she hoped to be dead. Kessler found the letter unbelievable, especially inasmuch as she quoted as an authority someone whose name she could not even remember. In his response, he asked whether this Herr Meutres or Leutres had more authority than Hans Vaihinger, Raoul Richter, Hofmannsthal, Strauss, D'Annunzio, or Hauptmann. If so, then she must find a way to repay the 60,000 marks used to purchase the land.[13]

Förster-Nietzsche again retreated in the face of Kessler's vehement response. Now Kessler turned to van de Velde's proposal, which did not please him. Van de Velde seemed to him incapable of transcending an interior design approach to the monument, working always from the inside out. His design, according to Kessler, resembled an English country house. He began to fear that the Belgian was out of his depth. In his diary, he noted that his friend had little appetite for the plan. Indeed, van de Velde's letters are full of a plaintive anxiety about the project, especially about the stadium. Aside from utter confusion about what sort of modern games could or should be played there, van de Velde also expressed his fear that such a facility would attract a mob to a sacred site intended for an elite. The crowd that we find so ugly today will not be so easily transformed as you believe, he wrote Kessler toward the end of October 1911: "Force, audacity, physical beauty—we know where modern life drags them and I believe I can say it will not be toward the stadium, a stadium that would be located in Weimar."[14] Offering his own brand of encouragement, Kessler wrote to his perplexed friend again, arguing that what was needed was a *"transposition of the personality of Nietzsche into a grand architectonic principle . . . .* It is an *expressive architecture* rather than a *constructive* which we need, a grand formula inspired by the *acute personality* of Nietzsche, such a grand musical motif as *Zarathustra* attempted to express." In other words, he elaborated helpfully, an "architecture absolutely *abstract,* purely rhythmic, like all musical architecture. Perhaps the sentiment of lightness, closer related *naturally* to architecture than that of joy, would give the ideal point of departure: a movement *light, soaring,* so to speak, on its height before the massive stadium, an almost aerial monument, . . . but nervous and strong and even slyly massive under the appearance of lightness, like the physiognomy of Nietzsche himself, with his formidable, Bismarckian bone structure under the exquisitely delicate Greek surfaces of his brow and mouth." [15]

One sympathizes with any architect confronted with the task of transcribing the very physiognomy of a philosopher into a building. In response to these criticisms, van de Velde moved even further from the standard Greek architectural vocabulary, explaining in a letter to a mutual friend interested in the project that Greek architectural forms were too exhausted to form the basis of a new, modern expressive architecture.[16] His third design called for a massive, hulking structure, quite accurately called "Assyrian" in its imposing grandeur. Kessler, however, had called for a very light temple—*presque aérien*—in front of the massive stadium. When he saw the new plans, he despaired: "He has proposed as the temple an enormously high Bismarcktower-like building, which despite an intricate arrangement of parts, has an oppressively heavy and empty effect." He did not hesitate to tell van de Velde his opinion and concluded that his failure to come up with a architectural design that could express "pure joy in life and lightness" was evidence of the lack of a modern tradition of decorative architecture. When he showed the plan to Bodenhausen the next day, Bodenhausen agreed, and Kessler suggested that van de Velde simply design a hall with four walls and a roof.[17]

Van de Velde did not resort to that expedient; instead, he prepared a fourth and final design, which was presented to the Nietzsche committee on June 9, 1912, and approved. Lacking any documentation, it is impossible to know why Kessler gave his support to the new design, after so thoroughly rejecting the one prior. If anything, the building had grown higher, not lighter, although the base had shrunk from a rectangle to a square. Perhaps it was the large arches on each side, the top half of which appears to be a concave surface, while the lower seems to present columns moving in toward the center, drawing the eye in with them. Whatever the reason, the committee was now faced with a staggering cost estimate of 2.03 million marks.[18]

Having come so far, the project seemed to remain in limbo for the remainder of 1912 and 1913. The enormous cost may have been a factor, but it does not seem to have dissuaded the financiers on the committee from voting for approval, so they must have thought it was feasible. Rather, the roadblock was Elisabeth Förster-Nietzsche. Having mismanaged the Archive, she needed money to cover her deficits and resented that the vast amounts she imagined were being assembled by Kessler were not available for her: "He chases a fantasy and it doesn't occur to him that I have suffered cares and anxieties for twenty years, and he could well come halfway to meet my wishes," she lamented. Neither Kessler, who by this time was deeply into the ballet business, nor Bodenhausen had the time or energy to deal with this issue until the very end of 1913. Then, after Kessler met with Förster-Nietzsche and Bodenhausen, it was agreed that only after the Archive was made solvent by raising 150,000–200,000 marks would the Nietzsche monument have priority. Later, she in fact tried to go back on this agreement, and the correspondence between Kessler and Bodenhausen on the subject gradually peters out in April 1914, by which time Kessler was fully preoccupied with *The Legend of Joseph*. Finally, the war ended any hope for a Nietzsche monument, especially one supported by the rest of Europe.[19]

It does not take a trained eye to notice the differences between van de Velde's final design and, say, the gargantuan Volkshalle proposed by Albert Speer for Berlin. Van de Velde's design eschews the long line of colonnades, the enormous cupolas, and other neoclassical clichés found in fascist, Nazi, and Soviet architecture. Nor is it accurate to imply that at the core of Kessler's conception lurked "an intimate relation between monumental architecture and ideological manipulation on a mass scale."[20] Something like the theatrical coordination and manipulation of masses of youths and of athletes, in huge arenas under spotlights and banners, all toward the purpose of exalting a leader, cowing dissenters, and exemplifying the unity of the nation, such as took place in the totalitarian regimes of the 1930s—what Walther Benjamin called "the aestheticization of politics"—all of this was beyond Kessler's ken in 1911. His emphasis on "rediscovering" the body, resurrecting a certain kind of religious sentiment and ceremony in public life, and emphasizing rhythm, dance, and feeling did not necessarily imply the "destruction of reason." Had it been pointed out to him, he probably would not have recognized any direct lineage from his plans for the Nietzsche monument to, say, the Nazi Party rallies in Nuremberg. After all, he passionately fought the politicization of the Nietzsche Archive in the 1920s and then, of course, chose exile when the Nazis came to power.

And yet . . . there is something equivocal about the plans for the Nietzsche monument. It is tempting to mock the effort to "monumentalize" the sharpest critic of nineteenth-century Germany's urge toward monumentalism. The blank inability of van de Velde to find a spatial analogue for Kessler's rhetoric suggests a deeper paradox: the urge for monumentality arose precisely in the nineteenth century against the background of a modern world seen ever more ephemeral, changing, and unstable. Monuments promised a return to order, to community, to origin. But, as Weber hinted, too often they failed to deliver on these promises, leaving only hollow monstrosities, huge not only in their dimensions but also in their irrelevance to the life that flowed around them.[21] Against this background, the whole endeavor of Kessler and van de Velde appears in retrospect as an immense effort of the will to overcome reality, a product of the "hothouse," a somewhat histrionic attempt to defy Weber's iron law. In this, it was a very Wilhelmian gesture.

CHAPTER 15

The Legend of Joseph

The tension between Austria and Serbia seems from here very disturbing. Will it really come this time to the world war? And what would then happen to *Joseph*? If only it doesn't shoot Nijinsky away from us!

Kessler to Hofmannsthal, *Briefwechsel*

"Only in dance do I know how to say the highest things," wrote Nietzsche. If the nineteenth century witnessed the great age of opera, the beginning of the twentieth century saw the rise of dance. From an activity once marginalized to ballrooms, dance halls, and popular festivals, it became the performing art perhaps most adapted to the modern age. In the process, it became, of course, purified of its popular roots, aestheticized, more ambitious. Interestingly, the craze for modern dance, which began approximately in the 1890s and culminated in the balletomania incited by Diaghilev's Ballets Russes in 1909, received its freshest impulse from two countries on the margins of European civilization, Russia and the United States. Starting from different points—the Russians from a sophisticated dance tradition, the Americans from nothing—both arrived at a form of modern dance, both sensual and symbolic, that was embraced with enthusiasm in Europe; nowhere more so than in Germany, where it seemed to be the embodiment of "life-philosophy." [1]

There was no more ardent fan in Germany, perhaps in Europe, than Harry Kessler. As early as 1891, after seeing a performance of a ballet called, significantly enough, *Joseph in Egypt,* he had prophesied: "The ballet, if the ballerinas got rid of their ugly costumes and let their hips be trained to a higher form of art, could display perhaps the most perfect example of the human shape in grace and beauty, of glowing and harmonious splendor of colors, and of beautiful scenery: one must however find a very great painter and a very great musician united in one."[2] When the Japanese actress-dancer Sada Yacco, who was a great influence on Ruth St. Denis, performed at the World's Fair in Paris in 1900, he went to see her five times, impressed by her lack of European sentimentality. A year later, he took van de Velde to see her and the American dancer Loîe Fuller.

About Isadora Duncan he had mixed feelings: when he and van de Velde first saw her dance, they were not impressed: "She is affected, with a sentimental expression of the eyes, has only one movement which she repeats ad nauseum, dances without rhythm and fire, and has in common with Greek art only what Philistines consider 'antique,' that is, barren emptiness and sugary beauty. Her chief attractions are that she dances naked and remains conventional, exactly the same charms as in academic art." Many years later, when he heard of her tragic death, he recalled how, having learned of his disapproval from Craig, she had invited him out to Neuilly in Paris to see her dance. When he expressed his sincere admiration, she replied in her Californian French: "*Oui, quand vous m'avez vue avant j'étais vertueuse, je ne savais pas danser: mais maintenant. . . !*" ("Yes, when you saw me before, I was virtuous, I did not know how to dance, but now. . . !") Even before then, he had visited her school for young girls in Berlin, along with Hofmannsthal and Reinhardt, and found that "a great freshness and grace reigns in everything . . . lightness and friendliness everywhere." Kessler believed strongly in dance and rhythm education for children; it was one way of "beautifying" the race, and he recommended to his sister that she enroll his nephew in Jacques Dalcroze's famous school.[3]

"At the moment," wrote Kessler to Hofmannsthal from Berlin in the fall of 1906, "there is one (great artist) here I would like to show you, a certain dancer St. Denis from Paris, who has realized what Duncan wants to do. It is as if she has climbed down from a Greek vase, in movement, beauty, rhythm exceptional." The sudden appearance of Ruth St. Denis at the beginning of her three-year European tour convinced Kessler that at last he had seen an artist who exploited the great potential of dance. Three days later, he again wrote to Hofmannsthal, insisting that he see her. His description stressed the two elements of his aesthetic, sensuality and symbolism: "An animal beauty and a mysticism without any intervening scale of spiritual or sentimental tones are present, the sexless Godhead and the purely sexual female, the contrast unleashing the effect of both to their greatest potency. She is an American and it is very curious and subtle how she is able to combine the sexlessness of her race with the practically sub-human, almost animal sexual feeling of the oriental woman. But you must see all of that; it will prove fruitful in you." St. Denis appeared to Kessler to be the same incarnation and confirmation of the modern American woman he had first noticed during his trip to the United States and whose type he thought so valuable as a cultural model. American too was the delightful way she sprinkled the most surprising insights with naiveté and girlish high spirits: "Every moment with her is a pure pleasure because she grasps all things always from out of her core."[4]

In her charming memoir, Ruth St. Denis described her reception by the Germans. Uncertain of her welcome in the wake of their enthusiasm for Isadora Duncan, she gave her first performance on October 6, 1906. "My great success in Paris had preceded me, and everywhere was an eager expectancy to discover what this new dancer had to offer. I immediately felt this atmosphere, and something in me began to open up and respond to this new country which was to give so much to me in joy and satisfaction." The conductor, it is true, refused, until ordered by the director of the Komische Oper, to alter the tempo of the music to suit her dancing, and the police had to look at her "tummy" to be certain it did not offend public morality (it did not). In general, however, she was treated as a serious artist, and, looking back, she wrote, "I believe I was never so happy as in these early days in Germany. Everything was wonderful. I had to work hard, but when I was free, the days were spent with delightful people, and I was taken to see all the wonders of modern artistic Berlin."[5]

Leading her to most of these wonders was Kessler. "I found Count Kessler a delightful companion. I knew him by reputation as a charming patron of the arts, a delightful social ambassador who spoke English like an Oxford man and had a genius for bringing people together for their mutual benefit." On November 18, 1906, Kessler whisked her off to a luncheon at the exclusive Automobile Club after a matinée performance at the Theater des Westens. There she met Munch, Hauptmann, and Hofmann. Hauptmann, quite taken by St. Denis, contemplated writing a pantomine for her, a fairy tale about the wanderer, the woodcutter, the tailor, the goldsmith, and the Brahman. It was all a very heady experience for the young American, who again was pleased to find herself regarded not as a mere entertainer, but as "an artist in the deepest sense of the word and the subject of earnest and critical analysis. To the German mind of that period the appearance of a new art form was a vital and significant thing, something that might have far-reaching effects upon their culture."[6]

Kessler certainly thought so. Among the people to whom he promised to introduce her was Hofmannsthal, who, he assured her, could write a *Salomé* in which dance would play a far more central role than it did in Wilde's play of the same name. He then wrote an excited letter to Hofmannsthal about the project: "To me it seems like a task made expressly for you. The scene before the dance can and even *must* be *poetically* enormously *strong,* breathtaking in the beauty of its language and mood, so that the dance emerges like a poisonous flower from it, out of this grandiose biblical language and scenery, and then overshadows everything. The stronger, greater, more primeval and Hebraic, this first scene, the higher it will hoist the dance. It is a very original division of drama into both of its elements: in the first part the element of the word prevails, in the second the element of movement and gesture."[7] He also asked Hofmannsthal to unmask as a fraud an imitator of St. Denis who was scheduled to appear in Vienna.

Hofmannsthal was intrigued enough to come to Berlin and see this phenomenon in person. When she did not show up in time at his hotel room to discuss the new Salomé, he was annoyed, exclaiming that he had had enough to do with unreliable people (thinking no doubt of Kessler's other discovery, Gordon Craig). His first question when she arrived was, " 'Now tell me one thing first: are you reliable?' The poor girl opened wide her eyes and then laughed, 'Why heavens yes!' And then they explained to each other at first, she in her amusing Yankee English and he in his very smooth but unmistakably Viennese English, what they understood by reliability." Despite this initial *contretemps,* the dancer and the poet became friends. In St. Denis's view at least there was an element of sexual attraction in their relationship.[8]

Hofmannsthal for his part wrote a glowing review of her performance in Vienna in *Die Zeit.* Only in a time as refined and complex as the present, he argued, could such dancing be possible. That Europeans could marvel at the pure beauty of the Indian dances by an American, without first traversing any detour of ethnographic interest or sentimental affectation, Hofmannsthal took for a sign of a modernity that was enveloping the world. "This girl and her temple dances are thoroughly a child of this moment in which the sons of Brahmans in the laboratories of Cambridge and Harvard wrest from matter the confirmation of ancient truths, in which, through the presses of Benares and Calcutta, Indians and Japanese enrich our libraries with masterful, wonderfully concentrated books in English. . . ." Borrowing from Kessler's letter, he went on to compare her with Isadora Duncan. Duncan was rather like a very charming professor of archaeology, passionately devoted to the beautiful. St. Denis, however, was "the Lydian dancer, climbed down from the relief."[9]

What, in the end, resulted from all of this enthusiasm? Hofmannsthal never finished his *Salomé*, Hauptmann never wrote his pantomime, and St. Denis returned, more or less permanently, to the United States in 1909. The reasons for this are not completely clear. Hofmannsthal apparently did begin a libretto for a version of *Salomé*, but had difficulty finding a composer. There is some suggestion that both Hofmannsthal and Kessler disapproved of St. Denis's (platonic) liaison with Hugo's brother-in-law, a dilettante painter. In her memoirs, she asserts that at one point the grand duke of Weimar offered to build her a theater if she would agree to stay in Germany, but from what is known of him, this seems most unlikely, and no trace of this project is mentioned in either Kessler's diaries or his correspondence. Her reception in Germany had given her artistic confidence, but she felt homesick for the United States and returned to become the founder, along with Ted Shawn, of American modern dance.[10] Although she dropped out of their sight, St. Denis had nevertheless sown a seed in the imaginations of both Kessler and Hofmannsthal that would later bear fruit.

The astonishing début of Diaghilev's Ballets Russes in Paris in the spring of 1909 was the greatest symbol of the ascension of dance to the throne previously held by opera. Uncharacteristically, Kessler missed the opening night, but not long after, he was writing to Hofmannsthal about the remarkable young male dancer, "truly like a butterfly, yet still with the greatest masculinity and youthful beauty: the ballerinas, who are just as beautiful, in comparison disappeared, the public was raving mad. If you ever write a ballet (with Strauss), we must have this young Nijinsky." He was in the midst of the exciting business of reading and making suggestions on the libretto for *Der Rosenkavalier* and envisioned a string of possible collaborations with Hofmannsthal. After the premiere of a new ballet, *Cléopatre* featuring Ida Rubenstein, Kessler returned to the charge: "I have not once dreamed of a *mimetic art* so beautiful, so refined, so 'beyond the theater.' Imagine a ballet corps that consisted of pure Ruth St. Denis. . . . It sounds almost strange but since my first performance of Tristan I have never had such a strong impression in the theater. . . . These women (Pavlova, Karasavina, Rubenstein) and these men, or rather boys, Nijinsky and a few others seem truly out of another, higher, beautiful world, like living young gods and goddesses." Kessler's insistence that Hofmannsthal abandon everything and come to Paris increased with each performance he saw. He vehemently assured the Austrian that it would be worth the trouble; Kessler would even—if in the worst case it came to that—give up his own tickets to the last performance. Hofmannsthal, of course, was in the midst of two important projects and so missed the first season. Kessler took Maillol instead.[11]

For someone like Kessler it was very easy to make the acquaintance of Diaghilev and the members of his entourage. One of the Russian's greatest patrons in Paris was Misia Edwards, the former wife of Thadée Natanson. In the spring and summer of 1911, Kessler came to be a regular of her circle of friends, which included the young Jean Cocteau (whom Kessler hoped would illustrate some Cranach Presse books for him), Reynaldo Hahn, José Maria Sert (soon to be Misia's third husband), and the Russians, Diaghilev, Nijinsky, Léon Bakst. At their midnight dinners at the Restaurant Larue, Marcel Proust would sometimes show up, as would Lucien Daudet, the right-wing critic of the *Action Française* who later would write savage things about Kessler during the war.[12]

It was a glittering crowd of socialites, writers, celebrities, déclassé aristocrats, and artists. The spirit in these gatherings, Kessler remarked, was that of Molière's *Precieuses Ridicules*. To his sister he wrote, "I have got into this set of people and shall continue in it for a time, till I get quite sick of it. They are amusing but silly *pantins* (puppets), and not really worth anything." Nevertheless, he found it increasingly difficult to resist the seductions of social life. Although he wrote to his sister about the progress he was making on his planned essay on Dehmel, he also complained of being sucked into society both in Berlin and in Paris: "I have been 'on the go' every day from eleven in the morning to two or three o'clock at night. It is quite impossible for me to give you any connected account of all these days; in fact I hardly remember what I have done, nor where I have been, myself, the next morning."[13]

An essay on Dehmel, whose standing as a writer had been slipping slowly in Kessler's mind since the turn of the century and whose attempt to turn to the theater he considered a failure, was pale stuff compared to the prospect of creating a scenario for the Ballets Russes. Rainer Maria Rilke, whom Kessler had introduced to Diaghilev, first suggested that they write a ballet together, something about a unicorn that could only be captured by a boy disguised as a maiden. Kessler having agreed "in principle," Rilke then asked him if he would support his application for a stipend from the Schiller Institute. A week later, Rilke seemed to have given up the idea and talked to Kessler instead about how he needed money to go to Bohemia and Germany in the fall and how he was reluctant to earn it through translations. "My attention today was fixed," wrote the disappointed Kessler, "almost the whole time on Rilke's enormously fat lips (namely the lower lip) and on the odor of fruits."[14]

When Nijinsky posed for Maillol that summer, Kessler promised Diaghilev a ballet. There was nothing left to do then but to get in touch with Hofmannsthal for whom Kessler had already done a favor by telling the Russian stage designer Léon Bakst of Hofmannsthal's interest in working with him on a new opera (*Die Frau ohne Schatten*). Kessler let Hofmannsthal know that Diaghilev would be interested in any ballets he might create. In return perhaps for the favor with Bakst, Hofmannsthal replied that he would love to write one; would Kessler, quite officially, like to work with him? Although inwardly delighted, Kessler coyly suggested that there was someone else with whom he was thinking of collaborating as well. The two corresponded about possible settings and atmospheres for the rest of the year. Discovering that Diaghilev was tired of themes from antiquity, Kessler suggested a Javanese ballet, only to discover that the impresario was already preparing a ballet on an Indian subject. Kessler informed Hofmannsthal that Diaghilev had very specific requirements and that they should wait to talk over the matter in person. "I have established very close relations with Diaghilev and Nijinsky," he assured him, "so that we can build upon them with almost as much security as you can with Reinhardt."[15]

Before they could meet, however, another incident disturbed their relationship. Hofmannsthal finally met Diaghilev and Nijinsky when the Ballets Russes came to Vienna in 1912. In Paris, Kessler received a short letter from Hofmannsthal, who, because he thought it would please Kessler, said that "since the evening of this Saturday I have actually only existed with no one else but Diaghilev and Nijinsky, evenings in the theater, breakfasting with them, sitting and speaking from breakfast until the theater again—nights either sleeping poorly or entranced—writing ballets for them, of which two, a tragic, antique and a macabre in the costume of Carpaccio now (have been) written, fixed, enriched, and modified. . . . The sketch goes today to Strauss, who is supposed to compose it. . . . That does not naturally prevent us at all, Harry, from doing a third." Kessler was shocked. "[I] considered carefully this mixture of bad conscience, cynicism, and sugar—moreover a masterpiece!—without finding immediately a reply," Kessler wrote bitterly, considering himself, with some justification, as having been used by Hofmannsthal in the crudest way. When Hofmannsthal arrived in Paris at the end of May, he noted Kessler's deliberate snubbing, and, guessing the reason, he wrote to say that his having already finished two ballets was "only a *façon de parler.*"[16] The two then patched up their differences, not without lingering suspicion and resentment, and went to work.

Years later, Kessler wrote a quasi-fictional account of the origin of *The Legend of Joseph.* The scene is a supper between midnight and three o'clock at the Restaurant Larue in the Rue Royale. Diaghilev, with the gesture of a pasha, asks for a biblical ballet but in the costumes, as painted by Paolo Veronese, of sixteenth-century Venice:

He turned to Jean Cocteau, who sat beside me, and then also to Hofmannsthal and me, if we did not wish to think of something for him and perhaps have Richard Strauss compose it? Immediately a complete series of biblical scenes emerged; Cocteau proposed David dancing before the Ark, another, Deborah, a third Judith and Holofernes. Nijinsky, Reynaldo Hahn, I believe also Proust, who, as an exception was present, wrapped in a thick scarf, participated in the conversation which now raced through the Bible like a raging fire. Bowls with monstrous strawberries stood on the table, glasses of champagne and liquors which glittered in all colors; the Aga Khan, the richest Muslim prince of India, sat, arriving from a masked ball, at the corner in an oriental costume completely covered with fabulous genuine pearls, and even larger rubies and emeralds. . . . A belated pair danced the tango. Out of this atmosphere the first scene of *Joseph* was born.[17]

On the way home, Kessler continued, he suddenly thought of Potiphar and his wife, their over-refined and decadent society confronted by the shepherd boy Joseph. Sure that this was the proper theme, he woke up at five o'clock and at eight took the scenario, finished except for the conclusion, to Hofmannsthal.

Aside from the improbability of Kessler waking up at five o'clock in the morning, this account compresses together a number of events spread out over several days. There was a supper at Larue after the premiere of *L'Après-midi d'une Faune* on May 29, 1912, and many of the luminaries Kessler mentions were present. But it was only on June 3 that Kessler and Hofmannsthal began to work on the ballet. Diaghilev had explained that he wanted a ballet for some costumes Bakst had designed in the manner of Paolo Veronese for a piece that was not worthy of such a beautiful wardrobe. Enchanted with the idea, Kessler discussed it the next day with Hofmannsthal. After a visit to the Louvre, where they admired Veronese's painting *Wedding at Cana*, they again came up with a theme from antiquity, a bacchanal in the Renaissance style. Stravinsky refused, however, to compose it, and Diaghilev rejected it as predictable: "One must always *surprise* the public," the impresario told them, "in that one presents it an unexpected side of an age, for example, the ascetic or mystical in the Renaissance." On the evening of June 5, 1912, he suggested a biblical theme, an idea that pleased Kessler immensely. The idea of a ballet based on the episode between Potiphar's wife and Joseph occurred to Kessler the next morning, and, having written out a draft, he arrived at Hofmannsthal's hotel room at eleven. Together, they strolled through the Tuileries and discussed it. When they had decided that the conclusion would have Joseph rescued by an angel, and Potiphar's wife committing suicide, they went straightaway to the Crillon, where Diaghilev was staying, and told it to him. He found it exceptional and immediately accepted it.[18]

If the details of Kessler's reconstruction of the origins of the ballet are partly wrong, the essence is correct: his description of the world of Potiphar's wife was undoubtedly based on his experience of the world of the *precieuese ridicules* as found past midnight in Larue. The content of the ballet is the contrast of two polar opposite worlds: "The one world—that of Potiphar—has reached its zenith, and has gathered up in itself all wealth, all power, all beauty and every art of life. But these elements, in consequence of their opulent development, have rounded each other off so fully, have become so satiated, that in such a world there remains hardly any possibility of further charm or stimulus: it is lavish, rank, sultry, impregnated with exotic perfumes alive with strange creatures, like a tropical garden, evenly balanced in itself, classical, hard, heavy—a world in which even the air seems charged with gold dust. What should strike the spectator in it is its wealth of gold and the greatness and grace of its gestures."[19]

Various forms of entertainment, dancers and boxers, are offered the bored royal couple. But it is only when the young shepherd boy Joseph is brought in, and performs his three dances that Potiphar's wife takes notice. Joseph represents, of course, a cleaner, purer world, "a world where everything is strong and light, blossoming and fresh, full of sur-prise and charm, where joyousness born of exuberant strength envelops all things in a shadowless light, but a world which in its aloofness has the effect of mystery and solemnity, almost of ghostliness, as a distant Paradise on mountain tops." [20] From the cautious, quite practical figure of the Bible, Joseph has become an *Übermensch*—or rather, an *Über-kind,* for the shepherd, Kessler insisted, has two faces, that of a child and that of the future. The future, vague but beckoning, lurks beneath the face and gestures of the boy. This double-sided aspect becomes star-tlingly evident to Potiphar's wife when he drops his cloak before her. Untouchable, unapproachable, really quite sexless, the "god of spring" stands before the court, an unanswerable challenge and provocation to them—archaic Greece before late Renaissance Venice. The mystery of his world, his relation to his God, first provokes Potiphar's wife to visit his room. There she undergoes a gamut of feelings, ranging from a desire to possess his secret to a fear that it will elude her to a moment of prayer in which she seems to wish for his forgiveness. Finally, there comes a moment, as she sees him sleeping, when her motherly feelings come to the fore and she thinks that she can absorb the future lying within him by a maternal embrace. Then, passion overwhelms her and she kisses him. He, of course, spurns the sudden physical contact, she becomes angry and ashamed, and she has her husband order prepara-tions be made for his torture and execution. In the last scene, however, she witnesses his apotheosis as his world becomes ever more radiant, while hers darkens, and when he is lifted into the clouds, she remains behind: "Then nothing is left for her but death." [21]

When he was trying to persuade Strauss to compose this ballet, Kessler took great pains to separate it from the theme of Salomé or Ju-dith and Holofernes. He convinced Strauss, but from a distance of more than seventy-five years, the work nonetheless bears the unmistakable, al-most unbearable, mark of the fin de siècle obsession with the femme fa-tale. The misogyny is too obvious to belabor. The character of Joseph resembles the male counterpart to the femme fatale Narcissus. However clichéd this appears now, the appeal of the subject matter to Kessler was deep-rooted. There had certainly been many cases when he had felt himself in the role of Joseph, starting with the episode on his first transatlantic crossing in 1892, when he was accosted by an older woman who reminded him of Potiphar's wife. Also, the curious momentary transformation of Potiphar's wife into an alarming mother figure, seek-ing to suck out, as it were, the boy's innocence, his secret, hints strongly at Kessler's ambivalence toward his own mother. But Kessler was also in part Potiphar's wife. Not simply because of his attraction to youth, whose will is stronger than their muscles, and to *Griechentum* (this Joseph is more Greek than Jewish), but also because he too felt himself a part of a culture where the air itself "seemed laden with gold." And a fatigue, perhaps not all that unlike the one that overcomes Potiphar's wife, gradually overcame Kessler too in these last years before the war.[22]

·   ·   ·

Reading his correspondence one can trace the erosion of Kessler's nerves, good humor, and strength due to the exasperating business of trying to realize his dream on the stage. During these two years, he confronted crisis after crisis, seeking to soothe ruffled feathers and to mediate raging arguments, while always pushing for his vision. He sent out a whirlwind of telegrams and letters, cajoling, pleading, encouraging, warning and was followed by a whirlwind of the same, as he dashed between Paris, London, and Berlin at an ever increasing tempo. A letter to his sister from Munich gives a glimpse of the way he ricocheted across Europe: "I shall leave here on Friday evening for Berlin, stay in Berlin Saturday and Sunday, go to Weimar on Monday, leave Weimar on Tuesday, arrive in Paris on Wednesday evening, stay in Paris Thursday . . . and leave for St. Honorine on Friday."[23] He could not come any sooner, he protested, because it would mean giving up *Joseph,* the Nietzsche monument, and the work on his papermaking for the Cranach Presse. All of this increasingly feverish activity took a toll.

First, he had to convince Strauss to accept the composition. A very long letter to Hofmannsthal outlined the arguments that should be used to persuade the composer, placing great stress on the austerity (*Herbheit*) of *Joseph* compared to the sultriness (*Schwüle*) of *Salomé.* Strauss was between operas and therefore accepted. "*Joseph* is exceptional: I have swallowed!" the composer wrote Hofmannsthal. "Have begun to sketch it already. The comments of Count Kessler do not quite convince me, it's true, but be that as it may, I will soon be over the stumbling block." By September, however, Strauss was encountering difficulties, and he informed Hofmannsthal: "*Joseph* is not going as quickly as I thought. The chaste Joseph doesn't sit well with me, and what bores me I have difficulty finding the music for. Such a Joseph who looks for God—I shall have to force myself damned hard. Ah well, perhaps in some atavistic corner of my gut lies a pious melody for the good

Joseph." When he heard of Strauss's comment, Kessler professed not to be alarmed; he thought it was even a hopeful sign because, he admitted, the character was complicated. To make his conception of Joseph clearer, he sent a long letter to Strauss. To his sister, he wrote, "Joseph must be *explained* in great part by the *music:* this is why I am giving myself the trouble of explaining him so copiously to *Strauss.*" When the composer played what he had written for Kessler in Berlin in December, however, Kessler was disappointed: he found the motif for Joseph's last dance exquisite, but the other pieces were "impossible, pretty little eighteenth-century dances."[24]

Trying to squeeze what he wanted out of Strauss was bad enough, but negotiating with Diaghilev and the prima donnas of the Ballets Russes proved even more aggravating. The business aspect proved to be relatively straightforward.[25] But Diaghilev, whose enterprise depended on a complicated web of patrons, was in danger of embroiling himself in a quarrel with his chief English patron, Lady Ripon. Only through Kessler's patient mediation was a fragile truce achieved. Worse was to come. Diaghilev had allowed Nijinsky, his most famous star and his lover, to choreograph the last several ballets, replacing Michel Fokine. Nijinsky's choreography was much more daring and modern than that of Fokine. After attending the notorious premiere of Igor Stravinsky's *The Rite of Spring* in Paris, which caused fistfights in the audience, Kessler wrote to Hofmannsthal: "What N. has accomplished here, sticks out from the choreography of Fokine, like a Gauguin from a Bouguereau. I have the feeling that we have before us in Nijinsky's choreographic fantasy something as surprisingly new, strong, and revolutionary as Poe for the literary, and Beardsley for the graphic fantasy, compared to what was before them."[26] As Nijinsky planned to choreograph *Joseph* next, Kessler confidently predicted that the production would be epoch-making. Clearly, Kessler had underestimated the role of Stravinsky's music and rather overestimated the revolutionary potential of *Joseph.*

Diaghilev, however, had lost his nerve temporarily in the face of the reaction to *The Rite of Spring* and wondered whether Nijinsky was not alienating his audience. Besides, he was tiring of his protégé. In the fall of 1913, just as Kessler was pleased with Strauss's reworking of the Joseph motif and thinking that all was going well, Diaghilev, after learning of Nijinsky's marriage to Romola de Pulszky, decided not to renew the dancer's contract. For Kessler, who had worked closely with Nijinsky on the choreography, the news was like a thunderbolt. He dispatched a flurry of letters, went to plead with Diaghilev in person, and, when that did not work, tried to get intermediaries such as Lady Ripon and Strauss to arrange a reconciliation between Diaghilev and Nijinsky. He soon, however, discovered the depth of the breach between impresario and dancer; "Everything goes much *deeper* than I thought. Diaghilev is mortified in his vanity, in his *sentiment,* in his pocket, in *everything.*"[27]

Kessler toyed with the idea of retracting the year-long monopoly on the performance of *Joseph* that he had granted the Ballets Russes; he considered having the ballet performed by Nijinsky, with Reinhardt as producer, in Germany. His vision of the central character was so thoroughly based on Nijinsky that he could not believe an adequate substitute could be found. "Joseph," he wrote Hofmannsthal, "is the being who through his perfection, through his godliness, disturbs others; Mephisto and God in one person. He incorporates the poisonous element of godliness, of perfect beauty of any kind (regardless physical or moral perfection). Nijinsky provided—could provide—exactly this terrible beauty; and no other mime, however pretty or clever, who is lacking the visible spark of genius, which entails the destructive element."[28] When he first saw Leonide Mjassin, the dancer who was to replace Nijinsky, Kessler was disgusted: "He is less 'pretty' than I feared, but has not the slightest charm or *rayonnment* . . . . He is as *terne* as possibly can be. . . . I feel indifferent about the whole thing; I have spent all the energy I had to put into it, and this uninspiring, heavy, not even disagreeable boy, has put out the rest of my interest."[29] This proved an exaggeration: only nine days later, he suddenly found that Mjassin "is *good, very good* as Joseph, intensely Russian. While Nijinsky is a Greek god, he is a strange, little wild animal from the Russian steppes."[30] He wrote in the same vein to Hofmannsthal, but this change of opinion did not prevent him from still trying to obtain Nijinsky for at least part of the performances. Up until the last minute, Kessler was scheming for the two dancers to alternate in the role. To his sister, he sighed, "What a droll, half unreal world, this world of the theatre is! *Petites causes, grandes emotions!*"[31]

Why did Kessler expend this truly stupendous amount of energy on *Joseph*? He outlined his reasons at the beginning of the project in response to a letter from Hofmannsthal urging calm. "You are certainly right *in abstracto;* we should all (we, I mean, who collaborate on the dance in Paris) be less excited, less nervous, more patient, more sedate, better balanced within, in a word, more *altdeutsch,* but over the long run one struggles against a certain atmosphere and rhythm of movement only with difficulty . . . . I take your friendly sermon *ad notam,* feel guilty, but cannot promise that I will improve. Moreover I plead in this special case for extenuating circumstances. That you, as an old stagehand with so many victories, do not have any lamplight fever, is truly nothing to brag about; that my first entry on the stage gives me pleasure, even *an unseemly* amount of pleasure, is in contrast forgivable . . . for me the first embodiment of my own creations in flesh and blood." As he gradually disappeared into the thicket of the ballet business, Kessler watched his innocent pleasure dwindle, until he could exclaim to his sister that "I have seen some ugly sides of human nature lately, I assure you, but what good comes of talking of it!"[32] What kept him going was the dream of finally seeing a work of his own upon the stage, and, to be sure, in a production by the Ballets Russes.

He was probably not aware of how his obsession was wearing upon the nerves of some of his friends. Hofmannsthal, who was happy enough to earn thousands of francs for what, he boasted to his father, had only cost him thirty-five minutes of work, kept his distance throughout the whole period of preparation, only doing what was necessary. A few days after the scenario had been drafted, he wrote to a friend, "With Kessler all is good. I see all at once that I feel terribly sorry for him. . . . The whole person, so full of gifts—and nevertheless without the decisive element—how horribly sad." By the time of the premiere, however, pity had turned to scorn: "Over Kessler I would rather say nothing: if one wished to be harsh, one would have to say, he is a fool and a poor fool, at times an insufferable fool. He has brought himself so low with his silly bumbling that he appears to be in a pitiful state. I hold my line against him and will hopefully maintain it until the end. It was completely stupid of me, what I did (draw him in out of unpsychological good will) but now it is a *tour de force* that I wish to endure decently and with generosity." Generosity, as Kessler had quite rightly noticed before, was not one of Hofmannsthal's qualities. After all, it was Kessler who had drawn Hofmannsthal into the ballet business and not the other way around. Furthermore, Kessler had tried to the best of his ability to both maintain the fiction of Hofmannsthal's coauthorship and, at the same time, protect him from the laborious, endless negotiations. As Kessler gently reminded him, "I . . . have had to fight for everything alone against these nervous, touchy people like Fokine, Nijinsky, Bakst, Sert, Mjassin."[33]

In any case, *The Legend of Joseph* opened before a very distinguished audience in the Paris Grand Opera on May 14, 1914, with Strauss conducting and Mjassin in the title role. Although the enthusiasm was generous, and Strauss was called to the podium ten times, the reception was not all Kessler had hoped for; he wrote to his sister that the performance in London at the Theatre Royal, Drury Lane, would be much better. The London audience for the Ballets Russes was, if anything, even more high-toned than that of Paris. The nobility, from the king down, made it a habit to attend, as did practically the entire political establishment, starting with the then prime minister, Herbert Henry Asquith. Kessler made his entrance into this society at the beginning of 1913, visiting Mrs. Asquith, "a little, dark, brisk, witty woman with hard lines in a once rather pretty face, no sentiment, but all 'push,'" and dining with Lady Randolph Churchill, mother of Winston, who he compared to "an elderly, but still curiously attractive, wicked Queen in a drawing of Aubrey Beardsley's." A few days later, he was presented to the king, who reminded him of "a capable, rather well-bred country solicitor," and the queen, whose conversation he compared to a watch that kept running down.[34]

It was important for Kessler to find his way into the upper strata of English society because the support, or at least the tolerance, of the leading society women was necessary for the success of *Joseph*. This was affirmed when a "*grand bataille des dames*" broke out just before the premiere. Lady Cunard, a born American, suddenly took umbrage at Strauss playing a sonata at a rival's home and swore revenge upon him, and the hapless *Joseph*. She tried to scuttle the production; when she saw it was to no avail, she changed tactics and threw herself upon Kessler, begging his forgiveness and promising to write Strauss a note of apology.

The Legend of Joseph was a popular, but not a critical success in London. The house was full for all the performances and the applause, according to Kessler, "enthusiastic and unending." The *Times* praised the scenario, writing that the contrast of two worlds "gave to the collaborators, Herr Hugo von Hofmannsthal and Count Hessler [*sic*], an absolutely free hand to make of the scenario what they would; by its means they have given opportunity to the designers of scenery, costume, and dance to provide something strikingly new just at the moment when historical epochs and topographical areas seemed near to exhaustion as a basis for the ballet's art, and they have provided the sort of stimuli which Herr Strauss needs for his art of the prodigious orchestra." Unfortunately, Strauss's music, the review went on, did not live up to the task: "The cumbersome interweaving of themes becomes in result terribly laborious and prosaic and leaves us oppressed by the murky

atmosphere of one world rather than impressed by the contrast between two." 35

The great critic Ernest Newman, in his review in *The Nation,* agreed
generally with this criticism, only excoriating Strauss as "one of the
dullest and at the same time one of the most pretentious composers
in Germany." The music for *Joseph* confirmed Newman's opinion that
Strauss had lost his avant-garde freshness and was now simply retread-
ing old themes. On the whole, Newman admired the staging and dancing, but he had very harsh words for the authors, accusing them of trying to overlay "with a typically Teutonic childishness, . . . the simple
story of Joseph and Potiphar's wife with a bastard sort of symbolism;
but on the stage the symbolism does not carry, even to those who have
taken the trouble to wade through Count Kessler's super-solemn preface to the score." The only interesting dramatic invention, Newman
claimed, was the dance of the women venting their rage upon Joseph.
Newman's article was written expressly to draw out his principle antag-
onist, George Bernard Shaw, who dutifully responded with a letter defending Strauss and *The Legend of Joseph.* In the wonderful exchange of
letters that followed, it cannot be denied that Newman bested Shaw, although, as Newman quite rightly put it, their difference of opinion
would only be settled by posterity's judgment of the composition. 36

That posterity has, on the whole, not been kind. Musically, critics
have agreed with the comments of Romain Rolland, who attended the
premiere in Paris: "The music seemed to me of a mediocre quality,
docile and rather flat, if always amusing." The author of the standard
work on Strauss goes so far as to call it "the first wholly unsuccessful
work Strauss wrote as a direct result of the mental lethargy which was
for many years to reduce his stature." Even as a dance spectacle, *The Legend of Joseph* has not fared well overall. The most recent historian of
the Ballets Russes writes of the works commissioned for 1914, "none
revealed so spectacularly the aesthetic malaise of the Ballets Russes
as Strauss's *Legend of Joseph.*" After the war, productions of the ballet
were given in Berlin and Munich in 1921; in Leipzig, Switzerland, and
Czechoslovakia in 1922; in Austria in 1924; in Italy in 1928; in Denmark
in 1931 (choreographed by George Balanchine); in Poland in 1937; and
in Argentina in 1938. On the whole, however, the ballet remained more
a curiosity or, as the Germans say, "hardly a cultural duty." 37

At least this was the received opinion until choreographer John Neumeier revived the ballet in Vienna in 1977 and then took it with him to
the Hamburg Ballet, where it became an important part of his reper-

toire. In 1983, *The Legend of Joseph* made its debut in New York with the Hamburg Ballet. Neumeier, who had hesitated to undertake the project, found his inspiration in the foreword by Kessler that had been so scorned as ponderously Teutonic; for Neumeier it was "much more layered, modern, philosophic and psychological" than the contributions of either Strauss or Hofmannsthal. In this new conception of the ballet, Joseph is not a static character but one that gradually in the course of the work understands his mission, "learns to fly." Interestingly enough, Neumeier eliminated Hofmannsthal's major contribution, allowing Potiphar's wife, performed by the magnificent Judith Jamison, to live at the end so she could watch as the angel bears off Joseph, bewildered at her inability to follow him.[38]

As a historical event, the premieres of *The Legend of Joseph* in Paris and London in 1914 marked the symbolic end of the fin de siècle. For the first time since 1870, a German work was premiered at the Paris Grand Opera. Written by a German and an Austrian, directed and conducted by an Austrian, danced by Russians, and performed in Paris and London, *Joseph* represented both the high-water mark and the end of prewar cosmopolitanism. Seen in this way, it is somehow fitting that the work was not as radical as, say, *The Rites of Spring,* but rather a bit passé. To the soaring tones of Strauss's huge orchestra and amidst the opulent oriental settings of José Maria Sert and the spectacular Venetian costumes of Bakst, the Belle Époque, unbeknownst to the jeweled and glittering audience, made its feverish final bow.

• • •

In a letter to his sister after the third performance of the ballet in London, Kessler wrote, "All the royalty were to be there but of course under the circumstances (the assassination of the Austrian Gr. Duke), they cannot." Kessler did not seem unduly alarmed and the rest of his letters until the end of July are concerned with his ballet and his social life. On the occasion of the Second Balkan War (which pitted Bulgaria against Serbia, Greece, Turkey, and Rumania), he exclaimed that "a war between the great nations on account of this Balkan squabble seems *utterly impossible.*" In fact, war between the great nations would not break out for a year, but that a "squabble" in the Balkans could and would indeed become a *causus belli* was something of which Kessler should have been well aware. For years, he had noted the growth of war fever on both sides of the alliances that were turning Europe into two armed and intransigent camps. He had greeted the replacement of Bülow by Theobald von Bethmann-Hollweg as chancellor in 1909 with enthusiasm, in part because the latter was the uncle of his good friend Gerhard von Mutius, who was soon to be second secretary in the French embassy. On February 11, 1911, Kessler attended dinner with the chancellor and had a long conversation with him. Kessler started by noting the rising chauvinism of the French, especially among the youth and the intellectuals of the *Action Française*. He considered reconciliation with the French impossible, but something might be possible with the English. Bethmann-Hollweg acknowledged this but opined that the way to better relations with England was through the application of pressure: that was the point of his effort to improve German connections with Russia. When Prince Lichnowsky, soon to become the German ambassador to England, chimed in that England would never go to war against Germany, the chancellor exploded that the encirclement of Germany, which he attributed to King Edward VII's intrigues, would have necessarily led to war. A little more calmly, he continued: "Yes sometime a pressure could develop that would cause us, perhaps over hastily, to our disadvantage, to strike. I don't mean against the legitimate interests of England, France, or Russia, but this block that, even when it has not interests, creates opposition to us all over the world, to destroy our position, in the long or short run that could lead to war." [39]

That summer, at the height of the Second Moroccan Crisis, triggered by the Germans in an effort to break the Triple Entente encircling them, Kessler wrote to his sister that he considered war not impossible but that there was a greater chance that all would be smoothed over. On the other hand, he wrote, "if there is a war, it will be necessary to take a side. It certainly will not last very long, and it will probably be the *last* war for generations to come. So it would not be an unmitigated evil." The fact that Kessler chose to say that war was "not yet" imminent implies that he considered it only a question of time. A few months after the crisis had subsided, Bodenhausen, by now an important figure in the great armaments firm Krupp, told him that war would come in five years: "Stinnes (Hugo Stinnes the industrialist) is preaching everywhere that the chief mission of industry is to prepare for war, enough supplies to fight for a year without imports. Financially too preparations are being made: the banks will learn how to operate without credits from France." [40]

As his remarks indicate, Kessler did not fear the prospect of war. In a September 8, 1911 letter to his sister, he made this very clear, remonstrating with her for thinking that toy soldiers were out of date: "There is no more hollow Utopia than eternal Peace, and a mischievous one into the bargain. All nations have become what they are by war, and I shouldn't give two pence for a world in which the possibility of war was abolished. Indeed, I cannot in the least doubt that we ourselves in our own lifetimes shall see another great war, for the reasons I once stated to you in Paris. And I cannot say I very much deplore this perspective." A few days later, he returned to the subject, writing that while a war would be unpleasant, on the whole it would be "healthier" for those who survived. About the same time, he fantasized about the coming war, which he considered inevitable because "the French (are) still convinced of their superiority, because in England the monied classes want a war between France and Germany, because we are tired of having our Western boundary always threatened."[41]

Kessler was not, of course, alone in his assumptions about both the inevitability and the nature of a future war. Nor was the palpable sense of relief and expectation with which he thought about the prospect uncommon. As early as 1908, he noted that he was hearing more and more often the sentiment that "a war, which would lead us out of the inner sump, would not really be so bad." Hofmannsthal too, at the time of the crisis over Austria's annexation of Bosnia-Herzegovina, half regretted that war had not broken out. Of all Kessler's companions, however, perhaps no one longed so much for a war as a solution to his own personal lack of purpose and direction than Alfred Walter Heymel. For years, the dilettante poet, Maecenas, and sexual adventurer had lead the distracted, hectic, aimless life of a wealthy debauchee. Kessler referred to him as Peter Pan, the boy who would not grow up. His escapades had been satirized viciously in two novels, one by Otto Julius Bierbaum and one by Heinrich Mann. As early as September 1910, Heymel had written to a friend: "All together, it's not going very well for me, not for my health, not for my soul, not for business, not really at all. . . . I believe it all has to do with that ridiculous comet, if only the beast would at least bring us a war next year! As cruel as this wish may be, imagine how pretty it would be, to simply sit up and ride away and receive no more letters, to read no newspapers, no stock market indexes, and not to know what the next day brings; to eat and drink and sleep and fight, to enjoy friendship and be dead tired, as tired as we have never been, in short to become a new Adam. The usual routine becomes somewhat shabby, at least with me."[42] Heymel got his wish. Mortally ill with tuberculosis, he summoned enough strength to join his regiment and witness the early battles in Belgium, before dying in November 1914.

For Kessler, the war offered as well something of the respite for which Heymel so longingly prayed. Although it put an end to the prospects for a German *Joseph* as well as to a number of other ballet projects he entertained, one wonders how he would have survived much more of the ballet business. He had come a long way from the dreams of a new culture with which he and van de Velde had inaugurated the Weimar experiment. As much as he might mock the "silly *pantins*" he frequented, he was in danger of becoming one himself. He seemed to recognize this on occasion: "My letters must give you the impression that I have become a frightful snob," he wrote to his sister at the height of the *Joseph* fever in the middle of July 1914. Although he tried to defend his interest in London society, he nevertheless concluded, "I must find time for serious things."[43]

It is doubtful whether he would have found this time were it not for the war. It put an end to the part of his life that reached its culmination in *The Legend of Joseph:* for the next ten years he would have time only for "serious things." On the evening of July 25, 1914, with the gravity of the international crisis becoming clear to everyone, he sailed from London in the company of Rodin on the night boat to Paris. As he parted from the sculptor to join his regiment in Germany, the old man called out to him, "I will see you next Wednesday at the Countess Greffullhe's then!" A whole world seems suspended in that phrase, which then faded in the din of a Parisian train station.

PART FIVE

War's Purifying Fire

CHAPTER 16

Furor Teutonicus

> The war is an aesthetic pleasure without compare.
> Ernst Glaeser, *Jahrgang 1902*

The July crisis, sparked by the assassination of Archduke Francis Ferdinand at Sarajevo, caught most of Europe unawares. Those who could
afford it were vacationing at the beaches and spas when suddenly it became apparent that a general war was imminent. Hurriedly, they packed
their bags and left for home. Kessler was particularly concerned both to
bring his family to safety and to secure his finances, spread out as they
were across the continents. As the trains and ferries crisscrossed Europe
in the last days of July, bearing excited and worried travelers, abruptly
wrenched from lazy summer vacations, and hustling them home, the
able-bodied men to report to recruiting stations and the women and
children to return to boarded-up houses, Kessler made hasty preparations. In an emphatic letter, written in Paris on July 28, he urged his
sister to take their mother and leave for England. Switzerland was too
dangerous, he argued, the Isle of Wight was better, although preferably
someplace in the interior of the island (no doubt he was thinking of the
dangers posed by a German naval raid). He left them 50,000 francs and
told them to write, through Switzerland, to his address in Berlin until—
not if—war between England and Germany broke out, a choice of
words that suggests that Kessler, unlike the German government, was
certain that England would fight. Nevertheless, as late as July 30, he apparently had hoped to return briefly to London, probably to arrange for

the last-minute transfer of funds, but this was no longer possible. Their letters to each other, he warned his sister in his last communication before the declaration of war, must never contain war news. He then inquired after his brother-in-law, about to don the French uniform, and wished him all luck. "If this great catastrophe happens, we must all bear up and not give way to nerves or sentiment. . . . I do not think that, anyhow, the war can last very long, the war itself perhaps two to three months, the peace preliminaries another three to four months; all should be over by next spring."[1] She could be grateful, he added, that the war had broken out when her boys were too young to fight; Jacques, even if he learned English, should not forget his German.

The war, of course, lasted four years, not two to three months. Kessler would not see his sister for five years. He would never see his mother again. The widespread conviction that the war would last only a few months, that it would be over by Christmas, accounts in part for that remarkable frenzy of war fever that consumed middle-class Europe in August 1914. For those caught abroad, crossing by train into the homeland seems to have triggered a tremendous emotional catharsis, a feeling of exultation that far transcended vulgar chauvinism and that, if they survived the war, they would remember fondly for the rest of their lives.

An important component of this euphoria was the exhilarating sense of the sudden and unexpected evaporation of all the class barriers that normally pervaded every aspect of prewar European society, enmeshing the individual in an inescapable and omnipresent net of distinctions and taboos. On these trains rushing home, with streams of travelers entering along the way, with the first soldiers and officers en route to their regiments, and with the passing villages and towns bedecked with flags and arrayed with cheering crowds, a carnival-like feeling of community was spontaneously celebrated. "I no longer recognize parties," declared the kaiser in his speech announcing the war, "I only recognize Germans." And for a moment, politics as usual—its rhetoric, its clash of interests, its acrimonious debates—did seem irrelevant, outdated, transcended by an immense wave of national solidarity and common purpose.[2]

Incidents of chauvinism and spy hysteria that represented the shadow side of this enthusiasm could not seriously mar the excitement Kessler felt at the approach of battle. As the "electrifying" news of the first German victories around Liege in the north and Mülhausen in the south reached Berlin, the unit Kessler commanded, the II Artillery Munitions

column of the Guards Reserve Corps, moved out from its Berlin barracks, adorned with flowers, and entrained for its destination, the battle
front in Belgium. Through every town, they passed an almost unbroken
line of people, women, children, workers, waving flags and handker-
chiefs and shouting "Wiedersehen." The soldiers stretched out com-
fortably in the hay and straw of the cattle cars, while the horses stuck
their heads out and watched as the fields passed by. Kessler, as the highest commanding officer, had a compartment to himself, and he traveled
in the greatest luxury, marveling at both the mood of the country and
the efficiency of the mobilization. Not even a slight concussion, the result of a fall from his horse when detraining near the Belgian border,
could dampen his spirits. The German people, over whom he had despaired so often, seemed reborn in a new and infinitely more beautiful
form. To Hofmannsthal, he wrote that "these first weeks of war have
brought forth something from unknown depths in our German people,
which I can only compare with a earnest and cheerful spirituality. The
whole population is as transformed and cast into a new form. This
already is the priceless gain of this war; and to have witnessed it will
certainly be the greatest experience of our lives."[3]

That this great adventure involved the invasion and partial devasta-
tion of Belgium, a small neutral country and the homeland of van de
Velde, receives no mention in Kessler's diary or letters during these
heady days. Taken aback by Belgian resistance to their plans and irritated by acts of sabotage and guerilla warfare committed by franc-
tireurs, the Germans deliberately pursued a policy of retribution, shooting hostages and burning villages. When, therefore, he caught up with
his regiment as it was fighting on the outskirts of the second great Belgian fortress of Namur, Kessler received the first intimation that this
would be a different kind of war than most Germans had imagined. The
sight of Belgian civilians shot for their alleged depredations shocked
Kessler. It seemed as if the war would be closer to the experience of the
Thirty Years War than to that of the 1870 campaign. He visited a village
of more than four thousand inhabitants that had been deliberately destroyed by the Germans for the "murder" of twenty German soldiers.
Not a house was left standing. A family—grandmother, daughter, son-
in-law, and little girl—wept silently and helplessly as they watched the
last roof timbers of their house burn and crash to the ground. "Cruel is
the people's war," Kessler wrote to a friend, "we are fired upon from all
the parks we pass through. Then they are punished, the place destroyed,
and despite it all, the peasants continue to shoot."[4]

At Namur, Kessler had a strange encounter that reminded him of how much the world had changed in a few short weeks. In the partially burnt city, he met the Duchess of Sutherland, who had brought a group of nurses from England to aid the Belgians and had been captured inside Namur. She described vividly the horrors of the bombardment by the heavy German siege artillery. Only a month before, she had sat at the same table as Kessler during that last hectic summer season in London. The Germans felt they could not let her return home immediately. "Somewhat uncomfortable" was how Kessler described the reunion under the circumstances. For her part, the duchess later wrote of their meeting that "it was exceedingly odd to meet him under such circumstances, after having discussed 'art' with him in London."[5]

From the very beginning of the war, Kessler was conscious of the terrible dissonance between the bureaucratic, routinized, faceless, distant, and even comfortable direction of modern war and its gruesome consequences. During the siege of Namur, he breakfasted with the captain of the Krupp 420 battery that was bombarding Fort Maizeret. Their leisurely meal was only interrupted every ten minutes or so by the captain calling a number into the telephone. They then could observe, from a safe distance, how another piece of the fortress collapsed, burning its inhabitants to death and burying them beneath rubble. These vulcanized corpses were the most frightful sight Kessler had yet seen: "Their faces looked mostly like a chocolate soufflé in which the eyes, quite small and white like almonds, were stuck." Modern war was anything but romantic, Kessler wrote to Dora von Bodenhausen. It resembled more the office of a large factory. "If one didn't know what was going on, one could assume that important orders and other office business were being settled. The corpses, the blood, even the thunder of battle, are distant. One sees in these orderly offices, in which so many officials go in and out, folders piling up and telephones ringing— nothing concerning the war."[6]

Yet, for all the implicit critique in these passages, it is clear from the long letters Kessler sent home to select correspondents, with the intention that they be circulated among his friends, that the war had seized his imagination. Indeed, it had almost literally swept him off his feet. His descriptions of warfare both in Belgium and in the East are rife with romanticism. "War's purifying fire," was how the great expressionist painter Franz Marc—who himself would perish in the conflagration— put it, and the pathos of this expression reverberates throughout Kessler's letters from the front. Commenting on a poem by Dehmel, which he felt had captured something of the spirit and rhythm of the war, he wrote, "Yes, in fact, most feel that the old world has disappeared and only this new existence, which Dehmel's verses express, this marching from one burning site to the next, from one field of corpses to the next, is possible any longer. . . . The entrance of the *Maikäfer* into Namur with the regimental bands at the head and the thousand young throats singing 'The Watch on the Rhine' will remain one of my most moving memories. All around the city burned but here from out of the flames and smoke emerged a new victorious life: forwards over the graves!"[7] Coming under fire was as exciting and arousing as champagne. Here, it seems, was the birth of a new world out of the ashes of the old, as Nietzsche had foretold—a quickening of life in the midst of death that made all other, earlier aesthetic pleasures pale in comparison.

The aestheticization of this most ugly of wars was not peculiar to Kessler or, for that matter, to the Germans, as it has been recently argued. Educated soldiers of all the combatant nations automatically dipped into the reservoir of literary and artistic traditions available to them to make sense of something so unexpected. The English, no less than the Germans, aestheticized the war, only they did so using the pastoral imagery—larks rising, roses and poppies—that made up such a large part of their poetic tradition.[8] If the Germans tended to use the vocabulary and assumptions of German romanticism, saturated with turn-of-the-century "life-philosophy," this does not prove that theirs was a particularly bloodthirsty culture.

Kessler's enthusiasm can be explained by the scent of victory. By August 26, 1914, as the massive right wing of the German army was streaming through the open plains of Flanders toward the French border, only weakly defended by the British Expeditionary Force and the French Fifth Army, Kessler predicted that Paris would be in German hands in a month and that the French and British armies would be annihilated. He knew, however, that he would not be among those who would parade, for the second time in forty-three years, under the Arc d' Triomphe. The army corps to which he was attached, the Guard Reserve Corps, as well as another, had just received orders from the head of the German General Staff, Helmut von Moltke, to move to East Prussia and help shore up the German army there, which was facing an invading Russian force twice its size. This represented a fateful decision, in the opinion of most military historians, because it weakened the German right wing just enough to enable the French counterattack at the Battle of the Marne to stop their advance and indeed to throw them back. As a result, the Germans would not come so close to Paris again until their last great offensive in the spring of 1918, and the western front would collapse into the bloody stalemate of trench warfare. Meanwhile, the two army corps would arrive too late in the East to play a role in the decisive battle there. Already on August 26, the Germans, under the new and vigorous command of Field Marshall Paul von Hindenburg and General Erich von Ludendorff, had engaged and destroyed the right wing of the Russian Second Army. The rest of General Alexander Samsonov's forces would be obliterated in the following days in the engagement known as the Battle of Tannenberg, the beginning of the great German advance into the heart of Russia.

•   •   •

The Unknown War was the title Winston Churchill gave to his account of the eastern front in his history of the First World War. The full story of the titanic struggle between the last three European empires has generally been told, if at all, from the German point of view, mostly because the sources have been much more accessible for Western scholars. The image of catastrophic Russian losses, of streams of Russian prisoners, of a nearly flawless German drive to the East dominates most lay knowledge of the eastern front, although recent scholarship has questioned the notion that the Russians were hopelessly outclassed.[9] Still, the First World War in Eastern Europe remains for Western readers largely "unknown" in an important way. Unlike the voluminous literature, memoirs, diaries, letters, and novels, much of it first-rate, concerning the day-to-day existence of ordinary soldiers on the western front, comparatively little of enduring value was apparently written on this topic in the East, and less has been translated or made accessible to Western audiences. This is true for the German public as well: the great German war novels and memoirs have almost all been set in the West. Thus, the emotional landscape of the eastern front remains largely uncharted. Kessler's diary and especially the long letters, which he later collected and published privately in 1921, provide therefore a valuable contribution to a sparse literature. Rilke praised them as "the most powerful and surest description of that unimaginable life that have ever come my way, ranking with the great example of Tolstoy's *War and Peace*, and carried along with a composure, presence of mind and narrative calm that seems inconceivable under such fearful conditions."[10]

Although he missed the battle of Tannenberg, Kessler arrived in time to participate in the so-called battle of the Masurian Lakes, where the

German army wheeled to the east and pushed the Russian First Army out of East Prussia. Kessler was with the vanguard of the new German IX army when it crossed over the border of southern Poland on September 22, 1914. The same day Kessler was introduced to both Hindenburg, with whom he exchanged a few words about the general's niece Helene von Nostitz, and Ludendorff, the inseparable duo who were just beginning to accumulate the power that would make them de facto dictators of Germany in the last two years of the war. Together, they seemed to Kessler to incorporate the two aspects of the German army at war, its Prussian military tradition and its modern business-like approach to the conduct of war. Kessler did his share to promulgate the myth of Hindenburg, writing to Hofmannsthal of the deep trust of the average German soldier in their leadership. Hindenburg seemed to embody the stolid virtues of the German *Soldatentum* in the East, mostly older reservists, who, while they lacked the beauty of the young regiments, made up for it in stoic dutifulness. In Kessler's words, "they stride heavily and powerfully into fire like workers moving at dawn through the streets of an industrial city to work. . . . Belgium and the Guards were aesthetically more beautiful but the qualities that will lead us in the end to victory are perhaps more clearly seen in our reservists." [11] After these inconclusive battles, Kessler's army saw little action in the last two months of 1914. As always in war, the lulls in the fighting allowed time for a flurry of rumors. One thing, however, was becoming more and more apparent: the war would last a lot longer than anyone had anticipated.[12]

Kessler tried without success to land a position on the western front. Instead, he was named orderly officer on December 12. As it happened, the decision turned out to be beneficial for him. Shortly afterward, he met and fell in love with a young staff aide named Schoeter. About the same time, he learned that his unit would be transferred south to Hungary to take part in a vast assault on the Russian positions in the Carpathian Mountains. Conrad von Hötzendorff, the vainglorious Austrian chief of staff whose strategic imagination far exceeded his tactical ability, had designed this operation. The aim was to surprise the exposed left flank of the Russians by an assault where and when they least expected, over the Carpathians in the dead of winter. Hötzendorff also hoped to relieve the Austrian garrison in the great fortress of Przemysl, which had been besieged by the Russians. A further strategic goal was to secure a success that would make the Italians pause before joining the Allies. Kessler's division was assigned to join the newly formed *Südarmee* that was to strike at the central passes.[13] He departed on January 16, 1915, Schoeter traveling with him. This winter campaign became thus a great romantic adventure for Kessler, an erotic idyll in the midst of death.

Down into the great Hungarian plain they traveled toward the eastern Carpathians. Together, Kessler and Schoeter galloped over fields of stubble: "The joy, which like a fluid of air and light streams from us, becomes elevated, through the attachment Schoeter and I feel for each other, into something personal." In Sziget, he and the "very dear, nice little Hussar" were greeted enthusiastically by the town and by their Hungarian officer counterparts as Hungary's saviors, and a great party was thrown for them. As the bottles of schnapps and Tokay emptied and the gypsy music swelled, the atmosphere grew thick with sentiment. At one point, a Hungarian Hussar gave Schoeter his military cap into which his mother had sewn an amulet to protect him. Later, as they moved into the mountains, he and Schoeter lived for a time in a tiny hut, buried in the snow, with an oven on which they could make tea and a table on which they could write. In the evening, Kessler read poems and his friend played the harmonica. "All day long march adventuresome looking columns in the snow past our hut," heading up to storm the Russian positions in the passes.[14]

In his letters home, Kessler stylized the Carpathian campaign as the triumph of Germanic will over the obstacles posed by a rugged landscape, a harsh climate, and a massive, if lethargic, foe entrenched in nearly impregnable positions:

Both our divisions have been fighting for three days successfully in the mountains and tomorrow we, that is, headquarters, will follow them. Since everything is deeply snowed in and for stretches mountain tracks high up in the massive cliffs must be used, we ascend on mules and sleds, but hoist our heavy artillery up ourselves. We have already fired them yesterday on the chief position of the Russians, the Kliwa, which dominates the road through the pass and then we stormed the fort, capturing many prisoners and much supplies. The mountains are almost empty of people. There is hardly any shelter, only huts. One climbs upwards through a grandiose desert of snow and cliffs. What it means to bring through there the masses of a modern army, along with munitions and supplies, what the cold, the lack of any kind of shelter, the deep snow, and the icy, in part almost vertically ascending, mountain paths demand in the way of endurance and courage from the troops, you can well imagine. Only an army like ours is capable of overcoming, in the face of the enemy, of enemy fire, such difficulties. Even Hannibal and Napoleon only crossed the Alps because the enemy was absent.[15]

Surely, he surmised, the Russians, already war weary, will be surprised by the boldness of the operation and will panic at the sight of the armies of the Central Powers streaming through the mountain passes. The battle would last six to eight weeks and then the enemy would collapse, Kessler prophesied to Hofmannsthal, like the characters in Dostoyevsky's novels (he was reading *The Brothers Karamazov*), suddenly, completely, and hopelessly.[16]

Only a few days later, however, Kessler noted laconically in his diary that the assault was losing men, who, sunk in the snow, made perfect targets. The snow that smothered the shells negated the customary advantage enjoyed by the Germans in artillery.[17] The Carpathian campaign was, in fact, a catastrophe. While Kessler and Schoeter read poetry and played music and enjoyed the view, the foot soldiers, consigned to a task that was not only heroic but also impossible, either froze to death or died of typhus. As the historian Norman Stone writes: "On two occasions, whole companies were found frozen to death, covered by snow. When either side attacked, it was a question of moving up steep slopes in conditions that would have exhausted a trained mountaineer, far less peasants from the plains or urban proletarians. All in all, the Carpathian offensives were a terrible experience for all who underwent them. They are the greatest blot on Conrad's record."[18]

The *Südarmee* to which Kessler was attached advanced at a rate of about one hundred yards per day, far slower than was planned or than one could surmise from Kessler's letters. Hötzendorff, however, worried about the looming capture of Przemysl, continued to hurl his armies forward, although their losses were appalling. One army corps lost 40,000 men in a week. Nearly 800,000 men were killed, wounded, deserted, or lost to sickness and the cold in the three months of the Carpathian campaign. And all for no appreciable gain, either strategic or tactical.[19]

In order to bolster the failing effort, Kessler was sent on his first leave toward the end of February in order to appeal for reinforcements and use his connections to get a reporter from the major Berlin papers to come and write about the Carpathian campaign. Traveling via Budapest and Vienna, he had time to think about the personal meaning of the war. "War is a situation which one gets used to unfortunately," he admitted, "one forms relations with an intensity and naiveté which one otherwise only finds in early youth. . . . The war has taught me to love and admire man, whom it has revealed in all his cruelty, baseness, greatness, and tenderness, infinitely more. It has shown him to me as god and beast." In Vienna, he met Hofmannsthal and together they discussed the postwar regeneration of Austria-Hungary and the future of Poland, as well as the failure of the Carpathian campaigns. The bitterness of the ballet business forgotten, at least briefly, due to the Sturm und Drang of the war, the two men got along well. Hofmannsthal noted how well the war seemed to sit with his friend. "Kessler was here," he reported, "from the Carpathians on a mission to Berlin. He looked unbelievably good and was never so handsome and manly as now. He is completely at one with the uniform and this entire condition of life, has much of interest to relate. Only that, admittedly, his army makes as little progress as the others (except for one in Bukovina) and the lovely, bold plan of an offensive from the southeast has so good as failed—despite the most enormous accomplishments and sacrifices." [20]

Then it was on to Berlin where, aside from problems obtaining bread because he did not yet have a ration card, he found that the war had made little impact on the life he had known before the war. Attending a performance in the Deutsches Theater, he found it difficult to believe that the packed, attentive house lay between two long lines of trenches in the West and East "that, covered with ditches, corpses, and blood stained snow, ward off the enemy in order that the public here will not be in the slightest disturbed in their enjoyment of the theater." In the capital of the beleaguered empire, Kessler found a very different atmosphere prevailing than on the front lines. The tension, fed by thousands of unsubstantiated rumors, particularly concerning Italy's decision whether to go to war or not, was nearly unbearable. For the first time, he encountered a deep pessimism about Germany's chances, even an incipient pacifism. Maxmilian Harden, for example, who had initially greeted the war with enthusiasm, now made the impression of a burnt-out volcano to Kessler. Harden was in favor of a status quo ante peace, made, if necessary, at the cost of Austria-Hungary, which, inasmuch as it could not be sustained over the long run, might as well be liquidated now, he argued. From the Nostitzs, Kessler learned of the small circle of pacifists in Leipzig centered around the expressionist writer Franz Werfel. Carl Sternheim, Max Reinhardt, and Richard Strauss also seemed less than enthusiastic about the war. On March 4, Kessler dined with Strauss, who termed the war a criminal atavism: The question of whether a "patch of land" like Alsace-Lorraine should belong to Germany or to France was fundamentally unimportant and not worth the loss of hundreds of thousands of people. [21]

More worrying than the pacifist opinions of his artist friends was the aimlessness and lack of direction Kessler found at the highest levels of the government. Bodenhausen, who was very worried about both the British blockade and the prospect of Italy's declaration of war, told his friend of the growing resentment against the kaiser. He was seen as protecting the unpopular chief of staff Erich von Falkenhayn and preventing the only generals who had won decisive victories, namely Hindenburg and Ludendorff, from taking over the military direction of the war. Kessler had recently had an interview with Bethmann-Hollweg to ask for reinforcements to prevent the fall of Przemysl: "He has become, since I saw him last, heavier, slower, and more tired, a weary colossus. He carries a heavy burden, has bags under the eyes, and loose folds in his face, is no longer the firm, still almost youthful, slender man of his first years as Chancellor." [22] To all these manifestations of pessimism and war weariness, Kessler responded with a vigorous and militant faith in the ultimate success of German arms. The only respectable peace, he argued, would be the German retention of the coast of Belgium, border expansions in Poland, a sufficient war indemnity, and the return and enlargement of the German colonies. Possession of the Belgian coast was especially important because only then could England be forced to acknowledge parity with Germany. He regarded public protests against the war, or other signs of war weariness, as a dangerous weakening of the nation's will to victory.

Upon returning to his unit in March, he found the battle lines pretty much as he had left them. Aside from an occasional incident, such as the time he was caught accidentally between the lines during some heavy shelling, the war on Kessler's front was relatively quiet, at times even tedious, in the spring of 1915. "This war would be, for me personally, a very fine and almost enjoyable adventure, if it was not for the being cut off from you and Mama, which keeps me in constant anxiety," Kessler wrote to his sister. He went on to describe the war as "an immense Cook's tour through a country where another touring party are (sic) trying to stop you. Of course those who happen to be in the front at any particular moment *can* get their skulls cracked; but the immense majority are *behind;* in places of absolute safety, and run no greater risks than ordinary travelers." [23] This was written of course to assuage the anxiety of his family but nevertheless seems an accurate description of at least part of Kessler's experience. If, in his political imagination, Kessler was rearranging the map of Europe to ensure the creation of a lasting Pax Germania, in his letters to his family in England, he continued to tend to the prewar international connections. In nearly every letter he wrote to his sister, he begged her to inquire after Colin and send money to his wife if they were in need. At the same time, he urged her to get in touch with Edward Johnston, Emery Walker, and John H. Mason, the English printers he had engaged on behalf of the Cranach Presse. He did not want their work to fall behind for the sake of a mere war. In the same vein, he inquired after both Maillol and Craig.

His family for their part plied him with rare gifts through neutral Switzerland. We have a description of the cosmopolitan at war. In April 1915, Heinrich Vogeler, one of the principal members of Worpswede artist colony, a friend of Rilke, and a collaborator with Schröder and Heymel on *Insel*, was assigned to the staff of Kessler's army corps as a war artist.* Vogeler was impressed with the palpable evidence of Kessler's international connections:

Soon the courier arrived with the mail. Horse, saddle, and he himself were covered with packages and tin cans. There were newspapers from Germany, France, England, and Switzerland. He brought wonderfully preserved fruits and conserves. Even English turtle soup in violet tin buckets was not lacking, and many other surprises for a man who was related by marriage to the French nation and whose closest friends sat in England. They provided their enemy brother-in-law and friend with the most beautiful things through neutral Switzerland. Kessler was an international figure. He had witnessed the outbreak of the war in London at the tea table with Asquith and Grey, who had advised him then to return as quick as possible to his own country.[24]

Vogeler, whom Kessler called a "earnest, intelligent man, rather self-possessed but not to the point of arrogance," brought a little of the vanished world of the 1890s into the military atmosphere at headquarters. Kessler, always the patron, sat for a portrait and commissioned the painter to do a sketch of the rooms he shared with Schoeter, which he bought for 500 marks.

---

*Vogeler was about to enter the decisive years of a strange and ultimately tragic life. The experience of war would radicalize this hitherto apolitical artist whose fashionably ethereal paintings epitomized Jugendstil. Brought into contact with Bolshevik propaganda in Rumania, he would, in the last months of the war, write a letter denouncing the war to the German High Command, a deed which would bring him temporary imprisonment in an insane asylum. He took part in the abortive communist revolution in Bremen after the war and then turned his house in Worpswede into a radical school for working-class children, a decision that split the art colony permanently. In the 1920s, Vogeler undertook a number of trips through the Soviet Union, and when Hitler came to power he fled there, somehow surviving Stalin's continual purges of his fellow German exiles, until 1942, when at the age of 69, he was evacuated before the German onslaught. He died of starvation in Kazakhstan.

Spring came to war-torn Galicia in Poland. Kessler, whose prewar moustache had been shaved off by accident by a Hungarian barber and was thus to remain clean shaven for the rest of his life, never felt healthier or stronger in his life. The rigors of the campaign, despite the consumption of turtle soup and other imported luxuries, had rendered him fit and trim. With Schoeter he went swimming in a river: "The whole day (we) lay naked on the meadows by the water, ran, jumped, and even rode horses naked . . . everywhere one saw between the willows, on the green banks, and in the sparkling water naked forms, bathing and sunning themselves." Kessler took advantage of this erotic interlude to photograph Schoeter naked, as he had once done with Colin. Even the local Ruthenian peasants pleased him. In appearance, he wrote to his sister, they are very English: tall, fair, and with blue eyes but more graceful and picturesque than northern peoples. Only the Jewish population displeased him. In one of the ugliest anti-Semitic thoughts he ever recorded, he described them as "louses" amidst the noble peasants.[25]

In the spring of 1915, the chief of staff Falkenhayn decided reluctantly to shift the German war effort from the western front to the east. They picked the most vulnerable section of the Russian front, the right flank of the Third Army, which, despite being the very center and lynchpin of the Russian lines, was only guarded by two isolated and inadequately equipped army corps, without reserves. When the German XI army, commanded by the redoubtable August von Mackenson and enjoying a two-to-one dominance in men and a much greater ratio in artillery, struck on May 2, the Russians reeled backward. After much anguish, the Russians decided to abandon all of Poland, Lithuania, and much of Byelorussia in a great retreat that lasted until the fall of 1915.

Shortly after Mackensen's attack, the German *Südarmee* moved to the attack. Kessler kept a detailed, almost hourly account of the fighting. He noted the corpses in front of the captured Russian trenches: "The faces quite black, like Negroes, already half rotten, and covered with dirt and earth. There's one lying on almost every tree. One still holds desperately a spade. Another thrusts a tightly clenched fist towards the sky." The sight of the wounded disturbed him much more. Choking on his tears, he left the hospital. From June 22 to June 29, he was involved in an exhausting battle to cross the Dniester River. One must not think, he warned Gustav Richter, that the pursuit of the retreating Russians was like chasing beaten troops. Rather, it was a continuously renewed assault on fortified positions in which the Russians defended themselves tenaciously. "Every 5 or 10 kilometers (according to the layout of the land) on a pond or a swamp or a stretch of hills, there runs through the countryside deeply sunk, shrapnel-secured, covered trenches, which have been built up for months, with barbed wire and flanking positions." Each one had to be almost besieged, using heavy artillery, infantry storms, and even sappers. Some of these Russian positions were so molded to their purpose and to the landscape that they seemed as well suited and beautiful in their environment as Greek temples or Roman villas. As liaison officer, Kessler was to help keep the pursuit from bogging down. In this role, he got caught again ahead of the German lines in no man's land. Pinned down by Russian gunfire, he crawled into a foxhole. "I sat on the sand in my hole, let the sun shine on me and waited, without being bored, on the contrary, with a not unpleasant tension." Shortly before noon, on August 11, 1915, after nearly six hours in that position, the German front lines moved up, followed by the artillery, which proceeded to shell the Russians. By evening, two companies of German infantry had successfully stormed the Russian lines. The Russians had not held out until the last, but they had held the German advance up for a day: "[T]he whole incident was typical of the Russian style of fighting: the surprising standing fast, the flexible resistance, which then immediately yields but only after first costing us losses and time, the clever vanishing into thin air in the fog and at night, the tenacious tiring and weakening of our troops who can never rest and must fight every day. A mixture of cunning and stubbornness over a background of weakness: snake and donkey as one finds in certain women." [26]

"This march into Russia," Kessler noted, "into the empty, holy, endless Russia [is] an experience quite uncannily different than the first in September. Something fairytale-like, like the penetration into Sleeping Beauty's castle." Step by step, deep into the endless Polish and Russian plains and swamps they advanced, through abandoned villages, where not a single person or animal was to be seen, only the rolling fields of wheat upon which the gray, drizzling, melancholy rain fell. Despite the sense of victory caused by the German advances, Kessler found the fighting increasingly depressing. For one thing, Schoeter was no longer by his side, having been transferred from his regiment on July 12. Only a month before, in the midst of exhausting battle, Kessler had queried, "Is it permissible to tell the being one loves of this love? Can both roles be combined?" The day he learned of Schoeter's transfer, Kessler spent a depressing afternoon with him. In the evening, they both sat listless at the table as Schoeter was toasted by the other officers. "With him disappears more than can be said from my life," wrote Kessler, and then a few days later, "he formed, in any case, an epoch in my life." [27] This personal misfortune was compounded only a day later when Kessler's train crashed into another on the way to Lemberg and derailed. His manservant, who had volunteered to follow Kessler into the war, broke his right leg and mangled his left arm horribly in the wreckage. [28]

Once it descended from the relatively uninhabited mountains to the flatland, the campaign lost the heroic luster. The quotidian sordidness of the war increasingly depressed Kessler: "The land east of the Bug (river) is dreary, a completely flat plain over which endless columns of refugees stream past our army. In this great expanse only ruins of villages, isolated trees, here and there a skinny woods, a pond. . . . Whole fields are covered with the corpses of cows, calves, pigs which complement the horses that have died along the path in a horrible, repulsive way. Everywhere, moreover, there is cholera, although it doesn't strike at us but rather at the backwards streaming population." [29] Outside of Kowel, Kessler was assigned to establish quarantine measures to prevent the cholera raging among the refugees from infecting the army. Not three hundred feet from staff headquarters in a lovely park lay an infected family in an isolated farmhouse. The mother and a three-year-old daughter were dead, and now another six-year-old girl was dying. Kessler went to investigate and the father lifted his daughter to the window: "The little, cheerful, pretty girl was now only a gargoyle, a waxen death mask with blue lips that hung over her tiny chest. She resembled medieval pictures of the crucifixion. The little blouse had slid up her body and the thin, dirt-covered little legs dangled lifelessly, as if broken, back and forth." Horrified at their lack of fresh straw and drinking water, Kessler berated the army doctor, who only laughed scornfully. Furious, Kessler went to his commander and had the doctor dismissed. At the same time, he saw to it that the family received water, straw, coffee, and brandy. In a letter to Richter, he wrote about the experience: "And we sit, I don't know if more foolish or numb, three hundred feet away in our park! I ask myself often what I myself feel in the face of all these horrors? One hardly knows one's own heart, let alone anyone else's." [30]

Shortly afterward, he again was confronted by another experience that undermined his earlier, Siegfried-like intoxication. Deep now in the Ukraine, he was given living quarters in an old country house— "some Rip van Winkle of a house, which should have disappeared long ago"—belonging to an old scholar. The ancient gentleman asked Kessler, "in an academic German with comical awkward expressions," if he could be permitted to stay in his corner of the house: "[H]e stood before me, so fearfully, so unworldly, so imperviously deaf to the 'greatness' of the war, yet still frightened out of his tranquility, that suddenly there came over me, prickling and tickling my consciousness, the grotesqueness of violence, the ridiculousness of my situation as the conqueror of this quiet scholar. Such sensations are like lightening, they last only a moment. Good that they are short, but also good that they come."[31]

That Kessler admitted having such moments, and even welcomed them, indicates how the spirit that had swept him away the previous August had ebbed under the pressure of more than a year of war. Perhaps the most prominent sign of the ineluctable withering away of heroic idealism was how the staff officers began to demand more comfortable, even luxurious surroundings, and meals. Whereas in December breakfast had consisted of only bread and at the most a glass of wine, now a second breakfast, complete with two warm courses, was insisted upon. In some cases, this process led to a scandalous "comfort gap" between the frontline troops and staff headquarters. Kessler, although worried about it, understood how it came about. It was difficult to remain heroic, at least in everyday life, for so long, and besides there were forces in people that resisted being subordinated to one overarching goal, no matter how noble, for too long.[32]

The question of leadership weighed heavily on Kessler's mind during this time. In the early months of the war, he seemed to suggest that Hindenburg and Ludendorff, embodying Prussian stolidity and strength of character coupled with the organization skills and energy of Imperial Germany, represented not only the best hope for a German victory, but also a cultural ideal. This mythic image would in fact only crumble for Kessler in the aftermath of Germany's defeat. Long before that, however, he had begun to worry about the cultural future of Germany precisely in the event of a military victory. Although he still refrained from criticizing either Hindenburg or Ludendorff, he increasingly found alarming signs that the war was indeed breeding a new kind of German cultural ideal. When he confronted the embodiment of this ideal in von Klewitz, the new commander assigned to his regiment in August, he balked. "An impudent, second-rate careerist. God protect us from being ruled by such people after the war. . . . That would be a costly victory," he noted. Unlike the philistines with whom Kessler had struggled over modern art, these new men did not even pretend to be the guardians of any tradition: they despised culture as a distraction to the hard business of conquering, governing, and ruling. Culture and religion, in their opinion, was something for the masses; the rulers did not need it. Indignantly, Kessler continued: "Why should a competent staff officer possess more talent to rule over a great people than a tailor or a painter who are competent in their professions? The fragility of this type (for fragile and not Cato-like and old-Prussian he is) rests on his ambition, his lack of character, the striving after superficial glory and advantages, his vanity and smugness. It lies in the fact that he nevertheless flirts with culture, which he despises, just as he does with the Christianity in which he does not believe. He is a type, but he has no style." [33]

Kessler's analysis of Klewitz's character is chillingly prescient. The spirit of ruthless military professionalism and Pan-Germania that the commander embodied was indeed a product of the atmosphere and values cultivated by the men around Ludendorff. A direct descent can be traced easily between this climate of opinion and the savage ethos of Hitler's Wehrmacht. Although he was not yet ready to expand this incipient critique to persons and institutions he still admired, Kessler, with his finely tuned powers of observation and his moral sense still intact, despite his adherence to a large part of the war party's agenda, intuited the presence of something ugly, something that would indeed shape the future of postwar Germany.

But Kessler was not yet ready to give up entirely on the idealism of August 1914. So many sacrifices, so many blackened corpses of young men, so much suffering required a compensatory raison d'être. If the leadership of the German army could no longer provide it, then he would look elsewhere. Personal sympathy and erotic inclination led him to find in the young combat officers the spirit that had so quickly sickened and died back in headquarters. The relationship with Schoeter was only the most intense and personal episode in Kessler's idealization of young officers. Others would follow in the later years of the war, and some of them would be deserters, war resisters, and pacifists. In a very important, but subtle way, this admiration for youthful idealism and energy would begin the process that would lead him from an enthusiastic supporter of annexations to becoming an ardent pacifist.

The great German advance came to a halt at the end of the fall. Once past the relatively developed area of Poland, the German and Austro-Hungarian armies entered the trackless wastes of western Russia, where there were even fewer serviceable roads and railways. Moreover, winter was approaching and the Central Powers were reaching the practical limits of their supply routes. Indeed, exhausted by the months of fighting, the soldiers were vulnerable to counterattacks if the demoralized

Russians could mount them. In one incident, a local Russian counter-attack in the Wolheynien region between Lutsk and Rovno threatened to crumple the Austrian divisions, composed mostly of Ruthenians who began to desert in large numbers. The heroic resistance of the Polish Legion, a force recruited by the Polish nationalist Josef Pilsudski to help liberate Poland from Russia, stemmed the potential rout. Kessler was commissioned by Klewitz to investigate the details of this battle, in part because the story of the Polish Legion would provide useful propaganda for the German and Austrian effort to raise a Polish army.[34]

Kessler visited the scene of the fighting and talked to the participants. According to Vogeler, who traveled with him, Kessler's report, which took him most of October to compile, angered headquarters because it exonerated the Austrian troops, blaming the setback instead on drunken German troops. Be that as it may, it was on this occasion that Kessler made the acquaintance of Pilsudski, the future leader of independent Poland. As Kessler and Vogeler arrived at the Polish trenches, a man in a gray sweater emerged. Pilsudski reminded Kessler more of a scholar than a warrior: "The head, large, yellow, long, and somewhat Mongoloid, with a long thin moustache and thin goatee, resembles that of Dostoyevsky. The gray eyes are thoughtful, but fix the object firmly upon which they are directed."[35] The two men spoke in French about the future of Poland. In the middle of their conversation, they were interrupted by an Austrian officer, who, Kessler assured Vogeler, had been sent by the Austrians to spy.

Kessler's meeting with Pilsudski would prove fateful for him. It was largely because of the mutual respect between the two men that Kessler would be chosen to liberate Pilsudski, in the hectic days just before the German revolution, from the prison to which the Germans had confined him in the last years of the war when he no longer served their purposes. And it was this connection again that caused Kessler to be named the Weimar Republic's first ambassador to Poland. The Polish question had preoccupied Kessler since his transfer to the East. It was through this debate that he began to participate in a serious way in the wartime politics of Germany. In the end, the engagement in politics would lead him away from the world of the front lines and into the world of diplomacy, propaganda, and espionage.

FIGURE 1. Alice, Countess Kessler, around 1868.

FIGURE 2. Adolph Wilhelm,
Count Kessler, 1894.

FIGURE 3. Harry Kessler, around 1880.

FIGURE 4. Kessler, greeting
Bismarck, August 10, 1891.

FIGURE 5. Kessler, 1898.

N. Perscheid
Königl. Sächs. Hof-Photograph etc.

Leipzig
Gellert-Strasse 2.

FIGURE 6. Elisabeth Förster-Nietzsche at the door of the Nietzsche Archive, after 1903.

FIGURE 7. Kessler, unidentified,
Ludwig von Hofmann (standing), Gordon Craig, Henry van
de Velde, 1904.

FIGURE 8. Aristide Maillol, *La Méditerranée*, 1905.

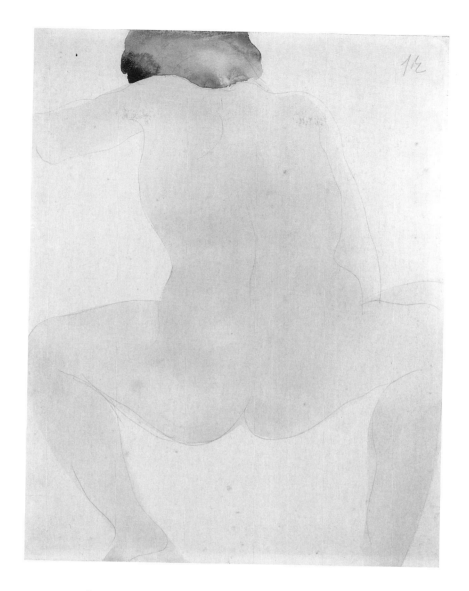

FIGURE 9. Auguste Rodin,
Weibe. Rückenakt.

FIGURE 10. Kessler's dining room, Weimar 1909, showing a frieze by Maurice Denis and a version of Auguste Renoir's *Marchande des pommes.*

FIGURE 11. Final version, Nietzsche monument.

FIGURE 12. Model, Nietzsche monument and stadium.

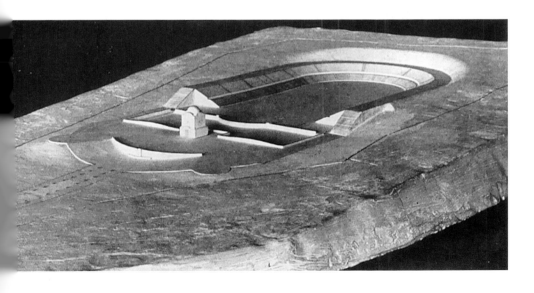

FIGURE 13. Leon Bakst, costume
design for *Potiphar's Wife*, 1914.

FIGURE 14. Ernst Oppler, sketch
of a rehearsal of *The Legend of
Joseph*. From right: Kessler,
Hofmannsthal, Diaghilev (seated),
Fokine.

FIGURE 15. Georg Kolbe, bronze
bust of Kessler, 1916.

FIGURE 16. Institute of Politics, Williams College, 1923. From left: Hue, President Gardiner, Abbé Dimnet; second row: Sir Edward Grigg, Dr. Estainides S. Zeballos.

FIGURE 17. Aristide Maillol, illustration for Virgil's *Ecologae*, Cranach Presse, 1926.

MÉRIS
Et ces vers qu'il n'a pas achevés et qu'il chantait à Varus
VARUS SI SEULEMENT MANTOUE NOUS RESTE
MANTOUE TROP VOISINE DE LA MALHEUREUSE

CRÉMONE Ô VARUS C'EST JUSQU'AUX ASTRES
QUE LES CHANTS DES CYGNES PORTERONT
TON NOM
LYCIDAS
Puissent tes essaims fuir les ifs de l'île de Corse; puis-
sent tes vaches, nourries de cytise, avoir leurs mamelles
gonflées de lait! Mais commence, si tu sais un chant.
Et moi aussi, les Muses m'ont fait poète. Moi aussi je

89

his enemies, and by the means to abandon the actions, gestures and apparel of a mad man, occasion so htly finding his turn, and as it were effecting it selfe, failed not to take hold therof, and seeing those drunken bodies, filled with wine, lying like hogs upon the ground, some sleeping, others vomiting the over great abundance of wine which without measure they had swallowed up, made the hangings about the hall to fall downe and cover them all over; which he nailed to the ground, being boorded, and at the ends thereof he stuck the brands, whereof I spake before, by him sharpned, which served for prickes, binding and tying the hangings in such sort, that what force soever they used to loose themselves, it was unpossible to get from under them; and presently he set fire in the foure corners of the hal, in such sort, that all that were as then therein not one escaped away, but were forced to purge their sins by fire, and dry up the great aboundance of liquor by them received into their bodies, all of them dying in the inevitable and mercilesse flames of the whot and burning fire; which the prince perceiving, became wise, and knowing that his uncle, before the end of the banquet, had withdrawn himselfe into

1. Priester Wir dehnten ihr begräbnis aus, so weit
Die vollmacht reicht: ihr tod war zweifelhaft;
Und wenn kein machtgebot die ordnung hemmte,
So hätte sie in ungeweihtem grund
Bis zur gerichtsdrommete wohnen müssen.
Statt christlicher gebete sollten scherben
Und kieselstein auf sie geworfen werden.
Hier gönnt man ihr doch ihren mädchenkranz
Und das bestreu'n mit jungfräulichen blumen,
Geläut und grabstätt'.

Laer. So darf nichts mehr geschehn?

Priester Nichts mehr geschehn.
Wir würden ja der toten dienst entweihn,
Wenn wir ein requiem und ruh ihr sängen,
Wie fromm verschiednen seelen.

Laer. Legt sie in den grund,
Und ihrer schönen, unbefleckten hülle
Entsprießen veilchen! – Ich sag dir, harter priester,
Ein engel am thron wird meine schwester sein,
Derweil du heulend liegst.

Ham. Was? die schöne Ophelia?

Königin (Blumen streuend)
Der süßen süßes: lebe wohl! – Ich hoffte,
Du solltest meines Hamlets gattin sein.
Dein brautbett dacht ich, süßes kind, zu schmücken,
Nicht zu bestreun dein grab.

158

FIGURE 18. Act V, Scene 1 of Cranach Presse *Hamlet*, translated by Gerhart Hauptmann, illustrated by Gordon Craig, 1928.

FIGURE 19. Kessler, just before
exile, 1933.

FIGURE 20. Kessler, signing the
French version of his memoirs,
October 26, 1936.

CHAPTER 17

Pax Germania

Concerning the Polish problem what the old Herr von Briest in Fontane's lovely novel liked to say still applies: "That is a wide field."

Bernhard von Bülow,
Aus dem Leben eines Optimisten

As soon as it became clear that Poland might fall into their laps, the Central Powers began to quarrel about its fate.[1] Fearful of granting the Poles an independence they saw as potentially dangerous to their own borders, the governments of Germany and Austria-Hungary were also unwilling to absorb more Poles into their populations. They vacillated for more than a year, both governments wanting to use the prospect of regaining Poland as a bait to entice Russia into a separate peace but at the same time concerned about each other's ambitions. There was, in fact, no clean solution to the conundrum, as time would prove.

From the very beginning, Kessler argued that the Germans should restore a Polish state that would be firmly enmeshed in Germany's military and economic sphere. Once the proper strategic strongholds and the right to use and build railroads had been secured, then Germany could allow the Poles "every freedom, even political, which they consider desirable: their own government, own parliament, own finances (even, as far as I am concerned, their own king, although I would prefer a personal union with the German emperor), perhaps even their own customs union, and naturally Polish as the national language, and above

237

all complete freedom for the church."[2] In return for this freedom, Kessler insisted that the new state give up definitively any claims to the Prussian province of Posen and West Prussia. In fact, he anticipated that the Prussian Poles would emigrate back to Poland thus solving permanently Germany's Polish problem.

This kind of Poland would, of course, be little more than a German satellite. Kessler doubted whether a truly independent Polish state would ever be viable. Although he found the Poles personally attractive, he shared the common German assumption that they were incapable of governing themselves. "Poland itself, even the population, I like very much. It is a beautiful, noble, (yet) unfortunately too idealistic and childish race," he wrote to Hofmannsthal, "while we fight for their land, they lie in the churches and pray. The Polish Legionnaires, very young, good looking lads, occupy themselves chiefly, as far as I can judge, by running around in the villages and admiring their pretty uniforms. I have yet to see one at the front. The Poles will never rule themselves. That is already clear to me. Just the Jews would make any complete independence of Poland into a complete disaster for the Poles."[3]*

Kessler's vision of Poland's future resembles, for the most part, the ideas of Ludendorff and others at OHL (Oberste Heeresleitung, or Supreme Headquarters), as well as the plans of ardent German annexationists, such as the Pan-Germans. Clearly, Poland's "independence" would be a facade, allowing the Germans to exploit Polish natural resources and, in fact, reducing that nation to a supplier of food and raw materials for Germany. The provisions for allowing the Poles the maximum amount of democracy within carefully determined confines seem intended actually to weaken Poland's autonomy even further by keeping the Poles fighting among themselves, although Kessler does not state this explicitly. Most chilling of all in the light of subsequent history, is Kessler's insistence on large-scale population transfers that would result in the final "Germanization" of the traditionally Polish provinces

---

* Kessler's remarks on the Jews he found in Poland are in general filled with loathing. As always, however, when he meditated on the Jews, Kessler expressed a somewhat grudging admiration for what he considered their tenacity and will. Perhaps the only really viable national state that had a chance in these territories would be a Jewish one, he speculated to Bodenhausen. "The Jews, it is true, are not in the majority, and represent only 30 to 40% of the population, but live everywhere, have the land economically in their hands, are ambitious and hardworking. Up to now they have only lacked the military and moral talent, and perhaps also the historical opportunity to rule." Simon, *Ein Briefwechsel,* August 25, 1915, 101–2.

of Prussia. Here too his ideas echoed those of Ludendorff, the younger staff officers at OHL, and the Pan-German fantasies.[4]

To what extent were Kessler's views at all influential? He certainly intended them to be. His long, carefully composed letters from the front, mixing firsthand accounts of the fighting with political reflections, were copied and distributed to friends, among them Gustav Richter; Gerhard von Mutius; Bodenhausen and his wife, Dora; Helene and Alfred von Nostitz; and Hofmannsthal. The two most influential among them were undoubtedly Bodenhausen and Mutius. The former, although already suffering from the effects of overwork and stress that would kill him in the spring of 1918, had an important position at Krupp Armaments Company and knew most of the leading German industrialists and bankers. Mutius, another friend of Kessler's from the university and the first years in Berlin, was the nephew of Bethmann-Hollweg and was eventually appointed councilor to the civil government that the Germans set up in Poland. Some of Kessler's circulated letters reached the chancellor therefore, either directly through Mutius or through Clemens Delbrück, the state secretary of the interior.[5] Bodenhausen informed him that he had given his letters to Gustav von Krupp, who in turn had shown them to Gottlieb von Jagow, the secretary of state. And, of course, Kessler met with Bethmann-Hollweg at the time of his first leave in Berlin.

It is impossible to determine what effect, if any, Kessler's opinions had on the chancellor's views regarding Poland, either directly or through his nephew. Other, far more powerful people than Kessler, advocated the same policy: namely, the creation of an "independent" Polish state. In any case, on November 5, 1916, the Central Powers announced in Warsaw and Lublin their promise to create a Polish state, with a hereditary monarchy and a constitution. The new state was to have its own army, the organization, training, and leadership of which was to be decided in joint consultation with Germany and Austria-Hungary.[6] By the time of the proclamation, Kessler had long since been transferred to the West, and his diaries and letters do not betray what he thought of it. The hopes that he and others put into the Polish state were not, however, to be fulfilled. The reasons are too many to enumerate, but eventually the Germans would be forced to imprison the very man around whom they had hoped to raise a pro-German army of volunteers, Josef Pilsudski. Only when the war was clearly lost, in October 1918, did they recognize the error they had made. Someone in the Foreign Office remembered that Kessler, now in Switzerland, had met

Pilsudski one cold morning in October 1915, and decided that it was up to Kessler to free the future leader of Poland from prison and to begin to make amends for a botched policy.

. . .

In one important respect, Kessler differed from the ardent, Pan-German, annexationists, a difference that would have far-reaching consequences. He recognized that long-term German domination of the East ultimately would have to rest on cultural, not military, hegemony. The lasting command of one people over another cannot rest on violence, "but rather only on a human type, which has developed within a dominant people and which is attractive to other peoples. . . . That is the problem of a German domination of the world." The more he looked, the more he despaired. The apparent coming triumph of men like Klewitz made the future of German culture itself problematic, not to mention the creation of a cultural ideal to which other peoples would be attracted. "Next to the superficial peace questions (new borders, new alliances and spheres of influence), there is an inner one; that is, through which inner values and creations will Germany retroactively justify her victory and her position, like Phidias justified Pericles . . . or Racine and Voltaire justified Richelieu and Louis XIV?" he mused in his diary. Earlier, he had written that victory on the battlefield, victory through violence, would not be enough. Germany must also overthrow the culture of its principal enemies. Here violence was secondary, even perhaps irrelevant, because such a cultural triumph, if at all possible, might have occurred without a war.[7] With an eye to the cultural justification of Germany's imminent victory, Kessler scanned the literary journals, the art exhibitions, and the theaters of wartime Germany. Eventually, he would find the avatars of a new and vibrant culture in the most unlikely of candidates: the deserters, war resisters, pacifists, and even drug addicts of the expressionist generation.

As the second winter of the war approached, no imminent end to the fighting seemed in sight. Perhaps, Kessler mused, by April the Germans would receive peace offers from their enemies, if the war went as well for them as it had in the last months. But to even think of it seemed presumptuous. Meanwhile, the eastern front had subsided into that quiet and uncomfortable tedium that is the background for war's horrors. Kessler's diary records no significant fighting during the winter, only the dispiriting business of occupying a foreign land. At the beginning of March, for example, he witnessed the execution of six young Russians for sabotage. One of them did not die easily, biting the rope so that another noose had to be brought and then biting the arm of the gendarme who wanted to hang him. Such incidents gnawed at the moral élan Kessler had felt during the great campaign of the 1915 summer. By the spring of 1916, the war news was dominated by the massive German offensive unleashed against the ancient French fortress of Verdun.

Kessler first learned of Verdun on February 22, one day after the methodically planned German attack began with an artillery bombardment of more than a million shells. At first, the news described dramatic German advances against a bewildered and demoralized French opponent. In the first five days of combat, the French lost 25,000 men, a rate of nearly three to one in favor of the attackers. Yet, by February 29, the Germans had lost more than 25,000 men as well. After the initial disarray, French resistance stiffened under the leadership of General Henri Pétain. French artillery struck back with deadly effect at the exposed German batteries, which, according to the German plan, had to be advanced to match the movement of the troops. Moreover, the advancing German infantry discovered that the bombardment had by no means eliminated French machine gun nests, which took a heavy toll. Verdun was well on the way to becoming the eponymous term for trench warfare hell.[8] Rumors of the slaughter quickly spread throughout the German army. By the beginning of March, Kessler found it difficult to concentrate on anything else, so great was the tension surrounding Verdun. A few days later, he learned of his regiment's imminent transfer to Verdun.

Before the transfer, he received leave to visit Berlin. He arrived in the middle of March 1916, and once again encountered the pessimism and fatigue he had discovered a year ago. Bodenhausen, whose experience of the war had not included the occupation of cities evacuated by a retreating enemy but rather the strain of industrial production in a time of blockade, was deeply worried about the economic course of the war. He expressed grave doubts as to whether Germany could continue longer than the coming fall. Walther Rathenau was only marginally more optimistic. Above all, the food situation was cause for concern. During his leave, Kessler was invited to the home of Prince Max Lichnowsky, the German ambassador in England at the time of the outbreak of the war. The prince, an independent and somewhat eccentric figure, expressed the most violent contempt for the conservative militarists and the Pan-Germans, arguing that the only political party with a correct view of the war was the Socialists. During the war, Lichnowsky would distribute a number of accounts of the July crisis that put the blame for the war squarely on the shoulders of the German government, a deed for which he would be roundly condemned as a traitor by most of his class but thoroughly exonerated by historians today.[9] Although in time Kessler too would have the experience of being attacked for betraying his class, at the time he considered Lichnowsky "cracked," a would-be Mirabeau of the German revolution but without the necessary gifts.

It was at the Lichnowskys, however, that Kessler met Johannes Becher. Lichnowsky's beautiful, unconventional, and talented wife, Melchtilde von und zu Arco-Zinneberg, shared with Kessler an interest in supporting young literary and artistic talent. Among her recent "finds" was the young expressionist poet Becher, ashen and drawn, not simply from literary exertion but as a result of his addiction to morphine. Kessler had read already his first volume of poetry, *Verfall und Triumph,* in Kowel in February 1916 and written an enthusiastic letter to Helene von Nostitz about his discovery. Upon meeting Becher in person, Kessler immediately felt the impulse to take him under his wing, just as he had done with Maillol. He invited the poet to see *Macbeth* together with Gustav Richter. After the theater, Becher, who was bit of a mythomaniac, regaled his new patron with Gothic tales of his family life, rife with savage hates and incest. All through the beginning of April, Kessler acted as the young man's cicerone, taking him to Berlin's museums and eventually inviting him to Weimar, where he made the acquaintance of van de Velde and Elisabeth Förster-Nietzsche.[10]

Becher's poetry belongs to the vatic, exclamatory school of expressionism that has faded so quickly in our literary evaluation, compared to the more sardonic, clipped, and ironic style represented by Franz Kafka, Frank Wedekind, Carl Sternheim, and others. Today Becher's willfully naive rhetoric rings hollow, inflated and flat at the same time. Seen from the point of view of his literary production, it comes as no surprise that the fragile, troubled morphine addict of the war years should metamorphose into the self-styled "proletarian" poet of the Weimar period and end up, having survived the Nazis and exile in the Soviet Union, the poet laureate of "the first German workers' state." The same rhapsodic pathos runs like a monotonous thread through his much too voluminous work. A few poems have survived the general debacle, but it seems safe to say that there will be no revival of Becher's work.

Such a literary judgment, however, obscures the historic reception of Becher in particular and prophetic expressionism in general. At the time, this ecstatic rhapsodizing, with its vague but ardent humanitarianism and its unqualified individualism, did seem different, fresher, more youthful, especially against the background of the reams and reams of pedestrian war poetry churned out by the older generation, the likes of Dehmel and Schröder. Although the expressionists would have denied it, at a deeper level their poetry did nevertheless share some of the same spirit as the "war poetry" they so despised. The common chord was *Aufbruch,* that evocative German word lacking any English equivalent ("awakening," "new beginning," "departure," and so forth are only approximations). At least some of the war poetry written in the aftermath of August struck the same note of liberation from a world gone stale and old.[11] Indeed, numerous artists and writers of the first expressionist generation marched off eagerly to battle, where many of them perished. If, after the first shock of combat, the survivors began to turn against the war, the rejection, in some cases, was that of bitterly disappointed lovers.

At any rate, this connection is what seemed to have attracted Kessler to Becher. Somehow, in this most unmilitary presence, he sensed a kinship with the young front-line officers he admired. Kessler had a long-standing weakness for prophetic poetry. In 1910, while working on the Dehmel essay he never finished, he rediscovered Walt Whitman. Earlier, he had stumbled on some dull passages, but, as he wrote to his sister, "now I have got the right thing and find him one of the most marvelous, most deeply human and moving writers of the nineteenth century, and a very great poet into the bargain. Get his 'Leaves of Grass' and read 'In cabin'd ships' and the 'Song of Myself' and tell me whether certain passages are not as fine as anything that has ever been written. The sense of *Life,* of the beauty and heroism of *all* life, no poet I think has ever expressed so grandly. Certain of his litanies are like those passages in Bach, where the whole universe seem to chime in." This same exultant pantheistic celebration of life he found in Becher, although he did not hesitate to criticize the more polemical poems as "empty declamation."[12]

In his autobiography, Becher credits Kessler with having saved him quite literally from starvation. Indeed, Kessler not only provided him with money, but also permitted him to stay at his home in Weimar while he was away, despite reports from his servants of his protégé's misbehavior. Breakfasting alone with Ilse Hadwiger, Becher's lover, Kessler learned that Becher was a pathological liar, that he beat her, and that he threw around too much money now that Kessler was supporting him, accusations that Kessler found all too believable. All of this, however, did not prevent Kessler from interceding on behalf of Becher with his old friend Anton Kippenberg, the head of the Insel publishing house. Although Kippenberg's wife Katherina was among the most generous and ardent supporters of both Becher and the new expressionist generation of writers, her husband had considerably more doubts about a literature so very far removed from the introspective aestheticism of Rilke, Hofmannsthal, and the others with whom Insel had made its mark. To allay these reservations and strengthen his nerve, Kessler wrote to assure him that, in Becher, the Insel Verlag had acquired the greatest talent in German literature since the appearance of Rilke. After praising Becher's poetry, he then played upon Kippenberg's anti-Semitic prejudices, particularly where the great expressionist publishing house founded by Kurt Wolff was concerned: "That, thanks to your intervention, this struggle and process of maturing can take place in a more peaceful, upright, and above all not in a *Semitic* atmosphere, is quite invaluable. He himself has, as you know, absolutely no Jewish traits, thank God; is a grandnephew of Bassermann and the painter Gussow, pure southern German, *allemannish-fränkisch,* from the race which has given us Goethe, Hölderlin, Mörike, Stefan George. All of this seems to me a good omen." [13] Kessler and the Lichnowskys had agreed to send Becher to a sanatorium for three months to be cured of his drug addiction. After that, they would provide him with 300 marks a month for the next three years. Thanks in part to Kessler's intervention, Insel agreed to pay Becher an additional 100 marks per month for the next four years in return for an option on any books he might produce in this period. There was no clause for repayment. In return for this generosity, the poet dedicated a number of poems to his patron:

> Tender of the sick. Consoles. Helper of the poor.
> Shepherds of the unsteady, lost people. The lamentably confused.
> Tirelessly teaching it. Raising it to a beaming
> Sun tower of the most fraternal community.

And so forth. Kessler does not record whether he was happy with this reward for his troubles. He did reflect on his relation to Becher as a patron. "I corrupt him, perhaps intentionally. His father is supposed to have said, 'Geniuses should starve.' I say the opposite: a genius must have money; only then can it be proven whether it is genuine, whether it has power." [14] Underneath Becher's hypersensitive and soft exterior lay a brutal core. His pacifism was only a way of disguising and repressing this brutality. Clearly, Kessler considered the man to be an unfinished product.

Most of Kessler's friends and contemporaries from the days of *Pan* could not share his enthusiasm, either for Becher or for expressionism. Kessler was quite astonished to learn that Bodenhausen, for example, rejected Becher utterly and had never heard the names of Franz Werfel or Theodor Däubler. Kessler's unconstrained surprise irritated his old friend. Troubled and angered, Bodenhausen wrote to Hofmannsthal expressing his dismay:

He (Kessler) is very fresh; for my feelings however a little too impetuous in relation to modern literature etc. He seems restlessly to experience what all but the fewest people can experience, and what I had always wished for myself: not to lose contact, even in advanced years, with the latest manifestations of artistic production. That he at the same time, as corresponds to his nature, even now exaggerates all of this, is probably the necessary pendant to such a talent. He has discovered a new poet, named Becher, with whom he is together uninterruptedly, either at his home or at the Lichnowskys. This man, with whom he wanted to bring us together, something I quite emphatically rejected, he considers a real genius. A long conversation, which I had with him recently, took place in the most cheerful form, but was nevertheless very disturbing for me and cost me around a night's sleep. He speaks of two persons, called Werfel and Deubler [*sic*], approximately like we speak of Titian and Rembrandt, or of Keller and Hebbel. That I had never heard both names, aroused his endless astonishment and pitying amazement. At the same time he doesn't think much of either, especially not of Werfel, but declares nevertheless that Werfel represents a turning point in the history of German literature, and considers now the production of Becher for a first example of perfection within this new literature. I myself have discovered in the stuff of Becher . . . some poems which appear to be strong. But exactly these appear, in the eyes of connoisseurs, to be more or less out-dated and full of clichés. Everything else fills me with the most honest disgust, and to be sure both regarding the content and the form. . . . (Kessler) concluded, in a worried manner, that my strenuous activity in the last 10 years had damaged my receptivity, especially in regards to my contact with vital life.[15]

There could be no better expression of the mixture of anxiety, bewilderment, and contempt with which the first generation of modernists in Germany looked upon the new rebels. Where once Bodenhausen could have exclaimed in Kessler's Weimar house, "We don't know nearly enough, what kind of spring in which we are living!" now it was quite apparent that, for Bodenhausen at least, spring was over. He was sensitive enough to regret it and to realize that there was a core of truth to Kessler's argument that his employment at Krupp had numbed his ability to remain in tune with the avant-garde. He still could not forgive Kessler for his still vital connection to the emerging art and literature. Neither, for that matter, could the recipient of his letter. Hofmannsthal, in his response to Bodenhausen, let himself go. Mockingly, he wrote of Kessler's "eternal understanding," of the "intimacy with the entire world, which such a Philinte summons for every, but every emerging form of art. I don't know, perhaps I am unjust, but he bets on *every* horse that's in the running—I find that deadly boring." More damning still was his assertion that "Kessler solves nothing, nothing in the spirit, because he, as sad as it is to say, does not live." [16]

Such a bitter accusation, which rehashes the old charge that Kessler was so open to the new that he lacked the character provided by the old, stemmed in large part no doubt from Hofmannsthal's own sense of growing estrangement from his time, an alienation only deepened by the increasingly evident futility of any regeneration of the Austrian state. This path would eventually lead him to embrace a conservative "return to tradition," the political consequences of which his death in 1929 would spare him from witnessing. Kessler, on the other hand, understood almost instinctively the moral value of not losing touch with the art and literature of the younger generation, even if he too, despite the comments of Bodenhausen and Hofmannsthal, could not fully embrace all of it. In a passage that reads like a response to the criticism leveled by Hofmannsthal, he wrote, "The coffeehouse culture (Café des Westens) is narrow and flat, but it lives; this little bit of life differentiates it, to its advantage, from all 'Bildung.' Deeper still would be a familiarity with culture, which would unite the range of our so-called Bildung with the liveliness of the coffeehouse. In Paris, Weimar, Florence, Athens (there was) such a fructification. To take culture personally, to penetrate with the look of hate and love, to be malicious and unjust, even confused, but to be a part with all one's heart." [17] Whatever his talents as a poet, Becher provided Kessler with many personal links not only to young artists and writers more important than himself, but to the pacifists working against both the war and the system that produced it.

Characteristically, at the same time that he cultivated these contacts with coffeehouse denizens, Kessler circulated at the highest level of the policy-making elite of Imperial Germany. Of course, he had known many of these people before the war, but now the relationship was formalized when, in July 1916, he was elected a member of the "Wednesday Society," an elite club, limited to seventy members, which met every Wednesday evening in the Hotel Continental in Berlin to discuss the direction of German politics. The discussions of the Wednesday Society were confidential and wide ranging. The club permitted a freer exchange of opinions than would have been possible in most other forums. The advantage of such clubs—several were formed during the war—according to Kessler was that they "established connections, in what was for Germany a completely new form, between the government on the one hand, and members of parliament, journalists, leaders of industry, bankers, and people from every department of public life on the other; and by means of these easy and unceremonious relationships they often exerted more influence on German policy and the direction of the war, especially in its critical moments, than did the censored press, or 'public opinion,' or even the houses of parliament, which after all sat within hearing of the Entente." [18]

On April 16, 1916, he departed Berlin for the western front and the battlefield of Verdun. His general impression of Berlin was that it was the economic, not the military, situation that was cause for concern. Although he anticipated that the coming months would be difficult, especially in terms of food supplies, he still thought the country would see the crisis through. Peace was another matter. He could not imagine it arriving in the fall, and Russia would not be ready until the Ukraine had been wrested from her.

The day before his departure, Kessler finished the last sitting for a bust that Georg Kolbe was making of him, at the sculptor's request. Three examples were cast, one of which Kessler bought for a thousand marks and eventually gave to Wilma. It is a very fine sculpture. With tightly pressed lips and sad eyes, he stares into an uncertain future.

The mood at the German headquarters in Charleville, behind the battlefield of Verdun, was a thousand miles away from the triumphant air that reigned on the eastern front. Falkenhayn's offensive had gone sour as the French rallied from their initial shock and the losses of the Germans mounted. No one at headquarters had a clue as to the commander-in-chief's intentions, Kessler discovered: the Germans exhausted themselves in little, seemingly pointless attacks. Indeed, the day before he arrived, the Germans had barely surmounted a crisis, one that nearly cost them the fort of Douaumont, their greatest conquest so far in the offensive. For the first time in his experience, he noted alarming rumors of demoralization among the frontline soldiers: "The fellows make very obvious preparations for attacking, stick their heads out of the trenches so that the French notice it, and then , when the red flare goes off above the enemy lines and the artillery and machine guns begin firing, they say: Spoiling fire, the assault is impossible, and everyone remains happily at home." Nor, on this front, were the generals behind the lines necessarily safe: several times in Charleville, Kessler was subject to the new and unnerving torment of aerial bombardment. Even the perennial optimist was daunted: "Everyone among us sees the madness of this mass slaughter," he noted two days after he arrived.[19] But how to end it?

Certainly, Germany's leadership did not inspire confidence. Aside from the grumbling about Falkenhayn, a general mood of discouragement prevailed at headquarters, where Kessler was constantly told that no decisive victory could be won in the West. At the end of April, the kaiser arrived to celebrate a field service with the troops. At close range Kessler observed his sovereign: "He has become very gray but looks healthy, even if, as it seems to me, less energetic and brutal than before." The service was not up to the occasion, "any depth or warmth of heart was missing in this otherwise so historical moment when a German emperor holds a service with his troops in his headquarters in France."[20]

In the middle of May, Kessler took part as an observation officer in the bitter fighting around Hill 304 and the eponymous summit known as Mort Homme. His diary entries are spare, laconically noting the high losses and the pessimism at headquarters. At this point, he appears to have suffered a nervous breakdown for by May 20 he was back in Germany, visiting Bodenhausen in Essen. He never would return to witness fighting again. Now forty-eight years old, Kessler for some time had felt the multiple physical and mental strains of the war. Verdun was the final straw then, not only because of the nature of the battle but because here he was fighting against the soldiers of one of his three "homelands." It must have often occurred to him that his former lover, Gaston Colin, to whom he was still sending money via his sister from time to time, may well have been serving in the trenches opposite. His highly placed connections on the home front had begun to concoct a plan to employ their cosmopolitan friend where his talents might be more gainfully employed. It took the summer to arrange matters, but at the beginning of September, he set out on a new task, as the cultural attaché to the German embassy in Switzerland. His real mission, however, was to explore the possibility of a separate peace with France.[21]

CHAPTER 18

Propaganda and Peace Feelers

Every moment in the life of an individual has become a
battlefield of the opposing parties. Nothing escapes politics.
                                                        Kessler, *Tagebuch*

It must have been initially a relief for Kessler to escape from the rumors,
unsubstantiated gossip, and idleness of his life in wartime Berlin and en-
train for Switzerland with the alluring prospect of undertaking a significant diplomatic mission for his country. He had spent an anxious
summer, worrying about such developments as the British offensive on
the Somme; the Russian "Brusilov" offensive in the Carpathians, which
threatened for a moment to crush Austria; the Rumanian declaration of
war on the Central Powers; and the replacement of Falkenhayn by Hindenburg and Ludendorff, which was, in Kessler's own words, a "coup
d'état," a de facto dictatorship.[1] In a Zurich seemingly untouched by
food rationing, he indulged himself in a beefsteak, accompanied by coffee with real cream. Characteristically, after dinner he tried unsuccessfully to find the Cabaret Voltaire in the Spiegelgasse, where for the last
several months Emily Hennings, Hugo Ball, and others had been inventing the Dada movement. Even before his appointment with Baron
Romberg, the German ambassador and Kessler's direct superior, he met
Louis Caillon, the young Frenchman with whom he had had a romantic epistolary relation during the last few months of peace. Caillon, now
an attaché at the French embassy, expressed his conviction that France
would win.[2]

As attractive as a post in Switzerland must have appeared at this point, Kessler was not willing to settle for anything. When he learned that Romberg wanted him to reside unofficially in western Switzerland (the French-speaking part) and establish connections, he rejected this as "smelling too much of espionage." As he had explained in an earlier letter to Bodenhausen, "sitting around in Switzerland, half as 'secret agent,' half as shirker is completely impossible for my feelings. . . . I also do not believe that it would be tenable over the long run, for it would quickly be seen through and therefore rendered useless." Instead, Kessler proposed that he receive an official appointment from the Foreign Office in Berlin that would not be made public, thus giving him the appearance of independence but at the same time the authority to enter into serious negotiations. To avoid upsetting Romberg, he offered repeated assurances that he would pass all his reports to the embassy in Bern rather than sending them directly to Berlin. The Foreign Office eventually agreed to this plan, confiding to Kessler, in its official if still secret appointment, a double mission: to prepare cultural propaganda inside Switzerland and to explore the prospects of a separate peace with whatever reliable French interlocutors he could find.[3]

Even during the war, many Germans believed that they were losing the propaganda battle. "Reuter rules the market, not Wolff; London makes foreign opinion not Berlin. We Germans have remained despite all our exertions as regards impressing foreign opinion, the same bunglers we always were," lamented a German newspaper in 1917. After the war, given the predilection of leading Germans to blame their defeat on domestic moral subversion rather than on the military strength of the Entente, this belief intensified. "We were hypnotized by Allied propaganda as is a rabbit by a snake," wrote Erich von Ludendorff in his memoirs. Like other ideas cherished by many Germans about the cunning British secret service, or the elaborate machinations of British diplomacy, the alleged diabolic efficacy of anti-German propaganda proves to be, upon objective examination, largely a myth. If, nonetheless, it is undeniably true that Allied propaganda was more effective in neutral countries than its German counterpart, it was largely because of certain fundamental advantages enjoyed by Germany's opponents rather than due to any innate cleverness on their part. For one thing, Great Britain and France controlled both the seas and the international cable network. Even more important, the German invasion of Belgium, and the scandals that accompanied it, including the destruction of the library at Louvain and the shooting of civilian hostages, put the Germans in a defensive position from the very beginning. Finally, egregious errors by the Germans, most notably the execution of the British nurse Edith Clavell and the ill-fated Zimmermann telegram, contributed in no small part to the success of the Allies in this field.[4] *

The Germans were becoming increasingly aware of these problems, and that is why Ambassador Romberg listened with interest to Kessler's proposal for a wide-ranging program of cultural propaganda, including theater, music performances, and art exhibitions but also variety shows and "pretty girls." Having received Romberg's approval, Kessler traveled to Berlin to seek the imprimatur from the Foreign Office, to arrange financing, and to enlist artists, directors, and agents. When he heard details of Kessler's plans, Jagow, the secretary of state in the Foreign Office, laughed and said, "I see you want a fund for the corruption of the Swiss." He granted him 500,000 marks as a beginning and warned him against inviting German professors to give lectures: "One can't let the German professor loose without him becoming tactless." As a sign of the new political arrangements in Germany, Jagow also informed Kessler that his plans would have to be approved by the High Command as well. The newly appointed military head for foreign propaganda, Captain Hans von Haeften, told Kessler that Ludendorff was especially keen on organizing film propaganda, especially in Switzerland where, in Ludendorff's opinion, "it was a quarter to midnight" due to Swiss sympathy for the Allied cause. Consequently, Kessler arrived at army headquarters in Pless at the beginning of November 1916 to discuss his plans with Ludendorff. Still under the sway of the man whom Bodenhausen was shortly to describe to him as "dictator Germanae," Kessler seemed to notice a change in Ludendorff's demeanor: "in place of his earlier, somewhat curt, hard manner, a glowing and mild amiability has appeared; he undergoes the transition from officer to *grand seigneur.* He listened smiling but with full attention to my proposal, followed it on the charts, which I had brought with me, asked questions which were always clever and trenchant, and finally approved the whole thing with enthusiasm.[5]

---

* Edith Clavell was a British nurse captured by the Germans in Belgium and executed for helping Allied soldiers escape. A statue of her stands near Trafalgar Square in London. The Zimmermann telegram refers to the message sent by German Foreign Secretary Arthur Zimmermann to the Mexican government urging them to join Germany in the event of war with the United States. Intercepted by British intelligence and made known in the United States, it contributed to the American decision to enter the war against Germany.

At the same time, Kessler was enlisting both old and new friends. Among the old was Max Reinhardt whose Deutsches Theater Kessler hoped to bring to Switzerland for a series of guest performances. In Weimar, he asked the beleaguered van de Velde to give lectures on non-political subjects, although privately he sneered that his old friend could not "despite all his desired and imagined cosmopolitanism eliminate this 'Belgianness' out of his blood."[6] The Grand Duke of Hesse was enlisted to send his court opera. Then it was down to Vienna to recruit Richard Strauss at the premiere of *Ariadne;* there he met Hofmannsthal and had to listen skeptically to the latter expatiate on the future of Austria.

All of this represented more or less the past. Kessler's new friends were much more interesting. Through his old friend from *Pan,* Julius Meier-Graefe, he met Annette Kolb, the novelist and writer, born of a German father and French mother, with whom he would become close friends in Switzerland and who would be his partner in the effort to foster reconciliation between France and Germany in the postwar world. "A very original, courageous, elderly person," Kessler described her to his sister, "She is very extreme and excitable . . . tremendously plucky and *payant de sa personne.*" Kolb in turn spoke to him of René Schickele, the Alsatian writer and editor of the avant-garde, expressionist journal *Die weissen Bättern,* which had moved to Bern from Leipzig to escape wartime censorship. The Entente had offered him, she said, 80,000 marks if he would take up a "J'accuse" standpoint against Germany, but he had refused. Back in Switzerland, Kessler caught up with Schickele: "He is small and blond, a small blond southwest German with a Gallic temperament; Alsatian in his views, *großdeutsch,* but anti-Prussian and friendly to the French. He wants the old Reich, an elected Kaiser with democratic and particularistic institutions; 'German intellectual world hegemony.' I objected that an intellectual imperialism without a political backbone would make the German into a kind of Jew."[7]

These differences aside, Kessler was looking precisely for someone like Schickele and for a journal such as *Die weissen Blätter.* Just prior to his meeting with Schickele, he had explained to a correspondent of the *Frankfurter Zeitung* that a journal founded for propaganda purposes must have a living kernel, must be entertaining, and must include very short articles from all of Germany's best writers.[8] Such a latitudinarian approach could easily accommodate the idiosyncratic political views of someone like Schickele. Even more surprising, however, were other objects of Kessler's patronage, both personal and official. One day in September, for example, Becher brought Wieland Herzfelde to Kessler's apartment for breakfast. A young man of twenty, Herzfelde had founded a journal entitled *Neue Jugend* (*New Youth*) in July. The name was guaranteed to attract Kessler's interest, but Herzfelde, who had suffered terribly as a soldier in Flanders during the first months of the war, made no secret of his bitter opposition to the war, believing it would end in a huge catastrophe. He did promise, however, when Kessler replied that he neither shared nor understood this view, to leave politics out of the journal entirely in return for financial support. Impressed by the energetic and good-looking Herzfelde, Kessler was assuaged by this rather weak promise and gave him 500 marks as a beginning. Comparing the two men, he noted, "Herzfelde is the stronger and harder: Becher seems in comparison like a soft and dreamy enthusiast." As hard as Herzfelde, at least in their radical opposition to the war, were his brother, Hellmuth, who would, under the name John Heartfield, become the most famous photomontage artist of the Weimar period, and their mutual friend and collaborator, Georg Grosz. Visiting Grosz in his studio, Kessler observed the "richness and thickness of the drawing and color. He says, Peter Breughel is his master, Seurat as well. . . . There is something of futurism in his works, but actually he is a naturalist, refuses to be abstract like so many today, to ignore reality. His figure drawings are in fact brutally true, a continuation of the northern German, Berlin tradition of Schadow, Menzel, Liebermann, in its ruthless ugliness completely unFrench. . . . I think highly of Grosz. There's something demonical in him."[9] Despite his enormous political differences with these young people, Kessler was ready, in a way scarcely imaginable for others of his generation, to recognize and support talent that pointed to the future. Just as he had with Becher, he would intervene to save them from the consequences of their anti-war activities, rescuing Herzfelde, for example, from being condemned to a penal battalion for "defeatism" and procuring for him a more comfortable job behind the lines as a radio announcer.*

* There Herzfelde spent his time, instead of transmitting information from the front lines, sending messages to the rear like "Where is our mail?" or dropping acid into the battery of a radio. When, predictably, this got him into trouble again, he wrote to Kessler once more for help, disingenuously claiming that his career in the radio may be over because "I have been sick a few times and too nervous to work, or perhaps am not mechanical enough"; see Herzfelde, *Immergrün*, 203; Herzfelde to Kessler, January 14, 1918, KN.

Soon word got out that the German attaché in Bern was unusually tolerant of political differences and supportive of avant-garde writers and artists. Romain Rolland noted it with envy: "The German consulate does not create trouble for their exiled, progressive compatriots like our consulates do. Count Kessler in Bern, who is responsible for German cultural propaganda, is a person of very fine taste and generous character, who takes German artists and intellectuals under his wings even when they are revolutionarily inclined." [10] In Annette Kolb's roman à clef about the war in Switzerland, *Zarastro,* a certain "Count Carry" is always willing to help exiles who are persecuted or threatened by military service, if he can find a way to bend the rules.

Naturally, the same acts praised as disinterested generosity by some appeared to others as bordering on treachery. Although the Foreign Office wanted its agents to maintain friendly relations with German pacifists for the sake of exploring contacts with the Entente, it soon received reports highly critical of Kessler's activities. Romberg felt compelled to defend his subordinate: "First one must remark that admittedly perhaps too much was done during the last year in the field of art propaganda. This is easily explained by the eagerness with which this new and certainly not unimportant area of our propaganda activity was tackled here. But, in my opinion, one shouldn't only criticize but rather acknowledge exactly that eagerness with which Count Kessler and his collaborators have dedicated themselves to this great and difficult task, and have the goodness not to overlook what has been accomplished." Romberg's defense did nothing to lower the increasing volume and bitterness of the criticism to which Kessler was subjected, as we shall see. Nevertheless, toward the end of May 1918, Kessler for a time imagined that he might actually be named chief of the entire German propaganda effort. "The work would be strenuous, the gratitude nothing, the personal slander doubtless enormous. I would approach the task with hesitation, without knowing whether I am really up to it. A catastrophe is possible at the end. But if I can accomplish it and can hold out, and peace negotiations come, this position is certainly of a scarcely measurable importance since public opinion depends on it." [11] Kessler would be, as he said, "spared" from this task when the General Staff chose someone else instead. Romberg tried to console him, blaming the decision on the military's virtual dictatorship of wartime Germany.

Kessler was able to get away with what he did in part because of his uniquely independent arrangement within the confused and overlapping German propaganda apparatus. Inasmuch as, in effect, his position had been created especially for him through the intervention of influential friends, he did not have to work through layers of bureaucracy, but instead not only reported directly to Romberg, but also had unusual direct access to the highest levels at the Foreign Office, the Chancellery, and Army High Command. Critical to all of this was his good relationship with Ambassador Romberg. Kessler discovered quickly his immediate superior's fundamental pessimism about Germany's chances in the war. He was in favor of making large concessions to France so that it could feel that it also had won the war. After listening to this speech, Kessler noted: "Romberg's perceptions are to a large extent perfectly correct; but he sees reality without having the power to shape events, without fantasy, passive, anxious, in the mirror of a temperament used up and tired by countless small details." A little later, the Ambassador returned again to this theme, complaining that Germany ought to have let the French sleep instead of marching through Belgium: "If we had been at war with Siam, we would still have marched through Belgium," he exclaimed. "I am of a different opinion than Romberg in so many points that I can only speak to him with difficulty," was Kessler's laconic remark.[12] His discretion paid off, however, and the two men worked together for two years without too much friction.

In the burgeoning Bern embassy, which eventually employed between 500 to 600 people, Kessler had his own tiny division, encompassing propaganda in the fields of art, theater, music, film, and varieté, with at first two, and then, three permanent employees. The small size of his department belies the large amount of activity Kessler generated, due largely to his excellent personal connections. After his meetings in Berlin, he reported back to Romberg that a company, the Internationale Gastspiel-Gesellschaft, funded with an initial capital of 100,000 marks, had been formed to finance the tours of leading German musicians and artists, to establish contact with other agencies and companies in Switzerland, and to disguise the German state's sponsorship of these events.[13]

By the beginning of 1917, Kessler's program was in full gear. Reinhardt's theater group gave guest performances in Zurich, Bern, Basel, and St. Gallen at the beginning of January and then returned in June. Richard Strauss directed *Elektra, Ariadne, Zarathustra,* and *Don Quixote* in Zurich and Bern during the second half of January. The following year, the conductor Oskar Fried gave a memorable performance of Mahler's Second Symphony. Although Kessler followed Jagow's advice and eschewed inviting German professors, Hofmannsthal nevertheless delivered his "Die Idee Europa," on March 31, 1917. The visual arts received their due with exhibitions of German art in Zurich, of recent German art in Basel, and an arts and crafts exhibition of the Werkbund in Bern. In 1918, Kessler put on an expressionist exhibition, an exhibition of Swiss painting in Berlin, and a joint exhibition of Swiss and German art in Mannheim.

Naturally, the Allies, particularly the French, responded in kind. Kessler must have been struck by the irony of the Swiss reception of two art exhibitions, the first German and the second French, that took place at the Kunsthaus in Zurich in 1917. With his penchant for the new and his growing interest in expressionism, Kessler had not hesitated to include a room devoted entirely to the latest expressionist art. According to one account, this had the effect of turning off most of the Swiss public: "An attempt was made to explain this partiality (in favor of expressionism) as an engagement on behalf of the newest and therefore most native talents of Germany (after the overcoming of impressionism). Nevertheless most visitors shook thoughtfully their heads and, if they sympathized with Germany, went back home disturbed. In short, the exhibition was a decided blunder; the concurrent Werkbund exhibition in Bern, which also contained some expressionist paintings, only strengthened the impression gained in Zurich." There then followed, in the same building, an exhibition of modern French painting since the nineteenth century, including such onetime controversial postimpressionists as van Gogh and Gauguin, but eschewing the more avant-garde and contemporary fauvists or cubists. The show also contained sculptures by Rodin and Maillol. Kessler was quick to note the irony of the glowing reception, on the part of the good Swiss burghers, of the very same artists for whose sake he had suffered such humiliation in Weimar: "Degas, Gauguin, Cézanne . . . self-evident classics. Where are the times when we fought for them as for outcasts?" Instead of feeling threatened by this example of French culture, however, he welcomed it, arguing that not only the French should send their best, but the Russians their ballet as well: "then the whole propaganda would change its face, (it) would be the beginning of a new, peaceful competition, of the new Europe which precisely we Germans are striving for after the war." [14]

Although it was the fine arts that undoubtedly attracted most of his energies, Kessler did pay attention to film propaganda. Here especially the Germans were alarmed at the superior production and distribution of Allied film propaganda. Given both the prevalent bias against film as entertainment for the masses and the prewar French domination of the German market, it was not until the summer of 1916 that the government mobilized to create the Deutschen Lichtbild Gesellschaft, on the board of which sat some of Germany's most powerful industrialists and politicians, including Hjalmar Schacht, Gustav Stresemann, and Alfred Hugenberg. Hugenberg became the effective power behind the scenes in the organization, eventually coming to rule as well the great film company UFA that would emerge at the end of the war to dominate the cinema in Weimar Germany. Shuttling back forth between Berlin and Bern, negotiating with film producers in both countries, Kessler played a significant role in the growing German effort in this field, although undoubtedly, given the aesthetic quality of the material concerned, his interests here were strictly subordinated to the German war effort.[15]

Nevertheless, Kessler's involvement with film propaganda did give him the opportunity to commission what is surely one of the most bizarre propaganda projects of the entire war. On November 18, 1917, Georg Grosz and Hellmuth Herzfelde approached Kessler with a plan, which he relayed to his superiors the next day. Describing Grosz as an "exceptionally witty draftsman," Kessler explained Grosz's amusing idea of producing a kind of news chronicle in the form of monthly cartoon films, which would presumably lampoon Germany's enemies. Through Kessler's influence, they obtained, astonishingly, funds for the project. Variously entitled *Pierre in St. Nazaire* or *Sammy in Europa,* it was intended to mock the arrival of the Americans in France. "I lay," wrote Wieland Herzfelde who assisted on the project, " . . . rather uncomfortably on my belly atop a ceramic stove, since the roof was right over me, and snapped photos of the work of Grosz and Heartfield. They moved with sticks individual limbs of the figures that Grosz had drawn and Heartfield glued to cardboard. The film was made from my photographs." One of the features of the film apparently was the way Grosz had skyscrapers shooting out of French soil the minute American soldiers landed. Because work on the film spared them from being sent back to the front, all three men delayed the production of the film as long as possible. Kessler did get a preview in February 1918 but did not record his impression. When the film was finally submitted for approval, it was rejected of course, and not only because the Americans had already arrived at the front line, but also—as was to be expected from a film made by some of the most bitter critics of Prussian militarism—because of Grosz's savage depictions of German soldiers.[16]

The entrance of the United States, with its film industry and its endlessly deep pockets for propaganda purposes, upped the ante considerably in Switzerland. "The propaganda war has become through the engagement of the Americans more vehement and complicated. They have more money, we have the craftiness of our Jews, which I put into motion, and our more precise work. Every moment in life, every individual becomes the battlefield of the enemy parties. Nothing escapes politics." [17] Kessler may be forgiven this burst of exaggeration; for someone with his responsibilities, the propaganda war would appear to be all-pervasive, all-important. In fact, it was largely a sideshow, certainly in Switzerland. Ultimately, no performance of Mahler's Second Symphony, no matter how moving, no matter how strongly reinforced by other examples of German culture, was in the position to change, in any fundamental way, the outcome of the war. What did promise—at least potentially—to determine the course of the war, were the secret negotiations concerning a separate peace in which each of the major belligerent powers felt compelled to engage, however cautiously. Here is where Kessler could play the "world-historical" diplomatic role that had eluded him up until now.

．．．

Surrounded by enemies who, when added together, overwhelmed it in both manpower and productive capacity, Germany had every reason to split the Allied coalition by concluding a separate peace with one of its members, especially after the entrance of the United States meant that time was working against the Germans. The great bulk of German wartime diplomacy was directed toward this end. The Treaty of Brest-Litovsk ultimately achieved the much-needed peace with Russia but, ironically, too late to make a difference. In the case of all three of its major opponents, the German government, pressured by annexationists not to yield an inch of occupied territory, overestimated its strength and failed to make the necessary concessions to achieve a separate peace that would have changed the course of the war. [18]

The control of Alsace-Lorraine would play the same role as stumbling block in the effort to establish a Franco-German understanding, as Kessler discovered for himself. The chief diplomatic gambit of the Germans regarding separate peace feelers with the French was always to make contact with leaders of the opposition they felt might be amenable to an "honorable" peace, albeit one that preserved the essence of German domination over France. At times they thought the French socialists would play this role; they also fondly hoped that somehow the disgraced former premier Joseph Caillaux, known to be a defeatist, would, perhaps after a great French defeat, come to power. But they estimated their most realistic chances were with Aristide Briand and Paul Painlevé, both of whom held ministerial posts, including that of premier, during the war. These two French politicians, while appearing to favor "war to the bitter end," seemed flexible enough to consider a more pacific solution if the right opportunity presented itself.[19]

Despite the obstacles, Kessler threw himself into his task with his usual enthusiasm, communicating indirectly with both Briand and Painlevé. In the last summer before the war, during the hectic ballet business, he had met frequently, at the salon of the Countess Greffuhle, Bertha Zuckerkandl, née Szeps, an Austrian whose sister had married the brother of Premier Georges Clemenceau. Nevertheless, it was not this connection, however interesting, that made Mme. Paul Clemenceau such a valuable contact, but rather the fact that Painlevé had become an intimate friend and frequent guest at her salon. Zuckerkandl, like so many other would-be peacemakers, greatly overestimated the influence of family connections. She was also, quite understandably, deeply anxious that her role as intermediary should be kept quiet, especially from the Austrian Foreign Ministry.[20] The connection with Painlevé was so valuable, however, that these things were easily overlooked.

The effort to approach Painlevé and discover how he envisioned a peaceful settlement of the war came to a head in the late summer and early fall of 1917. French morale had suffered greatly in the aftermath of the disastrous Chemin des Dames offensive of April, and the Germans hoped that this failure, coupled with the prospect of a final Russian collapse and the disappointment over the American contribution to the war so far, would bring to power a "reasonable" government in France. Indeed, throughout the spring, summer, and most of the fall of 1917, France was plagued by political instability. On September 12, a cabinet headed by Painlevé actually came into power. A few months earlier, Kessler had offered this description: "Painlevé presents himself as an intransigent proponent of war. This, however, appears to be largely a facade. . . . As I know from personal meetings and talks, Painlevé is clear-headed and enjoys a rich understanding, and is therefore armed through his intelligence against a one-sided interpretation of political and economic relations." Thus, when word arrived that the Frenchman was interested in sending a trusted confidante to meet Zuckerkandl's brother, representing the Austrian government, and Kessler, representing Germany, the excitement was palpable. Kessler wrote urgently: "It is therefore of the greatest importance that we do not come with absolute empty hands, but rather bring with us some kind of presentable discussion points. Such a favorable opportunity will hardly present itself again in the foreseeable future. The French negotiator who is under question is in fact one of the most skilled and least anti-German French government officials and stands in the closest personal and political connection with the man who gave him this mission. . . . Naturally the critical thing would be the possibility of establishing somehow a common ground for discussion of the Alsatian question."

Richard von Kühlmann, the new German foreign minister (and an acquaintance of Kessler), responded discouragingly, arguing that the present moment was not appropriate for talks and ordering Kessler, should a meeting not be avoidable, to listen passively to the French views and only speak in his private capacity as an acquaintance of Painlevé.[21] In any event, the proposed meeting was repeatedly delayed for one reason or another until finally, with the collapse in November of the Painlevé government and his replacement by an energetic and militant Georges Clemenceau, the opportunity passed forever.

Kessler did not have any better luck with his second principal interlocutor, Professor Emile Haguenin, a former lecturer at the University of Berlin. Haguenin was clearly an official representative of the French government and enjoyed the confidence of Aristide Briand. Although Kessler had known him fleetingly before the war, he was reintroduced to him in Switzerland by Annette Kolb and René Schickele. The discussions between Kessler and Haguenin, which the former carefully wrote down and submitted to his superiors, are amusing to read. They follow a neatly choreographed pattern in which Kessler played the role of the aggressive suitor and Haguenin that of the coquette, with both parties seemingly more concerned to avoid admitting any war weariness on their side than to advance concrete proposals.[22]

It became quickly evident to Kessler that some compromise on the question of Alsace-Lorraine would be necessary for discussions to lead anywhere. The return of the provinces to France was politically unthinkable, short of a catastrophic German defeat. Kessler, using a hint from Schickele, hit upon the formula of granting Alsace-Lorraine autonomous status within the German Empire. As part of this deal, both the leading personalities and parties within the two provinces, as well as the French government, would declare themselves content with that solution. The French government would in addition promise to prepare public opinion to accept the issue as settled. The notion that offering Alsace-Lorraine autonomy within Germany would somehow assuage French public opinion, or at least the French socialists, became an idée fixe with Kessler.

It is a measure of the underlying gulf between the two sides that even this anodyne proposal, so unlikely in hindsight to have achieved its goal, was still bitterly resisted by most of official Germany. True, when Kessler brought it up with the new secretary of state, Arthur Zimmermann, the latter did not dismiss it out of hand but pointed out the difficulties involved inasmuch as Bavaria had already been granted certain concessions in relation to postwar Alsace-Lorraine by the government. At the same time, Zimmermann recommended *"pas trop de zèle,"* not to give the impression that Germany was too eager to woo the French, "which would in no way correspond to the military and economic situation." Further, he demanded, as minimal demands upon the French, the cessation of the Briey basin, for the sake of its high-grade iron ore; a large indemnity, although perhaps disguised to placate French vanity; and colonial concessions.[23] This was hardly a promising starting point for all but the most defeatist of French statesmen.

When Kessler returned to the subject the following October he received much the same answer. Kühlmann, who certainly favored a negotiated settlement but with England, not France, informed Kessler that the war "was not about" Alsace-Lorraine. Kessler did not give up, writing to Kühlmann a few days later from army headquarters that the German declaration that Alsace-Lorraine was a republic, similar to Hamburg and Bremen, would turn the French socialists into an active peace party. He thought there might be a majority in the Reichstag for such a resolution if Kühlmann would put in the effort, although he also noted the strong opposition to any form of autonomy in army headquarters. In fact, Ludendorff had expressly told him that it was out of the question; "Germany must have Lüttich or she would cease to be a great power." Despairing of any movement in this matter, Kessler eventually went so far as to urge a German offensive in France to compel them to give up hopes of recovering Alsace-Lorraine. When he learned of German shelling of Amiens, Reims, and Paris during their last great offensive in the spring of 1918, he even exclaimed that "the entire northern French gothic was being destroyed in this war because of the stubbornness of Clemenceau and a few Frenchmen who want above all to reconquer Alsace-Lorraine!"[24]

By May 1918, Kessler learned from a professor at the University of

Strasbourg of the true political situation in Alsace: not only was there no possibility for autonomy, but also the bourgeoisie were solidly pro-French and resentful of the German attempt, instigated by the High Command, to destroy their influence. Nevertheless, during the last desperate days of the war, when Germany had already virtually admitted defeat, Kessler, in desperation, could fantasize about the revolutionary impact of sending Schickele into Alsace-Lorraine and proclaiming its neutrality. By then it was, of course, too late. In hindsight, it is clear that the fundamental refusal of the Germans to compromise on the issue of Alsace-Lorraine doomed all of Kessler's negotiations from the start. In the words of one expert: "In particular Germany was not willing at any moment during the peace fillers to cede anything at all on Alsace-Lorraine. . . . Thus the opposition between the war aims of France and Germany prove that none of the attempts at secret negotiations had a serious chance of succeeding." [25]

Kessler had one more opportunity to engage in an important diplomatic mission before the war ended. In March 1918, the new Bolshevik regime in Russia signed the Treaty of Brest-Litovsk. Kessler had followed the events since the November revolution with interest. He was surprised at how the mounting confusion and excitement of the war, with its myriad concerns and rumors, did not permit him or others to realize fully the astonishing fact of Russia's collapse: "Perhaps, like a cosmic catastrophe, it overwhelms the human capacity for understanding." In the following months, his diary is full of thoughts on the reorganization of the East. "No annexations, rather organization. . . . So a mutually fruitful and supporting German-Slavic-Byzantine world would emerge that would reach a political and economic agreement with the Anglo-Saxon-Latin world and be able to maintain a balance with it. The engagement of Japan in Siberia identifies the third factor in our future world history." [26] Command of the East would give Germany the wherewithal to hold out against the Anglo-Saxon command of the sea, an illusion that Kessler clung to even more tenaciously as the situation in the West deteriorated for Germany during the summer and fall of 1918.

The Brest-Litovsk treaty did not, however, fulfill these great hopes. Although Germany and Russia exchanged ambassadors, the peace inaugurated remained very much a "cold" one. Both sides distrusted and disliked the other, seeing the peace as a provisional agreement and not the final settlement in the East. For Lenin, who had staked all of his personal prestige by threatening to resign if the Central Committee did not approve the treaty, Brest-Litovsk represented only a "breathing space" to allow contradictions in the capitalist camp, by which he meant the struggle between Germany and the Entente, to permit the Bolsheviks to entrench themselves. Privately, he assured his comrades concerning the treaty, "I will neither read it nor fulfill its clauses." Later, he boasted of violating its provisions thirty or forty times.[27] The Germans were deeply divided over the correct way to handle both the Bolshevik regime in particular and the situation in the East in general, a division that mirrored the larger question about Germany's chances in 1918. Kühlmann thought Germany's best hope was a compromise peace and was therefore opposed to the High Command's dreams of pushing Russia's borders back hundreds of miles. He argued that Lenin's government was the only one both willing and capable of fulfilling the terms of Brest-Litovsk (the conditions of which he felt were too harsh and would need eventually to be revised). Ludendorff and his advisors for their part certainly despised the Bolsheviks both personally and ideologically; they were also convinced that they would not last the summer. The main strategic goal of Germany in the East should be the creation of a friend and ally that would be completely dependent on Germany.[28]

Into this bitter and unbridgeable gap Kessler wished to hurl himself as mediator, overestimating certainly his influence with Ludendorff. Fundamentally, however, Kessler supported Kühlmann's position of dealing with the Bolsheviks. Another proponent of this viewpoint was Gustav Stresemann, the influential Reichstag deputy, whom Kessler had first met when Stresemann invited him for tea at his house in the fall of 1917. Although he acquired a reputation during the war as an ardent annexationist, Stresemann was a far shrewder practitioner of realpolitik than many of his conservative friends and allies. Certainly, he realized that if the Germans were ever to profit fully from their success in overthrowing Imperial Russia then some kind of working modus vivendi would have to be worked out with the Bolsheviks. Such an accord could only be based on the mutual self-interest of both parties. This too was the view of many powerful German industrialists who wanted to resume the important trade links with Russia that the war had broken. Lenin and the other Bolshevik leaders, desperate in the spring and summer of 1918 to retain power, were all too willing to make the necessary ideological concessions to attract German capital, albeit with certain restrictions, back into the country.[29]

This was the background for the negotiations over the supplementary treaties that took place in Berlin and lasted through the summer of

1918, culminating in the signing of two treaties, one economic and one political on August 27. Kessler's exact role in these diffuse discussions is not easy to determine. On the one hand, he appeared to be participating as a member of the Foreign Office; on the other hand, he reported to Ludendorff through Haeften. His diary records pieces of the negotiations—for example, the Bolshevik threat that if the Germans were not forthcoming with economic aid, the Bolsheviks would be forced to turn to the United States. Kessler met frequently with Stresemann throughout the summer, advising him to keep Ludendorff's éminence grise, the sinister Captain Max Bauer, apprised of the progress, advice that Stresemann followed. The news of the murder of the German ambassador in Moscow shook him. "Mirbach belonged to my oldest acquaintances and contemporaries from the Spitzemberg, Harrach, and Richter circles, an aesthete out of which eventually emerged a skeptic and ironist. Very elegant, so that it is hard to imagine him with Trotsky and Lenin, but the last of whom would prophesize a tragic end." It must have surprised him to be asked by Stresemann a few weeks later if he would be willing to take Mirbach's place as ambassador in Moscow. As it turned out, Kessler's hopes were to be scuttled once again; the bitterly anti-Bolshevik Karl Helfferich was named instead, although the disappointment was cloaked by a telegram from Romberg in Bern that he would not want to lose the service of Kessler.[30]

Of most importance for Kessler's future political and diplomatic career was the contact with Stresemann, the greatest statesman of the Weimar period. Considering what close friends and allies the two men would become, it is interesting to see how cautiously their relationship began. At the end of June, just when the negotiations were beginning, Stresemann warned Kessler that conservatives in the Reichstag were preparing an attack on him because of his Swiss activity: "I am 'too modern' for them, namely in the matter of painting . . . . Stresemann himself stands by Anton von Werner: 'The Crown Prince at the Death Bed of General Douai:' Why do I prefer Liebermann? What is 'impressionism'? . . . These controversies, buried now for twenty years, live still in the parliament." Later, when he was being considered for the Moscow post, Kessler was subjected to further questioning about his prewar career. Kessler found this all too depressing: "Stresemann is despite a great rhetorical gift an amusing Dresden lawyer; a primitive."[31] The persistence of these issues he had long considered forgotten in the solidarity of the war effort. The ever more venomous opposition between the proponents of total victory and the growing peace movement within and without Germany, the precariousness of his self-styled position as mediator between these two positions, and the gnawing concern over the values of the postwar world, especially in the event of a German victory, all became obsessive subjects of reflection for Kessler, particularly in the last year of the war, perhaps the most conflicted and intense time of his life.

CHAPTER 19

Apocalyptic Times

Aestheticism and militarism are twin brothers, who embody
it in their enmity. It doesn't suffice that they recognize
each other as necessary evils, conclude sterile peace treaties;
they must meld into one another, as earlier, on the basis of
a common, compelling idea.

Kessler, *Tagebuch*

Almost from the very beginning of the war, Kessler was subjected to
personal calumnies from all sides in the conflict. For someone who
hoped to use his good name and contacts in France not only for the sake
of a separate peace but also to help heal wounds in the postwar world,
he must have been shocked by the scurrilous attacks on his reputation there during the war. Léon Daudet, the literary critic of the ultra-
nationalist *Action Française,* published a novel, charmingly entitled *La
Vermine du Monde,* about the supposed prewar penetration of France
by a German-Jewish clique of spies and agents. In it, Kessler, "Bavarian
[*sic*] gentleman, favored, then in disgrace, then favored again, who
prides himself on a distant resemblance to the Emperor while claiming
to despise him," makes a cameo appearance as an oily, sexually ambiguous, pseudo-Francophile.

Harry Kessler led in Paris the apparent existence of *d'esthete noceur,* only occupied by architecture, printing, and the Russian ballet. He played the Ma-
cenas [*sic*], protected artists and theater people. He passed for being indifferent to feminine attractions but nevertheless made a fuss over the beauties
in vogue. It was a subtle, gossipy, formidable, mobile personality. Even his

friends could not make sense of all his acts and his changing attitudes. Certain good Germans accused him of a lack of loyalty. Others winked their eye and asserted that one would see in the end. The Frenchmen who knew him considered him quite obviously as perfectly inoffensive and a sincere friend of our country."[1]

Daudet has Kessler play a pimp for the kaiser, summoning an Ida Rubenstein-like figure to dance for him. After one of his meetings with Kessler, Louis Caillon received a copy of the book anonymously with the parts about Kessler underlined. Even more absurd was the article in *Le Figaro* of January 1915 that alleged that, at the beginning of the war, Kessler had sent Maillol a telegram instructing him to "Bury the statues, we will be in Marly on August 15." The article goes on to assert that the paper factory built at Marly for the Cranach Presse was really made of concrete and intended to shelter the art that the Germans intended to plunder from France.[2]

Meanwhile, the attacks from right-wing circles on Kessler's propaganda activities continued. Annette Kolb warned him of the dangers of long absences from Bern; "the wild dogs have been let loose against me again." Dietrich Bethmann, the brother of the chancellor and assigned to the embassy in Bern, informed Kessler of the intrigues against him in Berlin. The campaign of innuendo and slander persisted up to the end of the war when it culminated in a grotesque incident. At the end of September 1918, on the day the Bulgarians announced their capitulation, foreshadowing Germany's own defeat, Kessler met Kurt Riezler in the streets of Berlin, just after the latter's return from Moscow. Riezler told him how Wilhelm von Bode, the distinguished art historian, director of Berlin's museums, and Kessler's colleague on the board of *Pan* years ago, had been writing letters to the kaiser accusing "the German-American" Kessler and others of "excessive attachment to foreign things (*Auslanderei*) and connections to modern art." The Cabinet then had demanded that the Foreign Office take a stand on the issue. Incensed, Kessler called the episode "a backstairs intrigue such as Bode had already woven against Tschudi earlier; only now he is senile and proceeds more ineptly, and that in wartime such selfish career-climbing and intrigues produce a more bizarre impression than in Tschudi's day."[3] The vindictiveness was not simply the echo of the bitter controversies over modern art ten years earlier; it also foreshadowed the personal calumny that would characterize the political campaigns of the Weimar Republic.

Such chicanery caused Kessler to brood more and more on the striking gap between the world of culture and the world of power inside

Germany, the same phenomenon he had first noticed on the eastern front. "In a time when Germany from the English Canal to the Don, from Finland to Persia stands as victor, German life between these more than Napoleonic war borders becomes ever pettier, ever more spied upon, ever more abnormal, and fatally paralyzed by poisonous, unnatural . . . gases. We, just like the other nations, are becoming morally hollowed out by the long war." Struck by the new aesthetic order he observed in an exhibition at the Zurich Kunsthalle of the expressionist Kirchner's paintings and woodcuts, he pondered on the opposition and affinity between the two worlds: "A monstrous gap yawns between this order and the political/military order. I stand on both sides of the abyss, into which one peers vertiginously. Earlier there were bridges—religious, mystic, priestly-political; today they are broken and one sees no longer any path, although the goal of both orders is the same, to enhance the power and freedom of man. . . . The values of both orders are without a common denominator, or this is, where some prophet erects one, laughably weak, such as pacifism: compare it with the sweeping power of the idea of God in earlier times. Can economic reorganization according to Marxist ideas create new bridges? Will out of it a new order emerge, reaching both sides, filling the abyss? Can one improve it for this purpose?"[4]

Increasingly, Kessler became aware that this distressing gap between culture and power had been the leitmotif of his life, at least from his early engagement on behalf of modernism. Every time he was criticized for his attachment to modern art or his support of young artists and writers, he arrived at a clearer understanding of this latent theme. So the remark that a German officer should not be named in the company of pacifists and emigrants inspired Kessler to muse that, "this frightful split between German power and German spirit that has lasted since Frederick the Great can perhaps only be overcome through a revolution . . . . These recognitions and conjectures are so much the more painful for me since I have actually spent my life trying to build a bridge between *Junkertum* and spirit, and now between Ludendorff and Europe." Confronted by yet another reactionary outburst, this time from a censor, Kessler concluded that such incidents justified the antipathy toward militarism. "The longer the war lasts, the more hateful the people who conduct it become. The spiritual tyranny of the military in their spiritless absurdity is preparing an explosion for later."[5]

The other gap that grew to preoccupy Kessler was generational. After a meeting with the members of the German colony in Bern, he expressed his disgust that so much young blood had been spilt to protect the existence of this characterless pack. A little later, he returned to the theme: "Today's twenty year olds will blame us for the war, even if they are also determined to extract what is useful in it for them. We are of less value and without authority like fathers who have sinned." During the talks with the Bolsheviks, Kessler speculated on the true revolutionary class in Germany, the youth. The conflict between father and son that was a staple of expressionist drama represented really a conflict between the capitalist and noncapitalist attitudes. That, Kessler speculated, was why resistance to the war emerged first among youth, whereas the workers, as a cog in the great capitalist machine, continued to fight with conviction. When Wieland Herzfelde came to him with reports about how the common soldiers increasingly resented the high living of the officers, Kessler not only passed this report on to Haeften so that it would reach the High Command, but he also paused to reflect on the young man: "To me a curiously interesting and sympathetic type, who would be of incalculable worth if he characterized the leaders of the trench generation. My little lieutenants and company leaders on the Styr were similar to him."[6]

Despite these signs of an incipient critique of the war and Germany's leadership, Kessler could still not completely reject both. In October 1917, Rilke paid him a rather odd visit in Berlin, ostensibly to ask his advice about what he should do during the war. "He asked me if I had experienced anything deep during the war, as deep as what I had experienced in my earlier life? And was deeply moved when I said that I had personally gone through out there a number of things which had moved me deeper than anything (seen) earlier. One could condemn the war in its totality as nonsensical and bestial. In its details . . . it harbors moments of spiritual beauty and revelations that can only be compared to those of love." Despite all his contempt for the lesser, technocratic cogs in the German military machine, he could not yet extend his critique to Hindenburg or Ludendorff. So, while he offered a trenchant criticism of the Fatherland Party, it was not because of their aggressive war aims propaganda but rather their reactionary domestic policy. Yet, as late as 1918, he seemed unaware of the forces behind the Fatherland Party and was astonished to hear Ludendorff criticized as its arch-reactionary leader.[7]

For Hindenburg, Kessler maintained the greatest admiration. "Every word from him," he gushed, "strikes the heart of the common man, completely unintentionally, and drives him forwards in victory and death. He is thereby almost as much as through his abilities a part of the demonic force that is constructing the German world mastery."[8] Contributing to Kessler's admiration was the news of the astonishing breakthrough of the Germans in the so-called "Emperor Battle," launched on March 21, 1918 which, employing new storm trooper tactics, pushed the demoralized British Fifth Army back an unprecedented forty miles in one week. Bodenhausen had informed him back in February of the forthcoming offensive, designed to take advantage of the temporary numerical advantage Germany enjoyed on the western front between the defeat of Russia and the arrival of large numbers of trained American soldiers. If it failed, Bodenhausen warned, Germany, exhausted, would be forced to conclude peace at any price. With Ludendorff directing it, however, both men were confident it would succeed. Eagerly, Kessler noted the successes of the German offensives throughout the spring and into the early summer.

The demonic quality of the war pressed itself ever more into Kessler's consciousness. The pressure cooker atmosphere resulted in striking scenes of unreal, carnival-like theater. One amusing incident, of which exist two separate descriptions, took place in Zurich at the beginning of 1918 after a very powerful performance of Mahler's Second Symphony directed by Oscar Fried. Trotsky had just broken off negotiations at Brest-Litovsk and called for world revolution. Following the concert and a late evening supper, there was a reception held in Paul Cassirer's rooms in the Hotel Schwert, rooms once occupied by Goethe. "The Van Goghs and Cézannes in Goethe's rooms, the peculiarly mixed, cosmopolitan party, almost as before the war, the time, the moment when Trotsky seeks to turn the Russian revolution into a world revolution, where the conflict at home between the military and the civilian authority becomes threatening, the echo of the monstrous Last Judgment depiction of Mahler, this jumble of so many different feelings, experiences, forebodings, people, has something dreamlike, unreal, fantastic about it." Of course, alcohol helped. René Schickele approached Kessler and told him that six people had the fate of the world in their hands, among them Trotsky and him. Kessler's time will come, he assured him, and then repeated the words of the French ambassador, "Schickele is a fanatic of Kessler." All that he did not qualify as strictly secret, Schickele hinted, Kessler should pass directly on to Kühlmann and Romberg. Schickele, in his diary, describes the "usual Kessler Souper at the *Baur au Lacu*," in the course of which Kessler explained to Annette Kolb that he divided the people he knew into three classes:

those that he loved, those that he trusted, and those that he used: "An-
nette asked with a nod in my direction to which class we belonged.
'Schickele, you know, often makes very difficult trouble for me . . . .'
Pause. Look in Annette's eyes: 'But in the end I trust him.' . . . .
Schlesinger took me by the arm to point out that the Count was drink-
ing to me. He does it with his loveliest, most affable mask."[9]

Some of the exiles, pacifists, war resisters, artists, and odds and ends
who had gathered in Switzerland to escape the war, to write and produce free from censorship, to dream and plan of a different future, must
have been intrigued by Kessler, this elegant representative of Imperial
Germany, who nevertheless used his power to protect artists and writers from the German war machine. One who seemed fascinated by
him was the poet Else Laske-Schüler, the friend of Gottfried Benn,
Franz Marc, and other leading expressionists. She began importuning
the count, trying to meet him, calling his office five times a day, sending him a birthday telegram with the message, "Immeasurable love,
burning desires." His laconic response: "Crazy great poet. But craziness
is gradually emerging into the light everywhere." Somewhat in the same
vein was his visit from Dr. Ernst Bloch, another friend of Schickele's. He
explained his philosophy to Kessler: "voluntaristic-mystic, according to
which each being, each thing, carries in itself a utopia, an unfulfilled
possibility, which seeks to complete itself, which redeems it and leads to
perfection. Novalis, Schopenhauer, Chassidim, A Thousand and One
Nights. As a person an almost shockingly powerful Jew, with a bull
neck, wild evil dark eyes behind a pince-nez and an untamed shock of
hair; a brutal force of nature who—not without vanity—has set himself
the task of rethinking the world . . . . He reminded me of the Jewish
boxers in the East End of London who were superior to the strongest
English rowdies."[10] Even though the Foreign Office was interested in
maintaining contacts with pacifists as a possible link to the Entente, it is
doubtful whether anyone else in Wilhelmstraße, or in any other foreign
service for that matter, would have listened as carefully to Ernst Bloch's
outline of his utopian philosophy.

As in all periods of fermentation and upheaval, the evident birth
pangs of something new and revolutionary subsisted with signs of decadence, confusion, and rot. Kessler may have recalled his studies of classical decadence back at the university when he looked around him in
Zurich or Berlin: "Genius, intellect, power, money, science are all per-
verted from their original goals in the blood thirst. Want and insanity
spread everywhere like a kind of mold on the surface . . . . Apocalyptic

times, whose pattern cannot be discerned. What affinity recalls the last centuries of the Roman Empire and the arrival of Christianity and all mysteries! Asexuality, world doom, mysticism unto madness, the sultriness of decay and growth. False prophets everywhere between the war profiteers and the martyrs: and still pressing forwards a youth, which, in the sight of death, has hardly become aware of sexual differences. The sex act becomes, where one can die the next morning, a simple exertion." Such "corruption" did not in his mind disqualify Germany from becoming a world power. It was rather the byproduct of the Nietzschean struggle for new values. What these would be, Kessler could not yet determine. In a discussion with Schickele and Oscar Levy, the English translator of Nietzsche, Schickele remarked that he feared the new idols. Kessler, however, "took the opposite standpoint, that new idols would be quite right with me, as long as they were new and fruitful. But I see only the old idols, 'Democracy, Freedom, Equality' rising up ghostlike." [11]

Nowhere, on the other hand, did he encounter more of a ghostlike evocation of the world that was lost than in his house in Weimar, where the cosmopolitan, sophisticated, indeed perhaps over-refined life of belle époque Europe lay preserved, as it were, in aspic, a relic of some infinitely remote time. Yet, he thought he could detect, wandering through these rooms, some still present freshness, some kernel of internationalism still capable of fructifying the future: "My house seemed in an almost miraculous way unchanged after years of such earthshaking events: young and light in the late hours, beneath the shining, turned on lights, awoken like Sleeping Beauty, the impressionist and neoimpressionist paintings, the French, English, Italian, Greek, German rows of books, the figures . . . of Maillol, his somewhat too stout, voluptuous women, his beautiful naked boy, modeled after the little Colin, as if it were 1913, and the many people, who were here and now are dead, forgotten, scattered, enemies, could return and begin again European life." Picking up each memento of that time—the dedication from D'Annunzio, a program of the Russian Ballet from 1911, books of Oscar Wilde and Alfred Douglas with a letter from Ross, the still unwrapped book of Robert de Montesquieu, "about the beautiful Countess of Castiglione whom he posthumously affected to love"—all of this threw into stark relief the doom that lay over this overripe culture, as the French Revolution had overhung the age of the Rococo. "That the times were headed not to an even more solid peace, but to war, all of us actually knew it, but at the same time did not know. It was a sort of suspended state, that burst like a soap bubble suddenly and disappeared without a trace, once the hellish forces, which were seething in its lap, were ripe." [12]

Such melancholy notes are sounded more often as 1918 stretched into the summer. The war, which he had greeted four years earlier as an immense relief from the nerve-wracking ballet business, now threatened to tear Kessler apart with its conflicting emotions, intrigues, overwork, and succeeding waves of jubilation and anxiety. His fiftieth birthday saw him sick in bed. Annette Kolb visited, flowers were sent, Romberg wrote a friendly letter, but all he could think of was "how pleasant and fundamentally indifferent it would be to slip, slowly and painlessly, into the eternally unconscious . . . . What is good in humans manifests itself officially in laws, foundations, conventions, phrases, but the canaille dominates and remains in reality the element upon which all else in society depends." Contributing to this despair were the personal losses brought by the long years of war. In May, he learned of the sudden death, from overwork, of Eberhard von Bodenhausen. "I was as if struck dead. One of my oldest, closest, best friends, one of Germany's best men, at the highpoint of his life cycle. . . . To me he was an absolutely reliable friend, the second along with Heymel that I have lost during the war. I owe it to him that I am in Bern, and how much intellectually and artistically from the very beginning." The same day he would visit Louis Caillon for the last time before the young man's transfer back to France. Three months later came the news of his death in the Spanish influenza epidemic: "the loyalist and most noble soul, without hate, a Frenchman of the most aristocratic and genuine character . . . . What will remain of him? My memory, that of his bride, a pair of beautiful poems; that as the remains of a young, rich, and ripening human life! In death everyone is completely alone." Added to these losses was the constant worry about his family, cut off from him throughout the war—he correctly intuited that he would never see his mother again. [13]

The "heightened sense of victory" Kessler noted with the news of the initial German victories in March had vanished by summer. Ludendorff's later offensives were never to achieve the same success, and by June these efforts had run out with little to show except the exhaustion of the best German troops. Behind the lines, the reserves and the garrison troops grew increasingly mutinous, as Herzfelde and others were able to warn Kessler. Meanwhile, the failure of unrestricted submarine warfare to strangle Great Britain or to prevent the arrival of the Americans was evident to all. In June 1918 alone, more than 275,000 American soldiers landed in France. The previous October, Ludendorff had personally expressed to Kessler his contempt for the American army. In early June, however, the U.S. Second Division stopped the Germans west of Chateau-Thierry and a Franco-American counterattack turned back his last offensive. All of the first-rate manpower had already been withdrawn from the East; what was left was fit only for police duties. Despite the efforts of Kessler, Stresemann, and others, no significant foodstuffs were coming in from the Ukraine to relieve the effects of four years of blockade. Meanwhile, the numerical and technical advantage had turned decisively to Germany's disadvantage in the West.[14]

Perhaps the single most important aspect of the First World War's conclusion was the abruptness of the collapse of the Central Powers. In March and April 1918, the frontline German troops came within sight of Paris again; by July, the Allies had begun a massive counteroffensive that, jerkily, ungracefully, by sheer brute force, would push the Germans back without respite until November. The seemingly sudden reversals, coming on the heels of supposedly imminent victory caught German public opinion, particularly that of the middle classes who had most ardently supported the war, by surprise. Their disbelief, coupled with the lack of time they had to adjust to the new situation, left a collective psychological wound. The seeds were sown for the pervasive myth of the "stab in the back" that would so profoundly poison the postwar political climate.[15]

As well informed as Kessler was, he too clung to the illusions of victory. At the beginning of June, he thought the war might continue until the next American presidential election in 1920 unless France collapsed before. Could the Anglo-Saxon powers continue the sea war for that long, he asked, thinking, one supposes, that Germany's own supply problems would be solved by the East. He believed he saw signs of war weariness in France and anticipated the victory of the socialists as a prelude to negotiations.[16] Later in July, a high-ranking source in the Foreign Office repeated and amplified this warning, informing him of the German lack of reserves and the increasing numbers of Americans. News of fresh retreats on the Marne later that month caused him to cling all the more tenaciously to the pipe dream of rebuilding the East. On the fourth anniversary of the beginning of the war, he tried to draw up a balance sheet. In favor of Germany, he was forced to put such dubious assets as the alleged threat to Egypt and India (at a time when the Ottoman Empire was near collapse), the incomparable experience of the Hindenburg-Ludendorff team, and German technical superiority: "Nevertheless the mood is bleak."[17]

And then the dam broke. On August 8, the "black day" of the German army, the British, French, American and imperial armies launched a massive offensive, spearheaded by great masses of tanks and aircraft. They advanced ten kilometers in a day and scooped up fifteen thousand German prisoners. Suddenly, Kessler was forced to admit that the Entente had not only caught up technically to the Germans, it had also, in tanks and their use, surpassed them. Under pressure, Germany's allies were crumbling. At the end of September, Kessler, still arranging for a campaign against enemy film propaganda, noted the mood of Berlin: "The slackening of will (*Vermarschuung*) is pervasive, but perhaps only temporary, the reaction to the first great defeat. This has the effect of an unaccustomed poison whereas the Entente is already over such things. But without a jolt we won't get up; the question is who or what will give us this jolt." The first jolt came the next day, but not in the manner Kessler hoped. The Bulgarians announced they were suing for peace, opening up the prospect of a southern invasion of Austria-Hungary and eventually Germany. Two days later, the Hertling government fell "and with it the entire inherited Prussian system. Since Jena (there's been) no such revolution." [18] And then the man whose iron nerves Kessler had admired almost without reservation lost his cool. Ludendorff had informed the civilian authorities that they must approach President Woodrow Wilson for an armistice, otherwise he could not vouch for the reliability of the army.

There could be no illusions now. On October 4, Kessler spent a "frightful" evening with Romberg in his office before the oven. There Kessler learned of the German note to Wilson accepting the conditions outlined in the Fourteen Points. "In other words we have capitulated. . . . Romberg was as annihilated. Has not slept for two days. 'But we are all great sinners.' His only hope is a later alliance of all of Europe against America's forthcoming world hegemony. . . . The mood between Romberg and myself was that of an enormous catastrophe; we sat silent alternatively following our sad thoughts in the oven fire. I was close to fainting: the blood pounded through my head and ears. As I left Romberg crossing at one o'clock in the morning over the bridges I had the wish to throw myself into the Aare. I was perhaps only dead inwardly to do it." [19]

Thus ended four years of hopes and illusions. Despite indulging in a series of quixotic daydreams of Germany joining the Russians in a revolt against the Entente and capitalism, Kessler *au fond* realized the hopelessness of the military situation. But every death foretells a rebirth.

Having lost one of the guiding poles of his conduct for the last four years, the faith in German victory, he flung himself with even more ardor on the one remaining, the hope in a revolutionary youth and a brave new world. So that even on that black day in Romberg's office, he could write, "for only if in reality that ideal arises, the free union of pure, free, peaceful peoples, equal in rights, are these days not the end of the German people? Will the thousand-year old kingdom be reality tomorrow? I read in the collection edited by Schickele, which was given to me today, Whitman's 'Salut au monde.' Perhaps the frightful predicament will produce in us the daemonic power which will make the paradise glimpsed by Whitman a reality?"[20] It was to be the project of his next years.

PART SIX

The Red Count

CHAPTER 20

The Lost Revolution

If I had come to Warsaw instead of Bern in 1916 I would have fulfilled my mission better.

Kessler, *Tagebuch*

"Communism," as I understand it, contains much that is good and human. Its goal is ultimately the total dissolution of the state (which will always be dedicated to power), the humanization and purification of the world by depoliticizing it. At bottom, who would be against that? To be sure, I too cross myself twice and thrice at the prospect of "proletarian culture."

Thomas Mann, 1919, *Letters of Thomas Mann*

The abdication of the kaiser on November 9, 1918, and the proclamation of a German republic from the balcony of the Reichstag on the same day marked an important turning point in modern German history. What would follow was not clear to anyone, least of all to the six-member Council of People's Representatives, composed of three members each from the Independent and the Majority Socialist Parties, which had stepped in to fill the void left by the collapse of the imperial government. The tasks confronting this provisional government were enormous: to conduct negotiations with the triumphant Allies, to fulfill the terms of the armistice, to prepare for the demobilization of more than ten million German soldiers scattered all over Europe, to begin the transition to a peacetime economy, to prepare a new constitution, and to prevent either the collapse of law and order or a Bolshevik-style sei-

zure of power by the radical left. Nothing could be foreseen, all was provisional, and the old certainties fell by the wayside. To some extent, how
one reacted to such a situation determined one's future politics. Those
who lamented November 1918 as an unmitigated disaster tended, by and
large, to support right-wing parties that promised to reverse its verdict.
Those who, quite apart from the immediate inconvenience and day-to-
day problems, recognized in the crisis the opportunity of beginning
again were more likely to support parties on the left.

Kessler was among the latter. Despite his ardent identification with
the cause of German victory and his membership in the Wednesday Society, his connections with Germany's ruling elite, he had always been,
in essence, an outsider. His attitude toward the expressionists, so baf-
fling for a Bodenhausen or a Hofmannsthal, was but one of the most
evident signs of this potential distance. Long exposure to the critical
voices of the younger generation, his own bitter experiences in Weimar,
his interest in the modern, perhaps even his homosexuality, all made it
impossible for him to share the nostalgia for Wilhelmian Germany indulged in by so many of the German elite. It took the painful shock of
defeat to cause Kessler to shuck off at last the old shell, but it was only
because something new had been growing inside for some years that he
could embrace the trauma of 1918 as—to a large extent—liberating.[1]
What exact shape his commitment to the new experiment in Germany
would take was still not clear—but that he was committed to the defense and strengthening of German democracy was evident almost from
the day the kaiser fell.

Before domestic politics could engage him, however, Kessler found
himself swept once again, with nary a respite, into the world of diplomatic intrigue. In February 1918, he had had the occasion to return to
Poland. He recalled the open plains of the East with nostalgia. "We in
the West are too predetermined and bourgeois. Here all possibilities—
Jewish, German, Slavic, Asiatic—are open. If I had come to Warsaw
in 1916 instead of Bern I would have fulfilled my mission better." He
would have his chance. On November 19, he was named the German
Republic's first ambassador to the new state of Poland. He left the same
day in a luxurious private train for the East "which I love, which has
some deep, impossible to define beauty for me."[2] The dream of becoming an ambassador that he had entertained years before as he waited
for acceptance into the foreign service had at last become a reality, albeit in a location and in circumstances that he could never have imagined back then.

It was his acquaintanceship with Josef Pilsudski that landed him in Warsaw. Arrested on the orders of the German military governor of occupied Poland in July 1917 because of his refusal to swear an oath of loyalty to the government installed by the Germans, Pilsudski had been languishing in a prison in Magdeburg for more than a year. His imprisonment was only the most evident sign of the bankruptcy of German policy toward Poland, a failure rooted, it has been shown, in deep German ambiguity toward an independent Poland, as well as in the arrogance and ambition of the German High Command-East. Because Germany now hoped to conclude a peace based on Wilson's Fourteen Points, the thirteenth of which called for an independent Poland with access to the sea, it was thought that Pilsudski, who had once fought on the German side, would be a better friend of Germany than the wildly anti-German, pro-Entente National Democrats, whose leader had spent the war in Paris.[3]

It was decided to send a representative to sound Pilsudski out and especially to discover his views on Poland's future relations with Germany. Someone, possibly Romberg, reminded the Foreign Office of Kessler's connections with Pilsudski, and on October 18, Kessler was asked if he would undertake the task. On November 6, the cabinet of Prince Max von Baden finally commissioned him to meet with Pilsudski and, if possible, convince the Polish leader to sign, as a condition of his release, a written declaration committing him to a pro-German policy. This absurd demand was dropped after Kessler learned that Pilsudski, understanding that time was on his side and the Germans were in no position to impose conditions, was not prepared to sign anything. Indeed, the Foreign Office, worried not only about getting its troops back through a Poland increasingly threatened by revolutionary chaos, but also about the impending German revolution, now informed Kessler that Pilsudski should be placed on a train to Warsaw as soon as possible.

By that time, the revolution inside Germany was growing more threatening. Bands of revolutionary sailors were making their way from the ports of Kiel, Cuxhaven, and Bremen toward Berlin. "The opposite of France," Kessler noted, "(here) the provinces revolutionize the capital, the sea the land: Viking strategy. Perhaps we will come against our will at the head of the slave uprising against England and American capital." The train link to Berlin was broken, so Kessler commandeered two cars to pick up Pilsudski and his aide and drive them from Magdeburg to Berlin. Because it was dangerous to appear in an officer's uniform, Kessler wore a civilian coat and hat as he drove up to the fortress. As his things were packed, Pilsudski noted the mounting chaos in Germany and told Kessler that he feared Germany was in for hard times, that Bolshevism did not suit well-organized lands like Germany, or even Poland for that matter. Kessler responded that both Poland and Germany needed a rest, and because he, Pilsudski, shared the same view, he was being released. The two cars then headed for Berlin, swiftly leaving a Magdeburg that was beginning to be engulfed in revolution.[4]

Thus, they were in Berlin the next day for the abdication of the kaiser. In the morning, Kessler went searching for a sword because Pilsudski had requested one. Unsuccessful in his search, he gave the Pole his own as a memento of their being brothers-in-arms. All together, Kessler did his best to strengthen his personal relationship with Pilsudski and to impress upon him the need for friendly relations with Germany. Neither man knew, of course, what borders the new Poland would receive from the victorious Entente, but Kessler insisted that the annexation of West Prussia by Poland could only lead to deep trouble between the two neighboring states. Pilsudski seemed to agree. After this discussion, Kessler returned to Wilhelmstraße for further instructions. The collapsing regime was eager to ship the Pole off, and a special train was arranged for him that evening. On the way back to the hotel, Kessler noted the kaiser's abdication in the special editions of the evening newspapers: "It grabbed me by the throat despite everything this end of the Hohenzollern house, so pitiable, so irrelevant, not even the center of events."[5]

On November 14, the Foreign Office asked Kessler if he would accept the post of ambassador to Poland. When he accepted under certain conditions,* he did so with open eyes. After receiving congratulations on his appointment, he noted, "In reality very few people would desire this post." His official appointment was delayed, however, for several days. Hugo Haase, a member of the Council of People's Representatives, apparently had wanted the first representative of the German republic to be a woman. Convinced that a woman could not handle the situation in Poland, Kessler enlisted his good friend Rudolf Breitscheid, at the time connected to the Independent Socialists and later to be one of the leading foreign policy experts of the Socialist Party, to exercise his influence. The final decision was taken by the Council of People's Representatives in the Reichs Chancellery while Kessler waited outside. "That the first ambassador of the German Republic should be a Count

---

* One of which was that his friend from the Polish campaign, Schoeter, with whom he had apparently kept in contact, should serve as his personal adjutant.

and a Calvary Guard officer is apparently uncomfortable and ticklish," Kessler noted as he watched them file in. Nevertheless, in the end, he was confirmed and the next day received his instructions. The big concern was the hundreds of thousands of German troops stranded in the Ukraine, where they had been guarding against the spread of Bolshevism. As soon as the Entente relieved them, they were to be brought home across Poland. To ensure their safe transport, Kessler would have to maintain good relations with Pilsudski and with the German army command in the East. Regarding the Polish-German border, Kessler was instructed to repeat privately and publicly that Germany had agreed to leave this question for the peace conference based on Wilson's Thirteenth Point.[6] On November 19, he departed for Warsaw, moving through the same countryside over which he had marched and fought only a few years ago.

Exactly how hopeless his position was he would soon find out. Nearly four years of military occupation had made the Germans unloved in Poland. A combination of arrogant disdain for the Polish population and susceptibility to corruption on the part of both the military and the civilian administration undermined whatever initial prestige they might have enjoyed as Poland's liberators. The anti-German sentiments thus engendered threatened not only Germany's relations with its neighbor but also the millions of ethnic Germans living in Poland. These tensions were further exacerbated by the looming question of Poland's future western border, especially in strategically and economically vital areas such as Upper Silesia and the port of Danzig. Indeed, nearly all of Poland's borders were in flux, and fighting had already broken out near Lvov (formerly Lemburg) with Ukrainian forces and in Vilna with Lithuanians.[7]

Adding to the confusion was the bitter political rivalry between Pilsudski, head of the Polish Socialist Party, and Roman Dmowski, the leader of the National Democrats. Dmowski, an ardent Catholic, who favored an ethnically pure Polish state, had placed his hopes in an Entente victory in 1914. As the imminent defeat of Germany became evident, Dmowski and the other National Democrats expected to return to Poland in triumph, in the baggage train of the Entente, as it were, much like Eduard Benes of Czechoslovakia had done. Instead, the Germans whisked Pilsudski out of prison and shipped him off to Warsaw, where he established a shaky provisional government. Dmowski was left stranded in Paris. The virulently anti-German National Democrats, who also were opposed to Pilsudski's comparatively tolerant vision of a multi-ethnic state as well as his moderate socialism, decided to make trouble for him before he could consolidate his power. There was no better way than to attack his connections with the greatly disliked Germans. Kessler had stepped into a hornets' nest.

As soon as he arrived in Warsaw, Kessler was besieged by representatives of the high command, journalists, and members of the German community. From a German manufacturer who had lived for fifteen years in Warsaw, the new ambassador learned the full extent of the ill feeling created by the occupation. Again, it was corruption in the much-vaunted officer corps that bore part of the blame. Drawing a parallel between the behavior of his countrymen in Poland and the moral collapse he witnessed in Germany, Kessler concluded, "it was a system that failed, not individuals, a system which finally relied entirely on brute force and broke down helplessly the moment this slipped out of its grasp."[8] When Kessler presented his credentials officially, Pilsudski reiterated his hopes that amity would replace enmity between the two countries. The two men maintained cordial relations when they met, but the Poles were eager to exploit the vacuum left by the Russian Civil War and advance as far east as possible. On November 22, shortly after he received a friendly personal visit from Pilsudski, now provisional dictator of Poland, Kessler was given a thinly veiled ultimatum by the Polish chief of staff: if the lines of communication to the Bug river were not evacuated immediately, Poland would call for the help of Entente troops. Kessler wired immediately to Berlin, asking for compliance with the Polish demand to prevent further animosities and perhaps even acts of sabotage, to strengthen Pilsudski's position, and to be able then to present the Poles with the request that the German army in the Ukraine be allowed to use the Polish railways to return to Germany. Although State Secretary Wilhelm Solf agreed with Kessler and sent copies of his request to the German High Command East, Kessler had not yet received any instructions from Berlin and felt himself completely isolated.[9]

Worse was to come. On Saturday, after making a number of visits— to the Archbishop of Warsaw, to some wounded and sick German troops in a hospital, and so forth—Kessler was dining late in his hotel when he and his companion heard the noise of large crowd in the hall: "We went to see what was the matter. A waiter rushed up and whispered, 'Take to your heels, here, through the back door.' I caught the crowd yelling. 'Down with Kessler.' They were preparing to storm my room. 'Kessler, out, out.' One or two of the pack's wild men ran up the stairs. Another, standing on a table gesticulating, made a speech that I did not understand. The manager approached and said that we must leave the hotel tomorrow before ten, or he would be shot." Kessler tried unsuccessfully to contact Pilsudski that evening but did extract a promise from one of his advisors that a military guard would be provided for the hotel. The following afternoon another crowd, several hundred strong, gathered again at his door, eventually breaking in and searching his room. Among the leaders was Wojciech Korfanty, leader of Polish resistance against the Germans in Upper Silesia and West Prussia, who made a glowing pro-Entente speech from the balcony of Kessler's hotel rooms and attacked Kessler in a newspaper article as a left-wing democrat and internationalist.[10] The Polish Foreign Ministry, embarrassed and apparently helpless, found a small apartment for Kessler to use as a temporary headquarters for the German embassy and provided a guard with a machine gun.

Despite these unnerving and difficult circumstances, Kessler moved ahead with arranging the negotiations for the evacuation of the Ukraine by German troops. His ability to negotiate was made very difficult, however, by the lack of instructions from either High Command East or from the Foreign Office and by the fact that he also had to deal with the elected representative of the German soldiers' council. Meanwhile the agitation against his presence continued. Unsigned posters appeared in the streets of Warsaw, urging war with Germany; Kessler had to leave restaurants by the side doors to avoid being accosted by troublemakers; a mob threatened to shoot the porter at the Legation offices if he did not tell them Kessler's private residence; and after Kessler moved yet again, his new landlady asked him to leave immediately: "The city mob is after me and there is no telling what may happen. Finally she returned my papers because she is not going to take the risk of registering me with the police."[11] When he had an opportunity, Kessler sent a message to Korfanty that he thought their efforts to drive the German Legation out would only have the effect of unleashing the tide of German soldiers stranded in the Ukraine onto Poland.

At last, on December 2, 1918, a courier brought word that Supreme Army Command had agreed both to the evacuation of the Bug lines of communication and to Polish forces occupying part of the area east of the Bug to forestall the Bolsheviks. Kessler greatly admired the dignified representative of the soldiers' council whose realism contrasted sharply with the mentality prevailing in High Command East. He received a copy of a telegram from High Command East to the Foreign Office, asking that Kessler "champion not merely Polish, but also German interests at Warsaw." Astounded by this insult, Kessler wondered, "whether narrow-mindedness or impudence has the upper hand among these braggarts and intriguers. Fortunately their teeth sit too loosely in their jaws to be much good for biting. These people, whose maneuvers have landed Germany in its present dreadful disaster, have the face to want to lay down rules of diplomatic procedure." [12]

Kessler's anxious tenure in Warsaw came to an abrupt end in the middle of December. Having kept the German ambassador long enough to settle the pressing problem of the troops, Pilsudski's government felt they could now yield to the tremendous pressure exerted by the National Democrats. On Sunday, December 15, Kessler was handed a final note announcing the break-off of diplomatic relations with Germany and Kessler's immediate departure. "It is the National Democrats, relying on France, who have brought it about. Here too France has shown itself to be insatiable in its desire for vengeance. Its demonic hatred has not by any means been pacified by our defeat, it seems." [13] Midnight the same day Kessler and the rest of the Legation left on the special train the Poles had put together for them. Kessler's first and only term as a German ambassador was over after only twenty-six days.

The main accomplishment of his mission, to arrange a reasonably orderly evacuation of German troops in the Ukraine, was a clear success. The evacuation was complete by the middle of February; only a few days later began the seesaw war between Poland and Soviet Russia that would last until 1921. It required enormous sangfroid on the part of Kessler to conduct successful negotiations in that atmosphere of chaos, failure of communications, and multiple physical threats. The longer term, more ambitious goal of keeping Poland from drifting into the Entente camp, however, was doomed from the very beginning. None of the "new" countries created by the breakup of the three Eastern empires could afford either to skip the upcoming peace conference in Paris or to proclaim their neutrality by maintaining friendly relations with the Entente's defeated archenemy, Germany. The official note Kessler received breaking off relations made this quite clear: it expressly stated the desire to regulate all Polish-German issues in the context of the conference and not in bilateral negotiations. [14] The accusation that Kessler overestimated the strength of Germany and his personal influence with Pilsudski is not really tenable. [15] It was not Kessler, hounded from apartment to apartment by Polish mobs, who overestimated the German position but the Foreign Office and the military, as witness the absurd accusation of the High Command East. Kessler quite legitimately strove to exploit his personal relations with Pilsudski—to ignore this connection would have been a dereliction of his duty—but in his discussions with the Polish leader, he always emphasized the concrete national interests of both states, warning quite clearly and, as it turns out, presciently about the dangers of poisoning relations. The deep antagonism dividing Poland and Germany in the interwar period can scarcely be placed on Kessler's door—here, as in so many other areas, he was fighting *auf verlorenen Posten*.

. . .

Kessler returned to a country on the brink of civil war. December 1918 and the first four months of 1919 would see intermittent but frequent, confused, and often bloody street fighting in cities throughout Germany. The monarchy had collapsed virtually without a struggle, so discredited was it by the war's end. The power that fell, more or less unexpected and unwanted, into the hands of the two branches of the Socialist Party, Independent and Majority, was by no means uncontested, however. The actual agents of the German revolution were the soldiers' and workers' councils that had spontaneously formed in most major cities. The divisions in the left that proved to be so fatal ultimately for German democracy had to do with a profound disagreement over the goals of the German revolution, and particularly over the role of the council movement. The Majority Socialists and their allies, the trade unions, had long since given up the notion of a violent convulsion that would usher in a revolutionary restructuring of society. Their chief goals were the creation of a genuine constitutional democracy to replace the pseudo-constitutionalism of Imperial Germany and the establishment, in partnership with the trade unions, of a social state that would guarantee such achievements as the eight-hour day.[16] Above all, Friedrich Ebert, the leader of the Majority Socialists, and his colleagues wished to end the awkward, not strictly legal, provisional government as soon as possible and turn power over to an elected National Assembly that would have the responsibility of drawing up a new constitution.

The Independent Socialists, who had split the Social Democratic party in 1917 because of their opposition to the war, were a more diffuse and loosely organized group. On the whole, however, the bulk of the party was much more sympathetic to the council movement than were the Majority Socialists. Some of the more radical leaders wanted to replace parliamentary democracy with a rather nebulous council democracy; nearly all hoped to make the workers' and soldiers' councils an institutional part of the new government. Still more frightening for any German wishing to avoid following in Russia's path was the presence of the Spartacus Union, a splinter group of radical socialists calling for an immediate social revolution. It was all too easy for a Majority Socialist like Ebert to see in the Spartacist leaders, Rosa Luxembourg and Karl Liebknecht, the specter of Lenin and the Bolsheviks and to worry that he might play the role of the doomed Kerensky.[17]

As the reluctance of the Majority Socialists to pursue a thorough restructuring and democratization of German society became increasingly evident in December 1918, distrust and impatience with their leadership grew in the ranks of the council movement and among Independent Socialists. The establishment of the Communist Party by Spartacists, concerned that the revolutionary opportunity was fading away, further polarized the left. The first stage of the German revolution concluded therefore in the middle of January 1919 when rank-and-file anger compelled the leadership of the Spartacists, against their better judgment, to launch an ill-timed and poorly organized insurrection in Berlin. The provisional government, now dominated completely by Majority Socialists, used the only means of coercion they had at their disposal, the *Freikorps*—in essence, private armies of former veterans commanded by right-wing officers—to crush the revolt. Rosa Luxembourg and Karl Liebknecht were murdered by the *Freikorps* in the white terror that followed. The "blood crime" had been committed and the German left would never recover.

Kessler was an omnipresent and sharp-witted observer of nearly all of these events in Berlin. His diary for the winter of 1918–1919 offers one of the most vivid descriptions of the German revolution available, cinematic in its detail, framing, and movement. Far from huddling in his apartment, he crisscrossed central Berlin continually like a peripatetic modern-day analogue to Restif de la Bretonne, the insomniac witness to the French Revolution. Always moving toward the sound of gunfire, seeking shelter now and then, engaging *Freikorps* soldiers and Spartacus agitators in conversation, using his various bona fides to pass roadblocks, and visiting an extraordinary range of acquaintances, he captured the chaos and confusion of street fighting in dozens of small details, incidents, and confrontations, little dramas without denouements. One such occurred during the so-called "sailors' revolt" two days before Christmas:

In the evening, towards ten, there was a rumor of shooting having broken out again and there being twenty dead. Some said that it had occurred at

Potsdamer Station, others said at Alexanderplatz. I drove to the latter to see
what had happened and was given the (correct) information that the shooting had taken place in the neighborhood of the Palace. A group of sailors
stood outside the Imperial Stables and told the tale of how their comrades,
having gone to the Commandant's office to demand pay, suddenly came
under fire from the direction of the University. Two of them were killed.
Hereupon they had put the City Commandant, Wels, under arrest and removed him to the Imperial Stables. That happened around eight.

As I passed down Unter den Linden, I met a unit in steel helmets. Big,
handsome fellows, it was some moments before I recognized the Third Battalion of the Uhlan Guards, my own regiment. Some young officers explained that Ebert had just now sent for them. While we were speaking,
other soldiers in half-tattered uniforms and civilians surged around the
troops and pestered them. Our men ignored the newcomers. After a few
minutes an order was issued and the contingent disappeared inside the University. I had not seen my regiment since August 1914, during the assault on
Namur. A sorry re-encounter, this, in a night of revolution fraught with the
danger of civil war and social dissolution.[18]

In the middle of the Spartacist insurrection from January 5 to January 13, Kessler had to go to a throat specialist for an unspecified operation. His trips took him across the center of the fighting. Again, one
of the most striking aspects of his descriptions is the juxtaposition of
panicked crowds, rumors, huddled soldiers, anonymous gunfire right
next to street vendors, overfilled cafés, trams running their accustomed
routes, and all the quotidian sounds of a big city.

Around four to the doctors in Karlstraße. Returning I passed through the
Friedrichstraße where there was a good deal of traffic and people discussing
matters. Suddenly gun fire broke out at the Unter den Linden end. The
crowd fled screaming into the Mittelstraße. I went down into the Linden
which was blocked off and darkened. Posts in combat helmets stood by the
house entrances; Wilhelmstraße was blocked but illuminated. The sentries
on the Wilhelmplatz say the houses in the Mohrenstraße are occupied by
Spartacists. In the Hotel Kaiserhof, which is closed and dark, lie government troops. The Leipziger Straße looks like normal, except for the closed
shops. On the Potsdamer Platz the great conditoreis—Josty, Fürstenhof,
Palastcafé, Vaterland—are open, brightly lit, and overflowing.[19]

Kessler's political attitude toward the revolution changed with events,
being particularly influenced by the bloody suppression of the Spartacists. If a summary can do justice to a complex assemblage of reactions,
predispositions, hopes, and illusions, then one could perhaps describe
Kessler as belonging formally to the bourgeois, democratic left, but
temperamentally to the utopian, socialist left. Where exactly he stood

within this spectrum depended on the issue at hand, and is hard to say with exactitude in any case. When he was accused of being a socialist, he always pointed to his membership in the German Democratic Party, one of the three pillars of the so-called "Weimar Coalition" that was home to many of Germany's leading liberal intellectuals, academics, and professionals, including Max Weber, Theodor Heuss, Theodor Wolff, and Friedrich Naumann. But he was never quite comfortable in this organization, swearing that he would never join a party that was simply the old prewar Progressive Party with a new label. Instead, he spoke of forming a left-wing opposition group within the DDP to change the party from the inside; "otherwise I will, if the experiment fails, shift much further to the left." [20] At the same time, he considered the Majority Socialists to be "outdated," concerned purely with piecemeal social reform and improving the material condition of their voters.

In fact, Kessler, like many left-wing intellectuals, viewed the politics and politicians of the Weimar Republic with undisguised distaste, even as he risked his physical safety in supporting the republic against the right. They lacked the stature needed to meet the historical demands of their time, he thought, and in this they continued the unhappy tradition of modern German political leadership in the aftermath of Bismarck. He would in time allow for two exceptions to the general mediocrity: Walther Rathenau and Gustav Stresemann. In a few other cases, most notably Josef Wirth and Friedrich Ebert, he would grudgingly revise his opinions and admit their good points. But by and large, his descriptions bristle with contempt. At the beginning of March 1919, he encountered Philip Scheidemann, the first chancellor of the Weimar Republic; Matthias Erzberger, the leader of the Center Party; and Hugo Preuss, the "father" of the Weimar Constitution in Weimar for the opening of the National Assembly. "Here the regal proletarian Scheidemann, inflated like a peacock in his brief glory, wandered round arm and arm with Preuss, and Erzberger, deliberating affairs of state. As they passed up and down, the Gothic trappings quivered slightly in the breeze, I joined them. Erzberger, with his baggy cheeks and sly, sensual lips, received me smilingly. He always looks like someone who has fed well and is in the process of giving a tip. What with Scheidemann being pompous in his concertina trousers and Preuss a sheer monstrosity, the three of them constituted the quintessence of German humdrumness." [21]

This was not simply an aesthetic judgment. It was also a moral one, and it expressed frustration over the results of the revolution. The events of November represented not a revolution but the collapse of a regime too rotten to withstand the strain of war. But collapse is only the precondition for revolution, not the revolution itself. Meditating on this subject on the day the Spartacist revolt was crushed, Kessler wrote, "[I]t will be a terrible thing if, for lack of any desire to bring it about, all this destruction and suffering does not prove to be the birth-pangs of a new era and it turns out that nothing better than a patchwork job can be done. The feeling that this is what would happen, the fear of such an outcome, has been the spur pricking the best among the Spartacists. Social Democracy of the old sort wants purely material changes, more equitable and better distribution and organization, but nothing new of an idealist nature. On the other hand it is this vision which inspires enthusiasts farther to the left, and it is true that only that could compensate for the war's awful blood-letting." [22]

Two points emerge from this comment. One is Kessler's unquestioned assumption that the "purely material" is less important than "idealism," an assumption deeply embedded in bourgeois German culture. Socialism, he would complain later, was a purely economic theory and lacked any substantial insight into politics, ethics, or aesthetics, which was why, in his opinion, political confusion had reigned since the socialists had been in power. A synthesis of Marx and Nietzsche was needed to make up for this lack as was a political party that would, on a socialist foundation, create the room for individual freedom and democracy. To forward this project, Kessler went so far as to fund, through the Nietzsche Archive, a 20,000 mark prize for works on individualism and socialism. [23] A rather vague conception of socialism seems to have taken the place in his mind formerly held by German military power as the outward bulwark protecting the inward development of the individual. The second point to note is how Kessler's hopes for the revolution, and his disappointment in its results in the spring of 1919, represent a displacement of that heady admiration for youthful idealism he first discovered in August 1914. The constant need to justify the sacrifice of so many young men explains his inability to recognize the modest achievements of the German revolution as anything but farcical unless they were a prelude to a real revolution led by the only revolutionary class in German society, youth. In March 1919, he noted bitterly, "what the revolution has brought to power is not the proletariat, but rather storekeepers and small party officials like Ebert, Scheidemann, Baake, Wissell, that is, the petite bourgeoisie [see Kotzebue and Sternheim]. Spartacus is the revolution of the proletarians and intellectuals against the philistines who are sitting illegitimately in the club seat. The philistine calls in the military with whom he has concluded a very shaky alliance."[24]

The savagery of the *soldestka,* not only during the Spartacist insurrection, but throughout the spring of 1919 turned Kessler's contempt to loathing. He intervened in two cases of brutality by the *Freikorps;* one of which he witnessed and the other brought to his attention by his left-wing friends. During a confused general strike called in March 1919 to protest the betrayal of the revolution by the embittered left, the defense minister of the government, Gustav Noske, a Majority Socialist, did not hesitate to declare martial law, announced that anyone found fighting against the government with a weapon in his hands would be summarily executed, and ordered the *Freikorps* to crush the strike, a task they performed with great zeal.[25] Kessler happened to be passing through the Wilhelmstraße as *Freikorps* soldiers were loading a truck with prisoners of the government. "Suddenly a soldier with a whip jumped on the lorry and several times struck one of the prisoners just before the lorry drove out into the street." Kessler immediately marched into the Chancellery and complained to an aide of the commanding officer. The lieutenant apologized but tried to explain that the *Freikorps* were deeply embittered by atrocities allegedly committed by the other side. A few days later, the commanding officer wrote to Kessler to say that the man he had seen with the whip had only used it to indicate the prisoner, not to hit him, something Kessler knew to be a lie. He attempted to let Captain Reinhardt know through an intermediary that this response was not satisfactory and that he would pursue the matter further, quietly if the crime was investigated properly, but publicly if not.[26]

A far more sinister event occurred only a few days later, March 11, 1919: the execution of twenty-four sailors by government troops under the command of a Captain Marloh in a courtyard of a Berlin house. Kessler could not shake "one of the most abominable civil war crimes I have ever heard" out of his head. Wieland Herzfelde, just released from a week in the Moabit and Plötzensee prisons, described to Kessler vividly the ill treatment accorded to the prisoners by the government troops; "his descriptions of them are so dreadful that I felt sick with nausea and indignation." A dehumanized military running amok could only be brought to heel by extreme measures. Kessler immediately arranged to have Herzfelde's account heard by leading members of the Democratic Party. When some present objected that the *Freikorps* were the only weapons the government had to maintain law and order, Kessler responded angrily that it would be the worst form of cowardice

to accept this argument, so similar to the compromises made continually during the war. Kessler then informed Stresemann of the crime
against the sailors and the conditions in the prisons. It was arranged to
have the government interjected into this matter.[27]

The upshot of all of this was the trial of Marloh in December 1919.
Much to Kessler's disgust, this "murderous marionette stuffed with
parade-ground rules and lacking either heart or intelligence" was ac-
quitted by the court, only one of many incidents where conservative
judges allowed right-wing assassins to escape with no or little punishment for their crimes. Half a year later, after the crushing of the so-
called "Red Army of the Ruhr" in the spring of 1920, Kessler wrote a
blistering newspaper account of the trial of another officer who ordered
fifteen prisoners to be shot "while trying to escape." In it, he warned of
the hatred and thirst for revenge that the accumulation of such atrocities aroused in the German working classes. Although the student "volunteers" who committed these crimes justified them through patriotism, it was not the kind of patriotism that was rooted in love of one's
people, Kessler noted. "The German Nationalist gentlemen have, it is
well known, in the place of this old fashioned patriotism, erected a
brand new one, whose most visible feature is that they declare the German people to be, because of the 'stab in the back' and other dirty
tricks, the most depraved people on earth. Which does not prevent
them in their great goodness of course to strive with every might to
make this people happy."[28] Through the German Peace Society, Kessler
met and collaborated with the lawyer and activist Emil Julius Gumbel,
who was collecting documentation of the grotesque right-wing bias in
the judicial system. Despite the overwhelming evidence Gumbel was
able to publish, nothing substantial was ever done to remedy the situation. The opportunity had already been lost when the Majority Socialists failed to purge the civil service and the army, as the Independents
had demanded.

Besides the reactionary officers, Kessler blamed the government for
the bloodshed. "At Weimar today," he noted in the midst of the March
disturbances, "Noske made a speech, boorish and utterly deplorable in
tone, predicting victory over the enemy at home. Repulsive! Every de-
cent-minded person must spurn a Government that so frivolously and
shamelessly plays with the lives of its fellow-citizens. During the past
week, thanks to its wanton lies and bloodshed, it has caused a breach in
the nation which decades will not suffice to mend. Tonight the popular
mood towards it fluctuates between loathing and contempt. The feel-

ing about Napoleon III after his *coup d'état* may well have been like that prevailing now against Noske and Scheidemann." In fact, Kessler did not think the Scheidemann cabinet could last long. Everywhere he saw a rising tide of revolution: in Hungary on March 22 a soviet regime under Bela Kun was proclaimed and on April 7 a similar revolution was announced in Munich, the capital of Bavaria.[29] Confusing the German workers with the German population as a whole, and relying on informants like Herzfelde for a picture of the situation, Kessler clearly overestimated the strength, resolution, and organization of the radical movement, which, in fact, was in the process of frittering away whatever power it may have once had in pointless and easily crushed rebellions. At the same time, he underestimated the long-term strength of the *Freikorps,* calling them mercenaries.

On the basis of such miscalculations, he became involved in an intrigue to topple the Scheidemann government and replace it with one that would include Independent Socialist ministers. To this end, he mobilized his connections to two of the most moderate and capable of the Independents, Rudolf Breitscheid and Rudolf Hilferding. The other pillar of this conspiracy was Count Brockdorff-Rantzau, the wartime ambassador to Denmark and now the foreign minister in the Scheidemann cabinet. Even though he had in common with Rantzau both homosexuality and a reputation as a radical democrat (eventually to earn both men the sobriquet "The Red Count"), Kessler at first was deeply scornful of him. When Rantzau gave a press conference in January 1919, asserting his hope for the ultimate victory of democracy in the world and that the "most vital requisite for membership in the League of Nations is moral conviction," Kessler could not contain his contempt: "Rantzau gives the impression of an old *cocotte* trying to persuade herself and others of her dewy virginity." Yet less than two months later Kessler approached Rantzau with the scheme, a coup d'état as he put it, of undertaking negotiations for a new government with the Independents. Such a reconstruction was "absolutely essential," Kessler pleaded, because the masses distrusted the government and because it was necessary for Germany's economic reconstruction to employ a system of workers' councils: "But the present Government . . . is . . . not in a position to implement the workers' council system to this extent. Consequently Scheidemann, Erzberger, and the Center Party as a whole must be forced to drop out and be replaced by the Independents, the stipulation being of course that the Independents guarantee work and quiet." [30]

When Rantzau expressed his interest, Kessler began a shuttle diplomacy between the foreign minister and Independents such as Hilferding, Breitscheid, and Haase. This desperate attempt to bring to power the council movement failed because there was no way to force the Majority Socialists to vacate their posts and because the left wing of the Independents was not interested in making the necessary compromises, especially in the wake of the brutal reprisals of March. Although it took Kessler some time to recognize it, the balance of power had shifted substantially to the right, and while the Independents would make huge gains at the expense of the Majority Socialists in the June 1920 Reichstag elections, the great bulk of these voters would shortly thereafter join the Communist Party, while the remnant would rejoin the old Socialist Party for the most part.[31]

Kessler's endeavor to be the éminence grise of the council movement, working behind the scenes to bring about the changes he thought necessary recalls his earlier efforts on behalf of aesthetic modernism in Imperial Germany. The same belief in the efficacy of informal networks composed of influential people motivated him in both instances. And yet, as his posting as ambassador to Poland had suggested, the revolution had brought outsiders like Kessler previously unimaginable opportunities for official careers in the Foreign Office. For a short while, during the uncertainty and confusion of 1919 and 1920, possibilities of obtaining positions were open, only to be eliminated as the professional diplomats closed ranks in the subsequent years. Kessler's diary records many instances of his name being bandied about as a possible candidate for important posts. As early as December 1918, the unreliable Ludwig Stein informed him that he was a possible successor as state-secretary; at the end of the same month, Hilferding, Breitscheid, and others approached him about the ambassadorship to Switzerland. Poland, because he had never resigned formally as ambassador, lay open when diplomatic relations should be restored. In June 1919, after Rantzau had resigned rather than sign the peace treaty, rumors that Kessler would be his successor floated through the foreign press. At various times, the ambassadorship to Belgium and as Germany's first ambassador to the League of Nations were mentioned in connection with his name. As always, Kessler posed difficult conditions as, for example, when discussing the post in Switzerland: "After declining several times, I finally declared myself prepared in principle to accept the appointment provided that I am relieved of attending to local affairs and of purging the Legation, whose staff has to be reduced to less than a tenth of its strength. My only real task, one of international importance, should be the establishment of relations with Britain and France" [32] The hubris is undeniable, but it was not merely an exaggerated sense of his own mission that was responsible for his attitude. Rather, it was the suspicion, probably correct, that he was not the man for a fixed, bureaucratic position, even one with such exalted opportunities as the reconciliation of former enemies. If it was an illusion that he could be more influential and come closer to the issues that really concerned him as an independent, but well-connected negotiator and "idea man," then it was a deep-seated one that he pursued all of his life.

The opportunities for informal leadership, on the other hand, seemed endless in those revolutionary years. "As in the French Revolution clubs are forming in which the politically important questions are debated first and decided upon," he noted at the beginning of the revolution. [33] He joined quite a few of these sometimes quite fleeting organizations. Among them was the so-called "November Club" composed of younger, more progressive members of the Foreign Office, including Friedrich Wilhelm von Prittwitz, later ambassador to the United States; Bernard Wilhelm von Bülow, who eventually would serve as state secretary; and Karl Riezler. There was a great deal of excited talk in this circle of the need to invent new approaches to foreign policy in the wake of the failure of Wilhelmian power politics, [34] but ultimately the majority of the members were content to pursue their careers in the conventional way.

Closely connected to the November Club was the journal *Deutsche Nation,* the editorial board of which Kessler joined in February 1919. Its members were the leading lights of the Democratic Party intelligentsia, among them Theodor Heuss, the future president of the Federal Republic of Germany, who recalled Kessler as "the most interesting figure" of the editorial board, "full of ideas but, as far as I can remember, somewhat vague in concrete judgments." Kessler remained on the editorial board throughout the journal's existence and contributed a number of articles on international politics, but he did not attend the editorial meetings regularly and in general kept his distance, especially after the journal refused to condemn the government for the violence of the *Freikorps.* "I come across like Gulliver," he noted revealingly, "compared with the others, but at the same time helpless because I lack the technical knowledge in so many questions, namely economics and law." The same ambivalence characterized his relations with the Democratic Party. [35] Typical of Kessler's preferred approach to politics was the idea he discussed in February with the poet Theodor Däubler and the financier Hugo Simon of creating "a club without political ties but for people of an independent frame of mind." The membership was to include virtually everyone of note on the left of the political spectrum, from politicians and journalists to artists, writers, and scientists, from Herzfelde to Albert Einstein to Kurt Eisner, the soon-to-be assassinated leader of the Bavarian revolution. This so-called "Club of Revolutionary Spirits," modeled in part after the Fabian Society in Great Britain, would unite, in Kessler's words, all who were willing to stand for the "destruction of the outdated or that which is unjustifiably hallowed in all areas." Of course, such a loose connection of individuals from disparate walks of life could not duplicate the role of the Fabian intellectuals with their close ties to the Labor Party, and after a few meetings the "Revolutionary Spirits" went their separate ways.[36]

It was about this time, however, that Kessler discovered the cause that would claim the great bulk of his time and energy in the next few years, pacifism. It was as a leading member of a number of interlocking pacifist organizations that he became known as "The Red Count" in the public eye. His pacifist connections and reputation would also encourage the Foreign Office to send him on informal missions to England and France to make contact with English and French counterparts. The issue that brought him into the pacifist fold was the League of Nations, particularly the hope of changing radically its structure, from one based on a "club" of victorious nation-states to one where international organizations of producers and consumers would make decisions. Certainly, the hope that a wave of public sentiment could compel the victorious Allies to abandon their own plans and adopt the blueprints of an international organization that transcended the nation-state was one of Kessler's most fanciful illusions. When it ebbed, however, it left him firmly in the camp of the pacifists who had mostly warmly embraced it.

CHAPTER 21

Pacifism and Its Discontents

> The world that we must seek is a world in which the creative
> spirit is alive, in which life is an adventure full of joy and hope,
> based rather upon the impulse to construct than upon the
> desire to retain what we possess or to seize what is possessed
> by others. It must be a world in which affection has free play,
> in which love is purged of the instinct for domination, in
> which cruelty and envy have been dispelled by happiness and
> the unfettered development of all the instincts that build up
> life and fill it with mental delights. Such a world is possible; it
> waits only for men to wish to create it.
>
> Bertrand Russell, *Roads to Freedom*

Kessler did not quite become a pacifist overnight, as a result of the shock
of the German defeat, as has been suggested.[1] If his remarks on pacifism
during the war are often scornful, they nonetheless betray an ever more
serious preoccupation with the issue. Given his growing alienation from
the extreme nationalism represented by the Fatherland Party and his increasing involvement with young war resisters such as Unruh, Herzfelde, and Grosz, it is not surprising that he tried to formulate a pacifism
he could support.

Neither of the two major strands of prewar German pacifism attracted
him. The so-called "ethical pacifism," represented best by Bertha von
Suttner, author of the best-selling antiwar novel *Nie wieder Waffen!*
(*Never Again Weapons!*), rejected war as simply immoral. Kessler found
this to be naive and flat: "Pacifism is weak because in the end it is purely

negative: 'No War,' 'No Violence,' without putting in the place of violence something creative."[2] The "organizational pacifism" of Alfred H. Fried—who, with Suttner, was awarded the Nobel Peace Prize—which asserted that war would become increasingly impossible in a world tied ever more closely together by trade, international treaties, and other forms of modern organization, had clearly received a major blow by the outbreak of the war and was, in any case, too passive for Kessler to accept. "Connections of the superficial kind such as Fried strives for," Kessler wrote one fine spring day in 1918 when he was impressed by the force of nature, "are torn apart like threads by such forces. A new faith, a new economic system, not purely legalistic formulas and debating clubs, are necessary."[3]

This critique is reminiscent of his criticism of orthodox socialism: he sought a more "muscular" version of pacifism, one that could successfully compete for the same idealism that drove men, especially youth, to war. Fritz von Unruh and Wieland Herzfelde both seemed to incorporate this kind of heroic pacifism; the more legalistic, traditional approach of the older generation struck Kessler as anemic in comparison. His willingness, however, to join a pacifist organization, organized by Wilhelm Herzog, the editor of the journal *Forum*, as early as February 1918, a full nine months before the end of the war, suggests that it was not merely the prospect of defeat that led him to embrace pacifism. He made both his reasons and his misgivings known on this occasion: "I fear a tendency to play games and coffeehouse pacifism. On the other hand the selection of leaders for the new world order and the fructification of the chaotic revolt created by the war is necessary."[4]

The last of Wilson's Fourteen Points calling for a vague "general association of nations" to secure peace and international order in the postwar world impressed Kessler at first as the purest charade. Lord Grey's pamphlet on this subject, which called for a league of four nations—England, France, the United States, and Germany, once it had successfully become a democracy—struck him as hypocritical because first, the other nations were not full democracies and second, it would serve as a fig leaf for Anglo-Saxon domination of the world. Only if Germany could achieve an alliance with Russia and possibly with Japan would a balance be possible within such an organization, he speculated.[5] Still, as early as October 21, 1918, before the German capitulation, he suggested to Romberg that a league of nations, provided it were established honestly, would open a great and beautiful future for the German people.[6]

Such a rosy vision depended on the goodwill and political imagination of the victorious Entente, something in which Kessler never had much confidence. Still, the publication in the German newspapers of the formal proposal for the League of Nations in the middle of February 1919 shocked him. "A bundle of barren legal paragraphs animated by the old spirit and barely disguising the imperialist intention of a number of states to enslave and pauperize their defeated enemies . . . a contract to be imposed on poor relations." Almost immediately he devised an alternative. "A mistake that leaps to the eye is that the plan has originated with states, political entities which are by nature rivals, rather than with those major economic and humanitarian interests and associations which inherently incline to internationalism. Those are the bodies (international labor organizations, international trading and raw materials federations, major religious communities, the Zionists, international banking consortiums, and so on) which should be furnished with power and sanctions *against* these political entities and become invested with ever more legal independence of any individual states. A framework and set of rules for that purpose is what is needed, and not one which will, just the other way around, provide the ridiculous old elite of Great Powers with even more ascendancy than before." With such a proposal, Germany, in alliance with Soviet Russia, could pursue a meaningful international policy, attracting popular support even in the Entente lands.[7]

Thus was born not only Kessler's plan for an alternate world organization, but also the agenda behind his future diplomatic activity. He asked Hilferding his opinion and, undaunted by the latter's rejection of the plan as impractical, proceeded to discuss it with Romberg, the editorial board of *Deutsche Nation,* Walther Rathenau, and others. The foreign minister Rantzau encouraged him to put his conception in draft form and offered him the services of the Foreign Office's legal department for the purpose. By February 26, a mere ten days after the first inspiration, the draft was completed and Kessler submitted it to his Cranach Presse for publication under the title "Plan for a League of Nations on the Basis of an Organization of Organizations (World Organization)."[8]

Several versions of his plan bear testimony to the evolution of his thinking, but the core idea was to transcend the nation-state by shifting the bulk of its economic functions to autonomous, self-governing, international corporations of producers and consumers. The underlying premise is that, in the modern industrial world, one's function as a producer, something over which one has some freedom to decide, is more essential to human identity than geographical place of birth, the result of mere chance. In an increasingly interconnected world economy, the individual's productive role within a certain branch of industry is rapidly becoming more important than his or her national identity. As banks, industrial enterprises, and workers begin to reach out across national borders and organize themselves internationally—whether in the form of syndicates, cartels, or unions—the international economy starts eroding the importance of the nation-state, so that both it and the nationalism connected with it look more and more like anachronisms. To reflect this reality, Kessler's plan calls for the creation of a central organ to which the already existing international organizations, as well as entirely new ones that would emerge, would apply for membership. This institution, which would be an integral part of the League of Nations, would have as its chief mission no less than the coordination of world economic production, distribution, and consumption with the aims of (1) increasing production, (2) meeting demand, (3) providing everyone the right to a decent job, and (4) and ensuring the greatest possible equality of economic opportunity. One of the chief causes of war, the unequal distribution of raw materials and markets, would thus be eliminated and the shattered world economy would be rebuilt along democratic socialist principles.

Kessler eventually came to believe that even the very unsatisfactory League of Nations as drawn up by the Allies offered the possibility for its reconstruction along the lines he envisioned.[9] He set forth the immediate steps to be taken, the first being the entrance of Germany, Austria, Russia, and the United States. The invidious distinctions between the states regarding military and legal rights must be abolished, and all members should enjoy equal rights and be equally disarmed. Those elements of the existing League that dealt with the rights of workers should be strengthened, particularly the International Labor Office and the planned international commissions to oversee the distribution of raw materials and the regulation of transportation and finance. Finally, a central organ for the self-administering, productive corporations—democratic and incorporating professionals as well as industrial workers—should be created. The ultimate goal of this transformation would be the autonomy of these organizations from the nation-state, resulting in, among other things, the dismantling of imperialism, of economic protectionism, and of national armed forces.

One source of inspiration for Kessler's proposals was Walther Rathenau. For years both the man and his ideas had intrigued him. During the war, Rathenau published two highly influential books on the coming postwar world: *Von kommenden Dingen* (*In Days to Come*), published in February 1918, sold out three editions in as many months, and *Die neue Wirtschaft* (*The New Society*), which appeared a year later, fared even better, selling 30,000 copies in a month. The success of these works depended on the credibility of their author, due to both his reputation as a prominent industrialist and, especially, his pioneering work in setting up Germany's wartime Raw Materials Section, established in August 1914 to confront the critical problem of assembling critical war materials. It eventually became one of the cornerstones of Germany's wartime mobilization and "undoubtedly the most successful economic organization created by Germany during the war."[10]

Rathenau's most important contribution to the success of the Raw Materials Section was the so-called *Kreigsgesellschaften* or "war companies," self-administering business enterprises organized by the state into syndicates controlling a particular vital branch of wartime industry. The resulting monopolies were operated on a day-to-day basis by private companies under the oversight of a government representative, who sat on the boards and exercised a veto right over any decision. Rathenau could thus argue that the prewar evolution of the company from the personal creation of a patriarchal founder-figure into a depersonalized, quasi-public, joint-stock company run by managers and technocrats foreshadowed its eventual further postwar transformation into a state corporation. This corporation would be similar to a private enterprise in that it would issue shares and have the freedom to close unprofitable enterprises, but it would be given monopolistic privileges by the state in return for a share in its administration, its social impact, and its profits.[11]

To any doubts about the efficiency of an economy run without competition, both Rathenau and Kessler pointed to the wartime experience not only of Germany but also of the Allies in regulating the economy. "It is," claimed Kessler, ". . . an established historical fact that industry systematically controlled by public bodies functioned on the whole satisfactorily on both sides for several years, and that both parties were thus led to recognize its superiority, at least in war emergencies, over the traditional type of private enterprise." But what about their effectiveness in peacetime? In the absence of a profit motive, what would provide the incentive for leadership, for risk taking, for responsibility, and for work itself? Would not the result be economic, technological, and social stagnation? "Rathenau replies that there is no cause for anxiety, for the leaders no less than the liberated proletariat would be moved by other impulses, by joy in creation, love for their work and the feeling of solidarity, and moved not only to jog along with the others, but to exert their influence as innovators, leaders and pioneers. And more important still, they would be moved by the true driving forces of the born leader: the will to power and the desire for responsibility, which impel him, quite apart from considerations of pleasure and profit, to great achievements and great risks." [12] At any rate, such considerations would have to substitute for material motives inasmuch as Rathenau called for the virtual elimination of private wealth through progressive taxation.

Rathenau's austere vision of a world of work for its own sake; of a collective capitalism divorced from its roots in luxury, ostentation, and personal ownership; of an economic democracy melded with a technocratic meritocracy appealed both to Lenin's economic advisors drawing up plans for a planned economy and to elements of the German right wing, who viewed his neocorporatist ideas as an effort to avoid class conflict by integrating the working class into a national community "beyond capitalism and communism." The Germans, with their special capacity for work and organization, would avoid both the soulless materialism and individual anarchy of Western liberal capitalism, shown by the war to be outdated anyway, and the regimented, brutal, primitive communism of Soviet Russia, not really suited to a *Kulturvolk* like the Germans.[13]

It was only one of Rathenau's many contradictions that he could propose a grim, gray, dutiful socialism, where the only really sanctioned joy would be joy in one's work and consumption strictly regulated, and at the same time lead a life of refined luxury himself. Inevitably, the question of his sincerity comes up, as it did for his contemporaries who noted the same contradictions. So too for Kessler. How can one reconcile the arts and crafts enthusiast, the aesthete who chose only the most refined furniture and furnishings for his residences, the bibliophile who did not hesitate to spend thousands of marks to have special typefaces cut for his printing press, the soldier who received turtle soup from abroad while serving on the eastern front with the man who cites the following passage from Rathenau approvingly? "The years of labor requisite for the production of some delicate embroidery, or some textile marvel, have been filched from the clothing of the poorest among us; the carefully mown lawns of a private garden could with less expenditure of labor have grown wheat; the steam yacht, with its captain and crew, with its stores of food and coal, has been withheld for the whole term of its existence from the possibility of playing a useful part in the world's commerce." [14] Granted even that Kessler's prewar lifestyle, however luxurious, had avoided the vulgarities of Wilhelmian ostentation, it is hard to imagine his endorsing the idea that the craft represented by, say, a fine tapestry represented merely theft from the poor. Did this signify a genuine change of heart due, perhaps, to the experience of the war or to his embracing socialism? Or was it a thoughtless hypocrisy never put to the test, the wishful thinking of the armchair socialist?

Rathenau would have responded by arguing that the underlying goal was freedom, defined as self-determination for the individual, "when he no longer accepts the forces that guide him, but creates them; when he no longer receives but freely chooses the values, ideals, aims and authority whose validity he will admit; when he begets out of his own being the relations with the divine which he means to serve." Or, as Kessler asserted, the real touchstone of any worthy revolutionary order would not be "whether it strengthens the state, increases production, or effects a more just and uniform distribution of the products of labor. All of these things are important, but not decisive. What is really vital is whether it makes men finer, deeper, spiritually richer, and freer from external and internal inhibitions." In short, the ultimate goals of Rathenau's socialism resemble nothing so much as those of the aesthetic state pursued by Kessler since the Weimar days. The entire apparatus of politics and economics should serve to give the individual the maximum opportunity for a Nietzschean "will to power" and "joy in creation." A joyful making of art would replace the sordid moneymaking of contemporary capitalism. "Man must be free," in Kessler's words, "not merely in general, as an individual, as a 'contemporary,' as like among like; he must be free also in a special sense as an *active* individual, specifically, as unlike among unlike, as one who performs a function along with others, as the member of a group engaged on some specific function within human society, in order that his energies may contribute in their full force to the strengthening of that function, to the strengthening of the group in its functional activity. . . . That is the conception of a universal functional democracy, which completes the one-sided purely political democracy, and whose aim can be summed up in Nietzsche's stirring words: 'To win freedom for renewed creation.'" [15]

These lines, repeated in Kessler's biography of Rathenau, were originally written for an article on the guild socialism, a movement that developed in Great Britain in the years just before and during the First World War. Guild socialism had its roots, of course, in the social thought of John Ruskin and William Morris and particularly in their admiration for the medieval craft organization of work, although it also drew inspiration from European syndicalism. The decade just before the outbreak of the war saw a flourishing of the guild socialist movement.[16] Among the most influential proponents were the philosopher Bertrand Russell and G. H. D. Cole, one of the most important leftist thinkers in twentieth-century British history. Cole's *Self-Government in Industry* (1918) was a key text in the movement. For Cole and other guild socialists, the poverty of the workers was not the main flaw of capitalism; rather, it was the enslavement of the workers in the form of wage labor. The guiding principle of guild socialism was not justice, but freedom: "freedom for self expression, freedom at work as well as at leisure, freedom to serve as well as to enjoy." Guild socialists opposed strongly the state-administered, distributive social policies favored by the Fabian Society and the Labour Party leadership, finding their attitude toward the workers to be patronizing and demeaning and distrusting their embrace of the state bureaucracy. Naturally, they also disagreed with the strategy of gaining power primarily through political campaigns and alliances. Rather, they favored "functional democracy," where workers of all kinds, including "brain workers," would be organized into national guilds based on their function in the economy.[17] These units of producers would be organized into a national guild congress, which, in some schemes, would have as its counterweight, a parliament, elected on a geographic basis, which would represent the interests of consumers and negotiate with the guilds over the prices and quantity of goods.

Many criticisms could be and were leveled at guild socialism of course, even from within the left.* Ultimately, however, what put an end to guild socialism's brief postwar efflorescence was not its theoretical deficiencies but the changing political and economic scene. The economic slump that struck Great Britain in 1921 threw British trade unions into a defensive stance, making the demand for workers' control

---

* Some Fabian intellectuals, for example, felt that the trade unions would never be able to perform the role vouchsafed them by the scheme—they were too conservative, too timid, too concerned with practical improvements. More generally, there is something unwieldy about the negotiation process that would establish the price and availability of goods. If the various guilds responsible for the production of the immense variety of goods and services needed in a modern industrial system have monopoly control over their bit of the economy, what leverage would the organizations representing consumers have in negotiations? If, further, the guilds are to be controlled democratically by the workers, what is to prevent their leadership from being dominated by political hacks rather than by competent professionals, especially given the absence of any possible competition within that branch of industry?

a secondary issue. At the same time, the split in the left engendered by
the Russian revolution made the middle ground staked out by guild socialists between the Soviet model favored by communist parties and the
moderate reformism of the social democrats untenable. And so guild socialism shared the same ultimate fate of the German council movement:
political irrelevance.[18]

That lay in the future, however. In 1919 and 1920, these ideas were
very much in the air. They appealed strongly to Kessler for a number of
deeply personal reasons. Their roots in the arts and crafts movement,
and in the visions of social transformation through aesthetics that un-
derpinned at least some of the impulse behind art nouveau and Jugendstil, recalled to him his youthful engagement on behalf of modern
art. The emphasis of both Rathenau and the guild socialists on injecting idealism, will power, and even spirituality into the socialist movement to rescue it from an overly intellectual passivity and scholastic
sterility came close to Kessler's call for blending Nietzsche with Marx.[19]
The democratization of Nietzsche's thought, the concept of providing
each citizen the maximum amount of self-determination in all spheres
of life, free from inherited or imposed constraints, rang a deep chord in
the part of Kessler's personality that remained an outsider, however well
connected to the establishment he was. Finally, both Rathenau and the
guild socialists gave the council movement a theoretical justification it
had lacked hitherto. Thus, while Kessler's open engagement for these
ideas represents a striking contrast with his prewar politics, there is,
nevertheless, a remarkable continuity between the goals he pursued as
an art critic, patron, and museum director before the war and those he
pursued as a diplomat and pacifist after. Although he was never required
to make the personal sacrifices, in terms of comfort and luxury, that
would have been necessary had the revolution triumphed in the way he
wanted, Kessler supported this brand of democratic socialism all the
more sincerely because he could both see its roots in his past and imagine a place for himself in the future it promised.

Not all those who professed their support for his reconstruction of
the League of Nations were firm believers in democratic socialism. The
government that adopted briefly Kessler's proposal as their own in April 1919 did so out of purely opportunistic grounds, as a gambit in the
chess game over the treaty negotiations in Versailles. By appearing *plus
Wilsonist que Wilson,* so to speak, the German government hoped to
convince the American president of its genuine conversion to his democratic and internationalist ideals and thus to drive a wedge between the

United States and its French and British allies. It further intended to play Wilson's game by appealing over the heads of the Entente regimes to their citizenries, which was the reason for the Foreign Ministry organizing and subsidizing, at a cost of 100,000 marks, a Deutsche Liga für Völkerbund, similar to the English League of Nations Union. The new organization engaged immediately in a feverish propaganda activity designed to prove Germany's bona fides.[20] When Walther Schücking, a longtime pacifist and law professor, informed Kessler on April 18 that his ideas had enjoyed "a great triumph" at the cabinet meeting the day before and would be adopted as the basis for the German government's counterproposal to the Allied draft, the latter could hardly contain himself. "I am really surprised how vigorously this idea, since I first ventilated it, is making progress: the notion of the state restrained by the universal forces of humanity. Born of despair, it can perhaps shape humanity's future and guide it to a fresh flowering. Good Friday magic. In the evening, listening to a folk song, only the contrast of the deep humiliation of our nation impinged painfully on me. Suddenly my nerves gave way almost completely."[21] Assured by Schücking that his authorship would be expressly acknowledged, Kessler made preparations for a speech before the upper house of the Prussian legislature, announcing his proposal and, for the accompanying publicity, including a full front-page spread in the prominent liberal newspaper *Vossische Zeitung*.

He was robbed of his triumph by the decision of the government to announce its own draft (the one supposedly based on his proposal) the very evening that he was scheduled to speak, April 22. This simultaneous publication caused some confusion in the foreign press as to which proposal was the official one, and it wounded Kessler's vanity, despite the success of his speech. He blamed the affair on a maneuver by Matthias Erzberger intended to steal the credit for Kessler's ideas. This accusation ignored the fact that Erzberger's engagement with the idea of a League of Nations long predated Kessler's; even more important, Kessler's pique overlooked the great differences between the two proposals. In fact, despite what Schücking had said, the government draft was much less radical than Kessler's and much closer in spirit to the Allied proposal. The final government proposal—stiff, legalistic, and inflexible—was never intended to do anything more than up the ante during the Versailles discussions on the League's Covenant, by shaming the Allies if they produced a draft less democratic or peace-loving than their own.[22]

In the end, all of the intrigue and maneuvering came to naught. The Allies simply brushed aside the German proposal when they presented the finished treaty to the German delegation on May 7. The shock of the terms, perceived by nearly all Germans of every political persuasion as draconian, overpowered all other discussion. It represented the final end of the fairy tales by which many Germans had assuaged their anxiety during the long months of waiting. Kessler was so crushed that he was unable to write in his diary for more than a month. Inasmuch as the Allies erected the League of Nations as an integral part of the Treaty of Versailles, to administer and enforce it, German public opinion, with the exception of the convinced pacifists, turned as swiftly against the League, now seen as a tool of domination, as it had embraced it when it hoped to salvage something from defeat. In the wake of this disappointment, the public debate over the League of Nations subsided and its mention aroused only derision and contempt in most circles.[23]

Kessler was among the few who did not abandon the idea, although he did put it on hold for the rest of the year. The brief flurry of publicity surrounding his proposal—he was photographed at his desk and interviewed by the foreign press—seems to have gone to his head. He had the pleasure of denying, in an interview with *The New York Times,* any intention of supplanting Rantzau as Germany's foreign minister and, when warned against being too ambitious, replied to himself: "To what should I aspire? As things are, I have more influence than if I were Minister of Foreign Affairs, the position to which the newspapers keep promoting me. Why should I, without serving myself or my country in the slightest, push myself forward to be Rantzau's successor?" When told of the rumors that he was a fire-breathing Independent or even a Spartacist sympathizer, he responded coyly that he was a registered member of the Democratic Party who preferred to avoid the class struggle. He seemed pleased, however, with his notoriety, as he was with the suggestion that he was being considered for the position of ambassador to Belgium.[24]

Nothing came of these rumors either, and meanwhile, Kessler confronted some deep political and personal tragedies in the summer and early fall of 1919. The final signing of the Versailles treaty was a bitter pill to swallow. When he learned that the German navy, interned at the British naval headquarters, had succeeded in scuttling its ships, he wrote "(T)his evening I have been indescribably depressed, as though the entire sap of life has dried up inside me." Despite desperate talk of resistance, it was the end of five years of struggle. At the same time, all hopes of a genuine revolution within Germany seemed dashed as well. At the beginning of September, Kessler delivered a shrewd postmortem. "It is my impression . . . that the revolution is provisionally over. Counter-revolution is on the march, with the monarchy clearly in the background. The revolution has come to a dead end through the incapacity of the Social Democratic Government team, the far greater experience and cunning of conservative civil servants . . . the difficulty of creating socialism in a ruined country, and the physical exhaustion of the famished proletariat. Nothing can stand permanently still, so we shall now have the retrogressive movement, counterrevolution. That will be Germany's real defeat."[25]

Another blow followed. For more than five years, he had been separated from his family. On September 21, 1919, he received a telegram from Wilma that their mother was seriously ill. The next day he was informed that she had, in fact, already died on the 19th. They had been planning for their first reunion in Switzerland. "This tragedy of poor Mama's death in the very moment where I could hope to see her after so many years, has simply crushed every possibility of utterance in me;" he wrote to Wilma in December, excusing his long silence, "it has literally struck me dumb. Something in me revolts, when I try to write. . . . I really care for *nothing* any more."[26]

He persevered. During the last half of 1919, he bided his time and gathered his strength for the strenuous public engagement that would characterize the next several years. After a trip to Switzerland and Italy to meet his sister, his first journey since the end of the war, he returned in the aftermath of the inept right-wing attempt, known as the Kapp Putsch, to overthrow the Republic. Its collapse was followed immediately by an equally disastrous leftist insurrection in the Ruhr, suppressed with bloody zeal by government troops, leaving Germany even more polarized and embittered than when he had departed.

Kessler was preparing for an ambitious lecture tour to promote his ideas on the League of Nations, on pacifism, and on international reconciliation. These speaking engagements, which began precisely in the same Ruhr valley that had witnessed bloody fighting between the *Freikorps* and the Red Army of the workers only weeks before, were to cement Kessler's public reputation as a pacifist and earn him the title, "the Red Count." True, he had already become a member of several pacifist organizations, among them the New Fatherland League, which he joined in January 1919, and the World Youth League, for which he served as honorary chairman of the German chapter. But it was the pub-

licity surrounding his lecture tour that was to prompt his election to the
board of the most prominent pacifist organization, the German Peace
Society, in 1921. Indefatigable on these trips, he honed his speaking
skills before all kinds of audiences. One day he might be addressing a
group of metal workers in Düsseldorf on "Workers and the League of
Nations," then, a month later, he could be found before the elite
Wednesday Society in Berlin discussing the subject "Should Germany
Join the League of Nations?" From the Ruhr to Berlin to Leipzig
(where he delivered a lecture on Poland) to Königsberg in East Prussia,
he traversed Germany. Often, he had to deal with hecklers from the
right and from the left. Such public engagement was potentially dangerous, too. In May, he learned of the murder of the pacifist Hans
Paasche and heard, via a right-wing acquaintance, that his friend Helmut von Gerlach, also a prominent pacifist, was next on a list of those
to be assassinated: "At present those in Germany who make themselves
politically unpopular stand in greater danger of their lives than they
would in the most disreputable South American republic or at Rome
under the Borgias." [27]

The high point of the campaign was undoubtedly the enthusiastic
adoption of his revised League of Nations plan by the Pacifist Congress
in Brunswick in October 1920. The German Peace Society, the most
prominent and oldest such organization in Germany, had invited all of
the numerous other pacifist groups that had sprung up as a result of the
war to this congress. Eventually, an umbrella organization, the German
Peace Cartel, would emerge from the effort.[28] One of the periodical
controversies that plagued the interwar German peace movement was
raging in Brunswick precisely at the time when Kessler's proposal was
scheduled to come up for debate, which at first alarmed him: "But my
success was enormous, far beyond what could be expected. The Congress was almost unanimous in voting to interrupt its debate so as to
pass my resolution. Schücking, who was in the chair, said that for years
he had not heard such a speech in the Reichstag. Afterwards, I was besieged from all sides with requests for lectures. Within half an hour I had
assumed engagements to speak all over Germany." Kessler had done
more than to provide the congress with a brief moment of unity; he had
also assisted materially by donating 100,000 marks to the German Peace
Society, the first of a number of financial contributions to German
pacifism. Ludwig Quidde, the long-term chairman of the Peace Society,
described him as one of "the relatively few persons . . . who supported
us with larger sums." [29]

Such services did not go unnoticed and Kessler was soon counted as one of the leaders of the pacifist movement. In February of the following year, he was recruited, along with Albert Einstein, to establish contact with the International Trade Union Congress headquartered in Amsterdam. The background for their mission was the meeting of the reparations committee in Paris to decide finally on the exact sum Germany would have to pay. On the train, Kessler queried the great physicist about his theory of relativity, the first of a series of affectionate encounters between the two over the next few years. Although more and more the issue of reparations came to preoccupy Kessler, as indeed it did international politics, in 1921, he still had not given up the promotion of his World League idea. In the spring and early summer, he traveled to Italy to visit with Wilma and her children in Florence as well as to work on an essay on Nietzsche. At the same time, he managed to secure an interview with the pope to discuss his plan. In the meeting, Benedict XV successfully evaded the subject of the League.[30]

In the last stage of his journeys on behalf of pacifism in 1921, Kessler traveled to Paris in December as part of a delegation of German pacifists to the International Democratic Congress hosted by the French League for Human Rights, led by Marc Sangnier, the most prominent French pacifist. Kessler had last seen Paris on July 28, 1914, only a few days before the war began. "Strange," he noted, "how seven so terrible years can be completely wiped out in a moment of unreflecting thought. I felt as though I was returning to the old familiar scene after but a brief absence." Kessler gave a speech emphasizing Germany's moral obligation to rebuild the areas of France devastated by the war, for which he reaped "frantic applause" from the audience. The contacts he made during the next days helped ensure him a role as a spokesman for Franco-German reconciliation. Thus it was that Kessler and Einstein were chosen as the speakers to greet a delegation of French pacifists visiting the Reichstag in June 1922. The speeches of Kessler, Einstein, and Victor Basch, one of the leading French pacifists, were received enthusiastically on that occasion. In his talk, Kessler confirmed the moral responsibility of Germany to rehabilitate northern France but drew the conclusion that German good will had limits and her payments and services should serve the purpose of European reconstruction, not the cause of French militarism.[31]

Despite his contributions to Franco-German understanding, his membership in the principal pacifist organizations, his financial support, and his public reputation as one of the leading German pacifists, Kessler never overcame completely his misgivings regarding pacifists, if not pacifism. The eternal squabbling among the pacifist organizations, the self-righteous posturing, and the general sense of unreality that accompanied each new resolution passed irked him. As early as January 1919, he remarked on the occasion of a meeting of the board of the New Fatherland League: "The discussion of a church committee in a village would have been, in terms of intellectual level and personal character, no different from this squabble between the martyrs of pacifism whose noble humanity is supposed to serve Germany as a beam of light . . . . The entire meeting was grotesque, especially if one considers the pompous claims of the League, that it, in a certain fashion, wishes to form a new and better humanity, and the personalities of those present who all consider themselves exalted over the rest of the German people because their noble character and high spirituality." If these remarks seem unfair, given the beleaguered condition of postwar German pacifism, they nevertheless echoed the sentiments of many observers on the left. Carl von Ossietzky, one of the leading Weimar leftist intellectuals and journalists, regularly ridiculed the German pacifists: "This movement is inundated by fanatics and sectarians of every conceivable denomination. Project makers with wonder drugs for all the ills of society; universal reformers who hate meat . . . . These people produce children only because they see no other solution, but they do it with a pronounced dislike. They would be happy only if they were allowed to prescribe a diet of kohlrabi for the entire human race."

Kessler himself once expressed the hope that "the German pacifists would be pacified." [32] Given the German Peace Cartel's broad range of membership, in terms of social class and political persuasion, conflicts over strategy, tactics, and issues were inevitable—it was the venomous, personal tone that seemed superfluous.

Kessler's own position within the movement was complicated. Although his background and his connections to official Germany placed him in the camp of the moderates, he was attracted temperamentally to the younger radicals on some issues. One contemporary put it this way: "One can not say that Count Kessler belongs to either the right or the left wing of pacifism. He has his own marching directions and a thoroughly independent position among the German pacifists. At the Leipzig Pacifist Congress of 1922 he came closer to the faction favoring resistance to conscription. But, if he sympathizes with their standpoint, resistance to conscription certainly is not the central plank of his platform." [33] Kessler also diverged from some moderate pacifists in his willingness to support the paramilitary organization formed by the Social Democrats to defend the Weimar Republic from its internal enemies, notably the Nazi brownshirts.

Yet, he could never endorse wholeheartedly the "fundamentalist" wing of pacifism. Quite apart from his ideological disagreements with them, he would have lost any chance of undertaking diplomatic missions on behalf of the Foreign Office had he been identified as a radical on this question. As it was, his reputation as a pacifist would cramp his diplomatic effectiveness on several occasions, most notably during the negotiations over Germany's entrance to the League of Nations in the fall of 1924. Although there was talk of nominating him for the Nobel Peace Prize (eventually awarded to Quidde), most Germans of his social background and education considered pacifism in the wake of Germany's postwar humiliation to be, at best, defeatist, at worst, sheer treachery. Thus, it was that Kessler in 1926 found himself called upon to resign from his old university fraternity, the Canitz-Gesellschaft, which met to discuss expelling him for his outspoken pacifism. In his appearance before the governing body of the fraternity, Kessler sought to justify his politics, explaining that in terms of domestic politics, he favored strengthening the current state, which happened to be a republic, and in foreign policy, he favored reconstruction (of Germany's power) without revenge or violence. Bismarck himself, he explained to his presumably incredulous audience, would have approved of this policy in view of Germany's postwar position. After his inevitable expulsion, he sadly remarked that it was a mistake to break the few links between the left and the right.[34]

As he tried to explain to his former fraternity brothers, pacifism and patriotism were not necessarily incompatible. Although his identification with an internationalist and pacifist foreign policy was sincere and entailed serious consequences—up to and including the threat of assassination by right-wing extremists—Kessler remained *au fond* a German patriot. The more far-sighted and discerning politicians and diplomats knew this. Gustav Stresemann conceded that Kessler was an "extreme pacifist" but did not doubt his "inner attachment to Germany." Within the pacifist movement, Kessler took pains to defend the official foreign policy of Weimar, whatever his personal reservations may have been. His support of the government's position concerning the Locarno security pact of 1925 upset the radicals who muttered angrily about falling victim to a plot by German nationalists.[35] Precisely this ambiguity, this position of having a foot in each camp, however, made Kessler suitable for sensitive, unofficial diplomatic missions in the tenacious struggle over the fulfillment of the Versailles treaty that ensued almost immediately after the war, and that culminated in 1923 with the French occupation of the Ruhr, the German passive resistance, hyperinflation, and Hitler's Beer Hall Putsch. In this crisis the Foreign Office mobilized all of its resources and Kessler found himself, for the first time since Warsaw and Switzerland, fully engaged in the struggle.

CHAPTER 22

Diplomatic Missions

Wars are seldom decisive . . . in the game of foreign policy
the protagonists have just so many counters as their economic
power provides, and . . . a nation can win and retain just so
much weight in foreign affairs as corresponds to its moral,
intellectual and economic resources.

Walther Rathenau, quoted in Kessler,
Walther Rathenau

In a very important sense, the titanic struggle between Germany and
the Western Allies did not conclude with the Treaty of Versailles, but
continued—fought this time on the diplomatic and economic plane—
until the Locarno treaties of 1925. Indeed, some would argue it really
only ended with the final capitulation of Germany in 1945 at the end of
the Second World War. Despite its military defeat, Germany remained
potentially the strongest state in Europe, with the principal source of
its strength, its immensely efficient industrial plant and highly educated
human capital, intact. Assuming that the nation could avoid collapsing
into anarchy in the short term, Germany could be confident that, over
time, its underlying strengths would redress the balance of power and
would restore her great power status. Meanwhile, absent the presence
of the United States, the supposed victors France and England were
exhausted financially, demographically, and economically. The Western
Allies could only hope to impose the results of Versailles if they acted in
unison and if they could rely on the cooperation of the real victor of the
war, the United States. Such hopes quickly proved illusory. Although

Allied public opinion was convinced that their side had won a total victory—so much so that making the Germans pay for their depredations seemed an easy matter—more farsighted French and English statesmen understood how fragile the Versailles settlement really was. It was this understanding that made what one might call the "second" half of the First World War, the struggle over reparations, so politically and emotionally charged.

Even in hindsight, there remains something unfathomably complicated about reparations. Concerning one absolutely central issue—the question of how much Germany could afford to pay—there has never been any consensus, not only among financial experts at that time, but also among historians today.[1] The sheer colossal costs of the war meant that its financial settlement presented statesmen and economists with problems of an unprecedented scale. But what really bedeviled the question was domestic politics. It was domestic politics that caused the British and French leaders to expand the definition of reparations and insist on a public figure that privately they never thought Germany would pay, that caused the U.S. Senate to reject the Versailles treaty twice, and that made the repayment of Allied debts to the United States a pillar of postwar American foreign policy.[2] Nowhere, however, were domestic politics and foreign policy more disastrously intertwined than in Germany.

Even before the final official figure of 132 billion gold marks ($32 billion) was settled by the Reparations Commission in May 1921, this issue had posed nearly intractable problems for the weak, unstable center-left ruling coalitions of the early Weimar Republic. Outright intransigence, as the right wing urged, was both impossible and irresponsible, but meeting Allied demands fully meant political suicide. In response, the center left coalitions coined a strategy called "fulfillment," a misleading name inasmuch as its chief goal was to prove to the Allied leaders, particularly in Great Britain and the United States, that a strict fulfillment of the reparations demands would lead to the destruction of the German economy and with it, the European and world economies. Although such a policy may well have been the only feasible solution to the dilemma, it required time, perseverance, and patience—all in short supply at the time—to work. It soon became apparent what a gamble it was. Because the damage wrought by inflation was a calculated part of the policy, as proof of the impossibility of paying such a high rate of reparations, and because it was politically impossible to increase taxes and balance its budget, the government met its obligations—grudgingly and with much foot dragging—by selling paper to foreign investors, printing marks, and liquidating Germany's gold reserves, all of which helped accelerate the already strong postwar inflation. To no avail. Unable to explain its intentions to the German public, the government was attacked both by German nationalists, who accused it of treachery, and by an increasingly intransigent French government, which, especially after Raymond Poincaré came to power at the beginning of 1922, threatened to occupy the Ruhr unless Germany fulfilled her obligations to the letter.

It was in this atmosphere that the German Foreign Office turned to comparative outsiders like Kessler. As the impossibility of working out an agreeable compromise with the French seemed confirmed, the Germans turned to Great Britain and the United States, hoping that leaders there would realize the importance of a vibrant German economy for their own economic health and would put pressure on the French to be reasonable. The Germans had, in fact, always counted on the eventual divergence of goals to help split the Allies and to give them room to maneuver, a policy that would indeed—over time—bear fruit. To make these approaches, however, was a delicate matter, as tricky as the negotiations over a separate peace during the war because an official démarche to either the British or the Americans could result in an embarrassing rebuff and aggravate French intransigence. What was required was unofficial interlocutors with good social and political connections, not only to the party in power but also to the opposition parties. In addition, one needed presentable, articulate, credible spokesmen for the German cause to help influence public opinion in both countries. For this kind of mission, Kessler—identified publicly as a pacifist, fluent in English, and with excellent connections, especially in England but also in France—was tailor-made.

Throughout 1920 and 1921, as he pursued his plans for a new League of Nations, he stayed in close contact with members of the Foreign Office, as well as with Allied representatives, and discussed reparation issues with them. Then in March 1922, shortly after his return from Rome, he obtained the reluctant blessing of Foreign Minister Rathenau to attend the upcoming international conference on European economic reconstruction to be convened in Genoa.[3] Largely the brainchild of Lloyd George, the conference was intended to address a number of problems that plagued postwar Europe: the continuing high unemployment, inflation and economic stagnation, the desperate Russian need for Western aid in the wake of a famine, the mounting mistrust between France and England over a number of issues, and the persistent struggle over the Versailles settlement.[4] Kessler's diary paints a vivid, blow-by-blow picture of the event—its setting, personalities, and intrigues—but he played only a minor role, serving as an unofficial intermediary between Rathenau and Jacques Seydoux, one of the more thoughtful and far-sighted officials among the French delegation who had long pursued Franco-German cooperation as a way of tying the German economy to France and resisting Anglo-Saxon economic domination.[5] In the end, the conference failed in part because of the announcement of the Rapallo treaty between Germany and the Soviet Union, which canceled prewar debts and cleared the path for closer trade relations but had the short-term effect of increasing both French and British suspicions of German trustworthiness. In two articles he wrote for the *Deutsche Nation,* Kessler gave the conference a more optimistic review than he did in private, describing it as a watershed. The most hopeful sign was the shift in British politics away from the close alliance with France to a pacifist politics aimed at establishing a viable peace on the European continent. Reparations remained the main stumbling block, but Kessler pointed to a possible solution, namely, a vast international loan. Five billion gold marks was the price of peace, he asserted. "But the peculiarity of the situation is that no regime has this sum available or can raise it for this purpose through compulsory taxes; it must be raised from the world's creditors. Europe must buy peace from the bankers. The power, to secure it at least for some time, lies with the millions of nameless capitalists disregarding nationality who represent international capital and who are advised and represented by the internationally connected banking world. Here, however, England no longer is the leader, but America."[6] Besides needing a loan from U.S. capital, Europe needed to provide the French with the security that nation craved so that it could begin disarming itself; in other words, a "non-aggression pact." In his recipe, Kessler outlined the basic elements of what eventually would become the Dawes Plan and the Locarno treaties, achievements that would help stabilize international politics until the onset of the Great Depression. Yet, in the summer of 1922, the time was not yet ripe for these plans.

The experience of Genoa seems to have at first whetted Kessler's appetite for diplomacy, perhaps because his League of Nations propaganda had run into the sand. That summer was marked by the assassination of Rathenau by right-wing extremists shortly after his return from Genoa. Kessler was thunderstruck by the news. In the emotional aftermath of the funeral service and the speeches in the Reichstag, he probably conceived the idea of writing the life of the enigmatic figure. He took his leave of Rathenau on the afternoon of June 25 as the Republican martyr lay in state in his home in Grunewald: "He lay in an open coffin in the study where I so often sat with him. His head was leant slightly back to the right, a very peaceful expression in the deeply lined face over whose shattered lower portion a fine linen cloth was laid; with nothing except the gray, closely cropped, disheveled moustache protruding. A few flowers were spread over his breast and hands. Kreuter and I added red and white roses. We were quite alone in the room. Complete silence reigned. From the dead, furrowed, wounded face emanated immeasurable tragedy. I felt it as I did at Nietzsche's bier." In the wake of the tragedy, the ever-optimistic Kessler, felt that the time for a cleansing backlash against the anti-republican right wing had finally arrived. Josef Wirth's speech in tribute to Rathenau in the Reichstag, which concluded by bringing "three fifths of the tightly packed Chamber to their feet, staring in the direction of the right who sat there pale and silent like accused in a dock," caused him to reevaluate his poor opinion of the man: "He is someone after all." In November, Kessler invited some of the leading lights of the republican parties to a dinner. "We decided on a weekly meeting between ten or twelve people who should act, to use Preuss's expression, as a sort of republican *camarilla*, influencing the responsible leaders of German politics." The idea was to undertake the step that the 1918/19 revolution had failed to do: purging the bureaucracy of reactionaries, particularly in the law and in the universities. "One has the feeling," wrote Kessler, "that now among the masses and the intellectuals the problem of democratization has been grasped for the first time on the right end and with the right energy. What has been unleashed through Rathenau's death is perhaps a second revolution which will shape the real power relations more fundamentally than the one of November 9."[7] Reminiscent of his other efforts at organizing cabals of progressive, influential individuals acting in secret consort, this organization also collapsed without much fanfare.

The hoped-for backlash against the right wing never materialized, in part, because the mounting international tensions exacerbated political extremism. Instead, the wave of physical assaults on prominent supporters of the republic by right-wing extremists continued. Shortly after Rathenau's murder, Kessler visited Maximilian Harden, who had suffered a brutal beating, in the hospital. "Can I live in this country any longer?" Kessler's old companion in the Palézieux affair exclaimed.

Everywhere were signs that the republic was beleaguered. Visiting his old friend Elisabeth Förster-Nietzsche, he was appalled to hear that she feared for Kessler's life because of the Bolsheviks who had murdered Rathenau, one more sign of the degeneration of the Nietzsche Archive into a right-wing institution. At a celebration in honor of Gerhart Hauptmann held at the University of Berlin, Kessler was disgusted by the behavior of the professorate and the students who had voted to boycott the event on the grounds that Hauptmann had declared himself to be in favor of the republic. At a breakfast at Stresemann's house, he noticed the contemptuous tone used by the conservative bankers and politicians gathered there: "All in all: one senses the coming of dawn in these circles. Revolution, socialization, leftist regimes lie like bad dreams behind them. We sail with swollen sails towards the right." The name of Hitler appears for the first time in the diary at this time as the leader of a well-organized and armed following capable of overthrowing the government.[8] The date was November 9, 1922, exactly one year before the Beer Hall Putsch.

. . .

Perhaps his distress with the political evolution, both domestically and internationally, motivated Kessler to pick up the threads of old projects and to renew old friendships. In August 1922, he visited Maillol for the first time since 1914 and found the artist considerably aged. In September, he traveled back to Rapallo to meet Gordon Craig, again for the first time since the outbreak of the war, and the two friends discussed renewing their prewar project of an illustrated *Hamlet* to be printed by Cranach Presse.

Although he hedged his bets by reviving plans for the Cranach Presse and renewing contacts with artists and writers, Kessler kept his political irons in the fire. He greeted with skepticism the news of the establishment of a new cabinet, dominated by non-party "experts" and right-wing politicians under the relative political novice Wilhelm Cuno. At the end of November, Stresemann sounded him out concerning how the parties of the left might view the return of the crown prince from exile. Stresemann also asked if Kessler would go as German ambassador to Brussels. Asserting his lack of ambition to be given another ministerial appointment, Kessler responded, "I am completely independent, I am thoroughly happy with the activities I already pursue, and I know from the experience the intrigues which sour life for everyone in the

Foreign Service. It would therefore mean a very great sacrifice for me to reenter the Foreign Service and I would only be prepared to make it if I was convinced that I could thereby render the country a service. Such a conviction would depend on whether the German Government, instead of confining itself to vague declarations of goodwill, at last came forward with firm proposals on the reparations question."[9] There is no reason to doubt his reservations about taking up another official post. The ambassadorship to Belgium, at a time when the Belgians were preparing with their French allies to occupy the Ruhr, would only have been a slightly less hopeless, arduous, and hazardous position than was the post of ambassador to Poland in the immediate aftermath of the war.

The fateful year 1923 began with the long dreaded occupation of the Ruhr on January 11 by sixty thousand French and Belgian troops. The Poincaré government, seeing in the German reparations policy only a Fabian strategy of delay and obstruction, felt compelled to exercise its trump card, namely, its overwhelming military advantage. The old plan to roll back Germany's western border by sponsoring a separate, French-controlled, puppet state in the Rhineland was revived. The Cuno cabinet, caught without a well considered plan, improvised by calling for passive resistance on the part of officials, railway men, factory workers, and miners. In retaliation, the French put their own officials in charge of civil administration, ran the railways themselves, seized bank reserves and factory inventories, and isolated the Ruhr economically from the rest of Germany. To keep the resistance going, the German government was compelled to support the Ruhr population with grants of money and goods, an enormous expense precisely when it could no longer count on either taxes or coal deliveries from its chief industrial region. The value of the mark, which stood at 18,000 per dollar in January, quickly evaporated, reaching more than four million per dollar by the summer and inaugurating the strange and catastrophic phenomenon of hyperinflation. The cold war between France and Germany now reached its climax, and, along with the German currency, the hopes for a stable and peaceful order in Europe careened toward the abyss.

Typically, Kessler made sure that he was a witness of the maelstrom. As early as April 1922, he passed on a warning from his French contacts that the Poincaré government would not hesitate to occupy the Ruhr unilaterally.[10] During his January visit to Paris, he noted the mood of resignation among the French, comparing the decision to occupy the Ruhr to the desperate gamble of unrestricted submarine warfare chosen by the Germans during the war. As he waited for the results of the last reparations conference (ultimately negative), he again ran into old acquaintances from before the war, this time the high society crowd, habitués of the Restaurant Larue in the days of the Ballets Russes. At a concert of music by Erik Satie and Francis Poulenc in the theater designed by van de Velde, he ran into Misia Sert and Diaghilev: "Our first encounter since the war. We were all deeply moved. Misia could hardly speak. To someone who greeted her, she replied, 'Excuse me, right now I am so upset!'" Later, when Kessler came to visit, she told him how "during the war you were for us the image which represented the other side. We thought of you when one said: Germany." Later however, when he met with Jean Cocteau and his newest *poet maudit,* Raymond Radiguet, Cocteau informed him that Misia had repeated the same words to him but added that she was also "disturbed (*genée*)" by the encounter with Kessler, suggesting that wartime suspicions and animosities had not died completely.

He continued to maintain his political contacts as well. Earlier in Berlin he had even struck up a friendship with Louis Barthou, the hardline French foreign minister upon whose performance as chief French delegate in Genoa Kessler had lavished such scorn. As it turned out, Barthou was a passionate collector of literary autographs, and Kessler showed him his copy of Verlaine's *Sagesse,* annotated by the poet himself. Besides ministers and senators, he also met with industry leaders such as Robert Pinaud, the general secretary of the Comité des Forges, the leading representative of French heavy industry. The range of Kessler's connections astonished Leopold Hoesch, the German ambassador to Paris. It was Hoesch who informed the Foreign Office that Kessler wished to convey in person the information he had garnered about the state of French politics and to outline his thoughts on the situation before he traveled on to London again. Back in Berlin at the end of the month, he reported to Foreign Minister Frederic Hans von Rosenberg as well as to the two leading figures in the Foreign Office, Carl von Schubert and Ago von Maltzan. With Schubert particularly he had been friendly since their days together at the Bern embassy during the war. As the nephew of Richard von Kühlmann and the husband of Helene, Countess Harrach, Schubert frequented the same social circles as Kessler, and the two men used the informal *Du* with each other. Now in charge of relations with England and the United States, Schubert was looking for ways to mobilize Great Britain to take a more active role in the crisis. The ambassador in London, Friedrich Sthamer, while intelligent and capable, lacked connections in British society and with the leaders of the left. Between Schubert and Rosenberg, it was agreed that Kessler's mission would be to sound out the leaders of the Labour and Liberal Parties.[11]

In the next six months, Kessler would shuttle continuously to and from London. His first visit at the very end of January 1923 brought him into contact with Ramsey MacDonald, the leader of the Labour Party, and Geoffrey Dawson, the pro-German editor of the *Times*. Over tea at his home, MacDonald informed Kessler that the Labour Party intended to pressure the government in the Ruhr matter. Kessler also took the opportunity to renew old prewar friendships with William Rothenstein and Roger Fry. The latter reminded him of their last meeting nine days before the outbreak of the war when Kessler gave his reconciliation meal with Lady Cunard but everyone cancelled due to the July crisis. "Even my war with Lady Cunard that summer, which concluded with the breakfast, called back to memory the radiance of that season of which Fry said: it was the first time he had the feeling that London was becoming European, cosmopolitan. Then suddenly the war, and I was compelled to take the Duchess of Sutherland prisoner in Belgium. All of that flooded back: how distant, how near!"[12] As a sign that wartime passions had not disappeared completely, however, Kessler had to confront rumors deliberately spread by the editor of the *Daily Telegraph* that he had been seen still in London several weeks after the outbreak of the war. The incident with the duchess in occupied Namur was all that he needed to refute that calumny.

As a way of bringing the issue of the French occupation to the fore and compelling the government of Prime Minister Bonar Law to justify their inaction, Kessler in the middle of February conceived of a plan to induce the opposition to ask the prime minister the following question: "Does His Majesty's Government know what proposals the German government is ready to make?" Such a gambit would then provide the Germans with an opportunity to propose a solution without appearing thereby to be capitulating to the French. Achieving this end proved to be a very complicated endeavor. Enlisting the support of the Labour Party was relatively easy, but the cooperation of both wings of the Liberal Party was needed to truly force a debate on the Ruhr in the House of Commons. Yet, the Liberal leadership was worried about appearing disloyal to the government if it collaborated too openly with the German government in provoking a debate. Above all, the strategy required the Cuno cabinet to come up with proposals for ending the crisis that would not be immediately rejected by the French, something that was not at all a sure bet.

For more than six weeks, Kessler played an immensely complicated game so that the opposition parties in the House of Commons would compel the government to respond to the new German proposals for a solution to the Ruhr crisis. The core idea called for submission of the reparations dispute to an independent committee of experts. His chief interlocutors in these maneuvers were Sir John Simon, as Herbert Asquith's right-hand man responsible for one branch of the Liberal Party, and the German ambassador, Sthamer. The anxieties and agendas of other players, however, affected the play: the German cabinet worried about the appearance of capitulation, their British counterparts fretted about going behind the backs of France, and all parties concerned feared that France, upon learning of the negotiations, would unleash a press campaign to discredit it. Time after time, the effort nearly foundered, only to be rescued at the last minute by Kessler's persistent efforts, now warning Berlin to come up with realistic proposals, now prodding Sthamer to inform the British foreign secretary of the these proposals, now allaying the suspicions of Simon that the Germans were not serious.[13] To his sister, he boasted, "I have during all these weeks been the real Ambassador here and . . . this is recognized not only at the Embassy here, but . . . still more in B (Berlin)." The key interview took place in Asquith's private room in the House of Commons—"an immensely ostentatious Gothic apartment with an open fire of medieval proportions burning away in the hearth"—when Asquith agreed to intervene under certain conditions. On March 28, he officially interrogated the government on their Ruhr policy, reading from notes drafted with Kessler's influence. With pride and some relief, Kessler recorded the triumph of weeks of patient effort: "Asquith and Macdonald have welcomed Rosenberg's (German foreign minister) proposals as a suitable basis for discussion. Thereby the German Government has won the support of both Opposition parties, a very important factor if the Ruhr occupation continues for long."[14]

His modest success here won him praise both in London and Berlin. After a public lecture on reparations in London he was told by a member of the German embassy that "formerly he was always asked, 'Do you know the Kaiser?', then 'Do you know Stinnes (the German industrialist)?', whereas now everyone's question is, 'Do you know Count Kessler?'" To this, Kessler, obviously flattered, added "Fine company one gets into!"[15] Upon returning to Berlin, he was greeted effusively by

Schubert, who considered Kessler's efforts to be "a very important complement to the entire situation," and Foreign Minister Rosenberg welcomed him with open arms: "'Well, here comes Kessler the Conqueror who shakes the position of British Prime Ministers and initiates in the Commons one Ruhr debate after another!'" Rosenberg then went on to explain how much influence Kessler's views had had in the formulation of German foreign policy. Kessler, who thought little of Rosenberg, found this praise hard to swallow, yet could still entertain the hope that his success might lead him to the one diplomatic post he would have accepted without hesitation, the ambassadorship to Great Britain. When Hilferding inquired whether he would go to Brussels or Paris (a hypothetical offer since Hilferding's party was not even in the government!), Kessler responded: "Paris, no. Brussels under conditions yes, if the current policy put me in the position to do something positive there and if I could regard this post as a springboard to London. My real place is London. Once Sthamer goes, I consider myself truly the best for that post and more suited than most others." To his sister, he confided, "I have a *very strong* position and great influence, such as I have never had before, but things may still have to go through a crisis, before we see any sort of light, yet on the whole I feel not quite hopeless."[16]

Kessler took an active part in the discussions over the official German Notes, the proposals to end the Ruhr crisis, of May 2 and June 7, arguing for a security pact that would guarantee borders and for the entrance of Germany into the League of Nations. When the Note of May 2 proved to be disappointingly vague, Schubert, in disgust at the timidity of the Cuno-Rosenberg government, concocted a plan, which, as he confessed to Kessler, bordered on treachery. Kessler was to return to London in order to persuade Sthamer to undertake an action that would provoke an angry reaction from Lord Curzon, which in turn would prove—so the strategy assumed—enough to overturn the Cuno cabinet or to move it toward more decisive action. Somewhat disturbed by the ambiguity of these instructions, Kessler nevertheless carried them out with the eventual result that the Cuno cabinet produced a much more forthcoming and flexible response on June 7. Schubert was delighted, letting his friend in London know that he had discussed his ideas about resolving the crisis with the foreign minister and that he should continue his soundings of the British position.[17]

Such a whirlwind of diplomacy may have led Kessler to imagine himself as the de facto ambassador and as the heir apparent for the official post, yet this was not his destiny. Instead, he left for the United States in July 1923 to accept an invitation to speak on the Ruhr crisis at the annual Institute for Politics held at Williams College in Williamstown, Massachusetts. The president of the college and founder of the institute, Harry A. Garfield—a son of James Garfield, the assassinated president of the United States—had made the offer to Kessler in March. Originally, Garfield had hoped to invite Rathenau. The conditions were generous: free round-trip tickets, his own house with servants, $1,500 for incidental expenses, and lodging for the entire five-week trip. Of course, at a time when the dollar was worth 20,000 marks and inflation was only accelerating, the prospect of earning hard dollars was an inducement, but there were other reasons to accept the invitation. As he explained to his sister: "Politically the (trip?) is important as the German point of view is very seldom heard in this part of American (not German-American) society." Yet, despite these enticements, he would probably have remained in London had not Schubert persuaded him to accept the American invitation, arguing that his further residence in London would only be "en vedette," a hint that the ambassadorship was not to be his, at least for the near future. And so, on July 11, 1923, he set sail—reluctantly and with second thoughts about returning to London—for New York after a twenty-seven-year absence.[18]

CHAPTER 23

American Interlude

Will America ever become deep?
Kessler, *Tagebuch*

"What is the source of this terrible wave threatening to wash all the color, everything particular out of life?" wrote Stefan Zweig in an article called "The Monotonization of the World," published in 1925. "Everyone who has ever been there knows: America. The historian of the future will one day mark the page following the great European war as the beginning of the conquest of Europe by America." For Zweig, as well as for many other German-speaking intellectuals, the journey to the United States was a trip into the future, one fraught with foreboding, with anxiety, and only occasionally with eager anticipation. A few visitors returned singing the praises of American productivity, optimism, and energy; most, however, had the same response as Zweig, finding the American cultural landscape to be alien, intellectually barren, obsessed with materialism, and dominated by a monotonous standardization, which, having already crossed the Atlantic, was now threatening to eradicate the fragile, European culture from which it sprang.[1] Cultural pessimism, therefore, almost always pervaded reflections on the United States.

Kessler shared much of this anxiety. He departed for Williamstown with every sign of reluctance, almost jumping ship at Cherbourg upon the news of a forthcoming speech on reparations by Stanley Baldwin, the new British prime minister. En route he prepared for the New World by reading Sinclair Lewis's *Main Street* and Ray Stannard Baker's biography of President Wilson. The sight of the Fire Island lighthouse, he confided in his diary, afflicted his heart with "an oppressive sense of frigidity. I have never truly felt at ease there. For me a layer of ice lies between Europe and America . . . in America I have never truly felt the warmth of a human heart (with perhaps the single exception of Walt Whitman)." About the Americans, he wrote to his sister: "They are, after all, *very different* from *Europeans* and I cannot say I quite enjoy the difference." Part of his anxiety may have been due to the fear that he would meet in the streets of New York "the ghost of my youth suddenly."[2]

Disembarking on July 20, he was overwhelmed by the reporters who swarmed aboard to interview and photograph him, as well as by the sight of New York. "New York is overpowering. I would never have believed that any impression could have had the power to so disorient me. I am staggered by the monstrous impact of this city. By contrast London is almost provincial. Here is the modern Rome, the colossal world capital, the city that has the appearance of being the center and the ruler of the modern world." His principal American contact, Oswald Garrison Villard, the prominent pacifist and publisher of the left-liberal journal *The Nation,* met his ship and introduced him to some of the leading lights of the American pacifist movement at the Villard home in Dobbs Ferry, New York. There followed a quick trip to Washington, where not only the German ambassador Otto Wiedfeldt, but also his entire family made a bad impression. Kessler met Secretary of State Charles Hughes, "a noticeably handsome, energetic man with a lively, piercing glance and a reddish-blond, graying beard," who belied his reputation as an "ice block." As Kessler correctly intuited, Hughes, although concerned about the mounting crisis, thought American intervention was premature. In any case, the death of President Harding at the beginning of August made any dramatic American diplomatic endeavor impossible that summer and fall. For his part, Hughes told the ambassador how much Kessler had interested him and was reported to have remarked to a colleague that "he (Kessler) will be a great success in Williamstown, he deals so nicely in generalities, and you know people like that very much."[3]

On July 28th, he traveled to Williamstown, Massachusetts, the site of the Institute of Politics, where he was lodged alone with a servant in a luxurious fraternity house on the leafy, wooded Williams College campus. In those first days, he had the opportunity to hobnob with the various American academics, reporters, foreign ambassadors, and wealthy visitors from the neighboring summer resorts, as well as to meet his fellow lecturers from Argentina, England, and France. One of the latter, the French representative Abbé Ernest Dimnet, described the crowd of around eight to nine hundred visitors who attended the Institute: "They were mostly elegant New Yorkers or Washingtonians summering at places like Lenox but anxious to give some seriousness to their vacation. . . . The general tone was Genevan, subdued and collected. . . . On the whole, the atmosphere at Williamstown was that of a Wisdom School where it was nice to be and where it would even be nicer to have been."[4] Still, the appearance of scholarly tranquility was deceptive and Kessler found his work on his lectures interrupted continually by reporters begging for interviews. American public opinion in general may have wished to ignore Europe and its seemingly intractable problems, but the interest among the American political and business elite provoked by the Ruhr crisis was keen.

Among the guests invited to speak at the institute were Lord Birkenhead, Winston Churchill's good friend and former lord chancellor, and Philip Kerr and Edward Grigg, both members of the influential Round Table group formed by Lord Milner to plan for the British imperial future. As Wiedfeldt reported later to Berlin, the focus of the well-heeled and influential audience was on the duel between Kessler, "brilliant and lecturing in marvelous English," and the "comparatively moderate and sympathetic" Dimnet, a professor of English literature at a Parisian lycée. Kessler, who later came to appreciate Dimnet's personal politeness, got it right when he described him as an "example of the little French school master, who distributes smugly grades to the left and right and keeps unruly children in check."[5] Dimnet, for his part, described Kessler as

(A) thoughtful, refined gentleman whose pensiveness was apt to be pathetic. I have never known whether or not he was exceptionally religious, but he often appeared to me as a monk who had gone back to evening clothes. He had an Irish mother and a French brother-in-law and the Keltic [sic] had largely eliminated the German ingredients in him. He could be full of animation as he recounted amusing experiences in three or four languages that he spoke like a native. Yet this internationalist was at heart an uncompromising German and his lectures showed it, even when he tried to make them appealing. His antipathy to Poland and his capacity for propagandizing against France—which he liked—revealed the nature of his patriotism. I noted in my Diary: 'It is frightening to reflect that Count Kessler is a real German Liberal; of course, there will be another war.'[6]

This perception led to a number of sharp public exchanges over the history of Franco-German relations in which, Dimnet confessed, neither he nor Kessler "was perfectly dignified." And yet, the Frenchman could still write "how much more European than the British Germans are. . . . A literary man like myself, Count Kessler seemed only separated from me by infinitesimal differences, yet dining, the same day, at the house of Sir Edward Grigg, I felt more *en rapport* with him and his wife and even with the avowedly pro-German Philip Kerr. The reason is no doubt that the French have never yet had with the Germans the kind of conversation which leaves no dark suspicious spot untouched, whereas they have had it, on several occasions, with the British."[7] And indeed, in the official picture of the lecturers taken with President Garfield of Williams College, Kessler, dressed austerely in a white linen suit, stands a little off to one side, aloof, his head slightly tilted as if he—like Germany itself—was still an outsider who has not yet shed his image of pariah.

Perhaps it was due to his excessive "pensiveness," but Kessler's six lectures, published as *Germany and Europe* in 1924, were the most thoughtful and penetrating of those that the Institute of Politics saw fit to publish in their series. Lively, passionate, responding to both the queries of listeners and to the points made by the other participants, but backed by extensive references to the most recent scholarship, they presented a delicate compromise between Kessler's own political views and those of the German government, making concessions about matters such as Germany's war guilt to gain credibility with an American audience and then using this as a lever to present the point of view of a "democratic" Germany. In the all-important matter of German responsibility for the war, for example, he conceded the role of the Imperial German government—an entity he continually sought to distinguish sharply from the German people themselves—in giving Austria a free hand to make war on Serbia, even when it knew the likely consequences would be a general European war. But he also pointed to the responsibility of both the Russian government in ordering general mobilization at a time when there was evidence that the Kaiser was looking for a diplomatic solution and the French ambassador in encouraging Russia to do so.

Seeking to place the issue of war guilt and such questions as whether the Germans were more or less brutal than their opponents against a larger background, he identified, in his first lecture, the long-term causes of the war in two forces: the tremendous demographic explosion of the nineteenth century that required all European nations to expand

their industrial capacities lest their populations starve and the concomi-
tant rise of nationalism, itself intensified by the growth of democracy.
The war with its terrible losses was the result of these impersonal forces,
rather than of the intentional malevolence of any one group of statesmen. But as calamitous as war was, the experience held out the hope for
a permanent solution to the problems that had engendered it, since the
experiments in wartime control of the economy illustrated how the
dangerous side effects of unfettered capitalism could be dampened.

In subsequent lectures, he examined the Versailles treaty and reparations. While careful to point out the potentially positive aspects of the
treaty, he underlined the importance of a healthy German economy not
only for European prosperity but also for the United States, suggesting
that the prosperity of Midwest agriculture depended on restoring normal trade and financial relations. Dismissing the 132 billion gold marks
figure as wildly unrealistic, he endorsed the American suggestion that a
committee of impartial experts should decide once and for all what exactly Germany could afford to pay. Turning to France, he excoriated the
Poincaré government for hoping to establish the Rhine as its eastern
border, a policy that had been the cause of nearly every war France had
fought. The real solution to French fears of Germany was to abandon
the failed policy of the past and to seek *"common interests recognized by
both countries and sufficiently powerful to minimize the risk of aggression
from either side*. German, and also French, foreign policy can do most
for reciprocal security by fostering the birth and growth of common interests, be they economic, social, or purely spiritual. It is this that gives
to schemes for cooperation between German and French industry, and
especially for a great Franco-German coal and iron trust, international
importance."[8] Anticipating by twenty-seven years the formation of the
European Coal and Steel Community, forerunner of today's European
Community, Kessler argued that such a trust must not be allowed to degenerate into a purely private cartel, but, if controlled democratically
and internationally, it could become the foundation of a true United
States of Europe.

In his final lecture, he addressed the future of democracy in Germany, stressing the ways in which the Weimar Constitution was even
more responsive to the people's will than either the American or British
system. Launching into the subject dearest to his heart, he described the
council movement and outlined his plan for transforming the League
of Nations, although what the wealthy, elegant audience made of this is
not clear. Finally, he painted a picture of the democratic and pacifist

forces to support the republic, most notably the trade unions and the pacifist movement. As far as the threat to democracy from extremists, he noted that neither the far right nor the far left had developed any dangerous leaders. In a judgment he would come to rue, he dismissed Hitler as "a local agitator endowed with some sort of magnetism for Bavarians."[9] But, he warned, if the process of social disintegration, of which the hyperinflation was but a symbol, continued, then the German people would inevitably turn to extremist solutions.

Kessler was pleased with the reaction to his talks, the first given by a German at the Institute of Politics since its organization. All of his lectures were interrupted by loud applause, he reported back to Schubert in Berlin, so much so that after his concluding talk, he had to return several times to acknowledge the audience's approval. Oswald Villard informed him that "nobody since 1914 has done such work in America." The response of many American listeners was direct, personal, and moving. An old woman came up to him in the street and told him that although her son had been killed in the war, she harbored no hate and thanked him for the work he was doing: "Certainly her dead son stood next to her, or in front of her—I was so moved that I could not speak a word." The same day, as he was walking along the street, two cars filled with members of the audience stopped and asked him if he would like to go on a picnic with them. In the wooded Berkshire hills, he was reminded of the Carpathian Mountains of Hungary, and of "murder in a similarly endlessly beautiful and indifferent nature. And now I sat with onetime enemies in a car to travel out to a country picnic." Everyone in the car related their war experiences; many of the women had served as nurses: "A profound mood spread through the group. How near we stood to each other, how similar in our humanity."[10]

Not all the responses were so genial, however. At one point, he received an urgent inquiry from the German embassy, asking if, as published in the Paris-based edition of the *New York Herald,* he had admitted both that Germany bore a great part of the guilt for the war and that, had it won the war, it would have imposed as harsh a peace as Versailles. Defending himself against the words taken out of context, he wrote to Schubert, "(I) would only say in general that before an assembly like yesterday's, where there are many who are in the know and many who as a matter of principle refrain from trusting any German right from the start, only absolute honesty and openness can work. Who wishes to peddle the kind of propaganda that immediately denies everything and sees in self-righteousness its only salvation, he should avoid at all costs such an audience." From the other side, Kessler was subjected to a constant barrage of sarcastic commentaries from the editorial page of *The New York Times*. The crescendo of their criticism reached a high point after Kessler's attack on French security policy. "In most of his previous lectures at the Williams Institute of Politics Count Kessler had shown himself as a German making a special effort to be restrained and conciliatory in his expressions. But on Monday something seems to have snapped inside him. Perhaps it was a deep and irrepressible Teutonic instinct for blundering that got the better of him for the moment. Whatever the explanation, he undertook to give to the United States two pieces of advice which were about as maladroit as ever entered into the heart of even a German ex-diplomat." The advice was for the United States to lower its tariffs on German imports and put economic pressure on France to help eject that nation from the Ruhr. The hostility of the *Times*, its blatant mangling of his position, puzzled Kessler, who was surprised to find, when he visited with its editorial board after the conclusion of the Institute, that they treated him with great kindness. Despite their editorial severity, the editors at the *Times* did not hesitate to quote him at length in two long flattering profiles of Gustav Stresemann and Rudolf Hilferding, chancellor and finance minister, respectively, of the new cabinet formed on August 12 to deal with the crisis.[11]

He had a better reception in the journals of the left. A long article by Andrew Ten Eyck on the Institute of Politics published in the *Outlook* was unstinting in its praise:

The greatest force on the lecture platform has been Kessler. Cold, logical, thorough, oblivious of the approval or disapproval of his audiences, which have been consistently large, and steering to his objective with the precision of a skillful pilot, he has had the hardest task and won the greatest victories. He said to me after speaking before a crowded house on the occasion of his first lecture: "I do not know whether they have come out of curiosity to see the 'Hun' or to hear the case: next time will tell." The next time saw no diminution in the number of those who came to hear him. There were few who felt bitterness over what he said. But the sum total of the impression Kessler made is, in my judgment, that the war psychology is gone, and that there is a real German case, attribute German default to what you will— inefficiency or dishonesty.[12]

The reports back to the Foreign Ministry in Berlin on Kessler's reception were also favorable, mentioning that press coverage from coast to coast had been about twice that of the other speakers at the institute.[13]

Just before his return trip to Europe, Kessler finished the manuscript of his lectures and shipped it to the publisher: "So, with painful effort, two months after my departure from Germany a book is finished. In every other way as well my trip [has been] successful; my lectures and their enormous publicity through the newspapers have doubtless made a greater impact in the United States than any other German presentation since 1914." Despite this mood of self-congratulation, there were other times when his experience of the United States drove him to despair. Returning to New York by ship down the Hudson, he mused over the alien cultural landscape: "America is a sleeping giant . . . . When one flies along the highways, flat and smooth like a racetrack, as I did today, meeting hundreds of autos, and right and left forever the same, small, white houses, which shelter eternally the same family in millions of examples from the Atlantic to the Pacific ocean, all of the them more or less well-to-do, all thoroughly content and satisfied, all with the same philistine, conventional prejudices, then one gets the full measure why America cannot be moved to do something for Europe. Why should it? What does anything outside of their Sunday sermon and their paycheck matter to these millions of narrow-minded families?" As with nearly all European visitors, he was most alarmed by the flatness of American culture: "Another impression that has grown ever stronger in me for six weeks: nothing here really has roots: not the Good, nor the Bad, not the houses, nor the people; neither the friendships nor the enmities. The soil, both the spiritual and the instinctual, is still too new and too loose. Feelings and judgments grow like asparagus and like asparagus are soon 'out of season.' . . . Will America ever become deep?" On board the *Martha Washington* heading home, he read Sinclair Lewis's great romance of philistinism, *Babbitt*, which reminded him of Gustave Flaubert's *Bouvard et Pécuchet*. To his sister, he summed up his feelings: "Although my stay in the States has been very interesting; the people extremely kind and courteous, and the country beautiful, I am looking forward to getting away with pleasure. I have had quite enough of this dead prosperity."[14] And yet, within months he would return for a much longer lecture tour across the entire country.

• • •

He delayed returning directly to Germany, which seemed likely to fall apart in September 1923, amid the effects of the hyperinflation, the separatist movement encouraged by the French in the Rhineland, the threatened Communist insurrection in Saxony, and the growing threat from Hitler's Nazis in Bavaria. Seeking a peaceful interlude from the volatile politics, he sailed instead to Lisbon en route to the Azores and the Canary Islands, where the climate and landscape charmed him. He spent October and the beginning of November in Paris and London. Stopping off in The Hague en route to Berlin to meet van de Velde, Kessler learned from his old friend on November 9 of Hitler's attempted coup d'état. "With this we stand directly before the collapse of Germany," Kessler jotted in his diary. A few hours later he noted with relief that the coup was collapsing due to the refusal of the top Bavarian leaders to play along. Buying German money for his return, he noted that twenty-five dollars brought him 10 billion marks in twenty, 500-million mark notes, each of which appeared about the same size as a 50 pfennig note used to be. A few days later, he took his friend Max Goertz and his bride to a cabaret and paid 16 billion marks, or about seven pounds, for a cup of soup, a steak, an omelet, coffee, and some schnapps. In contrast, the dinner for ten guests that he had given for Sthamer in London ten days earlier had cost only about eleven or twelve pounds, even when the French champagne was included. During a brief visit to Weimar, he was told by Elisabeth Förster-Nietzsche that inflation had wiped out the endowment of the archives. Like many in the German upper and middle class, she would blame the Republic for this loss. His home in the Cranachstraße, "which is an embodiment of so many dreams from the time of Germany's rise" made a troubling and melancholy impression on him.

In Berlin, nerves were frayed. Schubert complained that Germany was like a very gifted man who cannot get his life in order. Hilferding told Kessler of the imminent departure of the Socialists from Stresemann's coalition. It must have been with some relief, therefore, that he agreed with Maltzan to return to London and test British reaction to a German call for an international conference on starvation in the Ruhr.[15] Upon his return from London, he noted the first ray of hope following the November 15 introduction of the new Rentenmark designed to staunch the inflationary fever. The exchange value of the new currency climbed in the foreign markets and, as a result, the price of food fell sharply. In hindsight, historians can trace the beginning of economic stabilization to the Rentenmark, as well as to the almost simultaneous decision to establish a committee of experts—named the Dawes Committee after its American chairman, Charles Dawes—to determine what Germany could pay. To Kessler and his contemporaries, however, it was not at all clear that any corner had been turned. The new currency could easily collapse at the slightest bad news. The answer to the international crisis depended, in part, on finding a permanent solution to the Ruhr crisis, but, whether due to weariness or cynicism, German foreign policy appeared directionless at this critical juncture.[16]

Shortly before Christmas, Kessler attended dinner at the home of the Stresemanns and afterward had a rather remarkable interview with the foreign minister. Stresemann began by asking Kessler's opinion concerning a replacement for Sthamer, the current ambassador in London, who was becoming too old for the job. Would Prince Hatzfeldt be a good replacement? No, Kessler did not think so, and when Stresemann asked him what qualities a good candidate should have, he responded by providing his own résumé: "Someone who stands as close as possible to the Liberal and the Labour leaders. One of the advantages of the new turn in England is exactly that close personal contacts to the leading English politicians exist. I then sketched the leading men in the forthcoming Labour and Liberal governments." When Stresemann asked him directly if he would accept the post, Kessler replied he would on the basis of his precise knowledge of the English situation. Stresemann seemed to endorse this, saying that he needed someone in London whom he knew and trusted, someone with whom he could correspond confidentially. This had not been the case with Sthamer nor would it be so with Hatzfeldt. How long would Kessler be in the United States? "I said, I had promised to remain two months over there, but could interrupt my trip at any moment and return if he needed me. He need only telegraph and I would return immediately." They continued at some length on other foreign policy matters and there can be no doubt that when he left, Kessler felt he had come very close indeed to the one diplomatic post that mattered to him, the ambassadorship in London.[17]

These hopes received a douse of cold water on Christmas Eve in the course of a long interview with Schubert to discuss the instructions Stresemann wished to send to the Paris embassy via Kessler. Alluding indirectly to the possibility of Kessler becoming ambassador to England, Schubert averred that a Labour government would not last long; therefore, it would be a mistake for the Germans to become too attached to them. "I had the impression that Schubert wanted to push back for now my candidature for the London position. He will have spoken in this vein with Stresemann about it, in that he may have said to him that one should first proceed when the situation in England is clarified. I take from this at any rate that he would rather have Hatzfeldt, whose wife is a cousin. On the other hand he probably will not work against me if the Labour government is consolidated. . . ."[18] Kessler's supposition was not far wrong. Schubert, as the Foreign Office's expert on England, could not want his boss Stresemann to establish a confidential relation with his ambassador to England that would circumvent him. Precisely what Kessler imagined to be his strengths therefore worked against him, and it was a relatively easy thing for Schubert to sabotage his nomination.

Persistent nasty rumors circulating in the Foreign Office also worked against Kessler, as he discovered through Georg Bernhard, the chief editor at the *Vossische Zeitung,* on Christmas day: "In the Office an unbelievable campaign of smears and slander against me is always at work. One uses the vilest possible personal insinuations." The exact nature of these rumors is left unspoken, but they may well have concerned the strange remarks the ambassador to Washington, Wiedfeldt, made to Kessler about Baron von Steuben, the Prussian general who helped train George Washington's Continental Army. His homosexuality, Wiedfeldt sneered, made him a troubling symbol of Germany's services to the United States: "How would we look if it was discovered that Steuben was a pederast?" Kessler thought of reminding him of Frederick the Great but left off for fear that Wiedfeldt would misunderstand it. A few months later, Ludwig Stein would tell him that he would be the perfect replacement for Wiedfeldt if only Kessler would deign to marry.[19]

And so, although still hoping that a solidly established Labour government would yet result in his appointment as ambassador to the Court of St. James, Kessler nevertheless prepared—with enormous reluctance—to depart on the lecture tour of the United States at the beginning of 1924. The last passage of his diary for 1923 was a bitter summing up: "So the old year has come to an end. A very sad one. Perhaps the most lamentable aspect was the beggarliness and lack of dignity of the German middle class, which, in the wake of the financial catastrophe of the last six months, has developed in a repulsive manner. There exists hardly anyone who does not nauseate one. In Berlin now one is beleaguered, as if in the church plaza of a Spanish or southern Italian town, by beggars without any human dignity or shame. My correspondence has become for me revolting."[20]

. . .

Kessler arrived in New York on January 3, 1924. For the next four months, he crisscrossed the United States frenetically, visiting not only

New York, Chicago, and Washington several times, but also stopping off in Syracuse, Iowa City, St. Louis, Colorado Springs, Santa Fe, San Francisco, Los Angeles, San Diego, Seattle, Minneapolis, Buffalo, Pittsburgh, and Philadelphia. At the beginning of his stay, he participated in a debate before the Foreign Policy Association that was broadcast over the radio in New York and in another debate in Washington before the same organization at the end. In between, he spoke before audiences large and small, at Knights of Columbus and Y.M.C.A. halls, at breakfasts given by the League of Women Voters, in half-empty theaters, and in college lecture halls at the University of Iowa, Grinnell, Princeton, and the California Institute of Technology. At the same time, he experienced as much of American life and landscapes as he could, visiting with Jane Addams at Hull House in Chicago, attending a nightclub in Harlem, staying at the Phantom Ranch in the bowels of the Grand Canyon, touring a religious commune founded by German Mennonites in Iowa, residing as a guest with the theosophists in San Diego, examining a copper mine in Montana and a steel mill in Pittsburgh, and meeting the prominent names of the farm labor movement in St. Louis. All was grist for extensive reflections on the vast country that seemed to have the destiny of Europe, and ultimately therefore of the world, in its hands.

A number of themes and epiphanies stand out from the general whirlwind of faces, landscapes, and events. Some were recapitulations of impressions formed on earlier trips. One of the most salient was the dichotomy Kessler perceived between the grandiosity of the American landscape, particularly in the West, and the spiritual impoverishment of the people inhabiting this spectacular scenery. Like Dante descending into hell, Kessler descended into the Grand Canyon to stay at a little cabin on the Phantom Ranch, which recalled to him the blockhouse he shared with Schoeter in the 1915 Carpathian campaign. "Nothing can give any idea of its grandeur, majesty, and peacock-like beauty of color," he wrote to his sister describing the Grand Canyon, "Taking all in all, it is probably the most gorgeous sight in the world."[21] Yet, on the rim of this otherworldly beauty stood a tourist hotel "with hundreds of Babbitt families who, on the great car tour, want to buy two hours of sublimity. . . . Georg Grosz must draw this: 'Who buys sublimity?'" Such stark contrasts brought him to despair: "Between the flatness of Americans (I mean of course the average American) and the grandeur of America is a tension that continually gets on the nerves. Such power for such *Flachköpfe!* A somewhat superficial goodness cannot save the world if it is paired with so little spirit and depth. The first people of the world at the same time the shallowest? What a catastrophe!" Truly, he went on, one must be grateful to Russia that perhaps will one day create a different path.[22]

Partly responsible for the appalling wasteland of middle-class America was its crass religiosity and the avatar of this religious sentiment, the scourge of American culture, the American old maid. Kessler encountered the bizarre character of American fundamentalism during his debate against the lawyer Martin Lyttleton at the Hotel Astor sponsored by the Foreign Policy Association in New York. "He spoke, as I had expected from the depiction of his personality, poorly and irrelevantly. But the worst that he brought forth was Madame Lyttleton, next to whom I had the misfortune of sitting, a nutty old frump who, until I stood up and left, continually explained to me that all which was happening now, had been predetermined by Christ and foreseen in the book of Daniel and in the Revelation of St. John. . . . I nodded with my head and so unfortunately strengthened her in the belief that I agreed and this led her to make even crazier prophecies . . . until I could no longer stand it and fled." Expanding on these sentiments to his sister, he wrote: "I fear the old maids of both sexes will kill America like the priests killed and emasculated Spain. Nobody can have any conception of this moral oppression and tyranny who has not been here. The atmosphere of America, its shallowness, its self-righteousness, its fear and hatred of the truth are those of a tea party in the back parlor of a parsonage. There are a few faint signs of revolt; but up to date they do not amount to much considering the huge mass which takes its firm stand with the old ladies."[23]

Throughout his visit he was on the *qui vive* for those "few faint signs of revolt." If there was any hope for the birth of a native American culture worthy of the country's economic and political power then Kessler saw it transpiring on the Pacific coast, far from the old centers of culture and power on the eastern seaboard. Here he encountered a landscape and a spirit that enchanted him. Although he found San Francisco, despite its location, to be bitterly disappointing, with a street life "just as deathly boring and gray as in Leipzig," he had an entirely different impression of Los Angeles. Although the weather was rainy and the theaters merely provincial, Kessler felt a physical sense of well being there: "Nothing particular is happening, but the city is nevertheless not boring. Perhaps the superabundance of beautiful fruits and flowers in the shops and in the street commerce and the similar liveliness of the popu-

lation makes things amusing and engaging." Pasadena, where he lectured at the still unfinished California Institute of Technology, struck
him as particularly attractive. "The beauty of the gardens and alleys and
the pretty, clean fronts of the houses, which for the most part are built
out of adobe or stucco in the Spanish style, is astonishing." In the same
passage of his diary, he tried to express his astonishment: "The impression of prosperity, the entire endless rows of well-to-do and rich homes
and palaces, is overwhelming, and in the end here again one asks one's
self, as in New York, as in Chicago, as . . . in New England, where is this
all heading? . . . What will come forth this time from this wealth and this
power? Will spirit slip in? . . . . What will the 'third generation' here
in California look like? The children of these parents born and raised
in luxury? . . . I ask myself once again: what will take place in this
paradise?"²⁴

Nowhere did he sense the beckoning possibilities of California more
than in the theosophical community on Point Loma in San Diego. Invited there by Katherine Tingley, the leader of the community, who had
expressed an interest in having German children attend her school set
in a beautiful park by the ocean, Kessler initially was skeptical. While the
location was striking, the architecture seemed to emulate Monte Carlo
and he thought the environment was too luxurious. Nevertheless, he
agreed after some hesitation to attend a special performance by the children of *Eumenides* by Aeschylus in the middle of March. On his visit he
learned about the theosophical philosophy and practice of education.
Surprisingly, he did not find the conscious emulation of ancient Greece
to be off-putting or artificial. The school, both rigorous and progressive, struck him "as an almost ideal educational institute," the only jar-
ring note at Point Loma being the pervasive fear of any homosexual activity among the boys. "This sexual spying and anxiety is something
childish and revolting. . . . The great fear of masturbation among the
boys and of sexual commerce between them, for example, rests on pre-
conceived notions the unquestioned accuracy of which is not at all certain. Greek culture rested largely on a completely diametrically opposed
assessment of this urge and of the sexually colored friendship between
young people." Despite this misgiving, Kessler left Los Angeles for
Seattle, singing the praises of the City of Angels: "Los Angeles is sympathetic to me; the light, stimulating atmosphere, the clear sunlight,
the southern sky, the joyful life in the streets, engendered in me as a lasting musical theme a soft feeling of happiness. . . . The rhythm is American, even super-American; the atmosphere is that of the 'happy isles.'
It is perhaps the only city of America where happiness is endemic."²⁵

The second great theme that preoccupied Kessler during his trip was the question of immigration and the assimilation of races. This was indeed one of the burning issues in the United States during the 1920s, as he noted shortly after his arrival in New York. In Chicago, Robert E. Wood, the head of the Sears company, spoke to him at length about the danger of the "de-Americanization" of the United States through the immigration of unassimilable elements from southern Europe such as Italians, Greeks, Slavs, and Jews. Such a diatribe, coupled with doubts on the worth of democracy, was to be expected from the arch-reactionary Wood, who would later make a name for himself as the organizer of the America First isolationist movement during the Second World War and as a supporter of Senator Joseph McCarthy during the cold war. But Kessler encountered the same sentiments wherever he went. He was struck by the enormous variety of the country, and he made that variety the subject of the first of the two articles on the United States that he would publish in *Deutsche Nation*.[26]

His view was in many ways the exact opposite of men like Wood. In Seattle, reading in the newspapers articles about the immigration danger and about the growing support for the Ku Klux Klan, he took his stance against the nativist movement: "In all probability, a nationalism is springing up which would like to make all of America into an overgrown New England, Protestant, sectarian, narrowly moralistic, and Nordic blond." This effort was doomed, however, to failure, for "no great nation can grow on the shallow soil of contemporary New England-American culture." New Englanders, he concluded, "will have to content themselves with being but one element of a new, great American culture," as would the German-Americans, for most of whom he had the deepest scorn. Far from sharing the contempt so prevalent among American elites, Kessler actually credited the non-European elements of the melting pot with contributing what little culture of feeling the United States could evince. Whether it was the Indians in Taos, New Mexico, who, despite their shocking poverty, had what Anglo-Americans lacked, namely, "an aesthetic relation to the world," or a quartet from Fisk University singing spirituals, which he heard just when he despaired that anything "deep, simple, and soulful should ever be born out of American life and work," the outsiders and outcasts, he believed, were enriching American culture. After experiencing a bit of the Harlem Renaissance in a nightclub, he admired the style of the black audience: "In contrast our fat crooks with their women look far more run of the mill and behave themselves much more unmannerly. These Negroes and half-Negroes with their fine, slender bodies, their agile and precise dance steps, and their aristocratic matter-of-factness and calm have something of the nobility of unspoiled young animals." One recognizes the patronizing tone, but also Kessler's open-mindedness and receptivity to new experiences. For him, given his admiration of dancers from Ruth St. Denis to Nijinsky, to be an "unspoiled young animal" was no small achievement. The conclusion of his first article sounds uncannily like recent debates over multiculturalism. Even "100% Americans" were starting to realize, he argued, that "the goal of America in any case can no longer be to bind the American nation to a no longer viable past based on the example of backwards European nationalistic ideals, but that it must be the virtue and the fame of the American people to be a work in progress, forever pointing to the future, eternally reshaping itself and creating something new out of the best blood, to whom the task is given to bring forth on a new basis and through new means the unity of democracy and self-determination, of democracy and freedom in reality." He closed by citing Walt Whitman's great invocation of American diversity. The truly important question concerning this diversity was with what ideals and what forms, and on what cultural basis could America bind her great diversity into a functional unity that could face the future with confidence.[27]

A greater danger to American democracy than racial assimilation was the vast inequality of wealth, the theme of Kessler's second article. Writing at the time of the Teapot Dome scandals, he emphasized that overt cases of bribery and influence peddling were not the main threat to the American political system but, rather, the enormous funds that had to be raised for political campaigns. Relying on the historian Charles Beard's work, he noted that the preservation of property at the expense of real democracy could be traced indeed back to the founding fathers. However, he argued, in a highly developed industrial economy, where the personal fortune of Henry Ford alone was equal to the total amount of the American loan to Germany that was being currently debated in the Dawes Committee, the extremes of wealth had become even more glaring. Worse even than the corrupting influence of money on politics was its impact on American culture. "For the concentration of monied power coincides almost completely with the front that opposes any major change in intellectual life and wishes to protect the traditional and the existing. In this way the real aim of democracy, that which justifies its existence; namely, the continual and unrestricted adaptation of the institutions and the spirit of a people to its real needs and self-determined goals, the eternal freshness, the eternal blossoming and creation of the people's will according to its individuality, is suppressed in favor of the lifeless retention of traditional forms and an almost sick fear of any intellectual innovation." Concluding, Kessler pointed to one bright spot in this otherwise bleak picture, the effort by progressive forces around figures like Robert La Follette who were seeking to curb the power of big money and strengthen the forces of democracy by creating a third party.[28]

As a diplomatic venture, Kessler's tour seems to have been less successful than his appearance in Williamstown the previous summer. He did receive favorable press coverage in a number of cities. After one appearance before high society in Chicago, the *Tribune,* noting that Kessler appeared more British than German, surmised that if Kessler had come "to study our frame of mind and to make a silent plea for his native land he was very well selected for the job, as he is a capital talker and has an agreeable personality, the air of a man of the world who belongs to no especial country but is a citizen who would be at home anywhere," a surprisingly flattering portrait coming from a newspaper known for the xenophobic, anti-British stance of its publisher. Toward the end of his stay, he was able to mend fences with *The New York Times,* being invited to breakfast with the editorial staff and the publisher, Alfred Ochs, in the newly redecorated rooms of the newspaper, the Gothic interior of which reminded him of the House of Commons. Ochs agreed to relay personally to Poincaré, during his upcoming trip to France, Kessler's message that French security could best be maintained by a treaty with England, and then to convey Poincaré's response when Ochs would meet Kessler in London in May. The next day, in its Sunday section, the *Times* described Kessler as a "slender, young-looking man in a sack suit," who "resembles the athletic type of golf-playing American business man much more than the typical German diplomat or politician. He speaks excellent English and has acquired the American viewpoint in many things." While this latter assertion may have amused Kessler, the interview allowed him to assure the readership of the *Times*—just at a moment when American banks were preparing to lend Germany money as part of the Dawes Plan—of the fundamental stability of the Weimar Republic, despite the large gains that the extreme right and left were hoping to score in the upcoming Reichstag elections. The average German was no different from the average American and wants the same thing: humdrum work, stability, and normalcy. "We have our type of Babbitt in Germany and he dominates Germany," he declared, hoping, one supposes, that the readers would find that to be a good thing.

It is impossible, of course, to judge the effects of these bromidic statements on American public opinion, but they may have, in a small way, helped prepare for American reengagement in Europe. Many of his lectures, nevertheless, were poorly attended and the press coverage skimpy or nonexistent. The British ambassador to Germany, Lord D'Abernon, referring to Kessler's experience, wrote in his diary, "I gather from others that his tour was not a complete success, the most convincing speakers on behalf of Germany having been Cuno and Hermes." Perhaps part of the problem, Kessler conceded to D'Abernon, was that despite Americans' hospitality and their wish to be informed, "in twenty-four hours they have forgotten all the information they obtain. A propagandist who judges by the newspapers the day after his making a speech may be pardoned for imagining that he has powerfully influenced the opinion of the country. He will find, however, three days later that everyone has forgotten his name and no one remembers on which side he spoke." [29]

His private interviews with American leaders, principally Secretary of State Hughes and—at the very end of his visit—with President Calvin Coolidge, had less urgency in the spring of 1924 than they had had the previous summer. The nature of U.S. intervention had already been decided with the creation of the Dawes Committee. His interview with Coolidge on May 1 left him unimpressed: "All in all the impression of a conscientious, unimportant, hardworking clerk . . . . No trace of spirit or fire, or any original, constructive thought." [30]

But if Coolidge was a nonentity, then the German ambassador to the United States, Otto Wiedfeldt, became for Kessler a symbol of the dangers posed to Germany and Europe by a zealously nationalist German foreign policy. Relations between the men were bound to be strained, given Kessler's mission of nudging the ambassador out of his post. Wiedfeldt, an ardent nationalist, typical of those who had never really accepted Germany's defeat, revealed his character and at the same time struck a blow against Kessler and his efforts to enhance the image of German in the United States, when, on the occasion of former President Wilson's death in February, he refused to lower the flag on the German embassy. Fearful that Wiedfeldt could become foreign minister in a government dominated by the Nationalist Party, Kessler summed up his impression: "For us there is only the League of Nations and England or a war of revenge and Russia. Any middle path leads to the abyss just like our tacking back and forth between England and Russia under Wilhelm II." [31] The battle lines were clear as he prepared to return to Europe in time for the momentous debate over the adoption of the

Dawes Plan, an issue that pitted the two contending directions in German foreign policy against each other.

One glaring, fundamental fact, however, remained with Kessler as he prepared to leave the United States: if Europe were to ever escape American political, economic, and—most devastating of all—cultural influence, it would have to find a way to transcend its recent quarrels and unite. On the trip to the United States, more than four months earlier, he had read the work of Count Richard Coudenhove-Kalergi, *Pan-Europa*, in order to review it for the *Deutsche Nation*. The author's plan for a united Europe, excluding both England and Russia, was, Kessler thought, an impossibility. But that Europe must overcome its divisions struck him with even greater urgency when he arrived in England after his trip. After a few days in London, once the epitome of capitalistic modernism, he wrote, "An odd sensation of the smallness, the old-fashionedness, and the shabbiness of everything in England has accompanied me since the day before yesterday. London seems like a dirty, poorly laid out, superannuated village in comparison with New York . . . the shops even in Bond Street provincial compared to those on Fifth Avenue." The reasons for this usurpation were not hard for him to find: ever since the destruction of Germany with her progressive culture as a result of the war, time had been working for the United States and against Europe. In a way, it was Rockefeller, not Foch, who confronted Ludendorff at the battle of the Marne, and, in the final analysis, wrote Kessler in 1924, Ludendorff was preferable: "But now the struggle has been finally decided and it is only disastrous to put forth the old . . . Ludendorff. Now only *a united Europe* can still retain her control of the world. . . . The impression of the direct contrast between London and New York five years after the World War I will never forget. It is more than instructive, it's path breaking."[32] The task then was not to reverse the verdict of the Marne, an impossibility, but to work toward the unity of Europe.

CHAPTER 24

Retreat from Politics

Now I come at last to my real life's goal: to help, in the first
place and in a practical way, forge a united Europe.

Kessler, *Tagebuch*

When Kessler returned from his 1923 trip to the United States, Germany
stood on the brink of chaos. By the time of his return from the 1924
trip, the political situation was provisionally stabilized and the first, faint
signs of a general, European solution to the problems that had vexed
the postwar years were beginning to manifest themselves. The struggle
between France and Germany over the issue of reparations had led to
a dangerous and costly stalemate, and leaders of both countries were
looking for ways out of the cul-de-sac. The Dawes Plan, which, besides
clearing the way for a substantial American loan to Germany, called for
a four-year partial moratorium during which German payments would
be low enough to permit the stabilization of her economy. This represented a major defeat for France in its efforts to impose its solution to
the reparations problem.[1] The victory of the French left wing, led by
Édourad Herriot, in the legislative elections of May meant that France
was willing to swallow this bitter pill, if only because of the financial
pressure exerted by American bankers on the franc.[2] The formation of
the first Labour Party government in Britain under Ramsey MacDonald, committed to a policy of reconciliation and to strengthening the
League of Nations, also eased the way for a solution. However, the results in the May Reichstag elections went the other direction, leading

to a dramatic increase in the representation of political extremes: the Communist Party jumped from four to sixty-two delegates while the Nationalist Party and its allies emerged as the strongest bloc. Although upon arriving at Cherbourg Kessler had fired off a telegram to Stresemann urging him to reject the idea of bringing the Nationalists into the government, he learned later in London that it was not that easy. For Germany to accept those provisions of the Dawes Plan that required it to offer up its railways as collateral for the American loan, an amendment to the constitution requiring a two-thirds majority and thus the approval of at least part of the Nationalists was necessary.*

It soon became evident that one of the principal sticking points in the debate over the acceptance of the Dawes Plan would be the question of German violation of the disarmament provisions of the Versailles treaty. It was more or less an open secret that not only were substantial police forces, housed in barracks and receiving military training, being used as reserves for the armed forces, but also that the German army, the Reichswehr, had both established illegal caches of arms and provided military training to paramilitary bands. Stresemann could not afford to see his policy of rapprochement with the West sabotaged by the army and its head, the powerful, hard-nosed Junker, Hans von Seeckt. In the struggle, Kessler attempted to weigh in on the side of the foreign minister. In meetings with the Reichspresident Friedrich Ebert, with the Reichschancellor Wilhelm Marx, with Stresemann, with the British ambassador D'Abernon, and with Schubert and Gerhard Köpke in the Wilhelmstraße, he urged that the so-called Black Reichswehr paramilitary units be disbanded as the necessary first step to Germany's eventual admission into the League of Nations. In Paris, he lectured before the Comité National d'Études to a packed audience of dignitaries, including General Charles Mangin, victor at Verdun and one of the most ardent proponents of detaching the Rhineland from Germany. Noting the deep distrust of Germany, understandable in view of the abundant evidence of German contravention of disarmament, Kessler noted how the German paramilitary units "block our only road to peace and work, but can never suffice to carve us out a path through war and violence, even if this were a desirable goal: the narrow-minded people at home and the ghost-seeing here join hands in a *danse macabre*." [3] He reserved

---

* The election results also killed any remaining hopes Kessler might have harbored about becoming ambassador to Great Britain.

his deepest scorn, however, for the leadership of the German Nationalist party: "No aristocracy has gone under so cynically and treacherously
as the Prussian Junkers. For this attitude will be the cause of their destruction." In view of its eventual demise in 1944–45 at the hands of the
Nazis, the very party it so recklessly would help to power, the traditional German right wing would fulfill Kessler's prophecy to the letter.
To counter these forces required an equal but opposite fanaticism:
"Both here and there we must take up the fight with the same decisive-
ness and bitterness as our opponents or bury our hope for peace. Con-
tentious and reckless pacifists are needed, not whining." But he himself
felt "oddly flat and barren of thoughts."[4]

Returning to Berlin in the middle of July for a meeting of the Peace
Cartel, he also reported on the results of his Paris trip to Stresemann,
underscoring the French desire for peace but their fear of illegal German
rearmament. "It is therefore," Kessler emphasized, "the most pressing
patriotic task of the German government to wipe the intrigues of the
Reichswehr and the 'patriotic bands' off the map." Stresemann, in an
unusually good mood despite the constant stress, responded that the
paramilitary units were transforming themselves into less dangerous vet-
eran organizations and that this transformation should be allowed to
continue. About their activities in German schools and universities, he
professed to know nothing. But he reiterated the very strong resistance to any concession on these matters on the part of Seeckt and the
Reichswehr.[5]

In the latter part of the summer, Kessler had the opportunity to see
for himself the balance between "the forces of peace and the forces of
violence in Germany" when he attended a number of political rallies,
both as an observer and as a featured speaker. At the beginning of August, he spoke at a memorial rally in honor of the war wounded in Jena
and was encouraged by the response, which gave him the sense that the
republican movement was on the upswing. But only a few days later, at
a vast rally of more than 100,000 in Berlin, held in honor of the war
dead, he came away discouraged. As he thought back on the battlefields
and the dead he had seen, he found it outrageous that a service for the
victims of a cruel mass murder should take place under the aegis of the
most rigid nationalism. His next stop was the town of Holzminden in
central Germany, where he was scheduled to speak on the occasion of
Constitution Day. A clammy feeling of small town provinciality oppressed him. For one thing, he had forgotten his top hat, and he knew
that it would be inexcusable to appear hatless in public on a solemn oc-

casion in Holzminden. The thick atmosphere of the little city in the heartland of this *urdeutsch* landscape stifled him. "Tonight," he wrote, "I suffer from a *Grosstadt* pang, on the . . . longing for the spaces and the freedom of the big city! The river, which flows by in the moonlight like German romantic music, the barely visible line of hills sinking into the night, the clouds which like silver sheep pass in front of the moon, the small red lit windows of the houses in the gardens—I would trade it all for five minutes of Potsdamer Platz or Broadway."[6]

Presumably wearing a borrowed top hat, he delivered his speech the next day before a crowd of Socialist Party members, trade unionists, and members of the Reichsbanner, the paramilitary unit organized to defend the Republic. In his address, he hit all the themes dear to him, reminding his audience of the social and political rights the Republic had given them. Democracy meant self-determination and the personal responsibility of each individual for the commonweal. No longer could this responsibility be shirked, as it could under the old monarchy, where all one had to do was click one's heels and, by obeying without question, be absolved from the consequences of one's actions. True democracy, he reminded them, combined economic and political democracy and, without peace, there can be no true self-determination by the people, no true human dignity. He contested the right of the militarists to evoke the "spirit of 1914," claiming that the volunteers that summer were motivated by feelings of brotherhood and the sense of responsibility of each for everyone. They certainly did not fight and die to protect the divine right to rule of the Hohenzollern family, or to defend the privileges of the "upper ten thousand," or to submit to the bosses in the factories. Concluding, he read a telegram from Ebert and called on the crowd to demonstrate their allegiance to the Republic by acclamation. Despite the applause, a note of fatigue and a sense of futility began to creep into his diary. Thinking about the crowd at the memorial for the war dead in Berlin thrilling at the sight and sound of military bands and marching soldiers, he despaired: "When one notices how little even the most frightful war experiences . . . have altered the individual in his fundamental core and his views, one asks one's self if it isn't an untenable illusion to hope that a people, which, after all, is composed of all these individuals, should have been changed by the war in its fundamental direction."[7]

The most dispiriting evidence for this pessimistic assessment came in Weimar a few days later. For more than a decade, ever since the outbreak of the war, Weimar, once the site of so many hopes for a cultural renaissance, had been only the briefest of way stations for Kessler. His house there resembled a museum and was treated by him as such. The Rodin scandal must have seemed to him like an episode from the distant past, but he had never forgotten that encounter with the wrath of small town provincialism. Still, how it galled him to see what was, if anything could be called such, his hometown the site of a large Nazi Party rally. Wishing to see the enemy at first hand, he overcame his disgust and attended the event.

On the train, he observed the leader of the rally: "A small, old, fat, man with a straw yellow round skull and a roll of fat, a true rear line pig (*Etappenschwein*) . . . he had nothing in common with the noble, slender German, of the superman with the long, Nordic skull, nothing. Yet through this fat bastard from the German middle class the world is supposed to be restored." Laconically, he noted the words of the *völkisch* literary critic and Weimar resident, Adolf Bartels, in the past one of the bitterest critics of the New Weimar and destined to high office in the Third Reich: "I can no longer hear the damned word 'freedom' and wish that some one would finally come who would knock us on the head." Although he was angered by the large swastikas draped over the National Theater when he arrived, they soon disappeared and he professed to notice a lukewarm reception from the townspeople. Listening to Ludendorff address the crowd, he mocked the man he had once seen as the embodiment of the German will to power. His speech was "cautious, noncommittal, harmless, and empty." His listeners were so bored that they stared at an airplane circling until finally Ludendorff as well turned and stared, losing the thread of his talk, his voice trailing off. "No money and no spirit" was Kessler's contemptuous synopsis of the so-called German Day in Weimar.[8]

One last unpleasant duty remained. He visited Elisabeth Förster-Nietzsche and endeavored to keep away from the topic of politics, but could not avoid warning her against associating the archive with the cultural critic Oswald Spengler. The meeting was notable for an extraordinary falsehood on the part of Förster-Nietzsche. When Kessler asked whether any letters from her brother to Wagner still existed, she answered that Cosima Wagner had no doubt burned them all. To his astonishment, however, "instead of becoming indignant, she added in a mild tone: 'Ach, my dear friend, the more I penetrate into my brother's affairs, the more I see how thankful I must be that he was such a clean person. Cosima had so much retouching to do with Wagner that one must forgive her much. I did not have to burn or suppress anything.'"

The visitor today to the Nietzsche Archive can see on permanent exhibit all of the "retouching" she actually performed on her brother's work in order to make him presentable.[9]

Back in the capital, sultry in the August heat, he awaited the results of the vote on the Dawes Plan: it was adopted by 314 votes, 24 more than the two-thirds necessary. The battle had been won, it seemed. The way was now clear for Germany's reintegration into the community of nations. The next step seemed clear—namely, the admission into the League of Nations. A mere one and a half hours after the historic vote in the Reichstag, Kessler was called to the Wilhelmstraße to see Maltzan who informed him that Ramsey MacDonald had requested that Germany send a representative to Geneva for the next session of the League. Would Kessler go as an unofficial observer? From the Foreign Office's position, it was natural to turn to Kessler; a year earlier, at the height of the Ruhr crisis, Chancellor Cuno had sent him to meet Lord Robert Cecil, a member of the Conservative cabinet at the time and a noted proponent of the League, in part to discuss the issue of Germany's possible entrance into the League. The Foreign Office's offer was accepted with alacrity by a man who saw his whole life converging on this one mission: "Now I come at last to my real life's goal: to help, in the first place and in a practical way, forge a united Europe. Before the war I tried it on the all too thin and fragile level of culture. Now come the fundamentals. May it be a good sign that my appointment comes on the day where, through the acceptance of the (Dawes) report by Germany, a new era of peace perhaps begins."[10]

• • •

The issue of Germany's entrance into the League of Nations was only marginally less thorny than the reparations quagmire. The grandiose and unrealistic hopes some Germans had entertained about the League in 1919 quickly ebbed after the disappointment over the Versailles treaty. The Socialist Party remained an ardent supporter of Germany's entrance and the Foreign Ministry continued its subsidies to the *Deutsche Liga für Völkerbund,* albeit at a much reduced scale, but German public opinion in general treated the League with scorn. The Communists, echoing the judgment of Moscow, saw it as the embodiment of international capitalism, while the German middle class, with a few exceptions, considered it to be a mere vehicle for the ambitions of the Entente powers, particularly France. The fact that part of the responsibility entrusted to the League was to enforce Versailles only served to strengthen German distrust of the institution.[11]

Among the most important members of the German foreign policy establishment advocating a cautious, cool approach to the issue of membership in the League was the career diplomat, Bernhard von Bülow, a nephew of the former Imperial Chancellor, and the man responsible in the Wilhelmstraße for German policy toward Geneva. Although not unmindful of the potential advantages of membership, Bülow argued that Germany could only consider applying on two conditions: the immediate granting of a permanent seat on the League's council and an exemption from the provisions of Article 16, which called for compulsory participation of all members in sanctions ordered by the council against a renegade state. The first condition was indispensable for the sake of German pride and for domestic political reasons. Regarding the second proviso, the official argument was that a Germany disarmed by the Versailles treaty could not be expected to participate in any action that would put Germany at risk of being attacked. The real reason, however, was the German concern for friendly relations with the Soviet Union, the most likely target in the 1920s of any League-imposed sanction.[12]

Maltzan informed Kessler of these preconditions, emphasizing that Germany would never enter if application entailed any obligations regarding the enforcement of the Versailles treaty. Membership neither must be construed as German approval of the treaty nor stand in the way of the main goal of German policy, its revision. When the discussion turned to the issue of disarmament, Maltzan suggested that the goal should be mutual disarmament, not unilateral German disarmament. To Kessler's response that France would never permit that, Maltzan replied that the way to assuage French security concerns was to revive the idea first proposed by Chancellor Cuno of a mutual security pact on the Rhine that would establish Germany's western borders but leave her eastern borders open to revision. This plan would become, in a year's time, the Locarno Pact. For now, however, Maltzan, Bülow, and Stresemann felt that time was on Germany's side and that it would be a mistake to apply for League membership prematurely.[13]

It was with these instructions that Kessler arrived in Geneva to attend the fifth meeting of the League of Nations Assembly. The sight of the austere city on Lake Geneva reminded him of a happy six weeks he had spent there in 1921, working in the library. Such thoughts inspired one of the most remarkable passages of self analysis in Kessler's entire diary: "Perhaps the quiet, solitary life of the scholar would have been best for me. But no one can live out all of the personalities they contain, which is why no person (aside from quite primitive ones) is entirely happy. The more complicated he is, the more souls he contains, the more personalities he could and must be in order to live out his life fully, the more unhappy he is, at least relatively. Only for the very superficial or very primitive is it possible to exhaust all of the contents of one's soul in a short life span; for one must necessarily neglect a part of one's potential fulfillment." [14] Perhaps these reflections owe something to the awareness that his hopes for the ambassadorship in England, or any official post acceptable to him, were effectively at an end. All that realistically remained were the kind of vague, indeterminate diplomatic missions he was currently engaged upon, where the pitfalls were many and the rewards few. His bitter experience in Geneva would, it appears, sour him on undertaking many more of these.

In his first meetings, with Lord Parmoor representing the Labour government as well as with the French delegation led by Aristide Briand, Kessler kept to the letter of his instructions. He also quickly discovered that the note the German government intended to issue, explicitly refuting the war guilt clause of the Versailles treaty, caused deep distrust of her intentions. On the occasion of the Reichstag debate on the Dawes Plan, the Nationalist Party had insisted on this as a quid pro quo in return for their votes, but the prospect of such a note was not well received in Geneva. [15]

Just as it appeared that Kessler's mission was faltering, however, it was given even greater urgency by the dramatic speech of Ramsey MacDonald before the assembly on September 4, appealing to Germany to apply for admission during the current session. The invitation struck the German government like a thunderbolt. Because the British had not broached the subject of Germany's entrance into the League during the long London Conference that summer, the Germans had not anticipated MacDonald's gesture. Nor frankly did the policymakers in Berlin appreciate it. Kessler, however, embraced the possibility with his usual ardor, even if, in his private meetings with MacDonald, the British prime minister was more reserved and raised more problems than in his public speeches. The proposed German note on the war guilt question threatened to ruffle feathers, he warned, as did the discovery of weapons factories inside Germany. Kessler therefore fired off an urgent telegram to Maltzan, urging that the government refrain from issuing the note because it "must according to all of Germany's friends lead unavoidably to a catastrophic reverse in the foreign policy situation of Germany." He then hastened to Bern to confer with Adolf Müller, the German ambassador to Switzerland. Müller, one of the few Social Democrats to succeed in establishing a solid career within the Foreign Office, distrusted the League and was a bitter opponent of Germany's immediate entrance under all but the most advantageous conditions. He complained in his reports back to Berlin about the German personalities idling in Geneva who, ignoring the hard lessons of national dignity and interest politics, "display a limitless and ardent enthusiasm for entrance without regard for the issues of vital importance to Germany currently before the League of Nations." Kessler instantly sensed his opposition: "He is stuffed full of *ressentiments* and has aged and dried up greatly; outwardly and inwardly a fossil, who is only composed of nothing but petrifactions of his earlier cleverness." [16]

A further complication nearly put a premature end to Kessler's mission. Fridtjof Nansen, the well-known Norwegian explorer and a man whose stature as a humanitarian greatly impressed Kessler, suggested to him, as one who wished for Germany's entrance, that he become officially accredited by the German government; otherwise, the German government could deny whatever he said. Far from being able to take that step, however, the Marx government was forced to defend Kessler from public attacks by German newspapers questioning his status as Germany's observer and his pacifist background. The Geneva correspondent for the conservative *Deutsche Allgemeine Zeitung* observed that Kessler, contrary to his instructions, was telling everyone he met that he was authorized to negotiate Germany's entrance into the League of Nations to which the Stresemann's own paper, *Die Zeit,* responded that "the sufficiently well known pacifist Count Kessler, in case he really should have acted as a kind of official personality, was not authorized to do so." Newspapers in Switzerland and in France carried the story of the nationalist attacks on Kessler's presence in Geneva, and he was forced to telegram the Wilhelmstraße, urging them to put an end to the press campaign. [17]

The press campaign, the tepid public defense of his mission by the government, and the personal reports from Wilhelmstraße insiders indicated to Kessler that Stresemann and the rest of the cabinet were leaning against an early application. To clarify matters and try to shore up his crumbling position, Kessler decided to travel to Berlin. Certainly, one of his goals was to counteract the acidulous reporting of Müller, who did little to hide his personal and political hostility to Kessler. His first meeting was with Bülow, perhaps the most formidable opponent of entrance. He paid Kessler compliments but seemed cooler and more reserved than usual. He insisted on these minimal conditions before Germany could join: that an explicit declaration be made that joining the League would not mean acceptance of the war guilt clause of the Versailles treaty, that Germany would seek to revise unacceptable borders as foreseen in Article 19, and that the country would not be obliged to participate fully in the sanction process outlined by Article 16. Over a bottle of liebfraumilch, Kessler then sat alone with Stresemann and tried to persuade him of the need for Germany to apply during this session. The foreign minister asked Kessler to discover whether a special session of the League Assembly could not be called in December or January to consider Germany's admission, once the delicate negotiations regarding her reservations had taken place. Somewhat assuaged, Kessler awaited the decisive vote by the cabinet in their meeting devoted to the matter on September 23, 1924. In the cabinet meeting, the wisdom of appointing Kessler as Germany's unofficial observer was again raised. Stresemann defended him as a useful liaison with the British because of his connections with the Labour Party. Ebert reiterated that Kessler had already proven he had the qualities for these kinds of missions. In the end, the cabinet decided to reaffirm officially Germany's wish to enter the League but to insist on the following preconditions: the granting of a permanent seat; that entrance should not be seen as any endorsement of Article 231, the "war guilt" clause of the Versailles treaty; that German reservations regarding other treaty articles be acknowledged; and that Germany's right to colonies be addressed.[18]

Afterward, Stresemann asked Kessler whether he would make inquiries about the war guilt question in Geneva. Kessler agreed on the condition that he be legitimated by the German government vis-à-vis the League Secretariat and Müller: "I should not expose myself to the suspicion that I am acting on my own initiative." He participated in the discussions within the Foreign Office over how exactly to draft the memorandum. Once again, he encountered the opposition of Bülow, who clearly distrusted him: "He was noticeably stiff and dogmatic today. His 'good wishes' for the trip rang hollow. He considers me to be an ideologue whereas he is the ideologue who allows himself to be guided by a fata morgana Reich." Nevertheless, Kessler received his letter of accreditation to the secretary general of the League, which stated "Count Harry Kessler is in Geneva with the understanding of the Foreign Office and has the mission to discuss certain questions with certain delegates to the League of Nations." Feeling that "somehow the spring, despite everything, announces itself," he hurried back to Geneva.[19]

The city was tense with rumors about the content of the German memorandum. Adolf Müller, shown Kessler's letter of accreditation, could barely contain his bitterness. "He will give vent to his anger in some express telegram to Berlin. A comical, nasty gnome whom the times have left behind but who still seeks to bite at least," was Kessler's comment. The same day he met with Sir Eric Drummond, general secretary of the League of Nations, to go over the modalities of calling a special session of the League Assembly in January. All in all, despite some objections to the contents of the German memorandum, objections that Kessler privately shared, he had the feeling that progress was being made. After hearing through Nansen of the French reaction, he exclaimed "Not bad, it's working!" Contributing to his optimism was the news of the introduction by the British of the "Geneva Protocol," a document that sought to prevent the outbreak of war by imposing compulsory arbitration in all disputes and tightening the sanctions applied on renegade states. When the League Assembly approved the Protocol on October 2, Kessler called it "a world-historical day, or one that can be world-historical."

A letter from Bülow drove a stake through such tender illusions. The long, angry missive came in response to a letter Kessler had written him after their interview in Berlin, in which Kessler had argued that the best way for Germany to avoid being drawn into a blockade it did not support was to become a member of the League's council. "The blockade is a warlike action and irreconcilable with neutrality," Bülow replied. "But an unarmed state must cling to neutrality unconditionally even as a member of the League of Nations." Any concession from the Allies that Germany would not be obliged to provide a contingent of troops in the event of a League-sanctioned war was meaningless inasmuch as the provisions of the Versailles treaty forbade Germany from having any meaningful armed forces. In an unsigned internal memorandum addressing Kessler's mission in Geneva, Bülow vented his rage: "Unfortunately it cannot be hidden that Count Kessler overstepped by a wide margin his instructions as observer and through his enthusiastic meddling has had a negative impact. In this way he has diminished both Germany and his own personal standing. In this the judgment of all sober witnesses agrees. He observed everything in Geneva except the necessary discretion. Therefore it must be recommended that Count Kessler not be employed again in Geneva in these kinds of missions." When, at the beginning of October, Kessler returned to defend himself in person to Bülow, he argued that he had only been following the instructions of Foreign Minister Stresemann in his negotiations in Geneva. Bülow responded memorably: "Often one would do better to take into account the wishes of the department head, for ministers come and go, the department head remains." [20]

With these words, the case was closed. It was yet another disappointment for Kessler, who had begun his mission with such high hopes. At
one point in the complicated negotiations, he paused to reflect on the
reasons for the long chain of disappointments in his life. He recognized
that too often he underestimated the resistance of others but wondered
how to correct this in someone with his impulsive temperament: "It
doesn't suffice to see the right goal: one must also, if one wants to be
effective, estimate correctly the obstacles. . . . The most important
maxim for someone of my temperament: 'Don't rush!' But also see the
obstacles sharply: don't be satisfied with expecting some kind of obstacles; otherwise passivity and ossification." As so often in the past, he
turned to the cultural icon of the cool English statesman as the proper
model, "who in balance between fantasy and reserve moves forward.
Not the juste milieu that seeks as goal the mediocre but rather a wisdom
which chooses the correct path."[21] Even here, however, he exaggerated
the role of the individual and his willpower in shaping diplomacy, dis-
counting the institutional and structural limits. Bülow's words about
ministers coming and going, but civil servants remaining provide the
clue. Max Weber, not Nietzsche, would have been a better guide to the
question of how to bend the Foreign Office bureaucracy to one's will.

Yet, in this matter as well, Kessler's thinking would prove more prescient than that of a professional like Bülow. By the beginning of 1925,
the Foreign Office would be compelled to reconsider the value of membership in the League of Nations. The return to power of the Conservatives in the British parliamentary elections in October 1924, coupled
with the French refusal to evacuate Cologne in January 1925 due to their
concerns with secret German rearmament, meant that Berlin found itself confronting the renewed threat of an Anglo-Franco security alliance. To prevent that catastrophe, Stresemann and Schubert revived
an earlier German proposal for a Western security pact that would guarantee the borders in the West. An essential part of the ensuing complicated negotiations, culminating in the Locarno treaties, was that Germany would finally join the League of Nations as a permanent member
of the Council. This eventually came to pass on September 8, 1926. By
that time Kessler's political and diplomatic career was largely over, and
he was deathly ill in a hospital in London.

· · ·

One last political engagement awaited Kessler that fall. It was becoming evident that the government would fall and new elections would be

called. The May elections had strengthened extremists on both wings so much that the room for center coalitions had been considerably narrowed, especially when both the Center and the Democratic Parties refused to join with the Nationalists. Here Kessler saw an opportunity to push his policies in a different setting from the increasingly uncongenial Wilhelmstraße. On October 16, 1924, he approached the head of the Democratic Party, Erich Koch-Weser, about running on its list for the Reichstag. Koch-Weser promised to look for a vacancy but struck Kessler as less than enthusiastic. A few days later, he attended an editorial meeting of the journal *Deutsche Nation,* "the little paper that would not die or live," which served as the intellectual headquarters of the Democratic Party. The hotly debated question was whether the party should work with the Nationalist Party or, by refusing, compel the chancellor to dissolve the Reichstag and call for new elections. All in all, Kessler received the impression of a party in disarray, held together only by its leaders. Indeed, a revolt of the right wing of the party immediately ensued, although it proved to be rather easily squelched.

At the end of the month Kessler learned that the party, despite some misgivings about his pacifism, would ask him to be the head of their list in North Westphalia, a notorious stronghold of the Nationalist Party. For this privilege, he was expected to pay between 5,000 and 10,000 marks of the total cost of the campaign, estimated between 20,000 and 25,000 marks. He accepted the challenge and spoke at the party rally that kicked off the election campaign at the beginning of November. It was an unambiguous defense of pacifism, stressing how the services of British and French pacifists had made the conciliatory policies of MacDonald and Herriot possible. Despite the warm applause, there was still opposition within DDP circles in North Westphalia to his candidacy.

Undeterred, he began a month of grueling campaigning. All through towns such as Minden, Bielefeld, Bückeburg, and Münster, he traveled, giving speeches before audiences ranging in size from a couple of dozen to as many as eight hundred, sometimes speaking four times a day. From the beginning, the local press savaged his candidacy, denouncing his connections abroad to the international art world and to pacifism. He quickly discovered that he was more or less on his own, as the Democratic Party was very weak in this region and provided very little in the way of support. His campaign was almost a private organization therefore, and he relied heavily on his secretaries, Fritz Guseck and Max Goertz, as well as his sister who arrived from France to accompany him for part of the time. At one point, his rival from Stresemann's People's

Party lent him his automobile so that he could arrive in time for a rally. Twelve days into the campaign, he lost his voice; yet after a short respite in Berlin, he returned to the road.

Everywhere he encountered the same depressing message: middle-class Germany by and large rejected both democracy and pacifism. The youth in North Westphalia were almost completely organized into the Stahlhelm, the middle-class paramilitary unit. They did not join the Reichsbanner, the Socialist paramilitary wing, because they were uncomfortable with workers, not because of any firm political views. Those belonging to democratic parties were subject to a social boycott, a powerful weapon in Kessler's view. After a typical evening in Bückeburg toward the end of the campaign, in which he had to deal with the heckling of the Nationalists, Kessler brooded over the influence of such small princely capitals on German culture. On the one hand, a small town of six thousand had a good theater and orchestra, thanks to princely patronage; on the other, such cultural amenities seemed to come at the price of servility. "They have furthered culture but broken men. The misery of the German middle class is in large part due to the intensive development of servility through the many German courts. . . . Germany owes to its princes that it is the most educated but the most spineless people in Europe."[22]

The campaign closed at the beginning of December. Naturally, Kessler was optimistic, encouraged by the packed audiences for his last speeches and by the rumor that the assemblies of his political opponents to the right were less well attended. Germans went to the polls on December 7, for the second time in 1924. Rushing back to Berlin, Kessler visited the headquarters of the DDP: "The first results were favorable. From my electoral district an increase of thirty percent of the democratic votes was announced, which would guarantee my election." Later, at the Socialist Party headquarters where the reporting was more sophisticated, the news was somewhat less encouraging. The Socialist Party had indeed rebounded from its losses the previous May, while the extremist parties on both the left and right saw their vote total dwindle significantly. But the Nationalist Party posted moderate gains and the hopes of the Democratic Party were only partially fulfilled. Democrats did indeed gain four more Reichstag delegates, but their percentage increase was less than one. This modest amount was not enough to lift Kessler past the threshold. On December 9, after some days of uncertainty, he noted laconically in his diary: "It's now certain that I have not been elected."[23]

The Reichstag campaign represents not the end of Kessler's political engagement exactly, but its effective high tide. Ten years of a nearly constant preoccupation with politics—beginning with the outbreak of the war and proceeding through defeat, revolution, and the bitter postwar struggles—and the continual traveling, speaking, negotiating, and reporting had taken its physical toll. The ardors of the Reichstag campaign in particular seem to have exhausted Kessler, leaving him vulnerable to the illnesses that were nearly to kill him in the summer of 1925 and then again in 1926. For some time, an ebbing of his interests from politics back to the old prewar channels of culture had become evident.

The transition was gradual, of course. At first, he continued his political activity, almost out of habit. Thus, he found himself back in England at the beginning of 1925, in part to sound out his contacts concerning the German plan of a security pact, in part to give a lecture tour in the industrial region around Manchester and Birmingham.[24] This time, he was specifically warned by Schubert that he should not be seen in any way as an official emissary of the German government, a clear sign of his marginalization. Concerning the lecture tour through the north, Kessler was less than enthusiastic. Despite the large crowds who listened respectfully, and the decent publicity that accompanied his tour, he concluded that public opinion was largely apathetic: "Having now spoken in a number of large cities, my strongest impression is of the indifference to the League of Nations, the 'protocol,' international security, and the rest, which prevails among the vast mass of the public in this country. The problem of peace is of as little interest to it as in France or Germany. I, and those like me, remain preachers in the wilderness. . . . Seen in this light, though, these small, otherwise so dismal and intellectually wretched pacifist associations (leagues for human rights, peace societies, and so on) acquire a different aspect and significance."[25] Within Germany, he spoke at rallies of the Reichsbanner, participated in the unsuccessful referendum to deprive the former ruling German princes of their property, and continued to attend pacifist meetings. At the same time, he maintained his political connections abroad, spoke at meetings of PEN, the international organization of progressive writers.

Nevertheless, he slipped more and more from the role of a player, if a minor one, to that of an observer. With the exception of one last brief and unsuccessful mission to London in 1930, the Wilhelmstraße dispensed with his services. In part, he owed this retirement to his own work on behalf of peace and reconciliation. The passage of the Dawes Plan and then the signing of the Locarno treaties led to a pacification and stabilization of politics both within Europe and inside Germany. In hindsight, the period of relative prosperity and stability that ensued, sometimes called "the Golden Twenties," was all too brief and rested on an all-too-vulnerable foundation, the fragility of which would be demonstrated devastatingly in 1929 by Black Thursday on Wall Street. But for the time being, it must have appeared to Kessler that both the Republic and the cause of peace had been given a respite. He turned his attention to other matters, always keeping, however, a wary eye on politics.

PART SEVEN

The Path Downward

CHAPTER 25

The Golden Twenties

Perhaps Count Kessler should have invited Hindenburg with
Josephine Baker. As a host he failed here in any case.

Ruth Landshoff-Yorck,
Klutsch, Ruhm und Kleine Feuer

During the years of active political engagement, Kessler never lost sight
entirely of developments in art and culture. His connections with Herzfelde, Grosz, and Becher gave him access to the younger generation of
artists and writers, and his attitude of "Quoi de neuf?" that had so irritated Hofmannsthal did not desert him in the 1920s as the following
anecdote from Nicolas Nabokov, the young Russian composer (and distant cousin of Vladimir Nabokov), illustrates. Nabokov first made the
acquaintance of Kessler in the spring of 1921 at the Automobile Club as
a guest of a mutual friend:

He looked more German-Junkerish than I had expected, but, at the same
time, smaller and frailer than in the photographs I had seen in the papers.
His hair was brown-blond and was as carefully glazed as the shine in his light
blue eyes. His hands were small, with dainty fingers and well-manicured
nails. His clothes were dark, tweedy, and dapper. He spoke in a soft monotone, as upper-class Germans often do, and as he spoke his face did not
move at all, only his eyes blinked at rhythmic intervals, very fast, like cam-
era shutters.

When the waiter returned with the menus, Kessler began to grill the
young, nervous Russian about his acquaintances and his aesthetic pref-

erences: "Did I prefer Rilke to Valéry? I did not know who Valéry was. What was Meyerhold like? And Trotsky?" When Nabokov professed not to have met any of them, Kessler stopped talking to him. After his departure, Nabokov's friend tried to assure him that Kessler only *acted* like a snob, that in reality he was charming and full of concern for people he admired, a quality that Nabokov would in time come to appreciate.[1] John Rothenstein, the son of Kessler's old English friend William Rothenstein, caught something similar in Kessler's demeanor during an extended stay with him at Weimar in 1930: an admiring reference to a work of art of which Kessler happened to be ignorant inflicted upon his system a faint but evident shock, and one might be sure that his ignorance would be promptly remedied.[2] Both remembrances confirm the primacy to Kessler of the aesthetic way of approaching the world; the aesthete had survived the years of politics. Such an attitude could be interpreted as mere snobbery or hankering after novelty. In any case, Kessler's world in the second half of the twenties frequently combined high and low culture in a way that would have been unthinkable in the stuffier atmosphere of prewar Germany.[3]

Perhaps the most memorable instance of this took place at the beginning of 1926. Kessler, whose daily calendar was becoming as crowded as ever with social events, gave a dinner party expressly to have Josephine Baker, the American dancer who had taken Berlin by storm, dance, and, at the same time, to explain the pantomime he hoped to write for her. Around midnight, Josephine Baker was brought over, only to sulk in the corner, unwilling to dance. When Kessler described his scenario to her, however, she warmed up:

My plot is how Solomon, handsome, young, and royal (I have Serge Lifar in mind), buys a dancer (the Shulamite, Miss Baker), has her brought before him, naked, and showers his robes, his jewels, his entire riches upon her. But the more gifts he lavishes, the more she eludes him. From day to day he grows more naked and the Dancer less perceptible to him. Finally, when it is the King who is altogether bare, the Dancer utterly vanishes from his sight in a tulip-shaped cloud, first golden in color and composed of all the jewels and stuffs of which he had stripped himself to adorn her, then turning black. At the end of the scene, in the semi-gloom, there enters the young Lover, wearing a dinner jacket and. . . . For the present, I told them, I would keep the continuation to myself.[4]

Against the backdrop of Weimar culture, this scenario does appear an outdated concept, and one finds it hard to understand the enthusiasm it apparently inspired in Josephine Baker, who, as Kessler explained his ideas, began to dance around *La Mediteranné,* Maillol's massive statue of a crouched woman that was the centerpiece of Kessler's Berlin apartment. "She began to go into some movements, vigorous and vividly grotesque, in front of my Maillol figure, became preoccupied with it, stared at it, copied the pose, rested against it in bizarre postures, and talked to it, clearly excited by its massive rigor and elemental force. Then she danced around it with extravagantly grandiose gestures, the picture of a priestess frolicking like a child and making fun of herself and her goddess. Maillol's creation was obviously much more interesting and real to her than we humans standing about her. Genius (for she is a genius in the matter of grotesque movement) was addressing genius."[5]

Only a week before, the Maillol statute had attracted the admiration of a different sort of genius, Albert Einstein. Kessler, ever since meeting him on their joint pacifist expedition to Amsterdam, had cultivated the great scientist, in part because of their mutual pacifism but also because of the latter's famous genial, otherworldly image, which fascinated Kessler: "The ironical (*narquois*) trait in Einstein's expression, the *Pierrot Lunaire* quality, the smiling, pain-ridden skepticism that plays about his eyes becomes ever more noticeable," Kessler noted after one discussion. "Here and there, watching him as he speaks, his face recalls the poet Lichtenstein, a Lichtenstein who smiles not only at the superficial manifestations of human arrogance but at the causes of it too."[6]

Josephine Baker; Albert Einstein; Richard Strauss and his wife, Pauline; the British ambassador D'Abernon; the French ambassador Pierre de Margerie and his son Roland; the crowd around Misia Sert, Jean Cocteau, and Serge Diaghilev; the Lichnowskys; wealthy society women like "Baby" Goldschmidt-Rothschild; faded counts and countesses; old friends like Helene von Nostitz and Musch Richter; figures from the world of journalism such as Theodor Wolff and Georg Bernhard; politicians like Hilferding and Hans Luther; young writers and artists of all stripes—Kessler's diaries for the years 1926–30 offer a kaleidoscope of who was who in the Weimar Republic or even who aspired to be who. Neither did he miss many of the famous cultural premieres of the period, whether it was Sergey Eisenstein's film *Battleship Potemkin* ("Magnificent photography and highly effective dramatic construction. Best kind of popular art. I can understand that the right-wing parties and militarists loathe it.") or Bertolt Brecht's *Threepenny Opera* ("A fascinating production, with rudimentary staging in the Piscator manner and proletarian emphasis [apache style]") or Luigi Pirandello's

Six Persons in Search of an Author ("A piece of virtuosity which occasionally passes the bounds of staggeringly good craftsmanship and becomes real art. The problem of twirling together two or three plots simultaneously, and each time carrying the audience across the gaps without a break in the mood, has been solved by Pirandello with consummate nerve and confidence.") All of this activity came at a cost, of course. "You have no conception," he wrote to his sister in 1926, "of the social whirlpool into which I have been drawn; and I confess to being rather overwhelmed by it. Hardly a day without a lunch, a reception, a dinner and one or two balls, or routs. I never get to bed before 3 or 4 in the morning and am simply dried up. . . . Never has there been such a season here, everybody is dead beat."[7]

His relationship with Max Goertz, a young man whom he had met in the army in 1916, added a measure of stability to this otherwise hectic pace.[8] An aspiring writer, Goertz became Kessler's lover and served as his factotum, helping to run the Cranach Presse, nursing him through his various illnesses, and accompanying him on his travels. In return, Kessler sought to promote Goertz's work, an unrewarding task given his protégé's meager talents. In lieu of a more established commercial publisher, the Cranach Presse issued two short stories by Goertz, a slender work that disappeared quickly from view. As with Otto von Dungern and Gaston Colin before him, Goertz eventually married, but this did not end his relationship with Kessler. More burdensome was the inevitable tension caused by the younger man's realization that he had sacrificed whatever prospect he might have had of forging an independent career as a writer for the sake of a comfortable but dependent existence, and the older man's barely acknowledged understanding that his lover lacked serious talent.[9] Despite the occasional quarrels this conflict created, Goetz remained loyal to Kessler to the end, sharing, along with his wife, the older man's exile in Mallorca and performing invaluable service in smuggling his diaries and other documents necessary for the composition of his memoirs out of Nazi Germany.[10]

The social vortex of the late 1920s made it difficult for Kessler to find the time for his own work. He entertained for at least two years the idea of writing another ballet, switching from Josephine Baker to his old friend Diaghilev and his Ballets Russes and from the passé Richard Strauss to the jazzier Kurt Weill. Weill actually visited him in November 1927 to discuss the project, but although the composer expressed interest, he also reminded Kessler that he had a prior commitment to do a big opera (probably *The Threepenny Opera*), and in the end, nothing came of the project. Despite this disappointment, Kessler was nevertheless successful in two endeavors: he finally got his private press off the ground, publishing at least two monumental editions that have a secure place in the history of fine printing, and he wrote his brilliant biography of Walther Rathenau.

• • •

By 1922, Kessler had already reestablished contact with Maillol and Craig with a view to setting them to work for his Cranach Presse, the Frenchman on illustrations for an edition of Virgil's *Ecologues* and the Englishman on illustrations for a translation of *Hamlet* by Gerhart Hauptmann. His frenetic activity at the time of the Ruhr crisis and its aftermath had put these projects on hold, but at the beginning of 1925, with his gradual retreat from active politics, he returned to them. In January, he traveled to the south of France to visit Maillol in his hometown of Banyuls. Together, they worked on new woodcuts for *Ecologues* III and VII. On a subsequent trip at the beginning of April, Kessler encountered his old friend suffering from a bad cold and grumbling over the work of designing initials for each *Ecologue:* "All this, with a vain effort to conjure up a thoroughly hurt look, tumbled out with an artful, benevolent smirk, half that of a guilty schoolboy and half that of an old sage. . . . Horrible, setting a genius a task the way a schoolboy is set a lesson, but that is how it always has been between us. Without gentle pressure and ruthlessness in face of his continual complaints neither his great *Crouching Woman* nor his great relief nor the figure of Colin (also at the Orsay) would ever have been finished."[11*] Kessler marveled still at Maillol's apparently inexhaustible fertility. Asking him to ornament some of the capital letter alphabet that Eric Gill had carved, he was astounded to see Maillol complete the job, using a fine small Japanese brush, in only two hours: "When I think that Johnston simply does not trust himself to design an alphabet of ornamental capitals and would in any case take years to do it, while even Gill would be occupied for months on such a project, whereas Maillol has never seriously concerned himself with the decoration of literals but shakes them so to speak out of his sleeve, the profusion of forms alive in him appears miraculous."[12]

---

*The relief, entitled *Le désir* and originally in Kessler's Weimar garden, is now at the Musée d'Orsay in Paris, where the figure of Colin, *Le bicycliste,* also can be found.

Afterward, he took a side trip during his tour of England to visit Eric Gill in Wales in order to have him carve Maillol's initials. Gill had retreated, along with his abundant family, to a remote, barely accessible monastery in the mountains. After a car trip through a lonely valley that reminded Kessler of the Rio Grande, he arrived at "a dilapidated monastic building, passed along a cloister passage under repair, marched through an ante-room to where I could hear voices, and suddenly stood in a medium-sized room where a number of women and girls and two very dignified-looking monks were sitting in front of a large log-fire." A little while later, Gill arrived, "a Tolstoy-like figure in a smock and cloak, half-monk, half peasant." The two men were moved in their first meeting since the war and Gill explained why he was living a "squatter existence" in the wilderness; "for him and his friends, and evidently for me too, art has now taken second place to achieving a regeneration of life. Pre-war life was too superficial." After showing Kessler his work, Gill then looked at Maillol's woodcuts and agreed to carve his initials.[13]

The work on the *Eclogues*, already postponed by more than a decade, was delayed yet further by bouts of illness, one in late June, early July of 1925,[14] and a much graver bout of pneumonia that nearly killed Kessler the following summer. En route from Paris to London, he fell ill in the train and was immediately bedridden at the Hotel Cecil. As the crisis mounted, and he began bleeding internally, his family and friends gathered around him. His sister, Wilma, flew in from Paris: "For two months she remained day and night outside my door, hardly eating or sleeping, worn out by constant fear and anxiety, suffering more deeply than I did." Her sons, Jacques and Christian, came to London, as did Max Goertz and Kessler's secretary, Fritz Guseck. In the middle of July, he began hemorrhaging blood at an alarming rate and only a series of blood infusions and oxygen injections kept him alive but only barely. Because all other sedatives were useless, he was given morphine until he was moved to a sanatorium in the middle of August. Eventually, a regimen of injecting him with his own viruses was begun. In the middle of September, after a powerful injection that provoked an excruciating bout of coughing up blood and bits of tissue, giving him so much pain that not even the morphine relieved him, the crisis passed. The coughing had expelled much of the affected tissues in his lungs, and he dated his real convalescence from this episode.[15]

At the beginning of October, he felt well enough to travel at a leisurely pace. He arrived eventually at Capri, where he rented a villa, the C'a del Sole. There, high above the balmy bay of Naples, accompanied by his personal nurse and the faithful Guseck and Goertz, he recuperated. Old friends came to visit, such as Musch Richter, who spent Christmas of 1926 with Kessler. He planned to work on his biography of Rathenau but was hampered by trouble in his left eye, a consequence of the massive hemorrhages of the summer. This trouble required frequent consultations with the best eye doctors in Zurich, although in the end it was determined that the eye was inoperable. Not until the following May did he leave Capri permanently and return to Germany to attend the book fair in Leipzig. The return to his homeland, however, after a year's absence, brought no great joy: "Both Max and I were struck at Freiburg by the ugliness of the people crowding into the train. A nasty, gray, cold day too. Not a pleasant return home. A chilly feeling, both literally and metaphorically." [16]

Nevertheless, his return was a bit of a personal triumph, for the magnificent edition of *The Eclogues* produced by his Cranach Presse attracted the admiration of the fine book world gathered in Leipzig. Years of patient, tenacious prodding on the part of Kessler, gently but firmly shepherding such temperamental egos as Maillol, Gill, the calligrapher Edward Johnston, the letter-cutter Edward Prince, the printer Emery Walker, and others toward the goal he had in mind, resulted in one of the most striking printed books of the twentieth century. It also represented Kessler's tribute to his lifelong obsession with classical antiquity, with the Mediterranean world in general, and with a certain conception of the "total art-work" he had harbored since his Jugendstil youth.

An ideal of perfection animated the Cranach Presse from the time of its founding in 1913, leading to remarkable and frequently comic endeavors, most of which resulted in long delays. In the matter of finding the proper paper for the Virgil project, for example, Kessler and Maillol eventually decided the only solution was to manufacture their own, creating a factory in Monval outside of Paris for this purpose. The paper was produced by hand, avoiding purposely all chemicals in its manufacture; all impurities, which in most paper manufacturing were simply disguised by the bleaching process, were removed physically in "Maillol-Kessler Paper," yielding an absolutely pure product. In its most expensive version, pure Chinese silk rags were employed; when the civil disturbances in China disrupted the supply, printing had to be postponed until a new source could be found. In any version, the paper was very costly, so much so that Anton Kippenberg, Director of the Insel Verlag, refused to use it, much to Kessler's chagrin. And, of course, it was the factory in Monval that figured in the accusations of espionage leveled against Kessler in wartime France. [17]

Besides an original paper, Kessler required an original typeface. To this purpose, he employed Edward Johnston to design an italic alphabet based on the so-called Jenson Antique, an italic script created by Nicolaus Jenson and found in a 1476 edition of Pliny's *Natural History* published in Venice. Edward Prince was then to cut the letters based on Johnston's designs. What seems at first sight like a simple enough project proved to be an arduous exercise in diplomacy every bit as complicated as anything Kessler had undertaken for the Foreign Office and lasting years. Johnston worked very slowly, in part because his perfectionism required him to look at a problem from every angle and mull over it before beginning work. He also suffered from self-doubt and in long letters to Kessler, he expounded on the difficulty of conveying his conceptions to Prince and complained of the workload. To all of these, Kessler responded with long, patient, encouraging replies, sent from Paris, Berlin, London, Weimar, and other points of the compass, letters that however accommodating nevertheless pushed the reluctant Johnston toward completion.[18]

The text setting for *The Ecologues* began in 1913 when Maillol was already finished with the bulk of his illustrations, but it was interrupted by the war and then by Kessler's political preoccupations. During these years, Kessler sought to keep his press together by giving it various commissions, such as printing the private edition of his wartime letters or his proposals for a new league of nations. Gradually, he picked up the bits and pieces, and by 1925, he was only missing the four woodcuts that Maillol cut that year (for which he received 8,000 francs from his patron). Despite his illness in 1925 and other delays, Kessler was able to give Kippenberg the first printed copy in April 1926. *The Ecologues* was initially published in two editions, one with a German translation, by Kessler's old friend Rudolf A. Schröder, facing the Latin original, and the other with a French translation. A year later, an English version appeared.

A recent study of the Cranach Presse *Ecologues* posed the question of how Kessler, the pacifist and democrat, could have reconciled "the sinuous forms and perfect nudity of Maillol's designs for the *Ecologues* with his own political activism and tireless campaigning for the League of Nations." Had that question been asked of him, Kessler would have responded that there was no conflict or paradox at all. His political activity had always been motivated, at its most fundamental level, by an aesthetic vision of perfect harmony between man and his environment, by the same impression of *luxe, calme, et volupté* that pervades the pages of his Virgil. Certainly, Maillol's woodcuts of nymphs, naiads, and satyrs that "move contentedly in the sheer pleasure of existence" provided much of the atmosphere, yet the illustrations had always been seen as an integral part of the total book design. As early as 1905, Kessler had outlined the principles of illustration that he followed in the *Ecologues*. Illustrations "should be principally linear in so far as the text is composed out of lines. The thickness and thinness of their lines should hold exactly to the limits of the thick and thin lines of the letters, and the lines should be—as much as possible—distributed within in the white spaces of the picture square in the same way the letters are distributed on the page, so that there does not appear significantly greater white flecks and surfaces in the picture than there are in the text." [19]

In an article entitled "Why Maillol Illustrated Virgil's *Ecologues?*" Kessler once again summoned up the principal complaint against modernity first made by the pioneers of modern design, that of the dissonance between art and environment, or more specifically, between sculpture and architecture at the end of the nineteenth century. Once again, he used Maillol's friendly rival Rodin as a foil, claiming that the latter had, in his sculpture, simply turned his back on an ugly outside world and retired to "a 'delectatio morosa,' an entirely withdrawn, lonely enjoyment of the pleasures of his imagination and creative power, ignoring his environment." Maillol, by contrast, never separated his art from the environment within which it would form a part. Thus, his original name for the sculpture found in Kessler's Berlin flat had been *Statute for a Shady Park:* "he saw with the masses and lines of the figure, with her expression, with the play of light and shadows on her surfaces, at the same time the old trees, which would be her friends and protectors, yes even further, her justification before the world; for her name was not an attempt to create a mood such as mediocre artists give to their unsuccessful works in order to cloak their mistakes, but rather sprang out of the conception of the figure itself, whose calmness he from the very beginning saw in connection with other masses and lines, moved by light and wind, and which would only give their full meaning to the eye in this relation." The Jenson typeface was chosen as the natural complement to Maillol's illustrations, which Kessler depicted, much as he had done in his diaries, as emerging spontaneously from the sculptor's deeply personal connection to his landscape.[20]

One does not have to buy all of this, of course. As already noted, Maillol was not quite the "naïve" (in the sense used by Schiller in opposition to "sentimental") artist Kessler loved to portray. There was altogether more cunning and calculation in his presentation of himself, especially to his most important patron. Nor did Kessler seem to notice the irony that the "statue for a shady park" was now residing in an apartment in the middle of a huge metropolis in Germany, far from the landscape for which it had been putatively designed. The sculptor's response, when queried about his patron's article, was that naturally "this had nothing to do with it. Nevertheless he (Kessler) was not all that wrong after all." What disturbed him more, he complained years later, was how, after making the illustrations so that they would meld with the text, Kessler had undermined the effect by nevertheless leaving empty white spaces throughout the book. "He printed the book without informing me because he well knew that I would not agree. He fancies that he has taste. He has not sold a single copy."[21]

These and other unfair remarks do not disguise the fact that Maillol took the project seriously. When accused of having made naïve illustrations to accompany the text of an urbane, sophisticated poet, he responded: "But I did not at all attempt to do the same as Virgil. Who could imitate Virgil? . . . I tried to create something charming, something that would go well with the typography. I did not try to imitate Virgil. I didn't illustrate Virgil, I illustrated the paper. And for that one needs first of all a beautiful paper. Whether it is a book for kings, for students, or for whores, one needs always above all a beautiful paper." This attitude may explain why his illustrations often had only an indirect relation to the subject matter they were meant to illustrate. No matter. The book succeeds even today, for anyone lucky enough to come across a copy, as a potent evocation of that perhaps imaginary idea of Greece that has inspired Western civilization from the Renaissance to this day.[22]

The second great publication of the Cranach Presse provides an interesting counterweight to the *Ecologues*. If that book embodies a meridonal world of repose, of self-assurance, of calm, and of free play under southern skies, then the Cranach Presse *Hamlet*, illustrated by Gordon Craig, depicts a septentrional world of shadows, of suspicions, of uncertainty, and of dramatic gestures. Like the Virgil, the Shakespeare project set its roots before the war when Craig showed his sketches for his forthcoming production of *Hamlet* in Moscow to Kessler. The latter paid the designer two hundred and forty pounds for the seventy-five woodcuts. If the Virgil employed a typeface from the great Quatrocento Italian designs, it was only fitting that the Shakespeare would be printed with a typeface based on the gothic, Fraktur. Again, Johnston went to work—again, very slowly. The war came and Wilma, following her brother's instructions from the front, tried to keep the Englishman on task. Not long after the war the letter-cutter Prince died and a German replacement was found. The final typeface was not sent to the foundry for forging until July 1927.[23]

If the design of the *Ecologues* could be described as Apollonian, all clear lines and well-defined spaces, then the *Hamlet* could be described perhaps as Dionysian, following Craig's interpretation of Shakespeare, all suggestion and atmosphere. Whereas the margins of the former were kept clear, the ones in the latter were crowded, not just with the text of the play and Craig's illustrations but also with excerpts from two of Shakespeare's principal sources, the stories of Saxos Grammaticus and François de Belleforest's *Hystorie of Hamlet*. For the German edition, Kessler used a new, somewhat quirky, translation by Gerhart Hauptmann. He had gone to stay with Hauptmann at his home in Bad Liebenstein shortly after the book fair in Leipzig. The playwright, who was more or less consciously taking on the role of the elder statesman of German literature and who prided himself on a perceived likeness to Goethe, read to Kessler from his recent work *Till Eulenspiegel*. The pair also discussed German literature and Shakespeare, whereby Kessler learned of Hauptmann's version of *Hamlet* in which he altered the last two acts to conform with what he believed were Shakespeare's intentions and made Laertes, not Hamlet, the instigator of the uprising against Claudius. Kessler was impressed enough to suggest adding the emendations to the Cranach Presse edition. It proved an immensely complicated printing job to bring together all of these texts, sources, illustrations, and commentaries into a unified whole, but when it was finished, it was recognized as a masterpiece. The German edition won a prize at the 1929 Leipzig book fair.

The reputation of the Cranach Presse as one of the great private presses of the twentieth century rests firmly on the *Ecologues* and *Hamlet*. The press published other books, both under its own imprint and for other publishers, principally Insel. But the press was an immensely costly endeavor that could not break even and thus had to be subsidized by Kessler throughout its history. At its high point in the late twenties, the press employed more than twelve workers; also, Kessler's obsession with using only the finest materials, no matter the cost, did not help its profitability. The relationship with Insel Verlag eventually came to grief, partly over editorial differences, partly over Kessler's growing political estrangement from Anton Kippenberg, who was moving into the Nazi camp.

The Great Depression then finished it off. It is touching to see the tenacity with which Kessler clung to the press, hoping that it would yet prove his salvation from financial ruin. In Christmas 1930, he wrote to his sister, who had become an increasingly reluctant source of financing, of his hopes: "I am very sorry to put you to inconvenience and of course I quite understand that you should be anxious in the way you say about my finances. I do not dispute *que c'est un mauvais moment à passer* for me and my Press, but as I explained to you, it is a *momentary* crisis and it will certain be over when I can bring out my next two or three books which are practically ready for printing now." As the "momentary" crisis deepened, he desperately fought for a breathing space: "What I am trying to get is *time* to make a really *paying* concern of my Press which, I am only allowed time and a very small amount of liquid capital, is bound to be a paying concern with a short time. It has an immense reputation and if only I can run it quietly without constant money trouble for another year I am quite sure it will *repay amply*." But immensely costly fine editions do not sell well in a depression of such a magnitude. Still, even as he was forced to sell his priceless art for fire sale prices, he defended his independence as a publisher from his sister's increasingly frantic pleas that he find an investor: "If the worse comes to the worse, I should sell my house in Weimar, move the Press and myself to Berlin and live in my three rooms in the Köthnestrasse which are cheap and where I need only one or two servants. . . . Certainly the last thing I shall do, is to give up my Press. For then the only thing left for me to do would be to die." To Schröder, he wrote that "it would be exceptionally painful for me, and very regrettable as well for the public interest," he continued, "if the Cranach-Presse were forced to close its doors, I truly don't need to tell you . . . this concerns what is more or less my life's work and I must now fight so that it does not go completely to pieces." Even after the press was closed in October 1931 and Kessler forced into exile in March 1933 by the Nazi seizure of power, he continued to hope, dreaming of establishing the press again in Basel or Zurich. Sick, impoverished, living in a pension outside of Lyons, he wrote to his sister in June 1937 of the press, "I haven't the slightest intention it should be sold. That would be a real catastrophe for me." On August 10 of that year, he learned of its impending sale on the 19th: "All this is little less than a catastrophe for me, the final destruction of all I had built up in my lifetime."[24] He died only a few months later.

In the last analysis, there is something ironic about Kessler's achievements with the Cranach Presse. For someone whose identity had been bound up for so long with the avant-garde, he had ended his career publishing works that hearkened back to the opulent era of prewar aestheticism rather than works that embodied the more democratic, restless, and daring spirit of the 1920s. This becomes especially evident when one compares the *Ecologues* or *Hamlet* with the typography and book design generated by the Bauhaus. In a way reminiscent of how *The Legend of Joseph* was destined to be overshadowed by the more avant-garde *Rites of Spring*, it was Kessler's fate here too to be left behind, precisely in the creative field in which he was most accomplished, by the modernism that he had spent his life promoting.

• • •

The second big project of these years was his biography of Walther Rathenau. The exact date of his decision to undertake such a task is not clear, but he was among the contributors to an edition of *Die neue Rundschau*, published in Rathenau's honor shortly after his assassination in 1922. Three years later, he had his press publish a shorter version, containing tributes from himself, Hugo Simon, and Georg Bernhard, in the same month the Locarno treaties were signed, "which, through the evacuation of Cologne, the reestablishment of friendly relations between former enemies, and laying the foundation for a new, united Europe, justifies the foreign policy inaugurated by Rathenau." One can presume then that the thought of writing a fuller tribute to the man Kessler saw as the greatest martyr of the Republic had been with him for some time before he actually began his book research in the beginning of 1926. His illness that summer delayed him, but later in Capri, he was once again at work. Publishing business seems to have delayed him again for only a year later, in November 1927, did he begin writing. "Luckily," he wrote to Wilma, "Rathenau is really a fascinating subject, if only I can make people feel as I do about it," a sentiment recognized by any biographer. Throughout the spring of 1928, he worked furiously and there are scarcely any diary entries for this period. At last, on May 8, less than two months before the book was launched, he finished the last chapter. A potential last-minute crisis was averted when one of Kessler's principal sources, Lili Deutsch, the wife of a director of Rathenau's company and the closest thing to his lover, withdrew the threat of a lawsuit on the advice of her lawyer. Although she had been remarkably forthcoming with Kessler, even sending him her correspondence with Rathenau, she balked after seeing the draft, thinking Kessler had gone too far in citing personal passages. With that hurdle passed, *Walther Ra-*

thenau: Sein Leben und Sein Werk was published in June 1928 to a great deal of fanfare and publicity. It sold well, exhausting its first printing of five thousand copies in only three months, and a second appeared in October. Dutch and English translations arrived the next year, followed by a U.S. edition in 1930 and a French edition in 1933. Kessler, who expected the right to attack the book bitterly, was pleasantly surprised at the moderate reception it received in conservative newspapers and journals. In the left-liberal world, it was nearly universally praised.[25]

The energy and devotion that Kessler dedicated to this project is all the more remarkable considering that there was little in the earlier relationship between the two men to suggest that Kessler would ever undertake Rathenau's biography. They had first met in the salons of Berlin in the 1890s but had only really come to know each other in 1906 not long after Kessler's resignation in Weimar. After dinner at the home of the industrialist, he noted in his diary: "Rathenau is someone whom it pays to meet." They spoke of art and politics, and once, with Hofmannsthal, of Judaism, race, and mysticism. They met most frequently in 1911 at the Automobile Club in Berlin and enjoyed some wide-ranging discussions, and Kessler was able to obtain Rathenau's financial support for the Nietzsche Memorial.

Nevertheless, the two men, who shared a certain reserve within friendships, never were more than acquaintances. Kessler lamented Rathenau's disinterest in modern art and mocked his taste for the spare, Prussian classicism of the early nineteenth century as an affectation. Although reading *Von kommenden Dingen* in March 1917 renewed his interest in Rathenau's economic ideas, Kessler reserved his bitterest remarks for Rathenau's postwar thoughts and deeds. After outlining his alternative to the League of Nations in a long discussion in February 1919, Kessler was compelled to listen to Rathenau's lengthy rejection of this approach. Hurt no doubt by the abrupt dismissal of a plan that owed much to Rathenau's own thought, Kessler vented his spleen: "Rathenau spouted all this with a self-assured loquacity that often puts matters in a false light even when he is right. He is an adept at striking false attitudes and displaying himself in a freakish posture, as Communist ensconced in a damask-covered chair, as patronizing patriot, as ultramodernist strumming an old lyre. . . . His manner is a mixture of bitterness and conceit. No doubt his impenetrable attitude towards women plays a part in all this. There is something of a masculine old maid about him, his way of thinking and his arrogance."[26]

Despite these disagreements, however, Kessler was drawn to Rathenau's enigmatic presence. No doubt the assassination and the public funeral, which he described in detail in his diary, elevated Rathenau's stature in Kessler's mind, removing him to a certain extent from carping criticism. There can be no doubt that Kessler, on a deeply personal level, was fascinated by the tragic industrialist/visionary, partly because of personal affinities, partly because Rathenau represented for him so compellingly the Other. Both men were nearly the same age, both had fathers who belonged to the so-called founders' generation and embodied nineteenth-century liberal energy and empire-building, both had rather suffocating mothers who lived for society and cultivated a love of art in their sons. If Rathenau remained always, as a Jew, an outsider in Wilhelmian society, so too did Kessler, due to his family's recent—and, in some eyes, tainted—ennoblement. Finally, as Kessler's remark on Rathenau's "impenetrable attitude towards women" indicates, he suspected the industrialist of being a homosexual like himself, thus a double outsider. Yet, where Kessler had opted for forging a career in art and literature, Rathenau, despite much ambivalence, had plunged into the world of business, science, and technology, the forces that were most responsible for the creation of the modern world. In some ways, then, Rathenau represented for Kessler the man of action, the purpose-driven *Zweckmensch* similar to those he met in the army, especially Ludendorff, the difference being that part of Rathenau deplored this aspect of his personality and subjected it to a withering critique.

The tragic dualism in Rathenau's personality is the great theme of the biography. Borrowing perhaps from Proust, Kessler conceptualizes this duality as "the way of the intellect" and the "way of the spirit," the former referring to technocratic rationality and specialization, the latter to the search for an intuitive, visionary, holistic understanding of the world. Rathenau incorporated both of these paths in a particularly self-conscious and, through his books, public way but was never able to achieve a reconciliation between them. Of course, the conflict between these two worldviews lies at the heart of the crisis of modernity. Rathenau's life then was a microcosm that reflected the macrocosm: "Thus the struggle proceeded between the opposing forces of his soul. And as the conflict which raged under the smooth, or artificially smoothed, surface of his nature was the same as that which rages under the glittering surface of our western civilization, the revolt of his repressed spiritual forces against the crippling of his full humanity was transmuted into a revolt against the crippling of mankind through its bondage to material ends."[27]

Rathenau identified the way of the intellect with what he called "men of fear," of whom he considered the Jews to be most emblematic. The interpretation is soaked in Nietzsche. As a persecuted, relatively powerless minority, the Jews developed a hypertrophic intellect as a way to survive in a hostile world, but also an expression of the will to power. Although capitalism was a creation of Protestant Europe, pace Max Weber, it offered an immensely fertile and hospitable soil for the Jewish power of ratiocination, an elective affinity that accounts for their hugely disproportional presence in capitalist finance and industry, not to mention in the allied worlds of science and technology. But the avidity for knowledge, for material things, for power, makes the immediate joy in existence impossible for the rational man, regardless of ethnic or religious background. As Kessler noted, this description stemmed in part from Rathenau's self-analysis, and he devoted enormous energy and self-discipline in overcoming and transmuting those tendencies within himself that he attributed to the "man of fear." "He felt himself," Kessler wrote, "to be an experiment, one who was chosen out to test on himself how far a 'man of fear' can change himself into a 'man of courage,' 'a man fettered by purpose' into 'one whose soul is free.' "[28]

Opposed to the intellect is the soul. In *The Mechanism of the Mind*, Rathenau spoke of the "birth of the soul" in passages that Kessler traces back to impressions he gathered on his journey to Greece in May 1906. Not surprisingly, the landscape of Greece evoked once again a vision of wholeness, of harmony, of inner-directed contentment that could be held up against the relentlessly dissatisfied, Faustian world of modern Europe. To have a soul is to be capable of a transcendent, unselfish love, a love that grasps the world "but not with the talons of the intellect; rather it dissolves itself, is submerged, unites itself, becomes one and, in that it becomes one, comprehends. . . . 'Soul' is the collective name he (Rathenau) bestows on all those inner experiences which are alien and hostile to the schemer, the man enslaved by purpose; it is the rallying cry of all those faculties which Rathenau summons up within his own self to fight the dreaded and detested intellect: a cry to which they immediately respond in serried ranks."[29] The unabashed mysticism evident here was composed of various influences: Spinoza's philosophy, the idealism of Fichte, German and Jewish mystics. Rathenau applied himself to learning Hebrew and studied the Hassidim with Martin Buber during these years.

His ultimate failure to achieve this "sacrifice of the intellect," although a personal tragedy, nevertheless accounted for the perspicuity of

Rathenau's thought. Although generally he expressed overt scorn for the intellect, he still confessed to have a secret admiration for "men of fear," for their suffering and for their insight. Because he did not give up the business world, he could speak with authority, from within, about the macrocosmic forces allied with the way of the intellect. He subsumed these forces under the general rubric of "mechanization" and his passages on this phenomenon have a prophetic ring today. "Mechanization . . . is the amalgamation of the whole world into one compulsory association, into one continuous net of production and world trade." [30] The consequences of this process are both baleful and pervasive. For the industrial workers, it is soul-killing, dehumanizing, alienated labor, yet the managers, engineers, professionals, and others who service the capitalist machine are equally enslaved by the narrow goals imposed by mechanization. It also creates a homogenous world, where everyone increasingly resembles everyone else, while, at the same time, it subjects the individual to an unprecedented flood of information. "But does the inundation bring nourishment to the soul?" asks Kessler, only to then answer, in words that have only become more relevant since first written: "All this information, these visions, these ideas rush past us as though carried away by a roaring torrent. Very few ever succeed in taking hold; most of them whirl past, merely serving to provide man with moments of self-forgetfulness, to make him from day to day less intimate with himself, to draw him away more and more from the depths to the mere outer trappings of his soul." [31] There is no getting around mechanization, however—the modern world is doomed to it for it alone can produce the goods necessary to feed and clothe the massive increase in population that the industrial revolution inaugurated. The only hope is that, in a form of Hegelian dialectic, the mechanizing process will generate its own antidote.

In his book, Kessler also examines Rathenau's political views and record. Describing Rathenau as nearly the only German—indeed, the only European—who did not greet the outbreak of the war with enthusiasm, Kessler must have been aware of his own wartime correspondence, with its talk of a German imperium from Calais to Riga, and so these passages stand as a tacit critique of his own past. About Rathenau's biggest mistake, his letter to Ludendorff supporting the forcible deportation of seven hundred thousand Belgian workers to labor in Germany, Kessler is unsparing but fair, attributing it to the charisma of Ludendorff, something that Kessler knew well, having fallen for a time under its spell. "To explain his bewildering attitude in this matter," Kessler continued, "one must take into account other psychological motives besides his regard for Ludendorff: a clouding of his judgment, not by war psychosis—for from that he was immune—but by his Prussianism, his deep desire to be German to the core, which always disarmed him in the face of anti-Semitic attacks, and in this case proved stronger than the dictates of reason." Regarding the years following the German defeat, the two men shared the same perspective: anger at the sudden capitulation of the High Command, disappointment in the results of the German revolution, criticism of the deficiencies of Wilson's League of Nations, and reliance on a foreign policy of constructive engagement with the former enemies to obtain the space with which to revise the more unacceptable elements of the Versailles treaty. In general, Kessler sought to portray Rathenau's tenure both as reconstruction minister and as foreign minister as establishing the guidelines for what eventually become the policy of reconciliation associated with Stresemann.[32]

Rathenau, of course, would not live to witness the triumph. Even before the war, his books had earned him disdain and public notoriety, particularly in right-wing circles. "People found it comic that a business man should preach the birth of the soul; compromising that a rich man should attack luxury," writes Kessler. "But it was unforgivable, if not pathological, that a leader of industry should advocate the nationalization of monopolies, the abolition of the right of inheritance, the ruthless taxation of the wealthy, the liberation of the proletariat, a society without classes, and other Red impossibilities; that stamped him as a dangerous subject, against whom any steps were justified." Kessler's defense of his subject against these charges of hypocrisy is particularly heartfelt because he too was accused of being a wealthy armchair socialist. He admits Rathenau's contradictions but argues that they follow from the complexity of his nature. "But his ideas also followed from this complexity, and their value lay just in those contradictions in which they were rooted. For they were rooted in the same contradictions as is the world of the twentieth century, and for men who belong to this world the ideas that are valuable and redemptive are not those that come from simple souls. We cannot provide the soil of divine simplicity in which the ideas of St. Francis would blossom; at the best we cultivate such ideas like exotic plants, which may perhaps bear a few sickly blooms on alien soil, but no ripe fruit. Only those ideas are fruitful for us which are born in men whose souls are of our own type; only such ideas can find their accustomed climate and can develop to maturity."[33]

Be that as it may, in the distraught, overheated, labile atmosphere of postwar Germany, Rathenau's public persona, with its mysterious aloofness and its contradictions, attracted the virulent hatred of anti-Semitic, violent youth and veterans looking for a scapegoat for their country's disgrace. Rathenau, with a deep-seated fatalism Kessler ascribes to his Judaism, foresaw the violent death that awaited him shortly after his return from Genoa. The book closes with a moving account of Rathenau's funeral and, in an explicit comparison with the assassination of Abraham Lincoln, seeks to establish Rathenau as the first, great fallen hero of the German Republic.

It succeeds. The book has stood up well and is still considered the most satisfying biography of Rathenau, providing the kind of monument for its subject that still eludes other Weimar statesmen, most noticeably Gustav Stresemann.[34] There are several reasons for its quality. First, Kessler had access to invaluable sources, some of them lost now to future biographers: the letters of Lili Deutsch; private conversations with Josef Wirth, the chancellor who appointed Rathenau to his ministerial posts; and the reports of Ago von Maltzan, who died in an airplane crash just before Kessler began the project. For this latter source, he had to obtain special permission from the Foreign Office. Second, Kessler's own personal relations with his subject, his testimony as an eyewitness to many of the political events he describes, give his narrative an immediacy and authenticity denied forever to later generations. Most important, however, he had a clear plan, he had mulled these themes over in his mind for years, and he put himself into the book on nearly every page, without, however, diminishing his subject. In his *Rathenau,* Kessler did not just write someone else's biography, he left us his single most important political testament.

CHAPTER 26

Revenge of the Philistines

Mysterious, incomprehensible Germany.
Kessler, *In the Twenties*

Rathenau's assassination, along with the other murders, abortive revolutions, failed putsches, the occupation of the Ruhr, and the hyperinflation of 1923, could be seen, from the perspective of 1928, as belonging to the birth pangs of a republic that, although still vulnerable, was beginning to appear as if it might actually survive. In the aftermath of Constitution Day in August 1927, Kessler recorded his tentative optimism: "So there comes to be a not completely secure majority in favor of the maintenance of the Republic as a *pis aller*. Some kind of serious shift in the foreign or domestic political situation, which seemed to guarantee a restoration of the monarchy without a fight, could make today's pragmatic but reluctant republicans into active monarchists again. The problem for the republic is therefore whether the situation will stabilize itself, in which the restoration of the monarchy no longer is possible without a civil war." He estimated that approximately one-third of the Germans were true republicans; another third, so-called *Vernunftrepublikaner* (those who supported the republic with their reason, not their heart); and the final third rejected the republic completely. Therefore, the German democracy seemed guaranteed for the foreseeable future, "but too great a confidence is not appropriate either."[1]

The foreseeable future in this case ended, of course, with the stock market crash on Wall Street in October 1929. The Great Depression put an end to the fragile stabilization of the "golden twenties" and demonstrated the deep structural weaknesses within the Weimar Republic. In fact, the German economy had been in trouble even before the Wall Street crash. As early as 1927, Carl Schubert had predicted to Kessler an economic catastrophe, not just for Germany but for all countries. The winter of 1928–29 had witnessed a rise in unemployment that was attributed to the unseasonably cold temperatures, but the following spring did not bring the hoped-for reduction. By October 1929, the official number of jobless reached 1.6 million.[2] At the time, of course, the dimensions of the crisis were not immediately evident. There had been an even more dramatic drop in prices in 1925–26 as a result of the adjustment to the end of inflation, yet the German economy had come roaring back. As Kessler's letters to his sister, pleading for just a little more credit and a little more time, indicate, many felt the current recession would be a passing phase, a necessary correction that, by lowering prices, interest rates, and wages, would facilitate a renewed burst of prosperity. Indeed, at the beginning of 1931, it appeared that the economy was on its way to recovery.[3] The collapse of the well-respected Austrian bank, the Creditanstalt, in May and the ensuing credit crunch knocked the legs from under this recovery and turned what might have been a manageable crisis into a depression of unprecedented magnitude.[4]

The economic crisis and political developments accelerated the downward spiral. The last truly democratic government of Weimar—in the sense that it was based on a majority in the Reichstag—fell in March 1930 over the question of reducing unemployment benefits, something the Socialist Party would not endorse. The cabinets that followed were minority governments, forced to rely on the authority of Reichspresident Hindenburg to issue emergency decrees. Heinrich Brüning, the Center Party financial expert who became chancellor at this point, tried to apply the standard economic recipe for recessions: cutting government spending and raising taxes in order to free up capital for investment in private business, regardless of the short-term political consequences— disastrous measures politically. Political and economic developments, in a reciprocally negative fashion, worked together to deepen the crisis and undermine the republic. The single most decisive election in modern German history took place on September 14, 1930. A day later, Kessler wrote this analysis: "A black day for Germany. The Nazis have increased the number of their seats almost tenfold, from 12 to 107, and have become the second strongest party in the Reichstag. . . . We face a national crisis which can only be overcome if all those who accept, or at least tolerate, the Republic stand firmly together and furthermore demonstrate the ability to put straight the economic and financial situation before the next Reichstag dissolution. . . . National Socialism is a delirium of the German lower middle class. The poison of its disease may however bring down ruin on Germany and Europe for decades ahead."[5] Overnight, it seemed, the once unthinkable prospect of Adolf Hitler becoming chancellor loomed menacingly over the future.[6]

Few, if any, Germans were immune from the blows that struck their country in quick succession in the early 1930s. For Kessler, these years witnessed the destruction of his finances, leading to his nearly complete financial dependence on his sister and the obliteration of all that he worked for in the political and diplomatic arenas. Even without the political and economic crises, he had to deal with the death of friends and allies. His old ally in the struggles connected with modern art in Imperial Germany, the art dealer Paul Cassirer, shot himself in 1925. Even more disturbing was the death of Hofmannsthal at the funeral of his son, Franz, who had committed suicide. Ever since the disagreements over the ballet business, contacts between the two had been infrequent.[7] Shortly before his death, Hofmannsthal had written to Goertz to thank him for sending his book to him and then, added these lines: "If you see Harry Kessler, tell him that his image has never in all the years ceased to be close to me, but that his presence here a year ago and the wonderful biography of a contemporary by him which I was permitted to read, have deepened still further the pleasure of thinking frequently of him." Touched, Kessler meant to respond but put it off until it was too late. All that remained was to attend the funeral in Vienna, an event marred by crowds of spectators. "For a moment," he wrote, "as I scattered earth over it, I glimpsed the coffin in its vault. With that of the son who shot himself visible immediately below, it struck me how thin and frail it seemed. . . . A part of my own life is gone with Hugo von Hofmannsthal."* A day later, he recorded his final assessment: "With Hofmannsthal a whole chapter of German culture has been carried to the grave. He was the last of the great baroque poets, belonging to that same tree whose finest fruits were Shakespeare and Cervantes. Baroque—the grafting of genuine feeling upon consciously artificial matter. . . . He seeks matter to which he can transfer the expression of his own feelings (as in *Der Tor und der Tod*) and does not find it in re-

---

* Interestingly, in the fall of 1930, he attended a performance of Hofmannsthal's comedy *Der Schwierige (Hard to Please)* and claimed not only that the actor playing the title role had taken him as his model, but also that Hofmannsthal had based the central figures on his relationship with Helene von Nostitz; *Twenties,* October 10, 1930, 398–99 and Otto Friedrich's note on the implausibility of this hypothesis, 512–13.

ality. So he pursues his search for it in the arts, in literature, and creates his own artificial matter. That is genuinely baroque.[8] Only a month later, he read of Diaghilev's death: "A part of my world has died with him." And then, while sitting in the barber's chair in Paris, he heard of Stresemann's death. Struck by the expression of sincere grief over Stresemann's death in France and England, Kessler noted, "when I subscribed to *The Times* at my own expense so as to let him have a European perspective on affairs, neither he nor I foresaw such a close, such European *gloire,* for his career." Kessler tallied his losses: "This frightful year 1929 continues to garner its harvest. Hofmannsthal, Diaghilev, Stresemann. One landmark after another of the world, as I and my contemporaries knew it, disappears. Truly an *'Année terrible.'*"[9]

Worse was to come, especially in terms of Kessler's own finances. His spending habits had always been extravagant. In 1906, his mother wrote "I am very anxious and concerned in *every* way about you, knowing just so much of your financial disasters, and ignoring all the rest." A year later, she returned to the theme: "Since the *few* years of Baby's (Wilma's) marriage, with the 100 th(ousand) francs I gave you then, you have spent 420 th(ousand) frs. *C'est absolument terrifcant!* . . . My unfortunate child! You must seriously retrench." Such economies were not forthcoming, and, as a consequence, the fortune that had enabled him to send Stresemann the *Times* during the war (not to mention the other luxuries that Vogeler reports he received at the front) had already suffered severe attrition even before the Depression struck in full force. The British sequestered the part of his mother's money he expected to inherit upon her death in 1919 because he was German. The cost of maintaining two establishments, an apartment in Berlin and the house in Weimar; the subsidies he provided for the pacifist movement, the Nietzsche Archive, various artists and writers, including Maillol, Gill, Craig, Becher, Herzfelde, Grosz, and Nabokov; the monies he forwarded his past and current lovers, Gaston Colin and Max Goertz; and above all, the Cranach Presse swallowed what was left of his estate. As early as the middle of the 1920s, he was forced to sell off his art. The first major piece he sold was Seurat's *Les Poseuses,* the canvas van de Velde had wrapped around a scroll to make it fit into his Berlin apartment. "For nearly thirty years, I have enjoyed the serene charm of the picture's delicate tints and masses, so natural in effect. I part from it as I would from an individual dear to me. I should not have agreed to sell."[10]

By March 1930, he was writing to his sister that "things look very black economically. Nobody seems to have any money and there is a good deal of anxiety about the future." As already noted, his hopes for the time and money to make his press a paying concern came to naught. Step by step, he was forced therefore to take out loans, using his art treasures as collateral. Many of these loans came from his sister, who generously dipped into her half of their mother's fortune to keep her brother's various enterprises going. In the summer of 1930, for example, he asked for a loan of 50,000 francs to be added to the 360,000 francs she had already advanced him in order that Craig could be paid for his work on the *Hamlet* project. Naturally, she was anxious that such a large sum be paid back and pressed her brother to sell the paintings. Kessler wrote back, urging patience inasmuch as to sell valuable paintings in a hurry meant "throwing away between 200,000 and 300,000 Marks." Instead, he said he would call his chief creditor, Eduard von der Heydt, a banker and art dealer, and ask for an extension. Kessler expected an extortionist arrangement, but one that would cost him only 10,000 to 20,000 marks, not 200,000. Three days later, he returned to the theme, outlining a scheme to use the paintings as collateral for a bank loan so that he could pay off Heydt and escape his outrageous interest. But again he underlined the necessity for discretion: "Of course I intend to sell the Cézanne and the Renoir as soon as somebody offers me a decent and normal price. They are worth 100,000 Marks (600,000 francs) each under normal conditions. . . . The Van Gogh is of course worth much more, in fact, it is difficult to value it at all, as it is one of his outstanding and celebrated pictures and there are very few Van Goghs left in the market, most of them being already in public collections. It is certainly worth 200,000 M." But one had to be careful when showing paintings for sale because they depreciate too quickly. An English bank had demanded not only the English securities Kessler still hoped to retrieve from his mother's inheritance, but also the Cézanne, Renoir, Van Gogh, and the statute by Maillol in order to advance him the 10,000 pounds he needed—an absurd suggestion, he opined, inasmuch as the pictures alone were worth 20,000 pounds.[11]

Wilma continued to advance him money, 30,000 francs here, 5,000 there, but it was not enough. In August 1931, he received a letter from the once gracious Heydt: "It is couched in most menacing terms, announces that he is bringing legal proceedings against me." It was time, he concluded, for his nephew Jacques to sell the paintings, regardless of the price they would fetch. The Van Gogh sold that fall for $25,000, which halved Kessler's debt to Heydt, but still it was not enough. "I am going to Berlin today to try and sell some things (Maillol's small terracotta statuettes, as I risk having most of my furniture in Berlin sold within the next few days unless I can raise the money necessary to pay a number of bills, not very large bills, but the people have (seized?) the furniture and I am therefore absolutely forced to pay them. *Tout cela n'est pas amusant.*" When pressed by his sister, at the time of the liquidation of the press, to get rid of his secretaries and housekeepers, Max Goertz and Fritz Guseck among them, he refused at first, arguing that they were protected by a highly developed social legislation that made it impossible to dismiss them as if they were simply servants.[12] He did move out of his residence in the Köthnerstrasse into a smaller and more modest flat in Berlin; he thought of closing his house in Weimar for the winter; and he negotiated with Heinz Simon, one of the proprietors of the *Frankfurt Zeitung,* to receive a running subsidy for his memoirs. He finally dismissed Guseck only to be sued by him to which he responded with a countersuit over thefts he attributed to his former secretary. To no avail. In that horrible month, October 1931, he wrote again to Wilma that he owed 3,000 marks the following Monday or "have the library, the cupboards in my bedroom, and the chairs and table in the library and in my study sold." He could not pay the telephone, which was being stopped, and needed still to pay the rent. Could she please send 4,000 marks at the very least?

All of these requests and loans led to growing tension between brother and sister. Tormented by guilt and frustration, he groped for a solution: "I have gone almost mad over this situation, always having to ask you for this or that sum that was urgently needed, and never being able to set up with you some complete plan . . . . Of course I quite understand the situation is *quite intolerable* for you, and cannot go on. But I see only two ways out of it, either open bankruptcy on my part, making it practically impossible for me to take up a position again or earn money; or else some *plan d'ensemble,* which, in some reasonable time, will wipe out the debts and reduce the current expenses to proportions, which do not crush you and me. If I could free myself from debt and start a literary career, I think I could get on my feet again and need no longer be à ta charge *within two years.*"[13] He then concludes pathetically, asking for another 8,000 francs, saying that he does not even have coffee in the house, just a bottle of beer and a cup of tea.

In these desperate straits, he pursued several will-o'-the-wisps, among them, the prospect of recovering some of the sequestered English funds he lost during the war. The new and controversial program for reparations payments, the Young Plan, permitted, it appeared, the recovery of the profits, or some portion thereof, earned by sequestered German investments. In November 1929, he traveled to London, with the sanction of the German cabinet, to discuss the issue with the chancellor of the exchequer, Philip Snowden, in the new Labour government in power since May of that year. No doubt, he hoped that his connections to the Labour Party would help him, but the mission—his last on behalf of the Wilhelmstraße—turned out to be a disaster. Snowden, for all of his socialism, turned out to be a hard-nosed, penny-pinching treasurer, interested in making sure that Great Britain received every penny she could under the Young Plan. He received Kessler politely, listened attentively to his arguments, and then informed him: "You have touched my heart, but not my purse." Two days later, the *Times* published a brusque rejection of the claims to German property, in a manner that seemed deliberately insulting to Kessler. Kessler, who had planned to give a talk that day on the BBC on the subject of "German Youth," felt compelled to cancel the invitation. Worse, the German embassy informed him that Harold Nicolson, whom he knew fairly well, had denied any involvement on the part of the British government in the article published in the *Times* and went so far as to suggest that Kessler had leaked the information to the paper. The embassy now felt compelled to defend Kessler, who demanded an apology from the British foreign secretary and his old acquaintance, Arthur Henderson, and threatened to bring a libel suit if it was not forthcoming.[14] Eventually, Kessler did receive an apology "warm and upright" from the foreign secretary, but the affair was unpleasant and an official at the embassy wrote back to Berlin, harshly criticizing Kessler and urging the Wilhelmstrasse to finally cease with the "unhappy method" of sending half-official special envoys. When the British finally approved the Young Plan in the spring of 1930, it seemed that Kessler and his sister might finally recover something, and he returned to London, where he finally gave his broadcast on the radio on April 29. By October 1931, however, he despaired of recovering anything: "I'm now beginning strongly to doubt the good faith, if not the honesty of the English firm and think it possible that there may be some foul play by somebody," he wrote to Wilma.[15]

Another way of earning money was to write. He worked on a play about a Russian anarchist circa 1905 called *Ivan Kalïeff.* The fragments that remain read like warmed-over Dostoyevsky, and Kessler found it difficult to write. Nevertheless, he read the first act and the beginning of the second to Max Reinhardt and his leading lady, Helene Thimig, and discussed the possibility of producing it in the spring of 1933. Reinhardt's only criticism was that the language of the revolutionary hero of the play was too rhetorical and polished; "That is how revolutionaries talked in the French Revolution, but nowadays their utterances are briefer, more to the point, less oratorical. I protested that is precisely the way Kaliajeff actually spoke, but inwardly I was at once convinced that Reinhardt is perfectly right from a dramatic and production point of view. I must revise the scene." [16] Whether he would have actually finished it, and Reinhardt actually produced it, was rendered moot by political events. The conversation took place with Reinhardt on November 18, 1932 — the Weimar Republic had less than three months to live.

. . .

Even before the Great Depression struck Germany with its full force, the Nazi virus had been spreading among some of Kessler's oldest friend and acquaintances. Anton Kippenberg, for instance, remarked to him in 1925 that the "most important thing would be, to root the Jewish spirit out of Germany completely. I said: Whether he thinks that much spirit would be left in Germany afterwards? Whereupon, embarrassed: Yes, of course (but quite unsure of himself)." A year later, at dinner with both Kippenbergs, they began to criticize the republic, the League of Nations, and the Locarno treaties: "I didn't answer them but made it so clear in the end, how much their silly talk bored me, that they were rather embarrassed. . . . They are typical German philistines who know nothing about politics and understand nothing, yet always claim to stand on a Bismarckian pedestal high over all politicians and diplomats: nothing but little Bismarcks! The old man has poisoned all of German philistinedom deep into the fifth and sixth generation." [17] It was in 1926 that his old fraternity, the Canitz society, kicked him out for his political views.

Then came the long descent of the Nietzsche Archive into the Nazi camp. Impressed with the old woman's good cheer despite losing nearly all of the Archive's endowment in the inflation, Kessler gave Förster-Nietzsche a gift of 3,000 marks in 1926, even though her susceptibility to the right wing was already evident. A few months before she had bragged of Mussolini's support for the Archive and asked Kessler if he knew of it. "Yes, indeed, I said, I had both heard and regretted it, for Mussolini compromises her brother's reputation. He is a danger to Europe, that Europe which her brother longed for, the Europe of all good Europeans. The poor old lady became rather 'agitated,' but she changed the subject and the rest of the conversation passed off peacefully. She will be eighty soon and it is beginning to show." When Oswald Spengler was invited to lecture at the Nietzsche Archive in October 1927, Kessler tried to decline the invitation to attend politely but wound up listening anyway in the crowded hall: "The lecture proved a debacle. For an hour a fat person with a fleshy chin and brutal mouth (it was my first sight of Spengler) spouted the most trite and trivial rubbish." Still, although he told her the "unvarnished truth" about the lecture afterward, the two remained friendly, even while the archive became more nazified. On his last recorded visit in August 1932, Kessler witnessed the nadir. "The Nietzsche Archives are now, as she herself put it, 'right in the center of politics.' Emge, a Nazi professor of legal philosophy at Jena and a prospective Nazi Minister in the Thuringian Government, has been appointed chairman. Inside the Archive everyone, from the doorkeeper to the head, is a Nazi. Only she herself remains a Nationalist." She then described Hitler, who had visited the archive, and spoke of the crowd of Nazi literats who formed her circle in Weimar. "It is enough to make one weep," wrote Kessler, "to see what has become of Nietzsche and the Nietzsche Archives! . . . We talked in the small parlour on the first floor. Through the connecting door I had a view of the sofa where Nietzsche sat, looking like an ailing eagle, the last time I saw him; our conversation made a deep impression on me. Mysterious, incomprehensible Germany." With the breaking of the dam in the September 1930 Reichstag elections, the brown flood of Nazism spread everywhere. The Nostitzes, among his oldest friends, became fellow travelers. At a party in their Berlin home, Kessler noted "the atmosphere there reeks of Nazism. Helene told me that her sister-in-law, Marie von Hindenburg, an Englishwoman by birth, has become a zealous National Socialist and eager Party worker. Criticism of the Nazis is met by an embarrassed silence." [18]

He would have none of it. Although he was willing, for all of his scorn for Mussolini, to wait and see the results of the Italian fascist experiment,[19] his observations on Hitler and the Nazis seethe with contempt. His diaries for the period 1930–1933 resemble those covering the German revolution in 1918–19, with their vivid evocations of violent street demonstrations and fights suggesting an inchoate civil war. Attending the opening of the new Reichstag, with the Nazis as the second largest party, he observed the smashing of Jewish-owned department stores by the brownshirts: "In the main the Nazis consisted of adolescent riff-raff which made off yelling as soon as the police began to use rubber truncheons. I have never witnessed so much rabble in these

parts. . . . These disorders reminded me of the days just before the revolution, with the same mass meetings and the same Catilinian figures
lounging about and demonstrating. . . . The vomit rises at so much pigheaded stupidity and spite." In Hitler, he purported to see a resemblance with Wilhelm II, both loud-mouthed bullies but with "nothing
behind it when it comes to the point." The Nazi inroads among German youth alarmed Kessler especially, given his earlier hopes—dating
from the end of the war—in the young generation. Fritz von Unruh described to him the failure of the middle-class and republican parties to
appreciate the role of heroism in politics. "The same held good for the
SPD party bosses. These people failed because they see material welfare
as the sole object of political activity and make no allowance whatever for idealism and a faith worth sacrifices."[20] This diagnosis rang true
to Kessler who for years had urged the forces on the left to incorporate those elements of self-sacrificial idealism that he had witnessed in
the war.

If his reaction to the nazification of German youth was that of a
disappointed suitor, his attitude toward those members of the German
elite who contributed to the Nazi rise to power was scathing. When
Hindenburg replaced Brüning with Franz von Papen, an archconserva-
tive deputy from the Center Party, a Catholic nobleman, a dandy, and
an intriguer, Kessler commented on his policy declaration: "This almost
incredible document is a rottenly phrased distillation of darkest reaction
in comparison with which the declarations of Imperial Governments
would strike a reader as specimens of dazzling enlightenment. Social
insurance is to be scrapped, 'cultural Bolshevism' resisted, the German
nation steeled for a foreign policy struggle through re-Christianization
(i.e., cant) and 'concentrated' on the basis of extreme right-wing Junker
ideas. All other orientations of thought and party, social democracy,
bourgeois liberalism, Center sympathies, are pilloried as being not 'national' and morally undermining."[21]

Papen's government, dependent on Hindenburg like that of Brüning
before him, did its best to undermine the republic. Thus, shortly before
the Reichstag elections of July 1932, he lifted the ban on the Nazi storm
troopers but not on the Communist equivalent, with the predictable results. Given virtual carte blanche to attack their opponents, the Nazis
struck hard. "While we spent Sunday driving through the lovely countryside," wrote Kessler in the middle of July, "the unbridled, organized
Nazi terror has again claimed seventeen dead and nearly two hundred
wounded as its victims. It is a continuous St. Bartholomew's Massacre,

day after day, Sunday after Sunday." The elections were, nevertheless, a disaster for Papen and for Germany. The Nazis became, with 230 delegates, the largest party in the Reichstag, but they did not increase their popular vote total as much as they had hoped, the Communists making the greatest gains. The political question now became whether Hitler would be brought into the government and under what conditions. Tense negotiations broke down and the Papen government, unable to find a Reichstag majority without the Nazis, limped along, until forced by the prospect of a Nazi-organized no-confidence vote to call new Reichstag elections for November.[22]

The November 6, 1932, Reichstag elections represent one of the great "what ifs" of modern German history. "The outstanding features of the election results," noted Kessler, "are that the Nazis have lost thirty-five seats (nearly two million votes) and the Communists made strong gains." Perhaps the long-hoped-for ebbing of the Nazi tide had finally arrived. Membership cards were being turned in, strife within the party was increasing, and the financial situation was shaky. Catastrophically, there was no other party or statesman strong enough to take advantage of the Nazi discomfiture. With one hundred Communist and 196 Nazi delegates, nearly half of the Reichstag, the remaining deputies were split into multiple parties, some very small, with widely differing agendas and sharp antagonisms. After an abortive attempt by General von Schleicher to split off the "left wing" of the Nazi Party and put together some kind of governing coalition, the egregious Papen persuaded Hindenburg to do what he had refused to do in August. He invited Hitler into the government. All the important posts in the new cabinet, he assured his cronies, would be in the hands of the traditional conservatives, leaving only the chancellorship to Hitler and two other ministries to the Nazis. "In two months," Papen boasted, "we will have pushed Hitler so far into a corner that he will squeak." As one historian has noted, these remarks belong in any anthology of famous last words.[23]

The news of Hitler becoming chancellor struck Kessler like a thunderbolt on January 30, 1933: "I had not anticipated this turn of events, and so quickly at that." His diary records the carnival unleashed by the Nazis that evening. As part of the condition for entering the cabinet, they had insisted on calling new elections in March, elections in which they fully intended to win by using all the power now at their disposal, including licensing the storm troopers as auxiliary police. Rumors flew about a staged attempt on Hitler's life that would be the excuse for a true wave of terror. It was not an assassination attempt that provided the justification, but rather the burning of the Reichstag building at the end of February. Blaming it on the Communist Party, the Nazis, overwhelming Papen and his friends with their energy and brutality, outlawed the Communists, censored the opposition press, and stepped up their intimidation.

Kessler began to feel the heat himself. In February, he had been elected, without warning, to the main committee organizing a Freedom of Speech Congress at the Kroll festival hall in Berlin. Sitting on stage next to Ferdinand Tönnies, the renowned but aged professor of sociology, and Georg Bernhard, Kessler attended the meeting. A letter was read from Thomas Mann. Tönnies made a boring speech. And then, when the third speaker launched a fierce attack on the new government, Kessler told Bernhard that the meeting would be dissolved. Indeed, a police officer appeared with that order and the crowd dispersed, singing the "Internationale" and other revolutionary songs. "The situation was very moving," wrote Kessler. "Many, I am certain, had the same feeling as I did that for a long time to come this would prove the last occasion in Berlin when intellectuals would be able publicly to demonstrate on behalf of freedom. On news of the meeting's dissolution becoming known in my house, the wife of the concierge Schlöttke (he is a member of the SA) came out into the courtyard, shook her fist threateningly upwards, and shrieked, almost hysterically, 'That serves them right! There's a lot of other things coming to that pack of criminals up there!'"[24]

Indeed, Kessler began to receive warnings that he should leave the country, at least while the elections took place. His manservant, the son of a retired Nazi pensioner, asked permission nervously to leave his service. In Weimar, the old porter at the railroad station met him "with an utterly scared look on his face. Things are terrible in Weimar, he told me with 'auxiliary police' (SA) everywhere and nobody daring to speak a word." On February 25, 1933, he wrote to his sister (referring to himself in the third person for fear his mail was being read): "I need not tell you that the political situation here is serious, more so then since the war; I mean the national, not the international situation. I have seen *Boo* [Kessler's childhood name] lately and he told me he didn't think he could stay here. Very probably he will leave on Sunday or Monday. He said he would write to you and give his address, probably in Switzerland, as soon as he was fixed about it. So I don't think it is much good you writing to him before especially as he told me he thought he was being censored. Of course he is very amazed and much disturbed . . . ."

And so, on March 8, he left Germany for Paris. He had still hoped to return to Germany, but in Paris, ten days later, he learned, via the French ambassador, from his old friend in the Foreign Office, Gerhard Mutius, that the government, in order to "protect" him from young fanatics, might have to imprison him. Mutius advised him to prolong his stay in France. He never returned to Germany.[25]

CHAPTER 27

"And thus he left me"

A man, no matter how firmly rooted in his personality, can be exposed to two situations where one quickly degenerates: marriage or exile. Count Harry Kessler was a bachelor, but he was not spared exile.

Albert Vigoleis Thelen, *Die Insel des zweiten Gesichts*

And so they arrived, some by first-class coach with steamer trunks, others by the skin of their teeth having lost nearly everything. Among the exiles were the banker Hugo Simon; the publisher Gottfried Bermann; the journalist Georg Bernhard; the writers René Schickele, Annette Kolb, Wieland Herzfelde, Thomas and Heinrich Mann, and Siegfried Kracauer; the philosopher Hermann Keyserling; the pacifists Ludwig Quidde and Helmut von Gerlach; the politicians Heinrich Brüning and Rudolf Hilferding; socialists; pacifists; communists; and liberals; above all, Jews. "The whole of the Kurfürstendam is descending on Paris," Kessler noted. In some ways, he had it better than many of the refugees from Nazi Germany in that he spoke French and English fluently, knew France and England well, and had the support of his sister. Ironically, but understandably, the Germany that he had not hesitated to abandon for months and years at a time, which he often criticized upon returning, suddenly, now that the prospect of returning grew dim, beckoned to him. In June 1933, after several months of exile, a phone call from Max Goertz from Weimar, describing the garden, left him deeply moved. It was Goertz who sent him a small suitcase with papers and letters and

397

the information that his manservant Friedrich had been stealing his things and had betrayed him to the Nazis. Three Nazis had broken into his house, taken a banner from his attic (presumably a republican flag), and torn it to pieces in his courtyard. According to Goertz, Friedrich had expressed his satisfaction at this occurrence and had betrayed the whereabouts of Kessler's safe and the names of all those with whom he had been in contact. Kessler was stunned. "Sometimes I seem to be going through an evil dream from which I shall suddenly awake. These last few days have been grim. Yet life somehow continues, I work, I can concentrate on work, I talk to people, and I read. But all the time I am aware of a muffled pain throbbing like a double-bass." [1]

Not one of the refugees knew how long the Nazi regime would last or what would happen to Germany and Europe before it was over. Kessler initially thought Hitler could not last: "Undoubtedly a sort of Bolshevism lies ahead. Eventually it will be countered by a revolt among the preponderant part of the German nation—Socialists, Communists, conservatives, farmers, Catholics, Protestants, industrialists, and the merchant communities of the Hansa cities—which Hitler will be unable to handle. So far the Communists have proved the most active element, even though Hitler is fulfilling their object. But the others will also be galvanized into greater self-defense. And once the first spark of revolt has been struck, the whole ramshackle Hitler structure will go up in flames." Although Kessler called this prognosis gloomy, it discounted, as we know with hindsight, both the effect of the terror and control exercised by a totalitarian state and the legitimacy the regime would earn with a successful economic and foreign policy. [2]

From Kessler's perspective then, the thing to do was to find a way to survive while waiting for the collapse. His immediate concern was to find the space and time to finish his memoirs, the sole real chance he had of earning some urgently needed money. Two days before his departure from Germany, he had completed his revisions to the French translation of his book on Rathenau and was able to sign copies while in Paris. But he could not live on its sales. The memoirs were under contract with the Fischer Verlag, the most prestigious press of Weimar Germany, but one whose proprietors were Jewish. Over lunch, Sam Fischer had praised the chapters Kessler gave him, and the next day his wife had called to tell him how moved she was by his description of his mother's death.

That was in February 1933. By the spring, it was unclear how long the press could operate and what kinds of books it would be permitted to publish. For this reason then, and because he was still officially a German citizen and did not want to have his passport revoked, Kessler did not join any of the émigré circles that were involved in active opposition to the Nazis. From Prague, Herzfelde wrote about reestablishing his Malik Verlag and his plans for a new journal, apologizing for the apparently dominant position of Communists on the editorial board: "Quite apart from the impact of the propaganda abroad, I am convinced that a fruitful influence would transpire if the members of the editorial board were not all too *gleichgeschaltet* (ironic use of Nazi expression, meaning something like "put on the same track"). Moreover, that certainly many writers would be easier to win over if, for example, they were asked to participate by you. . . . If it would be possible for you to help me actively in the work and through the establishment of connections I naturally cannot judge. In any case it would be a pleasure for me. . . ."[3] Kessler could not take that step, however, and he kept his distance from such open resistance. Instead, he looked for some relatively peaceful refuge, far from the hectic, nerve-wracking world of exile politics, some place he could live cheaply and concentrate on writing his autobiography, a project that increasingly looked like it would take several volumes to complete.

The answer was Palma, the capital city of Mallorca, largest of Spain's Balearic Islands. He had long been attracted to the Catalonian part of Spain. In the spring of 1926, he visited the Catalonian coast, including Barcelona and Mallorca. "Barcelona is astonishingly *modern*," he wrote to his sister. "A fine, very lively, almost American city, or rather, half Paris and half Buenos Aires; but very little Spanish atmosphere. It is by far the most modern and animé part of the Mediterranean. The Italian parts, even Genoa or Naples, are old fashioned and romantic in comparison. The people too seem much more northern than southern: energetic, pushing, wide awake." Later, from Mallorca itself, he continued his paean of praise: "This island is a real paradise: all the beauty of rugged Alpine scenery and the *Üppigkeit* of the South. Much more beautiful than Italy. Besides the Hotels and Cooking *quite first class,* quite *modern* and as clean as in *Switzerland*. The air delightfully *fresh* and inspiring; splendid roads for motoring; in fact the *ideal*."[4] It was also very inexpensive at the time, so not surprisingly, Kessler decided to take up an offer from Hugo Simon to rent a property of his on the island. He arrived, along with Max Goertz and his new wife Uschi, on November 11, only to discover that the Simon house was quite impossible by his standards. It took him a few days to find the right house: "Plaza Iglesia 3, in the Bona Nova quarter, on the hill overlooking Palma and with a magnificent view out to sea, of the bay of Palma and the town. A pretty, one-storied modern house, pleasantly furnished, with large terraces and flower-beds facing south." While the Goertzes put the house in order, planting flowers and tending the poultry, he started to work again on his memoirs, under clear skies and warm temperatures.

Mallorca proved not to be quite the paradise for which he had hoped nor the inhabitants quite so energetic. "The people here are *very* slow and put off things from day to day (*mañana, mañana*) but are clean and tidy and I am told very honest," he wrote to Wilma in November. About two weeks later, however, he had changed his mind: "The country is miserably backward, the conditions incredibly bad, over 50% of the people are illiterate, the corruption of the officials past believing." Ominously, they had arrived in the midst of a general strike: "There is some shooting in the streets, and, as far as I can make out, a small number of people killed and wounded." He shared the island with many Americans, English, and Germans, "but I avoid the Germans, until I know exactly who they are, as a number of them are politically and for other reasons undesirable."[5]

One of these Germans was the ineffable Albert Vigoleis Thelen, author in later years of an autobiographical, picaresque novel of Mallorca in the 1930s, called *Die Insel des zweiten Gesichts,* a rambling, discursive, in parts wildly funny work that achieved status as an "underground classic" in the 1950s when it was published. Although also exiles from Germany and Switzerland, Thelen and his wife Beatrice had fled long before the Nazi seizure of power. Together, they scraped together a living by working as tour guides for visiting Germans and typing the manuscripts of resident authors. Beatrice, in fact, had typed the memoirs of Robert Graves, *Good-Bye to All That,* and Albert was eventually hired by Kessler to do the same for him. Kessler appears frequently in Thelen's "applied memoirs" under his own name, and if the book consciously defies any separation between truthful description and pure invention, the portrait of Harry is both amusing—and respectful, if gently ironic—and rings true. It also supplements the sparse diary entries and the few letters to Wilma for 1934.

Thelen and Kessler first met when Kessler asked Beatrice, whom he met in the streets, where he could find someone who could serve as a translator in a case of tax evasion that the Nazis had brought against him. Kessler appeared like an emissary from an older, more refined, more cosmopolitan world, yet, at the same time, his appearance confirmed the letters he wrote to his sister concerning the deterioration of his wardrobe. In Thelen's words: "His get up, it is true, looked a little shabby and dingy—one noticed that he had not been able to bring his manservant with him into exile—but in any case it was original. Where the Mallorcians use their picturesque scarves as belts for their pants, Count Kessler had his cotton underpants, which reached above the stomach, rolled rakishly into a ball around his waist, like a bullfighter. I thought at first it was a lifebelt, not a bad invention for a diplomat on the run. The hands of the Count were strikingly beautiful and of the kind which one finds described, even by good authors, as spiritual. That they were such could not be otherwise, for if a spirit like Harry Kessler did not have such hands, who could?" Thelen agreed to help the Count in his legal business, and shortly thereafter Kessler asked if he would serve as his typist.*

It was, as Kessler described it apologetically, "a task for slaves," as Thelen, typing with two fingers, transcribed the hundreds of notes, printed—not always legibly—in fastidious gothic letters on the fine linen, blue-tinted paper he used for his correspondence and, upon which, Kessler, surrounded by his diaries, wrote his memoirs. Returning the typed pages to the count, Thelen would then receive them back a few days later, covered with corrections that required whole pages to be retyped anew, thus giving rise to multiple versions: "Faces and Fatherlands [the title of Kessler's memoirs] began to turn around in my brain, so that I became dizzy; it was a leap frogging process, but with many steps backwards each time, and only a few that brought one further." Astonished that Thelen did not own a copy of Wustmann's *Allerhand Sprachdummheiten,* a famous guide to avoiding stylistic "stupidities," Kessler had a copy ordered only to discover that the guide had been revised to meet the stylistic demands of the Third Reich. "As I showed Count Kessler this genuflection of the German language before the German *Führer,* he was quite startled and, in a visible fit of discomfiture, said: naturally he couldn't give me something like that, this is truly an insult, a thousand apologies."[6] Gradually, the intimate and all-absorbing nature of their work brought the two men, so different in nearly every respect, together. Kessler came to call Thelen his "Wust-

---

* In their first two meetings, Kessler had interrupted Thelen while the latter was indulging in *Naktkultur.* The second time, deftly overlooking his host's nudity, the count remarked on the lovely view of the garden one noticed from the interior, a pure paradise: "That," I cried, "explains my situation," responded Thelen, *Insel,* 628.

mann" in wry appreciation for his editorial advice, and the latter claimed to discover over time Kessler's "true face beneath the mask of politeness."

From Thelen's account we learn that the memoirs were intended to come out in four separate volumes, only the last of which, covering the period up to his exile, would have contained material unacceptable to the Nazi censor. Although only the first, carrying Kessler up to the end of his university studies, was published, Thelen worked feverishly on the second volume, several excerpts of which were published in *Die Neue Rundschau,* and Kessler regaled him with many other stories from his life. Together, they discussed the political situation. Revising his earlier estimate, Kessler admitted now that the Third Reich would last for a long time still: "Years would go by like this, and only then would come the war, and then a denouement with still worse horrors."[7] Kessler paid Thelen regularly, mostly with money provided by Wilma, who, Thelen suggests, worshipped her brother like an idol.

Living like a recluse, as he described himself to Wilma,[8] and working—very much against his normal custom—at a café where old men played dominos, Kessler during 1934, in Thelen's words "lived only through the work of the memoirs, in which he wrapped himself up for an endless winter. Daily questions of politics and above all of the Nazi regime barely concerned him; that is, he kept them at arm's length, as much as he could, which frequently did not work."[9] He was frequently ill, and his anxieties over money did not cease. Nevertheless, the weather was good, the garden was beautiful, the Goertzes and the Thelens took care of him, and he immersed himself in the task for which, as Richard Dehmel had predicted years ago, he seem to have been born: to write the memoirs of his tumultuous times.

• • •

Decades before, in one of the first letters he ever wrote to Hofmannsthal, Kessler had remarked that autobiographies "are actually the only biographies which are not worthless, since for the individual it is not the fact in itself that is important but only the impression which a fact has made upon him, and only he himself can describe the ideas which he has derived from the facts." It has been suggested, although no direct proof exists, that Kessler always intended his extraordinary diaries to serve as the basis for the magnum opus that would provide the capstone to his life and to his times and endow both with a meaning that was not self-evident in his day-to-day existence. If that indeed was the long-term cause, the more immediate were his need for money and the posthumous publication, in 1930 and 1931, of the four-volume memoirs of von Bülow, the former chancellor of Imperial Germany. This at times droll, at times malicious work had, as noted earlier, maligned Kessler's father and especially his mother, spreading the rumors, already purveyed in society, that either he or his sister were the illegitimate offspring of an adulterous affair between the old Kaiser Wilhelm I and Alice Kessler. In discussing the memoirs, Heinrich Simon asked Kessler directly about these rumors, which if true, would have made him the half-brother of Wilhelm II. Even after Kessler refuted them, Simon insisted that the real theme of Kessler's autobiography should be how someone from his milieu ended up in the republican camp. "After this discussion with Simon, it is at any rate clear that the first chapter of my memoirs must be called 'My Mother' and once and for all do away with this idiotic gossip about my origins. To that degree the memoirs have become an essential act of piety."[10]

As he contemplated the task, aware of the advantages but also of the dangers that his exceptionally rich materials offered, he read widely in autobiographical literature and mused over the correct way to proceed:

On the technique of writing memoirs. Memoirs: the interpretation of the time through the perspective of a personality. Precisely therefore perspective, ranking of things and events in view of the personality and the drama, their changing situation, their tragedy or comic-tragedy. Through this the transcendence of mere chronicle, the ranking of personalities merely according to their "fame," therefore incorporation in the situation and the dramatic structure of the totality; organization of the material. . . .

The danger for the writer of memoirs (and the greater this danger, the richer and more lively the life of the writer has been)—the danger of the superior strength and viscosity of the material, which the author must knead and must limit through his art. In my opinion only he who has experienced dramatically, and to be sure passionately dramatically, can write good memoirs. That is the ultimate reason why the memoirs of the cold fish Bülow, despite all amusing, anecdotal polish and malicious character sketches, are not good and in the end only leave a feeling of disgust, as if one swallowed icy slime. St. Simon had his passionate noble pride, Casanova his passionate drive for love affairs, Bismarck his passionate hunger for power; they all have kneaded, through their passion, the material and given it a form. Bülow was flat and lazy and passionless (aside from the senile one of an impotent rabbit) and therefore he failed, despite all feuilletonist talent, and has only written a document for the archive of history (and a lying one at that).[11]

With those strictures in mind, he began his research. By the middle of January, he had finished the first chapter concerning his mother and reported with satisfaction the impression it made on Sam Fischer. He had done justice to their mother he wrote to Wilma: "She emerges as a great tragic noble figure. It was the best and only way to liquidate once for all the infamous aspersions in that disgusting scoundrel Bülow's *Memoirs*." [12]

The contract he eventually signed with Fischer called for a two-volume work, each of four hundred pages, the first to be delivered in September 1933 and the second in March 1934. For this he would be given the usual royalty of 15 percent of the bookstore price and, starting on March 1, 1933, an advance of 12,000 marks to be paid out over six months. Meanwhile, he had secured the English rights with Faber & Faber and signed a contract for a French translation with Plon, important steps given the uncertainty regarding his German audience. Needless to say, the book was delayed by ill health and by the difficulties of obtaining the necessary material, some of which had to be smuggled out of Weimar by the faithful Goertz, by the method of rewriting described by Thelen, and, above all, by the same overabundance of material against which he had warned. In no time, the two volumes became four. "It has been a tremendous piece of work," he informed his sister on December 7, 1934, "correcting and putting it into shape so that the first part can stand as a whole." Revisions that spring took more time than he wished because he was "thoroughly worried when anything strikes me that I have left out or said so that it could be misunderstood." Excerpts from the first volume appeared in *Die Neue Rundschau* in the February, March, April, and June issues, before the book finally was published in June 1935. [13]

A few positive reviews appeared within Nazi Germany, including one by his old friend, Rudolf Schröder, but in September the book was banned. The reasons were not given. Oskar Loerke, an editor at Fischer, noted in his diary: "The book of Count Kessler banned, not because it is 'dangerous,' but because he is supposed to have said something." It may have had to do with the unauthorized republication of a portion of the excerpts in an émigré publication, something that greatly upset Kessler for exactly these reasons. It may have had to do with the German spies on Mallorca and the report of the German consul in Barcelona, which, while confirming that Kessler was not active politically, also noted that "so far as I am informed, he has intentionally avoided taking a stand on the new Germany." [14]

Curiously, *Die Neue Rundschau* was permitted to publish portions of the planned next volume, covering Kessler's first trip to the United

States, in three installments from August through October, but the loss of his German audience made it imperative to make the French and English editions available. Kessler was distracted that fall by the effort to revise the miserable French translation: "I have had to redraft nearly every sentence, shaping it afresh, adapting it to the exigencies of the French language, and breathing fresh life into it, so that the French 'translation' stands alongside the German like an original piece of writing. And the labor involved! In six weeks I have nearly worked myself to death." [15] *Souvenirs d'un Européen* appeared finally in October 1936. Death intervened before the English translation was finished.

As noted, the ambivalence evident in his portrait of his mother in the first part, based on her fragmentary memoirs, threatens at times to subvert his pious intentions, as Wilma seems to have discovered, to her evident distress. [16] The second part begins the answer to Simon's question concerning Kessler's political trajectory. Two figures predominate: Nietzsche and Bismarck, representing, to use the same Proustian terms Kessler employed for his Rathenau book, the "way of spirit" and the "way of power," respectively. Naturally, Kessler projected retrospectively the ideas, themes, and meanings of his mature, postwar reflections into these portraits, editing and revising significantly his original attitude toward both men, something that can be easily ascertained by looking at the diaries. And yet, as Maillol said about Kessler's article on the *Ecologues*, he nevertheless got it right. The owl of Minerva flies at dusk, after all, and the question Kessler needed to answer was exactly the one he presented in the second half of the first volume: the vexed relation between *Macht* and *Geist*, power and spirit, in German culture, but also within Western civilization itself. It is a great pity—indeed, it is perhaps the outstanding tragedy of his life—that he could only pose the question; he was not vouchsafed the time to answer it.

Poor health plagued Kessler throughout his last years. He was sick enough to be hospitalized in April and August of 1930. Two days before Christmas 1933, while in Palma, he was sitting before the fire, reading a newspaper when he suddenly felt faint; "the blood began to ooze and then stream out of my mouth. I just called out to the Goertzes who were in the terrace and then lost consciousness." When he came to, blood was everywhere and Uschi Goertz was wiping his mouth. His right lung had hemorrhaged, causing him to lose about a liter of blood in fifteen minutes. "It was very disgusting as all my clothes and underclothes from top to bottom and the room were all drenched with blood." Had it not been for the Goertzes and the prompt appearance of the doctor, he would have died. "This is the fourth or fifth time I have been at the gates of death, but as Verlaine's Caspard Hauser says: *Death did not want me.*" A few months later, he even considered seeing a specialist in Bad Nauheim inside the Reich for a few weeks: "I do not think there is any serious reason for my not going there. I mean no serious political reason."[17]

For reasons of health, he was forced to return to the mainland in the summer of 1935. He intended to return and so left behind the bulk of his papers and notebooks. In August of that year, he reported that he had lost fourteen kilograms in two years and weighed only fifty-eight kilos now. A picture taken in October 1936 shows a gaunt, skeletal figure, with dark hollows for eye sockets and the skin of his face stretched taut over his skull. Friends remarked on how poorly he looked. Gordon Craig, who ran into him at the Café de la Paix in Paris, thought he was so altered as to be unrecognizable. Nicolas Nabokov saw him for the last time in 1934 when Nabokov invited Kessler and Misia Sert to see his ballet at the Paris Opera. He was despondent over what was taking place in Germany. Together, they attended vespers at St. Julien le Pauvre, the oldest church in Paris on the Left Bank.

After the service was over, we walked up and down the left bank, between Notre Dame and the Pont du Louvre, and he talked about the end of his hopes, his dreams, his efforts. His press in Weimar was closed and the furniture of his house was about to be sold. He was beginning to be short of money. His famous pictures and sculptures were gone.

"Now," he said, "I begin to understand what you Russians must have felt when you came to Berlin." And he added softly, as if talking to himself, "This thing in Germany will be long. I will not live to see the end of it."

We parted at dusk, I to my train to Salzburg, he to his homelessness.[18]

Indeed he was now homeless. In the spring of 1934 he could still write his sister that "I shouldn't wish to lose the house, which is the only little bit of home I have left in the world," but there was no escaping it. The local authorities took advantage of the fact that Kessler, in his haste to depart Germany but in the expectation that he would return, had failed to give his house staff permission to pay the taxes and other fines, things normally handled from Berlin. As the taxes and fines mounted, the authorities permitted, even encouraged, local merchants and craftsmen simply to take physically what the count owed them, or what they conceived to be a rough equivalent. In this way, he lost, among other things, the beautiful roses Goertz had described in full bloom. In July 1935, he noted "Today my poor domestic furnishings in Weimar are being auctioned. That closes the main chapter of my life and is the end of a home built up with great love." Although Wilma, as her brother's chief creditor, was able to save some of the books and furniture, when the rent for their storage was not paid, these too were lost. Servants, angry at not being paid their wages, stole some of the rest. "It was a great disappointment," he wrote to Wilma from London a month after the auction, "not to find either the Vuillard nor the Bonnard, nor any books from my Weimar library in *my study* which Goertz, I understood, said he had packed. I should very much like at least some of them with personal dedications, Rimbaud, Gerhart Hauptmann . . . ." A year later, the house was sold as well: "How many memories and how much of my life vanish with it." [19]

Nor could he return to Mallorca. By the time he was well enough and had his papers in order, the Spanish Civil War had broken out. Thelen wrote to him about their narrow escape: "We had to leave everything behind us, it is questionable whether we will ever get them back. When we left the island (end of September), the underground terror had taken on forms that mock any description. We were glad finally to escape the threat on an English cruiser." Some fifteen hundred people, including some anti-Nazi German exiles, were said to have been executed during the insurrection of Franco's supporters. Although he needed to return in order to secure the sources for his memoirs, he was constantly dissuaded from doing so by friends worried about his safety.* In lieu of returning to Palma then, he was set up by his sister in a boarding house that she owned, Hostellerie des Compagnons de Jéhu, at Pontanevaux between Lyons and Macon. From there, he sent plaintive letters to her asking to come to her home in Fournels; he promised that he would not bother her husband, he would work quietly on his English translation; he would require only a few warm vests, a thick sweater—"the one you bought me some years ago being rather thin and worn out"—a pair of snow boots, and a woolen scarf. Nor was the company at the Hostellerie all that it could be: "on the whole, one lives in a spiritual desert here, poor Faveri (the innkeeper) being hopelessly shallow, and Mme de Faveri, good and trusting creature, so dumb and mute as a cow. *À la longue,* it is rather trying, though the Faveris

* After the war, his sister was able to recover much of the material, but everyone had forgotten about the bank safe in which Kessler in 1933 had deposited the diaries from 1902 to 1914. It was only in 1983 that the safe was opened and the long sought-after diaries were discovered.

give themselves great trouble to be pleasant. But they can't change who they are." Wilma, however, who was having financial troubles of her own, was forced to sell the place in the summer of 1937, and the new owners wished to get rid of him for the season, he feared. By November, there was talk of moving to a nursing home in Cannes. In addition to the other ailments, he now had a bad heart: "I cannot go up stairs, cannot walk more than a few steps, just about the length of the garden, cannot hold any long conversations with anybody, and from time to time little heart attacks, which keep me in bed for a day. I am in bed most of the day anyhow, except part of it at midday."[20]

It was too much. The last entry of his diary, dated September 30, 1937, describes a visit to a small town near Fournels to have his heart x-rayed: "The little town, old-fashioned and picturesque, is reminiscent in style and atmosphere of Weimar, but is of a much more southern character." On November 30, 1937, his heart finally gave way and he died. Grief-stricken, his sister wrote the last entry in his great diary: "*Ainsi il me quitta.*"

He was buried in the family tomb in Père Lachaise in Paris. According to one newspaper report, barely sixty individuals attended the service in the Protestant chapel. One old friend was surprised that none of the artists Kessler had supported attended.[21] Julien Green, the Franco-American author befriended by Kessler in his last years, was among those present.

The death badge was noticeable against the black drapes: a white horse rearing, its feet on the summit of two white mountains, the background azure. The casket disappeared under a pile of roses whose scent reached as far as us. Just before me, Gide and Schiffrin. The pastor Boegner delivered a sermon on the "great wound in Europe." . . . Once I had the impression of a profound sadness, tearing, *racing* through the chapel, as if Kessler, rising, had grabbed on to us, like a drowning man who seizes a boat full of people. Gide, during the prayers, lowered his head and did not move. When one carried away the casket, there was a kind of general distress, I cannot express it any other way; one tore the poor Kessler from his friends. I returned shattered. I read the Bible. The entire day I felt ill with sadness.[22]

The obituaries praised him as a representative of the old, cosmopolitan Europe that was fast disappearing in a Europe torn by ideologies and girding for war.[23]

CONCLUSION

A World Forever Lost?

How to assess such a life? As already noted, the conventional yardsticks do not apply. Kessler was neither a professional politician nor a diplomat, neither an artist nor a professional writer, neither an academic nor a professional museum director, not quite a soldier and not quite a secret agent, not English or French, but not, in the end, fully German either. He had no firm vocation and no fixed abode. Kessler's life seems to lack clear contours, spills out over all banks, meanders, in places runs into the sand. The number and scale of his concrete achievements, while impressive enough, pale admittedly against the myriad unrealized or only partially realized ambitions, schemes, and projects, which, like a vast nimbus of potentiality, accompanied him up until the very last years. Those who knew him remarked, with frequent irritation, upon his mercurial nature, the difficulty they found in defining, identifying, fixing, or placing him. Nor can this view be attributed simply to the resentments of those more staid and stolid acquaintances Kessler left behind in his voyage: he himself provides the best evidence for this interpretation of him as a man without an authentic core in the passage where he describes his house in Weimar as the largely mythic center of an unusually fragmented life. Such a confession poses obvious problems for the biographer. If his subject has no qualms about admitting the arbitrary and imposed nature of his own self-definition, how can the biographer claim that his interpretation is any less arbitrary or imposed from without?

The great prophet of disintegration, Nietzsche, offers a way out of this dilemma. At the end of his essay, "On the Advantage and Disadvantage of History for Life," he addressed the emergence of a unified Greek culture from the "chaos of foreign, Semitic, Babylonian, Lydian and Egyptian forms and concepts." Rather than basking in this multi-cultural stew, however, the Greeks, Nietzsche wrote, "learned gradually *to organize chaos* by reflecting on themselves in accordance with the Delphic teaching, that is, by reflection on their genuine needs, and letting their sham needs die out. . . . This is a parable for each one of us: he must organize the chaos within himself by reflecting on his genuine needs."[1] So too did Kessler, profoundly influenced by Nietzsche, "organize his chaos" by inventing for himself a purpose, by telling himself a story, at first hesitatingly and then with growing conviction, that made sense of his life and his actions.

It is not difficult to discover this narrative. As he grew older, Kessler increasingly reflected upon a theme that he perceived to be the great axis of his life, namely, the agonistic relation between *Macht* and *Geist,* between power and spirit. As a young man coming to maturity in Wilhelmian Germany, he was confronted by the phenomenon of a vigorous, youthful, ascendant political power that seemed to advance hand-in-hand with a decadent, exhausted, imitative culture. Originally posed by Nietzsche, the question of how that gap could be bridged became Kessler's problem by adoption. The various conceptions of an aesthetic state that he pursued before and after the First World War were means to address this problem. In the same vein, it is striking to discover how often his apparently purely aesthetic judgments were rooted in a moral conception of the world. Thus, it is misleading to assert that the war represented a sharp break in his trajectory. As he himself acknowledged and as the detailed examination of his postwar pacifism reveals, the pre-war *Kunstpolitik* foreshadowed in remarkable ways the postwar political activity.

On another and more general level, Germany's power was obviously related to her mastery of science, technology, and industry, of *techne.* Throughout his life, Kessler worried about what Rathenau dubbed mechanization would portend for art and culture. "Men without leisure," he noted, thinking of his commanding officer on the Russian front during the war, "are men without hearts or souls and thus the most dangerous hindrance to culture. Precisely their competence makes them dangerous. The ancient Greeks had called such a man *Banausos* and had excluded him quite correctly, whenever the most important questions of politics, religion, or art were discussed."[2] Over and beyond the snobbery of the gentleman of independent means for those who must earn their living, one perceives here the lament of the dilettante, taking the word in its most generous sense, being crowded out by the rise of the specialist, the expert, the bureaucrat, the *Fachmann.*

Of course, the price the dilettante pays for his contempt for the expert can be ineffectuality. A recent biography of Kessler explains his fate as that of an amateur unwilling or unable to commit himself to playing by the narrow, professional rules that, in the modern world, represent the only real path to power. His friend Eberhard von Bodenhausen, it is suggested, by giving up his cultural ambitions and concentrating on his business career at Krupp, achieved the influence that would be always denied Kessler. It is worth dwelling on this comparison for a moment. Without wishing to deny that Kessler persistently overestimated the potential influence of gifted outsiders such as himself, it is important to examine the price his friend Bodenhausen paid once he buried his love of art beneath the grim, self-imposed duty of forging his way to the top of the armaments firm. Judging from his letters, he lived a kind of "death in life," deriving no enjoyment from his career, complaining constantly of the work, and becoming frequently sick. In the end, exhausted and alienated from the art he had once championed, Bodenhausen died prematurely, broken in spirit and body, without, in fact, ever achieving anything worthy of more than a footnote to a footnote.[3] Kessler, by contrast, because he remained until the end of his days open to the world, never lost contact with life. It is this quality, coupled with his attractive humanity, that makes him a figure of enduring interest, ensuring that his remarkable diaries will be read "so long as men can breathe, and eyes can see."

Undoubtedly, the type of individual Harry Kessler represented has not vanished completely. Both the preconditions necessary for such people and the needs they serve still exist; in this regard, society and culture have not changed quite as much as we are wont to affirm. But just as undoubtedly their numbers have dwindled as the bureaucratization of the world has proceeded. Concerning the cause to which he dedicated his life, the creation of a political order that would enshrine as its highest goal the free play of the human imagination, it does seem, here at the beginning of a new millennium, that such a goal is as remote as ever. Certainly, when one looks around the world, the only viable model appears to be one that subordinates all other aims, including cultural ones, to the overarching goal of maximizing the production and consumption of commodities.

But that is not the end of the story. In many important respects the world—or more accurately, the developed world—has come much closer to the realization of the ideals for which Harry Kessler fought. One need mention only the much freer and more open discussion and acceptance of sexualities once stamped deviant or, on the plane of international politics, observe the progress made by European integration. Many of the oppositions that bedeviled Kessler's political struggles have disappeared. In this way, Kessler can be read not simply for his brilliant evocation of a world forever lost to us, but also as a prophet, both of the world in which we live and of one that might yet come to be.

NOTES

Introduction

1. Annette Kolb, *Maß und Wert* 4 (1938): 630–31.

2. George Grosz, *Briefe* (Hamburg: Rowohlt, 1979), 305; Max Beckmann, *Tagebücher, 1940–1950* (Munich: Langen Müller, 1979). September 18 and 21, 1944, 98–99.

3. "A Saint-Simon of Our Time," *New York Review of Books,* August 31, 1972. Auden says that Kessler seems to have known everybody except T. S. Eliot and Winston Churchill. He, in fact, missed having met Churchill by a school term.

4. Kessler's postwar diaries, covering the years from 1918 to 1937, were published in German to wide acclaim in 1961 and are still in print; *Tagebücher,* (Frankfurt am Main: Insel Verlag, 1962) (henceforth *TB*). A great many of the entries for 1923 and almost all of those for 1924, both very important years in Kessler's life, were missing, as they were in the abridged English translation, published in the United States as *In the Twenties: The Diaries of Harry Kessler,* trans. Charles Kessler (New York: Holt, Rinehart and Winston, 1971). In 1983, bank employees in Mallorca discovered the long sought-after missing diaries from 1902 to 1914 in a bank vault where Kessler had stored them in 1933. Their recovery, along with the discovery of the missing diaries from 1923–1924, means that practically all of the diary is now available. The Deutsche National Literaturarchiv (DNLA) in Marbach am Neckar, the repository for Kessler's diaries, letters, and other papers, originally intended to publish the complete diary in a twenty-volume set but has since decided to issue it in CD-ROM form, a formidable work of scholarship. All references to the unpublished diaries and letters refer to those stored at the DNLA in the Kessler Nachlaß (henceforth KN).

5. As Arthur A. Cohen describes him in his novel, *An Admirable Woman* (Boston: D. R. Godine, 1983), 45.

6. For a study of this, see Josef Chytry's magisterial *The Aesthetic State: A Quest in Modern German Thought* (Berkeley: University of California Press, 1989).

7. John Willet, *Art and Politics in the Weimar Period: The New Sobriety, 1917–1933* (New York: Pantheon, 1978).

8. The discovery of Kessler's missing diaries has sparked a lively interest in both his life and his diary. Prior to this discovery, the chief sources were Renate Müller-Krumbach, *Harry Graf Kessler und die Cranach-Presse in Weimar* (Hamburg: Maxmilian Gesellschaft, 1969); and two editions of his correspondence: Eberhard von Bodenhausen/Harry Graf Kessler, *Ein Briefwechsel, 1894–1918,* ed. Hans-Ulrich Simon (Marbach am Neckar, 1978), and Hugo von Hofmannsthal/Harry Graf Kessler, *Briefwechsel, 1898–1929,* ed. Hilde Burger (Frankfurt am Main: Insel Verlag, 1968). The first major publication since the discovery was the catalogue accompanying an exhibition on Kessler's life mounted by the Deutsche National Literaturarchiv in Marbach am Neckar, the chief repository for Kessler's papers: Gerhard Schuster and Margot Pehle, eds., *Harry Graf Kessler. Tagebuch eines Weltmannes,* Marbacher Kataloge 43, (Marbach am Neckar, 1988) (henceforth *Weltmannes*). At the same time, his collected works were reprinted as Harry Graf Kessler, *Gesammelte Schriften* (Volume I: *Gesichter und Zeiten;* Volume II, *Künstler und Nationen;* Volume III: *Walther Rathenau*), ed. Cornelia Blasberg and Gerhard Schuster (Frankfurt am Main: S. Fischer, 1988). Additional recent literature on Kessler includes: Peter Grupp, *Harry Graf Kessler, 1868–1937* (Munich: C. H. Beck, 1995); Burkhard Stenzel, *Harry Graf Kessler: Ein Leben zwischen Kultur und Politik* (Weimar: Böhlau, 1995); Laird M. Easton, "The Red Count: The Life and Times of Harry Kessler, 1868–1914" (Ph.D. diss. Stanford University, 1991); Gerhard Neumann and Günter Schnitzler, eds., *Harry Graf Kessler: Ein Wegbereiter der Moderne* (Freiburg im Breisgau: Rombach, 1997); and L. M. Newman, ed., *The Correspondence of Edward Gordon Craig and Count Harry Kessler, 1903–1937* (London: W. S. Maney for the Modern Humanities Research Association and the Institute of Germanic Studies, 1995).

9. On the ambiguity of Wilhelmian culture, see Hermann Glaser's introduction to *Die Kultur der Wilhelminischen Zeit: Topographie einer Epoche* (Frankfurt: S. Fischer, 1982), 7–10.

10. The sigh of disappointment and frustration over this resilience of bourgeois society is very palpable in Peter Bürger's *Theory of the Avant-garde* (Minneapolis: University of Minnesota Press, 1980).

11. Gerhard Schuster, "Harry Graf Kessler. Tagebuch eines Weltmannes," *Jahrbuch der deutschen Schillergesellschaft* 32 (1968), 433.

12. Ibid.

13. Kessler, *TB,* April 30, 1932, 705.

14. Alexandre Kojève, *Introduction to the Reading of Hegel: Lectures on the Phenomenology of Spirit,* ed. Allan Bloom (Ithaca, N.Y.: Cornell University Press, 1969), 94–95.

Chapter 1

1. *Gesammelte Schriften I*, 31–33; Schuster and Pehle, *Weltmannes,* 9–12.
2. *Gesammelte Schriften I*, 33; *TB*, October 1, 1888. Kessler enjoyed a far more trusting relationship with his father than did his good friend and contemporary, Eberhard von Bodenhausen, whose father repeatedly backed down from his promises and thwarted his son's career plans.
3. *Gesammelte Schriften I*, 33.
4. Ibid., 39. The unmistakable Proustian ring to this passage was probably a deliberate allusion on Kessler's part. Not only was he an admirer and acquaintance of Proust, he also makes an appearance in *The Fugitive,* vol. 3 of *Remembrance of Things Past,* trans. Scott Moncrieff and Terence Kilmartin (New York: Random House, 1982), 662.
5. *Dictionary of National Biography,* vol.7 (London: Oxford University Press, 1975), 334.
6. Schuster and Pehle, *Weltmannes,* 19. For some malicious remarks on the status of the Kessler title as well as on the family, see Bernhard von Bülow, *The Memoirs of Prince von Bülow,* vol. 3 (Boston: Little, Brown & Company, 1931), 502–3.
7. *Gesammelte Schriften I*, 54–60. For the lifelong enmity between the Empress Augusta and Bismarck, see Edward Crankshaw, *Bismarck* (New York: Viking Press, 1981), 312, and Lothar Gall, *Bismarck: Der weisse Revolutionär* (Frankfurt a. M.: Propyläen, 1980), 244, 255.
8. For Kessler's version of the "Bülow Affair," see *Gesammelte Schriften I*, 76–78; see also Bülow, *Memoirs,* 502–3.
9. *Le Temps,* April 27, 1890; *TB*, April 28, 1890.
10. *Gesammelte Schriften I*, 83–86.
11. Ibid., 87.
12. *Gesammelte Schriften I*, 69.
13. Ibid., 89.
14. *TB*, September 22, 1919, 206–7.

Chapter 2

1. *TB*, June 16, 1880.
2. *Gesammelte Schriften I*, 98.
3. Ibid., 98–99.
4. Winston Churchill quoted in Randolph Churchill, *Winston S. Churchill: Youth, 1874–1900,* vol. 1 (Boston: Houghton Mifflin, 1966), 44; *Gesammelte Schriften I*, 103.
5. Churchill's insubordination and the punishment meted out to him by the headmaster were the stuff of legend at St. George's. Kessler recalled how Churchill's scampish manners, learned among his grandfather's stable boys, provoked Sneyd-Kynnersley to particular fury. Kessler must have picked this

up from another memoir or the anecdote of an acquaintance, for he had left St. George's the term before Churchill's arrival.

6. Maurice Baring, *The Puppet Show of Memory* (London: W. Heinemann, 1930), 100. As quoted by Virginia Woolf, Fry described one chilling scene: "In the middle of the room was a large box draped in black cloth and in austere tones the culprit was told to take down his trousers and kneel before the block over which I and the other head boy held him down. The swishing was given with the master's full strength and it took only two or three strokes for drops of blood to form everywhere and it continued for 15 or 20 strokes when the wretched boy's bottom was a mass of blood. Generally of course the boys endured it with fortitude but sometimes there were scenes of screaming, howling and struggling which made me almost sick with disgust." Virginia Woolf, *Roger Fry* (New York: Harcourt, Brace and Company, 1940), 31–33.

7. *Gesammelte Schriften*, 119. Kessler himself was never whipped—whether this was due to a secret agreement between his parents and the headmaster or simply because he was, as Roger Fry describes himself, "of such a disgustingly law-abiding disposition" that he was not likely to incur it, is unknown.

8. Ibid., 104–21, 120–21.

9. Ibid., 123–24.

10. Ibid., 125–28.

11. Ibid., 128–29.

12. Ibid., 132–35. Kessler's diary entry of September 26, 1888, mentions the suicide of Rodenwaldt and identifies his tormenter as Kießling. For a history of the Johanneum, including descriptions of the curriculum and reminiscences of Bintz, Kießling, and others, see Edmund Kelter, *Hamburg und sein Johanneum, 1529–1929* (Hamburg: Lütcke & Wulff, 1928), and the Festschrift published for the four hundredth anniversary of the school's foundation, *Kulturgeschichtliche Studien und Skizzen aus Vergangenheit und Gegenwart,* ed. Max Nonne and Fritz Ulmer (Hamburg: Broschek, 1929), 3–36.

13. *Gesammelte Schriften I,* 130, 135; André Gide, *Journals, 1889–1949* (Harmondsworth: Penguin, 1967), 80.

14. *Gesammelte Schriften I,* 139–40.

15. *TB,* September 13, 1888; January 16, 1889; January 1, 1892.

16. Ibid. On the literary use of the Salomé and Judith legends, see Wolfdietrich Rasch, *Die literarische Décadence um 1900* (Munich: C. H. Beck, 1986), 74–87, and Bram Dijaskrta, *Idols of Perversity: Fantasies of Feminine Evil* (New York: Oxford University Press, 1986).

17. *Gesammelte Schriften I,* 165–67.

18. On Jews and modern culture in Germany, see Peter Gay, *Weimar Culture: The Outsider as Insider* (New York: Harper & Row, 1968), as well as his *Freud, Jews, and Other Germans* (New York: Oxford University Press, 1978). Certainly not all homosexual members of the German elite were drawn to modernism—the aesthetic views of the Liebenberg Circle refute that notion; see Isabel Hull, *The Entourage of Kaiser Wilhelm II, 1888–1918* (New York: Cambridge University Press, 1982), 200.

19. Quoted in Grupp, *Harry Graf Kessler,* 30 (trans. from the German, the original in English, KN, New Additions, Adolf Wilhelm Kessler Folder, Harry to Alice, Ascension Day, 1888); Alice to Harry Kessler, May 18 and 23, 1889, KN, New Additions 26 and 125. In a letter dating from 1891, just as Harry was planning his world trip, she claimed her husband had informed her of being over a "million" poorer than a few years ago (presumably marks), blamed her husband's generosity toward his family, and warned Harry against visiting Australia.

Chapter 3

1. Daniel Fallon offers a useful, brief introduction to German higher education in *The German University: A Heroic Ideal in Conflict with the Modern World* (Boulder, Colo.: Colorado Associated University Presses, 1980). A more detailed account is offered by C. E. McClelland, *State, Society and University in Germany, 1700–1914* (Cambridge: Cambridge University Press, 1979). Konrad H. Jarausch concentrates on the social life and political views of students, *Students, Society, and Politics in Imperial Germany: The Rise of Academic Illiberalism* (Princeton, N.J.: Princeton University Press, 1982). On the history of the Friedrich-Wilhelm University, see the guide to German universities edited by Laetitia Boehm and Rainer A. Müller, *Universitäten und Hochschulen* (Düsseldorf: Econ, 1983), 78–81, and Friedrich von Bezold's *Geschichte der Rheinischen Friedrich-Wilhelms Universität* (Bonn: Marcus & Wehner, 1920), 1–89.

2. The Borussia Bonn became in fact more exclusive in the course of the nineteenth century. Whereas between 1827 and 1840, seventy-five of 170 members were non-noble, between 1840 and 1940, a mere twenty of six hundred members were non-nobles. See Peter Krause, *"O alte Burschenherrlichkeit:" Die Studenten und ihr Brauchtum* (Graz: Verlag Styria, Edition Kaleidoskop, 1979), 103; on this aspect of German academic life, see Jarausch, *Students,* 234–62, as well as Krause, "O alte," 74–159.

3. Kessler's description of Bodenhausen in *Gesammelte Schriften I,* 179–80. For Bodenhausen's autobiography, see *Eberhard von Bodenhausen: Ein Leben für Kunst und Wirtschaft,* ed. Dora von Bodenhausen-Degener (Düsseldorf-Köln: Eugen Diedrichs Verlag, 1955), 5–36. Hofmannsthal's phrase is taken from notes for his never completed essay on Bodenhausen, *Gesammelte Werke: Reden und Aufsätze III, 1925–1929* (Frankfurt: S. Fischer, 1980), 155–69. In his very insightful afterword to the Bodenhausen-Kessler correspondence, Hans-Ulrich Simon explores their relation. See Hans-Ulrich Simon, afterword to Simon, *Ein Briefwechsel,* 202–17.

4. James J. Sheehan, *The Career of Lujo Brentano: A Study of Liberalism and Social Reform in Imperial Germany* (Chicago: University of Chicago Press, 1966). For the conflict between the emperor and Bismarck over these issues, see J. Alden Nichols, *Germany After Bismarck: The Caprivi Era, 1890–1894* (Cambridge, Mass.: Harvard University Press, 1958), 12–26.

5. *TB*, November 5, 1886; *Gesammelte Schriften I*, 158; letter to Wilma von Kessler, February, 9, 1902, KN.

6. Among Springer's early admirers was the young Friedrich Nietzsche who wrote home to his mother and sister from Bonn (like Kessler, he attended first Bonn and then Leipzig), describing his classes: "Most of all I am happy to have made the acquaintance of Prof. Springer. A young, handsome, highly intelligent and artistic man, whose lectures are among the most attended," Friedrich Nietzsche, *Sämtliche Briefe*, ed. Giorgio Colli and Mazzino Montinari (Berlin: De Gruyter, 1986), 18; see also, Springer's autobiography, *Aus meinem Leben* (Berlin: G. Grote, 1892); Udo Kultermann, *Geschichte der Kunstgeschichte* (Vienna: Econ Verlag, 1966), 213–21; Michael Podro, *The Critical Historians of Art* (New Haven: Yale University Press, 1982), 152–58; and *Gesammelte Schriften I*, 192–93.

7. On Springer's theory and praxis of history, see Podro, *Critical Historians*, 154–58.

8. *TB*, September 20, 1889. On Kant and the critical historians of art, see Podro, *Critical Historians*, 6 ff., 9–11, 188 f.

9. *TB*, September 1, 1890. Springer had first called Kessler's attention to the significance of St. Francis, but Kessler owed the above interpretation of the importance of St. Francis for Italian art to the Heidelberg art historian Henry Thode, whose controversial book *Franz von Assisi und die Anfänge der Kunst in der Renaissance in Italien*, published in 1885, first put forth the argument that it was not the revival of classical learning in the fifteenth century that provided the impetus for the Renaissance, but the religious revival of the thirteenth century inspired by the teachings of St. Francis.

10. Henry Thode, *Franz von Assisi und die Anfänge der Kunst in der Renaissance in Italien*, 2d rev. ed., (Berlin: G. Grote, 1904), xviii, 60–63, 570–72. On Thode's place in the historiography of the Renaissance, see Wallace K. Ferguson, "The Reinterpretation of the Renaissance," in *Facets of the Renaissance*, ed. William H. Werkmeister (Los Angeles: University of Southern California Press, 1959), 9–10.

11. Quoted in *Die Berliner Moderne, 1885–1914*, ed. Jürgen Schutte and Peter Sprengel (Stuttgart: Reclam, 1987), 572; *Gesammelte Schriften I*, 194.

12. *TB*, December 31, 1890; January 17, 1891.

13. See Arthur Blumenthal, "A Reappraisal of Wilhelm Wundt," *American Psychologist* (1975), 1081–88 for a positive view; see also, Daniel N. Robinson, *Toward a Science of Human Nature: Essays on the Psychologies of Mills, Hegel, Wundt, and James* (New York: Columbia University Press, 1982), 128–68; D. B. Klein, *A History of Scientific Psychology: Its Origins and Philosophical Backgrounds* (New York: Basic Books, 1970), 829–78. Nevertheless, it is difficult not to concur with Egon Friedell that Wundt's "half-Kantian, half-Lebnitzian idealism gives the unavoidable impression of being a rather superfluous structure, not really intended to live in but rather for occasional solemn displays." Egon Friedell, *Kulturgeschichte der Neuzeit*, vol. 3 (Munich: C. H. Beck, 1931), 449.

14. *TB*, July 8, 1892.

15. There is an interesting hint in the diaries that Kessler's involvement in the affair may have had an erotic component. The tone of the following entry indicates, at least, that Kessler's disappointment over his friend's infidelity was more than ethical: "At home this afternoon, furious. The same old story, cherchez la femme. But Z(edlitz) has proven himself pitifully weak and false. Lies, lies, lies! I knew it but still trusted Zedlitz deaf to all warnings. . . . The case interests me psychologically, how Zedlitz has sunk, step by step, to this *baseness,* breaking his promise and then continuing to lie." *TB,* May 19, 1891; see his discussion of the incident in *Gesammelte Schriften I,* 201; see also Sander L. Gilman, "The Nietzsche Murder Case," *New Literary History* 14 (1983), 359–72.

16. *TB,* December 22, 1891.

17. Ibid., May 23, 1899.

18. Ibid., January 13, 1894.

19. Friedrich Nietzsche, *Beyond Good and Evil* (New York: Penguin, 1990), 185; *Gesammelte Schriften I,* 212.

20. *Gesammelte Schriften I,* 212–3.

21. Ibid., 213–14. This assertion has something of a retrospective insight about it. The evidence that Kessler at the time conceived of his diplomatic career in this way is scanty, although there are some hints. It is not even clear that he had actually read *Beyond Good and Evil* before he embarked on his world cruise. In his memoirs, he tends to backdate his reading of Nietzsche by several months; Nietzsche, *Beyond Good and Evil,* 138.

22. *TB,* July 23, 1891.

23. *Gesammelte Schriften I,* 221–23.

24. Ibid., 162; in October 1894, for example, Kessler jotted down in his diary the following note: "The problem of contemporary German history: if Bismarck simply created in the German Reich a body suitable for his powerful personality, or if he has created something living, that can survive and develop further without his sireship."

Chapter 4

1. *TB,* January 22, 1892.

2. Ibid., January 18, 1892; *Gesammelte Schriften I,* 251.

3. *TB,* January 30, 1892. See also the description of his White House visit in his memoirs, *Gesammelte Schriften I,* 242. This criticism of the United States could be found across the political spectrum in Germany; Heinrich von Treitschke alluded to it in his lecture, "The Democratic Republic," in *Politics,* ed. Hans Kohn, (New York: Harcourt, Brace, and World, 1963), 219.

4. *TB,* April 13, 1892.

5. Theodor Fontane, *Briefe, Volume IV, 1890–1898* (Berlin: Propyläen, 1968–71), 300; on the military's role in Wilhelmian Germany, see the essay by Wilhelm Deist in *Das kaiserliche Deutschland,* ed. Michael Stürmer (Düsseldorf, 1984), 312–39; also Martin Kitchen, *The German Officer Corps, 1890–1914* (Oxford,

1968), 22–63, 115–86; Gordon A. Craig, *The Politics of the Prussian Army, 1640–1945* (Oxford, 1978), v, 70; Fabricius, *Geschichte des 3. Garde-Ulanen-Regiments, 1860–1910* (Berlin: E. S. Mittler, 1910), for the regimental history as well as for the list of all the Jagows, Bülows, Westarps, and other prominent names who formed yet another network of connections for Kessler.

6. *TB,* December 10 and 12, 1907.

7. Otto von Dungern, *Unter Kaiser und Kanzelrn: Erinnerungen* (Coburg Veste Verlag, 1953).

8. *TB,* December 17, 1894, October 12, 16, and 17, 1895.

9. Ibid., May 4, 1902.

10. John Rothenstein, *Summer's Lease: An Autobiography, 1901–1938* (New York: Holt, Rinehart & Winston, 1965), 177.

Chapter 5

1. For how Berlin's population compared with other German cities, see Michael Stürmer, *Das ruhelose Reich: Deutschland, 1866–1918* (Berlin: Severin and Siedler, 1983), 53; on Berlin's industry, see Walther Kiaulehn, *Berlin: Schicksal einer Weltstadt* (Munich: Biederstein, 1958), 132–68, and Richard Dietrich, "Berlins Weg zur Industrie-und Handelsstadt," in *Berlin: Zehn Kapitel seiner Geschichte,* ed. Richard Dietrich (Berlin: De Gruyter, 1960), 161–98.

2. Quoted in Gerhard Masur, *Imperial Berlin* (New York: Basic Books, 1970), 10. In his seminal book, *German Home Towns: Community, State, and the General Estate* (Ithaca, N.Y.: Cornell University Press, 1971), Mack Walker argues convincingly that the peculiar experience of life in the many small towns scattered throughout Germany helped shape in myriad ways German political and social thought; Maximilian Harden, "Die Krisis," *Berliner Moderne,* 117.

3. *TB,* April 2, 1894.

4. Petra Wilhelmy, *Der Berliner Salon im 19. Jahrhundert (1780–1914),* Veröffentlichen der Historischen Kommission zu Berlin, vol. 73 (Berlin: De Gruyter, 1989), 1–32, 391–456.

5. On the Richter salon, see ibid., 343–44, 348–52, and 807–12.

6. See van de Velde's account in *Geschichte meines Lebens,* rev. ed., ed. Hans Curjel (Munich: R. Piper, 1986), 164–69, as well as the response of Elisabeth von Heyking in her diary: "In the afternoon quite a curious gathering at Frau Richters. All of Berlin's intellectual and noble elite before whom a Mr. van de Velde lectured on how we should decorate our homes and what actually is beautiful. According to him we should all burn our beautiful, comfortable pieces with their memories and replace them with modern furniture decorated with lines!" Heyking, *Tagebücher aus vier Weltteilen, 1886–1904* (Leipzig: Koehler & Amelang, 1926), 313.

7. *TB,* February 18, 1895.

8. On naturalism, see Richard Hamann and Jost Hermand, *Naturalismus*

(Munich, 1972), as well as the two essays by Jost Hermand in his *Der Schein des schönen Lebens* (Frankfurt a. M.: Athenäum Verlag, 1972), 11–38. For a counter-argument, see Wolfdietrich Rasch, *Zur deutschen Literatur seit der Jahrhundertwende* (Stuttgart: J. B. Metzler, 1967), 1–48.

9. *TB*, September 25, 1894; Robert Schmutzler, *Art Nouveau* (New York: Abrams, 1977), 35–124.

10. Schmutzler, *Art Nouveau*, 29–32.

11. Peter Stansky, *Redesigning the World: William Morris, the 1880s, and the Arts and Crafts* (Princeton, N.J.: Princeton University Press, 1985).

12. On bohemian life in Berlin, see Julius Bab, *Die Berliner Bohème* (Berlin: Seeman, 1904); on *Pan*, see Karl H. Salzmann, "PAN—Geschichte einer Zeitschrift," in *Jugendstil*, ed. Jost Hermand (Darmstadt: Wissenschaftliche Buchgesellschaft, 1971), 178–208. For a contemporary account, see Stanislaw Przybyszewski, *Erinnerungen an das literarische Berlin* (Munich: Winkler, 1965).

13. Bodenhausen, *Ein Leben*, 61; review in *Künste für Alle* quoted in Jutta Thamer, *Zwischen Historismus und Jugendstil: Zur Ausstattung der Zeitschrift "Pan" (1895–1900)* (Frankfurt a. M.: Lang, 1980), 24.

14. Letter of March 27, 1895, in Richard Dehmel, *Ausgewählte Briefe, Volume I, 1883–1902* (Berlin: S. Fischer, 1923), 195.

15. Dehmel, *Briefe*, 196; Hans-Ulrich Simon relates this idea to the organic thought of the turn of the century, characterized by the creation of innumerable "Secessions." See Simon, *Ein Briefwechsel*, 203.

16. *TB*, December 8, 1894.

17. Peter Paret, *The Berlin Secession: Modernism and Its Enemies in Imperial Germany* (Cambridge, Mass.: Harvard University Press, 1980), 50–52.

18. Kessler supported both the Polish writer and the Norwegian artist generously even though, at this point at least, he did not much care for their work. *TB*, February 9, 1895.

19. As Dominik Jost asserts in *Literarischer Jugendstil*, rev. ed. (Stuttgart: J. B. Metzler, 1980), 12.

20. Quoted in Simon, *Ein Briefwechsel*, 121; on Kessler's importance to *Pan*, see Gisela Henze, *Der PAN: Geschichte und Profil einer Zeitschrift der Jahrhundertwende* (Ph.D. diss, Freiburg, 1974), 96–97, and Salzmann, "PAN," 194.

21. Alfred Lichtwark, "Zur Einführung," *Pan*, III (1895), 173.

22. *TB*, May 31 and June 1, 1898; for Flaischlen's deference to Kessler on literary matters as well as his letter to Kessler regarding the Derleth contribution, see Henze, *Der PAN*, 362–63; 534–36.

23. *TB*, March 16, 1893.

24. The daughter of von Werner once complained to Kessler that her father found painting "ceremonial" pictures very boring. Kessler's laconic comment in his diary was "For the viewers as well." *TB*, March 28, 1895 and May 31, 1896.

25. Ibid., June 17, 18, and 20, 1895.

26. See Henze, *Der PAN*, 215–21 on the journal's financial problems.

27. Julius Meier-Graefe, "Der *Pan*," *Pan*, 1 (1910), 1.

28. Salzmann, "PAN," 181.

Chapter 6

1. The literature on decadence is endless. For a discussion of the term, see Richard Gilman, *Decadence: The Strange Life of an Epithet* (New York: Farrar, Straus and Giroux, 1979); also, David Weir, *Decadence and the Making of Modernism* (Amherst, Mass.: University of Massachusetts Press, 1995), 1–21. Robert M. Adams, *Decadent Societies* (San Francisco: North Point Press, 1983), offers a historical analysis; see also the essay by Clive Scott "Symbolism, Decadence and Impressionism," in *Modernism,* ed. Malcolm Bradbury and James McFarlane (Harmondsworth, U.K.: Penguin, 1976), 206–27; Rasch, *Décadence;* Matei Calinescu, *The Five Faces of Modernity: Modernism, Avant-Garde, Decadence, Kitsch, Postmodernism* (Durham, N.C.: Duke University Press, 1987), 149–221.

2. *TB,* November 24 and 29, 1894; June 17, 1897; see Grupp, *Harry Graf Kessler,* 55–56.

3. Ibid., January 30, 1894; see the description of Verlaine in the diary entries for July 7, 24, 26, 27, and 28, 1895.

4. Harry Graf Kessler, "Henri de Régnier," *Pan* 1 (October 1895), 244.

5. *TB,* November 29, 1893.

6. Kessler, "Régnier," 244.

7. Ibid.

8. Ibid., 246

9. Ibid., 249; see also Rasch, *Décadence,* 26.

10. *TB,* May 11 and 16, 1898.

11. Hugo von Hofmannsthal/Eberhard von Bodenhausen, *Briefe der Freundschaft* (Düsseldorf: E. Diedrichs, 1953), 13; *TB,* March 22, 1899. On the relationship between Kessler and Hofmannsthal, see the afterword to their correspondence by Hilde Burger in Burger, *Briefwechsel,* 433–45; Jürgen Haupt, "Harry Graf Kessler und Hugo von Hofmannsthal: Eine Freundschaft," in *Konstellationen Hugo von Hofmannsthals* (Salzburg: Residenz Verlag, 1970), 46–81; Alexandre Kostka, "Das 'Gesamtkunstwerk für alle Sinne': Zu einigen Facetten der Beziehung zwischen Hugo von Hofmannsthal und Harry Graf Kessler," in *Wegbereiter,* 1997, 135–51.

12. It was reprinted in 1903, 1921, 1929, 1962, 1988, and 1997. For an exhaustive—and exhausting—discussion of the book, see Alexander Ritter, "Der Dandy im Lande des Diktators Diaz: Harry Graf Kessler und seine asthetizistischen *Notizen über Mexiko* (1898)," in *Wegbereiter,* 1997, 227–79.

13. *Gesammelte Schriften I,* 337.

14. Quoted in Hamman and Hermand, *Impressionismus* (Munich: Nymphenburger Verlagshandlung, 1972), 29; *Gesammelte Schriften I,* 331–36; on fin-de-siècle travel literature, see Hamman and Hermand, *Impressionismus,* 27–30.

15. *Gesammelte Schriften I,* 351–52.

16. Ibid., 355–57.

17. Ibid., 397–98.

18. Georg Simmel, "The Ruin," in *Georg Simmel, 1858–1918,* ed. Kurt H. Wolff (Columbus: Ohio State University Press, 1959), 266.

19. *Gesammelte Schriften I,* 395.

20. Hans Taft, "Neue Schriften zur Völkerkunde," *Die Gesellschaft,* 1 (1900), 50–51.

21. Bodenhausen, *Ein Leben,* 178–79.

22. Simon, *Ein Breifwechsel,* June 24, 1900, 60–61.

23. *Gesammelte Schriften II,* 19–20.

24. Ibid., 22–24.

25. Ibid.

26. Simon, *Ein Briefwechsel,* December 27, 1899, 49.

27. Bodenhausen, *Ein Leben,* 135; Burger, *Briefwechsel,* July 26, 1900, 128.

Chapter 7

1. Alexandre Kostka, "Harry Graf Kesslers Überlegungen zum modernen Kunstwerk im Spiegel des Dialogs mit Henry van de Velde," in *Wegbereiter,* 1997, 161–80; idem, "Der Dilettant und sein Künstler. Die Beziehung Harry Graf Kessler—Henry van de Velde," in *Henry van de Velde: ein europäischer Künstler seiner Zeit,* ed. Klaus-Jürgen Sembach and Birgit Schulte (Cologne: Wienand, 1992); Peter Grupp, "Geteilte Illusionen: Die Beziehung zwischen Harry Graf Kessler und Henry van de Velde," in *Wege nach Weimar: Auf der Suche nach der Einheit von Kunst und Politik,* ed. Hans Wilderotter and Michael Dorrmann (Weimar: Böhlau, 1999), 195–204.

2. The best source on van de Velde's life and ideas remains his autobiography, *Geschichte meines Lebens,* ed. Hans Curjel (Munich: R. Piper, 1986). The French translation is *Récit de ma vie: Anvers, Bruxelles, Paris, Berlin,* ed. Anne van Loo, (Paris: Flammarion, 1992). See also Sembach and Schulte, eds., *Henry van de Velde,* the lavishly illustrated catalog, as well as Klaus-Jürgen Sembach, *Henry van de Velde* (New York: Rizzoli, 1989). Some of van de Velde's essays are collected in Hans Curjel, ed., *Zum neuen Stil* (Munich: R. Piper, 1995).

3. *TB,* January 30, 1898. This was not the only complaint about van de Velde. Kessler also agreed with Bodenhausen that van de Velde was not quite aboveboard in his financial dealings, a failing that they attributed to his concern for his growing family but that they still resented. See Bodenhausen's stern letter to van de Velde, Bodenhausen, *Ein Leben,* 201–2; Van de Velde, *Geschichte,* 159.

4. See H. F. Peters, *Zarathustra's Sister: The Case of Elisabeth and Friedrich Nietzsche* (New York: Crown, 1977).

5. Rosawitha Wollkopf, "Das Nietzsche-Archiv im Spiegel der Beziehungen Elisabeth Förster-Nietzsches zu Harry Graf Kessler," *Jahrbuch der deutschen Schillergesellschaft* 34 (1990), 125; Peters, *Zarathustra's Sister,* 150–51.

6. *TB,* August 7, 1897.

7. Ibid., August 8, 1897, October 2, 1897.

8. Ibid., August 27, 1900. On the so-called Nietzsche cult that developed in the 1890s, see Hubert Cancik, "Der Nietzsche-Kult in Weimar: Ein Beitrag zur Religionsgeschichte der wilhelminischen Ära," *Nietzsche-Studien* 16 (1987),

405–29, and Jürgen Krause, *"Märtyr" und "Prophet." Studien zum Nietzsche-Kult in der bildenden Kunst der Jahrhundertwende* (Berlin/New York: W. de Gruyter, 1984); also Steven Aschheim, *The Nietzsche Legacy in Germany, 1890–1990* (Berkeley, Calif.: University of California Press, 1992), 85–127.

9. Jane Block, "The Insel-Verlag 'Zarathustra': An Untold Tale of Art and Printing," *Pantheon* 45 (1987), 129–37.

10. *TB*, September 2, 1901; Simon, *Ein Briefwechsel,* September 6, 1901, 62.

11. *TB*, November 5, 1901; Kessler to Förster-Nietzsche, September 27, 1901, cited in Wollkopf, "Nietzsche Archiv" 151; ibid., 142–43; Kostka, "Der Dilettant," 261.

12. Förster-Nietzsche to Kessler, December 6, 1901, cited in Wollkopf, 155; quoted in Schuster and Pehle, *Weltmannes,* 119.

13. *TB,* April 20, 1902.

Chapter 8

1. The best introduction to the "golden age" of Weimar is W. H. Bruford, *Culture and Society in Classical Weimar, 1775–1806* (Cambridge: Cambridge University Press, 1961). See also, Ulrich Hess, "Beginn kapitalistischer Produktionsverhältnisse," in *Geschichte der Stadt Weimar,* ed. Gitta Günther and Lothar Wallraf, (Weimar: Böhlau, 1976), 441–43.

2. See the collection of accounts of visits to Weimar in *Weimar im Urteil der Welt,* ed. H. Greiner-Mai et al. (Berlin and Weimar: Aufbau Verlag, 1975).

3. Bruford, *Culture,* 394.

4. On Liszt's activities and ambitions in Weimar, see Hess, "Beginn," 400–4, and his letters to Karl Alexander and Maria Pawlowna in Greiner-Mai, *Weimar,* 231–38.

5. Liszt returned to Weimar in 1869 but gradually gave up hope of turning that state into the "Athens of the north." Alan Walker, *Franz Liszt: Volume II, The Weimar Years, 1848–1861* (New York: Knopf, 1989); Jürgen Krause, *"Märtyr,"* 101–8.

6. *TB,* August 1891.

7. Ibid., November 4, 1901; van de Velde, *Geschichte,* 224–25.

8. Nietzsche, *Beyond Good and Evil,* 99.

9. *TB,* November 26, 1897.

10. See Laird M. Easton, "The Rise and Fall of the 'Third Weimar': Harry Graf Kessler and the Aesthetic State in Wilhelmian Germany, 1902–1906," *Central European History* 29:4 (1997), 495–532; *TB,* January 10, 1903. On Kessler's elitism, see Hildegard Nabbe, "Mäzenatum und elitäre Kunst: Harry Graf Kessler als Schlüsselfigur für eine kulturelle Erneuerung um die Jahrhundertwende," *Deutsche Vierteljahrschrift für Literaturwissenschaft und Geistesgeschichte* 64 (1990), 652–79, although the author claims erroneously that Kessler's Weimar circle combined an interest in experimental modernism with an "outspoken conservativism." Kessler's political views at the time, as far as one can

discern them, come far closer to the nationalist liberalism of a Friedrich Naumann than to anything resembling "outspoken conservativism."

11. For Kessler's ambitions, see his letter to Bodenhausen of April 6, 1902, Simon, *Ein Briefwechsel,* 67–69.

12. *TB,* April 22, 1902.

13. Van de Velde, *Geschichte,* 226–27.

14. Simon, *Ein Briefwechsel,* December 25, 1901, 66. See also van de Velde, *Geschichte,* 209–13; on van de Velde's activity, see Karl-Heinz Hüter, "Hoffnung, Illusion und Enttäuschung: Henry van de Velde's Kunstgewerbeschule und das frühe Bauhaus," in Sembach and Schulte, *Henry van de Velde,* 285–337.

15. Quoted in Schuster and Pehle, *Weltmannes,* 110.

16. Rosenhagen's report, which appeared on July 15, 1903, is quoted in full in van de Velde, *Geschichte,* 245–50. For another report on Weimar, including pictures, see Max Hausen, "Das neue Weimar," *Die Woche* 6 (September 1904), 1641–45.

17. *TB,* November 8 and 13, 1903; on the imperial insult, see van de Velde, *Geschichte,* 238–39. For the report of the Prussian ambassador and the kaiser's marginal remarks, see Schuster and Pehle, *Weltmannes,* 133–35.

18. *TB,* December 19, 1901; Paret, *Berlin Secession,* 1–5. I am indebted to Paret's work in much of what follows. Other recent scholarship on art and politics in Imperial Germany include: Hermann Glaser, *Bildungsbürgertum und Nationalismus: Politik und Kulture im Wilhelminischen Deutschland* (Munich: Deutscher Taschenbuch Verlag, 1993); Peter Jelavich, *Munich and Theatrical Modernism: Politics, Playwriting, and Performance, 1890–1914* (Cambridge, Mass.: Harvard University Press, 1990); Wolfgang J. Mommsen, "Culture and Politics in the German Empire," in Mommsen, *Imperial Germany, 1867–1918: Politics, Culture, and Society in an Authoritarian State* (London: Edward Arnold, 1995); idem, *Bürgerliche Kultur und künstlerische Avantgarde: Kultur und Politik im deutschen Kaiserreich, 1870 bis 1918* (Frankfurt am Main: Propyläen, 1994); the elegant essay by Thomas Nipperdey, *Wie das Bürgertum die Moderne fand* (Berlin: Siedler, 1988); and Peter Paret and Beth Irwin Lewis, "Art, Society, and Politics in Wilhelmine Germany," *Journal of Modern History* 57 (1985), 696–710.

19. "Herr von Werner," in *Gesammelte Schriften II,* 79.

20. Paret, *Berlin Secession,* 109.

21. Ibid., 50–56.

22. Ibid., 43–49. See also the extensive catalogue *Max Liebermann in seiner Zeit* (Berlin: Staatliche Museen, National Galerie 1979), which, besides its essays on Liebermann, is especially interesting for its reproductions of his contemporaries.

23. Robert Jensen, *Marketing Modernism in Fin-de-Siècle Europe* (Princeton, N.J.: Princeton University Press, 1994); Paret, *Berlin Secession,* 69–79.

24. Ibid., 81–91.

25. *TB,* January 19, 1903. Simmel unknowingly found himself included among the barbarians when Kessler visited his rooms a few days later. Accord-

ing to Kessler, Simmel lived "in a gloomy, Philistine apartment, which was improved somewhat but not *essentially* through some good photographs and Japanese woodcuts. . . . I feel nevertheless that a man, who endures contentedly such a surrounding and considers it good, and who knows so little about art, represents a completely different station on the way to a new culture than me." Ibid., February 25, 1903, and October 22, 1903.

26. See Alfred Lichtwark, *Briefe an die Kommission für die Verwaltung der Kunsthalle,* ed. Gustav Pauli (Hamburg: Westermann, 1923), 66–68. Van de Velde's account mistakenly dates the procession at the time of the opening of the first *Künstlerbund* exhibition, *Geschichte,* 242–43. The news from Weimar was greeted warmly, if more soberly, by much of the press that had been following the controversy. For example, the journal *Kunstwart*—whose editor Ferdinand Avenarius was by no means an unequivocal supporter of modern art—greeted the *Künstlerbund* as a positive sign; "Der Deutsche Künstlerbund," *Kunstwart* 7 (January 1904), 473.

27. *TB,* October 23, 1903.

28. "Der Deutsche Künstlerbund," in *Gesammelte Schriften II,* 66–67.

29. Ibid., 72–75.

30. Ibid., 76–77.

31. On all of this see Paret, *Berlin Secession,* 152–62.

32. *TB,* September 20, 1905, June 1, 3, and 14, 1906; Kessler did not, however, take an active interest in expressionism until the war, and then it was first the expressionist poets who attracted him.

Chapter 9

1. *TB,* April 3, 1904.

2. Ibid., June 19 and 27, 1907.

3. Reprinted in *Gesammelte Schriften II,* 304–8.

4. Ibid., 58

5. *TB,* January 4, 1903.

6. On the Nabis, see Claire Frèches-Thory and Antoine Terrasse, *The Nabis: Bonnard, Vuillard and their Circle* (New York: H. N. Abrams, 1991), 13; Kessler, "Paul Gauguin," in *Gesammelte Schriften II,* 97; quoted in Frèches-Thory and Terrasse, *Nabis,* 22.

7. On the split within the Nabis, see Frèches-Thory and Terrasse, *Nabis,* 63–83; as well as Belinda Thomson's beautifully illustrated study, *Vuillard* (New York: Abbeville Press, 1988), 22–76.

8. *TB,* June 15 and February 20, 1903.

9. Kessler, "Aristide Maillol" in *Gesammelte Schriften II,* 263; *TB,* January 1, 1903; August 21, 1904; and September 2, 4, 8, 1904.

10. *TB,* September 3, 4, and 8, 1904.

11. John Rewald, *Maillol* (New York: Hyperion Press, 1939), 8–17; Frèches-Thory and Terrasse, *Nabis,* 52–54; and for his relation with Kessler, see Judith Claudel, *Maillol. Sa vie—son oeuvre—ses idées* (Paris: Grasset, 1937), 89–110.

12. *Gesammelte Schriften II*, 263–64.

13. Ibid., 267, 265.

14. Burger, *Briefwechsel*, April 26, 1909, 220.

15. On the Kessler-Maillol relationship, see James Fenton, "The Secrets of Maillol, *New York Review of Books* 43:8 (May 9, 1996), 47–55.

16. *TB*, May 31, 1905.

17. For Gide's visit to Weimar, see Claude Foucart, ed., *D'un monde à l'autre. La correspondance André Gide—Harry Kessler (1903–1933)* (Lyon: Centre d'études gidiennes, Université Lyon II, 1985), 35–54.

18. André Gide, *Pretexts: Reflections on Literature and Morality*, ed. Justin O'Brien (New York: Meridian Press, 1959), 57.

19. Foucart, *D'un monde*, 49; Hugo von Tschudi, "Kunst und Publikum," in *Gesammelte Schriften Zur neuren Kunst* (Munich: F. Bruckmann, 1912).

20. Kessler, "Kunst und Publikum," *Neue Rundschau* 17 (1906), 114–115; Kessler to Wilma de Brion, September 3, 1903, KN; Hofmannsthal's disparaging remarks about Weimar, about Kessler's rooms, his hypochondria, his unseemly snobbery about Viennese society, and his constant concern about earning money, wearied Kessler in the long run, no matter how much he forgave the poet the faults of the man, *TB*, August 25–September 1, 1903.

Chapter 10

1. *TB*, March 15, 1902, May 21, 1903.

2. Kessler in a letter to Poellnitz, quoted in Müller-Krumbach, *Kessler*, 20; on the Grand Duke Wilhelm-Ernst edition, see Schuster and Pehle, *Weltmannes*, 142–51; Heinz Sarkowski, "Zur Geschichte des Dünndruckpapiers und der Insel-Klassiker," *Das Inselschiff* 5 (March 1963), 1–3, 9; Müller-Krumbach, *Kessler*, 19–20.

3. Heymel to Kessler, February 27, 1905, quoted Schuster and Pehle, *Weltmannes*, 145.

4. See his reminiscences of Kippenberg in Kessler, "Reminiszenz," in *Navigare necesse est: Eine Festgabe für Anton Kippenberg* (Leipzig: Insel Verlag, 1924), 33–35.

5. Gordon Craig, quoted in Edward Craig, *Gordon Craig: The Story of His Life* (New York: Knopf, 1968), 99; William Rothenstein, *Men and Memories, 1900–1922* (London: Faber & Faber, 1932), 17.

6. *TB*, April 13, 1903; Kessler, "Ein neuer Englisher Künstler: A. E. John," *Kunst und Künstler* 2 (June 1904), 360–63.

7. Craig, *Craig*, 176, 178, 374.

8. For this argument, as well as a description of the production, see Denis Bablet, *The Theatre of Gordon Craig* (London: Eyre Methuen, 1981), 56–61, as well as Craig, *Craig*, 168–174.

9. Quoted in Bablet, *Theatre*, 47.

10. *TB*, April 17, 1903; Edward Gordon Craig, *On the Art of the Theatre* (Chicago: Browne's Bookstore, 1911), 157–59.

11. Craig, *Craig*, 31–46, 63–100; Bablet, *Theatre*, 1–29.

12. Craig, *Craig*, 84–87; Bablet, *Theatre*, 20–21.

13. Quoted in Rothenstein, *Summer's Lease*, 55. Indispensable for the relation between Kessler and Craig is their correspondence; see Newman, *Craig and Kessler*.

14. See Jelavich, *Munich and Theatrical Modernism*, 3, 17 ff; see also the letter of Kessler thanking Hofmannsthal for sending him the essay where he speaks of the "ideas that we discussed together . . . ." Burger, *Briefwechsel*, October 22, 1903, 57; Hofmannsthal, *Gesammelte Werke: Reden und Aufsätze I: 1891–1913*, 490–93.

15. Originally, the plan had been for Hofmannsthal to write a masque to be performed in an outdoor theater in the Belevedere Park at Weimar. That plan fell through when Kessler discovered that Craig would not stage any such production for less than a thousand pounds, far more than the grand duchess could afford; see the correspondence in Burger, *Briefwechsel*, February 28–December 24, 1903, 43–62, as well as *TB*, December 7, 1903.

16. L. M. Newman, "Gordon Craig in Germany," *German Life and Letters* 40 (October 1986), 11–14.

17. Bablet, *Theatre*, 71.

18. Bablet, *Theatre*, 68–73; Craig, *Craig*, 185–88; Burger, *Briefwechsel*, January 14, 1905, 75–76. Hofmannsthal intervened on behalf of Craig several times; see A. M. Nagler, "Hugo von Hofmannsthal and Theatre," *Theatre Research* 2 (1960), 11–13.

19. Craig, *Craig*, 200–2, 216–20; Bablet, *Theatre*, 85–89; *TB*, December 17, 1905; Newman, "Gordon Craig," 21; see also the complicated correspondence between Hofmannsthal and Kessler regarding Craig's work on *Elektra*, Burger, *Briefwechsel*, February 6–October 1905, 78–108.

20. Kessler, "Die Kunst des Theaters," in *Gesammelte Schriften II*, 92–93.

21. *TB*, November 1, 1911, January 28, 1912.

22. A good introduction to the Moroccan crisis is offered by A. J. P. Taylor, *The Struggle for Mastery in Europe: 1848–1918* (Oxford: Oxford University Press, 1977), 427–42; see also Paul Kennedy, *The Rise in Anglo-German Antagonism: 1860–1914* (London: Ashfield Press, 1980), 275–84, 287, and chapter 19.

23. *TB*, October 19, 20, and 23, 1905. Robert Koch, the scientist who discovered the cause of syphilis, signed only reluctantly: "The great mass of the English people are poisoned against us. Such a thing (the letter) can offer at best a palliative for a short time before it starts again." Ibid., December 20, 1905.

24. Schuster and Pehle, *Weltmannes*, 194; *TB*, December 8, 1905. Theodor Adorno, in his review of the Hofmannsthal-George correspondence, sneers at Hofmannsthal's letter, declaring that its pompous tone "has as much style as *The Legend of Joseph*" and praising George for refusing to sign it. Regardless of what one thinks of the sincerity and/or efficacy of the letter, to suppose that George had any greater insight into the international political situation seems doubtful. See Theodor Adorno, *Prismen* (Frankfurt am Main, 1955), 267–69.

25. Rothenstein, *Summer's Lease*, 75; Albert J. Beveridge, *What Is Back of the War* (Indianapolis: Bobbs-Merrill, 1915), 388; Rothenstein, *Summer's Lease*, 75–

76; Kessler to Rothenstein, December 28, 1905, William Rothenstein Papers, Houghton Library, Harvard University.

26. *Times,* January 12, 1906, 15; the German government welcomed Kessler's initiative to strengthen Anglo-German relations but did so with caution, not wanting to give the appearance of being too eager for a rapprochement; see the Politischen Archivs des Auswärtigen Amts (henceforth PA), 1A, England 78, Band 45 for a report of the German ambassador Paul Graf von Wolff Metternich's conference with his English counterpart, Lord Grey, as well as PA, 1A, England, 78, Band 46. According to Grupp, *Kessler,* 279 n. 109, Chancellor Bülow weakened the original wording of the congratulatory telegram somewhat.

27. Mrs. Maxwell Armfield (Constance Smedley), *Crusaders: The Reminiscences of Constance Smedley* (London: Duckworth, 1929), 142; Grupp, *Kessler,* 117–18.

28. Bodenhausen had just completed his doctorate at Heidelberg, but, unable to find an academic position that would support his growing family in the comfort he wished, he reluctantly accepted a job with the Deutsche Bank and thus began the business career that would take him to the highest echelons of German industry.

29. Gwinner, in fact, does not appear to have known that it was Kessler who spoke with Lynch or that they were cousins until Kessler himself told him. On the Berlin-Baghdad railway, see William L. Langer, *The Diplomacy of Imperialism, 1890–1902* (New York: Knopf, 1957), 629–50; for the period after 1903, see John B. Wolf, *The Diplomatic History of the Bagdad Railroad* (Columbia, Mo.: University of Missouri Press, 1936), 19–107, and Maybelle Kennedy Chapman, *Great Britain and the Bagdad Railway, 1888–1914* (Northampton, Mass.: Smith College Studies in History, 1948), 38–211. For the differences between German finance and the German government, see Helmut Mejcher, "Die Bagdadbahn als Instrument deutschen wirtschaftlichen Einflusses im Osmanischen Reich," *Geschichte und Gesellschaft* 1 (1975).

30. *TB,* August 7, 1905.

31. Ibid., July 9, 1905.

32. On the limits of cultural exchange, see the very astute comments of Kennedy, *Anglo-German Antagonism,* 389–400.

33. Van de Velde, *Geschichte,* 274; V. R. Berghahn, *Germany and the Approach of War in 1914* (New York: St. Martin's Press, 1973), 67 ff.

Chapter 11

1. *TB,* November 15, 1905.

2. Ibid., November 10, 5, 1905.

3. Simon, *Ein Briefwechsel,* April 6, 1902, and February 3, 1904, 68, 73; *TB,* November 4, 1905; on the opposition of Ruhland and on the Rodin scandal in general, see Renate Müller-Krumbach, "Kessler und die Tradition. Aspekte zur Abdankung 1906," in *Wegbereiter,* 205–25.

4. Peter Grupp makes the valid point that Kessler's appointment had been

approved by the Weimar authorities only because they thought he would introduce a technical modernization of the museum, not because they approved of
his wide ranging Nietzschean plans, Grupp, *Kessler,* 90–94.

5. *TB,* April 18, 1905. This outburst by Rothe qualifies the view that he was a
reliable supporter of Kessler and van de Velde, see Krause, *Märtyr,* 144; Müller's
report of February 8, 1904, PA, IA; Sachsen Weimar I (R 3309), 16–17.

6. *TB,* November 8 and 13, 1903; van de Velde, *Geschichte,* 222; according to
Hans-Ulrich Simon in the afterword to the Bodenhausen/Kessler correspondence, Simon, *Ein Briefwechsel,* 176.

7. Van de Velde to Kessler, October 31, 1904, January 2, 1905, KN. Peter
Grupp suggests that Kessler increasingly lost sight of the political realities of
Weimar, and especially of how dependent on the good will of the grand duke
his position was. Grupp further accuses him of an elitist contempt for his opponents and their sensitivity to the kaiser's feelings. This assumes, however, that
some fruitful compromise with Palézieux and his supporters was possible, a
questionable assumption given the almost immediate vituperation that greeted
even the most modest efforts at introducing modern art, see Grupp, *Kessler,*
122–23.

8. *TB,* December 10, 1908.

9. The editor of the local newspaper greeted the exhibition with enthusiasm:
"Rodin is a brilliant artist and has been recognized as such for a long time. We
have every reason therefore to sincerely thank the direction of the Grand Ducal
Museum on the Karlsplatz for the organization of this important and magnificent exhibition," quoted in Stenzel, *Kessler,* 101; Kessler, "Rodins Zeichnung,"
Gesammelte Schriften II, 86–87. Just before this exhibition was scheduled to
open, Kessler had met with Palézieux, who was very anxious about the reaction
of Berlin. "If something happens," he repeated, "then I will be dismissed. I risk
my entire position etc.," *TB,* April 22, 1904.

10. J. A. Schmoll, "Rodin's Late Drawings and Watercolors," in *Auguste
Rodin: Drawings and Watercolors,* ed. Ernst-Gerhard Güse (New York: Rizzoli,
1985), 211–31; for the plans of a Salle Rodin at the museum, see Kessler to van de
Velde, May 28, 1905; Bibliothèque Royale, Albert Première (Brussels) (henceforth BRA), van de Velde Archives; on Rodin's doctorate and the subsequent
scandal, see Volker Wahl, *Jena als Kunststadt, 1900–1933* (Leipzig: Seeman Verlag, 1988), 56–63.

11. *Deutschland,* February 17, 1906, quoted in Wahl, *Jena als Kunststadt,* 66.

12. Wahl, *Jena als Kunststadt,* 70; Paul Rieth, "Rodin in Weimar," *Jugend* 11
(1906), 234; Ferdinand Avenarius, "Die Schmach der Weimaraner," *Kunstwart*
19 (April 1906), 46–47. Avenarius was later taken to task by a reader for his patronizing defense of censorship, but the editor stuck to his position, "Zur
'Schmach der Weimaraner,'" *Kunstwart* 19 (September 1906), 622–23. For a
chronology of the "Rodin scandal," as well as examples of Rodin's controversial
watercolors, see Claude Keisch, ed., *Auguste Rodin: Plastik, Zeichnungen,
Graphik* (Berlin: Staatliche Museen, National Galerie, 1979).

13. On this effort, see Laird Easton, "The Red Count: The Life & Times of
Harry Graf Kessler" (Ph.D. diss., Stanford University, 1991), 313–22.

14. Von Below's report of February 22, 1906, PA, IA; Sachsen Weimar 1, (R 3309) also quoted in Schuster and Pehle, *Weltmannes,* 133–35.

15. The fact that Egloffstein does not mention the Rodin scandal in his fatuous memoirs, *Das Weimar von Karl Alexander und Wilhelm Ernst* (1934) may have to do with the rumor that Kessler heard some years later, according to which Egloffstein was physically struck by the grand duke and dismissed from his post when his role in the intrigue was revealed.

16. Van de Velde, *Geschichte,* 288, 284–90; *TB,* March 7, 1906; Burger, *Briefwechsel,* March 8, 1906, 115. Why he had been smiling for a week when he had only discovered the letter the day before is not clear.

17. Ute Frevert, "Honour and Middle-Class Culture: The History of the Duel in England and Germany," in *Bourgeois Society in Nineteenth-Century Europe,* ed. Jürgen Kocka and Alan Mitchell (Providence, R.I.: Berg, 1993), 232–33. In her book on the same subject, Frevert points out how "the honor code of the officer corps allowed the insulted officer no other option than to avenge the insult with a duel"; Frevert, *Ehrenmänner: Das Duell in der bürgerlichen Gesellschaft* (Munich: C. H. Beck, 1991), 102 and chapter 4. See also, Karl Demeter, *The German Officer-Corps in Society and State, 1650–1945* (New York: Praeger, 1965), 139–46, and Kevin McAleer, *Dueling: The Cult of Honor in Fin-de-Siècle Germany* (Princeton, N.J.: Princeton University Press, 1994).

18. See Wahl, *Jena als Kunststadt,* 72–73.

19. *TB,* June 7, 11, 12, July 3, 1906; van de Velde, *Geschichte,* 289.

20. *TB,* July 13, 1906.

21. Burger, *Briefwechsel,* February 17, 1907, 147; *Kunst und Künstler* 4 (1906), 531; *TB,* December 9, 1906. See *Die Zukunft* 15 (1906), 505–10 and 16 (1907), 153–56; *TB,* December 9 and 11, 1906.

22. Kessler to van de Velde, February 4, 1907, BRA.

23. Von Below's report of January 30, 1907, PA, IA; Sachsen Weimar 1 (R 3309); Wahl, *Jena als Kunststadt,* 74–76; *TB,* February 1 and 4, 1907.

24. Burger, *Briefwechsel,* February 17, 1907, 146–47; *TB,* February 19, April 1, 7, 24, 1907.

25. Much to the joy of some opponents of Kessler. The conservative writer Max von Münchhausen wrote to Elisabeth Förster-Nietzsche, "God, how merry we were often back then—before the horrible time arrived when we all wanted to make Weimar into a center of German culture with artificial means—and not only German culture!—How fortunate that we didn't succeed, that we blundered miserably, it would have certainly been solemn, but also terribly boring! How fortunate, that this Wahnfried remained a *Wahn,*" quoted in Wollkopf, "Nietzsche-Archiv," 132.

26. On the Nietzsche project, see chapter 14.

27. As Maria Makela has pointed out, the Bavarian state, eager to protect Munich's reputation as Germany's art capital from Berlin's encroachment, was rather more sympathetic to the rather tame modernism represented by the Munich Secession, see Makela, *The Munich Secession: Art and Artists in Turn-of-the-Century Munich* (Princeton, N.J.: Princeton University Press, 1990), 15, 21, 32, 58–67.

28. On the politicization of aesthetic issues see Paret, *Berlin Secession*, 198–99. The experience of Kessler in Weimar qualifies the optimistic view of Wolfgang J. Mommsen that the federal structure of the empire protected modern art from the wrath of its opponents; see Mommsen, "Culture and Politics in the German Empire," in *Imperial Germany, 1867–1918: Politics, Culture and Society in an Authoritarian State*, (London: Edward Arnold, 1995) 130, 136; see also, Mommsen, *Bürgerliche Kultur*, 55.

29. On the emergence of a right-wing cultural movement in Weimar, see Krause, "Märtyr," 142–47, and the articles by Justus H. Ulbricht: "Kulturrevolution von rechts. Das völkische Netzwerk 1900–1930," in *Nationalsozialismus in Thüringen*, ed. Detlev Heiden and Gunther Mai (Cologne: Böhlau, 1995), 28–48; idem, "'Wege nach Weimar' and 'deutsche Widergeburt': Visionen kultureller Hegemonie im völkischen Netzwerk Thüringens zwischen Jahrhundertwende und 'Drittem Reich,'" in *Die Weimarer Republik zwischen Metropole und Provinz*, ed. Wolfgang Bialas and Burkhard Stenzel (Cologne: Böhlau, 1996), 23–35; and idem, "Im Herzen des 'geheimen Deutschland': Kulturelle Opposition gegen Avantgarde, Moderne und Republik in Weimar 1900 bis 1933," in *Weimar 1930: Politik und Kultur im Vorfeld der NS-Diktatur*, ed., Lothar Ehrlich and Jürgen John (Cologne: Böhlau, 1998), 139–67.

30. For the bitter opposition to the Bauhaus within Weimar, see Éva Forgács, *The Bauhaus Idea and Bauhaus Politics* (Budapest: Central European University Press, 1991), 126–30; Gillian Naylor, *The Bauhaus Reassessed* (London: Herbert Press, 1985), 121–22; Reginald Isaacs, *Gropius: An Illustrated Biography of the Founder of the Bauhaus* (Boston: Little, Brown, 1991), 113–117; and, in the greatest detail, Barbara Lane, *Architecture and Politics in Germany, 1918–1945* (Cambridge, Mass.: Harvard University Press), 69–86.

Chapter 12

1. Burger, *Briefwechsel*, July 14, 1906, 121–22; Kessler to Förster-Nietzsche, October 6, 1906, GSA 72 1393; Burger, *Briefwechsel*, September 26, 1906, 126–27.

2. *TB*, November 19, 1903.

3. Richard Muther, author of *Die Geschichte der Malerei des 19. Jahrhundert* (1904). Kessler visited him in London to obtain his signature for the letter to the *Times* and was astonished to hear him ask who William Morris was; *TB*, September 9, 1906.

4. Burger, *Briefwechsel*, October 18, 1908, 203; July 30, 1906, 124.

5. *TB*, November 27, 1906.

6. Kessler to Wilma von Kessler, March 21, 1902, KN; *TB*, November 3, 1906.

7. Burger, *Briefwechsel*, September 26, 1906, 127.

8. See Wolfdietrich Rasch, "Harry Graf Kessler als Schriftsteller: Die frühen Schriften zur Kunst und Literatur," in *Zeit der Moderne: Zur deustchen Literatur von der Jahrhundertwende bis zur Gegenwart*, ed., Hans-Henrik Krummacher et al. (Stuttgart: A. Kröner, 1984), 331–32.

9. "Nationalität," in *Gesammelte Schriften II*, 117–20.

10. Ibid., 120–22.

11. Ibid., 130.

12. Helene von Nostitz, *Aus dem alten Europa*, 2d rev. ed. (Frankfurt a. M.: Insel Verlag, 1978), 100–4. For photographs of Kessler's rooms in Weimar and a more or less complete inventory of the artwork found in them, see Schuster and Pehle, *Weltmannes*, 214–24. On his private art collection, see Beatrice von Bismarck, "Harry Graf Kessler und die franzöische Kunst um die Jahrhundertwende," *Zeitschrift des Deutschen Verein für Kunstwissenschaft*, 42:3 (1988), 47–62; on the fascinating fate of Kessler's second most famous painting, see Cynthia Saltzman, *Portrait of Dr. Gachet: The Story of a Van Gogh Masterpiece* (New York: Viking, 1998).

13. Nostitz, *Europa*, 102; Van de Velde, *Geschichte*, 182.

14. Maurice Denis, *Journal*, vol. 2: 1905–1920 (Paris: La Colombe, 1957), 109.

15. Karl Scheffler, *Henry van de Velde: Vier Essays* (Leipzig: E. Reiss, 1913), 67 ff.

16. Osthaus, on the other hand, expressed admiration for Kessler's house in Weimar, which he visited in Kessler's absence. See *TB*, December 15, 1907; Heymel to Kessler, May 6, 1904, KN.

17. *TB*, June 24, 1907.

18. Ibid., August 23, December 7, 1907.

19. Kessler to Wilma de Brion, December 19, 1910, February 17, 1911, and March 22, 1911, KN. Kessler tended to mislead his sister, for perfectly understandable reasons, about the nature of his sexuality, referring occasionally to pretty women in whom he was interested and seeking to present his liaison with Colin in an acceptable light.

20. Colin to Kessler, November 24 and 29, 1908, April 20, October 23, 1909, KN.

21. Kessler to Wilma de Brion, January 27, 1915, KN; Colin to Kessler, January 14, 1928, KN.

22. *TB*, June 4 and 14, 1904.

23. Ibid., October 29, 1907.

24. Ibid., November 18, 1907.

25. Ibid., May 1, 1908. See the publication of Kessler's account of this trip, including portions from his and Hofmannsthal's correspondence, by Werner Volke, "Unterwegs mit Hofmannsthal: Berlin—Griechenland—Venedig," *Hofmannsthal Blätter* 35/36 (1987), 50–104.

26. *TB*, May 2, 1908.

27. Volke, "Unterwegs," 73; *TB*, May 5, 1908.

28. *TB*, May 7, 1908. One is curious, of course, to know the contents of the brochures.

29. Ibid., May 10, 1908; in "The Wanderer," the figure became a weird, *unheimlich*, and threatening creature, completely outside society, whose face, especially when Hofmannsthal imagines it reflected in the spring from which he drinks later, haunts him with its kinship to his own. See Hofmannsthal, "Mo-

ments in Greece," in *Selected Prose,* trans. Mary Hottinger and Tania and James Stern (New York: Pantheon Books, 1952), 176–80.

30. Volke, "Unterwegs," 86–87; see the charming, if inaccurate, account in Claudel, *Maillol,* 92–101.

31. *TB,* June 3, 1908.

Chapter 13

1. *TB,* December 20, 1908; Hugo von Hofmannsthal, "An Graf Kessler," first printed in the *Neuen Zürcher Zeitung,* July 15, 1959, reprinted in *Hofmannsthal Blätter* 21/22 (1979), 66–67. For an amusing exchange between Dehmel and Hofmannsthal regarding the wording *and* the nature of the gift, see *Hofmannsthal Blätter,* 49–52.

2. Burger, *Briefwechsel,* September 26, 1906, 126; Hofmannsthal, *Gesammelte Werke III* (Frankfurt a. M.: S. Fischer, 1980), 448.

3. Burger, *Briefwechsel,* September 5, 1907, 157–58.

4. *TB,* February 9, 1909. Kessler's extensive diary entries recording the genesis of *Der Rosenkavalier* provide an indispensable complement to the material provided in the volume on the opera in the critical edition of Hofmannsthal's works, *Sämtliche Werke XXIII, Operndichtungen I* (Frankfurt a. M.: S. Fischer, 1986), 105–13, 589–630. The most important passages from the diary have been published, along with excerpts from the letters of Kessler and Hofmannsthal, in Volke, "Unterwegs," 90–98 and Schuster and Pehle, *Weltmannes,* 249–58. For the sources, see Hofmannsthal, *Sämtliche Werke XXIII,* 701–19.

5. On the various contributions, see *TB,* February 10, 11, 12, 15, 1909; Kessler to Wilma de Brion, February 18, 1909, KN; quoted in Hofmannsthal, *Sämtliche Werke XXIII,* 589; *TB,* February 15, 1909.

6. Burger, *Briefwechsel,* March 24, 1912, 93.

7. Paul Robinson, *Opera & Ideas: From Mozart to Strauss* (Ithaca, N.Y.: Cornell University Press, 1985), 210–22, 239–61.

8. *TB,* February 8, 1909, December 6, 1907. Yes, Kessler replied, but you are not exactly a Lamartine, George Eliot, or George Sand.

9. Burger, *Briefwechsel,* May 20, 1909, 224–26.

10. Ibid., August 8, 22, 1909, 258–60; see Dirk Hoffmann, "Zu Harry Graf Kesslers Mitarbeit an 'Rosenkavalier,'" *Hofmannsthal Blätter* 21/22 (1979), 153–60, whose arguments are repeated in shorter form in Hofmannsthal, *Sämtliche Werke XXIII,* 719–21. Hoffman, who did not have Kessler's diaries available when he wrote the article, both exaggerates Kessler's resistance to Hofmannsthal's changes and understates the degree to which the skeleton of the opera was in fact developed in the scenario. Nevertheless, his main point is valid.

11. See the exchange of letters in Burger, *Briefwechsel,* July 5, 1910, and August 21, 1910, 296–98.

12. Ibid., October 29, 1910, 308.

13. Ibid., November 10, 11, 1910, 310, 313.

14. Kessler to Wilma de Brion, January 30, 1911, KN. A few days later, he wrote to her again: "As to Hofmannsthal, I think he has gone as far in trying to be just to me, as his nature (which is not generous) will allow him; but I do not think it very likely I shall ever *collaboré* with him again; certainly not on those terms." Kessler to Wilma de Brion, February 3, 1911, KN.

15. Quoted in Schuster and Pehle, *Weltmannes,* 263.

16. *TB,* June 27, 1911.

17. Ibid., June 27, 1911.

18. Burger, *Briefwechsel,* March 24, 1912, 94.

19. For a thoughtful discussion of the relation between Kessler and Hofmannsthal that stresses their political differences, see Haupt, "Kessler und Hofmannsthal," 46–81. Haupt does tend to overestimate the role political differences played prior to 1914.

Chapter 14

1. *TB,* February 8, 1911; see also Günther Stamm's article, "Monumental Architecture and Ideology," *Gentse Bijdragen tot de Kunstgeschiedenis* 23 (1973–1975), 305 ff. Stamm's suggestion that Kessler intended some ideological connection between the Blanqui monument and Nietzsche is most unlikely. See as well Hildegard Nabbe, "Im Zeichen von Apollo und Dionysos: Harry Graf Kesslers Pläne für eine Nietzsche-Gedenkstätte in Weimar," *Seminar: A Journal of Germanic Studies* 32:4 (November 1996), 306–24.

2. Kessler to Förster-Nietzsche, February 3 and 5, 1911, GSA 72 1393.

3. Ibid., April 15 1911; February 3 and 5, 1911.

4. *TB,* March 12, 1911; Stamm, "Monumental Architecture," 308.

5. Kessler to Förster-Nietzsche, April 15, 1911, GSA 72 1393.

6. Burger, *Briefwechsel,* April 16, 1911, 323–24.

7. Stamm, "Monumental Architecture," 313; for an overview of this issue, see Henning Eichberg, "Forward Race and the Laughter of Pygmies: On Olympic Sport," in *Fin de Siècle and Its Legacy,* ed. Mikulás Teich and Roy Porter, (Cambridge: Cambridge University Press, 1990) 115–31; *TB,* September 4, 1911.

8. *TB,* April 20, 1911; Kessler found more resistance, not surprisingly, among English intellectuals, who suspected that Nietzsche's influence in Germany was not all that pacific. Roger Fry felt that way, as did Gilbert Murray who signed anyway.

9. *TB,* August 9, 1911. Kessler was irritated later when Maillol said he could only start the statue in 1913; Kessler responded that the committee would not agree to such a long wait.

10. Max Weber, "Science as a Vocation," in *From Max Weber,* ed. H. H. Gerth and C. Wright Mills, (Oxford: Oxford University Press, 1946), 155.

11. Van de Velde's commission was contested because of his nationality, see van de Velde, *Geschichte,* 314–18, and Volker Wahl, " 'Kunstkämpfe' in Jena: Die Entstehung des Abbe-Denkmals von Henry van de Velde, Max Klinger und

Constanin Meunier," in Wahl, *Jena als Kunststadt,* 130–47; *TB,* September 5, 1911; Stamm, "Monumental Architecture," 318–21; van de Velde to Kessler, September 25, 1911, KN.

12. Förster-Nietzsche to Kessler, April 21, 1911, GSA 72 1798, and April 20, 1911, GSA, 72 1393.

13. Ibid., October 20, 1911, quoted in Stamm, "Monumental Architecture," 321; Kessler to Förster-Nietzsche, October 22, 1911, GSA, 72 1393.

14. Copy of letter of October 27, 1911, van de Velde Archives, BRA.

15. Stamm, "Monumental Architecture," 322; *TB,* November 29 and December 12, 1911; letter of December 12, 1911, van de Velde Archives, BRA.

16. Quoted in Stamm, "Monumental Architecture," 323.

17. *TB,* March 23, 1912.

18. Stamm, "Monumental Architecture," 325–30.

19. Ibid., 331–33; Simon, *Ein Briefwechsel,* December 7, 1913, January 4, March 4 and 6, 1914, 91–92, 95–98.

20. Stamm, "Monumental Architecture," 315. Stamm, who appears to know little about Kessler, misinterprets him as a kind of "Germanic" ideologue.

21. On these issues, see the very suggestive remarks by Andreas Huyssen, "Monumental Seduction," *New German Critique* (fall 1996), 181–201.

Chapter 15

1. Quoted in Wolfdietrich Rasch, "Tanz als Lebenssymbol im Drama um 1900," in his *Zur deutschen Literatur,* 65; Elizabeth Kendall, *Where She Danced* (New York: Knopf, 1979).

2. *TB,* October 21, 1891.

3. Ibid., January 26, 1903; *Twenties,* September 15, 1927, 328; *TB,* October 18, 1905, February 9, 1906.

4. Burger, *Briefwechsel,* October 26, 29, November 20, 1906, 130–1, 134. The comment about "the practically sub-human, almost animal sexual feeling of the oriental woman," while clearly reflecting a commonly held prejudice of the time, needs to be put into two contexts: first, Kessler's own, subconscious, ambivalence about female sexuality and second, his more manifest admiration for physicality.

5. Ruth St. Denis, *An Unfinished Life: An Autobiography* (New York: Harper, 1939), 89, 91.

6. Ibid., 95; see also *TB,* November 16 and 18, 1906.

7. *TB,* November 19 and 23, 1906; Burger, *Briefwechsel,* November 24, 1906, 138–39.

8. *TB,* December 10, 1906; Denis, *Unfinished Life,* 94–95.

9. Hofmannsthal, "Die unvergleichliche Tänzerin," in *Gesammelte Werke: I,* 497, 501.

10. For an excellent discussion of St. Denis, especially in comparison to Duncan, see Kendall, *Where She Danced,* 14–69.

11. Burger, *Briefwechsel,* May 28 and June 5, 1909, 234, 239–40.

12. On this milieu, see Arthur Gold and Robert Fizdale, *Misia: The Life of Misia Sert* (New York: Knopf, 1980), 125–61; Francis Steegmuller, *Cocteau: A Biography* (Boston: Little, Brown, 1970), 65–118; George D. Painter, *Marcel Proust: A Biography*, rev. ed., (London: Chatto & Windus, 1989), 160 ff.

13. *TB,* July 10, 1911; Kessler to Wilma de Brion, July 10 and February 17, 1911, KN

14. *TB,* July 4 and 12, 1911.

15. Burger, *Briefwechsel,* August 11, 1911, 329–34, 338.

16. Letter of March 8, 1912, quoted in *TB,* March 16, 1912; *TB,* May 25, 1912.

17. Kessler, "Die Entstehung der Josephs-Legende," in *Gesammelte Schriften II,* 277.

18. *TB,* June 5–6, 1912.

19. Kessler, "The Action of *Joseph,*" in *The Legend of Joseph* (Berlin and Paris, 1914), 13–14.

20. Ibid., 15–16.

21. Ibid., 25.

22. On Kessler's transformation of the biblical episode, see Gisela Bärbel Schmid, "Psychologische Umdeutung biblischer Archetype in Geiste des Fin de Siècle: Zur Entstehung der *Josephslegende,*" *Hofmannsthal Blätter* 35/36 (1987), 105–13.

23. Kessler to Wilma de Brion, August 6, 1912, KN.

24. Quoted in Schuster and Pehle, *Weltmannes,* 274, 276; Kessler to Wilma de Brion, September 21 and December 18, 1912, KN.

25. Diaghilev was to pay Strauss 100,000 marks in advance of which Hofmannsthal and Kessler would share 25,000, with an additional six percent royalty for each performance including certain guaranteed minimums (5,000 marks for each London performance).

26. Burger, *Briefwechsel,* June 4, 1913, 361.

27. Kessler to Wilma de Brion, October 13, 1913, KN.

28. Burger, *Briefwechsel,* undated fragment, 374.

29. Kessler to Wilma de Brion, March 19, 1914, KN.

30. Ibid., March 28, 1914.

31. Ibid., March 24, 1914.

32. Burger, *Briefwechsel,* June 28, 1912, 351; Kessler to Wilma de Brion, April 22, 1914, KN.

33. See Schmid, "Psychologische Umdeutung," 105; Hugo von Hofmannsthal and Ottonie Gräfin Degenfeld, *Briefwechsel,* rev. ed. (Frankfurt a. M.: S. Fischer, 1986), June 10, 1912, 227, and April 25, 1914, 307; Burger, *Briefwechsel,* April 11, 1914, 380. The discovery of Kessler's diaries has disproved many of the assertions about Hofmannsthal's role in the creation of the ballet, such as those advanced by Willi Schuh, "Hofmannsthal, Kessler und die *Josephslegende,*" *Hofmannsthal Blätter* 27 (spring 1983), 48–55.

34. On this, see Lynn Garafola, *Diaghilev's Ballets Russes* (Oxford: Oxford University Press, 1989), chap. 11; Kessler to Wilma de Brion, February 22 and 27, March 5, 1913, KN.

35. *Times,* June 24, 1914.

36. Ernest Newman, "The Strange Case of Richard Strauss," *The Nation*, June 27, 1914, reprinted in Bernard Shaw, *Shaw's Music: The Complete Musical Criticism in Three Volumes*, vol. 3: 1893–1950 (New York: Dodd, Mead, 1981), 648–75.

37. Schuster and Pehle, *Weltmannes*, 276; Norman del Mar, *Richard Strauss: A Critical Commentary on his Life and Works*, vol. 2 (Philadelphia: Chilton, 1969), 144 and see also, 124–50; Garafola, *Diaghilev*, 311; Ernst Krause quoted in Gerhard Brunner, "Richard Strauss und das Ballet," in *Richard Strauss, 1864– 1949* (Mainz, 1979), 93. For the performance history of *The Legend of Joseph*, see Günther Lesnig, "The 75th Anniversary of the *Josephs Legende*," *Richard Strauss Blätter* Neue Folge, 24 (December 1990), 6–36.

38. John Neumeier, "Mein Weg zu Josephs Weg," in *Programheft der Hamburgischen Staatsoper* (Hamburg, 1982), 8–9.

39. Kessler to Wilma de Brion, June 29 and 28, 1914, KN; *TB*, February 11, 1911.

40. Kessler to Wilma de Brion, August 19, 1911, KN; *TB*, December 11, 1911.

41. Kessler to Wilma de Brion, September 8 and 11, 1911, KN; *TB*, September 4, 1911.

42. *TB*, December 22, 1908; Burger, *Briefwechsel*, March 26, 1909, 216; quoted in *Rudolf Borchardt, Alfred Walter Heymel, Rudolf Alexander Schröder* (Marbach a. Neckar: Kösel, 1978), 178.

43. Kessler to Wilma de Brion, July 4, 1914, KN.

Chapter 16

1. Kessler to Wilma de Brion, July 30, 1914, KN.

2. See Eric. J. Leed, *No Man's Land: Combat & Identity in World War I* (New York: Cambridge University Press, 1979).

3. Harry Graf Kessler, *Krieg und Zusammenbruch aus Feldpostbriefen*, (Weimar: Cranach Presse, 1921), letter to Gustav Richter, August 13, 1914, 2–5; Burger, *Briefwechsel*, 17, August 1914, 384.

4. *Feldpostbriefen*, August 23, 1914, August 5 and 26, 1914, 7.

5. Ibid., August 26, 7; Millicent, Duchess of Sutherland, *Six Weeks at the War* (Chicago: A. C. McClurg, 1915), 42.

6. *Feldpostbriefen*, letter to Dora von Bodenhausen, August 25, 1914, 21–23.

7. Ibid., letter to Dora von Bodenhausen, November 25, 1914, quoted in Burger, *Briefwechsel*, 411–14. The Duchess of Sutherland also commented on the singing of the German troops in Namur: "I hear them singing as they march. They sing wonderfully—in parts as if well trained for this singing," Sutherland, *Six Weeks*, 30.

8. Modris Eksteins, *Rites of Spring: The Great War and the Birth of the Modern Age* (New York: Doubleday, 1989) 90–94; Paul Fussell, *The Great War and Modern Memory* (Oxford: Oxford University Press, 1975), 155–90, 231–69.

9. See particularly Norman Stone, *The Eastern Front, 1914–1917* (New York: Scribner, 1975). Following in Stone's path, W. Bruce Lincoln wrote an excellent popular history of the Russian front, *Passage Through Armageddon: The Russians in War and Revolution* (New York: Simon & Schuster, 1986).

10. Quoted in Donald Prater, *A Ringing Glass: The Life of Rainer Maria Rilke* (Oxford: Oxford University Press, 1986), 285.

11. Burger, *Briefwechsel,* November 25, 1914, 412.

12. *TB,* January 1, 1915.

13. See Norman Stone, "The Winter Carpathian Campaign," in *The Marshall Cavendish Illustrated Encyclopedia of World War I,* vol. 2: 1914–1915 (New York; Marshall Cavendish, 1984), 593–97.

14. *TB,* January 23, 1915; *Feldpostbriefen,* letter to Gustav Richter, February 1, 1915, 37.

15. Burger, *Briefwechsel,* January 28, 1915, 415.

16. Ibid., January 27, 1915, 390.

17. *TB,* February 6, 1915.

18. Stone, "Winter Campaign," 594.

19. Ibid., 109–14; Lincoln, *Passage,* 120–21.

20. *TB,* February 24, 1915; Hofmannsthal and Degenfeld, *Briefwechsel* March 7, 1915, 318.

21. *TB,* February 28 and March 4, 1915.

22. Ibid., March 10, 1915.

23. Ibid., April 25, 1915; *Feldpostbriefen,* letter to Helene von Nostitz, April 9, 1915, 49; Kessler to Wilma de Brion, November 18, 1914, KN.

24. Heinrich Vogeler, *Erinnerungen,* ed. Erich Weinert (Berlin: Rütten & Loening, 1952), 201.

25. *TB,* May 20, 1915. Fussell has a great deal of interest to say on the theme of soldiers bathing in English poetry and letters, *Great War,* 299–309; Kessler to Wilma de Brion, May 7, 1915, KN; *TB,* April 6, 1914.

26. *TB,* April 4 and 5, 1915; *Feldpostbriefen,* letters to Gustav Richter, August 11, 1915, 64, 71–76, and July 11, 1915, 76.

27. *TB,* July 20, 1915, and June 11, July 12, 1915.

28. *TB,* July 13, 1914; Kessler to Wilma de Brion, July 29, 1915, KN.

29. *Feldpostbriefen,* letter to Gustav Richter, September 12, 1915, 85.

30. *TB,* September 12, 1915; *Feldpostbriefen,* letter to Gustav Richter, September 12, 1915, 89.

31. *Feldpostbriefen,* letter to Gustav Richter, September 25, 1915, 91; Kessler to Wilma de Brion, September 29, 1915, KN.

32. *TB,* September 15, 1915.

33. Ibid., August 7–8, 1915.

34. Ibid., October 21, 1915.

35. Vogeler, *Erinnerungen,* 201–3. Vogeler, however, has his dates wrong here, claiming that Kessler was investigating the aftermath of the Brusilov offensive. This initially successful Russian offensive took place in July 1916, however, long after Kessler was in Switzerland; *TB,* October 29, 1915.

Chapter 17

1. On the history of Poland, see Norman Davies, *God's Playground: A History of Poland, vol. 2: 1795 to the Present* (New York: Columbia University Press, 1982) and the condensed version, *Heart of Europe: A Short History of Poland* (Oxford: Oxford University Press, 1984). On the relations between Germans and Poles, see William W. Hagen, *Germans, Poles, and Jews: The Nationality Conflict in the Prussian East, 1772–1914,* (Chicago: University of Chicago Press, 1980); Harry Kenneth Rosenthal, *German and Pole: National Conflict and Modern Myth,* (Gainesville, Fla.: University Presses of Florida, 1976). On the German approach to the Polish question during the First World War, see Werner Conze, *Polnische Nation und Deutsche Politik im Ersten Weltkrieg* (Cologne: Böhlau, 1958).

2. *TB,* November 18, 1914.

3. Burger, *Briefwechsel,* November 7, 1914, 386.

4. See, for example, the communications from General Headquarters to the Foreign Office, calling for, among other things, the expulsion of Polish Jews from the parts of Poland to be annexed by the Germans, the telegram of October 8, 1917, and memorandum of October 20, 1917, collected in *L'Allemagne et les Problèmes de la Paix pendant la Première Guerre Mondiale: vol. 2, De la guerre sous-marine a outrance a la révolution soviétique,* ed. André Scherer and Jacques Grunewald (Paris: Presses Universitaires de France, 1966), 495–96, 510–16.

5. According to Hans-Ulrich Simon in *Ein Briefwechsel,* 190. I have not been able to confirm this. See also *TB,* July 28, 1916.

6. See Conze, *Polnische Nation,* 106–24; 138–225.

7. *TB,* December 14, 1914. Kessler was influenced here by a book that his friend Mutius had given him, entitled *Essential Elements of World Politics in the Present (Grundzüge der Weltpolitik in der Gegenwart).* The author, while criticizing the ultra-German nationalists, holds up British history as a model for the proper path to world power. The secret of the success of the British Empire, as well as the key to its future, is that its domination is not based simply on brute force or economic interest, but comes also as a result of the attraction radiated by the ideal of the British gentleman. If Germany aspires to the status of a lasting world power, the author asserts, then it must reverse the cultural decline all too evident in the last decades; see J. J. Ruedorffer (Kurt Riezler), *Grundzüge der Weltpolitik in der Gegenwart* (Stuttgart: Deutsche Verlagsanstalt, 1915), 111–15; *TB,* October 1, 1915, April 2, 1915.

8. Alistair Horne, *The Price of Glory: Verdun 1916* (Harmondsworth: Penguin, 1984) is the best single volume in English on the battle.

9. See John Röhl's translation and introduction to Lichnowsky's text "Delusion or Design?" in *1914: Delusion or Design? The Testimony of Two German Diplomats* (New York: St. Martin's Press, 1973).

10. *TB,* April 13, 1916.

11. This is the argument of Eksteins, *Rites,* 84 ff, 257 ff. It would be inaccurate, however, to characterize the astonishing flood of war poetry as forward-

looking, revolutionary, or even vaguely avant-garde. Most of it was, in fact, deeply conventional and conservative, both in themes and in form.

12. Kessler to Wilma de Brion, December 12, 1910, KN; *TB*, August 8, 1916.

13. Kessler to Anton Kippenberg, May 2, 1916, KN.

14. *TB*, June 15, 1916.

15. Quoted in Schuster and Pehle, *Weltmannes*, 302–3.

16. Ibid., 301.

17. *TB*, August 21, 1916.

18. Kessler, *Walther Rathenau: His Life & Work* (New York: Harcourt, Brace & Company, 1930), 241; on the "Wednesday Society," see the article on the Mittwoch-Gesellschaft in *Lexikon zur Parteiengeschichte. Die bürgerlichen und kleinbürgerlichen Parteien und Verbände in Deutschland (1789–1945)*, ed. Dieter Fricke et al., (Leipzig: VEB Bibliographisches Institut Leipzig, 1983–86), 381–83.

19. *TB*, April 19, 20, 21, 26, and 30, 1916; for the fighting in April and May, see Horne, *Price of Glory*, 165–89.

20. *TB*, April 30, 1916.

21. Ibid., May 10, 12, and 14, 1916. I have not been able to find any evidence that indicates the exact reason for Kessler's abrupt departure from Verdun; some kind of nervous breakdown is the most reasonable conjecture; see also Grupp, *Kessler*, 166–68.

Chapter 18

1. *TB*, September 3, 1916.

2. Ibid., September 8 and 9, 1916.

3. Simon, *Ein Briefwechsel*, August 13, 1916, 112–13; Bodenhausen, *Ein Leben*, 326–27.

4. Michael Sanders and Philip M. Taylor, *British Propaganda during the First World War, 1914–1918* (London: Macmillan, 1982), 256; L. L. Farrar, Jr., "Nationalism in Wartime: Critiquing the Conventional Wisdom," in *Authority, Identity, and the Social History of the Great War*, ed. Frans Coetzee and Marilyn Shevin-Coetzee (Providence, R.I.: Berghahn Books, 1995), 138; For the British side, see especially Sanders and Taylor, *British Propaganda*; for Germany, see Peter Grupp, "Voraussetzung und Praxis deutscher amtlicher Kulturpropaganda in den neutralen Staaten während des Ersten Weltkrieges," in *Der erste Weltkrieg: Wirkung, Wahrnehmung und Analyse*, ed. Wolfgang Michalka (Munich: Piper, 1994), 799–824; see the judicious assessment in Sanders and Taylor, *British Propaganda*, 246–65.

5. *TB*, September 14, 18, October 2, and November 7, 1916.

6. Ibid., October 1, 1916.

7. Richard Lemp, *Annette Kolb: Leben und Werk einer Europäerin* (Mainz: Von Hase und Koehler, 1970); Kessler to Wilma de Brion, August 16, 1917, KN; In the context of 1916, "J'Accuse" referred to the 1915 pamphlet by the same title written by the peace activist Richard Grelling that accused the German

government of deliberately provoking the war in order to establish German hegemony within Europe and to preserve the political privileges of the Junker class. Grelling's jeremiad became an important weapon in the arsenal of Entente propaganda; see Friedrich-Karl Scheer, *Die deutsche Friedensgesellschaft (1892–1933): Organization, Ideologie, politischen Ziele* (Frankfurt a. M.: Haag & Herchen, 1981), 336–37; *TB,* November 28, 1916. On Schickele's political views, see the articles in *Elsässer, Europäer, Pazifist: Studien zu René Schickele,* ed. Adrien Finck and Maryse Staiber (Kehl: Morstadt, 1984).

8. *TB,* August 27, 1916. At the same time, he admitted that he himself was not—yet—a convinced democrat.

9. Ibid., September 28, 1916. Reprinted in part in Schuster and Pehle, *Weltmannes,* 310–11. Herzfelde himself has described both the journal *Neue Jugend* and his encounter with Kessler in his memoirs, *Immergrün: Merkwürdige Erlebnisse und Erfahrungen eines fröhlichen Waisenknaben* (Berlin/Weimar: Aufbau-Verlag, 1981) and essays entitled *Zur Sache geschrieben and gesprochen zwischen 18 und 80* (Berlin/Weimar: Aufbau-Verlag, 1976); *TB,* November 18, 1918; reprinted in Schuster and Pehle, *Weltmannes,* 311–12.

10. *TB,* October 1, 1917, and June 16, 1918; Schuster and Pehle, *Weltmannes,* 313; Romain Rolland, *Zwischen den Völkern: Aufzeichnungen und Dokumente aus den Jahren 1914–1919, vol. 2* (Stuttgart: Deutsche Verlagsanstalt, 1955), 489.

11. Peter Grupp, "Harry Graf Kessler als Diplomat," *Vierteljahrshefte für Zeitgeschichte* (1992), 64; *TB,* May 25, 1918.

12. *TB,* September 14 and November 23, 1916.

13. Grupp, "Kulturpropaganda," 811; letter dated November 8, 1916 from Kessler to Romberg, found in the collection "Essais de pacification" in the KN in Marbach; see also PA, Gesandtschaft Bern, Bde 1373–1377 for further details of Kessler's cultural propaganda activities in Switzerland.

14. *TB,* January 10, 1918. See also René Schickele's journal in his *Werke in drei Bänden, Dritter Band: Aufsätze und Reden, Tagebücher,* (Cologne/Berlin: Kiepenheuer & Witsch, 1959), 1013; Grupp, "Kulturpropaganda," 812; Grupp suggests that Kessler did not really hold expressionist art in high esteem, 171. But his early membership in *Die Brücke,* his support of Max Beckmann, the deep impression that the memorial exhibition for Franz Marc made on him, and his interest in Grosz, all prove the opposite; Schuster and Pehle, *Weltmannes,* 295–97; Jacob Ruchti, *Geschichte der Schweiz während des Weltkrieges 1914–1919, politisch, wirtschaftlich, und kulturell* (Bern: P. Haupt, 1928–29), 369; "The result of the two exhibitions was without a doubt a victory of France," in Ruchti, *Geschichte der Schweiz; TB,* June 11, 1918, and February 3, 1917.

15. Hans Barkhausen, *Filmpropaganda für Deutschland im Ersten und Zweiten Weltkrieg* (Hildesheim: Olms Presse, 1982). Evidence of Kessler's involvement in the organization of film propaganda may be found scattered throughout the diary, in the folder "Essais de pacification" in the Kessler Nachlaß, and in PA, Gesandtschaft Bern, 1373–76.

16. Barkhausen, *Filmpropaganda,* 110–11. According to Herzfelde, the last remaining copy of the film was stolen from his brother's room in the course

of a burglary in the 1920s—a very great loss, it would appear, to the history of film.

17. *TB,* January 12, 1918.

18. L. L. Farrar, Jr., *Divide and Conquer: German Efforts to Conclude a Separate Peace, 1914–1918* (New York: Columbia University Press, 1978), 10–12; passim. The most important documents concerning German diplomatic initiatives may be found in Scherer and Grunewald, *L'Allemagne.* On the general problems of secret diplomacy during the war, see Guy Pedronicini, *Les negotiations secretes pendant la grande guerre* (Paris: Flammarion, 1969). His pessimistic evaluations of the chances for either a separate or general peace settlement of the First World War are substantially echoed by David Stevenson, *The First World War and International Politics* (Oxford: Oxford University Press, 1991), 13–26, 181–82; Pedronicini, *Negotiations secretes,* 107.

19. Farrar, *Divide,* 35–56.

20. On this, see Kessler's report to Romberg, in Scherer and Grunewald, *L'Allemagne* #18, March 14, 1917, 28–31; see Zuckerkandl's memoirs, *Österreich intim; Erinnerungen, 1892–1942,* 2d ed., (Vienna: Amalthea, 1981); her letter to Kessler, September 23, 1917, reprinted in Schuster and Pehle, *Weltmannes,* 297–98; also Scherer and Grunewald, *L'Allemagne* #198, August 12, 1917, 330.

21. Several regiments of the French army actually mutinied in the spring of 1917, although the Germans never apparently learned of this. For the "crisis in morale," see Jean-Jacques Becker, *The Great War and the French People* (Leamington Spa: Berg Press, 1993), 217–35; Jean-Jacques Becker and Serge Bernstein, *Victoire et frustrations, 1914–1929* (Paris: Editions du Seuil, 1990), 118; see his long report of April 17 in Scherer and Grunewald, *L'Allemagne* #72, April 17, 1917, 119; #199, August 13, 1917, 331; and #204, August 14, 1917, 337.

22. Scherer and Grunewald, *L'Allemagne* #404, December 4, 1916, 594–97.

23. Ibid., #404, December 5, 1916, 598–99; #421, December 13, 1916, 616; and *TB,* December 12, 1916. Such conditions corresponded to Zimmermann's confidence in Germany's military position, see Farrar, *Divide,* 8.

24. *TB,* October 3, 1917; December 31, 1917; April 5, 1918.

25. Ibid., May 18, October 24 and 25, 1918; Pedronicini, *Negotiations secretes,* 25; Stevenson, *First World War,* 168.

26. *TB,* February 1 and March 3, 1918.

27. Winfried Baumgart, *Deutsche Ostpolitik 1918: Von Brest-Litovsk bis zum Ende des Ersten Weltkrieges* (Vienna: Oldenbourg, 1966), 27, 33. See also Richard Pipes, *The Russian Revolution* (New York: Vintage, 1990), 567–605; Fritz Fischer, *Germany's Aims in the First World War* (New York: Norton, 1967), 475–509; Hans W. Gatzke, "Zu den deutschen-russischen Beziehungen im Sommer 1918," *Vierteljahrshefte für Zeitgeschichte* (1955), 67–98.

28. See the record of the conference among the kaiser, the military, and civilian leaders at Spa, in which Ludendorff argues that the Germans cannot afford to antagonize the Cossacks of the Don basin for fear of losing the connection to the Baku oil fields, reprinted in Gatzke, "Beziehungen," 84–90.

29. *TB,* February 4, 1918; Baumgart, *Deutsche Ostpolitik 1918,* 262–70.

30. *TB,* July 5 and 22, 1918; July 8, 1918, Gatzke, "Beziehungen," 92–96; *TB,* July 6, 19, 23, and 29, 1918.

31. *TB,* July 29, 1918.

Chapter 19

1. Léon Daudet, *La Vermine du Monde: Roman de l'Espionnage Allemand* (Paris: A. Fayard, 1916), 55–59.

2. *TB,* November 29, 1916; Alexander Arsène, "Espions and Déménageurs," *Le Figaro,* January 5, 1915. See Daudet's repetition of this charge, "L'Art Boche," *L'Action francaise,* January 6, 1915.

3. *TB,* March 6 and September 27, 1918. See also Grupp, *Kessler,* 173.

4. *TB,* May 11 and March 27, 1918.

5. Ibid., August 3 and February 5, 1918.

6. Ibid., December 13, 1917; January 22, July 17, and February 16, 1918.

7. Ibid., November 1, 1917; see Prater, *Ringing Glass,* 285–86 for the impact of Kessler's remarks on Rilke; *TB,* September 26 and February 18, 1918.

8. *TB,* March 27, 1918.

9. Ibid., January 10, 1918; Schickele, *Werke,* 1017.

10. *TB,* January 12 and June 4, 1918.

11. Ibid., January 12, June 23, and March 27, 1918.

12. Ibid., August 17, 1918.

13. Ibid., May 23, June 9, and July 16, 1918.

14. Keith Robbins, *The First World War* (Oxford: Oxford University Press, 1984), 76; *TB,* October 3, 1917.

15. See Ulrich Heinemann, *Die verdrängte Niederlage: Politische Öffentlichkeit und Kriegsschuldfrage in der Weimarer Republik* (Göttingen: Vandenhoeck & Ruprecht, 1983).

16. *TB,* June 4 and 12, 1918.

17. Ibid., July 20, 24, and 31, 1918.

18. Ibid., September 26 and 30, 1918.

19. Ibid., October 4, 1918.

20. Ibid.

Chapter 20

1. Kessler's embrace of democracy, the Weimar republic, and pacifism did not quite happen overnight, as Grupp suggests, but had roots going back at least to his first contacts with Becher, and even beyond; Grupp, *Kessler,* 179–82.

2. *TB,* February 3 and 19, 1918.

3. On Kessler's mission to Poland, see Leon Grosfeld, "Misja Hrabiego Kesslera w Warszawie," *Dzieje Najnowsze Rocznik,* 2 (1970) (with summary in French), 17–30; and Kurt Georg Haussmann, "Pilsudski und die Mission des

Grafen Kessler in Polen," in *Geschichte und Gegenwart: Festschrift für Karl Dietrich Erdmann,* ed. Harmut Boockmann, et al. (Neumünster: Wachholtz, 1980), 233–73.

4. *TB,* November 7 and 8, 1918.

5. Ibid., November 9, 1918.

6. Ibid., November 14, 16, and 17, 1918.

7. Davies, *Heart of Europe,* 115–21; Richard M. Watt, *Bitter Glory: Poland and its Fate, 1918–1939* (New York: Simon & Schuster, 1979), 44–89.

8. *Twenties,* November 20, 1918, 15–16.

9. *TB,* November 22 and 23, 1918; Haussmann, "Pilsudski," 250–52.

10. *Twenties,* November 23–28, 1918, 19–23; on Korfanty's activities in Upper Silesia, see Watt, *Bitter Glory,* 157–60.

11. See Kessler's warning to the Foreign Office and related documents, #s 32 and 33 in *Akten zur Deutschen Auswärtigen Politik 1918–1945: Series A. Vol. 1: November 1918–March 1919,* (Göttingen: Vandenhoeck & Rupprecht, 1994); *Twenties,* November 28–30, December 1, 1918, 23–26.

12. *Twenties,* December 8–11, 1918, 29–30.

13. Ibid., December 15, 1918, 35.

14. Haussmann, "Pilsudski," 264.

15. See Grupp, "Kessler als Diplomat," 68.

16. For the definitive study of the German demobilization and the fears that it provoked among the experts, see Richard Bessel, *Germany After the First World War* (Oxford: Oxford University Press, 1993), 49–68 and passim.

17. The literature on the German revolution is enormous. I have relied on A. J. Ryder, *The German Revolution of 1918: A Study of German Socialism in War and Revolt* (Cambridge: Cambridge University Press, 1967); Ulrich Kluge, *Die deutsche Revolution, 1918/1919: Staat, Politik und Gesellschaft zwischen Weltkrieg und Kapp-Putsch* (Frankfurt a. M.: Suhrkamp, 1985); Reinhard Rürup "Problems of the German Revolution 1918–1919," *Journal of Contemporary History* 3 (1968), 109–35; Wolfgang J. Mommsen, "The German Revolution, 1918–1920: Political Revolution and Social Protest," in Mommsen, *Imperial Germany,* 233–54.

18. *Twenties,* December 23, 1918, 40.

19. *TB,* January 8, 1919.

20. Ibid., February 15, 1919.

21. On this phenomenon, see Istvan Deak, *Weimar Germany's Left-Wing Intellectuals: A Political History of the Weltbühne and Its Circle* (Berkeley, Calif.: University of California, 1968); *Twenties,* March 1, 1919, 78.

22. *Twenties,* January 14, 1919, 57.

23. *TB,* February 15 and 19, 1919; see also Grupp, *Kessler,* 189; Wollkopf, "Nietzsche Archiv," 137.

24. *TB,* March 19, 1919.

25. Ryder, *German Revolution,* 208–17; Kluge, *Die deutsch Revolution,* 107–29.

26. *TB,* March 31, 1919; *Twenties,* March 8 and 12, 1919, 83–86.

27. *TB,* March 14, 21–23, 25, and 29, 1919.

28. Ibid., December 4, 1919; Kessler, "Das Marburger Urteil," *Die deutsche Nation,* 2 (July 1920) in *Gesammelte Schriften,* vol. 2, 195.

29. *Twenties,* March 13, 1919, 86–87.

30. Both were destined to return to the Sozialistische Partei Deutschlands (SPD) and serve as its chief theoreticians, Breitscheid specializing in foreign relations and Hilferding, a brilliant economist, in finance. Sadly, both died at the hands of the Nazis. See the short sketches in Peter D. Stachura, ed., *Political Leaders in Weimar Germany* (New York: Simon & Schuster, 1993), 21–22; 81–83; *Twenties,* January 15, 1919, 57–58. In fact, Rantzau was both a committed democrat and a capable diplomat who served Germany well as ambassador in the Soviet Union from 1922 until his premature death in 1928, see Stachura, *Political Leaders,* 22–23. There is more than a touch of jealousy in Kessler's remarks; *Twenties,* March 4, 1919, 79.

31. For Kessler's negotiations, see the *TB,* March 4, 5, 6, 7, 9, and 12, 1919. Rantzau, forced to defend his role in this conspiracy before his fellow cabinet members, suggested that he had only wished to keep himself informed over domestic politics in order to function effectively as a foreign minister, hinting that Kessler had overstepped his instructions in the matter, see document 10b in *Das Kabinett Scheidemann. 13 Februar bis 20 Juni 1919,* edited by Hagan Schulze (Boppard am Rhein: H. Boldt, 1971).

32. See Grupp, "Kessler als Diplomat," 69; *TB,* December 17, 28, February 18, June 12, July 23, 1919; November 27, 1922; March 22, 1926; *Twenties,* December 28, 1918, 44.

33. *TB,* November 12, 1918.

34. Ibid., November 12 and December 23, 1918. For the November Club, see Peter Grupp, *Deutsche Außenpolitik im Schatten von Versailles: Zur Politik des Auswärtigen Amts vom Ende des Ersten Weltkrieges und der Novemberrevolution bis zum Inkrafttreten des Versailler Vertrags* (Paderborn: F. Schöningh, 1988), 15.

35. Theodor Heuss, *Erinnerungen, 1905–1933* (Tübingen: R. Wunderlich, 1963), 301; *TB,* February 15, 1919; see Grupp, *Kessler,* 184–90.

36. *Twenties,* February 8, 1919, 66; *TB,* February 18, 1919.

Chapter 21

1. See Grupp, *Kessler,* 179–84, although Grupp does acknowledge that there were antecedents.

2. *TB,* March 31, 1918.

3. Ibid., April 1, 1918.

4. Ibid., March 31, April 1, and February 5, 1918. On prewar German pacifism, see Roger Chickering, *Imperial Germany and a World without War: The Peace Movement and German Society, 1892–1914* (Princeton, N.J.: Princeton University Press, 1975); Karl Holl, *Pazifismus in Deutschland* (Frankfurt a. M.: Suhrkamp, 1988), 1–102; Friedrich-Karl Scheer, Friedengesellschaft, 11–235; *Pazifismus in Deutschland: Dokumente zur Friedenbewegung 1890–1939,* ed. Wolfgang Benz (Frankfurt a. M.: S. Fischer, 1988).

5. *TB*, November 1, 1918.

6. Ibid., November 1 and October 21, 1918.

7. *Twenties*, February 16, 1919, 68–69; *TB*, February 16, 1919.

8. For the text, see Schuster and Pehle, *Weltmannes*, 331–37.

9. See also his interview in the *Neues Wiener Abendblatt*, April 24, 1919 (reprinted in Schuster and Pehle, *Weltmannes*, 338–39) for further criticisms of the League of Nations. For a good introduction to the debates on the Allied side over the structure of the League, see Alan Sharp, *The Versailles Settlement: Peacemaking in Paris, 1919* (New York: St. Martin's Press, 1991), 42–76.

10. Kessler, *Walther Rathenau*, 221–22; Gerald D. Feldman, *Army, Industry, and Labor in Germany* (Providence, R.I.: Berg Press, 1992), 51; see also Wolfgang Kruse, "Kriegswirtschaft und Gesellschaftsvision: Walther Rathenau und die Organisierung des Kapitalismus," in *Die Extremen berühen sich. Walther Rathenau, 1867–1922*, ed. Hans Wilderotter (Berlin: Argon, 1993), 151–67.

11. Walther Rathenau, *Die neue Wirtschaft* (Berlin: S. Fischer, 1918), 56–58. Although officially designed to work on a nonprofit basis for the public good (defined in this case as helping Germany win the war), the war companies actually served, over the long run, the interests of the largest producers in each industrial branch, who were able to purchase the controlling interests in these war companies. Indeed, it was the high level of concentration in prewar German industry, its evolution into what Hilferding called "organized capitalism," that permitted the war companies to operate so effectively, as Rathenau himself acknowledged.

12. Kessler, *Rathenau*, 186, 200. See also Rathenau, *Wirtschaft*, 72–73.

13. The idea of a German *Sonderweg*, a "special path" between capitalism and communism, owed much to the wartime "Spirit of 1914." It was also attractive to radical right-wing thinkers, who spoke in terms of a "German communal economy" (*deutsche* Gemeinwirtschaft); see Kruse, "Kriegswirtschaft," 155–62. On the special role of work in German social thought, see Joan Campbell, *Joy in Work, German Work: The National Debate, 1800–1945* (Princeton, N.J.: Princeton University Press, 1989), including a discussion of Rathenau, 122–25. In his 1928 biography, Kessler, taking pains to distinguish Rathenau's ideas from the violent dictatorships associated with both communism and fascism, argued that "he himself had no belief either in the success of a sudden revolutionary transformation or of one brought about by over-hasty, though peaceful, means; because both the necessary increase of the means of production on the basis of economy, and the equally necessary change of mental attitude, must needs be slow to take effect. Thus the only transformation possible is a slow one; one which follows in the wake of increased production and changes in public opinion, though at the same time one which is consciously directed by its leaders and supported by the resources of the state," Kessler, *Rathenau*, 208–9.

14. Kessler, *Rathenau*, 194.

15. Walther Rathenau, *The New Society* (New York: Harcourt, Brace & Howe, 1921), 75. See also Kruse, "Kriegswirtschaft," 159; Kessler, *Rathenau*, 222, 227–28.

16. See Anthony W. Wright, "Guild Socialism Revisited," *Journal of Contemporary History* (1974), 165–80.

17. Kessler, "Gildensozialismus," originally in the *Vossische Zeitung*, August 8, 1920, now in *Gesammelte Schriften II*, 197–204; see also S. G. Hobson and A. R. Orage, *Guild Principles in War and Peace* (London: G. Bell and Sons, 1918). On Cole, see his *Self-Government in Industry* (Freeport, N.Y.: Books for Libraries Press, 1971, and Anthony W. Wright, *G. D. H. Cole and Socialist Democracy* (Oxford: Oxford University Press, 1979), esp. 13–101; Cole, *Self-Government*, 121; "Gildensozialismus," 199; Wright, "Guild Socialism," 173.

18. Wright, while summing up the reasons for its decline, argues that guild socialism nevertheless influenced mainstream British socialist thinking; Wright, *Cole*, 105–38.

19. Rathenau prophesied the triumph of spirit (*Geist*) over mechanization, and the guild socialists never made a secret of their belief in the necessity of idealism and of spirituality, see Kessler, *Rathenau*, 102–20; Hobson and Orage, *Guild Principles*, 86.

20. See Christoph M. Kimmich, *Germany and the League of Nations* (Chicago: University of Chicago Press, 1975), 1–22, as well as Ursula Fortuna, *Der Völkerbundsgedanke in Deutschland während des Ersten Weltkrieges* (Zürich: Europa Verlag, 1974).

21. *Twenties*, April 18, 1919, 96.

22. Ibid., April 22–24, 1919, 97–98; see Grupp's discussion in *Kessler*, 203–9; Kimmich, *Germany and the League of Nations*, 19–21; also Lothar Albertin, *Liberalismus und Demokratie am Anfang der Weimarer Republik* (Düsseldorf: Droste, 1972), 320–22.

23. Kimmich, *Germany and the League of Nations*, 23–32.

24. *Twenties*, June 12 and 24, 1919, 101, 104; July 23–24, 1919, 105–6.

25. Ibid., June 22, 1919, 102; September 2, 1919, 110.

26. Kessler to Wilma de Brion, December 5, 1919, KN.

27. *Twenties*, May 25, 1920, 126. See also the entries for May 16–18, 29, June 9, 16–18, and November 22, 24, 1920.

28. See the articles on the Deutsche Friedenskartell (German Peace Cartel), the Deutsche Friedensgesellschaft (German Peace Society), and the Deutsche Liga für Menschenrechte (German League for Human Rights) in Dieter Fricke et al., eds., *Lexikon der Parteiengeschichte: Die bürgerlichen und kleinbürgerlichen Parteien und Verbände in Deutschland (1789–1945)*, 4 vols. (Leipzig: VEB Bibliographisches Institut Leipzig, 1983–86), 347–57, 667–99, 749–59.

29. *Twenties*, October 2, 1920, 132–33; see Grupp, *Kessler*, 195, n. 66.

30. *Twenties*, June 23, 25, 1921, 141–43.

31. Ibid., December 11, 1921, 144; see also Reinhold Lütgemeier-Davin, *Pazifismus zwischen Kooperation und Konfrontation: Das Deutsche Friedenskartell in der Weimarer Republik* (Cologne: Pahl-Rugenstein, 1982), 207; *Twenties*, June 11, 1922, 181.

32. *TB*, January 21, 1919, quoted in Grupp, *Kessler*, 195; the intractable dilemmas facing pacifism are the theme of Karl Holl, *Pazifismus*, 138–219; quoted in Istvan Deak, *Weltbühne* 115–16; quoted in Scheer, *Friedengesellschaft* 508.

33. Hans Wehberg, *Voices of German Pacifism*, ed. Karl Holl (New York: Garland Publishers, 1972), 76.

34. *TB,* February 4, 19–20, 1926. Some members apparently conceded that thirty years hence they may recognize their error in expelling Kessler. One wonders how many who survived to 1956 recalled their decision at all. One fraternity "brother" who painted an unflattering portrait of Kessler in his autobiography published during the war was Joachim von Winterfeldt-Menkin, the president of the German Red Cross; see his *Jahreszeiten des Lebens,* (Berlin: Propyläen-Verlag, 1942), 126–27.

35. Quoted in Grupp, *Kessler,* 198–99.

Chapter 22

1. See Marc Trachtenberg, *Reparations in World Politics: France and European Economic Diplomacy, 1916–1923* (New York: Columbia University Press, 1980), Walter A. McDougall, *France's Rhineland Diplomacy, 1914–1924: The Last Bid for a Balance of Power in Europe,* (Princeton, N.J.: Princeton University Press, 1978). On the question of Germany's ability to pay, see Sally Marks, "The Myth of Reparations," *Central European History* 11 (1978), 231–55, as well as her exchange with David Felix: Marks, "Reparations Reconsidered: A Reminder," *Central European History* 2 (1969), 356–65; Felix, "Reparations Reconsidered with a Vengeance," *Central European History* 4 (1971), 171–79, and Marks, "Reparations Reconsidered: A Rejoinder," *Central European History* 5 (1972). For a defense of the earlier view on reparations, see Peter Krüger's review article, "Das Reparationsproblem der Weimarer Republik in fragwürdiger Sicht: kritischer Überlegungen zur neuesten Forschung." *Vierteljahrhefte für Zeitgeschichte* (1989), 21–47, as well as Krüger's extensive treatment of the subject in *Die Aussenpolitik der Republik von Weimar* (Darmstadt: Wissenschaftliche Buchgesellschaft, 1985). The Australian scholar Bruce Kent offers an interesting twist on the older position; see his *The Spoils of War: The Politics, Economics, and Diplomacy of Reparations, 1918–1932* (Oxford: Oxford University Press, 1991) 8–11 and passim.

2. A good summary can be found in Sharp, *Versailles Settlement,* 80–83; see also Kent, *Spoils of War,* 28–40, 66–74, and Trachtenberg, *Reparations,* 29–97.

3. For example, his discussions with Stresemann, with Lord D'Abernon, the British ambassador to Germany, and with Andre-François Poncet, the French ambassador to Germany, and Robert Pinaud, a leading French industrialist, *TB,* June 25, 1920, February 20 and December 23, 1921; *Twenties,* March 20, 1922, 155.

4. Carole Fink, *The Genoa Conference: European Diplomacy, 1921–1922* (Chapel Hill, N.C.: University of North Carolina Press, 1984).

5. On Seydoux, see Krüger, *Aussenpolitik,* 116–22; Kessler mentions this meeting in his diaries (*Twenties,* April 10, 1922, 159–60) and in his *Rathenau,* 326–28.

6. "Pax Britannica," originally published in *Deutsche Nation* 6 (June 1922), 429–32, now in *Gesammelte Schriften II,* 255. See also "Genua oder Bar-le-Duc?" published in *Deutsche Nation* (May 4, 1922), 286–90, now in *Gesammelte Schriften II,* 245–52.

7. *Twenties,* June 25, 1922, 184; November 7, 1922, 196; *TB,* July 1, 1922.

8. *TB,* November 10, 1922, 360; *TB,* November 9, 1922.

9. *Twenties,* November 27, 1922, 199.

10. *ADAP (Akten zur deutschen aüswartigen Politik: Series A. Vol. VI,* document #45, report of Mutius, April 6, 1922.

11. *ADAP: Series A. Vol. VII,* document #27, report of Hoesch, January 16, 1923; Grupp, *Kessler,* 213; see also the entry on Schubert in *Biographisches Lexikon zur Weimarer Republik,* ed. Wolfgang Benz and Hermann Graml (Munich: C. H. Beck, 1988).

12. *TB,* January 28, 1923.

13. See the correspondence between Sthamer and Berlin on the progress of these negotiations, *ADAP. Series A: Vol. VII,* documents #116, March 1, 1923, 149, March 17, 1923.

14. Kessler to Wilma de Brion, March 25, 1923, KN; *Twenties,* March 14, 1923, 217, March 28, 1923, 226.

15. *Twenties,* March 19, 1923, 220.

16. On Kessler's diplomatic activity in the spring of 1923 and Schubert's response see, in addition to the documents cited above, Schubert's correspondence with Albert Dufour-Feronce, a legation aide in the German embassy, *ADAP. Series A. Vol. VII,* documents #150, 168, and 171, of March 19, 29, and 31, 1923, respectively, where both men speak of Kessler's "very useful activity." See also Grupp, "Kessler als Diplomat," 72–73; *Twenties,* April 4, 1923, 228; *TB,* April 6, 1923; Kessler to Wilma de Brion, April 8, 1923, KN.

17. *ADAP. Series A. Vol. VII,* document #16, June 11, 1923. That Kessler's hopes of becoming ambassador were not entirely without foundation see Schubert's letter to Dufour in the embassy, complaining of Sthamer's inactivity and praising Kessler; ibid., document #38, June 25, 1923.

18. Kessler to Wilma de Brion, March 28, 1923, KN; *TB,* July 7, 10, and 11, 1923.

Chapter 23

1. Stefan Zweig, "Die Monotonisierung der Welt," *Berliner Bösen-Courier,* (February 1, 1925), quoted in *The Weimar Republic Sourcebook,* ed. Anthony Kaes, Martin Jay, and Edward Dimendberg, (Berkeley, Calif.: University of California Press, 1994), 397; the literature on the American image in Germany is enormous. For good introductions see, Detlev Peukert, *Die Weimarer Republik* (Frankfurt a. M.: Suhkamp, 1987), 178–90; Mary Nolan, *Visions of Modernity: American Business and the Modernization of Germany* (New York: Oxford University Press, 1995), especially chapter 6, "The Cultural Consequences of Americanization"; and the primary documents collected in Kaes, et al., *Sourcebook,* 393–411.

2. *TB,* July 19, 1923; Kessler to Wilma de Brion, July 19, 1923, KN.

3. *TB,* July 20 and 24, 1923; see Wiedfeldt's report of July 31, 1923, with the enclosure of Kessler's report in, PA, Abt. III, USA, Pol. 26, Vols. 4 and 5; see

also Melvin P. Leffler, *The Elusive Quest: America's Pursuit of European Stability and French Security, 1919–1933* (Chapel Hill, N.C.: University of North Carolina Press, 1979), 82–90, and Werner Link, *Die amerikanische Stabilisierungspolitik in Deutschland 1921–32* (Düsseldorf: Droste Verlag, 1970), 176–89.

4. Ernest Dimnet, *My New World* (New York: Simon & Schuster, 1937), 297.

5. Wiedfeldt report, September 1, 1923, PA, Abt. III, USA, Vols. 4 and 5; *TB,* August 3, 1923.

6. Dimnet, *World,* 300.

7. Ibid., 302.

8. Kessler, *Germany and Europe,* (New Haven, Conn.: Yale University Press, 1924), 137. Italics in the original.

9. Ibid., 129.

10. Kessler to Schubert, August 14, 1923, PA, Abt. III, USA, Vols. 4 and 5. Kessler's impressions were largely confirmed by Wiedfeldt who, although he was not present in Williamstown, followed the press reports carefully; *TB,* August 16, 1923.

11. Kessler to Schubert, August 14, 1923, PA, Abt. III, USA, Vols. 4 and 5; see also his report to Dieckhoff, August 14, 1923, PA, Abt. III, USA, Vols. 4 and 5, where he wrote, "It is a matter of attacking the chief position of the opponent; namely, the belief in the justice and the workability of the Versailles Treaty; in the particular wickedness of Germany and the nobility of the French policy of reparations. One cannot do this, however, if one attacks like a madman the entire line of the opponent, but only if one, as in war, applies a little strategy and diplomacy"; *The New York Times,* July 31, 1923, 16; August 8, 1923, 14; August 22, 1923, 14. See also the book review of Kessler's published lectures in *The New York Times Book Review,* February 24, 1924, 15; and August 19 and September 2, 1923.

12. Andrew Ten Eyck, "World Turmoil as Seen from Academic Shades," *The Outlook,* August 29, 1923, 660–61. See also the short remarks in the *New Republic,* August 8, 1923, 1.

13. Grupp, "Kessler als Diplomat," 75.

14. *TB,* September 8, 1923; Kessler to Wilma de Brion, August 30, 1923, KN.

15. *TB,* November 9–10, 13, 19, and December 14, 17, 1923.

16. Ibid., December 7, 1923. According to one expert, however, just about the only stable aspect of German policy in that turbulent month of November 1923 was the foreign policy of Schubert, Maltzan, and Stresemann, see Krüger, *Aussenpolitik,* 228.

17. *TB,* December 22, 1923.

18. Ibid., December 24, 1923.

19. Ibid., September 4 and December 25, 1923. On Schubert's opposition to Kessler, see Grupp, "Kessler als Diplomat," 75.

20. *TB,* December 31, 1923.

21. Ibid., February 21–24, 1924; Kessler to Wilma de Brion, February 23, 1924, KN.

22. *TB,* February 21, 1924.

23. Ibid., January 19 and March 18, 12, 1924; Kessler to Wilma de Brion, March 19, 1924, KN.

24. *TB*, February 26–29 and March 3–5, 1924.

25. Ibid., March 14, 1924. In a letter to his sister, Kessler described Mrs. Tingley as "an enthusiastic Germanophile, although 100% American (New Englander) and alltogether [*sic*] a most remarkable woman, especially when one takes into account that she is 72 and does and directs everything herself"; Kessler to Wilma de Brion, March 17, 1924, KN. On the theosophical movement in general and the Point Loma Institute in particular, see Bruce F. Campbell, *Ancient Wisdom Revived: A History of the Theosophical Movement* (Berkeley, Calif.: University of California Press, 1980), 131–40; Peter Washington, *Madame Blavatsky's Baboon: A History of the Mystics, Mediums, and Misfits Who Brought Spiritualism to America* (New York: Schocken Books, 1995), 108–14, 143–44. Pictures of the buildings and grounds of the Point Loma Institute may be found in the journal edited by Tingley, *The Theosophical Path* XII (May 1917), 445–48.

26. "Amerikanische Probleme: I. Der Schmelztiegel," *Deutsche Nation* 6 (July 1924), 36–41, and "Amerikanische Probleme: II. Die Geldmächte," *Deutsche Nation* 6 (August 1924), 102–7.

27. *TB*, February 1, 18, and March 20, 24, and 28, 1924; "Amerikanische Probleme: I," 40.

28. "Amerikanische Probleme: II," 105; *TB*, February 12, 1924.

29. Reports on Kessler's debate with Lyttleton (January 22, 1924) and his talk in San Francisco (March 6, 1924) may be found in, March 6, 1924, PA, Abt. III, USA, Vols. 4 and 5; *Chicago Tribune,* February 10, 1924; *TB,* April 25, 1924; "Kessler Expects Republic to Stand," *The New York Times,* April 26, 1924; Edgar Vincent, Viscount D'Abernon, *An Ambassador of Peace: Vol. 3: The Years of Recovery, January 1924–October 1926* (London: Hodder and Stoughton, 1930), 75.

30. *TB*, January 21, April 9, and May 1, 1924.

31. Ibid., February 6, 9, and April 30, 1924.

32. Ibid., January 6 and April 18, 1924; on Coudenhove-Kalergi, see Ralph White, "The Europeanism of Coudenhove-Kalergi," in *European Unity in Context: The Interwar Period,* ed. Peter M. R. Stirk (London: Pinter Publishers, 1989), 23–40; Kessler's review in *Deutsche Nation* 7 (March 1925), 182–89; *TB,* May 11, 1924.

Chapter 24

1. See Stephen A. Schuker, *The End of French Predominance in Europe: The Financial Crisis of 1924 and the Adoption of the Dawes Plan* (Chapel Hill, N.C.: University of North Carolina Press, 1976); also Becker and Bernstein, *Victoire,* 223–46.

2. Ibid., 180–97; Kent, *Spoils of War,* 245–86; Krüger, *Aussenpolitik,* 237–47; Leffler, *Elusive Quest,* 82–112.

3. *TB*, June 23, 30, and July 4, 1924.

4. Ibid., June 17–18, 1924; June 23, 30, and July 4, 1924.

5. Stresemann's position on the paramilitary units was ambivalent, as Kessler discovered; see Hans W. Gatzke, *Stresemann and the Rearmament of Germany*

(New York: Norton, 1954), 11–45; *TB,* July 25, 1924. See also the report of the German ambassador to Paris, Leopold Hoesch, on Kessler's impressions of French opinion in *ADAP. Series A. Vol. X,* document #118, June 3, 1924.

6. *TB,* August 9, 1924.

7. Ibid., August 10 and 3, 1924.

8. Ibid., August 14–17, 1924.

9. Ibid., August 11, 1924. On the politicization of the Nietzsche Archives in the 1920s and 1930s, see Justus H. Ulbricht and Frank Simon-Ritz, 'Heimstätte des Zarathustrawerkes': Personen, Gremien und Aktivitäten des Nietzsche-Archivs in Weimar 1896–1945, in *Wege nach Weimar,* ed. Hans Wilderotter and Michael Dorrmann (Weimar: Jouis, 1999).

10. *ADAP. Series A. Vol. VII,* document #19, Cuno's instructions, June 15, 1923; #35, Sthamer's report, June 23, 1923, and #42, embassy summary, June 27, 1923; *TB,* August 29, 1924.

11. See Kimmich, *Germany and the League of Nations,* and Jürgen Spenz, *Die diplomatische Vorgeschichte des Beitritts Deutschlands zum Völkerbund, 1924–1926* (Göttingen: Musterschmidt, 1966).

12. See Bülow's aide-mémoire prepared for the cabinet on the issue of Germany and the League of Nations in Abramowski, *Akten der Reichskanzlei,* 1044–50.

13. *TB,* August 28, 1924. See also Maltzan's telegram urging Kessler to be cautious in his discussions and expressing pessimism over the prospects of Germany being able to join the League in the near future, *ADAP. Series A. Vol. X,* document #62, September 3, 1924.

14. *TB,* August 31, 1924.

15. *ADAP. Series A. Vol. X,* document #63, Kessler's report on his meeting, September 3, 1924; the note was issued on August 29, see document #290 in Abramowski, *Akten der Reichskanzlei,* 1006–7.

16. *ADAP. Series A. Vol. XI,* documents #67, September 6, 1924; #90, September 21, 1924; and document #106, October 9, 1924; on Müller, see Karl Heinrich Pohl, "Ein sozialdemokratischer Frondeur gegen Stresemanns Aussenpolitik: Adolf Müller und Deutschlands Eintritt in den Völkerbund," in *Aspekte deutscher Aussenpolitik im 20 Jahrhundert,* ed. Wolfgang Benz and Hermann Graml (Stuttgart: Deutsche Verlags-Anstalt, 1976), 68–86; *TB,* September 4–7, 1924; on the German surprise at MacDonald's speech and on Müller and the League of Nations, see Kimmich, *Germany and the League of Nations,* 32–34.

17. *TB,* September 9–11, 1924. Both Spenz, *Völkerbund,* 28–29, and Kimmich, *Germany and the League of Nations,* 55–56, portray Kessler as a naïve enthusiast who, disregarding his instructions and cautionary telegrams from Maltzan, pressed for Germany's acceptance at a time when the ground was not yet prepared. Grupp, *Kessler,* 217–9, agrees but adds that Kessler was not operating with the same assumptions and rules as the career diplomats: he was looking for the dramatic gesture that would alter those rules entirely.

18. See Abramowski, *Akten der Reichskanzlei,* 1050–62 for the cabinet deliberations.

19. *TB,* September 23–25, 1924.

20. Quoted in ibid., October 3, 1924; *ADAP. Series A. Vol. XI,* document #62, footnote 2, October 13, 1924; *TB,* October 7, 1924.

21. *TB,* September 18, 1924.

22. Ibid., November 25, 1924.

23. Ibid., December 9, 1924, 413.

24. *ADAP. Series A. Vol. XII,* document #162, report of Kessler to Schubert, March 12, 1925, and *Vol. XIII,* document #107, report to Schubert, June 10, 1925.

25. Kessler to Wilma de Brion, February 1, 1925, KN; see the reports on his visit in the *Manchester Guardian,* February 28, 1925; and the *Yorkshire Observer,* March 3, 1925; *Twenties,* March 2, 1925, 253.

Chapter 25

1. The source is unreliable as Nabokov laced his lengthy recollections of Kessler with much free invention, but many friends confirm the gist of it; see Nicolas Nabokov, *Bagázh: Memoirs of a Russian Cosmopolitan* (New York: Atheneum, 1975), 120–22.

2. Rothenstein, *Summer's Lease,* 177.

3. For example, Detlev Peukert, *Die Weimarer Republik,* 8; Gordon A. Craig, *Germany 1866–1945* (Oxford: Oxford University Press, 1978), 470; and Gay, *Weimar Culture,* xiii.

4. *Twenties,* February 24, 1926, 283–84.

5. Ibid.

6. Ibid., December 18, 1924, 233.

7. Ibid., May 19, 1926, 295; September 27, 1928, 349; January 29, 1925, 247; Kessler to Wilma de Brion, March 5, 1926, KN.

8. Kessler visited Goertz while he was in a military hospital in Thorn in 1918 and referred to him as a young plant that flourished in military life, despite initial desperate resistance, *TB,* February 3, 1919.

9. For instance, in Capri one evening, after Kessler had finished reading to his guests one of Goertz's stories, a somewhat listless conversation ensued causing Goertz to suddenly shout, "I can't stand this boring chatter any longer!" and storm out of the room. A few days later, he worked himself into a rage over some poems by Becher that Kessler admired, *TB,* March 22 and April 9, 1927; Fischer Verlag rejected Goertz's stories, ibid., April 28, 1926.

10. After the Second World War, when he learned that van de Velde was making public inquiries into the whereabouts of Kessler's diaries, Goertz wrote to him several times and offered him a short reminiscence of Kessler. This pathetic and yet strangely poignant document is full of lies and misinformation, shocking in someone who knew both Kessler and his history so well. For example, he calls Edvard Munch, Munck, and claims he was Swedish; says that Kessler was educated at Harrow; that he had a pistol duel with Palézieux; that he loved

Switzerland; and so forth. As he wrote to van de Velde in 1948, allegedly await-
ing French naturalization along with his French wife and two small daughters,
he pleaded desperately with the Belgian for his assistance in publishing his reminiscence of Kessler so that he could "buy some additional foodstuffs." One
wonders what happened to Goertz in the tumultuous years between Kessler's
death and 1948; see Goertz to van de Velde, June 17, 1948, and "Zwischen zwei
Portraits: Erinnerungen an den Grafen Harry Kessler von Max Goertz," in
BRA, van de Velde Archives. Nabokov offers a vivid and wholly implausible account of the life Goertz and Kessler led together in Weimar; Nabokov, *Bagázh*,
132–43.

11. *Twenties*, April 1, 1925, 260–61.

12. Ibid., April 4, 1925, 262–63.

13. Ibid., January 20, 1925, 246.

14. The diary, which has a large gap from June to December, gives little evidence as to the nature of the illness. A letter to his sister, dated June 29, mentions his having a fever every evening between six and eight o'clock and feeling
physically depressed and ill. Later, he informs Wilma that the same doctor who
attended Lenin on his deathbed had given a consultation on the advice of
Hilferding; Kessler to Wilma de Brion, June 29, 1925, August 18, 1925, KN.

15. *Twenties*, entry entitled "My Illness," 305–7.

16. Ibid., May 25, 1927, 316.

17. Müller-Krumbach, *Kessler*, 16–17.

18. The Jenson italic was only completed in December 1913, and even then
not quite to Kessler's satisfaction. In the end, it was used exclusively in only one
book, a dual-language edition of Rilke's *Duino Elegies*, published in cooperation with the Hogarth Press of Virginia and Leonard Woolf. In the opinion of
John Dreyfus, the greatest expert on the subject, the relative failure of Kessler
in this matter can be traced back to the reluctance of nearly every acolyte of the
arts and crafts movement to employ machines, in this case, a pantograph. See
John Dreyfus's contribution to Müller-Krumbach, *Kessler*, 83–120, a German
translation of his *Italic Quartet*.

19. Annabel Patterson, *Pastoral and Ideology: Virgil to Valéry*, (Berkeley,
Calif.: University of California Press, 1987), 310; Müller-Krumbach quoted in
ibid., 312; quoted in Müller-Krumbach, *Kessler*, 46.

20. Kessler, "Warum Maillol Virgils Ekologen illustriert hat," in *Gesammelte
Schriften II*, 280–84.

21. Concerning Maillol's supposed inspiration by the landscape of Banyuls,
his friend and student, Henri Frère noted that the dance of the nymphs in the
fifth *Ecologue* had nothing to do with the famous ring dance that Kessler had
so admired when he visited Catalonia. Nor was there a well in Maillol's house,
which could have inspired the illustration in the ninth *Ecologue;* see Henri Frère,
Gespräche mit Maillol (Frankfurt a. M.: Societäts-Verlag, 1961), 162.

22. Müller-Krumbach, *Kessler*, 46–49.

23. Dreyfus in ibid., 111–17.

24. Kessler to Schröder, May 13, 1932, KN; Müller-Krumbach, *Kessler*, 65–70;

Kessler to Wilma de Brion, December 25, 1930, March 22 and 23, 1931, November 18, 1936, June 31, 1937, and August 10, 1937, KN.

25. *In memoriam Walther Rathenau 24 Juni 1922*, in *Gesammelte Schriften I*, 328; see Peter Grupp, "Distanz und Nähe: Harry Graf Kessler als Biography Walther Rathenaus," in *Die Extremen berühen sich. Walther Rathenau, 1867–1922. Eine Ausstellung des Deutschen Historischen Museums*, ed. Hans Wilderotter, (Bonn: Deutsches Historisches Museum, 1993), 109–116; Ernst Schulin, "Der Biograph und sein Held: Harry Graf Kessler und Walther Rathenau," in *Wegbereiter*, 307–25; and the remarks of Cornelia Blasberg in *Gesammelte Schriften III*, 353–65.

26. *Twenties*, February 20, 1919, 70–72.

27. Kessler, *Rathenau*, 58.

28. Ibid., 57.

29. Ibid., 77–78.

30. Walther Rathenau, *In Days to Come*, quoted in ibid., 93.

31. Ibid., 101.

32. Ibid., 243; see Grupp, "Distanz und Nähe," 115, who stresses that recent scholarship tends to confirm this judgment.

33. Kessler, *Rathenau*, 138, 141.

34. See Schulin, "Der Biograph," 308.

Chapter 26

1. *TB*, August 14, 1927.

2. On the causes and course of the Great Depression in Germany, see Fritz Blaich, *Der Schwarze Freitag: Inflation und Wirtschaftskrise* (Munich: Deutscher Taschenbuch Verlag, 1990), 58–116; Knut Borchardt, *Perspectives on Modern German Economic History and Policy* (Cambridge: Cambridge University Press, 1991), chapters 9 and 10.

3. Borchardt, *Perspectives*, 146; Blaich, *Schwarze Freitag*, 84.

4. Ironically, the credit crisis in Germany was a consequence of the linkage forged between the German and the American economies following the Dawes Plan. Short of capital, due to the depredations of inflation, the Germans had relied on American investment, usually in the form of short-term loans because U.S. banks were leery of the financial stability of the mark. Yet, most German businesses and banks had not hesitated to place these funds in long-term investments. When American banks collapsed, they began withdrawing their loans from abroad, hitting Germany particularly hard.

5. *Twenties*, September 15, 1930, 396–97; in a letter to his sister, he expressed the wistful hope that if the economy improved, the elections could prove to be the high-water mark of Nazism; Kessler to Wilma de Brion, September 15, 1930, KN.

6. Here too the literature is endless. Two excellent short discussions are Martin Broszat's *Hitler and the Collapse of Weimar Germany* (Leamington Spa:

Berg Press, 1989) and A. J. Nicholls, *Weimar and the Rise of Hitler* (New York: St. Martin's Press, 1992), chapters 10 and 11.

7. They met in 1921 for an unsuccessful revival of the *Legend of Joseph* in Vienna, and then in June 1928 with Richard Strauss. Hofmannsthal had sent his old friend a very warm letter of praise for the biography of Rathenau, and Kessler had designed for Insel a new edition of *The Fool and Death*.

8. Reprinted in Burger, *Briefwechsel, 1898–1929*, 407–8; Ibid., 410; 567–68; *Twenties*, July 19, 1929, 366.

9. Ibid., August 19, October 3 and 4, 1929, 366–68.

10. Alice Kessler to Harry Kessler, February 24, 1906, July 15, 1907, KN; *Twenties*, March 1, 1926, 285.

11. Kessler to Wilma de Brion, November 10, 1920, February 25 and 28, 1931, KN.

12. Ibid., March 22, 1931, September 17, 1931, October 1, 1931.

13. Ibid., February 9, 1932.

14. Ibid., November 13, 1929; it was Henderson who suspected Kessler of leaking the information to the *Times*, see *ADAP. Series B. Vol. XIII*, document #141, report of Sthamer, November 20, 1929; also ibid., documents #118, 131, 144, 145, 160.

15. Dieckhoff at the embassy, although claiming to like Kessler personally, wrote a sharp critique of his role in these negotiations. That the latter still had friends in the Foreign Office is proven by Schubert's disparaging marginal comments on Dieckhoff's report, *ADAP. Series B. Vol. XIII*, #144, November 21, 1929; See also *TB*, October 1 and 11, November 1, 4, 6, and 7, 19, 20–21; December 2 and 9, 1929; January 16, 1930; Kessler to Wilma de Brion, April 29, 1930, October 1, 1931, KN.

16. *Twenties*, November 18, 1932, 437–38; manuscript of play in KN.

17. *TB*, May 14, 1925; April 8, 1926. No doubt Kippenberg, as the head of Insel Verlag, felt the competition from Jewish-owned publishers.

18. Ibid., March 16, 1926; *Twenties*, April 20, May 15, 1925; February 11, 1926; August 7, 1932, 265, 267, 279, 426–27, July 14, 1932, 423.

19. See the long discussion about Italian fascism with Friedrich Prittwitz, the German ambassador in Rome (and later in Washington), *Twenties*, March 26, 1927, 312–13.

20. Ibid., October 13, 1930, 399–401; April 25, 1932, 415–16.

21. Ibid., June 4, 1932, 418–19.

22. Ibid., July 12, 1932, 423; Broszat, *Collapse*, 115–27; Craig, *Germany*, 560–63.

23. See the conclusion of Thomas Childers, *The Nazi Voter: The Social Foundations of Fascism in Germany, 1919–1933* (Chapel Hill, N.C.: University of North Carolina Press, 1983), 268–69; *Twenties*, January 28, 1933, 441–43; Craig, 568.

24. *Twenties*, February 19, 1933, 445–46.

25. Kessler to Wilma de Brion, February 25, 1933, KN; *Twenties*, February 22, 1933, 446–47; March 8 and 18, 1933, 449–50.

Chapter 27

1. *Twenties,* June 22, April 8, 1933, 460, 452.

2. Ibid., June 28, 1933, 460–61. Kessler was misled by reports from the ever-optimistic and ever-inaccurate Wieland Herzfelde, who told him of the organization of illegal resistance within the Third Reich, June 12, 1933, 457.

3. Herzfelde to Kessler, August 19, 1933, quoted in Schuster and Pehle, *Weltmannes,* 483.

4. Kessler to Wilma de Brion, April 18 and 27, 1926, KN; see also *TB,* April 26, 1926, 496–98.

5. Kessler to Wilma de Brion, November 29, December 12, 1933, KN.

6. Albert Vigoleis Thelen, *Die Insel des zweiten Gesichts* (Düsseldorf-Cologne: E. Diedrichs, 1953), 631.

7. It is the richness and accuracy of these anecdotes, many taken directly from the diaries, but written at the time, the early 1950s, when these were not available, that gives credibility to Thelen's account; ibid., 430, 629.

8. Kessler to Wilma de Brion, April 24, 1933, KN. True to his nature, however, by the end of the year he found himself sucked into the social whirl on the island.

9. Thelen, *Insel,* 635.

10. Burger, *Briefwechsel,* December 22, 1898, 13; *Twenties,* December 5, 1931, 406.

11. *TB,* April 28, 1932, 704.

12. Kessler to Wilma de Brion, February 8, 1933, KN.

13. Ibid., December 7, 1934, KN.

14. On the publishing history of his memoirs, see Schuster and Pehle, *Weltmannes,* 493–505; Kessler to Wilma de Brion, December 7, April 6, 1934, KN.

15. *Twenties,* August 15, 1935, 473.

16. To her criticism that Kessler left out a description of his mother's tenderness, Kessler responded that he had tried to express it; "Of course, I should have liked to quote words of hers shewing [*sic*] it, but had none," Kessler to Wilma de Brion, June 7, 1935, KN.

17. Ibid., December 23 and 29, 1933, April 27, 1934, KN.

18. Craig, *Craig,* 341; Nabokov, *Bagázh,* 144, as well as idem, "Der Mensch, der andere liebte: In memoriam Harry Kessler," *Der Monat* 170 (November 1962), 55–56.

19. Kessler to Wilma de Brion, August 18, 1934, August 31, 1935, KN; Schuster and Pehle, *Weltmannes,* 490–92; *Twenties,* July 6, 1936, 477.

20. Grupp, *Kessler,* 255–56; Kessler to Wilma de Brion, October 4, December 6, 1936, KN; July 18, November 22, 1937.

21. Maria van Rysselberghe, "Ce matin, obsèques de Kessler," *Cahiers André Gide: 6 Cahiers de la Petite Dame,* 3 (1975), 59.

22. Julien Green, *Oeuvres complètes: Tome 4,* (Paris: Gallimard, 1975), 452–53.

23. Among them, *Jeune Republique,* December 1937, *Aux Écoutes,* December 11, 1937; *Vendredi,* December 10, 1937, *The Times,* December 8, 1937; *The New York Times,* December 3, 1937.

Conclusion

1. Friedrich Nietzsche, *On the Advantage and Disadvantage of History for Life*, (Indianapolis, Ind.: Hackett, 1980), 64. Emphasis is Nietzsche's.
2. *TB*, September 6, 1915.
3. Grupp, *Kessler*, 257–58.

BIBLIOGRAPHY

Abbreviations

BRA	Bibliothèque Royale Albert Première, Brussels.
GSA	Goethe-Schiller Archives, Weimar.
PA	The Political Archives of the Foreign Office, Bonn.
PA, Abt. III, U.S.A.	The postwar records of the embassy in Washington at the Political Archives of the Foreign Office.
PA, Gesandschaft Bern	The records of the wartime embassy in Switzerland at the Political Archives of the Foreign Office.
PA, IA, Sachsen Weimar	Reports of the Prussian Ambassador in Saxony-Weimar at the Political Archives of the Foreign Office.
KN	Letters and documents found in the German National Literature Archive, Marbach am Neckar.
TB	Unpublished diaries found in the German National Literature Archive, Marbach am Neckar.

I. Archival Sources

Bibliothèque Royale Albert Première, Brussels. Van de Velde Archives.

The German National Literature Archive, Marbach am Neckar. The fundamental source for this biography is the extensive Kessler Nachlaß held here. All citations from the unpublished diaries are from this source. Letters and other documents found in the archives are cited with KN.

Goethe-Schiller Archives, Weimar. The Nietzsche Archive papers.

Houghton Library, Harvard University, Cambridge. William Rothenstein Papers, bMS Eng 1148 (826). Publication is by permission of the Houghton Library, Harvard University.

The Political Archives of the Foreign Office, Bonn. The principal collections consulted are the reports of the Prussian ambassador in Saxony-Weimar, the records of the wartime embassy in Switzerland, and the postwar records of the embassy in Washington.

Kessler's Writings

"Amerikanische Probleme. I. Der Schmelztiegel." *Deutsche Nation* 6 (July 1924).

"Amerikanische Probleme. II. Die Geldmächte." *Deutsche Nation* 6 (August 1924).

"Ein neuer Englisher Künstler: A. E. John." *Kunst und Künstler* 2 (June 1904), 360–3.

Germany and Europe. New Haven, Conn.: Yale University Press, 1923.

Gesammelte Schriften: Volumes I–III. Edited by Gerhard Schuster. Frankfurt a. M.: S. Fischer, 1988.

Harry Graf Kessler. Tagebuch eines Weltmannes. Edited by Gerhard Schuster and Margot Pehle. Marbacher Kataloge 43. Marbach am Neckar, 1988.

"Henri de Régnier." *Pan I* (October 1895), 243–49.

In the Twenties: The Diaries of Harry Kessler. Translated by Charles Kessler. New York: Holt, Rinehart and Winston, 1971.

Krieg und Zusammenbruch aus Feldpostbriefen. Weimar: Cranach Presse, 1921

"Kunst und Publikum." *Neue Rundschau* 17 (1906), 112–16.

"Reminiszenz." In *Navigare necesse est: Eine Festgabe für Anton Kippenberg.* Leipzig: Insel Verlag, 1924.

Tagebücher, 1918–1937. Frankfurt a. M.: Insel Verlag, 1982.

Walther Rathenau: His Life & Work. New York: Harcourt, Brace and Company, 1930.

and Hugo von Hofmannsthal. *The Legend of Joseph.* Berlin and Paris: Fürstner, 1914.

Sources and Memoirs

Abramowski, Günter, ed. *Akten der Reichskanzlei: Die Kabinette Marx I und II: Volume 2.* Boppard am Rhein: Boldt, 1973.

Aktenzur deutschen auswartigen Politik. Serie A: 1918–1945. Volumes I–XIV. Gottingen: Vandenhoeck & Ruprecht. 1966 ff.

Armfield, Mrs. Maxwell (Constance Smedley). *Crusaders: The Reminiscences of Constance Smedley.* London: Duckworth, 1929.

Arsène, Alexander. "Espions and Déménageurs." *Le Figaro,* January 5, 1915.

Avenarius, Ferdinand. "Der Deutsche Künstlerbund." *Kunstwart* 7 (January 1904), 473.

———. "Die Schmach der Weimaraner." *Kunstwart* 19 (April 1906), 46–47.

———. "Zur 'Schmach der Weimaraner.'" *Kunstwart* 19 (September 1906), 622–23.

Baring, Maurice. *The Puppet Show of Memory.* London: W. Heinemann, 1930.

Beckmann, Max. *Tagebücher. 1940–1950.* Munich: Langen Müller, 1979.

Beveridge, Albert J. *What Is Back of the War.* Indianapolis, Ind. Bobbs-Merrill Company, 1915.

Bierbaum, Otto Julius. *Gesammelte Werke.* Vol. 1. Munich: Müller, 1921.

Bodenhausen, Eberhard von. *Eberhard von Bodenhausen: Ein Leben für Kunst und Wirtschaft.* Edited by Dora von Bodenhausen-Degener. Düsseldorf-Köln: Eugen Diedrichs Verlag, 1955.

Bodenhausen, Eberhard von and Harry Graf Kessler. *Briefwechsel, 1894–1918.* Edited by Hans-Ulrich Simon. Marbacher Schriften 16. Marbach am Neckar: Klett, 1978.

Bourget, Paul. *Essais de psychologie contemporain.* Vols. 1 and 2. Paris: Librairie Plon, 1937.

Bunsen, Marie von. *Zeitgenossen die ich erlebte. 1900–1930.* Leipzig: Koehler & Amelangs, 1932.

Bülow, Bernhard von. *The Memoirs of Prince von Bülow.* Vol. 3. Boston: Little, Brown & Company, 1931.

Cole, G. D. H. Cole. *Self-Government in Industry.* Freeport, N.Y.: Books for Libraries Press, 1971.

Craig, Edward Gordon. *On the Art of the Theatre.* Chicago: Browne's Bookstore, 1911.

D'Abernon, Edgar Vincent, Viscount. *An Ambassador of Peace: Volume III: The Years of Recovery, January 1924–October 1926.* London: Hodder and Stoughton, 1930.

Das Kabinett Scheidemann. 13 Februar bis 20 Juni 1919. Edited by Hagan Schulze. Boppard am Rhein: H. Boldt, 1971.

Daudet, Léon. "L'Art Boche." *L'Action francaise,* January 6, 1915.

———. *La Vermine du Monde: Roman de l'Espionnage Allemand.* Paris: A. Fayard, 1916.

Dehmel, Richard. *Ausgewählte Briefe. Vols. 1 and 2: 1883–1902.* Berlin: S. Fischer, 1923.

Denis, Maurice. *Journal,* Vol. 2: 1905–1920. Paris: La Colombe, 1957.

Dimnet, Ernest. *My New World.* New York: Simon & Schuster, 1937.

Dungern, Otto von. *Unter Kaiser und Kanzelrn: Erinnerungen.* Coburg: Veste Verlag, 1953.

Egloffstein, Hermann Freiherr von. *Das Weimar von Karl Alexander und Wilhelm Ernst.* 1934.

Erdmann, Karl Dietrich, ed. *Kurt Riezler: Tagebücher, Aufsätze, Dokumente.* Göttingen: Vandenhoeck & Ruprecht, 1972.

Fabricius. *Geschichte des 3. Garde-Ulanen-Regiments. 1860–1910.* Berlin: E. S. Mittler, 1910.

464   BIBLIOGRAPHY

Feist, Günter and Ursula Feist, eds. *Kunst und Künstler: Aus 32 Jahrgängen einer deutschen Kunstzeitschrift.* Mainz: Florian Kupferberg Verlag, 1971.

Fontane, Theodor. *Briefe.* Vol. 4: 1890–1898. Berlin: Propylaen, 1968–71.

Foucart, Claude, ed. *D'un monde à l'autre. La correspondance André Gide— Harry Kessler (1903–1933).* Lyon: Centre d'études gidiennes, Université Lyon II, 1985.

Frère, Henri. *Gespräche mit Maillol.* Frankfurt a. M.: Societäts-Verlag, 1961.

Gide, André. *Journals. 1889–1949.* New York: Harmondsworth, Penguin, 1967.

———. *Pretexts: Reflections on Literature and Morality.* Edited by Justin O'Brien. New York: Meridian Books, 1959.

Gill, Eric. *Autobiography.* London: J. Cape, 1945.

Glatzer, Dieter and Ruth Glatzer, ed. *Berliner Leben 1900–1914. Vol. 1.* Berlin: Verlag Das Europäische Buch, 1986.

Green, Julien. *Oeuvres complètes: Tome 4.* Paris: Gallimard, 1975.

Greiner-Mai, H., et al., eds. *Weimar im Urteil der Welt.* Berlin and Weimar: Aufbau-Verlag, 1975.

Grosz, Georg. *Briefe.* Hamburg: Rowohlt, 1979.

Hausen, Max. "Das neue Weimar." *Die Woche* 6 (September 1904), 1641–5.

Herzfelde, Wieland. *Immergrün: Merkwürdige Erlebnisse und Erfahrungen eines fröhlichen Waisenknaben.* Berlin/Weimar: Aufbau-Verlag, 1981.

———. *Zur Sache geschrieben und gesprochen zwischen 18 und 80.* Berlin/ Weimar: Aifbau-Verlag, 1976.

Heuss, Theodor. *Erinnerungen, 1905–1933.* Tübingen: R. Wunderlich, 1963.

Heyking, Elisabeth von. *Tagebücher aus vier Weltteilen. 1886–1904.* Leipzig: Koehler & Amelang, 1926.

Hobson, S. G., and A. R. Orage. *Guild Principles in War and Peace.* London: G. Bell and Sons, 1918.

Hofmannsthal, Hugo von. "An Graf Kessler." *Hofmannsthal Blätter* 21/22 (1979), 66–67.

———. *Gesammelte Werke.* Frankfurt a. M.: S. Fischer, 1980.

———. *Poems and Verse Plays.* Translated by Michael Hamburger. New York: Pantheon Books, 1961.

———. *Sämtliche Werke XXIII. Operndichtungen I. Der Rosenkavalier.* Frankfurt a. M.: S. Fischer, 1986.

———. *Selected Prose.* Translated by James and Tania Stern. New York: Pantheon Books, 1952.

Hofmannsthal, Hugo von and Eberhard von Bodenhausen. *Briefe der Freundschaft.* Düsseldorf: E. Diedrichs, 1953.

Hofmannsthal, Hugo von and Harry Graf Kessler. *Briefwechsel, 1898–1929.* Edited by Hilde Burger. Frankfurt a. M.: Insel Verlag, 1968.

Hofmannsthal, Hugo von, and Ottonie Gräfin Degenfeld. *Briefwechsel.* Rev. ed. Frankfurt a. M.: S. Fischer, 1986.

Kolb, Annette. "Harry Graf Kessler." *Maß und Wert* 4 (1938), 630–31.

———. *Zarastro, Westlich Tage.* Berlin: S. Fischer, 1921.

Lichtwark, Alfred. *Briefe an die Kommission für die Verwaltung der Kunsthalle.* Edited by Gustav Pauli. Hamburg: Westermann, 1923.

————. "Zur Einführung." *Pan* III (1895).

Meier-Graefe, Julius. "Der *Pan*." *Pan* 1 (1910), 1–4.

Nabokov, Nicolas. *Bagázh: Memoirs of a Russian Cosmopolitan.* New York: Atheneum, 1975.

————. "Der Mensch, der andere liebt. In memoriam Harry Kessler." *Der Monat* 170 (November 1962), 41–56.

Newman, L. M., ed. *The Correspondence of Edward Gordon Craig and Count Harry Kessler, 1903–1937.* Bithell Series of Dissertations, vol. 21. London; W. S. Maney for the Modern Humanities Research Association and the Institute of Germanic Studies, 1995.

Nietzsche, Friedrich. *Beyond Good and Evil.* New York: Penguin, 1990.

————. *Nachgelassene Schriften. 1870–1873.* Edited by Giorgio Colli and Mazzino Montinari. Berlin: De Gruyter, 1973.

————. *On the Advantage and Disadvantage of History for Life.* Indianapolis, Ind.: Hackett, 1980.

————. *On the Genealogy of Morals.* Translated by Walter Kaufmann and R. J. Hollingdale. New York: Vintage, 1989.

————. *Sämtliche Briefe.* Edited by Giorgio Colli and Mazzino Montinari. Berlin: De Gruyter, 1986.

Nonne, Max and Fritz Ulmer, eds. *Kulturgeschichtliche Studien und Skizzen aus Vergangenheit und Gegenwart.* Hamburg: Broschek, 1929.

Nostitz, Helene von. *Aus dem alten Europa.* 2d rev. ed. Frankfurt a. M.: Insel Verlag, 1978.

Proust, Marcel. *Remembrance of Things Past.* Translated by Scott Moncrieff and Terence Kilmartin. New York: Random House, 1982.

Przybyszewski, Stanislaw. *Erinnerungen an das literarische Berlin.* Munich: Winkler, 1965.

Rathenau, Walther. *Die neue Wirtschaft.* Berlin: S. Fischer, 1918.

————. *The New Society.* New York: Harcourt, Brace and Company, 1921.

Rieth, Paul. "Rodin in Weimar." *Jugend* 11 (1906), 234.

Rolland, Romain. *Zwischen den Völkern: Aufzeichnungen und Dokumente aus den Jahren, 1914–1919.* Vol. 2. Stuttgart: Deutsche Verlagsanstalt, 1955.

Rothenstein, John. *Summer's Lease: An Autobiography. 1901–1938.* New York: Holt, Rinehart and Winston, 1965.

Rothenstein, William. *Men and Memories.* Vol. 2 1900–1922. London: Faber & Faber, 1932.

Rudolf Borchardt, Alfred Walter Heymel, Rudolf Alexander Schröder. Marbarcher Katalog 29. Marbach a. Neckar: Kösel, 1978.

Ruedorffer, J. J., (Kurt Riezler). *Grundzüge der Weltpolitik in der Gegenwart.* Stuttgart: Deutsche Verlagsanstalt, 1915.

Rysselberghe, Maria van. "Ce matin, obsèques de Kessler." *Cahiers André Gide: 6. Cahiers de la Petite Dame* 3 (1975), 59.

Scheffler, Karl. *Berlin: Ein Stadtschicksal.* 2d ed. Berlin: E. Reiss, 1910.

————. *Henry van de Velde: Vier Essays.* Leipzig: Insel Verlag, 1913.

Scherer, André and Jacques Grunewald, eds. *L'Allemagne et les Problèmes de la Paix pendant la Première Guerre Mondiale: Documents extraits des archives de l'office allemand des Affaires 'etrangères.* Paris: Presses Universitaires de France, 1962–78.

Schickele, René. *Werke in drei Bänden. Dritter Band: Aufsätze und Reden, Tagebücher.* Cologne/Berlin: Kiepenheur & Witsch, 1959.

Simmel, Georg. *Georg Simmel, 1858–1918.* Edited by Kurt H. Wolff. Columbus, Ohio: Ohio State University Press, 1959.

Spitzemberg, Hildegard, Baroness von. *Das Tagebuch der Baronin Spitzemberg,* Edited by Rudolf Vierhaus. Göttingen: Vandenhoeck & Ruprecht, 1960.

Springer, Anton. *Aus meinem Leben.* Berlin: G. Grote, 1892.

St. Denis, Ruth. *An Unfinished Life: An Autobiography.* New York: Harper & Brothers, 1939.

Sutherland, Duchess of, Millicent. *Six Weeks at the War.* Chicago: A. C. Mc-Clurg, 1915.

Taft, Hans. "Neue Schriften zur Völkerkunde." *Die Gesellschaft* 1 (1900), 50–51.

Ten Eyck, Andrew. "World Turmoil as Seen from Academic Shades." *The Outlook* (August 29, 1923), 660–61.

Thode, Henry. *Franz von Assisi und die Anfänge der Kunst in der Renaissance in Italien.* 2d rev. ed. Berlin: G. Grote, 1904.

Thelen, Albert Vigoleis. *Die Insel des zweiten Gesichts.* Düsseldorf-Köln: E. Diedrichs, 1953.

Times, January 12, 1906, 15.

Treitschke, Heinrich von. *Politics.* Edited by Hans Kohn. New York: Harcourt, Brace & World, 1963.

Tschudi, Hugo von. "Kunst und Publikum." In *Gesammelte Schriften zur neueren Kunst.* Munich: F. Bruckmann, 1912.

Van de Velde, Henry. *Geschichte meines Lebens.* Rev. ed. Edited by Hans Curjel. Munich: R. Piper, 1986.

———. *Zum neuen Stil.* Edited by Hans Curjel. Munich: R. Piper, 1955.

Vogeler, Heinrich. *Erinnerungen.* Edited by Erich Weinert. Berlin: Rütten & Loening, 1952.

Weber, Max. "Science as a Vocation." In *From Max Weber.* Edited by H. H. Gerth and C. Wright Mills. Oxford: Oxford University Press, 1946.

Wehberg, Hans. *Voices of German Pacifism.* Edited by Karl Holl. New York: Garland Publishers, 1972.

Winterfeldt-Menkin, Joachim von. *Jahrszeiten des Lebens.* Berlin: Propyläen-Verlag, 1942.

Zuckerkandl, Bertha. *Österreich intim: Erinnerungen, 1892–1942.* Vienna: Amalthea, 1981.

Secondary Literature

Adams, Robert M. *Decadent Societies.* San Francisco: North Point Press, 1983.

Adorno, Theodor. *Prismen.* Frankfurt a. M.: Suhrkamp Verlag, 1955.

Albertin, Lothar. *Liberalismus und Demokratie am Anfang der Weimarer Republik.* Dusseldorf: Droste, 1972.

Albisetti, James C. *Secondary School Reform in Imperial Germany*. Princeton, N.J.: Princeton University Press, 1983.

Aschheim, Steven E. *The Nietzsche Legacy in Germany, 1890–1990*. Berkeley, Calif.: University of California Press, 1992.

Auden, W. H. "A Saint-Simon of Our Time." *New York Review of Books*. August 31, 1972.

Bab, Julius. *Die Berliner Bohème*. Berlin: Seeman, 1904.

Bablet, Denis. *The Theatre of Gordon Craig*. London: Eyre Methuen, 1981.

Barkhausen, Hans. *Filmpropaganda für Deutschland im Ersten und Zweiten Weltkrieg*. Hildesheim: Olms Presse, 1982.

Baumgart, Winfried. *Deutsche Ostpolitik 1918: Von Brest-Litovsk bis zum Ende des Ersten Weltkrieges*. Vienna: Oldenbourg, 1966.

Becker, Jean-Jacques. *1914, comment les Francais sont entrés dans la guerre*. Paris: Presses de la Fondation National des Sciences Politiques, 1977.

———. *The Great War and the French People*. Leamington Spa Berg Press, 1993.

Becker, Jean-Jacques, and Serge Bernstein. *Victoire et frustrations, 1914–1929*. Paris: Editions du Seuil, 1990.

Benz, Wolfgang, ed. *Pazifismus in Deutschland: Dokumente zur Friedensbewegung, 1890–1939*. Frankfurt a. M.: S. Fischer, 1988.

Benz, Wolfgang, and Hermann Graml, eds. *Biographisches Lexikon zur Weimarer Republik*. Munich: C. H. Beck, 1988.

Berger, Ursel. "'Herauf nun, herauf, du großer Mittag': Georg Kolbes Statue für die Nietzsche-Gedächtnishalle und die gescheiterten Vorläuferprojekte." In *Wege nach Weimar: Auf der Suche nach der Einheit von Kunst und Politik*, edited by Hans Wilderotter and Michael Dorrmann. Weimar: Jovis, 1999.

Berghahn, V. R. *Germany and the Approach of War in 1914*. New York: St. Martin's Press, 1973.

Bessel, Richard. *Germany after the First World War*. Oxford: Oxford University Press, 1993.

Bezold, Friedrich von. *Geschichte der Rheinischen Friedrich-Wilhelms Universität*. Bonn: Marcus & Weber, 1920.

Bialas, Wolfgang, and Burkhard Stenzel, eds. *Die Weimarer Republik zwischen Metropole und Provinz*. Weimar: Böhlau, 1996.

Bismarck, Beatrice von. "Harry Graf Kessler und die französiche Kunst um die Jahrhundertwende." *Zeitschrift des Deutschen Verein für Kunstwissenschaft* 42:3 (1988), 47–62.

Blaich, Fritz. *Der Schwarze Freitag: Inflation und Wirtschaftskrise*. Munich: Deutscher Taschenbuch Verlag, 1990.

Block, Jane. "The Insel-Verlag 'Zarathustra': An Untold Tale of Art and Printing." *Pantheon* 45 (1987), 129–37.

Blumenthal, Arthur. "A Reappraisal of Wilhelm Wundt." *American Psychologist* (1975), 1081–88.

Boehm, Laetitia, and Rainer A. Müller. *Universitäten und Hochschulen*. Düsseldorf: Econ, 1983.

Bohnenkamp, Hans. "Jugendbewegung als Kulturkritik." In *Kulturkritik und Jugendkult*, edited by Walter Rüegg. Frankfurt a. M.: V. Kostermann, 1974.

Bonner Gelehrte: Beiträge sur Geschichte der Wissenschaften in Bonn: Philosophie und Altertumswissenschaften. Bonn: Bouvier, Röhrscheid, 1968.

Borchardt, Knut. *Perspectives on Modern German Economic History and Policy*. Cambridge: Cambridge University Press, 1991.

Broszat, Martin. *Hitler and the Collapse of Weimar Germany*. Leamington Spa: Berg Press, 1989.

Bruford, W. H., *Culture and Society in Classical Weimar, 1775–1806*. Cambridge: Cambridge University Press, 1961.

Brunner, Gerhard. "Richard Strauss und das Ballet." In *Richard Strauss, 1864–1949*. Mainz: Schott, 1979.

Bürger, Peter. *Theory of the Avant-garde*. Minneapolis: University of Minnesota Press, 1980.

Calinescu, Matei. *The Five Faces of Modernity: Modernism, Avant-Garde, Decadence, Kitsch, Postmodernism*. Durham, N.C.: Duke University Press, 1987.

Campbell, Bruce F. *Ancient Wisdom Revived: A History of the Theosophical Movement*. Berkeley, Calif.: University of California Press, 1980.

Campbell, Joan. *Joy in Work, German Work: The National Debate, 1800–1945*. Princeton, N.J.: Princeton University Press, 1989.

Cancik, Hubert. "Der Nietzsche-Kult in Weimar: Ein Beitrag zur Religionsgeschichte der wilhelminischen Ära." *Nietzsche-Studien* 16 (1987), 405–29.

Chapman, Maybelle Kennedy. *Great Britain and the Bagdad Railway, 1888–1914*. Northampton, Mass.: Smith College Studies in History, 1948.

Chickering, Roger. *Imperial Germany and a World without War: The Peace Movement and German Society, 1892–1914*. Princeton, N.J.: Princeton University Press, 1975.

Childers, Thomas. *The Nazi Voter: The Social Foundations of Fascism in Germany, 1919–1933*. Chapel Hill, N.C.: University of North Carolina Press, 1983.

Churchill, Randolph S. *Winston S. Churchill. Vol. 1. Youth. 1874–1900*. Boston: Houghton Mifflin, 1966.

Chytry, Josef. *The Aesthetic State: A Quest in Modern German Thought*. Berkeley, Calif.: University of California Press, 1989.

Claudel, Judith. *Maillol. Sa vie—son oeuvre—ses idées*. Paris: Grasset, 1937.

Cohen, Arthur A. *An Admirable Woman*. Boston, 1983.

Conze, Werner. *Polnische Nation und Deutsche Politik im Ersten Weltkrieg*. Cologne, 1958.

Craig, Edward. *Gordon Craig: The Story of His Life*. New York: Knopf, 1968.

Craig, Gordon A. *Germany, 1866–1945*. Oxford: Oxford University Press, 1978.

———. *The Politics of the Prussian Army, 1640–1945*. Oxford: Oxford University Press, 1978.

Crankshaw, Edward. *Bismarck*. New York: Viking Press, 1981.

Davies, Norman. *God's Playground: A History of Poland*. Vol. 2: 1795 to the Present. New York: Columbia University Press, 1982.

———. *Heart of Europe: A Short History of Poland*. Oxford: Oxford University Press, 1984.

Deak, Istvan. *Weimar Germany's Left-Wing Intellectuals: A Political History of the Weltbühne and Its Circle*. Berkeley, Calif.: University of California Press, 1968.

Del Mar, Norman. *Richard Strauss: A Critical Commentary on his Life and Works*. Vol. 2. Philadelphia: Chilton, 1969.

Demeter, Karl. *The German Officer-Corps in Society and State, 1650–1945*. New York: Praeger, 1965.

Dietrich, Richard. "Berlins Weg zur Industrie- und Handelsstadt." In *Berlin: Zehn Kapitel seiner Geschichte,* edited by Richard Dietrich. Berlin: De Gruyter, 1960.

Dijkstra, Bram. *Idols of Perversity: Fantasies of Feminine Evil*. New York: Oxford University Press, 1986.

Dilly, Heinrich. *Kunstgeschichte als Institution: Studien zur Geschichte einer Diziplin*. Frankfurt: Suhrkamp, 1979.

Easton, Laird. "The Red Count: The Life and Times of Harry Kessler." Ph.D. diss. Stanford University, 1991.

———. "The Rise and Fall of the 'Third Weimar': Harry Graf Kessler and the Aesthetic State in Wilhelmian Germany, 1902–1906." *Central European History* 29:4 (1997), 495–532.

Ehrlich, Lothar, and Jürgen John, eds. *Weimar 1930: Politik und Kultur im Vorfeld der NS-Diktatur*. Cologne: Böhlau, 1998.

Eichberg, Henning. "Forward Race and the Laughter of Pygmies: On Olympic Sport." In *Fin de Siècle and its Legacy,* edited by Mikulás Teich and Roy Porter. Cambridge: Cambridge University Press, 1990.

Eksteins, Modris. *Rites of Spring: The Great War and the Birth of the Modern Age*. New York: Doubleday, 1989.

Fallon, Daniel. *The German University: A Heroic Ideal in Conflict with the Modern World*. Boulder, Colo.: Colorado Associated University Presses, 1980.

Fancher, Raymond E., *Pioneers of Psychology*. New York: Norton, 1979.

Farrar, L. L., Jr. *Divide and Conquer: German Efforts to Conclude a Separate Peace, 1914–1918*. New York: distributed by Columbia University Press, 1978.

———. "Nationalism in Wartime: Critiquing the Conventional Wisdom." In *Authority, Identity, and the Social History of the Great War,* edited by Frans Coetzee and Marilyn Shevin-Coetzee. Providence, R.I.: Berghahn Books, 1995.

Feldman, Gerald D. *Army, Industry, and Labour in Germany*. Providence, R.I.: Berg Press, 1992.

Felix, David. "Reparations Reconsidered with a Vengeance." *Central European History* 4 (1971), 171–79.

Fenton, James. "The Secrets of Maillol." *New York Review of Books* 43:8 (May 9, 1996), 47–55.

Ferguson, Wallace K. "The Reinterpretation of the Renaissance." In *Facets of the Renaissance,* edited by William H. Werkmeister. Los Angeles: University of Southern California Press, 1959.

Finck, Adrien, and Maryse Staiber, eds. *Elsässer, Europäer, Pazifist: Studien zu Réné Schickele*. Kehl: Morstadt, 1984.

Fink, Carole. *The Genoa Conference: European Diplomacy, 1921–1922*. Chapel Hill, N.C.: University of North Carolina Press, 1984.

Fischer, Fritz. *Germany's Aims in the First World War*. New York: Norton, 1967.

Forgács, Éva. *The Bauhaus Idea and Bauhaus Politics*. Budapest: Central European University Press, 1991.

Fortuna, Ursula. *Der Völkerbundsgedanke in Deutschland während des Ersten Weltkrieges*. Zurich: Europa Verlag, 1974.

Frèches-Thory, Claire, and Antoine Terrasse. *The Nabis: Bonnard, Vuillard and their Circle*. New York: H. N. Abrams, 1991.

Frecot, Janos. "Von der Weltstadt zur Kiefernheide, oder: Die Flucht aus der Bürgerlichkeit." In *Berlin um 1900*. Berlin: Berliner Festspiele, 1984.

Frevert, Ute. *Ehrenmänner: Das Duell in der bürgerlichen Gesellschaft*. Munich C. H. Beck, 1991.

———. "Honour and Middle-Class Culture: The History of the Duel in England and Germany." In *Bourgeois Society in Nineteenth-Century Europe*, edited by Jürgen Kocka and Alan Mitchell. Providence, R.I.: Berg Press, 1993, 232–33.

Friedell, Egon. *Kulturgeschichte der Neuzeit*. Vol. 3. Munich: C. H. Beck, 1927–1932.

Fritz, Horst. *Literarischer Jugendstil und Expressionismus: Zur Kunsttheorie Dichtung und Wirkung Richard Dehmels*. Stuttgart: J. B. Metzler, 1969.

Fussell, Paul. *The Great War and Modern Memory*. Oxford: Oxford University Press, 1975.

Gall, Lothar. *Bismarck: Der weisse Revolutionär*. Frankfurt a. M.: Propyläen, 1980.

Garafola, Lynn. *Diaghilev's Ballets Russes*. Oxford: Oxford University Press, 1989.

Gatzke, Hans W. *Stresemann and the Rearmament of Germany*. New York: Norton, 1954.

———. "Zu den deutschen-russischen Beziehungen im Sommer 1918." *Vierteljahrshefte für Zeitgeschichte* (1955), 67–98.

Gay, Peter. *Freud, Jews and Other Germans*. New York: Oxford University Press, 1978.

———. *Weimar Culture: The Outsider as Insider*. New York: Harper & Row, 1968.

George, Waldemar. *Aristide Maillol*. London: Corey, Adams & MacKay, 1965.

Gilman, Richard. *Decadence: The Strange Life of an Epithet*. New York: Farrar, Straus and Giroux, 1979.

Gilman, Sander L. "The Nietzsche Murder Case." *New Literary History* 14 (1983), 359–72.

Glaser, Hermann. *Bildungsburgertum und Nationalismus: Politik und Kulture im Wilhelminischen Deutschland*. Munich: Deutscher Taschenbuch Verlag, 1993.

———. *Die Kultur der Wilhelminischen Zeit: Topographie einer Epoche*. Frankfurt: S. Fischer, 1982.

Gold, Arthur, and Robert Fizdale. *Misia: The Life of Misia Sert.* New York: Knopf, 1980.

Green, Martin. *Children of the Sun.* New York: Basic Books, 1976.

Grigoriev, S. L., *The Diaghilev Ballet. 1909–1929.* Harmondsworth: Penguin, 1960.

Grosfeld, Leon. "Misja Hrabiego Kesslera w Warszawie." *Dzieje Najnowsze. 2* (with summary in French). 1970, 17–30.

Grupp, Peter. *Deutsche Außenpolitik im Schatten von Versailles. Zur Politik des Auswärtigen Amts vom Ende des Ersten Weltkrieges und der Novemberrevolution by zum Inkrafttreten des Versailler Vertrags.* Paderborn: F. Schöningh, 1988.

———. "Distanz und Nähe. Harry Graf Kessler als Biograph Walther Rathenaus." In *Die Extreme berühren sich. Walther Rathenau 1867–1922. Eine Ausstellung des Deutschen Historischen Museums,* edited by Hans Wilderotter. Berlin: Argon, 1993, 109–16.

———. "Geteilte Illusionen: Die Beziehung zwischen Harry Graf Kessler und Henry van de Velde." In *Wege nach Weimar: Auf der Suche nach der Einheit von Kunst und Politik,* edited by Hans Wilderotter and Michael Dorrmann. Weimar: Böhlau, 1999.

———. *Harry Graf Kessler. 1868–1937. Eine Biographie.* Munich: C. H. Beck, 1995.

———. "Harry Graf Kessler als Diplomat," *Vierteljahrshefte für Zeitgeschichte.* (1992), 61–78.

———. "Harry Graf Kessler, das Auswärtige Amt und der Völkerbund." In *Harry Graf Kessler: Ein Wegbereiter der Moderne,* edited by Gerhard Neumann and Günter Schnitzler. Freiburg im Breisgau: Rombach, 1997.

———. "Harry Graf Kessler und das Auswärtige Amt. Funktionselite und elitärer Außenseiter." In *Eliten in Deutschland und Frankreich im 19. und 20 Jahrhundert,* edited by Rainer Hudemann and Georges-Henri Soutou. Munich: R. Oldenbourg, 1994, 293–302.

———. "Voraussetzung und Praxis deutscher amtlicher Kulturpropaganda in den neutralen Staaten während des Ersten Weltkrieges." In *Der Erste Weltkrieg. Wirkung, Wahrnehmung und Analyse,* edited by Wolfgang Michalka. Munich: Piper, 1994, 799–824.

Hagen, William W. *Germans, Poles, and Jews: The Nationality Conflict in the Prussian East, 1772–1914.* Chicago: University of Chicago Press, 1980.

Hamann, Richard, and Jost Hermand. *Gründerzeit.* Berlin: Akademie Verlag, 1965.

———. *Impressionismus.* Munich: Nymphenburger Verlagshandlung, 1972.

———. *Naturalismus.* Munich: Nymphenburger Verlagshandlung, 1972.

Haupt, Jürgen. "Harry Graf Kessler und Hugo von Hofmannsthal: Eine Freundschaft." In *Konstellationen Hugo von Hofmannsthals* (Salzburg: Residenz Verlag, 1970), 46–81.

Haussmann, Kurt Georg. "Pilsudski und die Mission des Grafen Kessler in Polen." In *Geschichte und Gegenwart: Festschrift für Karl Dietrich Erdmann,* edited by Harmut Boockmann, Kurt Jurgensen, and Gerhard Stoltenberg. Neumünster: Wachholtz, 1980, 233–73.

Heinemann, Ulrich. *Die verdrängte Niederlage: Politische Öffentlichkeit und Kriegsschuldfrage in der Weimarer Republik*. Göttingen; Vandenhoeck & Ruprecht, 1983.

Hense, Karl-Heinz. "Harry Graf Kessler. Eine biographische Skizze" *Liberal* 3 (1988), 127–34.

Henze, Gisela. *Der PAN: Geschichte und Profil einer Zeitschrift der Jahrhundertwende*. Ph.D. diss. University of Freiburg, 1974.

Hepp, Corona. *Avantgarde: Moderne Kunst, Kulturkritik und Reformbewegungen nach der Jahrhundertwende*. Munich: Deutscher Taschenbuch Verlag, 1987.

Hermand, Jost. *Der Schein des schönen Lebens*. Frankfurt a. M.: Athenäum Verlag, 1972.

———. *Jugendstil*. Darmstadt: Wissenschaftliche Buchgesellschaft, 1971.

———, ed. *Lyrik des Jugendstils. Eine Anthologie*. Stuttgart: P. Reclam, 1964.

Hermanik, Klaus-Jürgen, "Der Autor und sein Schreiberling. Die Zusammenarbeit von Harry Graf Kessler und Albert Vigoleis Thelen auf Mallorca." In *Harry Graf Kessler: Ein Wegbereiter der Moderne,* edited by Gerhard Newmann and Günter Schnitzler. Frieburg im Breisgau: Rombach, 1997.

Hess, Ulrich. "Beginn kapitalistischer Produktions verhältnisse." In *Geschichte der Stadt Weimar,* edited by Gitta Günther and Lothar Wallraf. Weimar: Böhlau, 1976.

Hildebrand, Klaus. *The Foreign Policy of the Third Reich*. Berkeley, Calif.: University of California Press, 1973.

Hillgruber, Andreas. *Die Zersörung Europas: Beiträge zur Weltkriegsepoche, 1914 – 1945*. Frankfurt a. M.: Propyläen, 1988.

Hoffmann, Dirk. "Zu Harry Graf Kesslers Mitarbeit an 'Rosenkavalier.'" *Hofmannsthal Blätter* 21/22 (1979), 153–160.

Holl, Karl. *Pazifismus in Deutschland*. Frankfurt a. M.: Suhrkamp, 1988.

Horne, Alistair. *The Price of Glory: Verdun 1916*. Harmondsworth, U.K.: Penguin, 1984.

Hughes, H. Stuart. *Consciousness and Society: The Reorientation of European Social Thought. 1890 –1930*. New York: Vintage, 1958.

Hull, Isabel. *The Entourage of Kaiser Wilhelm II, 1888 –1918*. New York: Cambridge University Press, 1982.

Hüter, Karl-Heinz. "Hoffnung, Illusion und Enttäuschung: Henry van de Velde's Kunstgewerbeschule und das frühe Bauhaus." In *Henry van de Velde: Ein Europäischer Künstler seiner Zeit,* edited by Klaus-Jürgen Sembach and Birgit Schulte. Cologne, 1992.

Huyssen, Andreas. "Monumental Seduction." *New German Critique* (fall 1996), 181–201.

Iggers, Georg G. *The German Conception of History: The National Tradition of Historical Thought from Herder to the Present*. Rev. ed. Middletown, Conn.: Wesleyan University Press, 1983.

Isaacs, Reginald. *Gropius: An Illustrated Biography of the Founder of the Bauhaus.* Boston: Little, Brown, 1991.

Jarausch, Konrad H. *Students, Society, and Politics in Imperial Germany: The Rise of Academic Illiberalism.* Princeton, N.J.: Princeton University Press, 1982.

Jelavich, Peter. *Munich and Theatrical Modernism: Politics, Playwriting, and Performance. 1890–1914.* Cambridge, Mass.: Harvard University Press, 1985.

Jensen, Robert. *Marketing Modernism in Fin-de-Siècle Europe.* Princeton, N.J.: Princeton University Press, 1994.

Jost, Dominik. *Literarischer Jugendstil.* Rev. ed. Stuttgart: J. B. Metzler, 1980.

Kaes, Anthony, Martin Jay, and Edward Dimendberg, eds. *The Weimar Republic Sourcebook.* Berkeley, Calif.: University of California Press, 1994.

Kaufmann, Walter. *Nietzsche: Philsopher, Psychologist, Antichrist.* 3d ed. Princeton, N.J.: Princeton University Press, 1968.

Kehr, Eckhart. *Economic Interest, Militarism, and Foreign Policy.* Berkeley, Calif.: University of California Press, 1977.

Keisch, Claude, ed. *Auguste Rodin: Plastik, Zeichnungen, Graphik.* Berlin: Staatliche Museen, National Galerie, 1979.

Kelter, Edmund. *Hamburg und sein Johanneum. 1529–1929.* Hamburg: Lütcke & Wulff, 1928.

Kendall, Elizabeth. *Where She Danced.* New York: Knopf, 1979.

Kennedy, Paul. *The Rise in Anglo-German Antagonism: 1860–1914.* London: Ashfield Press, 1980.

Kent, Bruce. *The Spoils of War: The Politics, Economics, and Diplomacy of Reparations, 1918–1932.* Oxford: Oxford University Press, 1991.

Kiaulehn, Walther. *Berlin: Schicksal einer Weltstadt.* Munich: Biederstein, 1958.

Kimmich, Christoph M. *Germany and the League of Nations.* Chicago: University of Chicago Press, 1975.

Kitchen, Martin. *The German Officer Corps. 1890–1914.* Oxford: Oxford University Press, 1968.

Klein, D. B. *A History of Scientific Psychology: Its Origins and Philosophical Backgrounds.* New York: Basic Books, 1970.

Kluge, Ulrich. *Die deutsche Revolution, 1918/1919: Staat, Politik und Gesellschaft zwischen Weltkrieg und Kapp-Putsch.* Frankfurt a. M.: Suhrkamp, 1985.

Kojève, Alexandre. *Introduction to the Reading of Hegel: Lectures on the Phenomenology of the Spirit,* edited by Allan Bloom. Ithaca, N.Y.: Cornell University Press, 1969.

Kostka, Alexandre. "Das 'Gesamtkunstwerk für alle Sinne'; Zu einigen Facetten der Beziehung zwischen Hugo von Hofmannsthal und Harry Graf Kessler." In *Harry Graf Kessler: Ein Wegbereiter der Moderne,* edited by Gerhard Neumann and Günter Schnitzler. Freiburg im Breisgau: Rombach, 1997.

———. "Der Dilettant und sein Künstler: Die Beziehung Harry Graf Kessler— Henry van de Velde." In *Henry van de Velde: Ein Europäischer Künstler seiner Zeit,* edited by Klaus-Jürgen Sembach and Birgit Schulte. Cologne: Wienand, 1992.

————. "Harry Graf Kesslers Überlegungen zum modernen Kunstwerk im Spiegel des Dialogs mit Henry van de Velde." In *Harry Graf Kessler: Ein Wegbereiter der Moderne,* edited by Gerhard Neumann and Günter Schnitzler. Freiburg im Breisgau: Rombach, 1997.

Krammer, Mario. *Berlin, im Wandel der Jahrhunderte.* 2d ed. Berlin: Rembrandt-Verlag, 1956.

Krause, Jürgen. *"Märtyr" und "Prophet." Studien zum Nietzsche-Kult in der bildenden Kunst der Jahrhundertwende.* Berlin / New York: W. de Gruyter, 1984.

Krause, Peter. *"O alte Burschenherrlichkeit:" Die Studenten und ihr Brauchtum.* Graz: Verlag Styria, Edition Kaleidoskop, 1979.

Krüger, Peter. "Das Reparationsproblem der Weimarer Republik in fragwürdiger Sicht: kritischer Überlegungen zur neuesten Forschung." *Vierteljahrsheft für Zeitgeschichte* (1989), 21–47.

————. *Die Aussenpolitik der Republik von Weimar.* Darmstadt: Wissenschaftliche Buchgesellschaft, 1985.

Krummel, Richard. *Nietzsche und der deutsche Geist.* Berlin: W. de Gruyter, 1974.

Kruse, Wolfgang. "Kriegswirtschaft und Gesellschaftsvision: Walther Rathenau und die Organisierung des Kapitalismus." In *Die Extremen berühren sich. Walther Rathenau, 1867–1922,* edited by Hans Wilderotter. Berlin: Argon, 1993.

Kultermann, Udo. *Geschichte der Kunstgeschichte.* Vienna: Econ-Verlag, 1966.

Lane, Barbara. *Architecture and Politics in Germany, 1918–1945.* Cambridge, Mass.: Harvard University Press, 1968.

Langer, William L. *The Diplomacy of Imperialism. 1890–1902.* 2d. ed. New York: Knopf, 1957.

Laqueur, Walter Z. *Young Germany: A History of the German Youth Movement.* New York: Basic Books, 1962.

Leed, Eric J. *No Man's Land: Combat & Identity in World War I.* New York: Cambridge University Press, 1979.

Leffler, Melvin P. *The Elusive Quest: America's Pursuit of European Stability and French Security, 1919–1933.* Chapel Hill, N.C.: University of North Carolina Press, 1979.

Lemp, Richard. *Annette Kolb: Leben und Werk einer Europäerin.* Mainz: Von Hase und Koehler, 1970.

Leppmann, Wolfgang. *Harry Graf Kesslers Urlaub von Deutschland.* Fürstenfeldbruck: Kester-Haeusler Stiftung, 1998.

Le Temps. April 27, 1890.

Lesnig, Günther. "The 75th Anniversary of the *Josephs Legende." Richard Strauss Blätter* Neue Folge 24 (December 1990), 6–36.

Lexikon zur Parteigeschichte: Die bürgerlichen und kleinbürgerlichen Parteien und Verbände in Deutschland (1789–1945). 4 vols. Edited by Dieter Fricke et al. Leipzig: VEB Bibliographisches Institut Leipzig, 1983–1986.

Lincoln, W. Bruce. *Passage Through Armageddon: The Russians in War and Revolution.* New York: Simon & Schuster, 1986.

Link, Werner. *Die amerikanische Stabilisierungspolitik in Deutschland 1921–32.* Düsseldorf: Droste Verlag, 1970.

Lütgemeier-Davin, Reinhold. *Pazifismus zwischen Kooperation und Konfrontation: Das Deutsche Friedenskartell in der Weimarer Republik.* Cologne: Pahl-Rugenstein, 1982.

McAleer, Kevin. *Dueling: The Cult of Honor in Fin-de-Siècle Germany.* Princeton, N.J.: Princeton University Press, 1994.

McClelland, C. E., *State, Society and University in Germany. 1700–1914.* Cambridge: Cambridge University Press, 1979.

McDougall, Walter A. *France's Rhineland Diplomacy, 1914–1924: The Last Bid for a Balance of Power in Europe.* Princeton, N.J.: Princeton University Press, 1978.

Makela, Maria. *The Munich Secession: Art and Artists in Turn-of-the-Century Munich.* Princeton, N.J.: Princeton University Press, 1990.

Mann, Thomas. *Buddenbrooks.* Frankfurt a. M.: S. Fischer, 1967.

Marks, Sally. "The Myth of Reparations." *Central European History* 11 (1978), 231–55.

———. "Reparations Reconsidered: A Reminder." *Central European History* 2 (1969), 356–65.

———. "Reparations Reconsidered: A Rejoinder." *Central European History* 5 (1972).

Masur, Gerhard. *Imperial Berlin.* New York: Basic Books, 1970.

Max Klinger: Wege zum Gesamtkunstwerk. Edited by Manfred Boetzkes. Mainz: Phillip von Zabern, 1984.

Max Liebermann in seiner Zeit. Edited by Sigrid Achenbach. Berlin: Staatliche Museen, National Galerie, 1979.

Mejecher, Helmut. "Die Bagdadbahn als Instrument deutschen wirtschaftlichen Einflusses im Osmanischen Reich." *Geschichte und Gesellschaft* 1 (1975), 447–81.

Meyer, Eduard. *Geschichte des wissenschaftlichen Vereins von 1817.* Halle: M. Niemeyer, 1925.

Modernism. Edited by Malcolm Bradbury and James McFarlane. Harmondsworth, U.K.: Penguin, 1976.

Moffet, Kenworth. *Meier-Graefe as Art Critic.* Munich: Prestel-Verlag, 1973.

Mommsen, Wolfgang J. *Bürgerliche Kultur und künstlerische Avantgarde: Kultur und Politik im deutschen Kaiserreich, 1870 bis 1918.* Frankfurt a. M.: Propyläen, 1994.

———. *Imperial Germany, 1867–1918: Politics, Culture, and Society in an Authoritarian State.* London: Edward Arnold, 1995.

Mosse, George L. *The Crisis of German Ideology: Intellectual Origins of the Third Reich.* New York: Schocken Books, 1981.

Müller, Lothar. "The Beauty of the Metropolis: Toward an Aesthetic Urbanism in Turn-of-the-Century Berlin." In *Berlin: Culture and Metropolis,* edited by Charles W. Haxthausen and Heidrun Suhr. Minneapolis: University of Minnesota Press, 1990.

Müller-Krumbach, Renate. *Harry Graf Kessler und die Cranach-Presse in Weimar.* Hamburg: Maxmilian-Gesellschaft, 1969.

———. "Kessler und die Tradition. Aspekte zur Abdankung 1906." In *Harry Graf Kessler: Ein Wegbereiter der Moderne,* edited by Gerhard Neumann and Günter Schnitzler. Freiburg im Breisgau: Rombach, 1997.

Nabbe, Hildegard. "Im Zeichen von Apollo und Dionysos. Harry Graf Kesslers Pläne für eine Nietzsche-Gedenkstätte in Weimar." *Seminar: A Journal of Germanic Studies* 32:4 (November 1996), 306–24.

———. "Mäzenatentum und elitäre Kunst. Harry Graf Kessler als Schlüssel-figur für eine kulturelle Erneurung um die Jahrhundertwende." *Deutsche Vierteljahrsschrift für Literaturwissenschaft und Geistesgeschichte* 64 (1990), 652–79.

Nagler, A. M. "Hugo von Hofmannsthal and Theatre." *Theatre Research* 2 (1960), 5–15.

Naturalismus: Manifeste und Dokumente zur deutschen Literatur. 1880–1900, edited by Manfred Brauneck and Christine Müller. Stuttgart: J. B. Metzler, 1987.

Naylor, Gillian. *The Bauhaus Reassessed.* London: Herbert Press, 1985.

Newman, L. M. "'Etwas sehr Schönes, ganz Neues . . .' Vorschläge des Grafen Harry Kessler für Max Reinhardts Inszenierung von Hofmannsthals 'König Ödipus.'" *Hofmannsthal Blätter* 35/36 (1987), 114–20.

———. "Gordon Craig in Germany." *German Life and Letters* 40 (October 1986), 11–33.

Nicholls, A. J. *Weimar and the Rise of Hitler.* New York: St. Martin's, 1992.

Nichols, J. Alden. *Germany After Bismarck: The Caprivi Era, 1890–1894.* Cambridge, Mass.: Harvard University Press, 1958.

Nipperdey, Thomas. *Wie das Bürgertum die Moderne fand.* Berlin: Seidler, 1988.

Nolan, Mary. *Visions of Modernity: American Business and the Modernization of Germany.* New York: Oxford University Press, 1995.

Painter, George R., *Marcel Proust: A Biography.* Rev. ed. London: Chatto & Windus, 1989.

Paret, Peter. "Art and the National Image: The Conflict over Germany's Participation in the St. Louis Exposition." *Central European History* 11 (1978).

———. *Art as History: Episodes in the Culture and Politics of Nineteenth-Century Germany.* Princeton, N.J.: Princeton University Press, 1988.

———. *The Berlin Secession: Modernism and its Enemies in Imperial Germany.* Cambridge, Mass.: Harvard University Press, 1980.

Paret, Peter, and Beth Irwin Lewis. "Art, Society, and Politics in Wilhelmine Germany." *Journal of Modern History* 57 (1985), 695–710.

Pascal, Roy. *From Naturalism to Expressionism.* New York: Basic Books, 1973.

Patterson, Annabel. *Pastoral and Ideology: Virgil to Valéry.* Berkeley, Calif.: University of California Press, 1987.

Pedronicini, Guy. *Les negotiations secrètes pendant la grande guerre.* Paris: Flammarion, 1969.

Peters, H. F., *Zarathustra's Sister: The Case of Elisabeth and Friedrich Nietzsche.* New York: Crown, 1977.

Peukert, Detlev. *Die Weimarer Republik*. Frankfurt a. M.: Suhrkamp, 1987.

Pipes, Richard. *The Russian Revolution*. New York: Vintage, 1990.

Podro, Michael. *The Critical Historians of Art*. New Haven: Yale University Press, 1982.

————. *The Manifold in Perception: Theories of Art from Kant to Hildebrand*. Oxford: Oxford University Press, 1972.

Pohl, Karl Heinrich. "Ein sozialdemokratischer Frondeur gegen Stresemanns Aussenpolitik: Adolf Müller und Deutschlands Eintritt in den Völkerbund." In *Aspekte deutscher Aussenpolitik im 20 Jahrhundert,* edited by Wolfgang Benz and Hermann Graml. Stuttgart: Deutsche Verlags-Anstalt, 1976.

Prater, Donald. *A Ringing Glass: The Life of Rainer Maria Rilke*. Oxford: Oxford University Press, 1986.

Rasch, Wolfdietrich. *Die literarische Décadence um 1900*. Munich: C. H. Beck, 1986.

————. "Harry Graf Kessler als Schriftsteller: Die frühen Schriften zur Kunst und Literatur." In *Zeit der Moderne. Zur deustchen Literatur von der Jahrhundertwende bis zur Gegenwart,* edited by Hans-Henrik Krummacher, et al. Stuttgart: A. Kröner, 1984.

————. *Zur deutschen Literatur seit der Jahrhundertwende*. Stuttgart: J. B. Metzler, 1967.

Rewald, John. *Maillol*. New York: Hyperion Press, 1939.

Ritter, Alexander. "Der Dandy im Lande des Diktators Diaz: Harry Graf Kessler und seine ästhetizistischen *Notizen über Mexiko. (1898).*" In *Harry Graf Kessler: Ein Wegbereiter der Moderne,* edited by Gerhard Neumann and Günter Schnitzler. Freiburg im Breisgau: Rombach, 1997.

Robbins, Keith. *The First World War*. Oxford: Oxford University Press, 1984.

Robinson, Daniel N. *Toward a Science of Human Nature: Essays on the Psychologies of Mills, Hegel, Wundt, and James*. New York: Columbia University Press, 1982.

Robinson, Paul. *Opera & Ideas: From Mozart to Strauss*. Ithaca, N.Y.: Cornell University Press, 1985.

Röhl, John, ed. *1914: Delusion or Design? The Testimony of Two Diplomats*. New York: St. Martin's Press, 1973.

Röhl, John C. G., and Nicolaus Sombart, eds. *Kaiser Wilhelm II: New Interpretations*. Cambridge: Cambridge University Press, 1982.

Rosenthal, Harry Kenneth. *German and Pole: National Conflict and Modern Myth*. Gainesville, Fla.: University Presses of Florida, 1976.

Rothblatt, Sheldon. *Tradition and Change in English Liberal Education*. London: Faber & Faber, 1976.

Ruchti, Jacob. *Geschichte der Schweiz während des Weltkrieges 1914–1919, politisch, wirtschaftlich und kulturell*. Bern: P. Haupt, 1928–29.

Rürup, Reinhard. "Problems of the German Revolution, 1918–1920: Political Revolution and Social Protest." *Journal of Contemporary History* 3 (1968), 109–35.

Ryder. A. J. *The German Revolution of 1918: A Study of German Socialism in War and Revolt*. Cambridge: Cambridge University Press, 1967.

Saltzman, Cynthia. *Portrait of Dr. Gachet: The Story of a Van Gogh Masterpiece.* New York: Viking, 1998.

Sanders, Michael, and Philip M. Taylor. *British Propaganda during the First World War, 1914–1918.* London: Macmillan, 1982.

Sarkowski, Heinz. "Zur Geschichte des Dünndruckpapiers und der Insel-Klassiker." *Das Inselschiff* 5 (March 1963), 1–3, 9.

Scheer, Friedrich-Karl. *Die deutsche Friedensgesellschaft (1982–1933): Organization, Ideologie, politischen Ziele.* Frankfurt a. M.: Haag & Herchen, 1981.

Schmid, Gisela Bärbel. "Psychologische Umdeutung biblischer Archetype in Geiste des Fin de Siècle: Zur Entstehung der *Josephslegende.*" *Hofmannsthal Blätter* 35/36 (1987), 105–13.

Schmoll, J. A. "Rodin's Late Drawings and Watercolors." In *Auguste Rodin: Drawings and Watercolors,* edited by Ernst-Gerhard Güse (New York: Rizzoli, 1985), 211–31.

Schmutzler, Robert. *Art Nouveau.* New York: Abrams, 1977.

Schorske, Carl. *Fin de siècle Vienna: Art and Culture.* New York: Knopf, 1980.

Schuh, Willi. "Hofmannsthal, Kessler und die *Josephslegende.*" *Hofmannsthal Blätter* 27 (spring 1983), 48–55.

Schuker, Stephen A. *The End of French Predominance in Europe: The Financial Crisis of 1924 and the Adoption of the Dawes Plan.* Chapel Hill, N.C.: University of North Carolina, 1976.

Schulin, Ernst. "Der Biograph und sein Held. Harry Graf Kessler und Walther Rathenau." In *Harry Graf Kessler: Ein Wegbereiter der Moderne,* edited by Gerhard Neumann and Günter Schnitzler. Freiburg im Breisgau: Rombach, 1997.

Schuster, Gerhard. "Harry Graf Kessler. Tagebuch eines Weltmannes." *Jahrbuch der deutschen Schillergesellschaft* 32 (1986), 432–39.

———. "Leben wie ein Dichter—Richard Dehmel und die bildenden Künste." In *Ideengeschichte und Kunstwissenschaft,* edited by Ekkehard Mai. Berlin: Gebr. Mann, 1983.

Schutte, Jürgen, and Peter Sprengel, eds. *Die Berliner Moderne, 1885–1914.* Stuttgart: Reclam, 1987.

Scott, Clive. "Symbolism, Decadence and Impressionism." In *Modernism,* edited by Malcolm Bradbury and James McFarlane. Harmondsworth, U.K.: Penguin, 1976.

Seeba, Hinrich C. *Kritik des ästhetischen Menschen: Hermeneutik und Moral in Hofmannsthals "Der Tor and der Tod."* Bad Homburg: Gehlen, 1970.

Sembach, Klaus-Jurgen. *Henry van de Velde.* New York: Rizzoli, 1989.

Sharp, Alan. *The Versailles Settlement: Peacemaking in Paris, 1919.* New York: St. Martin's Press, 1991.

Shaw, Bernard. *Shaw's Music: The complete musical criticism in three volumes.* Vol. 3. *1893–1950.* New York: Dodd, Mead, 1981.

Sheehan, James J. *The Career of Lujo Brentano: A Study of Liberalism and Social Reform in Imperial Germany.* Chicago: University of Chicago Press, 1966.

Silverman, Debora. *Art Nouveau in Fin-de-siècle France: Politics, Psychology, and Style.* Berkeley, Calif.: University of California Press, 1989.

Simpson, David. *The Origins of Modern Critical Thought: German Aesthetic and Literary Criticism from Lessing to Hegel.* Cambridge: Cambridge University Press, 1989.

Smith, Woodruff D. *The Ideological Origins of Nazi Imperialism.* Oxford: Oxford University Press, 1986.

Sokel, Walter H. *The Writer in Extremis: Expressionism in Twentieth-Century German Literature.* Stanford, Calif.: Stanford University Press, 1959.

Sontag, Susan. *Under the Sign of Saturn.* New York: Farrar, Straus and Giroux, 1980.

Spenz, Jürgen. *Die diplomatische Vorgeschichte des Beitritts Deutschlands zum Völkerbund, 1924–1926.* Göttingen: Musterschmidt, 1966.

Stachura, Peter, ed. *Political Leaders in Weimar Germany.* New York: Simon & Schuster, 1993.

Stamm, Günther. "Monumental Architecture and Ideology." *Gentse Bijdragen tot de Kunstgeschiedenis* 23 (1973–1975), 303–42.

Stansky, Peter. *Redesigning the World: William Morris, the 1880s, and the Arts and Crafts.* Princeton, N.J.: Princeton University Press, 1985.

Steegmuller, Francis. *Cocteau: A Biography.* Boston: Little, Brown, 1970.

Stenzel, Burkhard. *Harry Graf Kessler: Ein Leben zwischen Kultur und Politik.* Weimar: Böhlau, 1995.

———. "'. . . eine Verzauberung ins Helle und Heitere': Harry Graf Kesslers Ideen zur Kulturerneurung in Deutschland." In *Die Weimarer Republik zwischen Metropole und Provinz,* edited by Wolfgang Bialas and Burkhard Stenzel. Cologne: Böhlau, 1996.

Stern, Fritz. *Gold and Iron: Bismarck, Bleichröder, and the Building of the German Empire.* New York: Vintage, 1979.

Sternberger, Dolf. *Panorama of the Nineteenth Century.* New York: Urizen Books, 1977.

Stevenson, David. *The First World War and International Politics.* Oxford: Oxford University Press, 1991.

Stone, Norman. *The Eastern Front, 1914–1917.* New York: Scribner, 1975.

———. "The Winter Carpathian Campaign." In *The Marshall Cavendish Illustrated Encyclopedia of World War I: Vol. 2: 1914–1915.* New York: Marshall Cavendish, 1984, 593–97.

Stürmer, Michael. *Das ruhelose Reich: Deutschland 1866–1918.* Berlin: Severin and Siedler, 1983.

———, ed. *Das kaiserliche Deutschland.* Düsseldorf: Droste, 1984.

Taylor, A. J. P. *The Struggle for Mastery in Europe. 1848–1918.* Oxford: Oxford University Press, 1977.

Thamer, Jutta. *Zwischen Historismus und Jugendstil: Zur Ausstattung der Zeitschrift "Pan" (1895–1900).* Frankfurt a. M.: Lang, 1980.

Theweleit, Klaus. *Männerphantasien.* Frankfurt a. M.: Verlag Roter Stern, 1977.

Thomson, Belinda. *Vuillard.* New York: Abbeville Press, 1988.

Trachtenberg, Marc. *Reparation in World Politics: France and European Economic Diplomacy, 1916–1923.* New York: Columbia University Press, 1980.

Ulbricht, Justus H., and Frank Simon-Ritz. "'Heimstätte des Zarasthustrawerkes': Personen, Gremien und Aktivitäten des Nietzsche-Archivs in Weimar 1896–1945." In *Wege nach Weimar,* edited by Hans Wilderotter and Michael Dorrmann. Weimar: Jovis, 1999.

———. "Im Herzen des 'geheimen Deutschland': Kulturelle Opposition gegen Avantgarde, Moderne und Republik in Weimar 1900 bis 1933." In *Weimar 1930: Politik und Kultur im Vorteld der NS-Diktatur,* edited by Lothar Ehrlich and Jürgen John. Cologne: Böhlau, 1998.

———. "Kulturrevolution von rechts: Das völkische Netzwerk 1900–1930." In *Nationalsozialismus in Thüringen,* edited by Detlev Heiden and Gunther Mai. Weimar: Böhlau, 1995.

———. " 'Wege nach Weimar' und 'deutsche Widergeburt': Visionen kultureller Hegemonie im völkischen Netzwerk Thüringens zwischen Jahrhundertwende und 'Drittem Reich,' " In *Die Weimarer Republik zwischen Metropole und Provinz,* edited by Wolfgang Bialas and Burkhard Stenzel. Cologne: Böhlau, 1996.

Venturelli, Aldo. "Die Enttäuschung der Macht. Zu Kesslers Nietzsche-Bild." In *Harry Graf Kessler: Ein Wegbereiter der Moderne,* edited by Gerhard Neumann and Günter Schnitzler. Freiburg im Breisgau: Rombach, 1997.

Volke, Werner. "Unterwegs mit Hofmannsthal: Berlin—Griechenland—Venedig." *Hofmannsthal Blätter* 35/36 (1987), 50–104.

Wahl, Volker. *Jena als Kunststadt. 1900–1933.* Leipzig: Seeman Verlag, 1988.

Walker, Alan. *Franz Liszt: Vol. 2. The Weimar Years. 1848–1861.* New York: Knopf, 1989.

Walker, Mack. *German Home Towns: Community, State, and the General Estate.* Ithaca, N.Y.: Cornell University Press, 1971.

Washington, Peter. *Madame Blavatsky's Baboon: A History of the Mystics, Mediums, and Misfits Who Brought Spiritualism to America.* New York: Schocken Books, 1995.

Watt, Richard M. *Bitter Glory: Poland and its Fate, 1918–1939.* New York: Simon & Schuster, 1979.

Weir, David. *Decadence and the Making of Modernism.* Amherst, Mass.: University of Massachusetts Press, 1995.

White, Ralph. "The Europeanism of Coudenhove-Kalergi." In *European Unity in Context: The Interwar Period,* edited by Peter M. R. Stirk. London: Pinter Publishers, 1989.

Wilderotter, Hans and Michael Dorrmann, ed. *Wege nach Weimar: Auf der Suche nach der Einheit von Kunst und Politik.* Weimar: Böhlau, 1999.

Wilhelmy, Petra. *Der Berliner Salon im 19. Jahrhundert (1780–1914).* Veröffentlichen der Historischen Kommission zu Berlin. Vol. 73. Berlin; De Gruyter, 1989.

Willett, John. *Art and Politics in the Weimar Period: The New Sobriety, 1917–1933.* New York: Pantheon, 1978.

Wissmann, Ingeborg. *Die St. Galler Reformationschronik des Johannes Kessler (1503–1574).* Ph.D. diss. Tübingen University, 1972.

Wolf, John B. *The Diplomatic History of the Bagdad Railroad.* Columbus, Mo.: University of Missouri Press, 1936.

Wollkopf, Rosawitha. "Das Nietzsche-Archiv im Spiegel der Beziehungen Elisabeth Förster-Nietzsches zu Harry Graf Kessler." *Jahrbuch der deutschen Schillergesellschaft* 34 (1990), 125.

Woolf, Virginia. *Roger Fry.* New York: Harcourt, Brace & Company, 1940.

Wright, Anthony W. *G. D. H. Cole and Socialist Democracy.* Oxford: Oxford University Press, 1979.

———. "Guild Socialism Revisited." *Journal of Contemporary History* (1974), 165–80.

Zeldin, Theodore. *France. 1848–1945. Vol. 2. Intellect, Taste & Anxiety.* Oxford: Oxford University Press, 1977.

INDEX

Haldane, Lord, 142
Hamlet (Shakespeare), 138; Cranach
   Presse edition, 139, 320, 374–375, 388
Harden, Maximilian, 60, 153, 169, 170,
   228, 319
Hardenberg, Friedrich von. *See* Novalis
Harding, Warren, 328
Hardy, Thomas, 142
Harnack, Adolf, 142
Harrach, Hans-Albrecht, 34
Harrison, Benjamin, 49
Hart, Heinrich, 68
Hatzfeldt, Prince, 336
Hauptmann, Gerhart, 60, 62, 82, 140,
   176, 320; translation of *Hamlet,* 375
Hearn, Lafcadio, 79
Heartfield, John. *See* Herzfelde, Helmuth
Heckel, Erich, 115
Heimann, Moritz, 182
Heimatkunst, 144, 156
Heinrich XIV, Prince of Reuß, 17
Helfferich, Karl, 264
Henderson, Arthur, 390
Hennings, Emily, 249
Herriot, Édouard, 346
Herzfelde, Helmuth, 253, 257
Herzfelde, Wieland, 294, 458n2; in exile,
   397, 399; first meeting with Kessler, 253;
   during First World War, 269, 273; heroic
   pacifism and, 299; *Neue Jugend* journal
   and, 253; postwar imprisonment, 292;
   wartime film propaganda and, 257
Herzog, Wilhelm, 299
Hesse, Grand Duke of, 252
Heuss, Theodor, 290, 296
Heydt, Eduard von der, 388
Heymel, Alfred Walter, 68, 72, 131, 132,
   166, 214
Hildebrand, Adolf von, 110
Hilferding, Rudolf, 282, 294, 300, 325, 333,
   335, 397, 446n30
Hindenburg, Paul von, 224, 225, 234, 249,
   269–270, 385, 393, 394
Hitler, Adolf, 320, 332, 393, 394–395, 398
Hoesch, Leopold, 322
Hoffmann, Dirk, 434n10
Hoffmann, Josef, 63
Hofmann, Ludwig von, 121
Hofmannsthal, Hugo von, 3, 4, 159, 167,
   197, 221, 227, 238, 239, 245; on Eberhard
   von Bodenhausen, 34–35; Gordon
   Craig and, 137; criticism of Kessler's

writing style, 161; cultural propaganda
   in Switzerland and, 252, 255–256; death
   of, 386–387; in Greece with Kessler, 82,
   171, 172–174; Kessler and, 76–78, 176–
   184, 202–203, 208–210, 228, 246, 386–
   387, 427n20, 435n14, 457n7; on Kessler's
   "Art and Religion," 86; *The Legend of
   Joseph* and, 30, 202–203, 204, 206, 208,
   209, 437n25; letters for Anglo-German
   amity and, 140; *Der Rosenkavalier* and,
   178–181, 182; Ruth St. Denis and, 199–
   200; theater and, 136–137; Weimar and,
   128, 136–137, 146
Hogarth, William, 133, 178
Hogarth Press, 455n18
Hohenlohe, Chlodwig (Prince), 73–74
Hölderlin, Friedrich, 29
Holstein, Friedrich von, 96
Holzminden, 348–349
Homosexuality: Kessler's relationships
   and, 29–31, 53–55, 167–169; Moltke-
   Eulenberg scandal, 53, 169–170
Höppner, Hugo, 68
Hötzendorff, Conrad von, 225, 227
Houseman, Laurence, 132
Hugenberg, Alfred, 257
Hughes, Charles, 328, 344
Human, All too Human (Nietzsche), 42
Hungary, 225, 294
Huysman, Joris-Karl, 56
Hyacinth Forest, The (Denis), 119
Hyperinflation, 321, 335

Ibsen, Henrik, 19, 62
Immigration, in America, 341
Impressionism, 71, 103
Impressionisten (Kessler), 161–162
In Days to Come (Rathenau), 301
Independent Socialists (Germany), 287–
   288, 294, 295
Insel (journal), 72
Insel des zweiten Gesichts, Die (Thelen),
   400
Insel Verlag, 72, 93, 123, 243, 375, 457n7;
   Grand Duke Wilhelm-Ernst Edition,
   131–132
Institute of Politics (Williams College),
   Kessler's lectures at, 326, 328–334
Internationale Gastspiel-Gesellschaft, 255
International Labor Office, 301
International Trade Union Congress, 311
Irving, Henry, 134

Text: 10/13 Galliard
Display: Monotype Grotesque, Galliard
Compositor: G&S Typesetters, Inc.
Printer: Edwards Brothers, Inc.